HANDBOOK OF RESEARCH ON SPORT AND BUSINESS

Handbook of Research on Sport and Business

Edited by

Sten Söderman

Professor of International Business, School of Business, Stockholm University, Sweden

and

Harald Dolles

Professor in Sport Management, Molde University College, Specialized University in Logistics, Molde, Norway and Professor in International Business, School of Business, Economics and Law, University of Gothenburg, Sweden

Edward Elgar
Cheltenham, UK • Northampton, MA, USA

Published by
Edward Elgar Publishing Limited
The Lypiatts
15 Lansdown Road
Cheltenham
Glos GL50 2JA
UK

Edward Elgar Publishing, Inc.
William Pratt House
9 Dewey Court
Northampton
Massachusetts 01060
USA

A catalogue record for this book
is available from the British Library

Library of Congress Control Number: 2012951740

This book is available electronically in the ElgarOnline.com
Business Subject Collection, E-ISBN 978 1 78100 586 6

ISBN 978 1 84980 005 1 (cased)

Typeset by Servis Filmsetting Ltd, Stockport, Cheshire
Printed by TJ International Ltd, Padstow, Cornwall

Contents

v

PART VI   SPORT BRANDING AND SPONSORING

PART VII   REFLECTION

Contributors

Christos Anagnostopoulos is Lecturer within the Sport and Event Management Department at Coventry Business School, Coventry, UK, an associate member of the Centre for International Business of Sport (CIBS), and the head of the Sport Unit at the Athens Institute for Education and Research (ATINER). His doctoral dissertation (2008–2013) looked at the managerial decision-making process within the charitable foundations of the English football clubs. Christos' key teaching and research interests lie in organizational behaviour with a focus on issues such as decision making, influence tactics and interpersonal trust associated with the concept of corporate social responsibility in and through sport. He has presented papers at the European Academy of Management and the European Association of Sport Management and has published articles in *Business Ethics: A European Review, Soccer and Society and Sport, Business and Management: An International Journal*.

Tommy D. Andersson is Professor of Tourism and Hospitality Management in the School of Business, Economics and Law at Gothenburg University, Gothenburg (Sweden) where he is also coordinating a master programme in 'Tourism and Hospitality Management'. He received his PhD in managerial economics at Gothenburg University in 1989 and served from 1997 as a professor in Management Accounting at Bodø Graduate School in Norway and later on as Programme Director at the European Tourism Research Institute. His main research interests are managerial economics of the hospitality industry, economic impact analysis, event and festival management, restaurant management accounting, tourism economics and cost–benefit analysis. Most of his publications are in the area of event impact analysis and event management.

Anne-line Balduck finished her PhD in 2009 at the Department of Movement and Sports Sciences at Ghent University, Belgium, in sports management. Her research interests include organizational effectiveness, social impact, coach–athlete relationships and motivation in sports management. She has published extensively in international peer-reviewed journals and currently she supports the scientific research in sports management at Ghent University.

Nikolai Böhlke studied management at the University of Cologne (Germany) and the Pennsylvania State University (USA) as well as sport science at the German Sport University in Cologne. In 2002 he started working as a research and teaching assistant at the German Sport University before he joined the Institute for Sport and Leisure Policy at Loughborough University (England) in 2003 where he completed his PhD in 2006. From 2007 to 2013 Nikolai worked in the Research and Innovation Team at UK Sport (London). In 2013 he joined the Swiss Federal Institute of Sport, Magglingen.

Veerle De Bosscher is Professor at the Department of Sports Policy and Management (Faculty of Physical Education) in the Vrije Universiteit Brussel, Brussels (Belgium). She does research in the area of elite sport policies, international comparisons, measuring competitiveness and benchmarking of nations. Veerle is coordinating an international network of research cooperation in high performance sport, including over 15 nations, called SPLISS (Sports Policy Factors Leading to International Sporting Success), which was also the subject of her PhD. Since 2012 Veerle has been appointed as a Visiting Professor at Utrecht University (The Netherlands).

Maarten van Bottenburg is Professor of Sport Development at the Utrecht School of Governance of Utrecht University (The Netherlands). Prior to his full-time appointment as professor at this university in 2010 he was also Lecturer in Sport Business at Fontys University of Applied Sciences (2004–2009) and Research Director (2002–2006) of the W.J.H. Mulier Institute – a leading centre for research on sports in society in the Netherlands. Before 2002 he was managing director of a private social science research company specializing in matters of sports policy (1992–2002) and was attached to the University of Amsterdam and the Amsterdam School for Social Science Research (1988–1992). In his academic work, Maarten has focused on themes such as the globalization and commercialization of sport, elite sport policy, sport participation trends, the societal meaning of sport and sport management. Among many other books, Van Bottenburg is the author of *Global Games* (2001) and co-author of the *Global Sporting Arms Race* (2008). He has published articles in journals such as the *American Behavioral Scientist, Leisure Studies, Journal of Sport Management, Sport Management Review, European Sport Management Quarterly* and the *International Review for the Sociology of Sport*.

Ann Bourke is currently Head of Teaching and Learning at University College Dublin (UCD) Business School, Dublin (Ireland). In that role, she advises faculty on curriculum design, delivery and assessment and coordinates school policy on education and programme specific matters. Ann lectures in International Business, Services Management and Research Methods. Her main research interests include international trade in services, governance issues for sports organizations (professional and amateur), elite athlete development and continuing professional education. She has published extensively and presented at many international seminars and conferences. Ann is a former board member of the European Association of Sport Management (EASM).

Marc Buelens, PhD, is Professor at the Vlerick Leuven Ghent Management School and at the department of management, innovation and entrepreneurship of the University of Ghent (Belgium). His teaching focuses on management behaviour. His research interests are organization theory, change management and leadership.

Simon Chadwick is Professor of Sport Business Strategy and Marketing, and Director of the Centre for the International Business of Sport, at Coventry University, UK. He has published and commented extensively and internationally on the subject of sport. Among the outlets in which Simon's work has appeared or been quoted are the *Journal of Advertising Research*, the *Wall Street Journal*, Elsevier Publishing and Cable News Network (CNN). He has also worked with many of the world's leading sport organizations including Union of European Football Associations (UEFA), Mastercard, the International Tennis Federation, FC Barcelona and Octagon.

T. Bettina Cornwell (PhD in marketing, the University of Texas) is the Edwin E. and June Woldt Cone Professor of Marketing in the Lundquist College of Business at the University of Oregon, Portland (USA). She is also Director of Research for the Warsaw Sport Marketing Center at the University of Oregon. Prior to joining the University of Oregon, Bettina was Professor of Marketing and Sport Management at the University of Michigan. Her research focuses on marketing communications and consumer behaviour and often includes international and public policy emphases. Recent research on sponsorship-linked marketing has appeared in the *Journal of Consumer Research* and the *Journal of Experimental Psychology*.

Michel Desbordes is Professor of Sports Marketing at ISC School of Management (Paris, France). His research covers sports events, the marketing of football, sporting venues, and experiential marketing as applied to sporting events. Since 2008 he has been the scientific editor for the *International Journal of Sports Marketing & Sponsorship*. He has been visiting professor in Canada, China, the USA, the Netherlands, Spain, Finland, England and South Korea. In addition, he acts as consultant for a variety of organizations and firms, like UEFA, Adidas, New Balance, Tour de France, Rally Dakar, Paris Marathon, Reebok and Stade de France.

Mark Dibben, Dr, is Associate Professor and Head of the School of Management at the University of Tasmania, Hobart (Australia). His research adopts the metaphysics of Alfred North Whitehead to gain a processual understanding of (managerial) experience. To this end, he has published two edited books on applied process thought with the philosophy publisher Ontos and remains on the board of the International Process Network, the coordinating body of some 30 process philosophy research centres around the globe, having served as its Executive Director 2008–11. He is also co-editor of *Philosophy of Management*. He focuses on the nature and impact of trust, distrust and cooperation on managed interpersonal relations. He published on this topic across a variety of academic disciplines, from management sub-fields such as strategy, entrepreneurship and marketing, to accounting, information systems, medicine and philosophy. Throughout this work, he has obviously adopted longitudinal qualitative methods.

Harald Dolles is Professor in Sport Management at Molde University College, Specialized University in Logistics, Molde (Norway). He also holds a professorship in International Business at the University of Gothenburg in Sweden. Harald received his doctorate in international business/strategic management from the University Erlangen-Nuremberg in Germany, with a focus on East Asia. He has been Assistant Professor at Bayreuth University (Germany), where he taught on the University's sports management programme. From 2001 to 2006 he was assigned by the German Ministry of Education and Science to serve in official mission as expert on Japan and China at the economic section of the German Institute for Japanese Studies in Tokyo and taught as Visiting Professor at Chuo University (Tokyo, Japan). Harald frequently contributes to scientific development in the fields of international business, Asian studies and sports management. In this regard, he has a publication stream of articles and books, most recently スポーツ・マネジメントと メガイベント：Ｊリーグ・サッカー とアジアのメガスポーツ・イベント[*Sports Management and Mega Events: J-League Soccer and Mega-Sports Events in Asia*] (Bunshindo, 2012, with Takahashi, Hayakawa and Söderman); 'Evaluating and measuring: applying a management perspective on sports' (*Sport Business & Management*, October 2012, with Söderman); *Sport as a Business: International, Professional and Commercial Aspects* (Palgrave Macmillan, 2011, with Söderman); 'Managing sport: governance and performance' (*Sport Business & Management*, October 2011, with Söderman); 'Mega-sporting events in Asia: impacts on society, business and management' (*Asian Business & Management*, June 2008, with Söderman); 'Developing international sport' (*International Journal of Sports Marketing and Sponsorship*, October 2008, with Söderman); 'Addressing ecology and sustainability in mega-sporting events: the 2006 Football World Cup in Germany' (*Journal of Management and Organization*, September 2010, with Söderman). His book *Asian Inward and Outward Foreign Direct Investment: New Challenges in the Global Economy* (co-edited with Claes-Göran Alvstam, Patrik Strön and Rick Middel) will be published in 2013 with Palgrave Macmillan. Harald is Immediate Past-Chair of the European Academy of Management (EURAM) Strategic Interest Group on 'Managing Sport', a network of academics, practitioners, athletes and sport officials whose interests revolve around aspects of internationalization, professionalization and commercialization of sports in theory and in practice.

Bernd Frick, Dr, is Professor of Organizational and Media Economics in the Faculty of Management and Economics and Vice President with responsibility for strategy, finance and international relations at the University of Paderborn, Germany. He studied Sociology, Economics and Political Science at the University of Trier and at Clark University, Worcester, Massachusetts. Before joining the Faculty of Management and Economics at the University of Paderborn, Bernd held the Chair in Personnel and Organizational Economics at the University of Greifswald and the Reinhard Mohn-Chair in Organizational Economics and Leadership at Witten/Herdecke University. He is also Director of the Institute of Labor and Personnel Economics at Mobile Life Campus of Volkswagen AG in Wolfsburg and Research Associate at the Institute for Labour Law and Industrial Relations in the European Community at the University of Trier.

Hallgeir Gammelsæter is Professor in Social Change, Organization, and Management at Molde University College, Specialized University in Logistics, Molde (Norway). Before taking up sport studies, in particular the organization of football, ten years ago he conducted research on organizational change, management in professional organizations, knowledge diffusion, and innovation in private and public institutions. Hallgeir has co-authored several Norwegian books and *The Organisation and Governance of Top Football across Europe* (Routledge, 2011, together with Senaux). He also recently published on the organization of football in journals *Soccer and Society* and *European Sport Management Quarterly*.

Chris Gratton, BA(Econ), MA(Econ), PhD, is Professor of Sports Economics and Director of the Sport Industry Research Centre (SIRC) at Sheffield Hallam University, UK. He currently has five academic sports books in print, the latest being *The Economics of Sport Broadcasting* published in 2007. Chris's main areas of research include: the economic benefits of major sports events; measuring the economic importance of sport including the use of satellite accounts for sport; and the analysis and modelling of large sports participation surveys. He has represented the UK on the European Union (EU) Workshop on Sport and Economics since 2006.

Alessandro 'Chito' Guala is Professor of Citymarketing at the University of Torino (Italy), where he founded the Olympics and Mega Events Research Observatory (OMERO) in 2001. He served as City Councillor for Tourism of the Municipality of Genoa (1993–97) and was Visiting Professor at the Universities of Madison, Wisconsin, and San Diego, California. His main interests are social indicators, quality of life, mega events and urban regeneration. Since 2001 Alessandro carried out research on the Olympics, monitoring the Olympic Winter Games Torino 2006, and collaborating with the International Olympic Committee (IOC). He is also a consultant of severals institutions in the field of tourism and cultural planning.

Sean Hamil is a Lecturer in Management at Birkbeck College, University of London, where he is the programme director of the MSc Sport Management and the Business of Football, and a Director of Birkbeck Sport Business Centre, one of Britain's leading academic centres for the study of sport business. He is a member of the academic scientific committee of the Master in European Sport Governance. Sean has published extensively on the issue of corporate governance and regulation of sport organizations. Notably he is editor/author of *Managing Football: An International Perspective* (Butterworth-Heinemann, 2009) and *Who Owns Football? The Governance and Management of the Club Game Worldwide* (Routledge, 2010).

Kjetil Kåre Haugen is Professor of Logistics at Molde University College, Specialized University in Logistics, Molde (Norway). Kjetil holds a PhD in Management Science from the Norwegian Institute of Technology from 1991. Lately, his research interests have moved from operations management/logistics into sports economics/strategy. His main interest has been game theory applied in football, both as a tool to understand football economics as well as the game itself. Kjetil has published in journals such as *Journal of Sports Economics*, *European Sport Management Quarterly* and *Sport in Society*, among others. He is a massive supporter of Molde Football club.

Boris Helleu is a Senior Lecturer in Sports Management at Université de Caen Basse-Normandie, France, and has headed the Sports Management programme since 2010. He received a PhD in Sports Sciences from Université de Rouen and his thesis was devoted to the geographic aspects of the regulation of professional sport. His work looks at sport as an event combining contributions from economics (models of sports regulation), geography (the globalization and metropolization of professional sport) and marketing (fans and stadiums). Recently he has been working on the relationship between sports and social media. He was also the scientific adviser on the ministerial reports devoted to the competitiveness of French professional football (2008) and arenas (2010).

Patricia Hogan is Professor in Management of Health and Fitness at Northern Michigan University in Marquette, Michigan, USA. She researches and publishes in the areas of developing professional intellect in university students, inquiry-based and problem-based learning, professional ethics, prosumerism, social media applications (especially wikis) in education mission-central learning, and in Social Media for Health, Fitness, and Sport Business.

Hans Jansson is Professor of International Marketing at the Linnaeus School of Business and Economics at Linnaeus University, Kalmar (Sweden), where he is the

Head of the Linnaeus Baltic Business Research Center. He graduated from Uppsala University in 1981, and was previously professor at University of Lund and University of Göteborg as well as a senior fellow at National University of Singapore. Hans has an extensive research experience in international marketing and business in emerging markets, both on multinational corporations and small and medium-sized enterprises in Eastern Europe and South and East Asia, especially China. He has published eight books and a large number of articles and conference papers. The most recent are *International Business Strategy in Emerging Country Markets – The Institutional Network Approach* (Edward Elgar, 2007) and *International Business Marketing in Emerging Country Markets – The Third Wave of Internationalization of Firm* (Edward Elgar, 2007).

R. Burke Johnson is a Professor in the Department of Professional Studies at the University of South Alabama. He holds three masters degrees (psychology, sociology, and public administration). His PhD is from the REMS Program (Research, Evaluation, Measurement, and Statistics) at the University of Georgia. He is first author of *Educational Research: Quantitative, Qualitative, and Mixed Approaches* (Sage, 2011), and second author of *Research Methods and Design* (Pearson, 2010) and *Dictionary of Statistics and Methodology* (Sage, 2011). He is author or co-author of numerous articles and chapters on mixed methods research, was an associate editor of the *Journal of Mixed Methods Research*, was guest editor of a special issue on mixed methods research in *Research in the Schools*, and of another special issue on mixed methods research with the *American Behavioral Scientist*. His current interests are in research methodology (especially mixed) and the history and philosophy of social science.

Marc Maes passed away suddenly on 14th August 2010. He was Professor at the Department of Movement and Sports Sciences at Ghent University in sports management. Under his leadership, sports management at Ghent University developed into a full-fledged department. He combined both scientific research with his practical management experience. He was recognized as a leading expert in the areas of sports management and ethics.

Norm O'Reilly is a Professor at the University of Ottawa (Canada), specializing in sport business. Holder of BSc, MA, MBA and PhD degrees, as well as the Certified General Accountant (CGA) accounting designation, he has previously taught at the David Falk Center for Sport Management at Syracuse University, the Graduate School of Business at Stanford University, the School of Sports Administration at Laurentian University, and the Ted Rogers School of Management at Ryerson University. A former elite athlete and sport administrator, he has published five books, over 50 articles in refereed management journals and over 100 conference proceedings and case studies in the areas of sport management, tourism marketing, marketing, risk management, sport finance and social marketing. He is the lead researcher on the Canadian Sponsorship Landscape Study, a highlight of the annual Canadian Sponsorship Forum.

Leigh Robinson is a Professor of Sport Management at the University of Stirling (UK). Her research expertise lies in the field of organizational performance management and capacity development in the sport not-for profit sector. She works extensively with

Olympic sport organizations throughout the world, focusing on capacity building in developing sport systems. Leigh is author of *Managing Public Leisure Services* and co-editor of *Managing Olympic Sport Organisations* and *Managing Voluntary Sport Organisations*.

Andy Rudd holds a PhD in sport ethics from the University of Idaho. Additionally, he has a strong background in research methods and programme evaluation. His research interests are in the areas of character development, sportsmanship, ethical decision-making and spectator aggression. Andy also has methodological interests in mixed methods and scale development. Across these aforementioned topics, he has a publication stream of several articles. His articles can be seen in journals such as the *Journal of Sport Management, Sport Management Review* and the *International Journal of Sport Management*. He is currently on the sport management faculty at Belmont Abbey College in Belmont, North Carolina (USA).

James Santomier is Professor in the Department of Marketing and Sport Management, John F. Welch College of Business, Sacred Heart University, Fairfield, Connecticut, USA. He joined the faculty of Sacred Heart University in 1999. He received a PhD in Physical Education from the University of Utah. James has held academic positions at the University of New Haven, Hong Kong Institute of Education, New York University, the University of Oregon and the University of the Pacific. He has published extensively in the areas of sport management, sociology of sport, stress management, and psycho-social aspects of physical activity and sport. His research and publications reflect an interest in the organizational and social psychological dimensions of sport, fitness and physical education, the management dimensions of sport business and the integration of new media in sport.

Torsten Schlesinger is Research Assistant at the Department of Sport Sociology and Sport Management, Institute of Sport Science, University of Berne, Switzerland. He received his doctorate at TU Chemnitz in Germany in Sport Sciences. His research interests relate to different aspects of sports marketing (emotions in the context of sport marketing events, analysing sport sponsorship effectiveness), human resource management in voluntary sport clubs and sport club development. This actual research reflects a combination of individual and institutional perspectives for the investigation of individual decisions (multi-level analysis). He has published articles in journals such as *European Sport Management Quarterly, International Journal of Sport Management and Marketing, European Journal of Sport and Society*, and *European Journal of Sport Science*.

Benoit Senaux is Senior Lecturer and Director of the postgraduate programmes in sport management at Coventry University (UK). Prior to that, he was Associate Professor in Management Control at Reims Management School (France). His research focuses on institutional change and the commercialization of sport, and its impact on clubs' organizational identity and governance. He has published articles on the governance and organization of sport in *International Journal of Sport Management and Marketing, Soccer & Society* and *Sport, Business and Management*. Benoit has recently co-authored *The Organisation and Governance of Top Football across Europe* (Routledge, 2011, together with Gammelsæter).

Simon Shibli is Director of the Sport Industry Research Centre (SIRC) at Sheffield Hallam University, England. Simon is a graduate in Physical Education, Sport Science and Recreation Management from Loughborough University and also a qualified management accountant (ACMA). The SIRC team provide research and consultancy services to a range of clients such as national agencies, national and international governing bodies of sport and local authorities. The SIRC has been involved in elite sport related work since 1997 and with UK Sport (Jerry Bingham) is one of the founding members of the SPLISS consortium.

Eivind Å. Skille is a sport sociologist and Professor at the Norwegian School of Sport Sciences, Department of Culture and Society, and Hedmark University College, Faculty of Health and Sports, in Norway. His main research interests are sport policy, sport organization and sport participation. Eivind has a doctoral degree from the Norwegian School of Sport Sciences in Oslo, and he has published in journals such as *International Review for the Sociology of Sport*, *Sport Education and Society*, *Sport in Society*, *European Sport Management Quarterly* and *Sport Management Review*.

Aaron C.T. Smith is Professor and Deputy Pro-Vice Chancellor in the College of Business at Royal Melbourne Institute of Technology (RMIT) University, Melbourne, Australia. He was previously Director of Sport and Leisure Management and held the Chair of Sport Management at La Trobe University, Melbourne. Aaron has research interests in the management of psychological, organizational and policy change in business, and sport and health, and has authored or co-authored 13 books which examine these issues. Aaron also has an extensive background in organizational consulting. He has worked in the Asia-Pacific, Europe, North America and the Middle East in a diverse range of sectors and industries including multinational corporations, professional sporting clubs, national and state sport associations, media companies, sport and entertainment facilities, government and not-for-profit organizations.

Sten Söderman is Professor of International Business in the School of Business at Stockholm University, Stockholm, Sweden. Previously he was a professor at Luleå University of Technology and a business consultant specializing in startups (in Manila, Geneva and Brussels). His research has focused on market strategy development and implementation and is currently on the international expansion of European firms in Asia and the global entertainment economy. He is the author and editor of many books, case studies and articles. His most recent publications include *Football and Management: Comparisons between Sport and Enterprise* (Palgrave Macmillan, 2013); *Sports Management and Mega Events: J-League Soccer and Mega-Sports Events in Asia* (Bunshindo, 2012, with Takahashi, Hayakawa and Dolles); 'Evaluating and measuring: applying a management perspective on sports' (*Sport Business & Management*, October 2012, with Dolles); *Sport as a Business: International, Professional and Commercial Aspects* (Palgrave Macmillan, 2011, with Dolles); 'Managing sport: governance and performance' (*Sport Business & Management*, October 2011, with Dolles); 'Mega-sporting events in Asia: impacts on society, business and management' (*Asian Business & Management*, June 2008, with Dolles); 'Developing international sport' (*International Journal of Sports Marketing and Sponsorship*, October 2008, with Dolles); 'Sponsoring the Beijing Olympic Games – patterns of sponsor advertising' (*Asia Pacific Journal of Marketing and*

Logistics, January 2010, with Dolles), 'Addressing ecology and sustainability in mega-sporting events: the 2006 Football World Cup in Germany' (*Journal of Management and Organization*, September 2010, with Dolles). Sten currently chairs the European Academy of Management (EURAM) Strategic Interests Group on 'Managing Sport'.

Harry Arne Solberg is a Professor of Economics at Trondheim Business School, Sør-Trøndelag University College and Molde University College (all Norway). Harry Arne holds a PhD from Sheffield Hallam University, UK. His research interests have been related to economic analysis of various sporting activities, with special attention on sporting events and media-related issues. Together with Gratton he has published *The Economics of Sport Broadcasting* (Taylor & Francis, 2007). Harry Arne has also published a number of articles in scientific journals, such as *European Sport Management Quarterly*, *International Journal of Sports Marketing & Sponsorship* and *Journal of Media Economics*, among others. He has also published several book chapters.

Bob Stewart teaches sports studies in the School of Sport and Exercise Science at Victoria University, Melbourne, Australia. He is an Associate Professor of Sport Policy and Regulation, and has a special interest in sport ideology and its role in sustaining the values, myths and beliefs that drive sport's social development. Bob has written extensively on regulatory regimes and cartel practices in Australia's professional sport leagues, and is currently researching the regulation of drug use in sport, and how these regulations shape player and athlete behaviour. Bob is also undertaking research into the exercise industry, and has recently completed a study on 'body work' in gyms, where he examined the ways in which gym participants use their experiences to accumulate stocks of personal capital and social power.

Tim Ströbel, Dr, is Assistant Professor at the Department of Services Management at the University of Bayreuth, Germany. He teaches sport management, sport marketing and services management. His research focuses on several aspects of brand management, on value creation of organizations and on sport management in general. Especially, his dissertation deals with the measurement of brand equity in sports. Within this framework he made several conference contributions (for example, for the European Association for Sport Management [EASM], Sport Management Society of Australia and New Zealand [SMAANZ] or International Association of Sport Economists [IASE]). Furthermore, he is a member of EASM and board member of the Sport, Business & Law alumni association at the University of Bayreuth.

Jasper Truyens is working as a PhD student at the department of Sport Policy and Management at the Vrije Universiteit Brussel. He graduated as Master in Sociology in 2006 and successfully attained the postgraduate diploma in sport management (2007). His doctoral thesis (2008–11) is about the measurement of competitiveness in elite sport policies at a sport specific level. As a junior researcher he is developing new perspectives within the SPLISS consortium group on the measurement and comparison of elite development systems.

Douglas Michele Turco, PhD, has been professor and Associate Dean of Academic Affairs in the College of Global Studies at Arcadia University since 2012. An award-winning professor, Douglas teaches sport economics, sport tourism, globalization of sport, and research methods. He is also a visiting professor at the Rajiv Gandhi Indian Institute of Management, IMC FH-Krems (Austria), Romanian American University and National Taiwan Sport University. He has authored over 40 articles in *Sport Marketing Quarterly, International Journal of Sport Management, Journal of Travel Research, Journal of Sport and Tourism* and others, and has written several books. His recent research involves the 2011 Women's Tennis Association Championships, the 2010 Delhi Commonwealth Games, the 2010 FIFA World Cup, the US Open Golf Championship and the Cricket World Cup.

Geoff Walters is a Lecturer in Management at Birkbeck, University of London and a director of the Birkbeck Sport Business Centre. He graduated from Lancaster University Management School and the University of Manchester before completing a PhD at Birkbeck on corporate governance in the football industry and the relevance of stakeholder theory. He has since published numerous articles and book chapters on governance, regulation, and corporate responsibility in the sport industry. In 2010 he was funded by UEFA through the Universities Research Grant Programme to undertake research on corporate social responsibility (CSR) in European football and more recently has been involved with the development of the Voluntary Code of Good Governance for the Sport and Recreation Sector, an initiative led by the Sport and Recreation Alliance in the UK in 2011.

Mathieu Winand is Lecturer in Sport Management in the School of Sport at the University of Stirling (Scotland, UK). He is also involved as associate researcher in the Olympic Chair Henri de Baillet Latour and Jacques Rogge in Management of Sport Organizations from the Université Catholique de Louvain in Belgium. Dr Winand's expertise is in the area of organizational performance of sport governing bodies, organizational change, innovation of non-profit sport organizations and in the development of mixed-method designs, particularly Qualitative Comparative Analysis.

Herbert Woratschek, Dr, is Professor and Dean of the Faculty of Law, Business and Economics as well as Head of the Department of Services Management at the University of Bayreuth, Germany. He is also Board Member of the University's Sports Institute and responsible for the Sport Management programmes at the University of Bayreuth. His research focuses on the measurement and management of the service profit-chain and on sport fan behaviour. In these fields he published numerous academic articles (for example, in *Journal of Service Research, European Journal for Sport Management, Journal of Relationship Marketing, Australasian Marketing Journal*) and made several conference contributions. Herbert is Vice-President of European Association of Sport Management (EASM) and member of the Editorial Board of *European Sport Management Quarterly, International Journal of Sport Finance, International Journal of Sports Marketing and Sponsorship and Marketing ZFP.*

Thierry Zintz is Dean of the Faculty of Sport Sciences at the Université catholique de Louvain, Louvain-La-Neuve (Belgium). He is Professor of Sport Management and Holder of the Olympic Chair Henri de Baillet Latour and Jacques Rogge in Management of Sport Organizations at the Université catholique de Louvain. His research interests include configurational approaches, strategies and governance of sport organizations. Thierry is also Vice-President of the Belgian Olympic and Interfederal Committee and Director of the Executive Master in Management of Olympic Sport Organizations (MEMOS).

Preface and acknowledgements
Sten Söderman and Harald Dolles

It started in Stockholm at a conference in international business more than ten years ago when we, Harald Dolles and Sten Söderman, together visited a Swedish football match between Djurgården IF and Malmö FF, and discovered a shared interest in how management concepts could be applied and might function (or not) in sports. Before this evening at Råsunda Stadium we had met at several conferences. Our backgrounds were rather similar, focusing on sensitivity and pre-understanding of sports based on own experiences combined with several years of academic research, writing and teaching on international business and industry experience from working abroad, especially in Asia. We agreed that despite the well-documented economic impact of sports in media and the mismanagement at club level often reported by journalists, academic research papers on sports management were rarely seen at top management conferences. Sport management and research on the nexus between business and sports simply had not made its way to well-established business schools' management curricula and research agendas.

Our early ambition was to bring sport management research from a specialist niche market and focused conferences into international management conferences as the industry increasingly developed towards internationalization, professionalization and commercialization. By doing so, we aimed to develop and establish research on sports and business as a serious new stream of management research in the hope that it would later be broadly accepted in leading business schools. We have been fully aware that a lot of qualified research in sports has been done and is visible, for example, in economics, sociology and physical education, but not within business administration. In the following years we presented our research on sport and business with posters, interactive and competitive papers not only at sports conferences (in order to get feed-back from sports specialists) but also at various highly ranked management conferences worldwide (to relate to the latest theoretical research in the field). We also organized well-received panels, for example on 'Sport businesses and sport: facing the challenges of internationalization' in 2008 (Academy of International Business Conference, Indianapolis) and on 'Targeting the international audience: challenges facing sports managers' (Academy of International Business Conference 2009, Milano). Special issues on 'Mega-sporting events in Asia: impacts on society, business and management' (*Asian Business & Management*, just ahead of the Bejing Olympic Games in 2008) and 'Developing International Sport' (*International Journal of Sports Marketing & Sponsorship*, 2008) were published by us subsequently.

In 2008 our competitive proposal to organize an academic track on 'Sport as a business: internationalisation, professionalization, commercialisation' was accepted for the European Academy of Management (EURAM) Annual Meeting at the University of Liverpool, Liverpool (UK). For the first time in the history of EURAM a track on the business and management aspects of sports was accepted. At the actual conference in spring 2009 the track was well received, far beyond our expectations. Plenty of high-profile papers, interesting discussions and a stimulating atmosphere during the conference constituted the most important platform in our knowledge-development endeavours. This achievement and the fulfilment of the organizational requirements stated by EURAM has led to the founding of a strategic interest group (SIG) named after the initial track on 'Sport as a business'. By encouraging this development, the EURAM board concluded that the main topics chosen for the track ('internationalization, professionalization and commercialization in sports') were promising emerging areas of research. In a seemingly parallel development we have been approached by Francine O'Sullivan from Edward Elgar about editing this research handbook about sport and business.

The EURAM SIG on 'Sport as Business' was renamed in 2012 into 'Managing Sport'. The group has in the meanwhile defined itself as a network of academics, practitioners, athletes and sport officials whose interests revolve around aspects of internationalization, professionalization and commercialization of sports in theory and in practice. The group, which is chaired since its inauguration by ourselves, functions as a catalyst for building and disseminating new ideas around the business of sports, by particularly aiming at: (1) promoting research and education in the fields of sports business and management in Europe, with special emphasis on international comparisons; (2) fostering an understanding of the role of professionalization and commercialization of sport in European economy and society; (3) encouraging the exchange of research results, practical experience, and ideas; (4) supporting the development of international research collaborations; and (5) disseminating research results through a variety of channels. This *Handbook on Research on Sport as a Business* is one of the outcomes and the result of three years of hard work.

ACKNOWLEDGEMENTS

We would like to thank Francine O'Sullivan, Jennifer Wilcox and Caroline Cornish for their patience with the process and for their continuous encouragement and support. We also would like to express our sincere gratitude to the broad and highly competent group of contributors to this lengthy project. All contributions benefited tremendously from the peer-reviewing process of chapter drafts applied among all chapter authors and the helpful comments and careful advice on how to improve the chapters. Even if this process was time-consuming, it also helped enormously to interrelate the chapters towards each other to reinforce the handbook's efforts to link various perspectives on research on sport as business in ways that will undoubtedly support further research efforts and classroom use. While working on the project for several years, we talked to many people about the handbook and received encouragement and appreciation of undertaking such a challenging academic endeavour. We are extremely happy that this long-lasting editing and authoring production process has come to an end. The journey was enabled thanks also to support from colleagues and friends from Stockholm University, School of Business, Luxembourg Business Academy, the School of Business, Economics and Law at the University of Gothenburg and the EURAM SIG on 'Managing Sport'. The book cover graphic was designed and provided by Monika and Charlotte Dolles by using the research methods showcased in the book as inspiration. Thank you both; you created a terrific piece of art, even including a match game to challenge our observation skills.

Finally, and most of all, we would like to express our sincere gratitude to our families. They have had to suffer long periods of our physical and mental absence. Our family members also helped tremendously to cope with the seemingly never-coming-to-an-end pressure of open tasks associated with editing such a comprehensive volume. This handbook is dedicated to all of you.

We and the Publishers also wish to thank the following who have kindly given permission for the use of copyright material:

Elsevier and the editor of *Sport Management Review*, Tracy Taylor, for the articles: Andy Rudd and R. Burke Johnson (2010) 'A call for more mixed methods in sport management research', *Sport Management Review*, **13**, 14–24. © Elsevier 2010; Aaron C.T. Smith and Bob Stewart (2010) 'The special features of sport: a critical revisit', *Sport Management Review*, **13**, 1–13. © Elsevier 2010.

Emerald Group Publishing Limited for the article: Simon Chadwick (2009) 'From outside lane to inside track: sport management research in the twenty-first century', *Management Decision*, **47** (1), 191–203. © Emerald Group Publishing Limited 2009.

M.E Sharpe, Inc for the article: T. Bettina Cornwell (Fall 2008) 'State of the art and science in sponsorship-linked marketing', *Journal of Advertising*, **37** (3), 41–55. © 2008 by American Academy of Advertising. Reprinted with permission of M.E. Sharpe, Inc.

MANZ'sche Verlags-und Universitätsbuchhandlung GmbH for parts of the article: Harald Dolles and Sten Söderman (2008) 'The network of value captures: creating competitive advantage in football management', *Wirtschaftspolitische Blätter Österreich* [*Austrian Economic Policy Papers*], **55** (1), 39–58.

Every effort has been made to trace all the copyright holders but if any have been inadvertently overlooked the publishers will be pleased to make the necessary arrangements at the first opportunity.

PART I

INTRODUCTION

1 Research on sport and business
Harald Dolles and Sten Söderman

The purpose of the handbook is to present the current frontier of research on sport and business in theory and in practice. It is designed to function as a catalyst for building and disseminating new ideas around the variety of methods being applied in research on the business aspects of sports as well as of sport-related industries. It can be read and used by academics, PhD students as well as sports practitioners looking for useful ways of expanding knowledge, conducting research or searching for insights into the challenges of managing sport. We have also attempted to make the handbook useful and accessible to master's and bachelor students who prepare their thesis projects. Although such students will normally be expected to complete their thesis projects in months rather than years, they face the same problems of finding a thesis topic, how to design their research project, the choice of appropriate methods and summarizing their findings as analysed and demonstrated in the chapters in this handbook.

This introductory chapter explains how and why this handbook is structured in thematic clusters, and presents some of our thoughts and observations on cross-links between the research methods and chapter topics by introducing the chapters. We also provide graphs and summaries of the main research themes (see Figure 1.1), some of the main theoretical concepts being applied (see Figure 1.2) and the key research methods and approaches (see Figure 1.3) across all chapters in the field of research on sport and business. We hope this will enable the reader to make quick use of the handbook. Our concluding 'outlook' chapter at the end of this handbook provides a summary of future research areas on the nexus between sport and business.

1 STARTING WITH THEMATIC CLUSTERS IN SPORT MANAGEMENT RESEARCH

The handbook is divided into five thematic clusters 'Governance and performance', 'Media and technology', 'Place, time and spectators', 'Club management and teams', 'Sport branding and sponsoring' as well as an introduction and a reflection chapter cluster. Figure 1.1 provides the main areas of research covered in this handbook, which we will further explain in the following.

Chapter 2 by Andy Rudd and R. Burke Johnson, in the introduction cluster, explores how mixed methods have been applied in sport management research and demonstrates ways in which the application of mixed methods can help to improve the validity of research findings. The basic idea is to select, in a systematic way, a combination of qualitative and quantitative approaches that will effectively cover the objective of a study and to do it in a way that eliminates overall research design weaknesses associated with an either/or approach. As research in sport management is often concerned with causal questions, it is argued that mixed methods provide designs for improving

Note: The numbers in brackets indicate the chapter numbers.

Figure 1.1   Main research topics addressed in the handbook

causal inference. Examples are provided from three areas of sport management research, including marketing, organizational behaviour and finance. Further examples of mixed methods approaches are to be found in other chapters of the handbook.

1.1   Thematic Cluster 'Governance and Performance'

The first thematic cluster, on 'Governance and performance', includes seven chapters in a fast-expanding area of sport research. We might state that existing research into the comparison and analysis of top sport has led to a convergence in the design of top or elite sport systems, as many countries have attempted to copy what has been perceived to contribute to the performance of those nations who have a history of elite sporting success. This view dominates Chapter 3 by Leigh Robinson and Nikolai Böhlke. However, despite this, it is obvious there are countries that perform consistently better in some sports than other countries do, such as British cycling, German rowing, and so on. Thus, while most elite sport systems now have similar infrastructure and practices, it can be argued that the management and operational delivery of the factors that make up an elite sport system is now a more crucial differentiator for success. Thus, if a sport wish to improve its success, managers of elite sport systems should focus on improving the processes they follow, rather than simply increasing the support infrastructure they provide to athletes. Since its emergence in the 1980s, the concept of benchmarking has been used as a framework for researching best practice in a range of industries in an attempt to understand, compare and improve performance. Within sport management, for example, benchmarking has been used to compare public sport facilities, as a framework for investigating the management of sport teams or, in the context of elite sport systems, to identify the factors that need to be considered to facilitate international sporting success. In this chapter a number of the processes of the elite systems supporting the Swedish Athletics Association and the Norwegian Cross Country Skiing National Team are investigated using the process benchmarking methodology for comparative analysis.

In sport management literature, researchers need to understand and explain a phenomenon or outcome by comparing a limited number of cases. Comparisons between top-level sport clubs in a country (such as English Premier League football), same national sport organizations from different countries (such as cross-national study of national Olympic Committees) or staff behaviour in a specific sport organization (such as volunteers in a sport governing body) are examples of research areas where the maximum number of cases is, of necessity, quite limited. To address this gap, Mathieu Winand and Thierry Zintz in Chapter 4 suggest applying a mixed method design named qualitative comparative analysis (QCA). This innovative configurational comparative approach allows researchers to analyse small samples (that is, from three up to 60 cases) and to develop a conception of causality that includes complexity. Indeed, combinations of necessary and sufficient variables, rather than net effect of individual independent variables, are related to a phenomenon of interest (dependent variables). Winand and Zintz show how QCA is applied in the area of organizational performance of sport governing bodies in Belgium. They highlight patterns that are observed in highly performing organizations and illustrate the QCA approach and technique. Results show that three combinations of key determinants are linked with high performance of communities' sport governing bodies.

Benchmarking is considered in Chapter 5 by Veerle De Bosscher, Jasper Truyens, Marten van Bottenburg and Simon Shibli. This chapter illustrates how a scoring system is developed in order to compare objectively elite sport policies of six nations and thus to move beyond the descriptive level of comparison. Mixed research methods were found to be the most appropriate approach with which to collect a wide range of data on elite sport policies whereby both qualitative and quantitative data are transformed into a score. This chapter exemplifies a scientific approach to measuring the determinants of competitiveness influenced by economic competitiveness measurements. In sport, the issue is even more convoluted because sports systems are closely enmeshed with the culture of a nation and, therefore, each system might be considered as unique. In the USA for example, sport is highly embedded in the school system, which is designed to feed athletes into the university system. There is no sport club tradition in the United States that is comparable to the kind found elsewhere in the world. These and other differences between nations make comparison of sport determinants, and elite sport in particular, in an international context extremely difficult. Cultural factors shape the environment surrounding sports: they are integrated with the determinants and not isolated from them. Bearing in mind the arguments outlined above, the authors present a measurement system that allows objective comparison of quantitative and qualitative data on elite sport policies in different nations. This method is based on three essential features: (1) the development of a theoretical model of success determinants (or pillars) in elite sport with the identification of clear critical success factors that are used for international comparison (called SPLISS model); (2) the use of mixed methods research and the development of a scoring system to measure competitiveness of nations in elite sport for each dimension of the theoretical model and thus to move beyond the descriptive level of comparison, and (3) the involvement of the main stakeholders in elite sport – the athletes, coaches and performance directors – as the evaluators of policy processes in elite sport. This methodology is explained by comparing elite sport policies and systems in six nations: Belgium (separated into Flanders and Wallonia), Canada, Italy, the Netherlands, Norway and the UK.

Competitive sport in Ireland is largely played on a semi-professional or amateur basis, but there is a professional layer within rugby union and golf. The sports infrastructure in Ireland might be considered as less developed than that of other European Union (EU) countries, however, in recent years, facilities have been improved largely due to government and other funding. A key feature in this development is the role of national governing bodies (NGBs). Sports bodies are mainly trusts, and ownership is difficult to define, which complicates governance matters. Two other characteristics of NGBs, are emphasized by Ann Bourke in Chapter 6, are that while NGBs operate on a not-for-profit basis, many transactions are completed with for-profit entities, and NGBs need to make effective use of organizational resources (financial, physical and human). This chapter outlines a research agenda on identifying governance procedures and principles, the main changes that have occurred and key drivers of these changes. Insights are gathered by taking Ireland as an example and using secondary and primary data. The chapter reveals a shift towards a corporate approach to governance, largely due to the competitive dynamics between the NGBs but also resulting from Irish government policy on sport. Within sports there are more than 60 NGBs in Ireland, and based on a comparative multiple-case study approach, evidence exits of good governance practice. Some governance areas which need attention include the selection and recruitment of board (executive committee) members, the assignment of roles and the evaluation of performance.

The use of cases as a teaching strategy has a long history dating back to the 1920s. At that time, Harvard Business School adopted the use of case studies as a way to prepare students for management roles by using case examples as a way to learn theories and principles relevant to business. The use of cases as a strategy to develop a research topic is also found in Chapter 7 by Geoff Walters and Sean Hamil. The authors emphasize how a case study approach contributes to knowledge and demonstrates the relevance of a particular theory. The chapter begins by providing an understanding of theoretical issues underpinning case study research. It discusses how the case study strategy can be applied across competing epistemological positions before demonstrating that a variety of different data collection methods can form part of a case study strategy. The chapter also discusses reasons why the case study can be considered a relevant approach to sport management research. Following the theoretical discussion, this chapter uses the English football industry as an example. Through the use of interview data and documentary sources, Walters and Hamil present a descriptive case that provides a detailed background to the financial problems in the English football industry. This is followed by setting out the range of regulatory measures that have been introduced by the football authorities. The objective of this chapter is twofold. First, it illustrates when, why, and how the case study strategy can be a relevant approach for sport management research. Second, it discusses how a case study strategy can be applied across competing epistemological positions and how a case study can also draw on multiple data collection methods.

If governance is about influencing the fate of the game, then it is basically about intentions, initiatives, efforts, events and processes that impact on its well-being. The term 'governance', according to Hallgeir Gammelsæter and Benoit Senaux in Chapter 8, can be reserved for the intentional strategies, actions, structures and systems created by sports' mandated organizations, directors, leaders and managers – which is usually the case in sport management studies. More broadly, governance can also be seen as the outcome of processes that designated managers do not always fully understand or control, although, or perhaps because, they are deeply immersed in them, for instance institutional organization theory. The most defining characteristic of competitive sport is the need to balance cooperation and competition. While the focus of contestants is to win competitions, competition is premised on the ability of contestants to cooperate in organizing the competition and to make sure that it is sustainable, that is, keeping a critical mass population of more or less equal competitors. The main purpose of governance, then, is to ensure the popularity of the game, which, as long as a balance between competition and cooperation is maintained, can happen in many ways encompassing different views of what the game should be. In accepting these terms it follows that the issue of governance in sport particularly pertains to two levels: the organization and management of the competing unit (the club and national team), and the organization and management of the sport which aims at ensuring continuous cooperation and competition between competing units (the football authorities). Although these two levels are closely connected, in this chapter the authors focus on the latter. This chapter provides a review of the literature on the governance of football at the national and international level (not the club level). It identifies key features and outlines the deviation from the idealized archetype set-up of football as a members' game.

The case study approach in conducting research in sport management is emphasized and grounded in its epistemological and ontological dimensions in Chapter 9 by Eivind Å. Skille. He demonstrates the applicability of a case study approach by providing an example of a study of Norwegian sport policy-making and implementation through local sport clubs. The author first argues that case study research relies on phenomenological perspectives of individual perceptions and intentions of reality, and the researcher's ability to focus on the phenomenon. Second, he argues that case study research relies on the hermeneutical acknowledgement of earlier understanding, and the ability to both explain and understand through interpretation. The empirical example shows how these philosophical ideas are utilized in real-life research, for example through purposive sampling and closeness to the field of study. Finally, the approach presented and the utilization of it in the empirical example are discussed in relation to traditional concepts of construct validity, internal validity and external validity. The chapter conclusion is that the qualitative case study approach is particularly strong on internal validity. The strength of the approach when it comes to descriptions and explanations of phenomena of reality and society (and the lack of possibilities for creating controlled experiments of such phenomena), makes case study research specifically apt for research into sport management (for example, investigating sport policy and sport organization).

1.2 Thematic Cluster 'Media and Technology'

Information technology and media have over past decades had an enormous impact on the development of the relationship between sport and business. Media has become a major source of income for all kinds of sport events, and the proliferation of information technology has made it possible to serve the needs of sport fans all over the world. They can consume an event either in real time or recorded from virtually anywhere. As a result of this, the opportunities for the promotion of sport, and the benefits for sport and its partners, are significant (Dolles and Söderman, 2011).

In the first of three chapters in this cluster James Santomier and Patricia Hogan discuss 'Social media and prosumerism: implications for sport marketing research' (Chapter 10). Web 2.0 and social media are making it possible for millions of sport fans to become prosumers. Fans, along with athletes and sport organizations worldwide, can directly correspond and interact using social media. For example, fans are empowered to participate on sport-specific organization or team wikis, homepages, blogs, microblogs, pictures, podcasts, video sites, Twitter, Facebook, iTunes, and so on. In the near future it may be possible for fans to use tele-immersion technologies to insert themselves into sporting events on their high definition/three-dimension (HD/3D) televisions or mobile devices, and, given empathetic social media now being developed, to actually feel the atmosphere in sports events. We might argue social media is changing the way businesses, including sport businesses, communicate in the pursuit of brand building and commerce, and is compelling these businesses to create new and innovative ways to capitalize on the prosumer (co-creator of value) economy. Yet, despite the rapid development and integration of social media into the marketing strategies of many sport and sport-related brands worldwide, many organizations have neither developed an efficacious social media measurement strategy nor determined how well social media compares to other marketing initiatives relative to important metrics (return on investment and return on objectives) of sport business. As such, there is a need to rethink approaches and metrics related to sport marketing with social media as it is proposed in this chapter. Based on the current frontier of research in theory and practice in social media and marketing, suggestions by the authors are made for research ideas in this fecund area. Social media and the techniques and processes related to marketing using social media are changing at an incredible rate and will require continual monitoring for those involved in social media research. As such, Santomier and Hogan identified the need for sport marketing researchers who are abductive thinkers who can design and use innovative research methodologies as stimulated by the continually evolving technology. Research prospects related to social media and sport marketing, however, are vast for scholars and marketing professionals alike, and are replete with opportunities for using newer and newer technology and for designing new research methodologies.

Throughout the 1990s, the growth of pay-television (TV) channels raised concerns regarding the general public's ability to watch popular sport. European politicians were alarmed in 1996, when News Corporation almost bid the Olympic rights away from the European Broadcasting Union. As Chris Gratton and Harry Arne Solberg explain in Chapter 11 the politicians' fear increased when the International Federation of Association Football (FIFA) in the same year sold the 2002 and 2006 World Cup Soccer finals to the German Kirch corporation and the Swiss ISL marketing agency, and not to the European Broadcasting Union as in the past. As consequence of this, it was assumed that viewers in many nations would not be able to watch the entire tournament on free-to-air broadcasts anymore. This chapter focuses on direct regulations in sport broadcasting that control which channels are allowed to broadcast specific sport events. Examples of such regulations are the European Listed Events legislation and the Australian Anti-Siphoning List, which prevent pay-TV channels from broadcasting events that are of special value for society. The chapter specifically concentrates on the UK since in 2009 an independent review of the UK listed events legislation was carried out by a committee of experts appointed by the Minister for Culture, Media and Sport. One of the authors of this chapter was an invited member of this committee and was present at all the sessions where evidence was presented. This committee received evidence from broadcasters, national and international governing bodies of sport, and media experts over a four-month period. Qualitative and quantitative evidence on the views of the public was also collected by a major market research company. This chapter uses that recent evidence (or at least that part of it that is in the public domain) to examine the question of whether or not in the coming digital age of broadcasting it is still necessary for governments to intervene in broadcasting markets to ensure that major sports events are shown on channels available to the whole nation, or at least to a high percentage of it.

In recent years, many clubs, event organizers and sport governing bodies have earned substantial revenues from the sale of media rights. These revenues can be affected by many factors, where the strategy of rivalling buyers is one example elaborated by Harry Arne Solberg and Kjetil Kåre Haugen in Chapter 12. The major reason behind the strong inflation of sports rights has been the fierce competition between commercial broadcasters. However we have also seen incidents where the rights fees have declined instead of continuing to grow. This chapter analyses the sale of media sports rights by applying game theory. First the authors look at a situation where there are two television broadcasters operating at the demand side. Both are interested in buying the media rights from upcoming events in two different sports. The popularity of the sports varies, and this also reflects the values of the rights. At the supply side are the event organizers in the two sports mentioned. The sellers and the buyers can choose between two alternative strategies: playing tough and playing soft. An event organizer who adopts a tough strategy will demand a high price and be unwilling to reduce it. A television broadcaster who follows the same strategy will offer the seller a moderate price, and be unwilling to increase the offer. A soft strategy indicates the sellers/buyers initially will come up with more moderate offers and will be willing to reduce/increase these offers. In the second situation there is only one broadcaster operating at the demand side, while there is only one event organizer; in other words, a bilateral monopoly. The authors assume the broadcaster will compare its revenues from broadcasting the event with the revenues it can earn from other programmes. The event organizer will consider if sponsorship revenues are reduced if the event is not on television. Lastly, Solberg and Haugen also analyse to what degree the strategy of the event organizer will be affected in case television programmes from the event reduce gate receipts. Additionally, it can also help consumers (which in this case are television viewers) to understand when the sellers and/or buyers are bluffing as a part of the negotiations.

1.3   Thematic Cluster 'Place, Time and Spectators'

In the new millennium the arena has become a centre of urban living, incorporating spaces for all kind of leisure activities, stores, cafés, restaurants and offices, which ensued from a new way to manage the modern facility, regarded as a public area and open seven days a week. The new multi-purpose sporting venues also host shows, concerts, or even weddings, and the centre space is structured to accommodate multi-purpose use by different sports and other kinds of events. The sports competition, the show or concert itself is the centre of a 'package event' sold by event organizers: the pre-phase, break(s), and post-phase are occasions for a variety of attractions offered in the arena, intended to not only appeal to the single spectator or visitor but the whole family, to encourage the spectators/visitors to arrive earlier, leave later, and to consume more in merchandising shops or shopping areas and in bars or restaurants. Today's modern arenas and large-scale events, and the perception of spectators and residents about arenas and events constitute an important field in sport management research – a thematic cluster comprising five chapters in the handbook.

Impacts of sport events, as explained by Tommy D. Andersson in Chapter 13 may appear in many forms, and research in the area of impact assessments is at present developing wider perspectives rather than being limited to economic impact assessments. Concepts like social and cultural capital, environmental care, 'ecological footprint analysis' and 'triple bottom line' are now appropriate, and traditional cost–benefit analysis is regaining momentum. Another important dimension for an analytical framework to research the impact of sport events is the subject of analysis, that is, from whose perspective impacts are assessed. A stakeholder analysis reveals a large number of stakeholders affecting and being affected by a sport event. The event-makers, the industry as well as the community are all relevant spheres of stakeholders for an impact assessment. The overall ambition of this chapter is to demonstrate how impacts of sports events can be assessed from a broad social science perspective with a focus on sustainability. The major objectives are, first, to examine analytical frameworks related to sustainability of sport events, second to discuss analyses related to the triple bottom line framework, that is, economic, sociocultural and environmental impacts, and third, to review implications and challenges for future research. Although focus in this chapter will be on sport events, a triple bottom line perspective is applicable to a wide range of sports and business activities.

French professional football is considered the fifth biggest in Europe for its economics and sports performances, according to Boris Helleu and Michel Desbordes in Chapter 14. Even though brand new sports facilities are reputed to increase revenues and retain fan loyalty, French stadia are old and poorly run. Consequently, French football clubs have less attendance than their German or English counterparts. The business model remains, then, widely dependent on broadcasting rights. So, to be more successful economically and sportily, clubs have to consider their facilities as a new source of profit. That is why, the authors argue, France was bidding to host the final round of the UEFA Euro 2016 tournament and to take advantage of this opportunity to build or renovate stadiums. This chapter, bridging contributions of geography, marketing and economy, analyses the strategy of reform of French stadiums by focusing particularly on the process of political legitimization. Indeed, even if in the planning there is a will to favour private rather than public financing, the influence of central French government and regional bodies remains strong. A case study dedicated to the new Grand Stade of Lille in France concludes and illustrates this chapter.

In Chapter 15 Anne-line Balduck, Marc Maes and Marc Buelens examine the social impact of the arrival of the Tour de France in Ghent. More specifically, residents' perceptions towards the impact of the arrival of the Tour de France in Ghent (Belgium) are studied before and after the arrival of the cyclists. In contrast to the Olympic Games and the World Cup in football which take place every four years, the Tour de France is a major annual cycling event and the majority of the stages starts in one city and ends in another hosting city. A stage of the Tour de France, therefore, lasts only two days (finish during the afternoon, start during the morning of the following day). There is strong competition between cities and communities to host one stage of the Tour de France. The main reason why cities compete against each other to host such events is that it is expected this will generate benefits for the community. Most impact studies have focused on the economic outcomes of hosting major sport events; however, more recently, the social and cultural impacts have gained interest. This chapter contributes to the latter line in research by exploring the perceptions of residents living along or near to the cycling route towards the impact of the arrival of the Tour de France. A quantitative research technique was applied using questionnaires. A drop-out analysis was performed to reveal whether there was a selection bias between respondents who participated in the survey ahead and after the event and respondents who only participated in the pre-event survey. Overall, results revealed that residents' perceptions of impacts have changed over time.

Residents were also consulted in Chapter 16, by Alessandro 'Chito' Guala and Douglas Michele Turco, where the results of a longitudinal study of Torino residents are explained and presented to reflect the attitudes of the population towards the 2006 Winter Olympic Games. Four polls were conducted before the Games and two more polls followed after the Games. The questionnaire was divided into two main parts, with a conclusive appendix dedicated to socio demographic variables. The first part dealt with the Games, the bidding, the pride to have received the nomination, the expectations and the fears linked to the organizational problems, the concerns about the impact of the works for the Games on the everyday life of the population. The second part of the questionnaire was related to the future of Torino, its international image, its hopes and preparations for a new town devoted to culture and tourism. The authors discovered that public opinion changes, before, during and after the event, offering a wide sample of concerns and expectations; pride at the nomination, concerns during the works in preparation for the Games, happiness during the event and a more rational evaluation one year after the event. The 'four steps' evolution of the public opinion is discussed in the chapter, and is useful to predict the effects of the Games on local identity. Worth noting also are shifts in public perceptions corresponding with the identity change for Torino from the 'capital of the Fiat company' to an Olympic city now devoted to culture, sport and tourism.

There are a number of reasons why sport businesses conduct market research. Sport spectator market profiles, economic impact studies and sponsorship effectiveness research allow organizations to understand consumer behaviours, quantify sport benefits and determine the value of their operations. Field research in Chapter 17 is explained by Douglas Michele Turco as the most direct approach to gathering data from sport consumers, and is conducted where the action is – at the sport setting. Spectator market profiles, economic impact assessments and sponsorship effectiveness measures are but a few of the sport business studies completed using field research. In this concluding chapter to the cluster on 'Place, time and spectators' the aim is to provide an overview of common research procedures, research issues and proper ways to address them. An array of sampling techniques for sport field research is described. Five key steps to field survey research for sport businesses are highlighted: (1) developing the problem (defining and delimiting it); (2) formulating hypotheses or research questions; (3) research design; (4) data gathering, treatment and analysis; and (5) reporting. Several mini-cases in sport business research are interspersed throughout the chapter to demonstrate the application of key steps in the research process, on, for example, the Pocono 500 NASCAR race, the Cricket World Cup Super Eight matches in Guyana; the Bassmaster Elite 50 Series fishing tournament, the Little Leagues Baseball World Series and the cycling race, Tour de Georgia. The research procedures presented in this chapter are based on several theoretical approaches including input–output and cost–benefit analyses, transaction-cost analysis, balanced scorecard and diamond framework.

1.4   Thematic Cluster 'Club Management and Teams'

Why is European football of increasing importance to ongoing research in the nexus between sport and business? Because it is a huge and fast-growing business, operating worldwide – but still in need of more systemized knowledge. If this is a bold statement, it is backed by many arguments as argued earlier, for example by Söderman et al. (2010: 86):

> Football is highly popular (this in itself should generate interest in research); it has rabid fans (whose sociology is well researched); it involves high uncertainty (the outcome of a game is not always the same as winning a game); and it is an activity where ethnic, gender, social, and economic backgrounds are irrelevant to its practice (but still of great interest to spectators). The skilful team or the talented football player are visibly obvious; this is intuitively perceived by all spectators. The game has become famous because it is generally linked to our childhood, and its professional teams are on top of pyramid-like organisations of several leagues, with amateur players at all levels, from silver aged teams to kid's teams.

Football today has emerged to become an international business, as players are transferred frequently around the globe, international professional leagues are created and the European Cup finals or the FIFA World Cup finals are top media events. We might say the world of football has been referred to increasingly as an industry in its own right and with its own characteristics – which could be transferred to many other team sports as well – will be the focus of this thematic cluster and featured in four of the five chapters in this part.

Models of management are known to render decision making less complex and more certain when implemented properly and in a timely fashion by experienced managers, and have therefore been the topic of frequent discussion. Akin to other businesses, professional sport managers need to make complex decisions in a variety of areas. In Chapter 18 Norm O'Reilly explores how portfolio theory contributes to the management of professional sport clubs. Specifically, this chapter introduces an extensive case study on the largest sport entertainment organization in Canada, Maple Leaf Sports and Entertainment. The purpose of this chapter is to assess this professional sport conglomerate as a portfolio of assets. Based on six categories of organizational assets, the case study looks at the entire portfolio of assets of the conglomerate and assesses each based on the input of the senior management. At the end a management model for professional sport clubs is introduced, which considers the breadth of assets for such organizations, including players, management, contracts and facilities. It is argued by O'Reilly that team management personnel can use these risk assessments in order to optimize the team's performance, structure their team around the salary cap, and build a strong brand image or market individual players.

In addition to earning profits, professional sport clubs have to satisfy the needs of the audience, whether this is an individual member's idealistic orientation or more specific requirements by certain stakeholder groups, such as supporter associations or the local community. In Chapter 19 the analysis by Hans Jansson and Sten Söderman identifies and describes relevant marketing theories for sport clubs, which differ from those normally found for typical commercial organizations and firms. For non-profit organizations, it is a question of creating value for their members by living up to various expectations which aid the club in creating a legitimate image in the eyes of these stakeholders. The key issue is how to relate such profit and non-profit approaches to each other, that is, to solve the dilemma between being profitable and being legitimate. In this respect, marketing is not only of importance for sports clubs which offer experiences to various audiences, but also very complex. Major viewpoints on the relationship between the market, the organization and marketing are analysed in the chapter. From monopolistic competition to marketing practice the authors develop an overall relationship marketing theory for football clubs, which might also be relevant for other sports. There are four typical relationship designs for sport clubs: marketing management, customer-focused relationship marketing, network marketing and institutional network marketing. The logic of consequence and the logic of appropriateness are two important concepts assisting in the analysis concluding that all four designs are examples of logic of consequence and only the institutional network marketing is applicable as a logic of appropriateness.

The contribution by Harald Dolles and Sten Söderman in Chapter 20 is the systematic exploration of the business parameters in professional team sport, described as a network of value captures. Targeting a top performance on the football pitch, the handball field or the ice hockey rink is related to top management performance today. Driving forces are technology and the interplay between television and sponsors, as well as the increasing international impact. The proposed network of value captures supports the club management to analyse specific activities through which clubs in professional team sport can create value and competitive advantage. By identifying eight value offerings and six customer categories, up to 48 value capturing activities are identified in professional team sport, reflecting the complexity of this industry. Competitive combinations of these value captures are preceded by the management's strategy intent and strategies on different levels of aggregation. The chapter builds upon strategic management research on how to create and maintain competitive advantage as well as research in marketing on value and its co-creation. This chapter ends by providing conclusions for the management of professional team sport as well as ideas on how the network of value captures could be applied in further research.

Over the past decades, a large number of empirical studies on labour economics of the team sport industry have been published in leading economics journals. The evidence presented by Bernd Frick in Chapter 21 provides a critical literature review on the topic and demonstrates the potential of econometric analyses to answer two particularly important questions: first, is it possible to field a championship team by outspending competitors and, second, what are the factors that determine player salaries? The answers are not only of academic value, but have obvious managerial implications. Team owners and/or presidents wishing to maximize the sporting performance of their clubs are well advised to take the results into account when purchasing talent in the relevant labour market. The growing acceptance of sports economics research in the 'mainstream' of the discipline is certainly due to the high standards of both the theoretical contributions and the empirical papers. The combination of rigorous modelling and state-of-the-art econometrics is required to gain the recognition of the social science community. Presenting the findings in a way that is accessible to the public is another step that has yet to be taken. Moreover, a lot of research awaits to be done: individualistic sports (such as tennis, boxing, and track and field athletics) are interesting subjects to study, comparative analyses (across leagues and countries) are still scarce and the (economic) consequences of many rule changes (such as the recent 'de-regulation' of the labour market) still need to be analysed and documented. Advanced quantitative methods are used to analyse the very detailed and reliable longitudinal data that are available both at the club and the individual level. A particular study that uses longitudinal information on individual players in the German first professional league in football (the Bundesliga) is presented in the chapter.

Despite the fact that grounded theory is becoming a methodology with a growing appeal to mainstream business management research, it has somehow failed to penetrate the sport management field of study. Chapter 22 by Christos Anagnostopoulos addresses this issue by having three specific aims in mind. First, as an introduction to grounded theory methodology for sport management researchers, it hopes to encourage more grounded theory-based research projects. Second, the broader philosophical difficulties associated with the different variants of grounded theory have often brought early-career researchers up short; addressing these difficulties here should remove this potential stumbling block. The author attempts to address this shortfall. Third, by way of illustration, all these philosophical arguments are contextualized in the chapter, with reference to a project that looked at the ways managers in English football developed and implemented corporate social responsibility programmes. The discussion in the chapter is in dialogue with a consideration of the researcher's role when employing grounded theory.

1.5 Thematic Cluster 'Sport Branding and Sponsoring'

The area of marketing communications has experienced a quiet, yet significant transformation during the past three decades. Sponsorship has become a vital revenue source for sport organizations. It has also become a core marketing activity, often complementing advertising, of many companies and service providers (Söderman and Dolles, 2008). The sponsorship of sports, arts and charitable events today is a mainstream marketing activity no longer in need of extensive introduction or justification. There is, however, a recognized need to account for the progress made to date in the integration of sponsorship-linked marketing into management theory and research. Moreover, as emphasized by Cornwell (Chapter 24 in this volume) there is a need to open a discussion of realignment in our thinking regarding the role sponsorship and other indirect marketing communication currently play and will play in the future. Up to this point, sponsorship, product placement, advergaming and other new approaches have been considered as uniquely interesting areas at the intersection of advertising and entertainment. As argued in this thematic cluster on 'Sport branding and sponsorship' that holds four chapters, it is time to consider these trends holistically as a move towards a new era in communications, one that could be called 'indirect marketing'. However some risks and uncertainties needs to be considered and careful preparations are needed before strategic sport sponsorship investments are carried through (Söderman and Dolles, 2010).

Chapter 23 by Torsten Schlesinger examines the impact of fan identity with a sport team or club on consumers' attitudes towards the sponsor and consumers' purchase intentions. To evaluate this relationship, a cause-and-effect chain is developed by the author to show the triangular relationship between sport club, fan and sponsor. In the chapter, hypotheses derived from the model were proven empirically on the basis of two questionnaires among supporters and fans of two sport clubs in different top sport leagues and different form of sports (football and ice hockey). The empirical findings in both cases reveal that fan identity positively influences the attitude towards the club sponsor, but takes no direct effect on the purchase intention. In turn, the attitude towards the club sponsor correlates very strongly with the purchase intention. The results support the assumption that highly identified fans are more likely to exhibit several positive effects related to sponsorship. We might therefore conclude that sport fans are a highly attractive target group for marketers of sport clubs. However, as this study clarifies, this is only the case for products connected directly with the club and not whether these effects might also be found related to offers indirectly associated with the sports club.

Chapter 24 by T. Bettina Cornwell offers a summary of the development of sponsorship towards mainstream marketing communication. Arguments are made for the entrenchment of sponsorship in a new evolving indirect marketing mix, and the progress in understanding the art of management and the science of communication measurement is examined. There are many perspectives that can be taken on sponsorship. In this chapter the perspective of the firm or organization that might use sponsorship in a marketing and communications programme is considered. It concludes that advances in technology and changing lifestyles are also related to the growth of sponsor activities, such as product placement, viral marketing, buzz, ambient marketing and, even, guerrilla marketing. All these approaches stem from the need to be where the consumers are and the need to be embedded in experience, thus circumventing technologically enabled avoidance on the part of the consumer. Cornwell argues for a need to open a discussion of realignment in thinking regarding the role that sponsorship and other indirect marketing communications play and will play in the future. She concludes by introducing a research agenda in the field of sponsorship-linked marketing focusing on the following issues: sponsorship and reconstructive memory, leveraging and activation of sponsorship, sponsorship portfolios, sponsorship's role in market entry, sponsorship and social considerations, sponsorship policy as a company instrument, sponsorship termination and ambushing.

The handling of promotional marketing issues, the structure and organizational culture of organizations in sport are identified by Mark Dibben and Harald Dolles in Chapter 25 as critical success factors in perusing entrepreneurial driven activities in motorsports. Based on a case of how a charismatic entrepreneur prepared for and finally was able to break the world land speed record for motorcycle and sidecar combination, the authors explore a close-knit team identity and a clear goal that translated vision, communication, planning, feedback and learning. Ongoing evaluation of goal achievement was a significant aspect of organizational learning and thus strategy development which 'morphed' successfully from a marketing organization (to gain sponsorship) into a manufacturing organization (to build the record-breaking vehicle) and then an event management organization (to actually run the attempt), all to deliver a unique and ultimately tangible 'product' of a world land speed record. Those insights are gained by applying a participant observation method in research, which enabled otherwise unavailable access to the complexities, privations and core values of the people involved. The chapter concludes by arguing that participant observation allows otherwise unavailable access to the ephemeral and the personal, where the value that is inherent within sports scenarios resides. Dibben and Dolles suggest a number of other related topics, notably sports volunteerism, that would benefit from studies utilising the method. This chapter furthermore aims to introduce the participant observation technique as a method taken from ethnography into the field of research on sports management. The vast majority of sport management research uses questionnaires and interviews or relies on secondary data. A careful observation of ongoing behaviour by the researcher is often ignored, in most cases due to the lack of access. It is emphasized that what an observer will see shall be conditioned by her or his personal knowledge, and will depend largely on his or her particular position in a network of not purely academic relationships.

The measurement of brand equities has a tradition of several decades and became one of the hottest topics in business administration literature during the last years according to Tim Ströbel and Herbert Woratschek in Chapter 26. Besides price determination in the case of mergers and acquisitions, the measurement of brand equity is, for example, essential in the context of international accounting standards. This becomes also relevant in sport business as more and more football clubs are changing their legal form to corporate entities looking for investors. Brand equity is a decisive figure for these potential investors, like sponsors, that still represent one of the most important income sources in sport business. Another field of interest for the measurement of brand equity derived from the so-called trademark piracy, since it must be possible to define the financial damage to a sport brand, for example. Recent studies about the brand equity of football clubs revealed very diverse results. According to this great variety of brand equities and the consequent uncertainty of the measurement techniques and its results, a critical analysis of the existing brand equity models is necessary. Therefore this chapter presents a categorization of brand equity models. Each category is discussed by the underlying theoretical background, to give a basic understanding, and introduces representative models of each category. The authors provide some specific implications for the use of brand equity models in professional sport.

1.6 Concluding Cluster 'Reflection'

Major changes have taken place in sport in recent years, which have led to the emergence and development of an associated sport management literature. A literature review is provided by Simon Chadwick in Chapter 27 exploring the multitude of opportunities existing today for academics and practitioners to address the most pertinent issues facing sport management. This chapter summarizes the following fundamental elements of sport that mark it out as being different from other products or industrial sectors: the uncertainty of outcome; competitive balance; contest management; collaboration and competition, and performance measurement. It also considers the management issues pertaining to the models of sport employed in, for example, the USA and Europe. Following on from this, the internationalization and globalization of sport, linked to developments in new media technology, are examined. The history of sport is arguably richer than any other form of human activity. Sport has variously developed across the world as a ceremony, a celebration, a physical pursuit, a leisure activity and now, increasingly, a business. In the world of contemporary sport it is claimed by the author that, at its elite end at least, sport's management is complex because the product it delivers to participants and fans is so idiosyncratic. This claim is accompanied by the view that while professional sport is, in large part, just another form of business, it has a range of special features that demand a customized set of practices to ensure its effective operation.

The perspective that while professional sport is in large part just another form of business, it has a range of special features that demand a customized set of practices to ensure its effective operation is re-examined in Chapter 28 by Aaron C.T. Smith and Bob Stewart. It initially proposes that while both business and sport are concerned with widening market share, building profits and strengthening brands, the presumption that sport has a monopoly over the delivery of intense emotional experiences, tribal belonging and strong interpersonal relationships is difficult to defend. The chapter concludes that while sport's economic and social progress has created an industry that is built around complex bureaucracies that turn over many thousands of millions of dollars every year, it has also created a more diverse and heterogeneous system of structures and experiences that are difficult to conflate to a handful of neat special features. The management of sport has traditionally been divided between two contrasting philosophical approaches. At one extreme, sport is viewed as a unique cultural institution with a host of special features wherein the reflexive application of standard business practices not only produces poor management decision-making, but also erodes its rich history, emotional connections, tribal links and social relevance. At the other extreme, sport is seen to be nothing more than just another generic business enterprise subject to the usual government regulations, market pressures and customer demands, and is best managed by the application of standard business tools that assist the planning, finance, human resource management and marketing functions. Over time these divisions have been blurred because of sport's corporatization, and through the emergence of sport management as an academic discipline. Sport is additionally complicated by the fact that it exists in both commercial and not-for-profit forms like other cultural services, such as theatre, art, music, health care and education. On the other hand, it is also distinctive in the sense that despite its growing commercialization and corporatization, it ostensibly possesses many special features thus challenging research in the field.

Chapter 29 by Harald Dolles and Sten Söderman concludes this section and the handbook. It, provides a research agenda in sport management research based on own research and the insights by the various authors contributing to this handbook.

2   RETHINKING THE CHOICE OF THEORIES AND METHODOLOGY IN SPORT MANAGEMENT RESEARCH

We choose to organize the handbook in thematic clusters in an effort to go beyond the 'qualitative versus quantitative' debate that takes place (not only) in sport management research, and take the approach that particular research methods needs to be chosen to suit a specific research problem. It is the research topic and the question by the researcher 'what should be achieved by conducting this research?' that leads to the choice of the theoretical approach and a suitable research method. There is no fixed preference or pre-defined evaluation of what is a 'good' or at least 'appropriate' and a 'bad' or 'inappropriate' theory and research method. No theoretical reasoning and no research method, qualitative or quantitative, is intrinsically better than the other, and in some cases we might end up in a struggle to choose between different theoretical approaches, multiple or competing methods, or might apply mixed methods to suit our research needs. As research problems are not neutral, the choice of theory and the research design depends on the problem and what the researcher wants to find out.

How a research problem is framed – and there are many examples to be found in the handbook – however, will inevitably reflect a commitment to a particular point of view as to how science is perceived, executed and evaluated. Two main approaches to theory-building that are not mutually exclusive need to be mentioned in this regard (see also Chapter 20 by Dolles and Söderman on value captures in football club management, in this volume, for further discussion).

The *model-based approach* to theory-building abstracts the complexity of the research topic to isolate a few key variables based on certain selection criteria of the researcher whose interactions are examined in depth in research. This implies the creation of a wide range of situation-specific scenarios or, in other terms, several mathematical models of limited complexity. The normative significance of each model depends on the fit between its assumptions and reality. Game theoretic models of competitive interaction seeking to understand the consequences of patters of choices over a variety of strategic variables (for example, as applied by Solberg and Haugen, in this volume) or the applications of various economic concepts to sporting activities (for an overview see *Handbook on the Economics of Sport* by Andreff and Szymanski, 2006) might serve as examples for this approach.

Porter (1991: 97) argues on the limits of this approach 'no one model embodies or even approaches embodying all the variables of interest, and hence the applicability of any model's findings is almost inevitably restricted to a small subgroup of firms or industries whose characteristics fit the model's assumptions'. It might be summarized, that this 'classical view' (Kjellén and Söderman, 1980) of theory-building and research is characterized by principles derived from the natural sciences and based on the language of mathematics. The emphasis on understanding the world using mathematical tools has often been used to argue against other approaches. Godfrey-Smith (2003) claims this has been done because people have thought that mathematics shows us that there must be another route to knowledge beside experience; experience might be *a* source of knowledge, but not the *only* important source. What makes science special is its attempt to quantify phenomena and detect mathematical patterns in the flow of events. And science is especially successful because it is organized, systematic and especially responsive to experiences – on the one hand, learning from experiments and, on the other, learning from practical life.

Based on a mere holistic understanding of contextual factors in which a research topic is embedded, the *framework-based approach* to theory-building is constructed as an alternative. A framework-based approach seeks to capture much of the complexity and it encompasses many variables. Michael E. Porters framework of the five competitive forces, the value-chain perspective of the firm or the diamond framework exploring the competitive advantage of nations are prominent examples of this approach. Porter (1991: 98) argues in favour: 'frameworks identify the relevant variables and the questions which the user must answer in order to develop conclusions tailored to a particular industry and company. In this sense they can be seen as almost expert systems'. However, it needs to be mentioned that all relations among the variables incorporated in a framework cannot be rigorously drawn or calculated. A framework-based approach, on the contrary, does not even intend to do so; rather it seeks to help both the practitioner and the researcher to better analyse the problem by understanding the main actors and forces in a general research setting.

This principle is further explained by Godfrey-Smith (2003: 8) as 'scientific thinking and investigation have the same basic pattern as everyday thinking and investigation. In each case, the only source of real knowledge about the world is experience'. But already Kant (1787) has argued that all our thinking involves a subtle interaction between experience and pre-existing mental structures that we use to make sense of experiences. Not everything can be derived solely from experience, because a person must already have key concepts in mind, like time, space or causation, in order to use experiences to learn about the world. When taking the framework-based approach to theory-building the researcher must therefore avoid overly simple pictures of how experience affects belief. The mind does not passively receive the imprint of facts. The active and creative role of the mind must be recognized. Gummesson (2003) argues, when we are dealing with complex research questions, we have to act ad hoc, both manually and intellectually, even if bits and pieces within a research project can be standardized. 'We have endless options, none offering a self-evident choice. They all require judgment calls and the major source to excellence is our own experience, wisdom and inventiveness' (ibid.: 483).

As a matter of consequence we need to be aware that, when taken, the framework-based approach might be considered trivial, as knowledge is based on experience, but that tells nothing about what makes science different from other human thought. We also need to admit that the framework-based approach to the equilibrium concept is not precise. The development of frameworks embodies the notion of optimization, but not equilibrium in the normal sense of the word. Instead, and emphasized by Porter (1991) earlier, there is a continually evolving environment in which a perpetual competitive interaction between competitors takes place.

A constructive tension with each other could be stipulated between both approaches. The model-based approach is particularly valuable in ensuring logical consistency and exploring the subtle interactions involving a limited number of variables. Porter (ibid.: 98) writes:

> Models should challenge the variables included in frameworks and assertions about their link to outcomes. Frameworks, in turn, should challenge models by highlighting omitted variables, the diversity of competitive situations, the range of actual strategy choices, and the extent to which important parameters are not fixed but continually in flux.

In the rather confusing landscape that confronts PhD students and novice researchers intending to employ a consistent epistemology in research, it might be added that the model-based approach to theory-building is commonly related to deductive reasoning, whereas the framework-based approach corresponds with inductive logical argumentation. In addition to both common approaches, 'abductive reasoning' or 'systematic combining' (Dubois and Gadde, 2002) gained attention as a combining third way to generate explanations.

The abductive approach corresponds to the intertwined nature of different activities in the research process and applies to research settings in which, seemingly parallel to data collection and guided by the empirical findings, the search for complementary theories continues. In real life a standardized conceptualization of the research process as consisting of a number of planned subsequent 'phases' might be difficult to execute. On the contrary, the researcher might constantly move 'back and forth' from one type of research activity to another and between empirical observations and theory aiming to expand his or her understanding of both, theory and the empirical setting. This continuous movement between the empirical world and theory might be the main characteristic of this approach, as emphasized by Dubois and Gadde (2002). During this process the research issues and the analytical framework are successively reoriented when they are confronted with the empirical world. Thus theoretical framework, empirical fieldwork and analysis evolve simultaneously in the research process.

> This stems from the fact that theory cannot be understood without empirical observation and vice versa. The evolving framework directs the search for empirical data. Empirical observations might result in identification of unanticipated yet related issues that may be further explored in interviews or by other means of data collection. This might bring about a further need to redirect the current theoretical framework through expansion or change of the theoretical model. (Dubois and Gadde, 2002: 555)

We might conclude that abductive reasoning involves merging models or creating new frameworks to creatively develop new options for solving problems of the industry, addressing issues or creating opportunity especially in a fast-developing field of research like sport and business. An abductive approach is applied, for example, in the chapters by Santomier and Hogan, and Jansson and Söderman – both in this volume – and implicitly used in all chapters in the final cluster on 'reflection'.

One of the key assumptions of the 'classical way' and of methods based on natural sciences is that the researcher should be objective, aiming to maintain a complete independence from the object of study by applying 'objective' criteria and methods. Among others, the chapters by De Bosscher, Truyens, van Bottenburg and Shibli or by Schlesinger – both in this volume – might serve as examples. Obviously such claims of the researcher's independence are much harder to sustain in research on sports, as we all have our own sporting experiences, interests and knowledge. Hence it is not surprising that a wide range of research methodologies exist in which the researcher are part of the research process itself. Such constructionist research designs seeks understanding through description of the continually changing social phenomena by applying research methods such as interviews, case discussions or direct observation. The objective is to gain rich descriptions of the subject of study by being as faithful as possible to the meanings attributed to the experience by the participants. The role of the researcher in this process is twofold: on the one hand, to assist the participants in the research to explore their experience and, on the other, without imposing his or her own biases and interpretations of the data, to seek to identify core themes and essences within the data gathered. This requires a sufficient degree of self-awareness of the researcher to be able to 'bracket out' those biases and preconceptions which might have caused his or her interests in conducting this research or redirecting the research process. Most of the chapters in this handbook might be summarized within this approach, and its benefits and shortcomings are especially discussed in the chapters by Anagnostopoulos, Dibben and Dolles, and Skille in this handbook.

The following questions (extensively amended from Punch (2005)) might be used in the beginning by the novice researcher to structure the decision-making process between frameworks and models, different theories and research methods:

1. What exactly do I want to find out?
2. What kind of focus on my topic do I aim at? Do I want to study this topic in detail or am I mainly interested in making standardized and systematic comparisons concerning this topic?
3. How have other researchers dealt with this topic? What limitations did other researchers face by applying particular theories or methods? To what extend is it necessary to align my research project with this literature?
4. Will certain theories help me to structure the research object? Consider the benefits/shortcomings when applying a model-based or a framework-based approach to theory development in research.
5. Will we learn more about the topic using qualitative, quantitative or mixed methods? What will be the knowledge pay-off of each method? Are certain theories aligned with specific research methods?
6. Will a deductive, inductive or abductive approach suit the generation of new knowledge on the research object? How can I ensure reliability (how far each research instrument can be relied upon to produce the same score for each occasion that it is used) and validitiy (will the same patterns observed in the data also hold true in other contexts and settings) in the research project?

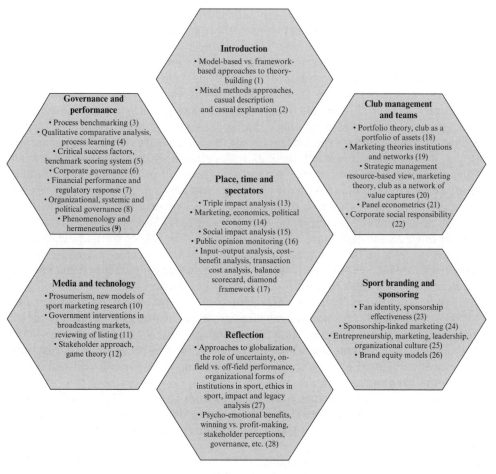

Note: The numbers in brackets indicate the chapter numbers.

Figure 1.2   Selection of the theories addressed in the handbook

7. What practical considerations are affecting my choice? For example, how long is my time budget to finalize the study? Do I have the resources to study it that way? Might I get access to the single case I would like to study in depth? Are databases readily available and affordable for being used in the proposed research?
8. What will work best for me? Do I feel comfortable with a particular method of data collection, such as developing a questionnaire or conducting interviews via telephone or face to face? Do I favour certain methods for data evaluation, for example statistical calculations versus qualitative content analysis?

This handbook aims to reflect the range of theories (see Figure 1.2) and research methodologies (see Figure 1.3) to be applied to research in the field between business and sports. It is obvious that the selection in the handbook just provides some insights and might be considered as an 'appetizer' to conduct research in certain areas, and

Note: The numbers in brackets indicate the chapter numbers.

Figure 1.3   Selection of research methods addressed in the handbook

there might be other research methods and theories also available to be considered in the research on sport and business. The authors provide as much information on their approach as possible, and considered, in close cooperation with the editors when designing their chapter, for example: level of aggregation (individual level, team or group level, club or corporate actors level, national level, international or global level); theoretical framework or theory applied (such as input–output analysis, cost–benefit analysis, resource-based view, transaction-cost analysis, dynamic capabilities, network view and diamond framework); sampling technique applied (such as qualitative research and quantitative research); sample size (such as single case study, multiple case study and large-size sample), and originality and value of your contribution (method used and findings). The central approaches used in the chapters in the handbook can be clustered in a way to provide the reader/user quick access (see Figures 1.2 and 1.3). A brief overview on various research methods applied in the handbook is provided in the following.

2.1   Research Methods Applied in the 'Introduction Cluster'

Andy Rudd and R. Burke Johnson point out that a popular objective in sport management research is to gain an *understanding of cause and effect*. When these causal studies are conducted they are almost always done with quantitative approaches based on a single method. Specifically, it is argued in the chapter that many sport management researchers seeking causal relationships may fail to recognize an important distinction between causal description and causal explanation. Causal description and causal explanation are both important for testing and unpacking causal relationships. Only a small percentage of empirical studies in sport management currently are adopting mixed methods approaches. Experiments should be designed to explain the consequences of interventions and not just to describe them. Causal description identifies an overall, molar causal relationship between an independent and dependent variable; however, such relationships tell the researcher little about the underlying causal mechanisms responsible for the causal relationship. Causal explanation is therefore an important route to the generalization of causal descriptions because it tells the researcher which features of the causal relationship are essential to transfer to other situations. This benefit of causal explanation helps to elucidate its priority and prestige in all sciences and helps explain why, once a novel and important causal relationship is discovered, the bulk of basic scientific effort turns towards explaining why and how it happens.

2.2   Research Methods and Selected Theories Applied in the Thematic Cluster 'Governance and Performance'

The challenges in using benchmarking as a method for learning about the processes that may improve the management and delivery of certain sport systems are emphasized by Leigh Robinson and Nikolai Böhlke. Managers should understand process benchmarking as a method for innovation, idea generation and general inspiration based on the descriptive benchmarks that emerge from the research exercise. It appears crucial to employ an extensive and flexible data collection strategy, to carry out a careful and intensive data analysis, as well as a sensitive and critical evaluation of the observed best practices and their transferability, in order to bring a benchmarking exercise to a successful conclusion.

A *mixed method research design* summarized as *qualitative comparative analysis* (QCA) is introduced by Mathieu Winand and Thierry Zintz, and refers to the research subject with all its richness and specificity. QCA furthermore relies on the rigorous and transparent selection of conditions made by the researcher and supported by theoretical arguments. Reliability is considered according to the theoretical validation of QCA (that is, ratio between variables and number of cases, absence of contradictory configuration showing the coherence of the data and absence of contradictory simplifying assumption when using logical remainder(s)) and the proper interpretation of the solution (that is, confronting the solution with the narratives of cases and, when possible, with individuals' own interpretation). The researcher is therefore able to refer back to the complexity of the case analysed and its narratives. There are methodological limitations to consider when taking this approach: the time dimension is not integrated by the QCA, researchers therefore need to re-examine cases in a qualitative way. The dichotomous calibration of the measures, however, should not be seen as a limitation.

Based on *critical success factors* and standards, a *benchmarking scoring system* called SPLISS is developed by Veerle De Bosscher, Jasper Truyens, Marten van Bottenburg and Simon Shibli, enabling the researcher to deliver an objective comparison of nations and policies. This can be regarded as a potentially useful means of helping policy-makers and institutions to assess the performance of their sport system in comparable terms and to undertake appropriate remedial strategies. To date, however, in economic studies as well as in this chapter, there has been limited critical interrogation of how valid and useful these measurements are with respect to their ability to provide insights into what drives competitiveness and to generate robust predictions of future performance. While objective scores can be calculated in the elite sport climate survey, the definition of standards in the overall sport questionnaire is somewhat arbitrary because of the absence of clear standards to rate objectively an elite sport system. The survey is based on comparative country data (where more is often better) and on the opinions of experts. The small sample of nations does not allow statistical techniques similar to the economic studies to identify the standards for comparison and weights, for example the deviation between the four highest and lowest ranked nations (min-max method), quartiles, normalizations or other transformations. Therefore, the method needs to be further explored in terms of its construct validity. In contrast to existing sport studies, the unique feature of this study is that it assesses processes by means of an elite sport climate survey (both objective and subjective data) with the main stakeholders in elite sport and that these responses are included in the scoring system.

A *comparative case analysis* is applied by Ann Bourke as it forces the researcher to try to remain detached and throws up plenty of surprises on which to reflect. The resistance to making certain information available (confidentiality is always respected) was a surprise, but the author then tried other sources. The interviews 'degenerated' into conversations, at first the author was unhappy, but soon realized that to get insights on values, culture, processes, relationship management, power and hierarchy, a two-way discussion is more valuable (while difficult to write up). Following her 'conversations' (interviews) contact was made with a number of other informants to seek clarification and confirmation on certain matters. But the interviewees in the field of sports seem to be very passionate about their sport (not always the representing institution) which complicates data interpretation. There are more procedural issues which need attention in a comparative case analysis, that is, the use of external/independent sources to comment critically on or monitor key processes, web page management and resource availability.

To illustrate when, why, and how the *case study strategy* can be a relevant approach for sport management research is pointed out by Geoff Walters and Sean Hamil. The reason for undertaking a case study is not only to get insights into an individual sport's organization, a group of sports' organizations or a particular sport industry, but also to gain an in-depth contextual understanding of the research subject. The case study in the chapter builds on interviews and documentary sources of evidence, therefore it is hoped that the triangulation of multiple data sources reduces the potential for misinterpretation. It also demonstrates the flexibility of the case study strategy in that multiple methods can be used. However, the inability to gain access to the relevant people/organizations can be a potential weakness of the case study strategy. This case study is largely descriptive, rather than explanatory or exploratory in regards to theory building, and is used to provide a deeper understanding of a particular industry addressing a specific issue of regulation, thus introducing the field for further research.

A *critical literature review* is provided by Hallgeir Gammelsæter and Benoit Senaux on football governance at national and international level (not at club level). The review is primarily based on empirical and conceptual studies in the field. It maps and coarsely classifies research areas, research questions and findings, by identifying key forms of governance and relate them to transnational and national levels of the organization of football. The review is focused on studies appearing roughly during the past decade, arguing on the development in football in the last era, and most of the academic material on the topic published in English, that also dates back to the last decade. The authors, however, admit, there are historical, sociological, and economic studies appearing before this time that have a bearing on governance, organization, and management issues. Whereas the authors hope their synopsis does right to the research that has been done in the field, their synopsis does not fully testify that research on this issue still has big leaps to take. To the extent that football governance constitutes a research field in its own right, it is fragmented and comprises as yet few studies which target football from a governance perspective. However, while many of the studies reviewed here suffer from not being situated in an explicit governance context, this does not mean that they are flawed. Rather it reflects that many of them happen to fill a vacuum by providing descriptions and analyses that are relevant for conceptualizing how football changes. It also reflects a lack of engagement in studying football in more typical governance disciplines such as management and organization studies. Therefore the contribution to the understanding of governance often comes from disciplines that are dedicated to pursue other research questions than governance, such as ethnography, sociology, history and, in part, marketing.

How a *case study research* might positively respond to the challenges of validity – construct, internal and external – is explained by Eivind Å. Skille. *Construct validity* asks whether the instruments are accurate measures of reality; internal validity asks whether research design is capable of eliminating bias and the effect of extraneous variables, and external validity requires definition of the domains to which the results of the study may be generalized. Construct validity, or measurement validity, is about how the terms used describe the reality in which we are conducting research. *Internal validity*, or credibility, may have slightly different meanings in qualitative research (about interpreting statements meanings and presenting different perspectives) compared with quantitative research (about causality), but overall it is about how to describe, explain and understand the object of study. *External validity*, or transferability, is about how the findings could be generalized to populations outside the sample from which the data is taken. This is particularly important in relation to case study research, because the logic of transferability differs from a classical notion of generalization. First, one might argue case study research is more about particularity and contextualization than about generalization. Second, case study research adheres to analytical generalization (and not statistical generalization, such as in quantitative studies). In that respect, prejudice comes into play again, in terms of the theoretical approach applied. Theory must be tested by replicating the findings from one case on other cases. Thus, one method of increasing external validity in case study-based research is to conduct a multiple case study. In that respect, the sampling procedure – or, more precisely, the specific cases chosen – also increases external validity; the ideal types together probably represent a significant proportion of the total population of the research subject. Construct and internal validity are highly reduced in qualitative research in general, for two inter-related reasons. First, there is little reason to disbelieve the informants' expressions of their understanding of their own environment or institution. Second, the constructs applied relate as much to the researcher's approach to the analysis through a conscious use of prejudice.

2.3 Research Methods and Selected Theories Applied in the Thematic Cluster 'Media and Technology'

The explorative chapter by James Santomier and Patricia Hogan discusses three basic types of *research questions (descriptive, correlational and causal)* that can be applied (usually in combination) to research in social media sport marketing:

1. Descriptive: when a study is designed primarily to describe what is going on or what exists. For example, 'How are sport enterprises using social media in their marketing efforts?'
2. Correlational: when a study is designed to look at the relationships between two or more variables. For example, 'What is the relationship between the level of social media used in a marketing campaign and team (or athlete) brand awareness or brand recognition?'
3. Causal: when a study is designed to determine whether one or more variables (for example, a social media campaign) causes or affects one or more outcome variables (such as ticket sales). For example, 'What is the effect of a new pre-season social media campaign on the number of season tickets sold?'

According to the authors the basic research process may still be able to function as the fundamental framework for any research study related to social media and sport marketing, whether from the perspective of a scholar or a marketing professional. It is obvious, however, that the fast-paced, constantly changing, networked, integrated and relentlessly competitive (but simultaneously cooperative) business environment of today, in which the business of sport has to act, has changed and appears to demand a change in thinking in order to more successfully navigate through the current milieu in order to collect data, address problems and capitalize on opportunities. It is contended that *deductive and/or inductive thinking* are necessary but not sufficient for this rapidly chang-ing world, and suggests the addition of *abductive conceptualization* – integrative or design thinking that builds its own way of understanding what is going on and then goes on to develop ways to address the research problem. As argued by the authors, the 'webifying' of the world ushers in the need for changes in the way that research is conducted and asks for innovative ideas to collect data using interactive media and for sparking new ideas for 'what might be'.

Since the early 1990s the price of sports broadcasting rights for major sports events has increased tremendously. In 1984, whether an event was on the government's list of public service or not made little difference to the income of the governing body.

Now, for many governing bodies the majority of their income comes from the sale of broadcasting rights, and therefore the listing has become an important factor. By means of a *case study approach* Chris Gratton and Harry Arne Solberg explain what the listed events regulation looks like across countries. The case study provides detailed insights into how the UK list was generated and reviewed, thus explaining the methological steps applied in the process. In the UK, the main criterion for listing in the review in 1998 was that the event had a special national resonance, not just a significance to those who ordinarily follow the sport concerned; an event which serves to unite the nation, a shared point on the national calendar. For a sporting event, both the following categories were also considered: it is a pre-eminent national or international event in the sport; and/or it involves the national team or national representatives in the sport concerned. The terms of reference for the Independent Advisory Panel's Role for the UK review in 2009 are explained in the chapter: (1) the principle of listing; (2) the criteria against which events were currently, or might in the future be listed, and (3) the events which make up the current list, and those which should do so in the future. The authors explain in detail the methodology applied by the Independent Advisory Panel to reach a recommendation, for example, launching a formal consultation, seeking information, reviewing other listing regimes and conducting focus group discussion.

The objectives of the *stakeholders* involved in sport and sporting activities have been thoroughly discussed in the sports economic literature. As for team sports, there has been a consensus that North American teams behave like profit maximizers, whereas in Europe and other continents, some kind of utility maximization seems to be the objective. In recent years, many clubs, event organizers and sport governing bodies have earned substantial revenues from the sale of media rights. These revenues can be affected by many factors, where the strategy of rivalling buyers is one example. By analysing this topic, Harry Arne Solberg and Kjetil Kåre Haugen argue that *game theory* has grown into a mature scientific toolbox to explore such situations. Central to game theory are concepts like players, preferences, pay-offs, strategies and information. Through careful definition of such concepts, best reply functions or correspondences can be derived as optimizing behaviour for each player as functions of all other players' possible strategies. The central solution concept, 'Nash equilibrium', can then be defined as 'intersecting points' on such best replies. Game theory can help both the sellers and buyers to get an insight into the processes affecting the terms of trade. It can improve the ability to foresee the strategies of rivals, and also the consequences of these strategies. As for the case investigated, it can help the owners of sports rights to better analyse the alternative strategies of the television channel(s), as well as their consequences, and vice versa. Additionally, it can also help consumers (which in this case are television viewers) to understand when the sellers and/or buyers are bluffing as a part of the negotiations. For example signalling to 'the outside world' that there is a risk of not being broadcast can be used as instruments during the sales processes. Television broadcasters may hope it will put pressure on the seller to lower the price, and vice versa. Non-commercial and semi-commercial public service broadcasters may use the uncertainty whether the sports events will be broadcast or not, to persuade politicians to give them more favourable conditions, for example more funding. Indeed, such strategies have been observed on several occasions in Europe over the past decade.

2.4 Research Methods and Selected Theories Applied in the Thematic Cluster 'Place, Time and Spectators'

The purpose of the chapter by Tommy Andersson is to discuss how impacts of sports events can be assessed from a wide social science perspective with a focus on sustainability. Sport events have impacts on individuals, social life and society at large in many different ways. Tangible impacts such as improvement of local infrastructure, urban regeneration or 'architectural pollution' are common for sport mega-events. But intangible effects may be at least as important. Sport events are manifestations and often celebrations of sports values such as competitiveness, fairness and loyalty. Such values are important for the social fabric and have an impact on social life not only in the short run, but also on the accumulated social capital of the community. The author introduces the *triple bottom line approach*, that is, a framework to analyse the economic, sociocultural and environmental impacts of events. The triple bottom line framework may owe part of its success to the magic number three and to the fact that three perspectives provide an acceptable complexity. It covers a great deal of perspectives on event impact analysis but does not provide a complete coverage, which is important to keep in mind when the scope of a triple bottom line approach is discussed. A *cost–benefit analysis* is all inclusive, but only implicitly so. A cost–benefit analysis should include all aspects and 'externalities' that are affected by the sport event, but for practical reasons all cost–benefit studies are limited and, unfortunately, in different ways. Thus cost–benefit analyses, although in theory more inclusive, lack the clarity of presentation that a triple bottom line approach has. The scope of a cost–benefit analysis is also related to the time horizon. An analysis of the complete life cycle of a sport event is desirable in order to describe not only cash flows over the life cycle, but also how other tangible as well as intangible impacts are distributed over time. Another issue related to scope is to what extent an impact assessment should describe not only direct but also indirect effects. This is explicitly discussed in economic assessments and, if calculated, there are theoretically well-developed methods to do so. *Socio-cultural* impacts, if measured by instruments using attitude scales, can be considered as direct impacts. The next question may be how these attitudes affect local residents' peace of mind and happiness, which may later on also influence local residents' desire to continue living in the area and so on. Although these chains of sociocultural impacts should be relevant for an impact assessment, it may be too difficult theoretically to describe with any certainty these chains of impacts. It is, however, worth pointing out this difference in scope between an economic and a sociocultural impact assessment.

A detailed analysis of the status of French football stadia is provided by Boris Helleu and Michel Desbordes. The aim of this contribution is to describe how a country negotiates its transition to stadia designed as true recreational spaces and profit centres. The marketing, economic, and political issues in refurbishing old stadia and building new stadia are identified and evaluated by using both second-hand quantitative data, and qualitative data obtained via discussions with experts. An *inventory map* of French league 1 and league 2 stadia is developed and explains, together with a *case study* on the Grand Stade Lille Métropole project to build a new stadium in Lille, the needs and the discourse that legitimizes the public support for new stadia in France. In order to strengthen the legitimacy of public assistance, the authors refer to studies of the *impact on the economics* of football clubs, and the additional income for the clubs as well as the fiscal and social revenues for the State, which could be produced by the refurbishing of French stadia.

A *social impact analysis* is provided by Anne-line Balduck, Marc Maes and Marc Buelen by exploring residents' perceptions of the impact of the arrival of the Tour de France in Ghent before and after the arrival of the event. As the city of Ghent hosted a stage of the Tour de France for the first time, researchers were aware of a possible novelty effect. Besides the strengths of the study, a number of limitations or concerns might be considered for further research in the field. First, although the sample strategy has a number of strengths (for example, demographic profile, survey ahead and after the event, drop-out analysis), the nature of the sample limits generalization of the findings. Since only residents of Ghent who lived in the selected survey area were allowed to participate, the findings could not be generalized to all residents of Ghent. Second, since only a quantitative approach was used, it was not possible to obtain a richer and in-depth data-set that could be obtained by using a mixed method approach by adding qualitative interviews. A qualitative approach might reveal other perceived benefits and costs that were not taken up in this survey. Researchers have stated that the social value of major sport events should earn more attention. Sport events are more than only entertainments, they are social events that allow for adding a social value to the event. Other researchers support this, arguing that social impacts are a core source of potential significance or a core source of potential troubles. The social impact of sport events should not be left to coincidence and should be managed. In this study, half of the residents indicated that the Tour de France was like a social event to them. The importance of the cultural interest and consolidation factor also indicated that the social aspect of hosting the Tour de France was the surplus value for residents, as they did not perceive any economic benefits.

In a *longitudinal study on residents perception* of mega-sporting events, Torino residents were asked by Alessandro 'Chito' Guala and Douglas Michele Turco between 2003 and 2007 to evaluate the overall experience of hosting the Olympic Winter Games. It included a series of studies that were conducted in the two primary areas that hosted the event in 2006: Torino and the Alp Valleys. The monitoring of public opinion involved information, recommendations and expectations which were acquired from the population by means of different techniques for collecting survey information from residents. They are implemented through interviews or questionnaires (telephone interviews are currently used, in particular) with respect to a representative sample of the population; in some cases, the samples may be 'designed' or 'by quota'. In certain cases, surveys are conducted for specific purposes that are not connected to other studies; in other cases, longitudinal surveys are implemented in order to periodically gauge the moods of the population, and is generally the best solution. Surveys may be implemented with respect to the same population sample, monitored over time (a panel) or different samples may be selected each time so long as they are created on the basis of the same criteria. The latter solution – which is simpler from an organization aspect– is a real longitudinal study and allows the changing attitudes of the population to be verified over time. People were questioned about positive effects (urban regeneration, new infrastructures, sport facilities, public transportation system, new image and visibility, and tourism) and negative effects (heavy expenditures for new buildings, high costs for maintaining the ice facilities, political corruption and inflation). The questions were balanced between a new local development, based on sport, tourism and culture, and the scenario of rust monuments and white elephants, considering the Games only an 'intermezzo'. The general principle of social research – that the subject's perceptions are a 'moving target' – also applies to research on public opinion on events that may change over time and must be captured through the use of new measurement tools, new questions and new response modalities.

To familiarize the reader with *sport business field research*, Douglas Michele Turco describes the following key steps to research success: (1) developing the problem; (2) formulating hypotheses or research questions; (3) research design; (4) data-gathering, treatment and analysis, and (5) reporting. Several data collection approaches for field research in sport business were described, including on-site interviews, door-to-door, e-surveys and the skier lift technique. It must be remembered that research in the field is fluid and dynamic, and requires, at times, flexibility by the researchers. The reader should also be aware that sport event economic impact studies are sometimes commissioned to justify a political position rather than to search for economic accuracy, resulting in the use of questionable procedures that produce bloated numbers. Questionable research procedures include: local resident spending; appropriate aggregation; inclusion of time-switchers and casuals; abuse of multipliers; ignoring costs borne by the local community; ignoring opportunity costs; ignoring displacement costs; expanding the project scope; exaggerating visitation numbers; and inclusion of consumer surplus. Regardless of the motives for conducting research, what is most important is that sound, systematic and ethical procedures are followed for data-gathering and analysis. *Internal validity*, or the extent to which an instrument accurately measures what it purports to measure, is critical to any field study. Estimates or projections of sport tourist activity generally come from attendance figures, room occupancy rates or some other system to measure tourism demand. Internal validity is threatened from poorly constructed and formatted questionnaires that produce responses of little worth. The accuracy of spectator studies may be limited by the amount of time that transpires between a subject's event attendance and the survey, inducing what is termed recall bias. *Recall bias* is particularly acute in economic impact studies with mail-back surveys when a lengthy time lag between the event and survey has occurred. Visitors tend to underestimate their expenditures when asked for information after a considerable time has elapsed from their visit. They also tend to perceive their travel experiences more positively as time transpires. To address the issue of recall bias, visitors should be queried as soon after their experiences as possible; at least within one to two weeks of their visit. The flipside of recall bias is *projection bias*, which can occur when subjects are asked to estimate their spending early in their trip or visit. To address projection bias, visitor samples should be drawn near the end of, or immediately after, the event. A split-method research approach may also be employed, that is, on-site interview and post-event e-mail survey, permitting spending comparisons based on when the surveys were conducted.

2.5   Research Methods and Selected Theories Applied in the Thematic Cluster 'Club Management and Teams'

The development of a management model specific to professional sport clubs is featured by Norm O'Reilly. More specifically *portfolio theory* is used to develop a professional sport club management model that considers the club to be a portfolio of assets.

The numerous assets of Maple Leaf Sports and Entertainment were articulated by the author in a *detailed case study* to support theory development. Applied in accounting, investment banking, finance and strategy, the portfolio theory uses the perspective of an investor and seeks to optimize investment benefits through the diversification and risk management of the investor's portfolio. It considers the portfolio problem, where the risk of a given investment is determined based on each investor's preferred portfolio. The level of risk is based on the investor's risk aversion, the overall composition of the investor's portfolio and sought return objectives. Over time, changes to a portfolio that maintain the same level of expected return, but with reduced risk, are sought. The separation theorem is an important aspect of portfolio theory that considers the implications of a riskless asset and how it compares to the risk/return outcomes of alternate investment options Optimization, or finding the optimal mix of high- and low-risk assets, is a common aspect of portfolio theory. In practice, portfolio theory typically guides investment portfolio decisions by considering the expected return and the unique risk of a given asset as part of a larger portfolio of assets. Defining a professional sport club as a series of assets forms the basis for applying portfolio theory as a foundation for a model for professional sport club management.

Marketing is important for sports clubs which offer experiences to various audiences. A major purpose of a professional elite club is to earn money and be profitable, but clubs also have to satisfy non-profit needs. In practice it is difficult to separate profit issues from non-profit or social issues. Hans Jansson and Sten Söderman offer, as a conclusion taken from industry and the *literature review*, four typical relationship designs for sport clubs, thus applying an abductive reasoning to theory-building: *marketing management, customer focused relationship marketing, network marketing and institutional network marketing*. In order to market a sport product, a marketer has to consider several influencing factors that are unique to sport marketing. The most distinctive and challenging factors are that sport is product led. A sport is all about the uncertainty of outcome, and sport customers help to produce the product (or service) and sports fans are unlikely to purchase products from a rival sport organization. A coherent link exists between the market as a social arena and marketing activities. The institutional-network model focuses on factors which influence the happenings within a specific market, while the practice-based approach focuses on creating the market and its opportunities through the marketing practices. It is important to note that there is no hard and fast rule about adopting a specific approach. In fact, the adoption of approaches varies with the task/activity at hand, and considering a hybrid approach might be the most beneficial: first, marketing management theory and, second, customer-focused relationship marketing theory which caters to a narrow range of stakeholders and activities. Pivotal attention is only aimed at relationships and making profits through them. Access to multiple markets enables an enterprise to cover a broader spectrum of stakeholders and activities as it includes relationship marketing. The networking marketing theory is another broad relationship marketing theory, where marketing takes place through a set of network relationships. Since it is based on the markets as networks approach and sociology, the market is viewed as a social arena. The decisions are made on the basis of actual happenings in the market and outside it. In the institutional-network theory, the logic of appropriateness and logic of consequence go hand in hand. The logic of appropriateness is used to find alternatives to a problem as the word 'appropriate' rightly suggests.

On the other hand, the logic of consequence plays a critical role in solving the problems outlined and maximizing the social values from an economic point of view. This logic therefore goes a step further by translating social values into economic consequences, for example, the competitiveness of the club. It is therefore concluded by the authors that the logic of consequence is valid for all four marketing theories, while the logic of appropriateness is only included in the institutional network marketing theory.

A *framework-based approach* to theory-building is applied by Harald Dolles and Sten Söderman in developing the network of value captures as a management model specific to professional team sport clubs. Built on *multiple-cases*, a *critical literature review* and *interviews with experts* the authors construct three dimensions of professional sport club management: (1) the product and its features; (2) the customers, and (3) the business process, strategic vision and intent. The following possible 'offerings', termed 'value captures' are explored and it should be noted that all value offerings are interlinked and might also be considered as bundles of a club's value captures: team; sporting competitions; club; players; team-sport services; event, facilities and arena; merchandise; and other commercial activities. This broad consumer approach addresses the following customer groups: spectators and supporters (fan base); club members (club membership); media; sponsors and corporate partners; local communities, and other clubs. Combining the eight 'offerings' with the six groups of 'customers', 48 relationships appear, showing the competitive scope of a professional club in team sports. Each of these relationships constitutes a value-capturing activity through which a club can create value and competitive advantage. This understanding of value captures is founded in *strategic management* and the *resource-based view*. A club's resources can only be a source of competitive advantage when they are valuable and recognized by the customer. Resources are considered to be value captures when they enable a particular club to implement strategies (value-capturing activities) that improve its efficiency and effectiveness. Valuable club resources possessed by a large number of competing clubs cannot be sources of sustained competitive advantage, if a club is not differentiating upon them. A club only enjoys a competitive advantage when it is implementing a unique value-creating strategy combining bundles of valuable club resources (value captures) recognized and accepted by the customer (by the customer's groups).

The potential of *econometric analyses* to answer two particularly important questions that arise in the context of the team sports industry is featured by Bernd Frick: first, is it possible to field a championship team by outspending the competitors and, second, what are the (main) determinants of player salaries? The answers are not only of academic value, but have obvious managerial implications. Team owners and/or presidents wishing to maximize the sporting performance of their clubs are well advised to take the results into account when purchasing talent in the relevant labour market. *Advanced quantitative methods* are used in this chapter to analyse the very detailed and reliable *longitudinal data* that are available both, at the club and the individual level.

Grounded theory, featured next by Christos Anagnostopoulos, is a systematic inductive and comparative methodology for conducting inquiry with the purpose of developing theory. Three main reasons are often given for why grounded theory has proved popular in management research: (1) it is useful for developing new theory or fresh insights into old theory; (2) it generates theory of direct interest and relevance for practitioners, and (3) it can uncover micro-management processes in complex and unfolding scenarios.

Surprisingly, the application of grounded theory in the sport management field has been relatively sparse. Sport management research that wishes to employ grounded theory methodology needs to specify from the outset the unit of analysis the inquiry will use. A grounded theory-based inquiry (in particular one that adopts the Straussian variant) should not be considered as an a-theoretical research engagement. The example used throughout this chapter and based on *interviews* gathered through *snowball and purposive sampling*, for instance, is located in the broad field of organizational strategy. The decision-making by the author to concentrate on *corporate social responsibility* in English Football was an emerging sense-making process developed over a period of time, shaped by a series of (non-)intentional choices and actions by various actors and influenced by a changing set of conditioning and intervening factors. Thus sport management researchers must always keep in mind that their 'substantive theory' lies in a broader field of study, and this is why, for example, a modest review of the literature can be justified; it can actually provide the platform upon which further 'knowledge' on the matter can be acquired.

2.6   Research Methods and Selected Theories Applied in the Thematic Cluster 'Sport Branding and Sponsoring'

A theoretical model of the influence of fan identity on the attitude toward sponsors and the intention of purchasing the sponsors' products is developed by Torsten Schlesinger. It introduces several concepts and models which analyse different *psychological (attitudinal and behavioural) facets* and components for assessing the connection between spectators and fans with their team or club. A strong bond between fans and their teams or clubs can be described by different dimensions: emotional achievement, self-connection and intimate commitment. Emotional achievement represents the feeling of personal achievement and pride of the fans when their team is successful. In this context the effective influence of fan identity on parameters crucial for success like attitude or purchase intention of sponsor's products is of special interest. The sponsorship effect model is empirically tested by two quantitative *single case studies* with sport clubs in different top sport leagues and one of its sponsors (sponsors are dealt with anonymously). An *online survey* is generated, having the advantage that it is possible to generate a big sample within a very short time. However, it is only possible to question persons with a specific interest in a discipline and specific habit of media use, so that a control on representativeness with regard to age and sex is limited. The data is tested in a two-staged process. First, the measurement model is assessed via *confirmatory factor analysis* to evaluate the reliability and unidimensionality of the scales used in the studies. Further, a *structural model* is estimated to allow for an assessment of the overall model fit and the hypothesized relationships. Owing to the fact that there are two different sponsoring situations on hand, the established model is analysed for each sport club separately.

A *critical literature review* is applied by T. Bettina Cornwell offering the reader a summary of the development of sponsorship as a mainstay of marketing communications, exploring the theoretical propositions made in research and how sponsorship works, and making arguments for the entrenchment of sponsorship in a new evolving indirect marketing mix. Managerial implications are discussed and a future research agenda is proposed.

Participant observation as a legitimate method of engaging in sports management research is highlighted by Mark Dibben and Harald Dolles. It is notwithstanding the limitations of sample size that are inevitably associated with participant observation that the sorts of insights sought in the adoption of participant observation as a research method are different to those feasible through more traditional methods. It is argued that participant observation allows otherwise unavailable access to the ephemeral and the personal, that is where the value inherent within sports scenarios resides. The sorts of insights gained from applying participant observation are not readily available from more traditional studies of sports business; there is a degree of intimacy required to yield such sensitivities. In the case investigated, the implications of the hard financial reality for the World Landspeed Record Attempt project were felt every day; there was no prospect of obtaining materials without having the necessary cash and it was being run on a 'hand-to-mouth' basis. Yet to the outsider there would be nothing to suggest anything other than a paid team working in a well-funded environment. Indeed, it was not in the project's interests to make the privations known; this would have caused sponsors and officials to doubt the potential success of the project to the extent it would have ceased to retain the necessary credibility. As such, it seems that it is only through participant observation that one is able to discern just precisely what the drivers are behind a sports project or event; the data is not as readily available from more traditional methods as it is in other ventures with (for example) publicly available financial information. Further, sports events, teams and projects exist precisely as a result of a camaraderie among the individuals that is not fully observable from the outside. Particularly in motorsport, the true *raison d'être* is held within the team; it is a fallacy to believe that all teams are only there to win, because teams are realistic as to their chances. Getting behind the sponsorship and the vehicle, to sit 'inside the caravan' of the team and, indeed, each member of the team in 'the circus' is the only way to access the personal lived reality of the participants and their families. It is for this reason that participant observation is suggested as a valid method for sports management research and the authors argue that the standard normative scientific methodological questions regarding 'objective validity' and 'replicability' are rendered obsolete in those research settings.

The discussion about the *evaluation of brand equity* should, according to Tim Ströbel and Herbert Woratschek in the next chapter, be referred to two main issues: (1) one should always differentiate between brand equity and brand strength. Although this separation is not entirely persevered in literature and the expression brand equity dominates the discussion, there is a common understanding of the existence of both finance-oriented and customer-based brand equity. (2) Based on that first conclusion, one should distinguish between the three main models of brand evaluation: finance-oriented models, customer-oriented models and integrative models. With reference to those two main issues it can be summarized that the evaluation of brand equity belongs to one of the most discussed and most important management topics, and this is specifically apparent in the field of sport. It is extremely important for sport organizations to evaluate both brand strength and brand equity. This is practically proven by the increasing numbers of evaluations done in several sports. By following that discussion, the reader should keep in mind that *finance-oriented models* usually ignore the influence of different stakeholders, especially the sport spectators' perspective. In that case, psychological variables like fan loyalty or image are completely out of scope. *Customer-oriented models* include, on the other hand, those psychological variables, but ignore more or less financial figures. These two perspectives are combined in integrative models that measure brand equity by scoring models where the weights of brand key drivers are subjectively determined. This is the reason why the results of different brand evaluations of one and the same brand usually differ extremely. Therefore, it is important to differentiate brand strength and brand equity.

2.7   Research Methods and Selected Theories Applied in the Concluding Cluster 'Reflection'

Sport has today emerged as an industrial sector in its ownright, with a number of studies and estimates that it makes a major contribution to economic and commercial activity both within and across national boundaries. At the same time, sport continues to have a profound influence on the social, cultural, health and psychological spheres of human existence. The *literature review* by Simon Chadwick reveals that the appeal of sport might even increase in the future and a wide range of institutions, organizations, bodies, clubs, teams and individuals are both affected by and involved in sport. As such, there is a multitude of challenges facing managers in sport, many of which have only emerged over the last two decades. There is a real need to understand the challenges faced by sport managers, and what the most effective ways of managing them are. The author encourages the starting of a debate – and we are sure this handbook contributes to this process – about the extent to which sport should draw from existing theories and concepts in the management literature. At one level, this implies that sport is an industrial sector similar to any other and that the generic implications of the established management literature are equally as applicable in the sports setting. Adopting such a viewpoint would clearly be beneficial, as it would allow those with an interest in sport to engage in a process of applying established management theory to sport. However, this rather denies the specificity of sport, most notably the importance of managing in the essential context of uncertainty (of outcome). Given this core characteristic of the sector, some argue that sport requires special attention and is not a vehicle to which one can simply apply management theory that is evolved in other, often less distinctive, settings.

Over the past 10 to 20 years professional sport has been interrogated from various perspectives, with sociologists, historians, lawyers and management theorists leading the charge. On balance they found that sport is both commercially special and culturally unique. The *review of these special and unique features* of sport by Aaron C.T. Smith and Bob Stewart indicates that (1) the distinctiveness of some of them have been overstated, (2) a number of new and novel features have emerged, while (3) other features have been eroded in line with sport's relentless corporatization. While it is inappropriate to conclude that the features discussed above demand a specialized form of management practice, the analysis here suggests that sport leagues and competitions still have many idiosyncrasies that demand considered and strategic responses. First, sport is still characterized by fierce, loyal and passionate fans, who experience a strong, vicarious identification with their favourite players and teams. It remains one of the few products to deliver engaging experiences that become part of our collective memory. However, even the most strident sport fans are also motivated by other benefits of the sport product, including aesthetic appeal, entertainment and social interaction. It is further argued in the chapter that, traditionally, the major difference between business and sport was the importance of profit and return on investment for business, and the preference for winning and on-field success for sport. While it is clear that winning is sovereign in professional sport, there is a growing recognition that revenue and profits, and the resources that money attracts, are the keys to successful performance. Moreover, the evidence suggests that winning is also the fastest route to profitability. This means that it is no longer a case of either or, but of both aims being met through an interdependent managerial strategy that builds a strong platform of quality resources from which to launch a high win–loss ratio.

While the corporatization of sport over recent years may have resolved the dilemma of how to balance profits against performance, no such solution has been secured for the issue of quality in sport. The ambiguous nature of sport quality is exemplified in the ways in which different stakeholders approach it. For example, many club officials and diehard fans view quality primarily in terms of consistent winning, whereas regulators and run-of-the-mill sport followers are more likely to perceive quality in terms of competitive balance and outcome uncertainty. Added to this ambiguity is the complicating fact that the core sport product is now surrounded by services and merchandise that are used to provide a more consistent and multifaceted sport experience. Finally, professional sport is embedded in a fundamental structural and operational paradox which complicates its management at every strategic turn. It arises out of the fact that sport's commercial progress and subsequent corporatization is a two-edged sword. While, on one the hand, it allows sport to tap into new markets by changing its shape and features, on the other hand it fractures all those traditions that made it attractive to fans in the first place.

3　OTHER AIDS TO SEARCH IN THE HANDBOOK

An additional figure which aims to aid the reader when searching for specific content of the handbook is Figure 1.4. It will assist the search for specific sports featured in the chapters. As future research in the field strongly benefits from bridging or comparing different sports settings as well as contextual factors, such as regions or different forms of how sport is organized, we strongly encourage the readers to take the indications mentioned in the chapters merely as a starting point to develop their own research journeys by exploring changes in sport and/or contextual settings.

4　CONCLUSION

This handbook provides a substantial overview of the range of theories and methodologies applied in the five thematic clusters on current frontiers in sport management research. It encourages reflection by established scholars, practitioners, novice researchers and students on the different stages of the research cycle – selecting a topic, research design, data analysis and interpretation – and represents the diversity in approaches as practised by sport management researchers. As with other handbooks aiming to

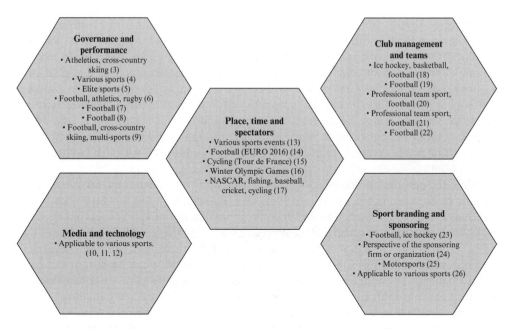

Note: The numbers in brackets indicate the chapter numbers.

Figure 1.4   Selection of specific sports addressed in the handbook

summarize theory and research in a certain field, this handbook is also more than simply that; it involves careful analysis and rethinking, by ourselves and all chapter contributors, of how a particular area of research is constituted. The following chapters in the handbook therefore not only provide insights into different research topics, theories and methodology, but also different conceptions about the sub-areas of research on the nexus between sport and business by the community of sport management researchers. Our aim in assembling these contributions is not to advocate a single methodology or one particular theoretical approach; rather it is to explore existing practices and alternative paths to advance the understanding of the research field. An outlook and research agenda on sport and business will be provided in the concluding chapter as a further attempt to provide inspiration for future research in the field.

REFERENCES

Anagnostopoulos, C. (2013), Examining corporate responsibility in football: the application of grounded theory methodology, in S. Söderman and H. Dolles (eds), *Handbook of Research on Sport and Business*, Cheltenham, UK and Northampton, MA, USA: Edward Elgar, pp. 418–32.

Andreff, W. and Szymanski, S. (eds) (2006), *Handbook on the Economics of Sport*, Cheltenham, UK and Northampton, MA, USA: Edward Elgar.

Cornwell, T.B. (2013), State of the art and science in sponsorship-linked marketing, in S. Söderman and H. Dolles (eds), *Handbook of Research on Sport and Business*, Cheltenham, UK and Northampton, MA, USA: Edward Elgar, pp. 456–76.

De Bosscher, V., Truyens, J., van Bottenburg, M. and Shibli, S. (2013), Comparing apples with oranges in international elite sport studies: is it possible?, in S. Söderman and H. Dolles (eds), *Handbook of Research on Sport and Business*, Cheltenham, UK and Northampton, MA, USA: Edward Elgar, pp. 94–111.

Dibben, M. and Dolles, H. (2013), Participant observation in sport management research: collecting and interpreting data from a successful world land speed record attempt, in S. Söderman and H. Dolles (eds), *Handbook of Research on Sport and Business*, Cheltenham, UK and Northampton, MA, USA: Edward Elgar, pp. 477–94.

Dolles, H. and Söderman, S. (2011), Sport as a business: introduction, in H. Dolles and S. Söderman (eds), *Sport as a Business: International, Professional and Commercial Aspects*, Basingstoke: Palgrave Macmillan, pp. 1–12.

Dolles, H. and Söderman, S. (2013), The network of value captures in football club management: a framework to develop and analyse competitive advantage in professional team sports, in S. Söderman and H. Dolles (eds), *Handbook of Research on Sport and Business*, Cheltenham, UK and Northampton, MA, USA: Edward Elgar, pp. 367–95.

Dubois, A. and Gadde, L.-E. (2002), Systematic combining: an abductive approach to case research, *Journal of Business Research*, **55** (7), 553–60.

Godfrey-Smith, P. (2003), *Theory and Reality: An Introduction to the Philosophy of Science*, Chicago, IL: University of Chicago Press.

Gummesson, E. (2003), All research is interpretive!, *Journal of Business and Industrial Marketing*, **18** (6/7), 482–92.

Jansson, H. and Söderman, S. (2013), Proposing a relationship marketing theory for sport clubs, in S. Söderman and H. Dolles (eds), *Handbook of Research on Sport and Business*, Cheltenham, UK and Northampton, MA, USA: Edward Elgar, pp. 350–66.

Kant, I. (1787), *Kritik der reinen Vernunft [Critique of Pure Reason]*, Akademie Textausgabe Kants Werke vol. 3, reprint of the 1904 issue, Berlin/Leipzig: DeGruyter.

Kjellén, B. and Söderman, S. (1980), *Praktikfallsmetodik [The Methodology of Case Studies]*, Malmö: SIAR/ Liber.

Porter, M.E. (1991), Towards a dynamic theory of strategy, *Strategic Management Journal*, **12** (special issue): 95–117.

Punch, K. (2005), *Introduction to Social Research: Quantitative and Qualitative Approaches*, 2nd edn, Thousand Oaks, CA: Sage Publications.

Santomier, J. and Hogan, P. (2013), Social media and prosumerism: implications for sport marketing research, in S. Söderman and H. Dolles (eds), *Handbook of Research on Sport and Business*, Cheltenham, UK and Northampton, MA, USA: Edward Elgar, pp. 179–201.

Schlesinger, T. (2013), A review of fan identity and its influence on sport sponsorship effectiveness, in S. Söderman and H. Dolles (eds), *Handbook of Research on Sport and Business*, Cheltenham, UK and Northampton, MA, USA: Edward Elgar, pp. 435–55.

Skille, E. (2013), Case study research in sport management: a reflection upon the theory of science and an empirical example, in S. Söderman and H. Dolles (eds), *Handbook of Research on Sport and Business*, Cheltenham, UK and Northampton, MA, USA: Edward Elgar, pp. 161–75.

Söderman, S. and Dolles, H. (2008), Strategic fit in international sponsorship – the case of the Olympic Games in Beijing 2008, *International Journal of Sports Marketing & Sponsorship*, **9** (2), 95–110.

Söderman, S. and Dolles, H. (2010), Sponsoring the Bejing Olympic Games – patterns of sponsor advertising, *Asia Pacific Journal of Marketing and Logistics*, **22** (1), 8–24.

Söderman, S., Dolles, H. and Dum, T. (2010), Managing football. International and global developments, in S. Hamil and S. Chadwick (eds), *Managing Football: An International Perspective*, Amsterdam: Butterworth-Heinemann, pp. 85–101.

Solberg, H.A. and Haugen, K.K. (2013), The sale of media sport rights: a game theoretic approach, in S. Söderman and H. Dolles (eds), *Handbook of Research on Sport and Business*, Cheltenham, UK and Northampton, MA, USA: Edward Elgar, pp. 219–34.

2 A call for more mixed methods in sport management research

Andy Rudd and R. Burke Johnson

Many social and behavioral science researchers have promoted the use of mixed methods to more effectively answer research questions (Brewer and Hunter, 1989; Johnson and Onwuegbuzie, 2004; Tashakkori and Teddlie, 1998, 2003). Such an approach has generally been defined as the combining of at least one quantitative method and one qualitative method (e.g., Hanson et al., 2005; Jick. 1979; Maxwell and Loomis, 2003). Combining quantitative and qualitative data in a single study can be beneficial in a variety of ways. For example, the researcher can triangulate which involves combining quantitative and qualitative methods to produce a set of data that has complementary strengths and nonoverlapping weaknesses (Brewer and Hunter, 1989; Johnson and Onwuegbuzie, 2004; Johnson and Turner, 2003; Tashakkori and Teddlie, 1998).

This concept of combining approaches for complementary strengths and non overlapping weaknesses has been called the fundamental principle of mixed research (Johnson and Turner, 2003). The idea is to strategically select a mixture of quantitative and qualitative approaches that will effectively cover the objective or set of objectives of a research study and to do it in a way that eliminates overall study design weaknesses. According to Onwuegbuzie and Johnson (2006) this fundamental principle can be adapted to multiple purposes including initiation (discovering contradictions), expansion (attaining a deeper and broader understanding), complementarity (examining overlapping parts of a phenomenon), and development (using results from one method to inform the use of a second method) (see also, Greene et al., 1989).

The potential benefits of using mixed methods approaches has stimulated its adoption in a variety of fields including sociology, nursing, psychology, management, health sciences, evaluation and education (Tashakorri and Teddlie, 2003). Yet, despite the popularity and strong advocacy for combining quantitative and qualitative approaches, few mixed methods studies can be found amid extant sport management research. As evidence, empirical articles were reviewed by the first author for the presence of mixed methods approaches in three major sport management journals: *Journal of Sport Management (JSM)*, *International Journal of Sport Management (IJSM)*, and *Sport Management Review (SMR)* during the period of 2000–2007.[1] The analysis identified the following number of mixed methods articles: *JSM* (10), *IJSM* (15) and *SMR* (2) (Rudd, 2007). Comparatively, Quarterman et al. (2006) reviewed 299 articles (conceptual and empirical) published in the *Journal of Sport Management* from 1987 to 2004. From their analysis, only 6 of the 299 articles (2%) employed a mixed methods approach, 27 out of 299 (9%) were qualitative, 165 of the 299 (55%) were quantitative, and 101 of the 299 (34%) were conceptual. As well, Barber et al. (2001) assayed 42 empirical articles published in the *Journal of Sport Management* during the period of 1991–95 and found the majority of articles to be survey research (73%). Other types of methods employed included content analysis (19%) and mixed methods (9%). Overall, these analyses suggest that when it comes to empirical studies, the majority in sport management employ quantitative monomethods (a single method).

Additionally, although there are many different types of mixed methods designs (Creswell and Piano Clark, 2007; Johnson and Onwuegbuzie, 2004; Teddlie and Tashakkori, 2006), many of the mixed methods articles uncovered in our analysis involved limited or weak use of mixed methods. According to Johnson and Christensen (2008), research methodology can be viewed on a continuum ranging from monomethods (far left of the continuum) to fully mixed studies (far right of the continuum). The majority of the mixed methods studies observed in sport management journals would arguably fall to the left on the research continuum, representing relatively weak use of combining quantitative and qualitative methods. For example, 10 of the 15 mixed methods articles found in *IJSM* simply involved a questionnaire with open and closed questions. Other examples of weak to moderate mixed methods included eight articles involving content analysis (within *JSM* and *IJSM*) and five articles across *JSM, IJSM* and *SMR* that used mixed methods for instrument development (i.e., using qualitative data from interviews or focus groups to develop items for a questionnaire).

In sum, the results from our analysis as well as others (Barber et al., 2001; Quatermen et al., 2006) suggest that few employ mixed methods approaches in sport management and when they do, they are not strongly mixed designs (i.e., a substantial amount of both quantitative and qualitative strategies and data in single studies). The purpose of this chapter, then, is to demonstrate additional, more fully mixed methods approaches that can be useful to the sport management researcher. In particular, given that much research in sport management is concerned with causal questions, our chapter focuses on applying mixed methods to studies dealing with causation. Because we are focusing on the question of causation, the type of mixed methods research we are discussing in this chapter generally involved complementing quantitative research with qualitative approaches. The reason is that quantitative epistemologies are explicitly interested in identifying nomological (causal) relationships in their literatures.

For example, in the area of sport marketing, researchers are often interested in the factors that affect purchasing behavior of sport fans (e.g., Kwon and Armstrong, 2002; Kwon et al., 2007; Trail et al., 2003). Or, concerning organizational behavior, studies have examined variables that influence organizational commitment or turnover intention (e.g., Cunningham and Sagas, 2006; Kent and Chelladurai, 2001; Whisenant, 2005). As well, in the domain of finance and economics, researchers commonly ask causal questions related to economic impact. For example, a professional sport team's effect on public goods (Johnson et al., 2007a) or a star player's effect on fan attendance (DeSchriver, 2007). To probe cause and effect relationships, many of these studies employ correlational or causal modeling techniques rather than experimental or quasi-experimental designs. This is presumably because it is difficult to control or manipulate naturally occurring causal variables such as team identity, the location of a professional sport team, or the procurement of star players.[2]

Regardless of the method one uses to ascertain cause and effect, an important consideration is the distinction between causal description and causal explanation. The former simply allows one to suggest that there is a causal relationship or covariance between the independent and dependent variable. The latter involves an explanation of the causal mechanisms responsible for a particular causal relationship as well as the conditions under which the relationship holds (Cook, 2002; Shadish et al., 2002) (see a more extensive explanation later in this chapter). Obtaining this explanatory knowledge allows researchers to make more accurate conclusions (increases internal and external validity) and provides clearer applicability and utility to practitioners.

Although causal or structural equation models (SEM) take into consideration mediating and moderating variables that may help explain a causal relationship, these models may fail to capture additional important mediating or moderating factors. This problem is known as specification error which refers to misidentifying or omitting important variables that are involved in a causal relationship (Shadish et al., 2002). Specification error also occurs when the researcher incorrectly identifies the direction of a causal relationship or mistakes correlation for causation (Shadish et al.).

As an example of specification error, Kwon et al. (2007) examined the mediating effect of perceived value in the relationship between team identification and intent to purchase collegiate team-licensed apparel. In their discussion they acknowledged that they were surprised not to find a direct significant relationship between team identification and purchase intention. They surmised that the failed relationship may have been related to including the price of the t-shirt whereas past studies had not. The researchers theorized that perhaps price sensitivity had a moderating effect on purchase intention. Kwon et al.'s study is a prime example of how the addition of qualitative data may strengthen causal explanation. Specifically, qualitative methods including focus groups, one-on-one interviews, and field observations could have been used to expand their understanding of various unanticipated moderating or mediating factors. This chapter will therefore provide specific strategies for adding qualitative data to quantitative data to increase causal explanation in cause and effect related studies. However, it is important to note that we do not intend to suggest that the addition of qualitative data can overcome all of the weaknesses involved in making causal inferences with correlational techniques like SEM. Rather, the point is to show how the addition of qualitative data can expand and improve one's understanding of causal relationships. Additionally, we advocate the use of mixed method approaches for not only correlational techniques but also experimental designs (see Cook, 2002; Shadish et al., 2002).

Before describing the mixed methods approaches, it is important to familiarize the reader with several key foundational components. First, we introduce the historical debate between quantitative and qualitative researchers and how mixed methods evolved into a legitimate research paradigm. Second, we present some of the basic characteristics of quantitative and qualitative research and how they can be used in a complementary fashion. Third, we show the reader how our mixed methods strategies fit within a larger typology of mixed methods designs. Doing so will hopefully stimulate more thinking about the use of mixed methods for studies not only dealing with causation but for other research objectives as well (e.g., prediction, description, and exploration). Fourth, we provide a brief overview of mixed methods data analysis strategies that will aid in ascertaining causation. We then present our mixed methods approaches for causation along with specific illustrations that are based on real life examples of sport management research. Examples come from three major areas of sport management which include marketing, organizational behavior, and finance. The chapter is concluded with a discussion and future directions.

1 THE PARADIGM WARS AND THE EMERGENCE OF MIXED METHODS RESEARCH

Throughout the latter part of the 20th century, social and behavioral scientists engaged in a fervent debate over the supremacy of quantitative versus qualitative research (e.g., House, 1994; Johnson and Onwuegbuzie, 2004; Tashakkori and Teddlie, 1998). Each side argued from two distinct paradigmatic perspectives (i.e., a researcher's world view of how best to obtain knowledge) (Tashakkori and Teddlie, 1998). Quantitative purists, held to a positivist paradigm which makes a variety of assumptions including the following: there is a single objective reality, cause and effect relationships can be known (especially when a randomized experiment is conducted), time and context free generalizations are possible and desired, the observer and the observed are sufficiently independent for objectivity to be approximated in a research study, and the focus of research should be on the empirical testing of hypotheses and theories (House, 1994; Johnson and Christensen, 2008; Tashakkori and Teddlie, 1998). Alternatively, qualitative purists, espouse a constructivist (or naturalistic/interpretivist) paradigm with the following assumptions: there are multiple realities, cause and effect relationships are difficult to discern and generally not of interest, the observer and the observed are inseparable, context free generalizations are neither possible nor desired, research is value-laden, and when there is interest in theory the focus is on the inductive generation of theory rather than the testing of previously specified theories (House, 1994; Johnson and Christensen, 2008; Tashakkori and Teddlie 1998).

These divergent paradigms caused some researchers to eschew the combining of quantitative and qualitative methods in a single study. To the methodological purist, combining quantitative and qualitative methods means illogically conflating two wholly distinct paradigms for obtaining knowledge and truth (Cuba and Lincoln, 1988; Smith and Heshusius, 1986). This belief is known as the 'incompatibility thesis' (Howe, 1988; Johnson and Onwuegbuzie, 2004; Tashakkori and Teddlie, 1998).

Despite some of the arguable differences between quantitative and qualitative research, the emergence of two philosophical schools of thought have helped overcome the incompatibility thesis. The first is the postpositvist paradigm which has generally replaced the 'positivist' thinking of most quantitative researchers (e.g., Garrison, 1986; Johnson and Onwuegbuzie, 2004; Phillips and Burbules, 2000; Tashakkori and Teddlie, 1998; Trochim, 2007).[3] Postpositivism takes a quantitative approach but rejects positivist principles such as the notion that there is a single external reality that can be infallibly known (Reichardt and Rallis, 1994; Trochim, 2007). Instead, postpositivsts strive for objectivity but believe that observations are fallible, that research is both theory and value-laden, and that a study's results can be partially explained by multiple theories (Reichardt and Rallis, 1994; Tashakkori and Teddlie, 1998; Trochim, 2007). Postpositivists also believe that subjective reality is, in part, individually constructed (via Piagetian schemas), which is counter to the naïve realist's belief in a single, directly visible external reality (Reichardt and Rallis, 1994; Tashakkori and Teddlie, 1998; Trochim, 2007). These tenets have some similarities to the constructivist views of qualitative researchers (e.g., value and theory ladenness of inquiry, multiple types of realities, fallibility of knowledge, and the use of multiple theories) which consequently makes quantitative and qualitative research more compatible (Reichardt and Rallis, 1994;

Tashakkori and Teddlie, 1998). According to mixed methods research, quantitative and qualitative research should thus not be considered incompatible but rather, complementary and strength forming.

The second philosophy is called pragmatism which is popular among many mixed methods researchers and has significantly influenced the acceptance and increasing use of combining quantitative and qualitative approaches. One of the major tenets of pragmatism is the notion of 'what works', which is premised on the idea that researchers should make methodological choices based on research questions rather than world views (Howe, 1988; Tashakkori and Teddlie, 1998). Thus, adopting a pragmatic philosophy which involves dropping dogmatic adherence to a single paradigm and instead focusing on research questions has stimulated many researchers to use whatever methodology will best answer their research questions including the combining of quantitative and qualitative data.

Additionally, Patton (1988), from the field of evaluation, and Johnson and Onwuegbuzie (2004), from education, also propose a pragmatic philosophy but from a slightly different perspective. Rather than completely removing the paradigms from consideration, Patton suggests it is possible to shift back and forth between paradigms depending on the situation. Attempting to fuse this position with pragmatism, Teddlie and Johnson (2009) call this back-and-forth movement, *dialectical pragmatism*. Using what Johnson and Onwuegbuzie (2004) (and also Johnson et al., 2007b) call the *contingency theory* of research, some research questions/situations may call for a qualitative, constructivist approach while in other cases a quantitative, postpositivist methodology may be more appropriate; and many questions call for mixed methods research. In essence, authors such as these argue for flexible and responsive thinking among applied researchers. Doing so opens up the door for more creative research methods, particularly in the form of combining quantitative and qualitative methods in a single study (c.f. Hanson et al., 2005; Maxwell and Loomis, 2003).

In sum, many social and behavioral science researchers no longer take an either-or-approach; that is, that one cannot be a quantitative and qualitative researcher at the same time. Instead, it is now commonly accepted that combining quantitative and qualitative research is a beneficial practice.

2   CHARACTERISTICS AND COMPLEMENTARY STRENGTHS OF QUANTITATIVE AND QUALITATIVE RESEARCH

Appreciating the utility of mixed methods approaches requires the reader to understand basic methodological distinctions between quantitative and qualitative research and how they can be complementary. Much, but certainly not all, quantitative research is characterized by deductive hypothesis testing, the controlling or manipulating of variables, and generalizing from one's data (in the form of numbers).[4] Popular research objectives include explanation (cause and effect), prediction, or description. Methodologically, quantitative researchers advocate the use of standardized instruments, large random samples for generalization, statistical analysis, and the use of various types of experimental or quasi-experimental designs (and sometimes nonexperimental designs) (Cuba and Lincoln, 1988; Johnson and Christensen, 2008; Patton, 1987).

Qualitative research is characterized by in depth naturalistic description and exploration and inductive theory construction (generating theory from the data). The main objectives are exploration, discovery, description, and theory development. Methodologically, qualitative researchers typically conduct in depth interviews or do extended field observations (words and pictures are collected rather than numbers). Focus groups, open-ended questionnaires, and document analysis are also sometimes used (Guba and Lincoln, 1988; Johnson and Christensen, 2008; Patton, 1987).

Although there are distinct methodological differences between quantitative and qualitative research, these differences can be combined advantageously. For example, qualitative data (e.g., interviews or focus groups) could be added to an experiment to attain a deeper understanding of the cause and effect relationship (expansion). Or, in a quantitative survey design, the researcher could add a qualitative component (interviews or open-ended questions on a questionnaire) to corroborate or expand the findings from the quantitative data (triangulation). Alternatively, following a qualitative exploration one could develop a questionnaire (sequential) to broaden understanding of emerging patterns and themes (expansion) to seek contradictions in the differing forms of data (initiation), to test a grounded theory that was qualitatively generated (also sequential).

3   MIXED METHODS TYPOLOGIES

Researchers from a variety of disciplines have worked to advance the application of mixed methods. One of these advancements has been in the development of mixed methods design typologies (Creswell and Piano Clark, 2007; Greene et al., 1989; Hanson et al., 2005; Johnson and Onwuegbuzie, 2004; Maxwell and Loomis, 2003; Morgan, 1998; Morse, 2003; Tashakkori and Teddlie, 1998; Teddlie and Tashakkori, 2006). A mixed methods typology provides a useful framework for thinking about how to design mixed methods studies for a variety of purposes. Notably, many of these proposed typologies/designs contain a great deal of overlapping similarities. As such, we have chosen to adopt Johnson and Onwuegbuzie's mixed methods typology on the basis of its understandability and because it generally represents the underlying concepts of various mixed methods typologies.

Johnson and Onwuegbuzie's (2004) typology is premised on two key dimensions: time order and status of the quantitative and qualitative study components. The first dimension, *time order*, refers to when the quantitative and qualitative phases are carried out in a study. The researcher may collect data sequentially, (i.e., quantitative and qualitative data are collected in phases) or the quantitative and qualitative components may be conducted concurrently (i.e., at approximately the same time). The second dimension, *status* or *priority* (i.e., equal status versus dominant status) refers to the emphasis on the research approaches. Depending on the study, one might believe that the quantitative component is more important and thus place more emphasis and effort on the quantitative methods, while in another study the qualitative component may be viewed with more importance.

To explain further, priority or status is used in two somewhat different ways in the literature. First, priority can refer to the amount of time and effort devoted to the qualitative and quantitative approaches in answering the research questions. In practice, this refers to whether the researcher spent more time collecting qualitative or quantitative data. Second, priority is used more at the epistemological level to refer to whether qualitative or quantitative paradigmatic assumptions are dominant. Here, dominant status implies that either the full qualitative or the full quantitative paradigmatic approach was used while the other was de-emphasized and equal status would mean that both paradigms were fully used. Using two different epistemologies can be difficult; however, one can get around this problem by extensive training in both paradigms and applying strategies and techniques for alternating between paradigms. The dialectical method (Greene, 2007) has specifically been developed for mixed methods research as a way of 'listening' to both qualitative and quantitative perspectives. As the name suggests, it involves moving back and forth between qualitative and quantitative paradigm perspectives, carefully listening, and generating a complementary synthesis of perspectives. If a researcher is not able to shift epistemologies in this way, we recommend the use of a research team composed of a qualitative and a quantitative researcher. The key for equal-status mixed methods research is that both perspectives are equated in power and emphasis and that both perspectives are represented in the final report.

Given these two dimensions, Johnson and Onwuegbuzie (2004) offer nine different designs. To depict these designs the following notation is used: qual refers to qualitative research, quan refers to quantitative research, uppercase letters (QUAL or QUAN) represent dominant status, lowercase letters (qual or quan) represent subordinate status, arrows represent sequential staging of the approaches, and a plus sign (+) represents concurrent conduct of the qualitative and quantitative approaches. Using this notation the following designs are obtained:

- Equal-status concurrent designs (i.e., QUAL + QUAN)
- Equal-status sequential designs (i.e., QUAL → QUAN and QUAN → QUAL)
- Dominant-status concurrent designs (i.e., QUAL + quan and QUAN + qual)
- Dominant-status sequential designs (i.e., QUAL → quan, qual → QUAN, QUAN → qual, and quan → QUAL)

These nine designs by no means capture all of the mixed methods possibilities because design typologies can be constructed on several additional dimensions. A few additional dimensions that have been offered for design typology development include a research continuum dimension (monomethods to fully mixed) (Johnson and Onwuegbuzie, 2008), the transformative dimension (e.g., the use of different advocacy theories such as critical or emancipatory theory) (Hansen et al., 2005), the purpose or rationale of the research study (Creswell and Piano Clark, 2007) and the use of a theoretical perspective in the study (Creswell and Piano Clark, 2007). For the interested reader, Teddlie and Tashhakkori (2006) have offered a more complex but dynamic design typology based on the dimensions of number of methodological approaches, number of strands or phases in the study, type of implementation process, and stage of integration. The main point here is for the reader to see the variety of ways in which quantitative and qualitative approaches can be combined as one constructs the design that is most appropriate for his or her needs.

4   DATA ANALYSIS

According to Caracelli and Greene (1993), data from mixed methods research can be analyzed and interpreted separately or in an integrated fashion. Specific to the latter, one might for example employ the use of data transformation which involves the conversion of one type of data into the other to be used in the overall analysis (e.g., convert the qualitative data into quantitative variables which can then be used with other quantitative data in a regression analysis). Or, one could identify 'extreme cases' from quantitative data that are investigated in depth with qualitative interview data, i.e., extreme case analysis (see Caracelli and Greene, 1993 for other integrative approaches). On the other hand, a questionnaire (quantitative data) might be used to increase breadth and expand one's understanding of the qualitative findings. Or, following the measurement of a set of predetermined variables, interviews could be conducted to attain more depth and detail and to discuss process variables. In these cases, the quantitative and qualitative data are analyzed separately and then integrated at the level of interpretation.

Tashakkori and Teddlie (1998) proposed a similar analytical framework also acknowledging that data from mixed methods can be analyzed and interpreted independently or in a more integrated fashion. However, their framework is somewhat different in that they categorize their mixed analyses into two major groupings referred to as concurrent versus sequential. Concurrent mixed analyses involve either separate (parallel) analyses on each data type or the use of data transformation techniques. Sequential mixed analyses are executed in a particular order and are ultimately integrated at the level of analysis. Arguably, many of the analytical approaches identified by Tashakkori and Teddlie are identical to the ones proposed by Caracelli and Greene (1993) with different labeling. They do however, offer a couple of sequential approaches that are different than that of Caracelli and Greene and that are germane to our interest in causal studies. One approach is a sequential QUAL → QUAN analysis in which a theoretical order of causal relationships is developed first from qualitative data and then confirmed through quantitative analyses such as SEM or path analysis. Alternatively, they suggest the same concept can be applied through the opposite order, i.e., beginning with QUAN SEM analysis and confirming through a QUAL analysis (see Tashakkori and Teddlie for additional analytical approaches that are slightly different from that of Caracelli and Greene).

5   CAUSE AND EFFECT AND MIXED METHODS RESEARCH

Considering a major objective of this chapter is to provide mixed methods approaches for causal studies, it is important to explain the notion of cause and effect as well as two types of causal evidence: causal description and causal explanation. Shadish et al. (2002) noted that people easily intuit a variety of cause and effect relationships in their everyday lives. For example, one might say that poor study habits were the 'cause' of a student's low test grade. Or, one might declare that their favorite football team's losing season was 'caused' by a number of injuries to marquee players. In each case, an individual has inferred a cause and effect relationship which according to Johnson and Christensen (2008) can be thought of as the following: 'A cause and effect relationship between an independent and dependent variable is present when changes in the independent variable tend to cause changes in the dependent variable' (p. 39). These methodologists further remind us that to make a credible causal claim, one must demonstrate evidence of (a) relationship between the causal and outcome variables, (b) proper time ordering of these variables (i.e., the cause must occur before the effect), and (c) elimination of all plausible alternative or rival explanations for the observed relationship (p. 362). Importantly, qualitative data can supplement quantitative data in all three of these domains.

Although the notion of cause and effect might seem rather straightforward, Shadish et al. (2002) and others (Cook and Campbell, 1979; House, 1991; Russo and Williamson, 2007) have pointed out that cause and effect relationships in actuality can be very complex. This is largely due to what can be considered the 'cause' of a particular effect. Shadish et al. illustrated with an example of a lighted match as a potential cause of a forest fire. A lighted match has the capability of starting a forest fire only if other important conditions are satisfied. The match must stay hot enough, leaves in the forest must be dry, a sufficient amount of oxygen is needed for combustion to occur, and the weather conditions must be suitable. Additionally, there are many other ways to start a forest fire including lightening, an unattended campfire, a burning cigarette, and so forth. Therefore, there can be a variety of required conditions for a particular effect to occur even when the independent variable is known generally to produce changes in the dependent variable.

Cause and effect relationships are also complex because a cause can be thought of as a molar (consisting as a whole rather than in parts) package consisting of various molecular components (Cook and Campbell, 1979; Shadish et al., 2002). For example, sport participation as a medium for character development can be thought of as a molar cause consisting of various molecular components in the form of coaches' behavior, the features of the sport played, and characteristics and actions of teammates and opponents. Concurrently, the outcomes or effects from the cause can be considered as a molar package or in individual molecular components. Rudd (2005) for example argued that character consists of two key dimensions (moral and social character). At the molar level one would examine overall character; at the molecular level, one would examine different dimensions of character. Cause and effect relationships, then, can be examined as molar wholes or in their molecular parts.

The distinction between molar and molecular causes and effects parallels the concepts of causal description and causal explanation respectively. Causal description is concerned with cause and effect on a molar level whereas causal explanation seeks to understand the underlying molecular causes and effects relationships (Shadish et al., 2002). Cook and Campbell (1979) also argue through the concept of 'activity theory' that the strongest evidence of cause and effect is obtained when the independent variable is actively manipulated by the researcher. For example, to demonstrate causal description, a randomized experiment may be conducted in which the treatment group outperforms the control group. The researcher then has evidence of a causal relationship on a descriptive or moral level (i.e., the treatment package produced changes). Here the researcher is able to 'describe' the consequences of purposely varying or withholding the treatment (independent variable). However, results from a basic experiment do not clarify the underlying mechanisms or molecular parts that are responsible for the causal relationship; that is, evidence of explanatory causation (Shadish et al., 2002) or what Russo and

Williamson (2007) refer to as mechanistic evidence (see also, Maxwell, 2004b; Salmon, 1998) is lacking.

The difference between causal description and causal explanation can be further understood by comparing two associated philosophies: the 'standard view' versus scientific realism. A key aspect of the standard view entails causality as a matter of 'regularities' in one's data (House, 1991; Manicas and Secord, 1983; Maxwell, 2004a). In other words, when x then y, when no x then no y; this approach comes from the perspective that causal laws can be established in relationship to the observed regularities in one's data. However, such a view assumes that causation can be examined within a closed-system or laboratory-like setting that is devoid of influences from extraneous variables. Additionally, as Maxwell (2004a), states, 'This view treats the actual process of causality as unobservable, a "black box", and focuses on discovering whether there is a systematic relationship between inputs and outputs' (p. 4). The discovery of a relationship between inputs and outputs is very much inline with notion of causal description.

On the other hand, a philosophy of science known as scientific realism (House, 1991) is more congruent with the concept of causal explanation. This is because scientific realism posits that reality is more than what we merely see, 'but also of the underlying causal entities that are not always directly discernible' (House, 1991, p. 4). Therefore, according to a scientific realist, causation is more than just observed regularities; causation involves underlying structural causal mechanisms that produce observed effects (House, 1991; Manicas and Secord, 1983). This also means that scientific realists do not believe causal relationships can be fully known because we do not operate in a closed system. Causation is presumed to take place within a complex, multilayered world (Manicas and Secord, 1983). Thus, the context may have a significant effect on the nature of the causal process that is responsible for producing a given effect (House, 1991; Maxwell, 2004a, 2004b).

6 EXAMPLES OF MIXED METHODS APPROACHES FOR STUDIES DEALING WITH CAUSATION IN SPORTS MANAGEMENT

In this section we provide several examples of mixed methods approaches that might be useful for sport management studies concerned with causation. These approaches involve a consideration of both causal description and causal explanation and operate under the notion that quantitative approaches are well suited for studying causal description while qualitative approaches lend themselves to causal explanation (see Cook, 2002; Maxwell, 2004b; Shadish et al., 2002). The proposed mixed methods designs are derived from multiple sources (Hanson et al., 2005; Johnson and Onwuegbuzie, 2004; Morse, 1991; Tashakkori and Teddlie, 1998). Considering our interest in causal explanation, the proposed methods are, perhaps, most appropriate for the purpose of expansion – attaining a deeper and broader understanding of a given phenomenon.

To facilitate better understanding we have included examples of real life sport management research that originally used monomethod quantitative designs in order to illustrate the application of mixed methods approaches. Examples of research were selected in the areas of organizational behavior, marketing, and finance given that these are areas in which researchers seek an understanding of causal relationships. However, there could certainly be other areas in sport management that involve studies concerned with causation. Further, the methods proposed here by no means exhaust the possibility for other additional mixed methods causal studies.

6.1   Sport Marketing – Dominant-status Sequential Design (QUAN → QUAL)

A study by Kwon et al. (2007) is the first example of how mixed methods can be beneficial for ascertaining causation on a deeper and broader level (i.e., both causal description and causal explanation). Kwon et al. studied the mediating effect of perceived value in the relationship between team identification and intent to purchase team-licensed apparel. To clarify, team identification refers to the way in which an individual shares a common bond with their favorite sports team (Kwon et al.). Perceived value has been defined as 'the consumer's overall assessment of the utility of a product based on perceptions of what is received and what is given' (Zeithaml, 1988, p. 14). Purchase intention relates to an individual's decision to buy a particular product (Kwon et al.).

With a sample of 110 undergraduate and graduate students, structural equation modeling was employed to understand how team identification and perceived value affect consumers' intent to purchase collegiate team-licensed apparel. Quantitative attitude scales were used to measure each construct. Respondents then received a score on each measure which was then analyzed in the SEM analysis.

In general, results from the SEM analysis showed that perceived value had a moderate mediating effect between team identification and purchase intention. More significantly, Kwon et al. (2007) were particularly surprised not to find a direct significant relationship between team identification and purchase intention. They surmised that the failed relationship may have been related to including the price of the t-shirt whereas past studies had not. The researchers theorized that perhaps price sensitivity had a moderating effect on purchase intention. Additionally, Kwon et al. were puzzled by the low scores on the perceived value and purchase intention scales.

In response, an improved research design in this case would be a dominant-status sequential design (i.e., QUAN → qual). For the improved study suggested here, the quantitative methods are considered the dominant approach while an additional qualitative component is added to obtain a deeper understanding of the quantitative findings and to explore the nature of the causal relationships.[5] In this case, a combination of repeated case observations based on a logic model, one-on-one interviews with some of the respondents, and the use of focus groups could be added to shed light on the reason or reasons why there was not a stronger relationship between team identification and purchase intention. Repeated observations could be conducted to help untangle the direction of cause and effect in specific instances. Yin (2009), for example, recommends logic models as part of case study research focused on causation. He points out that 'The logic model deliberately stipulates a complex chain of events over an extended period of time. The events are staged in repeated cause–effect–cause–effect patterns, whereby a dependent variable (event) at an earlier stage becomes the independent variable (causal event) for the next stage' (p. 149).

Additionally, interviews could be used to attain a better understanding of why respondents scored low on the perceived value and purchase intention scales. In the interviews, the researchers could ask respondents some pointed questions about their level of team identification and their intent to purchase as well as how their perceived value of the t-shirt (in relationship to its price) moderated their intent to purchase. Questions about participants' reasons for their actions could be explored (Davis, 2005; Dretske, 1989) as well as ordering of contextual and intentional factors. A qualitative data analysis could then be conducted on the qualitative data for emerging themes or categories as well as information about sequencing of events (Creswell, 1998; Patton, 1987). Spradley (1979) explains how to locate causal language in written/transcribed text, and Miles and Huberman (1994) demonstrate the strategy of drawing network diagrams of events occurring over time to document local or particularistic chains of causation. These themes and network diagrams could be used to expand the researchers' understanding of how perceived value mediates or moderates the relationship between team identification and purchase intention.

6.2   Organizational Behavior – Equal-status Sequential Design (QUAL → QUAN)

A study by Cunningham and Sagas (2006) in the context of organizational behavior serves as a second example of how mixed methods can improve causal inference in sport management research. Cunningham and Sagas conducted a quantitative study to examine the effects of person–organization fit ('P–O fit') and leader–member exchange ('LMX') on turnover intentions among a sample of $N = 235$ male intercollegiate basketball coaches ($n = 74$ African American; $n = 161$ White). Organizational commitment was included as a mediating variable. To clarify terms, P–O fit refers to a person's compatibility with an organization (Kristoff, 1996). LMX is concerned with a leader's relationship with their subordinates (Graen and Uhl-Bien, 1995). Organizational commitment refers to an individual's psychological attachment to an organization (Meyer et al., 1993). Last, turnover intention refers to a person's desire to leave their place of employment (Cunningham and Sagas, 2006). Attitude scales were used to measure each variable. Structural equation modeling was used to statistically test the hypothesized causal model.

Results from the SEM analysis supported the researchers hypothesis that P–O fit and LMX has an effect on turnover intention and that the relationship is mediated by organizational commitment. As well, the results provided evidence to support their hypothesis that the relationship between P–O fit and organizational commitment would be stronger than the relationship between LMX and the same outcome variable. Results however, did not support their hypothesis that P–O fit would have a stronger relationship with turnover intention than would LMX and turnover intention. Rather, P–O fit and LMX had an equal relationship with the outcome variable.

An improved research design in this case would be an equal-status sequential design (i.e., QUAL → QUAN). Here, the qualitative and quantitative data would be given equal priority. The qualitative part of the study would be conducted first to dig deeply into the nature of the constructs and the appropriate model to be tested in the second, quantitative, phase of the study. This design is recommended given the complexity of the causes Cunningham and Sagas (2006) sought to examine. For example, they point out that P–O fit may entail 'congruence between an individual's *values, beliefs*, and *norms* [italics in original quote] with the organization's culture' (Cunningham and Sagas, 2006, p. 33). This statement suggests that P–O fit may be a complex molar package consisting of various molecular components.

Similarly, LMX is characterized by unique relationships between leaders and their subordinates and therefore may also involve a molar package that includes various molecular components. For example, in describing the nature of LMX, Cunningham and Sagas (2006) state, 'high-quality relationships are marked by mutual trust, obligation, support, and respect. On the other hand, low-quality relationships are marked by a relatively low level of mutual influence' (Cunningham and Sagas, 2006, p. 34). Additionally, they posit that subordinates in high quality relationships with their superiors are considered 'ingroup members whereas followers in low quality relationships are outgroup members'. These descriptions suggest that LMX is a complex construct.

Cunningham and Sagas (2006) argue that it is important for managers and organizations more generally to know which variable or variables (i.e., P–O fit and LMX) contribute the most to employee turnover. Additionally, they include organizational commitment as an important mediating variable and thus argue that organizational commitment may also play a role in turnover intention. We contend however, that it is just as important to obtain a deeper and clearer understanding of the specific causal mechanisms that are involved in the relationship between P–O fit and turnover intentions and LMX and the same variable (before statistically testing the grounded theory obtained). Therefore, it is suggested that equal priority be given; that is, the full power of both approaches should be used in this study, including the qualitative approach that would allow for an in-depth investigation and uncovering of important causal processes and a quantitative approach for testing the model obtained from the qualitative phase and from study of the previous research.

Specifically, interviews and focus groups could be conducted on multiple levels with a sample of assistant coaches and head coaches to attain a more in depth and expansive understanding of how LMX impacts organizational commitment and turnover intention. Collection of data from different levels or sources (e.g., head coaches and assistant coaches and other key organization members) has been referred to as multi-level use in the context of mixed methods (Tashakkori and Teddlie, 1998). Questions could be asked specifically about the types of circumstances and antecedents that relate to either high or low quality relationships between assistant and head coaches and how those relationships impact organizational commitment and turnover intention. As well, long-term field observations could be conducted to attain a deeper understanding of head coach–assistant coach relationships and to attempt to determine variable ordering from studying particular cases (Maxwell, 2004b; Patton, 1987; Yin, 2009).

A similar methodology could be used to better understand the overall relationship between P–O fit, organizational commitment, and turnover intentions. Specifically, one-on-one interviews or focus groups could be conducted with a sample of participants. Within the interviews, the researchers could ask certain questions about the specific causal mechanisms involved in the P–O fit, organizational commitment, and turnover intention relationship. Additionally, questions could also be posed that might help the researchers understand which causal variables play a stronger role, if any, toward influencing turnover intention, i.e., P–O fit, LMX, and organizational commitment.

Interviews could also be conducted with comparative or extreme cases (Maxwell, 2004b; Patton, 1987). That is, those with lower levels of LMX and P–O fit could be compared to cases with higher levels of the same variables. These cases could be identified from scores on the quantitative measures used by (Cunningham and Sagas, 2006). This would contribute to the QUAN component of the mixed methods design.

For analysis, emerging themes or categories could be gleaned from the qualitative data as well as the use of rich data or thick description (i.e., the use of data that provide a detailed account of events or processes experienced by the participants (Creswell, 1998; Maxwell, 2004a, 2004b; Patton, 1987). The quantitative phase of this study would employ Cunningham and Sagas's original quantitative methods (use of attitude scales and SEM) to statistically test the broader causal model incorporating causal relationships between P–O fit, LMX, organizational commitment, and turnover intention. However, based on emerging themes from the qualitative study, some changes or additions (more variables) might be made to the statistical model. Taken all together, the qualitative and quantitative data and findings could be integrated at the level of interpretation to obtain both a deep-particular and broad-general understanding of the causal relationships.

6.3   Finance – Equal-status Concurrent Design (QUAN + QUAL)

A study by DeSchriver (2007) provides a final example of how mixed methods can expand and deepen one's understanding of causal relationships. In the context of sport economics, DeSchriver examined the causal influence of a professional athlete's star status on fan attendance. Specifically, DeSchriver chose to focus on Freddy Adu of DC United in Major League Soccer (MLS). Adu was selected for two major reasons. First, his contract was the largest in MLS history at the time of his signing in 2003 ($500,000 × 6 years). Second, Adu was extremely young – only 14 years old with no prior professional playing experience. Thus, DeSchriver was interested in determining what level of impact a young inexperienced athlete with worldwide recognition would have on fan attendance. Additionally, MLS was selected among other major professional leagues because it is considered a young league that operates on a minor league level. The study's ultimate purpose, then, was to ascertain the effect of a young callow athlete with star status on fan attendance in a less established professional sport league.

DeShriver used multiple regression analysis to statistically examine the hypothesized causal relationship between Adu and fan attendance. Included in the analysis were a variety of other variables that might also explain changes in fan attendance including home versus away games, promotional activities, weather conditions, star players on opposing teams, home team performance, previous season visiting team performance and market specific characteristics (population size, racial composition, income and ticket prices). The data were collected across the 2004 MLS season. The total sample size was 150 games.

Results showed that the overall model was statistically significant and explained 67% of the variance in fan attendance. Of the 22 explanatory variables, 9 were statistically significant. The variable involving Adu and DC United as the visiting team was the third largest explanatory variable suggesting a strong relationship between Adu and fan attendance after controlling for the other variables in the equation. It was estimated that an additional 10958 spectators attended games when Adu and DC United were the visiting team. The two stronger explanatory variables were promotional activity variables – United States of America National Team double headers (20577 additional spectators) and Fireworks Night (14566 additional spectators).

An improved research design in this case would be an equal-status concurrent design (i.e., QUAN + QUAL). DeSchriver's (2007) discussion of results points to a couple of areas in which the addition of qualitative data could have expanded his understanding of the causal relationship between Adu and fan attendance. For DeSchriver's study, we believe the additional qualitative data should be given priority equal to that of the quantitative. This is because there are some areas within DeSchriver's study where qualitative data could make a significant contribution to the causal relationship between Adu and fan attendance.

First, DeSchriver noted that Adu saw little playing time during the 2004 season (his first) suggesting that many fans attended games to see Adu, the celebrity rather than Adu, the player. DeSchriver compares the phenomenon to the likes of former professional tennis player, Anna Kournikova who has been highly marketable despite a lack of on court success. To better understand fans' attraction to Adu, interviews could have been conducted with a sample of fans during pre-game festivities (e.g., tailgate barbecues). Fans could be asked to explain their attraction to Adu as well as their interest in other star players. Perhaps the reason for fans' attraction to star players varies in relationship to the particular player. This could be brought to bear in the qualitative analysis in which the researcher would look for emerging patterns or themes in the data. These emerging themes would help explain the meaning and nature of the relationships suggested in the original regression model. Because a basic multiple regression model only investigates direct effects and usually only checks for main effects (i.e., interaction effects typically are not examined), the qualitative data could help the researcher theoretically order the previously unordered set of independent variables and determine if any complex interaction terms should be included in the regression model. Additionally, the qualitative interviews might uncover some other reasons for fan attendance that were not originally specified in the regression analysis.

DeSchriver (2007) also noted that Adu's presence did not seem to have a lasting effect. Fan attendance across MLS games dropped in 2005 (the year subsequent to Adu's first). A clearer understanding of why many fans did not continue their interest in Adu could be obtained by conducting interviews with a sample of fans and asking questions about Adu's lasting appeal in 2005. Questions could also be posed to fans concerning their sustained attraction to other star players. It could be that there are certain athletes that maintain the ability to draw additional fans to games whereas other so-called star athletes do not. Information as such could be obtained by analyzing the qualitative data for emerging patterns or themes related to the qualities of star athletes. These themes could also be used to develop a questionnaire concerning qualities of star athletes. Administration of the questionnaire would allow for collection of data from a larger sample and thus a broader understanding. Doing so however, would change our original concurrent design to a sequential one.

7 CONCLUSION

It has been pointed out in this chapter that a popular objective in sport management research is to gain an understanding of cause and effect. When these causal studies are conducted they are almost always done with monomethod, quantitative approaches. Specifically, we argued that many sport management researchers seeking causal relationships may fail to recognize an important distinction between causal description and causal explanation. Causal description identifies an overall, molar causal relationship between an independent and dependent variable; however, such relationships tell the researcher little about the underlying causal mechanisms responsible for the causal relationship. This latter type of causal information has been referred to as causal explanation (Maxwell, 2004b; Salmon, 1998; Shadish et al.) or evidence of mechanisms (Russo and Williamson, 2007).

It was argued that both causal description and causal explanation are important for testing and unpacking causal relationships. We agree with Cook (2002) in his acknowledgement of the importance of both causal description and causal explanation when he states, 'Experiments should be designed to explain the consequences of interventions and not just to describe them. This means adding more details to an experiment's bare bones measurements and sampling plan, thus abjuring black box experiments' (p. 189). In the same vein, Shadish et al. posit:

> So causal explanation is an important route to the generalization of causal descriptions because it tells us which features of the causal relationship are essential to transfer to other situations. This benefit of causal explanation helps elucidate its priority and prestige in all sciences and helps explain why, once a novel and important causal relationship is discovered, the bulk of basic scientific effort turns toward explaining why and how it happens (p. 10).

However, despite the importance of causal explanation, Maxwell (2004a) and others have suggested that historically the standard view in philosophy of science has dominated scientific thinking, and this has resulted in dominance of only one approach to the study of causation and a lack of qualitative approaches for studying causation in local or particular contexts.

We explained what we believe the mixed methods research position to be with regard to causation, which essentially says to use multiple forms of causal evidence, multiple logics of cause and effect, and to study causation locally (i.e., in particular contexts) as well as more broadly (based on larger samples). We explained that the use of both quantitative and qualitative data will allow researchers to obtain a better understanding of both causal description and causal explanation. Such use of mixed methods is wanting in the field of sport management considering the small percentage of empirical studies in sport management currently adopting mixed methods approaches (Barber et al., 2001; Quarterman et al., 2006; Rudd, 2007).

We hope that this chapter will motivate sport management researchers to examine the many different ways that mixed methods can be used to improve their understanding of the phenomena they study. This type of open-mindedness and creativity requires sport management researchers to bracket their current research paradigm and creatively consider how the adoption of mixed methods approaches might help the advancement of research in sport management which is something that will benefit us all.

NOTES

1. It is acknowledged that mixed method approaches have been employed by researchers since at least the latter half of the 20th century (Brewer and Hunter, 1989; Greene et al., 1989). Therefore, it is possible that the journals we reviewed carry articles employing mixed method approaches prior to the 21st century. However, we felt a review of recent empirical articles over the last seven years would provide a reasonable estimation of how often mixed methods are used in sport management research.
2. Some of the studies identified employed correlational or statistical modeling techniques and use language such as 'relationship' rather than 'effect'. We argue that many of these studies are essentially interested in a cause and effect relationship rather than a correlation. For example, Kent and Chelladurai (2001) studied the 'correlation' between transformational leadership and organizational commitment. A personal communication with Kent revealed that he and his colleague were interested in a cause and effect relationship but refrained from such language given the lack of an experimental design and the ability to control or manipulate the independent variables (A. Kent, personal communication, 16 November 2007). We surmise that many other studies may operate under a similar rationale, and in fact, some research methods textbooks sometimes encourage writers to do so. We recommend that authors use language appropriate to the purpose of the study while simultaneously admitting and discussing the weaknesses of the research design.
3. Virtually no philosophers of social science or any quantitative researchers currently regard themselves as 'positivists'. We therefore use the more accurate term 'postpositivists' that recognizes that most quantitative researchers no longer fit the caricatures often associated with the label positivism.
4. Distinctions between qualitative and quantitative research should be viewed critically because there is a great deal of intra-paradigmatic variation. Nonetheless, our focus in this section is on inter-paradigmatic distinctions because mixed methods research attempts to mix quantitative and qualitative data and/or approaches. We do not imply that all quantitative or all qualitative research follows any single research or philosophical style. We also do not imply that all mixed methods researchers are alike (see Johnson et al., 2007b).
5. Although its not the focus of this manuscript, if possible, randomized experiments causally linking specific pairs of causes and effects is a quantitative research approach that would add to this (sport marketing) line of research.

REFERENCES

Barber, E.H., Parkhouse, B.L and Tedrick, T. (2001), A critical review of the methodology of published research in the *Journal of Sport Management* from 1991 through 1995 as measured by selected criteria, *International Journal of Sport Management*, **2**, 216–36.

Brewer, J. and Hunter, A. (1989), *Multimethod Research: A Synthesis of Styles*, Newbury Park, CA: Sage.

Caracelli, V.J. and Greene, J.C. (1993), Data analysis strategies for mixed-method evaluation designs, *Educational Evaluation and Policy Analysis*, **15** (2), 195–207.

Cook, T.D. (2002), Randomized experiments in educational policy research: a critical examination of the reasons the educational evaluation community has offered for not doing them, *Educational Evaluation and Policy Analysis*, **24** (3), 175–99.

Cook, T.D. and Campbell, D.T. (1979), *Quasi-experimentation: Design and Analysis Issues for Field Settings*, Boston, MA: Houghton Mifflin.

Creswell, J.W. (1998), *Qualitative Inquiry and Research Design: Choosing among Five Traditions*, Thousand Oaks, CA: Sage.

Creswell, J.W. and Plano Clark, V.L. (2007), *Designing and Conducting Mixed Methods Research*, Thousand Oaks, CA: Sage.

Cunningham, G.B. and Sagas, M. (2006), The influence of person-organization fit, leader-member exchange, and organizational commitment on organizational turnover intentions, *International Journal of Sport Management*, **2** (1), 31–49.

Davis, W.A. (2005), Reasons and psychological causes, *Philosophical Studies*, **122**, 51–101.

DeSchriver, T.D. (2007), Much adieu about Freddy: Freddy Adu and attendance in Major League Soccer, *Journal of Sport Management*, **21** (3), 438–51.

Dretske, F. (1989), Reasons and causes, *Philosophical Perspectives*, **3**, 1–15.

Garrison, J.W. (1986), Some principles of postpositivistic philosophy of science, *Educational Researcher*, **15** (9), 12–18.

Graen, G.B. and Uhl-Bien, M, (1995), Relationship-based approach to leadership: development of leader-member exchange (LMX) theory of leadership over 25 years: applying a multi-level multi-domain perspective, *Leadership Quarterly*, **6** (2), 219–47.

Greene, J.C (2007), *Mixing Methods in Social Inquiry*, San Francisco, CA: Jossey-Bass.

Greene, J.C, Caracelli, V.J. and Graham, W.F. (1989), Toward a conceptual framework for mixed-method evaluation designs, *Educational Evaluation and Policy Analysis*, **11**, 255–74.

Guba, E.G. and Lincoln, Y.S. (1988), Do inquiry paradigms imply inquiry methodologies?, in D.M. Fetterman (ed.), *Qualitative Approaches to Evaluation in Education: The Silent Scientific Revolution*, New York: Praeger, pp. 89–115.

Hanson, W.E., Creswell, J.W., Plano Clark, V.L, Petska, K.S. and Creswell, J.D. (2005), Mixed methods research designs in counseling psychology, *Journal of Counseling Psychology*, **52** (2), 224–35.

House, E.R. (1991), Realism in research, *Educational Researcher*, **20** (6), 2–9.

House, E.R. (1994), Integrating the quantitative and qualitative, in C.S. Reichardt and S.F. Rallis (eds), *The Qualitative-Quantitative Debate: New Perspectives*, San Francisco, CA: Jossey-Bass, pp. 13–22.

Howe, K.R. (1988), Against the quantitative-qualitative incompatibility thesis or dogmas die hard, *Educational Researcher*, **17**, 10–16.

Jick, T.D. (1979), Mixing qualitative and quantitative methods: triangulation in action, *Administrative Science Quarterly*, 24, 602–11.

Johnson, B.K., Mondello, M.J. and Whitehead, J.C. (2007a), The value of public goods generated by a National Football League team, *Journal of Sport Management*, **21** (1), 123–36.

Johnson, R.B. and Christensen, L. (2008), *Educational Research: Quantitative, Qualitative and Mixed Approaches*, 3rd edn, Thousand Oaks, CA: Sage.

Johnson, R.B. and Onwuegbuzie, A.J. (2004), Mixed methods research: a research paradigm whose time has come, *Educational Researcher*, **33** (7), 14–26.

Johnson. R.B. Onwuegbuzie, A.J. and Turner, LA. (2007b), Toward a definition of mixed methods research, *Journal of Mixed Methods Research*, **7** (2), 1–22.

Johnson, R.B. and Turner, L.A.(2003), Data collection strategies in mixed methods research, in A. Tashakkori and C. Teddlie (eds), *Handbook of Mixed Methods in Social and Behavioral Research*, Thousands Oaks, CA: Sage, pp. 297–319.

Kent, A. and Chelladurai, P. (2001), Perceived transformational leadership, organizational commitment, and citizenship behavior: a case study in intercollegiate athletics, *Journal of Sport Management*, **15**, 135–59.

Kristoff, A.L (1996), Person-organization fit: an integrative review of its conceptualizations, measurement, and implications, *Personnel Psychology*, **49** (1), 1–49.

Kwon, H.H. and Armstrong, K.L (2002), Factors influencing impulse buying of sport team licensed merchandise, *Sport Marketing Quarterly*, **11** (3), 151–63.

Kwon, H.H., Trail, G. and James, J.D. (2007), The mediating role of perceived value: team identification and purchase intention of team-licensed apparel, *Journal of Sport Management*, **21** (4), 540–54.

Manicas, P.T and Secord, P.F. (1983), Implications for psychology of the new philosophy of science, *American Psychologist*, **38**, 399–413.

Maxwell, J.A. (2004a), Causal explanation, qualitative research, and scientific inquiry in education, *Educational Researcher*, **33** (2), 3–11.

Maxwell, J.A. (2004b), Using qualitative methods for causal explanation, *Field Methods*, **16** (3), 243–64.

Maxwcll, J.A. and Loomis, D.M, (2003), Mixed methods design: an alternative approach, in A. Tashakkori and C. Teddlie (eds), *Handbook of Mixed Methods in Social and Behavioral Research*, Thousands Oaks, CA: Sage, pp. 241–71.

Meyer, J.P., Allen, N.J. and Smith, C.A. (1993), Commitment to organizations and occupations: extension and test of a three-component conceptualization, *Journal of Applied Psychology*, **78** (4), 538–51.

Miles, M.B. and Huberman, A.M. (1994), *Qualitative Data Analysis: An Expanded Source Book*, Thousand Oaks, CA: Sage.

Morgan, D.L. (1998), Practical strategies for combining qualitative and quantitative methods: applications to health research, *Qualitative Health Research*, **3**, 362–76.

Morse, J.M. (1991), Approaches to qualitative-quantitative methodological triangulation, *Nursing Research*, **40**, 120–23.

Morse, J.M. (2003), Principles of mixed methods and multimethod research design, in A. Tashakkori and C. Teddlie (eds), *Handbook of Mixed Methods in Social and Behavioral Research*, Thousands Oaks, CA: Sage, pp. 189–208.

Onwuegbuzie, A.J. and Johnson, R.B. (2006), The validity issue in mixed research, *Research in the Schools*, **13** (1), 48–63.

Patton, M.Q. (1987), *How to Use Qualitative Methods in Evaluation*, Newbury Park, CA: Sage.

Parton, M.Q. (1988), Paradigms and pragmatism, in D.M. Fetterman (ed.), *Qualitative Approaches to Evaluation in Education*, New York: Praeger, pp. 89–115.

Phillips, D.C. and Burbules, N.C. (2000), *Postpositivism and Educational Research*, Oxford: Rowman & Littlefield.

Quarterman, J., Jackson, E.N., Kim, K., Yoo, E., Yoo, C.Y., Pruegger, B. and Han, K. (2006), Statistical data analysis techniques employed in the *Journal of Sport Management*: January 1987 to October 2004, *International Journal of Sport Management*, 7(1), 13–30.

Reichardt. C.S. and Rallis, S.F. (1994), Qualitative and quantitative inquiries are not incompatible: a call for a new partnership, in C.S. Reichardt and S.F. Rallis (eds), *The Qualitative-Quantitative Debate: New Perspectives* San Francisco, CA: Jossey-Bass, pp. 85–92.

Rudd, A. (2005), Which 'character' should sport develop?, *The Physical Educator*, **64** (4), 205–11.

Rudd, A. (2007) Analysis of mixed-method studies in the *Journal of Sport Management*, *International Journal of Sport Management*, and *Sport Management Review* for the years 2000–2007, unpublished raw data.

Russo. F., and Williamson, J. (2007), Interpreting causality in the health sciences, *International Studies in the Philosophy of Science*, **21** (2), 157–70.

Salmon. W.C. (1998), *Causality and Explanation*, New York: Oxford University Press.

Shadish, W.R., Cook. T. and Campbell, D. (2002), *Experimental and Quasi-experimental Designs for Generalized Causal Inference*, Boston, MA: Houghton Mifflin Company.

Smith, J.K. and Heshusius, L. (1986), Closing down the conversation: The end of the quantitative-qualitative debate among educational inquirers, *Educational Researcher*, **15**, 4–12.

Spradley, J.P. (1979), *The Ethnographic Interview*, Fort Worth, TX: Holt, Rinehart, & Winston.

Tashakkori, A. and Teddlie, C. (1998), *Mixed Methodology: Combining Qualitative and Quantitative Approach*, Thousand Oaks, CA: Sage.

Tashakkori, A. and Teddlie, C. (2003), *Handbook of Mixed Methods in Social and Behavioral Research*, Thousand Oaks, CA:Sage.

Teddlie, C. and Johnson, R.B. (2009), Methodological thought since the 20th century, in C. Teddlie and A. Tashakkori (eds), *Foundations of Mixed Methods Research: Integrating Quantitative and Qualitative Techniques in the Social and Behavioral Sciences*, Thousand Oaks, CA: Sage, pp. 62–82.

Teddlie, C. and Tashakkori. A. (2006), A general typology of research designs featuring mixed methods, *Research in the Schools*, **13** (1), 12–28.

Trail, G.T., Fink. J.S. and Anderson, D.F. (2003), Sport spectator consumption behavior, *Sport Marketing Quarterly*, **12** (1), 8–17.

Trochim, W. (2007), *The Research Methods Knowledge Base*, Atomic Dog Publishing.

Whisenant, W. (2005), Organizational justice and commitment in interscholastic sports, *Sport, Education and Society*, **10** (3), 343–57.

Yin, R.K. (2009), *Case Study Research: Design and Methods*, Thousand Oaks, CA: Sage.

Zeithaml, V.A. (1988), Consumer perceptions or price, quality, and value: a means-end model and synthesis of evidence, *Journal of Marketing*, **52**, 2–22.

PART II

GOVERNANCE AND PERFORMANCE

3 Researching elite sport systems using process benchmarking

Leigh Robinson and Nikolai Böhlke

1 BENCHMARKING AND SPORT MANAGEMENT

The concept of benchmarking emerged in the management literature as a consequence of a series of successful organizational development projects conducted by the management of the US copier manufacturer Rank Xerox. Since its emergence in the 1980s, benchmarking has been used as a framework for researching best practice in a range of industries in an attempt to understand and improve performance. Within sport management for example, benchmarking has been used to compare the performances of public sport facilities and as a framework for investigating the management of sport teams (Böhlke, 2002). In the context of elite sport systems, research carried out to identify the factors that need to be present in order to facilitate international sporting success (de Bosscher et al., 2006, 2008; Green, 2007; Green and Oakley, 2001) has similarities to, or makes direct reference to, the process of benchmarking.

The existing research into the comparison and analysis of elite sport systems has led to a convergence in the design of those sport systems as many countries have attempted to copy what has been perceived to contribute to the performance of those nations who have a history of elite sporting success (Green and Oakley, 2001). However, despite this, it is clear there are countries that perform consistently better in some sports than other countries do, such as British cycling. Thus, while most elite sport systems now have similar infrastructure and practices, it is possible to argue that the management and operational delivery of the factors that make up an elite sport system are now more important differentiators for success than the mere existence of such a system. Thus, if sports wish to improve success, managers of elite sport systems should focus on improving the processes they follow, rather than simply increasing the support infrastructure they provide.

Knowledge of how to do this is limited, however it can be argued that benchmarking not only provides a method for obtaining information on what elite sport systems should consist of, but also how elite sport systems need to be delivered. Therefore, this chapter contains the results of research which used 'process benchmarking' as a research framework in order to understand how elite sport systems might be delivered. Benchmarking, and, in particular, process benchmarking, was chosen as the framework for this research as it provides a structure for systematically identifying as well as describing and analysing best practice in organizations that are performing highly. Process benchmarking requires a consideration of exemplar work processes and superior-performing comparison partners. Consequently, a number of the processes of the elite sport systems supporting the Swedish Athletics Association and the Norwegian Cross Country Skiing National Team were investigated using a generic process benchmarking methodology.

The chapter begins by presenting an overview of the method of benchmarking, followed by an outline of the approach used in the study. It ends with a discussion of the usefulness of benchmarking as a research tool for understanding the delivery of elite sport systems.

2   THE CONCEPT OF BENCHMARKING

The general idea that underpins the benchmarking approach constitutes an intuitive element of everyday life. Instead of developing a new solution for a specific problem, it is common to find an individual who has already developed a successful solution to the problem and to seek to understand the nature of that solution. Today, the term 'benchmarking' is prevalent in the management literature, where a wide range of different perceptions of the concept and its terminology have developed over the years (Böhlke, 2002). A review of the literature in this field highlights a large number of definitions of the concept, although most only differ in terms of the terminology they use, or the amount of information they include. For the purposes of this research the definition of Bogan and English (1994: 4) was adopted which states that: 'Benchmarking is the continuous process of measuring products, services and practices against the toughest competitors or those companies recognised as industry leaders.' Consequently, benchmarking can be considered as a structured process that leads to understanding of superior performance in the delivery of services and products (Camp, 1998; Lankfrod, 2002; Marwa and Zairi, 2008).

There are four other key terms to be found in the benchmarking terminology (Camp, 1995). First is the 'benchmarking object', which describes the organizational elements or practices and processes that are to be benchmarked. Second is the 'benchmarking subject', which refers to the organization that demonstrates superior performance in the delivery of the selected benchmarking object. These organizations serve as the comparison partner in a benchmarking project. Third is the concept of 'a benchmark', which describes an exemplar process or a level of performance. Finally, 'best practice' describes the processes or activities that lead to this benchmark. In other words, best practice refers to the practice a benchmarking subject uses to deliver a benchmarking object, which creates a benchmark.

Camp (1995: 18) further differentiates between a quantitative and a descriptive benchmark. The former refers to the actual performance best practice creates and that a benchmarking subject achieves. In the context of this study, this could be the number of gold medals that the athletes of an elite sport system win. A descriptive benchmark refers to the specific set of practices and methods which lead to, or create, the quantitative benchmark, such as the processes and structures applied in the superior-performing organization. Consequently, quantitative benchmarks can be used to identify performance levels as well as help to identify benchmarking subjects. Descriptive benchmarks are, however, the actual result of the data collection of a benchmarking project as they describe and explain how a superior performance has been achieved. Thus the terms best practice and descriptive benchmark can be used interchangeably. The obtaining of descriptive benchmarks was considered to be the key outcome of this particular research as these help to explain superior performance which may then be transferred to other elite sport systems.

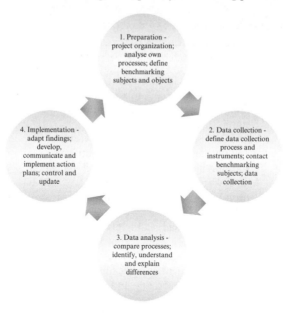

Source: Adapted from Böhlke (2002: 17).

Figure 3.1   The benchmarking process model

3   THE BENCHMARKING PROCESS

Several different models exist in the benchmarking literature which provide a structure for benchmarking research. The different models vary predominately in the way they structure the sub-phases of a benchmarking project. Horváth and Herter (1992) distinguish between three main phases, Shetty (1993) uses five and Kinni (1994) identified seven distinct stages of a benchmarking project. The differences in these research models are, however, mainly of a rhetorical nature (Keller, 1996) as they tend to include the same sub-elements. Hence, due to its proven practical and didactical potential (Böhlke, 2002), the four-step model summarized in Figure 3.1 was used as a research framework to guide this particular research.

3.1   The Preparation Phase

After considering the administrative matters required for every management project, such as the members of the project team or defining the general project and budget restrictions, Balm (1992) and Keller (1996) have noted that one of the key tasks in the first phase of a benchmarking project is the identification of the processes that require improvement – the benchmarking object. For an elite sport system this might be its coach education scheme or its talent identification programme, as these support structures are an established part of an elite sport system (see Table 3.1).

Once the benchmarking object is defined the next step in the preparation phase is the identification and selection of the comparison partner(s) for the benchmarking project

Table 3.1   Factors contributing to elite sport success

Oakley and Green (2001)	Digel (2002a, 2002b)	UK Sport (2006)	Green and Houlihan (2005)
An excellence culture	Support, especially financial, of the state	Financial support	Support for 'full-time' athletes
Appropriate funding		Participation in sport	
Clear understanding of the role of the different agencies	Economic success and business sponsorship	Scientific research	A hierarchy of competition opportunities centred on preparation for international events
Simplicity of administration	A media-supported positive sports culture	Talent identification and development system	
Effective system for monitoring athlete progress	Talent development through the education system	Athletic and post-career support	Elite facility development
Talent identification and targeting of resources	Talent development through the armed forces	Integrated approach to policy development	
Comprehensive planning system for each sport	A sport science support service	Coaching provision and coach development	
Lifestyle support		International competition	
Well-structured competition programmes		Training facilities	
Well-developed specific facilities			

Source: Houlihan and Green (2008).

– the benchmarking subject. As stated earlier, the benchmarking subject is considered to demonstrate best practice concerning the identified benchmarking object. Benchmarking subjects can come from a number of sources. For example, for an elite sport system with an inadequate coach education programme, a benchmarking subject could be a different elite sport system in the same country, a system in a different country in the same sport, a system in a different country and in a different sport, or even an organization outside the sport sector with a highly developed staff education programme (Stork, 2001). The careful selection, application and analysis of quantitative benchmarks can support the selection process of the benchmarking subject.

The selection of the benchmarking subject is the most decisive element in the preparation of a benchmarking project, as there are a number of factors to be considered in identifying a benchmarking subject. First, the benchmarking project team has to consider which organizations, worldwide, might provide the best practice of the benchmarking object they would like to improve. In addition, the identified organization(s) need to be willing to participate in the benchmarking project. Finally, and this is one of the most important as well as difficult steps in a benchmarking project, a decision has to be made as to which potential benchmarking subject might demonstrate the best practices that are most likely to be transferable to the organizational context faced by the organization that carries out the benchmarking exercise – the 'benchmarking' organization.

3.2   The Data Collection Phase

The main aim of data collection in a benchmarking project is to create a detailed understanding of the way the benchmarking subject achieves its performance (Krell, 2003; Lankfrod, 2002; Stork, 2001). In other words, the goal of data collection is to identify descriptive benchmarks (Camp, 1995). In the process of data collection, benchmarking requires a mature and close relationship between the organization which initiated the benchmarking exercise and the benchmarking subject. The information which is required to truly understand the nature of the processes which constitute best practice is detailed and might even be sensitive. Hence, such information can only be collected in an atmosphere of partnership. It cannot be collected through espionage or based only on publicly available documents (Boxwell, 1994). This constitutes a key difference between the benchmarking approach and other comparative management tools (Crook et al., 2003; Dresen, 1997). For example, a competitor analysis tends to be based on publicly available information about an organization that could come from strategy papers, annual reports or reports of analysts. Thus, a competitor analysis can be conducted without the direct contribution or even the knowledge of the organization which is the focus of the investigation. Benchmarking, on the other hand, requires the open and extensive cooperation of the benchmarking subject in order for the researcher or manager to understand the story behind the success of a benchmarking subject (Krell, 2003).

One of the challenges that arises at this stage is the issue of *tacit knowledge* which emerged from the work on organizational knowledge by Nonaka and Takeuchi (1995). This may mean the actual nature of a specific practice cannot be measured, verbalized or documented (Desouza, 2003; Smith, 2001). For example, in the field of elite sport services, this tacit knowledge might refer to the 'eye' of a talent scout and, if benchmarking a talent identification scheme, it must be considered whether the success of this scheme is based on the scouting protocols that are in place or if it is the result of the experience of specific individuals.

3.3   The Data Analysis Phase

Once a detailed understanding of the nature of the processes which underpin best practice has been developed, the goal of the data analysis phase is to develop recommendations for improving the processes in the organization that initiated the benchmarking project. These recommendations are established through identifying gaps between the practices of the organization looking to benchmark and those that have been observed in the benchmarking subject. One crucial element in this analysis process is the evaluation of the transferability of the identified practices. For this evaluation, it is important to develop an understanding of the degree to which the observed best practices are linked to the organizational context of the benchmarking subject, and how far this differs from the context of the benchmarking organization – a challenge which can be defused by careful selection of the benchmarking subject. For example, specific legal conditions might prohibit the transfer of an otherwise successful human resource and recruitment policy, for instance, due to the different employment laws in the USA and Great Britain, a 'hire and fire' strategy cannot be transferred from North America to the UK.

In this third phase it must also be critically evaluated if, and to what extent, the observed practices are actually responsible for the superior performance of the benchmarking subject. A detailed analysis of the data might reveal that the superior performance of the benchmarking subject is not due to any consciously made management interventions, but a result of specific environmental factors. For example, instead of being due to superior management practices, success may be due to a high level of resources which may not have been obvious when selecting the benchmarking subject.

The analysis of the nature of the observed best practices leads to the development of specific action plans upon which the organization that initiated the benchmarking project will try to improve its own processes. At this point, it is important to emphasize that benchmarking should not be misunderstood as simply a copying process. The action plans should consider the specific situation faced by the organization which initiated the benchmarking project and they have to take into account how this situation differs from that of the benchmarking subject (Krell, 2003; Lankfrod, 2002). In short, consideration needs to be given to whether or not the observed best practices constitute useful lessons for the benchmarking organization, leading to realistic action plans.

3.4   The Implementation Phase

The closing stage of a benchmarking project requires these action plans to be carefully integrated into an organization's culture and management infrastructure. It is critical that these plans are not regarded simply as a 'quick fix' troubleshooting or 'copy and paste' exercise. The challenge of transferability, or the comparison of 'apples' with 'pears', underpins all benchmarking projects and should be considered at all stages. Benchmarking is based on the comparison of one organization with that of another. As both organizations may have a different corporate history, culture and environment, there is a danger that benchmarking is not a comparison of 'like with like' and leads to the identification of non-transferable management practices (Fernandez et al., 2001; McGonagle and Fleming, 1993). Fernandez et al. (2001) doubt whether practices in their entirety can be successfully adopted by other organizations. They note that this is particularly an issue when trying to transfer practices across cultures (internationally). Furthermore, they go on to comment that although transferability is a tacit condition of benchmarking in that it is assumed that the processes investigated can be transferred to other contexts. This cannot be guaranteed, as processes can be culturally and socially embedded. This means that from the outset, benchmarking should be viewed as a source of innovation and new ideas, rather than a method of identifying practices that can be directly copied into the organization.

4   THE APPROPRIATENESS OF BENCHMARKING IN SPORT MANAGEMENT RESEARCH

The purpose of benchmarking is to reduce organizational learning costs by trying to benefit from the experiences of the benchmarking subject instead of developing new solutions for a given problem. The discussion above indicates that benchmarking is not a resource-neutral exercise. On the contrary, there are substantial hurdles to be overcome in the application of the concept, and overcoming these requires the investment of a substantial amount of resources and, even then, there is no guarantee of success. Research using a benchmarking approach must be carefully planned; it must be founded on an extensive data collection process; and the analysis of the data is a time-consuming and resource-intensive process. Despite this, there is no guarantee that the research will lead to the identification of tangible and transferable best practices. As argued previously, this might be due to fundamental differences in the organizational environment of the benchmarking party and the benchmarking subject, or due to the fact that the performance of the benchmarking subject is not the result of specific processes, but a result of the unique characteristics of specific key staff members. However, these threats and risks can be reduced through careful planning, especially in the selection of the benchmarking subject, by gathering a wide and detailed set of data, and by analysing this data carefully and critically.

4.1   The Research Context: Elite Sport Systems

'Elite sport system' is the term used to describe the infrastructure and processes used by a sport to identify, develop and prepare athletes for international sporting success. The emergence of international comparative studies of elite sport systems that show similarities to the benchmarking concept (de Bosscher et al., 2006, 2008; Green, 2007; Green and Oakley, 2001) was initiated by the success of the Australian Institute of Sport (AIS) in the build-up to the 2000 Olympic Games. As the main elements of the AIS were based on the former East German system, this suggested that it was possible to achieve success by copying the elements to be found in other successful sporting nations.

Research in this field has revealed a number of different elements and factors that have become common components of many successful elite sport systems (see Table 3.1; also refer to Chapter 5, by de Bosscher et al., 2013, in this volume, which sets out a significant study in this field.) First are contextual factors, such as a need for the general professionalization and further development of the infrastructure of an elite sport system. Second are factors which are not directly related to the actual support of individual athletes and coaches but which improve the management of different elite sport systems. This cluster of support activities includes comprehensive planning for individual sports and a clear prioritization of sports in the allocation of resources (Deloitte and Touche Sport, 2003; Green, 2007). Finally, there are a number of support services which directly affect athletes and coaches in their daily training, such as the presence of a talent identification scheme which leads promising youngsters on to an athlete development pathway. It is these services that are the focus of the research, using a benchmarking methodology, which is described below.

4.2   Benchmarking Elite Sport Systems

Although elements or factors that are common to successful elite sport systems have been identified through previous research, little evaluation has been carried out to assess the role of benchmarking as a method for producing descriptive benchmarks in the field of elite sport systems. Such an evaluation of the benchmarking concept is necessary to see if it can be used as a research tool to improve understanding of why some sports and nations continue to be more successful than others despite the convergence of elite sport system structures. For example, the All Blacks rugby team is consistently number one in the world, despite the similarity of the elite sport systems of other rugby playing nations to the system in place in New Zealand rugby. This suggests that the All Blacks are managing and operating their system in a manner that is different from other countries. Process benchmarking has particular value as a method for gaining this understanding, as research of this type should result in the emergence of descriptive benchmarks which provide explanations of how high performance is achieved. What follows is a description of research that aimed to assess the potential of process benchmarking when applied to the field of elite sport management to develop descriptive benchmarks, as well as to analyse their origins and transferability. The results of this project can be used to inform researchers and managers about the actual nature of best practise, as well as to improve knowledge of the general applicability of benchmarking in this field.

4.2.1   The preparation phase

The starting point of this project was the selection of the benchmarking objects. This was based on the findings of the meso-level research carried out by authors like Digel (2002a, 2002b), Green and Houlihan (2005), Green and Oakley (2001) and UK Sport (2006) which is set out in Table 3.1.

While there is no evidence to suggest a hierarchy concerning the importance of these different factors, resource constraints meant it was not possible to consider all elements of an elite sport system in the width and depth required when using process benchmarking methodology. An expert panel comprising Professor Barrie Houlihan, who is an expert in the policy associated with elite sport systems, Professor Leigh Robinson, who is an expert in the management of National Governing Bodies, and Dr Mick Green, who had carried out extensive research investigating the development and constituent parts of international elite sport systems, selected the following five factors or structural elements as benchmarking objects:

- the squad system to determine if and in how far this creates a long-term athlete development pathway;
- the hierarchy of coaches within this squad system to evaluate what different types of coaches exist, their educational requirements, and how the athlete–coach relationship develops in this system;
- the coach education programme, its general administration and the way it balances the delivery of theoretical and practical knowledge;
- the delivery of sport science support available to coaches and athletes;
- the design and delivery of the lifestyle support programme that is provided to athletes

These benchmarking objects were selected on the basis of the following selection criteria:

- Direct support services: as the aim of the research was to establish if process benchmarking can be used to describe the actual nature of best practice in the specific fields of sport systems and their management, only direct support services were considered for this research as they are arguably unique to the field of elite sport systems.

- Fundamentality: certain elements of an elite sport system require investigation in order to understand the working of the system as a whole. For example, a detailed analysis of the athlete development pathway and associated coaching structure was considered fundamental to understanding the delivery of any other support service around this structure.

- Structural interdependency: similar to the above, the choice of one factor leads to the choice of another factor. For example, investigating coaching structures within an elite sport system leads to consideration of its coach education scheme in order to explain how the structure works.

- Topicality: certain questions dominate debates surrounding contemporary elite sport systems and were thus considered worth investigating. For example, the appropriate structure for an athlete development pathway is frequently discussed by policy-makers, leading to the selection of this service for study.

Although other services set out in Table 3.1 meet some of these criteria, the five selected services were felt, by the expert panel, to be most appropriate for this research as they are the focus of extensive research literature, perceived to be easy to identify and describe and often interdependent, facilitating data collection.

Once the benchmarking objects were identified the next decisive step was the selection of the benchmarking subject(s). The following selection – respectively exclusion – criteria were utilized to identify potential benchmarking subjects for this research:

- A democratic political environment with a stable economy: when considering the transferability of the factors to be investigated, it appeared appropriate to consider only sport systems which are embedded in a democratic environment and a stable, strong economy as these factors provide an element of contextual consistency. For example, although countries like Cuba and Kenya show extraordinary sporting success, it was argued that their unique political and economic environments make it unlikely that their practices are transferable to other contexts.

- Discipline specific success: different countries demonstrate success in different sports and no one country can claim to be successful across all sports (de Bosscher et al., 2008). Therefore it was considered necessary to focus on success of specific sports, rather than the overall sporting success of a country. As the research also aimed to investigate whether this methodology would allow the detailed investigation necessary to understand how different factors of an elite sport system are delivered at an operational level, it was decided that the benchmarking process should focus on a sport-specific base. For example, the Norwegian sport system would not have been a potential comparison partner if its position on the medal table of the Summer Olympics was taken into account, however, its success in the sport of cross-country skiing is outstanding. Thus, it was decided to investigate how the chosen benchmarking objects were delivered to the Norwegian Cross Country Skiing Team, rather than in the Norwegian sport system as a whole.

- Recent and continuous success: a nation can be successful in a sport due to the emergence of one talented athlete or as a result of extensive investment as a consequence of being selected as a host city for a major event such as the Olympics. Such success is not necessarily the result of a system that systematically produces winning athletes and, therefore, potential comparison partners were required to not only show recent sporting success, but also a history of success.

- Sporting success per capita: as a crude measure of efficiency, sporting success was considered in the context of the available human resources and medals per capita was used in the final selection.

The research team applied the above selection criteria to the medal tables of a number of major international sporting events held over the past decade, including Winter and Summer Olympics, World and European Championships. Based on the information gathered, the Swedish Athletic National Team, represented by the Swedish Athletic Association (SAA), and the Norwegian Cross County Skiing National Team, represented by the Norwegian Skiing Federation (NSF), were selected as comparison partners for this research. The same panel of experts that confirmed the final selection of the benchmarking objects also supported this selection, as it was found that the above processes provided a practical and traceable rationale for choosing the benchmarking subjects.

4.2.2   The data collection phase

Semi-structured interviews were identified as the most appropriate data collection tool for the purpose of this study. This technique provided the necessary flexibility to investigate best practice which was anticipated to be innovative and varied from context to context. Conducting questionnaires or structured interviews would not have allowed this flexibility to investigate the actual nature of the processes under investigation. It was necessary to interview individuals such as the general secretaries of the two investigated federations, the head coaches of national teams or representatives of the management of the general national elite sport support centres in Norway and Sweden in order to develop a basic understanding of the more general elite sport support policy and infrastructure the two benchmarking subjects operated within. However, these individuals were not in a position to provide the detailed insights on the operational provision of the elite sport support service that this research required, i.e., the nature of the day-to-day interaction between athletes, coaches and support staff members in the delivery of the chosen benchmarking objects. Hence, this study differentiated between three different clusters of interviewees:

- Strategic design: this included interviewees from the general management of the elite sport system such as the general secretary of a federation or leaders of the different service units such as a sport science support coordinator or coach education officer.
- Operational delivery: this included those individuals who were working in the actual delivery of the different support services; for example, regarding the delivery of sport science support, this referred to the sport scientists and diagnosticians in the laboratories.
- Recipient: this included individuals such as coaches and athletes who received the support services the elite sport systems provided.

This system made it possible to triangulate interviewees and led to a more valid picture of the broader context conditions of the investigated elite sport systems, the general design of the actual elite sport support infrastructures, and the operational provision of the different support services which were chosen as benchmarking objects for this study.

Data collection was carried out in 2005, during two separate study visits that were timed to suit the elite sports systems involved in the study. In total, 50 individuals were interviewed (22 in Sweden and 28 in Norway) and nearly 65 hours of interviews were analysed. Guidelines for the interviews were devised by a review of the micro-level research in which subject experts, such as sport sociologists, psychologists or physiologists have investigated problems in the delivery of the specific elite sport support services. Based on this literature it was possible to become familiar with the operational issues and challenges concerning the delivery of the selected benchmarking objects and to design the guidelines for the semi-structured interviews. The findings from the interviews were supported and triangulated by an analysis of pertinent documents made available by the benchmarking subjects.

4.2.3   The data analysis phase

The processing and analysis of the data was done in two steps. The purpose of the first phase was to develop a detailed understanding of the nature of the two investigated sport systems and the practices that they use. The two cases were handled, in this first phase, very much in isolation. The second phase of the analysis process was of a more comparative nature in order to identify common themes between the two systems.

All interviews were recorded and transcribed. The transcripts were imported into the software NUDIST (an earlier version of NVivo) which was then used to structure and manage the data. Once all data was processed, a report was written for each of the two case studies and sent back to key interview partners in Norway and Sweden for the purpose of respondent validation. These reports provided a detailed overview of the nature of the investigated service delivery practices as applied in the two benchmarking subjects as perceived by the researcher.

The reports also included a discussion of the background and origin of the observed practices. Here an attempt was made to analyse whether the practices which were observed in Sweden or Norway depended on the respective cultural, social, economical or geographical context; if they were a result of clear managerial interventions or if they were a result of the intangible competence of, or the personal relationships between, key staff members. In other words, the discussion in the report sought to evaluate the context dependency of the observed practices.

For full results see Böhlke (2006; 2007), however, the research showed that both benchmarking subjects provided the support services which were selected as benchmarking objects. It was also possible to identify and describe the processes which underpin the delivery of these different support services in great detail. This suggests the strong potential of process benchmarking as a method for generating descriptive benchmarks. Furthermore, several interviewees indicated that the investigated support services, and the way these are delivered in the Swedish and Norwegian sport systems, were essential factors contributing to the sporting success of the two systems. Therefore, this research suggests that benchmarking has potential as a research tool to identify and describe descriptive benchmarks in the specific context of elite sport systems that have clear relevance for performance. Both were achieved even though the design of the different processes observed in Norway and Sweden often turned out to be unconventional when compared with the expectations which can be derived from the contemporary elite sport management and policy literature regarding the design of best practice.

First, in some areas, services appeared to be less extensive than expected from reading the literature and compared to what is common in other sport systems. For example, there was little evidence of the systematic physiological assessment or the psychological support associated with many elite sport systems and set out in Table 3.1. Even more importantly, for this research, is the fact that many of the investigated services were, at first, difficult to identify and describe as they were integral to, or included in, other practices. For example, coaches appeared to cover many of the tasks that a lifestyle support manager would be responsible for in other systems. Most importantly, however, was that some functions were satisfied by the wider sport context, rather than being specific to the elite sport system. Neither comparison partner had a detailed athlete development pathway or a sophisticated selection system for the national team. Thanks to a substantial, volunteer-led club structure and an extensive national competition framework, the national team manager seemed to simply select the winners of the respective national championships to be members of the team. This suggests that without the thorough and comprehensive data collection procedures followed in this research, obtaining descriptive benchmarks and understanding their background may be problematic in the context of elite sport systems as there seems to be the potential to overlook the presence of key processes if the investigation is superficial.

4.2.4   The implementation phase

As stated earlier, the final stage of research using a benchmarking methodology requires new practices and processes to be carefully implemented into an organization's culture and management infrastructure. Although this research did not attempt this phase, it does suggest that there may be problems with this, echoing concerns expressed by others regarding the potential challenges of this final phase. On the one hand, it was possible to obtain detailed data on the benchmarking objects, to describe their impact on performance and reveal the five interdependent factors that are set out below that helped to explain the emergence of the practices observed in Sweden and Norway and why they work well in these contexts. However, these factors also indicate that a successful, direct transfer of these practices to other sport systems may not, in many cases, be fully possible. This poses a challenge to the application of the benchmarking methodology in elite sport systems, if the intention is to simply copy what has occurred in the benchmarking subject.

Factor 1: Sociocultural context. Many of the practices and structures observed in Norway and Sweden reflected elements and characteristics of their general socio-cultural contexts as suggested by Fernandez et al. (2001). This suggests that their application may be difficult in other sociocultural contexts (See factor 3 for example).

Factor 2: Strong club competition infrastructure. Both sports have an extensive, volunteer-led club infrastructure with a strong club competition environment. Although the use of local clubs and racing teams to provide an athlete development pathway is, as the Scandinavians illustrate, a highly effective strategy for success, it can only be a successful solution if a sport system has a similarly strong club environment to rely on.

Factor 3: Working atmosphere in the sport environment. The research also found that the working atmosphere in the two sport systems had a significant and positive impact on their success. Interviewees felt that this system had emerged as a reflection of the traditionally short hierarchical distance between the elite and the 'average people' which can be found in many areas in the two Scandinavian societies (factor one). As this may not exist in other countries, the transfer of some of this practice may be difficult.

Factor 4: Personality and knowledge of key agents. The inherent or tacit knowledge (Desouza, 2003; Smith, 2001) and personality of key managers, coaches and athletes were identified as key factors in the success of the different initiatives identified by the research. Even though an attempt was made in the research to describe how key individuals interacted with their colleagues, as Desouza (2003) and Smith (2001) have argued, it remains difficult to fully understand all 'tacit' elements which made their behaviour so successful.

Factor 5: Conscious interventions. A number of interventions had been introduced in order to change and improve the atmosphere in the two systems, and these interventions may have the potential for introduction into other elite sport systems. However, although these interventions can be described in detail it remains difficult to evaluate to what extent the general cultural context in Norway and Sweden (factors 1 and 3), the specific structure of and atmosphere in the two sport environments (factors 2 and 3), and the personality and knowledge of key agents (factor 4) provided the required foundation for the initiatives to work (Böhlke, 2007).

5   CONCLUSIONS AND IMPLICATIONS FOR MANAGERS

The findings of the research lead to the conclusion that there are challenges in using benchmarking as a method for learning about the processes that may improve the management and delivery of elite sport systems and transferring these lessons to other systems. The research identified a number of practices that probably have limited, direct transferability to other elite sport systems due to high dependence on the cultural background, structural design or staff of the Swedish and Norwegian elite sport systems. For example, the research suggested that the use of local clubs to provide an athlete development pathway can be a highly effective strategy for success, however, it will only be successful if an elite system has a similarly strong club environment as its foundation. It was also shown that the enthusiasm, openness, personality and background of key coaches, managers and practitioners were more important for the successful cooperation between the national teams and the central support systems in Norway and Sweden than contracts and formal agreements.

Thus, the findings of the research lead to the conclusion that although benchmarking is a valuable methodology for understanding the nature and complexity of the structures of elite sport systems, it does not necessarily mean that the descriptive benchmarks generated by the research can be directly utilized by managers of other elite sport systems. Thus, from a management perspective, process benchmarking should not be carried out in an attempt to identify a ready-made solution for a specific benchmarking object.

Rather, managers should understand process benchmarking as a method for innovation, idea generation and general inspiration based on the descriptive benchmarks that emerge from the research exercise.

This is only possible, however, with the thorough methodological approach followed in this benchmarking exercise. It appears crucial to employ an extensive and flexible data collection strategy, to carry out a careful and intensive data analysis, as well as a sensitive and critical evaluation of the observed best practices and their transferability, in order to bring a benchmarking exercise to a successful conclusion. Although this is time-consuming and may be expensive, it is the only way of understanding how best practice is possible. At a more general level, benchmarking requires a high degree of honesty and openness as only due to the willingness of the interviewees to share their knowledge and experiences was it possible in this project to identify descriptive benchmarks. Managers should gain this commitment from their benchmarking partners before embarking on the data collection.

This study showed that benchmarking is not a methodology that will provide a universal remedy for the problems managers of elite sport systems face. The approach, however, has the potential to inform managers and researchers about new and alternative ideas in order to design elite sport systems and operational processes within them. Thus, it also has potential in other sport contexts such as investigating why the quality of one sport facility is higher than another, or understanding how a professional league maintains its spectator numbers when another is experiencing a reduction in spectators. Overall, it seems appropriate to conclude that, based on this research, benchmarking is a useful research framework for improving understanding of good and innovative practice in the management of sport organizations, including elite sport systems.

REFERENCES

Balm, G.J. (1992), *Benchmarking: A Practitioner's Guide for Becoming and Staying Best of the Best*, Schaumburg, IL: QPMA Press.
Bogan, C.E. and English, M.J. (1994), *Benchmarking for Best Practice: Winning through Innovative Adaptation*, New York: McGraw-Hill.
Böhlke, N. (2002), Benchmarking im Sportmanagement [Benchmarking in sports management], diploma thesis, University of Cologne, Cologne.
Böhlke, N. (2006), Benchmarking of elite sport systems, unpublished doctoral thesis, University of Loughborough, Loughborough.
Böhlke, N. (2007), New insights in the nature of best practice in elite sport system management – exemplified with the organisation of coach education, *New Studies in Athletics*, 21 (1), 49–59.
Boxwell, R. (1994), *Benchmarking for Competitive Advantage*, New York: McGraw-Hill.
Camp, R. (1998), *Global Cases in Benchmarking*, Milwaukee, WI: ASQ Quality Press.
Camp, R. (1995), *Business Process Benchmarking – Finding and Implementing Best Practices*, Milwaukee, WI: ASQ Quality Press.
Crook, T., Ketchin, D. and Snow, C. (2003), Competitive edge: a strategic management model, *Cornell Hotel and Restaurant Administration Quarterly*, 44 (3), 44–53.
De Bosscher, V., De Knop, P., van Bottenburg, M. and Shibli, S. (2006), A conceptual framework for analysing sports policy factors leading to international sporting success, *European Sport Management Quarterly*, 6 (2), 185–215.
De Bosscher, V., De Knop, P., van Bottenburg, M. and Shibli, S. (2008), *The Global Sporting Arms Race*, Oxford: Meyer and Meyer Sport.
De Bosscher, V., Truyens, J., van Bottenburg, M. and Shibli, S. (2013), Comparing apples with oranges in

international elite sports studies: is it possible?, in S. Söderman and H. Dolles (eds), *Handbook of Research on Sport and Business*, Cheltenham, UK and Northampton, MA, USA: Edward Elgar, pp. 94–111.

Deloitte and Touche Sport (2003), *'Investing in Change' – High Level Review of the Modernisation Programme for Governing Bodies of Sport*, London: Deloitte & Touche, UK Sport, available at: http://www.lsersa.org/modernisation/Report_Master_22_July.pdf (accessed 19 September 2011).

Desouza, K.C. (2003), Barriers to effective use of knowledge management systems in software engineering, *Association for Computing Machinery*, **46** (1), 99.

Digel, H. (2002a), *Organisation of High-performance Athletes in Selected Countries*, final report for the International Athletics Foundation, Tübingen: University of Tübingen.

Digel, H. (2002b), A comparison of elite sport systems, *New Studies in Athletics*, **17** (1), 37–49.

Dresen, P. (1997), *Benchmarking in der Beschaffung [Benchmarking in Procurement]*, Cologne: Hundt Druck.

Ferdenandez, P., McCarthy, I. and Rakotobe-Joel, T. (2001), An evolutionary approach to benchmarking, *Benchmarking: An International Journal*, **8** (4), 281–305.

Green, M. (2007), Olympic glory or grassroots development? Sport policy priorities in Australia, Canada and the UK 1960–2006, *International Journal of the History of Sport*, **24** (7), 921–53.

Green, M.J. and Houlihan, B.M.J. (2005), *Elite Sport Development: Policy Learning and Political Priorities*, London: Routledge.

Green, M. and Oakley, B. (2001), Elite sport development systems and playing to win: uniformity and diversity in international approaches, *Leisure Studies*, **20** (4), 247–68.

Horváth, P. and Herter, N.R. (1992), Benchmarking: Vergleich mit den Besten der Besten [Benchmarking: compare with the best of the best], *Controlling*, **4** (1), 4–11.

Houlihan, B. and Green, M. (2008), *Comparative Elite Sport Development: Systems, Structures and Public Policy*, Oxford: Butterworth-Heinemann.

Keller, T. (1996), *Benchmarking – Methoden und Techniken [Benchmarking – Methods and Techniques]*, Chemnitz: Univation.

Kinni, T.B. (1994), Measuring up, *Industry Week*, **12**, 27–8.

Krell, E. (2003), Why benchmarking does not always lead to best practices, *Business Finance*, October, 20–27, available at: http://www.businessfinancemag.com/magazine/archives/article.html?articleID=14008 (accessed 29 April 2011).

Lankfrod, W.M. (2002), Benchmarking: understanding the basics, *The Coastal Business Journal*, **1** (1), 57–62.

Marwa, S. and Zairi, M. (2008), A pragmatic approach to conducting a successful benchmarking expedition – case of Dubai Holding Group, *The TQM Journal*, **29** (1), 59–67.

McGonagle, J. and Fleming, D. (1993), New options in benchmarking, *The Journal for Quality and Participation*, **16** (4), 60–68.

Nonaka, I. and Takeuchi, H. (1995), *The Knowledge-creating Company*, New York: Oxford University Press.

Oakley, B. and Green, M. (2001), The production of Olympic Champions: international perspectives on elite sport development systems, *European Journal for Sport Management*, **8** (1), 83–105.

Shetty, Y.K. (1993), Aiming high: competitive benchmarking for superior performance, *Long Range Planning*, **26** (1), 39–44.

Smith, A.E. (2001), The role of tacit and explicit knowledge in the workplace, *Journal of Knowledge Management*, **5** (4), 311–22.

Stork, K. (2001), Benchmarking 101, *Purchasing*, **130** (10), 18.

UK Sport (eds) (2006), *Sport Policy Factors Leading to International Sporting Success: A Comparative Study*, London: UK Sport.

4 Qualitative comparative analysis of sport governing bodies: a tool on ways towards high performance
Mathieu Winand and Thierry Zintz

1 INTRODUCTION

Organizational performance is usually seen as the combination of efficiency and effectiveness within organizations (Madella et al., 2005). Several scholars have analysed this central topic in the sport management literature (Bayle and Madella, 2002; Chelladurai et al., 1987; Frisby, 1986; Koski, 1995; Madella, 1998; Madella et al., 2005; Papadimitriou, 1999, 2002, 2007; Papadimitriou and Taylor, 2000; Shilbury and Moore, 2006; Vail, 1985; Winand et al., 2010; Wolfe et al., 2002). Their approaches primarily consist of the identification of dimensions of performance and the range of indicators measuring them. However, little research in this field has focused on ways that facilitate high performance. The main reason for this is that it is difficult to understand how organizational aspects of sport governing bodies act and interact to produce high performance (Bayle and Robinson, 2007). This might deal with causal complexity.

To address this gap, we suggest applying an innovative method called Qualitative comparative analysis (QCA) (Ragin, 1987). This configurational comparative approach develops a conception of causality that leaves room for complexity (Berg-Schlosser and De Meur, 1994; Rihoux and Ragin, 2008). It is a valuable method for strategic management researches (Greckhamer et al., 2008). Throughout this method, we argue that complex combinations of factors might lead to performance in the sport organization sector, in line with suggestions of Wolfe et al. (2002). Furthermore, a call for such mixed method approaches has emerged in the sport management literature. They are considered to lead to a 'better understanding of both causal description and causal explanation' (Rudd and Johnson, 2010: 23; 2013). Our research intends to highlight combinations of the key determinants linked with high performance of sport governing bodies. We apply QCA in order to test a conjecture and to develop new theoretical arguments (Rihoux and Ragin, 2008) in the area of organizational performance in the sport governing body context. Qualitative comparative analysis could also be used to test hypothesis or existing theories, or simply to summarize data and check their coherence according to the cases studied (Rihoux and Ragin, 2008).

This chapter considers the 49 competition-oriented (versus leisure-oriented) sport governing bodies from the French-speaking community of Belgium (called CSGBs hereafter). These are small-sized non-profit sport organizations. Owing to the organization and coordination of sport by communities in Belgium – from which they receive grants – they are in charge of the tasks and activities usually assigned to national sport governing bodies. The system of regulation and environment they all share make it possible to compare these sporting organizations.

First, we briefly introduce the notion of organizational performance to highlight the strategic goals and the potential determinants of performance of CSGBs. This is followed by a presentation of the methodology – performance measurement, internal functioning assessment and QCA – and its application to the organizational performance of CSGBs. Finally, building upon crisp-set QCA (Ragin, 1987, 2008; Rihoux and Ragin, 2008), we highlight combinations of key determinants that are linked with high performance, and discuss the results and the application of QCA for further research.

2   ORGANIZATIONAL PERFORMANCE OF CSGBS

Madella et al. (2005) proposed a definition of organizational performance in the sport management literature we selected. It refers to 'the ability to acquire and process properly human, financial and physical resources to achieve the goals of the organization' (ibid.: 209). As a result, organizational performance should be understood as the combination of 'means and ends' of organizations. The 'means' group the determinants of performance, including the human and managerial skills. The 'ends' group the strategic goals of the organization, which are the *raison d'être* of the organization.

2.1   Strategic Goals of CSGBs

According to the multidimensional models of organizational performance of Bayle and Madella (2002), Chelladurai et al. (1987), Frisby (1986), Madella et al. (2005), Papadimitriou and Taylor (2000) and Shilbury and Moore (2006), there are three main strategic goals for sport governing bodies: elite sport, sport for all and customers strategic goals. These strategic goals are also those determined by authorities for all the 49 sport governing bodies we study (Government of the French-speaking Community of Belgium, 1999). In the next step, we illustrate how to measure their ability to achieve these strategic goals in comparison with one another.

The elite sport strategic goal refers to the strategic objectives 'to obtain international sport results' and 'to increase athletes' participation in international sport competitions'. The sport for all strategic goal includes the strategic objective 'to increase sport activities for members'. The customers strategic goal groups the non-sport strategic objectives of CSGBs including 'to sustain sport values in society' and 'to increase their membership figures'. We assume that achieving these three strategic goals will result in high organizational performance in CSGBs which can be reached through key determinants.

2.2   Potential Determinants of Performance for CSGBs

Ten potential determinants related to high organizational performance were selected from the literature on non-profit organizations and sport governing bodies. All the relevant determinants which might play a role in high performance have to be selected. Afterwards, we would be able to reduce the number of determinants so to focus on key determinants. We present each potential determinant – numbered from 1 to 10

– according to the non-profit literature strengthened by the specific literature on non-profit sport organizations (that is, centralization, governance of volunteer(s), task orientation and supervision, vision, external relations, financial independence, innovative activities, elite training structure, size and sport objectives). We did not take into account the age of CSGBs because a great majority of them was created in 1977 and 1978, as a consequence of the organization and coordination of Sport by Communities. Content analysis of a focus group discussion involving experts (that is, two chairs and the administrative director of different CSGBs and the Vice-President of the Belgian Olympic and Interfederal Committee) was performed to confirm the relevance of the potential determinants selected and to adapt them in the CSGB context. The 10 determinants are presented here.

2.2.1   Determinants 1 and 2: centralization and governance of volunteer(s)

Glisson and Martin (1980: 33) underlined the fact that a 'highly centralized human service organization is likely to be highly productive'. They highlight the involvement of paid staff in the decision-making processes as a key criterion of governance. In the sport governing-body context, Bayle (1999) argued that the character of the chair (usually a volunteer) has an effect on performance. Is he or she a leader, or are there several volunteers and/or paid staff involved in the decision-making processes? Thus, centralization refers to the number of decision-makers in CSGBs, and governance of volunteer(s) refers to the role of the decision-maker(s) in the organization.

2.2.2   Determinant 3: task orientation and supervision

Schmid (2002) linked the decentralization/centralization of management to the professionalization of the staff of human service organizations. Decentralized management is most appropriate where the staff are primarily professional, so organizational structure and patterns of management tend to be relatively informal and flexible, whereas centralized management is most appropriate where high levels of supervision are required and there is formalized decision-making (Crittenden et al., 2004; Schmid, 2002). The sport management literature (Bayle, 1999; Papadimitriou, 2002; Thibault et al., 1991; Zintz, 2004) focuses on the role played by technical paid staff (in charge of the organization of sport activities) and the delegation of tasks. As CSGBs are very small organizations with few staff (60 per cent have two or fewer paid staff), their organization chart is flat and therefore some structures overlap and formalism is reduced (Zintz and Camy, 2005). Thus, task orientation and supervision focuses on the presence of someone in charge of the division of labor and supervision of paid staff

2.2.3   Determinant 4: vision

Several researchers pointed to the involvement of board members of non-profit organizations in strategic planning as a key factor related to performance (Bradshaw et al., 1992; Siciliano, 1997). Also, Brown (2005) identified the adherence of the board to the organization's mission as one factor of success. In the sport organization context, Bayle and Madella (2002) and Madella et al. (2005) underlined not only the role of board members in high performance, but also the organizational atmosphere created by the paid staff – and the involvement of sport clubs which form part of the vision of CSGBs.

2.2.4   Determinant 5: external relations

The connection to influential funders developed by board members of non-profit organizations (Brown, 2005) or the connection of sport governing bodies to national or international partners (Madella et al., 2005; Papadimitriou and Taylor, 2000), as well as their ability to promote their sport (Bayle, 1999), might affect their revenues and reputation, and thus their performance. In addition, these external relations affect each other, given that partnerships make it possible to invest in promotion which might attract additional new partners.

2.2.5   Determinant 6: financial independence

The ability of board members of non-profit organizations to attract resources has been emphasized by researchers (Brown, 2005; Smith and Shen, 1996) as a factor, combined with others, that is linked to organizational effectiveness. In the CSGB context, this is demonstrated mainly by independence from public funds, because significant sponsorship resources are rare (Zintz, 2004). A CSGB which receives less than 40 per cent of its funding from public resources is considered to be financially independent, whereas a CSGB which receives more than 40 per cent of its funding from public resources is considered to be financially dependent (Winand, 2009; Zintz, 2004). The latter CSGB is likely to be weak at self-financing (Winand, 2009).

2.2.6   Determinant 7: innovative activities

Innovation refers to the development of a new idea which will be of benefit to the organization (Camisón-Zornoza et al., 2004; Damanpour, 1987; Read, 2000). It can lead to higher performance (Deshpande et al., 1993). Sport governing bodies support services and programmes to increase mass participation in sport and to develop sport activities (Madella et al., 2005; Slack and Parent, 2006). Thus, innovative activities focus on the innovative processes CSGBs could put in place in their sport and non-sport services to satisfy their members.

2.2.7   Determinant 8: elite training structure

According to researchers (Deloitte and Touche Sport, 2003; Madella et al., 2005; Papadimitriou and Taylor, 2000), services sport governing bodies provide to their elites might help them to develop elite performance. Elite training structure concerns strategies and programmes implemented to identify talented members, to develop their sport potential and to support their training. Owing to the size of CSGBs in comparison with national sport governing bodies (NSGBs) from other countries, their elite training structures are small-scale.

2.2.8   Determinants 9 and 10: size and sport objectives

Size has long been linked with performance. It can be interpreted as the number of customers or staff (Papadimitriou, 2002; Slack, 1985; Smith and Shen, 1996). In the CSGB context, size is of course crucial, as well as whether the sport they promote is an Olympic or non-Olympic sport, revealing their sport objectives. These are the criteria authorities refer to in order to allocate grants. Large size (5000 members according to Communities' Decree) and/or Olympic-oriented CSGBs (their sport is enrolled in the Olympic Games) receive more grants than other CSGBs.

Each determinant emphasized may play a crucial role in the achievement of the three strategic goals of CSGBs. However, specific determinants might also be key success factors. In order to analyse the link between the possible key determinants and performance, we use QCA. Qualitative comparative analysis represents one method by which the exploration of complexity in organizations, such as CSGBs, can be conducted (Kogut and Ragin, 2006). We first measure the achievement of the strategic goals of the 49 CSGBs in order to distinguish high-performing CSGBs from low-performing ones. In the next step, we assess the determinants that CSGBs possess. This mixed method design is presented in the next section.

3   METHODOLOGY

Qualitative comparative analysis constitutes both an approach and a technique. First, we explain the QCA approach representing the essence of this innovative method. Afterwards, we detail the preliminary steps of measuring the dependent variable (performance), selecting cases and assessing the independent variables (determinants). Finally, we give guidance to properly use one of the specific QCA techniques: crisp-set QCA (csQCA).

3.1   The Qualitative Comparative Analysis Approach

Qualitative comparative analysis aims to identify the different combinations of causally relevant 'conditions' linked to an outcome (Ragin, 2008). It is a configurational comparative approach. It considers each case as a complex combination of dynamic characteristics. Even if QCA should fundamentally be considered as a case-oriented tool (Rihoux and Lobe, 2009), the primary aim of Charles Ragin (1987), initiator of this new research methodology, was to 'integrate the best features of the case-oriented approach with the best features of the variable-oriented approach' (Ragin, 1987: 84).

Fiss (2007: 1180) argues that configurational analysis takes a 'systemic and holistic view of organizations, where patterns or profiles rather than individual independent variables are related to an outcome such as performance'. Consequently, QCA enables the highlighting, according to 'causal regularities', of key combinations of properties (independent variables called 'conditions' in QCA terminology) leading to a phenomenon (the dependent variable called 'outcome' in QCA terminology). These properties are necessary – the invariable aspect through cases – and/or sufficient – the contingent aspect of phenomena – 'causes' (Rihoux and Ragin, 2008). Therefore, QCA allows for causal complexity (equifinality, multifinality). Multiple causes combined with each other (conjunctural causation) could lead to the presence of a phenomenon the absence of which could require different explanations (asymmetric causality).

Qualitative comparative analysis enables researchers to analyse more than a handful of cases (from 3 up to 60, or even more). So, it is particularly relevant in fields where the maximum number of cases is of necessity quite limited, such as one can face in sport management literature when studying, for instance, national sport organizations from different countries or volunteers in a specific sport organization.

Qualitative comparative analysis also enables, as much as possible, each case to be interpreted individually. It considers each and every case as being relevant. Therefore, cases, which follow a distinct pattern are treated with interest. They show paths leading to the presence of the outcome that statistical analysis would have hidden (Rihoux and Ragin, 2008). This makes QCA sensitive to cases, so that new cases could change the solution resulting from QCA. However, QCA takes into account 'logical remainders' which are configurations of conditions researchers do not observe as cases because they were limited in their selection or because such cases do not (yet) exist (Ragin, 2004). So, every possible path (according to the conditions considered) leading to the outcome could be analysed. In our study, every possible combination of potential determinants we have highlighted from the literature and leading to high performance could be considered.

3.2 Performance Measurement of CSGBs

The 'dependent' variable (outcome) we studied is the ability of CSGBs to achieve their three strategic goals in 2005. The year 2005 was chosen because it follows a four-year cycle corresponding to an Olympiad during which the pressure on Olympic sport governing bodies is very high. In line with the literature, a quantitative measurement model was developed in order to identify high-performing CSGBs. The model includes eight quantitative performance indicators which together measure the achievement of the strategic objectives of each strategic goal. These indicators were identified by a specific group of experts from sport or management (that is, the Vice-President and the General Secretary of the Belgian Olympic and Interfederal Committee and two university professors) who employ performance indicator assessment techniques. The values of the indicators in 2005 were calculated for each CSGB for which quantitative data was collected. According to standard normalization, we obtained a performance score from 0 to 10 for each indicator: the higher score, the more a CSGB performed in comparison with the other CSGBs in 2005. We computed an average performance score for each objective and strategic goal. Therefore, each CSGB obtained one performance score for each of their three strategic goals. Afterwards, we computed two complementary clustering methods – hierarchical ascendant classification with the Ward method and K-means (non-hierarchical) clustering (Fiss, 2011; Ketchen and Shook, 1996) in order to highlight group(s) of high-performing CSGBs which had a tendency to achieve their strategic goals according to the three performance scores of each CSGB.

3.3 Case Selection

In order to analyse the CSGBs in details, we selected a sample of them. The method we chose is configurational, so that each case refers to a specific combination of determinants. To enlarge the scope of the analysis, cases should represent dissimilar combinations of determinants. This is crucial. Similar cases do not bring information about new kinds of configurations of determinants, but more about frequency emergence, which is not particularly the point here (but might be interesting when paying attention to consistency and coverage of the results, see Ragin, 2006, 2008; Schneider and Wagemann, 2007). For that reason, we selected a few CSGBs whose internal functioning differs. We used three distinguishing criteria. The CSGBs we selected cover different sizes, different sport objectives and different levels of performance. Also, it is advised to select a group of cases about which researchers have good knowledge (Ragin, 2008; Rihoux and Ragin, 2008).

3.4   Assessment of the Determinants of CSGBs

Semi-structured interviews were conducted with the chair and the administrative manager of each selected CSGB in order to understand their perceptions of their organization, respectively volunteer and paid staff. Content analysis of the interview transcripts was performed to assess the way these CSGBs were operating, according to the potential determinants highlighted (also called conditions hereafter for csQCA), before the year 2005 (the Olympiad 2000–2004). Each determinant was assessed according to the criteria they refer to and which are presented in the theory section and in Table 4.1. Afterwards, we were able to analyse the link between (high-) performance and potential determinants (key success factors) using one of the three main QCA techniques. These main QCA techniques are: crisp-set QCA (csQCA), multi-value QCA (mvQCA) and fuzzy-set QCA (fsQCA). We explain them in the next section.

3.5   QCA as a Technique: Crisp-set Qualitative Comparative Analysis (csQCA)

The QCA techniques are based upon the matching and contrasting of cases which eliminates negligible conditions (no matter if a condition is present or absent, the phenomenon occurs anyhow) or trivial conditions (a condition is present, or absent, for almost all cases) in order to highlight the minimum necessary and sufficient conditions that can 'explain' (non-) occurrence of the outcome. This process of reducing, through Boolean or set-theoretic algorithms, complex expressions into shorter combinations of conditions is called the 'minimization' (Rihoux and Ragin, 2008).

Three QCA techniques could be used. In csQCA, data treated are dichotomous so that only the presence and the absence of the conditions and the outcome are showed. In mvQCA, the conditions can display more than two values in order to reflect more fine-grained empirical differences (for instance, a distinction between leadership governance, governance involving a handful of key individuals and governance involving the whole staff). In fsQCA, data are located in a continuum between 1 and 0, so that the degree of presence or absence of the conditions and the outcome is computed. In this research we focused on crisp-set QCA (csQCA) in which quantitative or qualitative data is converted into dichotomous data. This process is called 'calibration'. Therefore, according to the criteria selected, researchers have to justify how they decide to convert their quantitative or qualitative data into dichotomous data (1/0). The advantage of this technique is its transparency. Indeed, all steps are clearly defined and explained including the calibration. The first step of the csQCA (Figure 4.1) is thence to calibrate the outcome (performance) and each condition (determinant).

The aim of this study is to highlight key determinants high performing CSGBs possess in comparison with those possessed by low performing ones. Therefore, we compare high-performing CSGBs with low-performing ones. The high-performing CSGBs (outcome value [1]) are considered to be those which achieve their three strategic goals (sport for all, elite sport and customers) whereas the low-performing CSGBs (outcome

Table 4.1   Calibration of the potential determinants of performance for communities' sport governing bodies (CSGBs)

Name	Calibration criteria	Symbol {1}or {0}
Centralization (1)	One or two decision-makers	[CEN{1}]
	More than two actors take part in the decision-making processes	[CEN{0}]
Governance of volunteer(s) (2)	The decision-maker(s) is (are) volunteer(s). No paid staff is involved in the decision-making processes	[GOV {1}]
	One or more paid staff are involved in the decision-making processes	[GOV {0}]
Task orientation and supervision (3)	Someone is in charge of the supervision of the employees. They are being supervised and managed	[TOS {1}]
	Nobody is in charge of the staff. They are not really supervised	[TOS {0}]
Vision (4)	The relationship between volunteers and paid staff (and sport clubs) is not conflicting. They share the same strategy	[VIS {1}]
	There is organizational conflicts or volunteers do not share the same strategy but serve personal interests	[VIS {0}]
External relations (5)	Development of partnerships (local and national or international or commercial) and sport promotion support	[EXR {1}]
	No partnership or no involvement in the sport promotion	[EXR {0}]
Financial independence (6)	Financial dependence under 40% of public resources in comparison with total resources. Perception of financial autonomy	[IND {1}]
	A large part of the resources is coming from public funds (more than 40%). A weak self-financing capacity is perceived	[IND {0}]
Innovative activities (7)	Development of various or adapted activities for membership satisfaction	[INA {1}]
	No involvement in new and different activities	[INA {0}]
Elite training structure (8)	Development of programmes and strategies to detect talent and to support elites, directly or through their clubs	[ETS {1}]
	No involvement in elite detection or support	[ETS {0}]
Size (9)	More than 5000 members (French Community Decree)	[SIZE{1}]
	Less than 5000 members (French Community Decree)	[SIZE {0}]
Sport objectives (10)	Sport is enrolled in the Olympic Games	[SPORT {1}]
	Sport is not enrolled in the Olympic Games	[SPORT {0}]

value [0]) are considered to be those which fail to achieve at least one strategic goal. The calibration of the determinants is presented in Table 4.1. Calibration criteria for each determinant are explained in line with the theory section. They lead to the numeric transformation of the data into dichotomous data in which '{1}' shows the presence (strong)

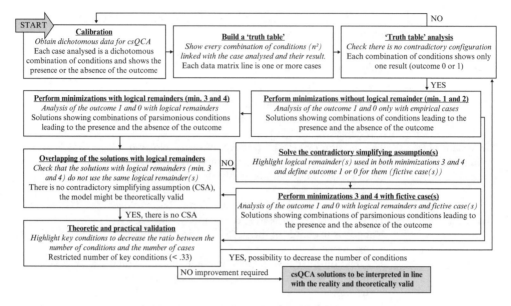

Figure 4.1   Crisp-set qualitative comparative analysis process

of the determinant and '{0}' its absence (weak). Blind review of the calibration has been performed by one independent researcher in sport management.

According to the calibration of the outcome and the conditions (performance and determinants), a dichotomous data matrix can be built. It summarizes the configurations of determinants of the cases selected, linked with their performance. This matrix is called a 'truth table'. Each line refers to one or more CSGBs, that is a configuration of determinants and the performance of the latter.

The next step of the csQCA is to check each configuration (combination of conditions) displays only one outcome value. No contradictory configuration – the same configuration shared for different empirical cases which display different outcome values (Ragin, 2008; Rihoux and Ragin, 2008) – is allowed (they could be solved, see Rihoux and Ragin, 2008). Afterwards, two minimizations without logical remainder are computed for the outcome value [1] and for the outcome value [0] (usually researchers use the free softwares Tosmana or fsQCA). These minimizations only take into account the combinations of conditions of the cases we selected (empirical cases). This can lead to interesting results but, most of the time, it tends to be descriptive and not parsimonious.

Afterwards, we perform two other minimizations with logical remainders, which are logically possible combinations of conditions – absent in the empirical cases – for which an outcome has been chosen in accordance with the configurations and outcomes of the empirical cases. The assumption made on the outcome values of logical remainders are called 'simplifying assumptions'. Therefore, the same logical remainders could be used in both the minimizations of the outcome values [1] and [0] according to the assumptions. In that case, there are 'contradictory simplifying assumptions'. The analysis of the overlapping between the minimal solutions of the outcome values [1] and [0] is essential when the minimizations with logical remainders are performed. We have to check no logical remainder is used in both the solutions of the outcome values [1] and [0]. To solve these, Rihoux and Ragin (2008) suggested to identify which logical remainders set problems and to define for them a single outcome [1] or [0]. This amounts to create fictive cases to be added in further minimizations (but without forgetting they are fictive). The process is redundant (minimizations 3 and 4 with fictive cases) until no more contradictory simplifying assumption emerges.

According to Marx (2006), in order to obtain a (theoretically) valid model, the ratio between the number of variables (conditions + outcome) and the number of cases has to be limited to 0.33 or less. So, we should highlight key determinants to decrease the number of determinants according to the number of empirical cases analysed. If no determinant (condition) could be neglected and with respect to the ratio suggested by Marx (2006), the csQCA solutions can be interpreted.

4 RESULTS

Table 4.2 shows the performance scores corresponding to the achievement, in 2005, of the three strategic goals (sport for all, elite sport and customers) for each of the 49 CSGBs, the higher the better. Two CSGBs (multisports adapted and labour table tennis) are not measured for the elite sport strategic goal owing to a lack of data concerning their sport results and their elite sport expenses in 2005.

No strong correlation emerges between these strategic goals. It shows their relative interdependence which allows to perform the clustering methods (Ketchen and Shook, 1996). Table 4.2 shows three emerging clusters. We distinguish CSGBs which performed relatively lowly in achieving their three strategic goals in 2005 (cluster 1) from those which performed relatively highly (cluster 3). Moreover, we also distinguish CSGBs which performed relatively lowly on some strategic goals, such as elite sport strategic goal, and highly in others (cluster 2). Thus, we obtain a clear picture of the performance of the 49 CSGBs. Eighteen of them were selected (underlined within Table 4.2) according to our case knowledge, our data and the methodological imperative to obtain various types of CSGBs. They have different levels of performance, different sizes and sport objectives. These CSGBs in clusters 1 and 2 were considered low-performing (n = 11), their outcome value for csQCA is [0], whereas those in cluster 3 were considered high-performing (n = 7), their outcome value for csQCA is [1] (athletics, jiu-jitsu, archery, wheelchair sports, petanque, fencing and swimming).

Thirty six interviews were carried out to assess the way these 18 CSGBs were operating before 2005, according to the 10 potential determinants highlighted. No contradictory configuration emerges from the dichotomous calibration of the 10 determinants assessed in the 18 CSGBs selected and their performance, each configuration of conditions shows only one outcome value (1 or 0).

We computed the minimizations of the outcome value [1] with logical remainders with the software Tosmana 1.3. We do not show the minimization without logical remainders because it does not go much beyond the description of CSGBs. Five determinants linked with high performance emerged: innovative activities [INA], elite training structure [ETS], centralization [CEN], governance of volunteer(s) [GOV] and size [SIZE]. Arguably, they are sufficient – according to the cases selected – to 'explain' the

Table 4.2 Performance score of the three strategic goals of the 49 communities' sport governing bodies (CSGBs) in 2005

	CSGBs 2005	Customers	Elite sport	Sport for all
Cluster 1	Yachting	3.41	2.96	5.22*
	Canoe	3.48	2.95	4.91
	Scuba diving	2.96	2.93	3.76
	Weightlifting/power lifting	2.70	3.63	4.48
	Shooting	1.45	5.59*	3.25
	Clay shooting	3.85	4.92*	5.42*
	Gliding	1.18	3.11	2.81
	Fishing	5.19*	4.84*	0.73
	Labor athletics	3.21	0.00	1.88
	Labor swimming	3.66	0.57	1.56
	Futsal	4.53	0.00	2.69
	Baseball	2.13	0.00	5.09
	Motorcycling	2.33	1.14	3.75
	Automobile	0.33	0.00	3.23
	Roller-skating	2.82	0.00	3.75
	Multisports adapted	3.60	/	0.00
Cluster 2	Squash	7.33*	2.28	6.71*
	Handball	6.90*	2.99	6.95*
	Ice-skating	6.35*	1.96	6.91*
	Gymnastics	6.27*	2.74	4.44
	Basketball	7.37*	2.50	4.36
	Lifesaving	9.25*	1.96	6.25*
	Skiing	8.57*	2.57	4.76
	Triathlon	3.87	2.35	8.45*
	Orienteering	4.79	3.19	9.44*

	CSGBs 2005	Customers	Elite sport	Sport for all
Cluster 2	Volleyball	4.33	3.07	6.97*
	Rugby	5.85*	2.78	6.44*
	Parachuting	5.97*	0.28	5.05
	Wrestling	4.76	0.28	7.70*
Cluster 3	Taekwon do	5.33*	7.67*	3.57
	Petanque	5.28*	7.37*	3.92
	Swimming	4.68	8.36*	6.10*
	Table tennis	3.83	8.25*	4.75
	Tennis	5.96*	9.10*	4.49
	Karate	4.49	10.00*	3.82
	Labor table tennis	7.77*	/	0.00
	Judo	3.33	6.51*	7.56*
	Cycling	5.32*	5.76*	7.48*
	Climbing	4.78	7.49*	8.91*
	Athletics	7.38*	7.60*	5.63*
	Rowing	6.68*	5.69*	4.99
	Wheelchair sports	6.73*	8.16*	9.51*
	Water-skiing	7.48*	5.72*	6.58*
	Horseback riding	8.18*	5.61*	5.46*
	Fencing	7.34*	6.50*	4.10
	Badminton	6.71*	7.15*	6.58*
	Archery	6.50*	7.08*	5.86*
	Savate	6.79*	7.52*	7.64*
	Jiu-jitsu	9.00*	7.43*	7.45*
Means of the scores of the 49 CSGBs		*5.14*	*4.27*	*5.13*

Notes:
CSGBs are identified according to the sport they promote.
* Performance score greater than the mean: high achievement.

Table 4.3   *'Truth table' with the five key determinants for the 18 Communities' sport governing bodies selected*

Communities' sport governing bodies	CEN	GOV	INA	ETS	SIZE	OUTCOME
Athletics, swimming	1	1	1	1	1	1
Jiu-jitsu	1	1	1	0	0	1
Archery, wheelchair sports	1	1	0	0	0	1
Petanque	0	0	1	0	1	1
Fencing	0	0	1	1	0	1
Handball, triathlon	1	0	0	0	0	0
Canoe, rugby, gliding	0	1	0	0	0	0
Scuba diving	0	1	1	0	1	0
Futsal, shooting	1	1	0	0	1	0
Baketball	1	1	0	1	1	0
Orienteering	0	0	1	0	0	0
Gymnastics	0	0	0	0	1	0
Logical remainder 1/fictive case 1	0	1	1	1	–	? →1

Notes:
The coordination dichotomies are all coded in the same direction with a score of 1 signalling the presence (high or strong) of the condition and a score of 0 signalling the absence (low or weak) of the condition ('–' is 1 or 0).
[CEN]: centralization; [GOV]: governance of volunteer(s); [ETS]: elite training structure; [INA]: innovative activities; [SIZE]: size; [OUTCOME]: achievement of the strategic goals.
Logical remainders are the combinations of conditions we do not have in our selected cases, but may be possible.
The arrow symbol [→] represents the assumptions made on the outcome values of the logical remainders (fictive cases).

performance of CSGBs. Indeed, the 'truth table' utilizing only these five key conditions (Table 4.3) showed no contradictory configuration, but 12 configurations of conditions, each with a unique outcome value (1 or 0). Furthermore, with 18 CSGBs, a maximum of six variables (five conditions and one outcome) can be analysed in order to obtain a ratio of 0.33 between the number of cases and the number of variables (Marx, 2006). However, we did not neglect the fact that the CSGBs have several others conditions affecting their internal functioning.

We continued the csQCA process with the five key determinants highlighted. The minimizations of the outcome values [1] and [0] with logical remainders showed one contradictory simplifying assumption (logical remainder 1 in Table 4.3). One logical remainder is used in both of them. This contradictory simplifying assumption has to be solved in order to obtain theoretically valid results. Rihoux and Ragin (2008) suggested assigning to logical remainders an outcome present or absent based on case knowledge. Then, they advise to compute the minimizations with this fictive case (the logical remainders for which an outcome is assigned are called fictive cases). Outcome value [1] is assigned to the fictive case 1 because it shows present elite training structure and innovative activities which have been identified such as crucial for CSGBs to perform high. The following minimizations with the five key determinants and with logical remainders will use this fictive case 1 (Table 4.3).

Figure 4.2(a) represents the minimization with logical remainders and fictive case of

(a)

INA{1} * ETS{1} +	GOV{0} * INA{1} * SIZE{1} +	CEN{1} * GOV{1} * SIZE{0}	→ OUTCOME {1}
Athletics	Petanque	Jiu-jitsu	
Swimming		Archery	Achievement of the three strategic goals
Fencing		Wheelchair sports	(High performance)

(b)

INA{0} * SIZE{1} +	CEN{0} * GOV{1} * ETS{0} +	GOUV{0} * ETS{0} * SIZE{0}	→ OUTCOME {0}
Basketball	Canoeing	Handball	Low achievement of the three strategic goals
Futsal	Rugby	Triathlon	
Shooting	Gliding	Orienteering	(Low performance)
Gymnastics	Scuba diving		

Notes:
The [*] (multiplication) symbol represents the logical 'AND'.
The [+] (addition) symbol represents the logical 'OR'.
The arrow symbol [→] represents the link (usually casual) between the combinations of conditions and outcome.
The coordination dichotomies are all coded in the same direction with a score of 1 signalling the presence (high or strong) of the condition and a score of 0 signalling the absence (low or weak) of the condition.
[CEN]: centralization; [INA]: innovative activities; [GOV]: governance of volunteer(s); [ETS]: elite training structure; [SIZE]: size; [OUTCOME]: achievement of the strategic goals.

Figure 4.2   Solutions for high performance (a) and low performance (b): minimizations of the outcome value [1] and [0] with logical remainders

the outcome value [1]. The conditions, expressed by their symbol, are followed by the values {1} or {0} according to the dichotomization. Basic logical operators are used to express the connections between the conditions. The [*] (multiplication) symbol represents the logical 'AND'. The [+] (addition) symbol represents the logical 'OR'. Finally, the arrow symbol [→] represents the link (usually causal) between the combinations of conditions and outcome.

The solution of the minimization for high performance can be read as follows:

the outcome value [1], high attainment of the three strategic goals of CSGBs (sport for all, elite sport and customers) is observed: in CSGBs that combine innovative activities [INA{1}] *AND* presence of an elite training structure [ETS {1}] *OR* governance of volunteer(s) and paid staff [GOV{0}] *AND* innovative activities [INA{1}] *AND* large size [SIZE {1}] *OR* centralization [CEN {1}] *AND* governance of volunteer(s) [GOV {1}] *AND* small size [SIZE {0}].

This solution highlights three combinations of key success factors that are linked with high performance. Afterwards, we analysed the outcome value [0] with the five key determinants. The combinations of determinants linked with low performance could not be observed in high performance. Eleven CSGBs showed low achievement of their strategic goals (clusters 1 and 2). Figure 4.2(b) represents parsimonious formulas from the minimization of the outcome value [0] with logical remainders and fictive case. It can be read as follows:

the outcome value [0], low attainment of the three strategic goals of CSGBs (sport for all, elite sport and customers) is observed: CSGBs that combine no innovative activity [INA

{0}] *AND* large size [SIZE {1}] *OR* weak centralization [CEN {0}] *AND* governance of volunteer(s) [GOV {1}] *AND* an absence of an elite training structure [ETS {0}] *OR* governance of volunteer(s) and paid staff [GOV {0}] *AND* an absence of an elite training structure [ETS {0}] *AND* small size [SIZE {0}].

These parsimonious formulas show paths leading to low performance which differ from the paths leading to high performance. The solutions with logical remainders for the outcome values [1] and [0] do not overlap. Therefore, this csQCA leads to theoretically valid results (Rihoux and Ragin, 2008). Furthermore, according to Marx (2006), the model combining the achievement of the three strategic goals (elite sport, sport for all and customers) of CSGBs and five key determinants is theoretically valid.

5 DISCUSSION AND CONCLUSION

An innovative method called qualitative comparative analysis is introduced for the analysis of the organizational performance of sport governing bodies. This approach deals with causal complexity so to highlight combinations of conditions linked to an outcome. Five key determinants have emerged: elite training structure, centralization, governance of volunteer(s), innovative activities and size. Using crisp-set qualitative comparative analysis we observed three combinations of these key determinants in high-performing communities' sport governing bodies (CSGBs) but not observed in low-performing CSGBs: those which develop innovative activities for their members and an elite training structure to detect talent (1) might achieve their strategic goals, as well as large-sized CSGBs which develop innovative activities and are governed by volunteers with the involvement of paid staff (2), and small-sized CSGBs which are governed by one or two volunteers (3).

Innovative activities and elite training structure refer to services CSGBs are able to provide to their members and elites. Athletics, swimming and fencing detect elites within sport clubs and support their training, which may have some effects on their elite sport strategic goal. At the same time, they develop new or adapted activities to satisfy their members in order to achieve their sport for all and customers strategic goals. However, not all CSGBs have the opportunity to provide so many services, because these need large human and financial resources. Owing to their sport specificities, athletics, swimming and fencing attract a large number of members and/or are enrolled in Olympic Games. They are financially dependent on public funds. Their revenues allow them to invest in services for members and elites. The development of innovative activities seems to be particularly crucial for large-sized CSGBs to attain high performance.

According to Schmid (2002), involvement of paid staff in the decision-making processes might be most appropriate where the level of professionalism among the staff is high. Patterns of management in petanque tend to be relatively informal and flexible. Furthermore, the lengthy experience of its paid staff makes it possible to develop activities in line with members' expectations. Indeed, knowledge they hold about the organization is often greater than that of board members. Thus, they organize themselves and are involved in the decision-making processes. This trust between volunteers and paid staff results in a shared vision leading to a common strategy revealed by the development of innovative activities.

Small-sized CSGBs governed by one or two volunteers might attain high perform-ance. The presence of a leader has an effect on performance (Bayle, 1999), and this might be true for (very) small sport governing bodies. Jiu-jitsu, archery and wheelchair sports do not attract a lot of members owing to their sport specificities. They are not able to invest in an elite structure and/or innovative activities. However, they rely on devotee volunteer(s) and delegate activities they are not able to deliver to their sport clubs. Nonetheless, we would not advise this configuration for large governing bodies. Although we have highlighted that small-sized CSGBs which have no elite training structure and a governance mix of volunteers and paid staff might perform lowly, we need to qualify this result. Indeed, three CSGBS (handball, triathlon and orienteering) performed highly in the sport for all strategic goal and lowly in the elite sport strategic goal, primarily due to weak elite structure. Therefore, the involvement of paid staff in the decision-making processes is advised no matter the size of a CSGB, even if volunteer leaders can easily manage small CSGBs.

In line with this research, we argue that the added value of QCA relies on five key points. Qualitative comparative analysis makes it possible to treat small-N sample (1) one could often be confronted with in the sport management literature (for example, the limited number of Olympic organizations, top level sport clubs, sport governing bodies, volunteers, staff or managers in a small sport organization or cross-national studies). It also enables causal complexity analysis (2) when highlighting necessary and sufficient conditions linked to an outcome of interest. Transparency (3) is one of the key advantages of QCA. Researchers have to justify each methodological choice (for example, selection of cases and conditions, calibration). They make a clear inter-pretation of the solutions resulting from QCA according to their case knowledge, but also their dialogue with the cases (back to the narrative of cases is common in QCA). Qualitative comparative analysis is replicable (4) due to its formalized techniques and processes, and is case sensitive (5). Indeed, contrary to statistical analysis, discrete cases, which do not follow the usual pathways, are underlined (such as petanque in this research). They could show interesting ways to reach the phenomenon studied (performance in this research).

5.1   Limitations and Implications for Further Research

There are methodological limitations to consider in this research. Some CSGBs included in methods presenting an outcome value [0] have achieved one or two of their three strategic goals. Therefore, every solution emerging from QCA has to be carefully inter-preted. Furthermore, because the time dimension is not integrated by QCA, research-ers have to re-examine cases in a qualitative way. The dichotomous calibration should not be seen as a limitation, as we do not neglect the qualitative assessment of the cases. Indeed, as Rihoux and Ragin (2008: 14) stated, we could refer 'back to the cases with all their richness and specificity'. We can, therefore, refer back to the complexity of the cases analysed and their narratives in the discussion (Rihoux and Lobe, 2009). Qualitative com-parative analysis relies on the rigorous and transparent selection of conditions made by researcher and supported by theoretical arguments. The reliability is considered accord-ing to the theoretical validation of the QCA (that is, ratio between variables and number of cases, absence of contradictory configuration showing the coherence of the data and absence of contradictory simplifying assumption when using logical remainder(s)) and the proper interpretation of the solution (that is, confronting the solution with the narratives of cases and, when possible, with individuals' own interpretation).

This study suggests that researchers should analyse combinations of factors leading to phenomena of interest and not only the net effects of variables. Indeed, factors are interconnected and thus affect each other to produce results. Their presence (or absence) might lead to different results according to the factors with which they are combined. We argue that it is particularly relevant for complex organizations such as sport organizations growing in a complex internal and external environment. Generally speaking, we also advise researchers to engage in mixed method designs. The combination of quantitative and qualitative data could be useful to strengthen researchers' analysis/studies. Qualitative comparative analysis has proven to be an adequate method to understand which combination favours performance in sport governing bodies. The key success factors leading to high performance have been identified according to this csQCA. Moreover, QCA could be applied in other research areas to test existing theories, to identify (dis)similarity between cases and to highlight new arguments or theories not exploited (niche).

REFERENCES

Bayle, E. (1999), Management et performance des organisations à but non lucratif. Le cas des fédérations sportives nationales [Management and performance of the non-profit sport organizations. The case of the national sport federations], unpublished doctoral dissertation, Université de Limoges, Limoges, France.

Bayle, E. and Madella, A. (2002), Development of a taxonomy of performance for national sport organizations, *European Journal of Sport Science*, **2** (2), 1–21.

Bayle, E. and Robinson, L. (2007), A framework for understanding the performance of national governing bodies of sport, *European Sport Management Quarterly*, **7** (3), 249–68.

Berg-Schlosser, D. and De Meur, G. (1994), Conditions of democracy in interwar Europe: A Boolean test of major hypotheses, *Comparative Politics*, **26** (3), 253–79.

Bradshaw, P., Murray, V. and Wolpin, J. (1992), Do nonprofit boards make a difference? An exploration of the relationships among board structure, process, and effectiveness, *Nonprofit and Voluntary Sector Quarterly*, **21** (3), 227–49.

Brown, W.A. (2005), Exploring the association between board and organizational performance in nonprofit organizations, *Nonprofit Management and Leadership*, **15** (3), 317–39.

Camisón-Zornoza, C., Lapiedra-Alcami, R., Segarra-Cipres, M. and Boronat-Navarro, M. (2004), A meta-analysis of innovation and organizational size, *Organization Studies*, **25** (3), 331–61.

Chelladurai, P., Szyszlo, M. and Haggerty, T.R. (1987), System-based dimensions of effectiveness: the case of national sport organizations, *Canadian Journal of Sport Science*, **12** (2), 111–19.

Crittenden, W.F., Crittenden, V.L., Stone, M.M. and Robertson, C.J. (2004), An uneasy alliance: planning and performance in nonprofit organizations, *International Journal of Organization Theory and Behavior*, **7** (1), 81–106.

Damanpour, F. (1987), The adoption of technological, administrative, and ancillary innovations: impact of organizational factors, *Journal of Management*, **13** (4), 675–86.

Deloitte and Touche Sport (2003), *'Investing in Change' – High Level Review of the Modernisation Programme for Governing Bodies of Sport*, London: Deloitte & Touche, available at: UK Sport. http://www.lsersa.org/modernisation/Report_Master_22_July.pdf (accessed 19 September 2011).

Deshpande, R., Farley, J.U. and Webster, F.E. (1993), Corporate culture, customer orientation and innovativeness in Japanese firms; a quadrad analysis, *Journal of Marketing*, **57** (1), 23–37.

Fiss, P.C. (2007), A set-theoretic approach to organizational configurations, *Academy of Management Review*, **32** (4), 1180–98.

Fiss, P.C. (2011), Building better causal theories: a fuzzy stet approach to typologies in organization research, *Academy of Management Journal*, **54** (2), 393–420.

Frisby, W. (1986), Measuring the organizational effectiveness of national sport governing bodies, *Canadian Journal of Applied Sport Science*, **11** (2), 94–9.

Glisson, C.A. and Martin, P.Y. (1980), Productivity and efficiency in human service organizations as related to structure, size, and age, *Academy of Management Journal*, **23** (1), 21–37.

Government of the French-speaking Community of Belgium (1999), Decree of the 26th April 1999 organizing sport in the French speaking community, *Moniteur Belge*, 23 December 1999.

Greckhamer, T., Misangyi, V.F., Elms, H. and Lacey, R. (2008), Using qualitative comparative analysis in strategic management research: an examination of combinations of industry, corporate, and business-unit effects, *Organizational Research Methods*, **11** (4), 695–726.

Ketchen, D.J. and Shook, C.L. (1996), The application of cluster analysis in strategic management research: an analysis and critique, *Strategic Management Journal*, **17** (6), 441–58.

Kogut, B. and Ragin, C.C. (2006), Exploring complexity when diversity is limited: institutional complementarity in theories of rule of law and national systems revisited, *European Management Review*, **3** (1), 44–59.

Koski, P. (1995), Organizational effectiveness of Finnish sports clubs, *Journal of Sport Management*, **9** (1), 85–95.

Madella, A. (1998), La performance di successo delle organizzazioni – spunti di riflessione per gestire efficacemente le societa di atletica leggera [Performance success of organizations – Reflection point to manage effectively athletics clubs], *Atleticastudi*, **1**, 2–3.

Madella, A., Bayle, E. and Tomé, J.-L. (2005), The organisational performance of national swimming federations in Mediterranean countries: a comparative approach, *European Journal of Sport Science*, **5** (4), 207–20.

Marx, A. (2006), Towards more robust model specification in QCA: results from the methodological experiment, *COMPASSS Working Paper 2006–43*, available at: www.compasss.org/files/WPfiles/Marx2006.pdf (accessed 20 June 2011).

Papadimitriou, D. (1999), Voluntary boards of directors in Greek sport governing bodies, *European Journal for Sport Management*, **6**, 78–103.

Papadimitriou, D. (2002), Amateur structures and their effect on performance: the case of Greek voluntary sports clubs, *Managing Leisure*, **7** (4), 205–19.

Papadimitriou, D. (2007), Conceptualizing effectiveness in a non-profit organizational environment. An exploratory study, *The International Journal of Public Sector Management*, **20** (7), 571–87.

Papadimitriou, D. and Taylor, P. (2000), Organisational effectiveness of Hellenic national sports organisations: a multiple constituency approach, *Sport Management Review*, **3** (1), 23–46.

Ragin, C.C. (1987), *The Comparative Method: Moving Beyond Qualitative and Quantitative Strategies*, Berkeley, CA: University of California Press.

Ragin, C.C. (2004), La spécificité de la recherche configurationnelle [The specificity of configurational research], *Revue Internationale de Politique Comparée*, **11** (1), 138–44.

Ragin, C.C. (2006), Set relations in social research: evaluating their consistency and coverage, *Political Analysis*, **14** (3), 291–310.

Ragin, C.C. (2008), *Redesigning Social Inquiry: Fuzzy Sets and Beyond*, Chicago, IL: University of Chicago Press.

Read, A. (2000), Determinants of successful organisational innovation: a review of current research, *Journal of Management*, **3** (1), 95–119.

Rihoux, B. and Lobe, B. (2009), The case for QCA: adding leverage for thick cross-case comparison, in D. Bryne and C.C. Ragin (eds), *Handbook of Case Based Methods*, Thousand Oaks, CA: Sage, pp. 222–42.

Rihoux, B. and Ragin, C.C. (2008), *Configurational Comparative Methods: Qualitative Comparative Analysis (QCA) and Related Techniques*, Thousand Oaks, CA: Sage.

Rudd, A. and Johnson, R.B. (2010), A call for more mixed methods in sport management research, *Sport Management Review*, **13** (1), 14–24.

Rudd, A. and Johnson, R.B. (2013), A call for more mixed methods in sport management research, in S. Söderman and H. Dolles (eds), *Handbook of Research on Sport and Business*, Cheltenham, UK and Northampton, MA, USA: Edward Elgar, pp. 40–58.

Schmid, H. (2002), Relationships between organizational properties and organizational effectiveness in three types of nonprofit human services organizations, *Public Personnel Management*, **31** (3), 377–95.

Schneider, C.Q. and Wagemann, C. (2007), *Qualitative Comparative Analysis (QCA) und Fuzzy Sets: Ein Lehrbuch für Anwender und jene, die es werden wollen* [*Qualitative Comparative Analysis (QCA) and Fuzzy Sets: A Guide for Current and Future Users*], Opladen and Farmington Hills: Verlag Barbara Budrich.

Shilbury, D. and Moore, K.A. (2006), A study of organizational effectiveness for national Olympic sporting organizations, *Nonprofit and Voluntary Sector Quarterly*, **35** (1), 5–38.

Siciliano, J.I. (1997), The relationship between formal planning and performance in nonprofit organizations, *Nonprofit Management and Leadership*, **7** (4), 387–403.

Slack, T. (1985), The bureaucratization of a voluntary sport organization, *International Review for the Sociology of Sport*, **20** (3), 145–66.

Slack, T. and Parent, M.M. (2006), *Understanding Sport Organizations: The Application of Organization Theory*, 2nd edn, Champaign, IL: Human Kinetics.

Smith, D.H. and Shen, C. (1996), Factors characterizing the most effective nonprofits managed by volunteers, *Nonprofit Management and Leadership*, **6** (3), 271–89.

Thibault, L., Slack, T. and Hinings, B. (1991), Professionalism, structures and systems: the impact of professional staff on voluntary sport organizations, *International Review for the Sociology of Sport*, **26** (2), 83–98.

Vail, S.E. (1985), Organizational effectiveness and national sport governing bodies: a multiple constituency approach, unpublished doctoral dissertation, University of Ottawa, Canada.

Winand, M. (2009), Déterminants de la performance organisationnelle des fédérations sportives: une analyse comparée des ligues sportives de la Communauté française de Belgique [Determinants of organizational performance of sport federations: a compared analysis of sport governing bodies from the French speaking Community of Belgium], unpublished doctoral dissertation, Université catholique de Louvain, Louvain-la-Neuve, Belgium.

Winand, M., Zintz, T., Bayle, E. and Robinson, L. (2010), Organizational performance of Olympic sport governing bodies. Dealing with measurement and priorities, *Managing Leisure: An International Journal*, **15** (4), 279–307.

Wolfe, R., Hoeber, L. and Babiak, K. (2002), Perceptions of the effectiveness of sport organisations: the case of intercollegiate athletics, *European Sport Management Quarterly*, **2** (2), 135–56.

Zintz, T. (2004), Configuration et changement organisationnel des ligues et fédérations sportives belges. Typologie et perspectives d'évolution [Configuration and organizational change of Belgian sport federations and leagues. Typology and progressing perspectives], unpublished doctoral dissertation, Université catholique de Louvain, Louvain-la-Neuve, Belgium.

Zintz, T. and Camy, J. (2005), *Manager le changement dans les fédérations sportives en Europe* [*Managing Change in Sport Federations in Europe*], Bruxelles: De Boeck Université.

5 Comparing apples with oranges in international elite sport studies: is it possible?
Veerle De Bosscher, Jasper Truyens,
Maarten van Bottenburg and Simon Shibli

1 INTRODUCTION

International comparative studies are one of the most complicated areas of research (for example, da Costa and Miragaya, 2002; Haag, 1994; Henry et al., 2005; Porter, 1990). In sport the issue is even more convoluted because sports systems are closely enmeshed with the culture of a nation and therefore each system is unique. In the USA, for example, sport is highly embedded in the school system that is designed to feed athletes into the university system (Sparvero et al., 2008). There is no sport club tradition in the USA that is comparable to the kind found elsewhere in the world. These and other differences between nations make comparison of sport determinants, and elite sport in particular, in an international context difficult. Cultural factors shape the environment surrounding sports: they are integrated with the determinants and not isolated from them. Such factors change only gradually and are difficult for outsiders to replicate (Porter, 1990).

Furthermore (elite) sport development is dominated to a large degree by a nation's political system. Politics determines policies (Houlihan, 1997; Houlihan and Green, 2008). In addition, processes of governmentalization and commercialization influence sport considerably, yet they vary greatly among nations. These are all extraneous and uncontrollable factors that make comparability problematic. Accordingly much discussion exists about the suitability of nations as components to be compared (De Bosscher et al., 2007). As a result, there are not many comparative sports studies, except those that exist mainly on a descriptive basis and which examine general trends and similarities among nations. Oakley and Green (2001) developed the research agenda by indicating that there was also a general need to investigate differences between nations. Furthermore Bergsgard et al. (2007) indicate that many international comparative studies fail to establish analytical relationships between variables. There appears to be a lack of standardization of research methods used to make comparisons, as well as limited publicly available and quantifiable data on sport policies (Henry et al., 2005).

This chapter addresses these issues and explores a method to compare elite sport policies of nations on a mixed quantitative and qualitative basis. We endeavour to simulate debate in the field of international comparative sports research by quantification of data and the introduction of 'measurement' on a subject (comparing elite sport policies and systems) that is essentially qualitative in nature. In this respect we illustrate how a scoring system was developed in order to compare objectively the elite sport policies of six nations and thus to move beyond the descriptive level of analysis. This study is part of a large-scale project, called the SPLISS study (Sports Policy Factors Leading to

International Sporting Success) which aimed to compare the determinants of competitiveness in elite sport (De Bosscher et al., 2007, 2008).

As far as we know, there are no studies that actually measure competitiveness in the sports sector. While governments and other institutions worldwide intervene directly in elite sport development by making considerable financial investments, there is a gap in literature on the determinants of competitiveness and how to measure and compare these factors. Useful methodological insights can be observed when considering research beyond the sport sector, for example, in the economic sector where the concept of competitiveness is more developed, notably in the fields of international trade, industrial organization and business economics (Siggel, 2003). Hence this chapter compares economic methods with the methods used in this study on high-performance sport. According to Porter (1990), it is far more difficult to compare nations than firms, because firms compete but governments, to a large extent, influence the preconditions of these firms. Furthermore, in economics, very few studies have considered the issue of multi-country competitiveness (Önsel et al., 2008). Competitiveness inherently refers to the relative position of an organization vis-à-vis its competitors (ibid.), which are – in the context of competiveness in elite sport – by definition other nations. Therefore, international comparisons are the only way to identify and compare the determinants of national competitiveness.

Elite sport is international by definition. Competition in high performance sport has increased considerably during the past decades, reinforced by increasing internationalization and globalization (De Bosscher et al., 2008). As nations strive for success, there are diminishing returns on investments such that it is necessary to continue investing in elite sport simply to maintain existing performance levels. The central tenet of this global sporting arms race, as described by Oakley and Green (2001), is that elite sporting success can be produced by investing strategically in elite sport. Accordingly, this chapter focuses on the national level of comparison (and not the individual level of athletes or individual sports) and on the determinants that can be influenced by policies.

Bearing in mind the arguments outlined above, the aim of the present chapter is to develop a measurement system that allows objective comparison of quantitative and qualitative data on elite sport policies in different nations. Drawing its influences from economic competitiveness measurements, this method is based on three essential features:

1. The development of a theoretical model of success determinants (or pillars) in elite sport with the identification of clear critical success factors that are used for international comparison (called SPLISS model).
2. The use of mixed methods research and the development of a scoring system to measure competitiveness of nations in elite sport for each dimension of the theoretical model and thus to move beyond the descriptive level of comparison.
3. The involvement of the main stakeholders in elite sport – the athletes, coaches and performance directors – as the evaluators of policy processes in elite sport.

This methodology was used to test a conceptual model in an empirical context in a pilot study, where elite sport policies and systems were compared in six nations: Belgium (separated into Flanders and Wallonia), Canada, Italy, the Netherlands, Norway and the UK. This chapter is structured as follows. This study was part of a large-scale project, called SPLISS. The first section describes the theoretical framework that has been used. The core of this chapter consists of the methods used to translate the critical factors into scores. Finally, the discussion section focuses on the strengths and limitations of these methods.

2   A CONCEPTUAL FRAMEWORK FOR INTERNATIONAL COMPARISON: THE SPLISS MODEL

Referring to (macro)economic studies the concept of competitiveness, or competitive advantage, has been given numerous interpretations and tends to be inconclusive (for example, Krugman, 1996; Önsel et al., 2008; Porter, 1990; Siggel, 2003; Sigel and Cockburn, 1995). As Porter points out 'instead of seeking to explain "competitiveness" at the national level, we must first understand the determinants of productivity' (1990: 9). Porter (1990) identified and aggregated the characteristics of national competitive advantage into a systemic model, called the 'competitiveness diamond', consisting of four determinants that are compared in the ten most competitive nations. Reflecting this seminal work of Porter (1990), De Bosscher et al. (2006) developed the first elite sport conceptual model, called the SPLISS model.

This model, based on previous research (De Bosscher et al., 2006, 2009) is used as a basic framework for international comparison and the methods presented in this chapter. This conceptual model aims to identify the determinants of productivity in elite sport at the meso level, or those determinants that can be influenced by human impact. Macro-level factors (such as population, wealth, cultural factors, religion, urbanization and natural resources) are not included in this study. Inductive procedures were used to consolidate all relevant sources from a comprehensive body of literature. It was concluded that all factors in sport policy that may increase the chances of elite sporting success, can be distilled down to nine key areas or 'pillars'. These are situated at three different levels according to the effectiveness literature (Chelladurai, 2001; Chelladurai et al., 1987), as shown in Figure 5.1.

'Inputs' are reflected in pillar 1, as the financial support for elite sport. Having the financial resources in elite sport does not guarantee success. There is need for a strong support structure which is willing to invest its resources in the most efficient and effective way (De Bosscher et al., 2007). This is reflected in pillars 2 to 9 as the 'throughputs', which refer to the efficiency of sport policies, that is, the optimum way that inputs can be managed to produce the required outputs.

The focus of the model presented in Figure 5.1 is nine general elite sport policy dimensions for which it can be assumed that all the factors that can be influenced by sport policies can be classified under one of these pillars. It was indicated in this research that: 'its function is not deterministic: rather it aims to identify pivotal issues and to generate crucial questions in a benchmark study of elite sport systems' (De Bosscher et al., 2006: 209). This model therefore provides only a tentative theoretical conclusion on sports policy factors leading to international sporting success, or the competitiveness factors of an elite sport policy. It was concluded that it is impossible to

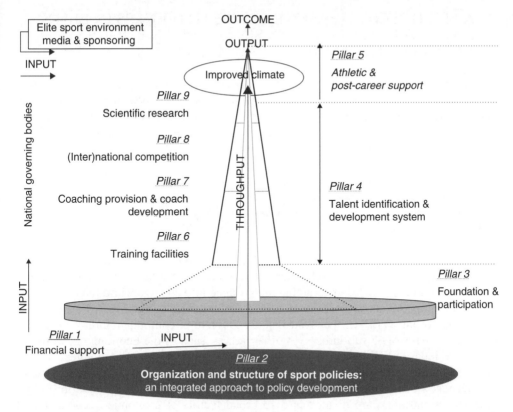

Source: De Bosscher et al. (2006). We acknowledge EASM for their permission to reuse this figure after publication in ESMQ.

Figure 5.1   SPLISS model: a conceptual model of 9 pillars of Sports Policy factors Leading to International Sporting Success

create one single model for explaining international success and that different systems may well all be successful (De Bosscher et al., 2007). Nevertheless, it was a useful analytical framework, based on a comprehensive body of literature and preliminary research.

The SPLISS model is multidimensional, based on input and throughput indicators and was operationalized into 144 detailed critical success factors (CSFs) that allowed a more analytical and objective comparison of the pillars than previous studies. Critical success factors are elements that are vital for a strategy to be successful. These CSFs have been compared in an international context in order to test and validate the model. The aim was to explore a method for comparing nations' elite sport systems less descriptively by measuring and comparing the critical success factors of elite sport systems – or the determinants of national competitiveness (Depperu and Cerratu, 2008; Porter, 1990) – both quantitatively and qualitatively.

3   A METHOD TO MEASURE COMPETITIVENESS IN ELITE SPORT: A PILOT STUDY IN SIX SAMPLE NATIONS TO VALIDATE THE CONCEPTUAL MODEL

For more than 25 years measuring the economic competitiveness (and economic growth prospects) of countries and their underlying factors has been a focus for research (Ochel and Röhen, 2006). Although a sport policy setting differs from an economic setting, notably because its goals are not financially focused, the basic principles of competitiveness studies are quite similar in design (Linssen, 1998):

- generating the determinants of competitiveness;
- expressing relevant factors in indicators and sub indicators;
- scoring each indicator and in some cases applying weightings;
- comparing the scores and, if possible, explaining differences between nations.

For example in the World Competitiveness Yearbook (WCY, from IMD, International Institute for Management Development, Lausanne, Switzerland), 55 economies are analysed and ranked on 331 criteria that are grouped into 20 factors and then regrouped into four competitiveness determinants (Rosselet and McCauley, 2008). In the World Economic Forum (WEF) (Lopez-Claros et al., 2007), three component indices are calculated on the basis of 35 sub-indices. In other indices, such as the Economic Freedom of the World index (EFW index, by the Fraser Institute, 2005), the 21 components in five major areas are incorporated into the index, made up of several sub-components. And in the Heritage Foundation Index of Economic Freedom 50 (Heritage Foundation, 2005) independent variables are divided into 10 broad factors of economic freedom (Ochel and Röhen, 2006). Each of these indices uses different scoring methods, standardization methods and weightings, but essentially the construction of the indices is very similar. In these studies, both hard data and soft data (surveys) are used to collect the data. These data are scored and then aggregated into a final score for each dimension, possibly after weightings. A comparison of the methods used in the four economic measurements mentioned above, is provided in Table 5.1.

Consistent with these studies, this chapter details how the critical success factors of the SPLISS nine-pillar model were transformed into measurable units that are individually scored and aggregated into a final score for each pillar. One main difference from these economic studies is related to the scale of the research, as only six nations have been compared. This implies that methods other than statistical analyses have been used to determine scores and weightings. These were based mainly on expert opinion and constant comparison of meanings. Therefore, the SPLISS study was coordinated by an international consortium group of seven researchers from three countries (Belgium (Flanders), the Netherlands and the UK). As the members were all internationally recognized researchers in elite sport, and in close contact with elite sport policy agencies in their nations, they acted as a group of experts throughout this research. Their role was to validate and refine the conceptual model, to operationalize the CSFs, to supervise the objectivity of the data analysis, to assure internal validity and reliability, to ensure the international comparability of data and to discuss the standards for comparison (De Bosscher et al., 2008). As a result of this extensive process, the research took four years.

Table 5.1 Comparison of four economic competitiveness indices with the SPLISS method in elite sport

Economic indices	WEF GCI	IMD	EFW (Fraser)	Heritage Foundation Index of Economic Freedom	SPLISS
Objective	Tries to measure national competitiveness; *the ability of countries to attain sustained economic growth*	Ranking the ability of nations to create and maintain an environment that sustains the competitiveness of enterprises and promotes economic growth	Measures the degree of economic freedom present in five major areas	Systematic, empirical measurement of economic freedom	Develop a tool for objective evaluation of competitiveness of elite sport at the meso-level, or the sports policy factors leading to international sporting success; is not an index
Theory/concept	3 component indices, calculated on the basis of 35 sub-indices (= unweighted average of data if weights are not given)	4 main competitiveness factors that are broken down into 5 sub-factors. 241 competitiveness criteria	21 components in five major areas are incorporated into the index; made up of several sub-components	50 independent variables divided into 10 broad factors of economic freedom	9 pillars, operationalized into 144 critical success factors
Nations	More than 100 nations	51 nations (9 regions)		155 nations	6 nations
Data collection	14 hard data and 21 survey data (e.g. in 2004 2100 executives from 30 OECD member countries)	128 hard data and 113 survey data (e.g. in 2005 4000 executives from 60 economies)	19 hard data and 19 survey data supplied by WEF and IMD surveys		54 hard data combined with 18 hard survey data and 31 soft survey data or perceived data

Table 5.1 (continued)

Economic indices	WEF GCI	IMD	EFW (Fraser)	Heritage Foundation Index of Economic Freedom	SPLISS
Standardization and scoring	(1) *Score classes method*: scale with scores ranging from 1 to 7 (based on linear interpolations to normalize the indicators within a scale) (2) *Continuous scaling methods* transform the underlying indicator values into a continuous, uniform scale that retains the relative distances between the original values. The distance from the best and worst performer to transform the original indicators into	*Continuous scaling method*: – Transforms all original indicators into a common scale. Converts data from a 1–6 scale to a 0–10 scale and then calculates standard deviation values to determine rankings (Rosselet and McCauley, 2008) – slightly different linear interpolation. All original indicator values are transformed into a standardized distribution with mean 0 and standard deviation of 1 (Ochel and Röhen, 2006)	(1) *Score classes method*: scale with scores ranging from 1 to 10 (based on linear interpolations to normalize the indicators within a scale) (2) *Continuous scaling methods* transform the underlying indicator values into a continuous, uniform scale that retains the relative distances between the original values. The distance from the best and worst performer to transform	The 50 independent variables are analysed to determine for each of the 10 factors a score on a scale running from 1 to 5. *Score classes method* (or categorical scaling method), using expert assessments to determine final score	*Score classes method*: – Scale with scores ranging from 1 to 5 for each CSF are aggregated into one final percentage score for each pillar – These scores are categorized into five scales in order to get an overall perspective on each nation and pillar – There are no overall rankings (or indices) made and pillars are not aggregated into one final score – The allocation of scores is based on quantitative data (survey) and qualitative data (overall sports policy questionnaire); for the latter, scoring is based on arbitrary scaling according to expert's opinion

Criterion	WEF – GCI	IMD	EFW	SPLISS
	a range between 0 and 1. In a second step, GCI linearly transform these values to lie within a range of 1 and 7. (Min-max method)		the original indicators into a range between 0 and 1. In a second step, EFW linearly transform these values to lie within a range of 0 and 10. (Min-max)	– Objective and subjective information is deliberately kept separate
Weighting	Statistical techniques to determine weights: regression analysis with the average growth rate as the dependent variable to establish the weights of its three sub-components as well as the weights within these sub-components	In the first step, the universe of basic indicators are grouped into 20 sub-indices. In the second step all sub-indicators are assigned equal weights in the composite index. *Sub-factors do not necessarily include the same number of criteria*	In the first step, the universe of basic indicators are grouped into five sub-indices. In the second step all sub-indicators are assigned equal weights in the composite index	In the first step, the universe of basic indicators are grouped into 10 sub-indices. The 10 factors are weighted equally. In the second step all sub-indicators are assigned equal weights in the composite index. Weightings are only allocated to aggregate CSFs into one final percentage score according to their relative importance following expert opinion

Notes: WEF: World Economic Forum – GCI: Global Competitiveness Index from the Global Competitiveness Report; IMD: International Institute for Management Development; EFW: Economic Freedom of the World index (Fraser Institute); SPLISS: Sports Policy factors Leading to International Sporting Success.

Sources: Information on economic indices adopted from Ochel and Röhen (2006); information on SPLISS adopted from De Bosscher (2007; De Bosscher et al., 2008, 2009, 2010).

The methodological approach of involving experts is proposed in several works on qualitative research methodologies (for example, De Pelsmacker and Van Kenhove, 1999; Gliner and Morgan, 2000; Gratton and Jones, 2004).

A mixed methods triangulation design was used to compare the nations. This is a type of design in which different but complementary data are collected concurrently and analysed against the conceptual model of nine pillars (Creswell and Plano Clark, 2007).

3.1   Sample Selection

The six countries involved in the pilot study were: Belgium (separated into Flanders and Wallonia,[1] Canada, Italy, the Netherlands, Norway and the UK (De Bosscher et al., 2008). The selection of these nations was initially based on (1) the sport performances including good, medium and poorly achieving nations with the aim of observing differences in policies, (2) the countries' socio-economic nature (Western industrialized countries) and (3) a broadly comparable cultural background (general social development and population, sociology and ethnography). We tried to provide an even distribution of typical welfare states, as differentiated by Esping-Andersen (1990) in his research. In the end, the selection was merely pragmatic, owing to limited research funds, and the need for reliable and engaged researchers in each nation who were sufficiently familiar with the elite sport structures in their own country and who were able to obtain funding to undertake the research (De Bosscher et al., 2009, 2010).

3.2   Data Collection

Two research instruments were used in SPLISS to collect both hard (objective) and perceived (subjective) data: the 'overall sport policy questionnaire' and the 'elite sport climate survey'.

In the 'elite sport climate survey' (ESCS) (Van Bottenburg, 2000), all participating countries were asked to undertake surveys of athletes, coaches and performance directors, using self-completion questionnaires prior to the 2004 Athens Olympic Games. The use of surveys is also derived from the marketing and services literature, which assumes that it is the consumers who best know the quality of a service as they experience it (Chelladurai and Chang, 2000). It is also widely accepted in effectiveness literature that the primary stakeholders in sport organizations should be involved (Chelladurai, 2001; Papadimitriou and Taylor, 2000; Shilbury and Moore, 2006).

A second instrument was used to measure hard data, called the 'overall sport policy questionnaire' (OSPQ). Here, the SPLISS researchers in each country completed an extensive semi-structured questionnaire on objective indicators or 'facts', with 84 open-ended and closed questions in the nine pillars, including their evolution over the past 10 years. The degree of detail required to complete the policy questionnaire by the researchers was such that, for each nation, the task was a large-scale research project in its own right, for which researchers had to search for existing national surveys, analyse secondary sources and policy documents (De Bosscher et al., 2008, 2010). Furthermore, depending on the data available and on the knowledge of the researcher, interviews with members of the National Olympic Committee and national governing bodies of sport (NGBs) were conducted in order to provide answers to all of the CSFs.

Table 5.2   Overview of hard data and perceived data measured in the pilot study

Pillar	Number of CSF on 'facts' (hard data)		Number of CSF on 'assessment' (perceived data)
	OSPQ	ESCS	ESCS
1. a. Financial support	8		No assessment
b. Financial support for NGBs	5		
2. Sport policy structures and organization	7	3	4
3. Participation in sport	14		No assessment
4. Talent identification and development system	4	2	5
5. Athletic and post career support	3	3	5
6. Training facilities	2	2	6
7. Coaching provision and coach development	4	7	7
8. International competition	3		4
9. Scientific research	4	1	No assessment
Total		72	31

Source: De Bosscher (2007).

Similar to the economic indices, qualitative and qualitative data were used and were subsequently compared through the collection of both hard data (or objective data) and by means of surveys for perceived data (or subjective data). Similarly, the WEF uses 14 hard data inputs (from secondary data sources) and 21 survey data inputs, the IMD (World Competitiveness Yearbook) uses 128 hard data inputs and 113 survey data inputs, and Fraser (Economic Freedom of the World Index) uses 19 hard data inputs and 19 survey data inputs (Ochel and Röhen, 2006). More information about these studies is detailed in Table 5.1. To operationalize the CSFs into nine pillars, the SPLISS study used (a) 54 hard data inputs (from the OSPQ) combined with 18 hard survey data inputs (from the ESCS) (which means data that provide objective information from secondary sources and from a survey) and (b) 31 perceived survey data inputs (or subjective information from the survey). For example when athletes are asked what kind of support services they receive from their governing bodies, this is identified as a hard (objective) data input. When athletes are asked to assess these services using a 1–5 Likert scale this is identified as a soft (perceived or subjective) data input. Table 5.2 provides an overview of the number of hard and soft CSF for the nine pillars.

In total 103 CSFs were measured (on a total of 144 CSFs as mentioned before). Some other CSFs were not included, because the study was limited to the overall national sport level and they require sport-specific analysis, or because some CSFs required too much supplementary research within a nation. For example, this was the case with respect to data on expenditure on sport by local government or private investors. Such data needed to be gathered at levels which fell beyond the scope of this research (De Bosscher et al., 2010). Furthermore the number of CSFs differed by pillar, as some determinants required more factors to go into sufficient depth. Consequently, the SPLISS study did not calculate scores embracing all the pillars, because there is no information available on the relative weight of each pillar.

Table 5.3   Overview of response rates from athletes, coaches and performance directors in the six sample nations

	Athletes		Coaches		Performance directors	
	Response	%	Response	%	Response	%
The Netherlands	421	34%	62	28%	28	52%
UK	279	47%	23	8%	x	x
Flanders	140	43%	119	51%	26	100%
Canada	132	16%	x	x	11	32%
Wallonia	63	41%	16	20%	06	19%
Norway	55	58%	x	x	x	x
Italy	x	x	32	64%	x	x
TOTAL	1090	34%	253	29%	71	45%

Sources: De Bosscher et al. (2008: 35; 2010: 580).

3.3   Response

For the elite sport climate survey, the targeted response rate from athletes, coaches, and performance directors was 30 per cent which is a reasonable return for postal surveys (De Pelsmacker and Van Kenhove, 1999). Table 5.3 provides an overview of the responses by nation, respondent type and response rates (De Bosscher et al., 2008: 35). A total of 1090 athletes, 253 coaches and 71 performance directors in six nations responded to the questionnaires.

As can be seen in Table 5.3, the elite sport climate surveys from the six nations (seven regions) working together on this research differ significantly in terms of sample sizes. As the research was highly dependent on the cooperation of sport authorities and national Olympic committees, which had not necessarily commissioned the research, practical difficulties arose in accessing all three target groups (athletes, coaches and performance directors). Despite the limitations of the sample, and bearing in mind that all six sample nations also conducted lengthy overall sport policy questionnaires (on which the major-ity (two-thirds) of the 103 CSFs are based), the research could be regarded as a useful step towards understanding the issues involved in making cross-national comparisons of elite sport systems. The study was therefore a pilot study to test and validate the conceptual model. The unique feature of the research is that in addition to measur-ing easily quantifiable variables, such as inputs (for example, money) and outputs (for example, medals), it has also delved into understanding the 'black box' of throughput both in terms of the existence of various system components and the rating that athletes, coaches, and performance directors provided to these system components (De Bosscher et al., 2008, 2010).

3.4   Data Analysis: Development of a Scoring System

Similarly to the economic competitiveness studies, all CSF were allocated a score on a 1 to 5 point scale, with 'one' indicating little development and 'five' for a high level of development. There is no general consensus on the use of scales (Ochel and Röhen, 2006). For example the World Competitiveness Yearbook converts data from a 1–6 scale to a 0–10 scale and then calculates standard deviation values to determine rankings (Rosselet and McCauley, 2008). The World Economic Forum converts the data to a scale of 1–7 (Önsel et al., 2008) and for example Sledge (2005) used a Likert scale of −1 to +2 to assess firms' strategies. The rationale for a 1 to 5 scale in this research was arbitrary but nonetheless consistent with the answers obtained on the elite sport climate survey.

Depending on the source (elite sport climate survey, or overall sport policy questionnaire) and type of question (open-ended, dichotomous or assessment), the standards for this five-point scale differed. Generally there were three types of ratings (De Bosscher et al., 2010: 582).

1. The most complex ratings were derived from the OSPQ, because qualitative information on the elite sport systems for each pillar had to be transformed into a score for a five-point scale. These (mostly) open-ended questions were grouped into categories to define the standards. Generally, the existence of specific aspects of the elite sport system were assessed in terms of 'availability of the criterion in a stronger or weaker form', to indicate the level of development. For each CSF, the standards and ratings were discussed within the consortium group until consensus was reached and, if necessary, further clarification of answers was sought from the researchers concerned.
2. In the ESCS, quantitative data were available based on two types of questions: dichotomous questions (yes/no) and ratings on a five-point Likert scale (ordinal). For the dichotomous questions absolute standards were used. When the CSFs contained several sub-indicators the scores were aggregated taking into account the non available answers. For the Likert scale questions 'net ratings' (i.e., positive answers minus negative answers) were calculated.

Next, the 1–5 scores on all the CSF were aggregated into one final percentage score, by taking into account the number of 'not available' (n/a) answers, given that not all countries achieved a score on the same number of criteria (De Bosscher et al., 2010: 582). When two-thirds of the answers were not available for any nation, a score for that pillar was not calculated. When only two nations responded to a criterion, the criterion was deleted. A final percentage score was then calculated which ranged from 20 per cent to 100 per cent. Scores lower than 20 per cent are not possible as each nation received at least one point for each CSF. This was a deliberate choice because seldom is there 'no development' at any level of sport policies (ibid.). In this respect, the scoring system aims to express the general assessment of each pillar for each nation. An overview of this aggregation is given in Figure 5.2, for pillar 5 (athletic career and post-career support) as an example. Figure 5.2 shows how six CSFs on the objective scale and five CSFs on a subjective scale are aggregated into a final percentage score. A similar approach was taken for the other eight pillars.

Finally, the CSFs were weighted to reflect the consortium's view of their relative importance. These weightings were needed primarily because each CSF was not measured by the same number of questions, and to 'lock in' the impact of each CSF on the overall score. In order to enhance the internal validity of our scoring system

(a) *General score of pillar 5 on facts or hard data*

W	Weights for each CSF / Critical success factors (CSF)	CAN	FLA	ITA	NED	NOR	UK	WAL
	Stage 1: the career of elite athletes: individual lifestyle support							
2	Athletes receive direct financial support (a monthly wage) to become a professional/full time athlete	4	Scores on a 1–5 scale; questions deriving from the overall policy questionnaire (black text)		5	4	4	5
2	Coordinated support programme for elite level athletes (apart from financial support)	5			5	4	5	2
1	*Total gross annual income (non-student athletes)*	*3*	Scores on a 1–5 scale; questions deriving from the elite sport climate survey (grey text): dichotomous questions	*5*	*4*	*5*	*na*
1	*Gross annual income from sport activities of athletes (non-student athletes)*	*2*		*na*	*3*	*5*	*na*
1	*Kind of facilities that athletes can make use of (according to athletes)*	*na*		*2*	*3*	*na*	*na*
	Stage 2: the post-athletic career							
3	Support for athletes at the end of their career	4	1	3	4	4	4	1
	Sum of (the points for each nation × weight) TOTAL points	35	21	27	39	38	40	17
	Maximum score that each nation can have, taking into account the number of 'non available' answers (= weight for each CSF × 5) MAX Number of times NA	45 / 1	45 / 1	35 / 1	45 / 1	50 / 0	45 / 1	35 / 3
	Percentage scores = total points/MAX Total score for pillar 5	77,78	46,67	77,14	86,67	76,00	88,89	48,57

(b) *General score of pillar 5 on perceived data or assessment*

W		CAN	FLA	ITA	NED	NOR	UK	WAL
5	*General satisfaction with the support package that athletes receive*	*4*	*3*	*na*	*5*	*4*	*na*	*na*
1	*Rating level of sport specific coaches (acc. to athletes)*	*na*	Scores on a 1–5 scale; questions deriving from the elite sport climate survey: based on net ratings		*5*	*5*	*na*	*na*
1	*Rating level of (para)medical coaches (acc. to athletes)*	*na*			*5*	*4*	*na*	*na*
1	*Rating level of social & business support (acc. to athletes)*	*na*	*4*	*na*	*3*	*1*	*na*	*na*
1	*Satisfaction with attitude of the employer (acc. to athletes)*	*5*	*5*	*na*	*5*	*5*	*na*	*na*
	TOTAL points for assessment	25	34		43	35		
	MAX	30	45		45	45		
	Number of times NA	3	0	4	0	0	4	4
	Total score for assessment of pillar 5	83,33	75,56	NA	95,56	77,78	NA	NA

Notes:
CAN: Canada; FLA: Flanders; ITA: Italy; NED: The Netherlands; NOR: Norway; UK: United Kingdom; WAL: Wallonia.
na: data not available; W: weight.
Italic text: results from elite sports climate survey; non-italic text: results deriving from the overall sport policy questionnaire.
(a) Wallonia supplied data on relatively few criteria; (b) Canada supplied data on relatively few criteria and scores were not calculated for the UK, Wallonia and Italy due to the low number of responses from coaches in the survey.

Figure 5.2   *An illustration of pillar 5: aggregation of scores of several CSFs into one overall percentage score*

(De Pelsmacker and Van Kenhove, 1999), the consortium group held several meetings devoted to the verification of the standards used to categorize the nations into five classes and to agree the weightings for each CSF. Nonetheless, these weightings remain a subjective interpretation of a relative value of certain CSFs and, therefore, need to be explored in greater depth in future research.

It follows from Figure 5.2 that the different response rates obviously influence the scores of each nation for each pillar. Nonetheless, the method shows how different nations can be evaluated against pillar 5. However, the limitations in this pilot stage need to be taken into account and are indicative of the fact that policy evaluation cannot solely be based on these measurements. Descriptive qualitative information in this respect remains a valuable contribution and the key point is that both methods should be mixed. This will be shown in the next section.

4 RESULTS ON PILLAR 5: ATHLETIC AND POST CAREER SUPPORT

This section provides only a summary of the results for pillar 5 as an example, since the intention of this chapter is to explore a method for measuring the competitiveness of elite sport policies, rather than comparing the policies themselves. For more detailed information, we refer to De Bosscher et al. (2008: 99–105). Importantly, it should be noted that quantitative measurements and descriptive evaluation should complement each other.

To simplify the presentation of results and to identify any specific characteristics and trends, each nation (for each pillar) was allocated a colour-coded score or 'traffic light' (black and white in this book), varying from a policy area being 'very well developed' to having 'little or no development' according to a five-point scale with a range of 16 percentage points between each category (80 per cent range divided over five categories). Figure 5.3 presents the results for pillar 5, only for the hard data inputs (objective evaluation) as an illustration.

All of the sample nations, apart from Belgium, perform particularly well against the criteria in the competitive and post-career stages of an elite athlete's career. It is apparent that sports authorities are taking a holistic view of athletes' careers. Talented athletes pursuing their sport are recognized and treated as employees, for example in the Netherlands and Belgium. Funding for living and sporting costs linked to the minimum wage is in place and athletes can also access a range of other lifestyle support services. This differs from the UK where there is no bottom limit to means-tested awards; therefore almost half of UK athletes (46 per cent) were in some form of employment to supplement their income.

The only nation which is rated as having a fairly low level of development in Figure 5.3 is Belgium (both Flanders and Wallonia). Both regions have minimal lifestyle support

		CAN	FLA	ITA	NED	NOR	UK	WAL
Evaluation		○	◑	○	○	○	○	◑
	Key							

	○	Policy area very well developed	84.1–100%
	○	Good level of development	68.1–84.0%
	○	Moderate level of development	52.1–68.0%
	◑	Fairly low level of development	36.1–52.0%
	●	Low level of development	20.0–36.0%

Note: Adapted from De Bosscher et al. (2008).

Figure 5.3 *Competitive analysis (traffic light, here in black and white) of six nations for pillar 5: athletic career and post career support*

mechanisms (except from financial support), and support for athletes at the end of their careers is considered to be poor.

5   DISCUSSION

The key point of this chapter is that it shows how the methods developed by the SPLISS group are highly comparable with economic studies. This final section discusses the advantages and disadvantages of these methods by running through the theoretical framework, the scoring system and the interpretation of the results.

5.1   The SPLISS Model

The SPLISS model attempted to offer a first conceptual framework of the Sports Policy factors Leading to International Sporting Success. The SPLISS study distinguishes itself from other elite sport policy studies (for example, Bergsgard et al., 2007; Digel et al., 2006; Green and Houlihan, 2005; Houlihan and Green, 2008) because of the identification of concrete critical success factors for each pillar, as well as the consolidation of a wide range of literature and experts both at the meso- and micro-levels. This model was developed because of the absence of a coherent competitiveness framework in elite sport, despite the large sums of money being invested in international sporting success worldwide. Despite our efforts to be rigorous, the SPLISS model is in no way comprehensive. Even more critically, the model relies very heavily on expert judgement and ad hoc empirical analysis. Ochel and Röhn (2006) gave a similar critique about the IMD where the expert knowledge of many business leaders has been used in order to select the main determinants of competitiveness and growth. Their choice of factors for inclusion seems to have been carried out quite subjectively. Consequently, the SPLISS model needs to be refined and validated further.

An econometric approach can be used in future research in order to identify the most important factors and the weights to be used for each pillar. Using additional questionnaires, factor analysis or principal component analysis offers alternative methods to establish weights for each CSF. Furthermore, in order to aggregate variables into a composite indicator the variables need to be normalized or standardized to a common scale. Thus, the SPLISS model needs to be explored in more nations and for specific sports (or 'industries'). These are the aims of future SPLISS research. This SPLISS group is currently extending its activities on a wider scale, both at the overall and sport-specific levels, in order to validate and develop theories on the key determinants of success and to explore validated methods in international comparative research.

5.2   Scoring System

The scoring system in this study was developed with one belief in mind, that is, it can deliver an objective comparison of nations and policies, based on concrete CSFs and standards. This can be regarded as a potentially useful means of helping policy-makers and institutions to assess the performance of their sport system in comparable terms and to undertake appropriate remedial strategies. To date, however, in economic studies as well as in our study, there has been limited critical interrogation of how valid and useful these measurements are with respect to their ability to provide insights into what drives competitiveness and to generate robust predictions of future performance (Ochel and Röhn, 2006). While objective scores can be calculated in the elite sport climate survey, the definition of standards in the overall sport questionnaire is somewhat arbitrary because of the absence of clear standards to rate an elite sport system objectively. It is based on comparative country data (where more is often better) and on the opinions of experts.

The small sample of nations does not allow statistical techniques similar to the economic studies to identify the standards for comparison and weights, for example, the deviation between the four highest and lowest ranked nations (min-max method), quartiles, normalizations or other transformations. Therefore, the method needs to be further explored in terms of its construct validity. In contrast to existing sport studies, the unique feature of this study is that it assesses processes by means of an elite sport climate survey (both objective and subjective data) with the main stakeholders in elite sport and that these responses are included in the scoring system.

5.3   Interpretation of Data

The beginning of this chapter started with some points of interest that should be addressed when making international comparisons. Many of these points are related to the interpretation of the results: when data are isolated from their broader cultural and historical context; the search for cause and effect; and the search for differences that are not there. It was therefore of major importance in this study that quantitative findings alone were not sufficient to assess the quality of elite sport systems. The scoring system is a supportive and tangible way of understanding elite sport policies more broadly in relation to sporting success, rather than an isolated competitiveness measurement or ranking system. Unlike laboratory experiments, studies on elite sport policies do not take part in a closed system. Qualitative descriptions of elite sport policies and how they are formed remain essential units, even in a quantitative sport comparison. In this respect the scoring system is merely a guiding system as part of an overall qualitative and quantitative evaluation.

ACKNOWLEDGEMENTS

The authors would like to thank the dedicated researchers who joined this study: Jerry Bingham (UK Sport), David Legg (Canada), Berit Skirstad and Torkild Veraas (Norway), Alberto Madella and Lorenzo Di Bello (Italy), Bas Rijnen (the Netherlands), Chris Gratton (UK), Luc van de Putte and Thierry Zintz (Wallonia). The coordination of the research was funded by the Vrije Universiteit Brussel as part of doctoral funding and by the other members of the consortium. Expenses for the research in the respective nations had to be covered by the researchers themselves. Financial constraints were the main barrier for more nations to be involved. We want to acknowledge the following organizations providing financial support: Olympiatoppen (Norway), CONI (Comitato Olimpico Nazionale Italiano, Italy), UK Sport (UK), NOC*NSF (amalgamation of the

Netherlands Olympic Committee and the Netherlands Sport Federation), Sport Canada (Canada), the ministers for sport from Flanders and Wallonia and the BOIC (Belgian Olympic Interfederal Committee).

NOTE

1. Flanders is the northern, Dutch-speaking part of Belgium, Wallonia the southern, French- and German-speaking part. In Belgium, the Flemish community (Flanders) and the French/German-speaking community (Wallonia) have separate sport policies at each level, from local to national (including three separate ministers of sport). Apart from the Olympic Committee (BOIC), whose main task is to select athletes for the Olympic Games, there is no national (federal) policy or structure for sport, nor are there expenditures on sport at federal level. Therefore, Flanders and Wallonia have participated in this research as if they were two distinct nations. As the study includes to a large extent qualitative data, it is not possible to consider policies of Wallonia and Flanders in one final evaluation. Instead of excluding Belgium as a nation, it was decided with the consortium group to separate the two regions.

REFERENCES

Bergsgard, N.A., Houlihan, B., Mangset, P., Nødland, S.I. and Rommetveldt, H. (2007), *Sport Policy. A Comparative Analysis of Stability and Change*, London: Elsevier.
Chelladurai, P. (2001), *Managing Organizations, for Sport and Physical Activity. A System Perspective*, Scotsdale, AZ: Holcomb Hathaway.
Chelladurai, P. and Chang, K. (2000), Targets and standards of quality in sport services, *Sport Management Review*, **3** (1), 1–22.
Chelladurai, P., Szyszlo, M. and Haggerty, T.R. (1987), System-based dimensions of effectiveness: the case of national sport organisations, *Canadian Journal of Sport Sciences*, **12** (2), 111–19.
Creswell, J.W. and Plano Clark, V.L. (2007), *Designing and Conducting Mixed Methods Research*, London: Sage.
Da Costa, L. and Miragaya, A. (2002), *Worldwide Experiences and Trends in Sport for All*, Oxford: Meyer & Meyer Sport.
De Bosscher, V., De Knop, P. and van Bottenburg, M. (2007), *Sports Policy Factors Leading to International Sporting Success*, published doctoral thesis, Brussels: VUB Press.
De Bosscher, V., De Knop, P., van Bottenburg, M. and Shibli, S. (2006), A conceptual framework for analysing sports policy factors leading to international sporting success, *European Sport Management Quarterly*, **6** (2), 185–215.
De Bosscher, V., Bingham, J., Shibli, S., van Bottenburg, M. and De Knop, P. (2008), A *Global Sporting Arms Race. An International Comparative Study on Sports Policy Factors Leading to International Sporting Success*, Aachen: Meyer & Meyer.
De Bosscher, V., De Knop, P., van Bottenburg, M., Shibli, S. and Bingham, J. (2009), Explaining international sporting success. An International comparison of elite sport systems and policies in six nations, *Sport Management Review*, **12** (3), 113–36.
De Bosscher, V., Shibli, S., van Bottenburg, M., De Knop, P. and Truyens, J. (2010), Developing a methodology for comparing the elite sport systems and policies of nations: a mixed research methods approach, *Journal of Sport Management*, **24** (5), 567–600.
De Pelsmacker, P. and Van Kenhove, P. (1999), *Marktonderzoek: methoden en toepassingen* [*Market Research: Methods and Applications*], 3rd edn, Leuven – Apeldoorn: Garant.
Depperu, D. and Cerrato, D. (2008), Analysing international competitiveness at the firm level: concepts and measures, *Studies in Business and Economics*, no. 126, available at: http://www3.unicatt.it/unicattolica/dipartimenti/DISES/allegati/wpdepperucerrato32.pdf (accessed 15 August 2008).
Digel, H., Burk, V. and Fahrner, M. (2006), *High-performance Sport. An International Comparison*, Weilheim/Teck: Bräuer.
Esping-Andersen, G. (1990), *The Three Worlds of Welfare Capitalism*, Cambridge: Polity Press.
Fraser Institute (2005), *Economic Freedom of the World: 2005*, Annual Report, Vancouver.
Gliner, J.A. and Morgan, G.A. (2000), *Research Methods in Applied Settings: An Integrated Approach to Design and Analysis*, Mahwah, NJ: Lawrence Erlbaum Associates.

Gratton, C. and Jones, I. (2004), *Research Methods for Sport Studies*, London: Routledge.
Green, M. and Houlihan, B. (2005), *Elite Sport Development. Policy Learning and Political Priorities*, London: Routledge.
Haag, H. (1994), Triangulation: a strategy for upgrading comparative research methodology in sport science, in R. Wilcox (ed.), *Sport in the Global Village*, Morgantown, WV: Fitness Information Technology, pp. 501–7.
Henry, I., Amara, M. and Al-Tauqi, M. (2005), A typology of approaches to comparative analysis of sports policy, *Journal of Sport Management*, **19** (4), 520–35.
Heritage Foundation (eds) (2005), *The 2005 Index of Economic Freedom*, Washington, DC: Freedom House.
Houlihan, B. (1997), *Sport, Policy and Politics. A Comparative Analysis*, London: Routledge.
Houlihan, B. and Green, M. (2008), *Comparative Elite Sport Development*, London: Butterworth-Heineman.
Krugman, P. (1996), Making sense of the competitiveness debate, *Oxford Review of Economic Policy*, **12** (3), 5–23.
Linssen, G.W.J.M. (1998), Benchmarking. De concurrentietoets 1997: Een voorbeeld van benchmarken [An example of benchmarking], *Beleidsanalyse*, **1**, 14–22.
Lopez-Claros, A., Porter, M., Sala-i-Martin, X. and Schwab, K. (2007), *Global Competitiveness Report 2007–2008*, World Economic Forum, New York: Palgrave Macmillan.
Oakley, B. and Green, M. (2001), The production of Olympic champions: international perspectives on elite sport development systems, *European Journal for Sport Management*, **8** (1), 83–105.
Ochel, W. and Röhen, O. (2006), Ranking of countries. The WEF, IMD, Fraser and Heritage Indices, *CESifo DICE Report*, **4**, 48–60.
Önsel, S., Ülengin, F., Ulusoy, G., Aktas, E., Kabak, Ö. and Topcu, I. (2008), A new perspective on the competitiveness of nations, *Socio-Economic Planning Sciences*, **42**, 221–46.
Papadimitriou, D. and Taylor, P. (2000), Organisational effectiveness of Hellenic national sports organisations: a multiple constituency approach, *Sport Management Review*, **3**, 23–46.
Porter, M.E. (1990), *The Competitive Advantage of Nations*, London: Macmillan Press.
Rosselet, S. and McCauley, S. (2008), *Methodology and Principles of Analysis*, IMD World Competitiveness Yearbook, available at: http://www02.imd.ch/wcc/yearbook (accessed 2. August 2008).
Siggel, E. (2003), Concepts and measurements of competitiveness and comparative advantage: towards an integrated approach, paper presented at the International Industrial Organization Conference, Northeastern University, Boston, MA.
Siggel, E. and Cockburn, J. (1995), International competitiveness and its sources: a method of development policy analysis, discussion paper, no. 9517, Concordia University, Department of Economics, Montreal.
Shilbury, D. and Moore, K.A. (2006), A study of organizational effectiveness for national Olympic sporting organizations, *Nonprofit and Voluntary Sector Quarterly*, **35** (1), 5–38.
Sledge, S. (2005), Does Porter's diamond hold in the global automotive industry?, *Advances in Competitiveness Research*, **13** (1), 22–32.
Sparvero, E., Chalip, L. and Green, C. (2008), United States, in B. Houlihan and M. Green, *Comparative Elite Sport Development*, London: Butterworth-Heinemann, pp. 243–93.
Van Bottenburg, M. (2000), *Het topsportklimaat in Nederland* [*The Elite Sports Climate in the Netherlands*], Hertogenbosch: Diopter-Janssens and Van Bottenburg bv.

6 Sports governance in Ireland: insights on theory and practice
Ann Bourke

1 SETTING THE SCENE

Competitive sport in Ireland is largely played on a semi-professional or amateur basis, but there is a professional layer within rugby union and golf. The sports infrastructure in Ireland is less developed than that of other countries, however, in recent years, facilities have been improved due largely to government and other funding. Houlihan (1997) asserts that until the early 1990s, sports policy in Ireland was fragmented and focused mainly on tourism and the Gaelic Athletic Association (GAA). At that time, a number of sports (football: World Cup 1990 and boxing: Olympic Games, 1992) achieved international competitive success which led to increased pressure on the Irish government to take a more active role in providing facilities and the necessary resources for Ireland's sporting programme. In 1999, the Irish Sports Council (ISC) was established and its remit set out by statute. Its main role is the implementation of government policy, ensuring that government investment in sport provides 'value for money' and leads to effective use of resources. The ISC also supports national governing bodies (NGBs) in providing core services and managing key activities. There are over 60 NGBs in the Republic of Ireland (a complete list is available from the Irish Sports Council, see www. IrishSportsCouncil.ie for details).

Many theories and disciplines have influenced corporate governance practice (Mallin, 2004), in addition to institutional history, culture and administrative heritage (see also chapters in this volume, for example Gammelsæter and Senaux, 2013; Walters and Hamil, 2013; Winand and Zintz, 2012). The distinction between corporate and non-profit governance is pertinent in the sports context. While NGBs' main activities (delivering sports programmes, facilities, competitions, and so on) are performed on a not-for-profit basis, the completion of many transactions necessitate competing and collaborating with commercial and public sector enterprises on a for-profit basis. The research question posed for the study outlined in this chapter was, 'Are Irish Sports NGBs adopting a "corporate" approach to governance matters?' In deciding on a research strategy, reference was made to business and sports management research. When the purpose of a research study is to provide insights on procedures, processes in business enterprises or organizations, qualitative case studies are commonly used (Blumberg et al., 2008; Piekkari et al., 2009; see also in this volume Dibben and Dolles, 2013; Gratton and Solberg, 2013; O'Reilly, 2013; Skille, 2013).

Governance continues to be a 'hot topic' in the business domain which is largely due to corporate failures and/or unethical behaviour by some executives. Many public and private service entities (government departments or agencies, healthcare providers, education bodies, and so on) pay attention to defining and managing their service

Table 6.1 *National governing bodies (NGBs) in Ireland – key facts on the cases (as at 2008)*

	FAI	GAA	IRFU
Founded	1921	1884	1879
Domain	Republic of Ireland	All Ireland and overseas	All Ireland
Games	Football (soccer)	Gaelic football hurling, handball, camogie	Rugby union
Player status	Semi professional and amateur	Amateur – government grants	Professional and amateur
Main stadium	~	Croke Park Capacity 82 300	Lansdowne Road (*now Aviva Stadium*)
Main revenue sources	Senior internationals	All Ireland Championships	Six Nations [home games]
Main domestic competition(s)	FAI Eircom National League	All Ireland Championships	AIB National League
Gross revenue	€38.3 million (2008)	€64.3 million (2008)	€56.9 million (2008/09)
Leading sponsor(s)	Eircom, Umbro	Bank of Ireland, Guinness	O2, Puma, AIB, Guinness

and communicating clearly the organization's service concept to all stakeholders. The *service concept* is a clear statement about the nature of the service – the service experience, outcome, operation and value provided to customers (Johnston and Clark, 2001; see also in this volume Dolles and Söderman, 2013; Jansson and Söderman, 2013. Sports NGBs provide a very diverse service which requires effective and efficient management, coordination, given the high investment and revenue potential. Management personnel are responsible for the coordination and configuration of the organization's activities, employing an organizational structure designed to attain objectives and targets. As management are not the owners, the *agency problem* arises and corporate governance provides a structure through which an entity sets its *objectives* and its *performance* is managed – in other words, it is really the management of management. It is generally acknowledged that enterprises operate more efficiently when 'good' governance principles apply. Convincing certain sports organizational personnel (where profit motivation does not exist, but value for money does) that governance is important can be a challenge. In recent years, increased attention has been given to sports governance research and practice in Ireland, and this study seeks to identify the procedures and processes applied and the key changes which have occurred.

To provide insights on sports governance arrangements and practices, its complexities and the external and internal influences in NGBs, a multiple case study approach was adopted. The cases selected for the study are the three leading (in terms of membership and participation) sports' NGBs in Ireland – the Football Association of Ireland (FAI), the Gaelic Athletic Association (GAA) and the Irish Rugby Football Union (IRFU) – see summary profiles in Table 6.1. The objectives for the study were as follows: (1) to identify, compare and contrast governance arrangements in Irish sports NGBs; (2) to examine the extent to which individual/team roles and responsibilities are delineated within such organizations, and (3) to ascertain the main governance changes which emerged during the period 2000–2008. The chapter comprises five sections. In the following section the theoretical strands informing the study are considered and section 3 describes the methodology used. Section 4 sets out the main research discoveries, while in section 5 reflections on the topic, process and discoveries are provided.

2   THEORETICAL UNDERPINNINGS

The literature on corporate governance centres on definitions, theoretical and discipline influences, the development of governance codes, their communication to stakeholders and the extent to which different entities comply (Mallin, 2004; Monks and Minow, 2004). The composition and role of the board of directors in ensuring performance effectiveness (Chait et al., 2005; Stiles and Taylor, 2002) is also examined along with the role of executive and non-executive directors. Nadler (2004) asserts that the key to better corporate governance lies in the working relationships between boards and managers, in the social dynamics of board interaction, and the competence, integrity and constructive involvement of individuals.

A frequently cited definition of corporate governance is that of the Organisation for Economic Co-operation and Development (OECD, 2004: 11) 'as set of relationships between a company's board, its shareholders and other stakeholders. It also provides the structure through which the company objectives are set, and the means of attaining those objectives and monitoring performance are determined'. According to Mallin (2004), corporate governance is the exercise of power over and responsibility for corporate entities. The Cadbury Report (Cadbury, 1992: 15) defines corporate governance 'as the management of Management' while Luthans and Doh (2009) state that an organization's corporate governance specifies the distribution of rights and responsibilities among different participants in the corporation – board, managers, shareholders and stakeholders – and spells out the procedures for making decisions on corporate affairs. Sports NGBs stakeholders are many and varied, that is, sponsors, funding agencies, members, the general public, affiliated organizations, staff, board members, venues, government agencies and suppliers. A major challenge for NGBs is relationship management and, in addition, blending voluntary input with that of paid professionals may complicate organization decision-making procedures and outcomes.

Hoye and Cuskelly (2007) examine the applicability of various theories (agency, stakeholder, institutional, resource dependency and network) to governance in sports organizations and conclude that apart from agency theory, the others provide mechanisms for sports bodies to examine their governance assumptions, processes, structures and outcomes. These authors summarize the essence of governance in sport as: (1) establishing a *direction or overall strategy* to guide the organization and ensuring the organization members have some say in how that strategy is developed and articulated; (2) *controlling the activities* of the organization, its members and staff so that all are acting in the best interest of the organization and working towards an agreed strategic direction, and (3) *regulating behaviour* which entails setting guidelines or policies for individual members or member organizations to follow.

Governance systems and processes vary across borders due to institutional differences and cultural variations (McCarthy and Puffer, 2002). Some countries have well-developed systems in place (the UK, the USA, Germany and France) which are influenced by culture, history and legal dimensions, while others are in the process of development (Russia and former Eastern bloc countries). According to McCarthy and Puffer (2002) emerging governance systems will reflect a more *cultural embeddedness model*, incorporating additional influences from the home country culture, history and traditions. Luthans and Doh (2009) refer to the 'insider' and 'outsider' systems used which reflect the dispersal of corporate equity. The codification of sport in Britain during the 1860s influenced developments in Ireland, with many soccer, rugby and hockey clubs being established in the larger towns. The GAA was established in 1884 to promote Irish games and pastimes, and stimulate cultural and political resistance to Britain and things British. The influence of tradition, culture and history is evident in GAA governance, as the *parish club* is the key organization unit. Both the FAI and the IRFU had their origins in Northern Ireland; the FAI the result of a split from the Irish Football Association and the IRFU from a merger between Irish Football Union and the Northern Football Union. The Irish Football Association (IFA) governs soccer in Northern Ireland which comprises six northern counties and is part of the UK. The GAA and the IRFU are 32 county bodies, while the FAI operates within the Republic of Ireland only. In addition, the IRFU and the FAI are subsidiaries of global bodies – the International Rugby Board (IRB) and FIFA – unlike the GAA which can be labelled a global sports organization (Forster, 2006) and has a cultural remit in addition to promoting Gaelic games (www. gaa.ie, accessed 18 March 2010).

Hums and Maclean (2009) note that there is a certain language, terms and concepts associated with corporate governance. In the sports arena, the terms used to denote the inner workings of sports bodies and organizational units have a variety of titles such as general assembly, executive committees, standing committees and ad hoc committees. These arrangements are often not clearly understood outside the sports context. The official guide by the GAA or the rulebook (FAI) outline the organizational specifications regarding the sport, membership and the like. The IRFU operational details focus on facilities and events, child welfare and the games, and are covered in a variety of documents available in its resource library (www.irishrugby.ie, retrieved 20 March 2008).

An organizational chart normally sheds light on how a firm does its business and organizes key tasks, operations and activities. In business entities the structure is likely to be a functional, multidivisional or matrix system (Grant, 2010), while in sports organizations the structure is likely to be one or a mix of the following: (1) a simple, (2) a bureaucratic, (3) a matrix and (4) a team structure, depending on the organization size, its technology and the environmental uncertainty (Hoye and Cuskelly, 2007). Irish people are keen sporting spectators (Cronin, 1999), who hold and express their views on sporting matters including NGB governance. Many sports governing bodies in Ireland operate using a simple or 'ad hoc' structure and, over the years, have engaged little in strategic planning or communicating their mission and vision to stakeholders. Since the establishment of the Irish Sports Council in 1999, Irish NGBs have been urged to formalize and manage their governance procedures and processes. The three NGBs which are the focus of this study would be considered by some sport analysts in Ireland as having a progressive approach to governance matters, noting that the level of progression does vary.

Sport has become increasingly global and commercial and the alterations to geopolitical boundaries, technological advancements, and greater competition in the sport industry and marketplace, have all resulted in pronounced changes to many organizations, often over very short periods of time (Amis et al., 2004). Some sports bodies (particularly voluntary bodies) do not have the facility to respond quickly to market, competitive or game developments. Tradition, culture and fear of the unknown are often cited by sports administrators as reasons not to change the product, policy or procedures. In the following part, the research methodology used for the study is described, explained and justified.

3   METHODOLOGICAL MATTERS

Case studies are the method of choice when a phenomenon under investigation is difficult or impossible to distinguish from its context (Yin, 2003), with realism the preferred paradigm for this type of research. As the focus of this research is organizational processes, procedures and policies, a qualitative case study approach was used. The purpose of the study is to illustrate new and changed practice and use corporate governance theory to explain these changes. In that sense, the case study can be labelled illustrative and explanatory (Collis and Hussey, 2009). Comparative cases are used, not to identify the most advanced NGB from a governance perspective, but rather to provide valuable and trustworthy insights, avail of the learning potential and provide pointers for governance enhancement. As noted by Stake (2005), there is a risk associated with comparative case studies, in that emphasis may centre more on the comparison and overtake the discoveries such as the organizations' specific features, unique practice or complexities. It would have been possible to use a survey approach, but that would fail to capture the complexities of governance in sport entities (ownership, membership, stakeholder management, and so on) plus the role and extent of interdependency ties and relationships (internal and external).

The merits of case study research normally focus on the ability to get a rich understanding of the context of the research (Flyvbjerg, 2006; Remenyi et al., 1998; Saunders et al., 2009). Other merits include the fact that case studies produce first-hand information, in that they work in natural settings; and employ methods that encourage familiarity and close contact with informants (Sarantakos, 2005). Critics of case study research assert that it is hierarchically inferior to other forms and lacks validity and reliability. Other weaknesses cited include the difficulty in replicating case study research, and that the findings often entail personal impressions and biases, hence there is no assurance of objectivity, validity and reliability (Li et al., 2008). While NGB information and statistics are pertinent in assessing governance arrangements, understanding the role, mission and context of each governing body is vital. How this was achieved is explained in the following paragraphs.

Both secondary and primary data were gathered to complete this study. Secondary source materials draw on documentary evidence from multiple sources – internal and external, paper based and electronic. The *internal* source materials used included the

Table 6.2   Brief profile of interviewees

Respondent ID	Affiliation	Respondent ID	Affiliation
R1	FAI	R7	Irish Sports Council
R2	FAI	R8	Official – Department of Sport
R3	GAA senior executive	R9	FAI Regional Development
R4	GAA former senior official		Officer
R5	IRFU Head Office –	R10	IRFU Club (board member)
	executive	R11	GAA Club officer
R6	IRFU (former executive)	R12	Board member (FAI Club)

Note: N = 12.

NGBs' annual reports; strategic plans; association newsletters and official magazines – *In Touch* (IRFU) and *Hogan Stand* (GAA); various handbooks and rulebooks; guidelines and codes of practice, and web pages. The *external sources* comprised newspaper articles; journal articles; Irish Sports Council (ISC) documents and newsletters; independent consultant reports, and so on; fanzines and independent web pages. Insights with respect to organizational (re)design, committee structure and terms of reference, board operations, and so on, are primarily drawn from organization publications, reports and commentaries. *Descriptive content analysis* was used to organize the data which involved examining the main content of the documentary data chronologically, designed to explain 'how' and 'why' each NGB's mission, vision, strategy and governance procedures evolved.

Primary data were gathered by way of in-depth personal interviews. Interviewees were drawn from the three NGBs (central, regional and local units); the Department of Arts, Sports and Tourism and the Irish Sports Council. To be eligible to contribute, individuals must have been employed at senior management level in the pertinent sports organization for at least three years, and be knowledgeable (as opposed to being passionate) about sport, sport governance and sport policy development. *Purposive sampling* was used to identify interviewees who are 'experts' to ensure that more than information was gathered. Brief details of the 12 interviewees are provided in Table 6.2. The interview schedule was developed drawing on the documentary review phase (described earlier), supplemented by theory and secondary source materials. These interviews were also used to gauge the usage and understanding of key corporate governance concepts in the sports setting.

The semi-structured interviews were conducted between April and August 2008, and were recorded with each interviewee's permission and later transcribed. Following their completion, interview transcripts were reviewed, with the removal of non-pertinent data and the search for information that fittingly describes the essence of NGB governance. Interviewees were advised about the purpose of the research in advance and assured that data would be used for academic purposes only. Participants in this research project clearly have an interest in and influence on governance procedures and processes, but as none was a member of the management/executive board, their influence was more advisory than implementer. It was interesting to observe that many study participants in addition to outlining current strategic operations and roles, were keen to learn about and/or reflect on possible alternative arrangements, so in many instances the 'interview' was more a two-way conversation.

A general suspicion exists among certain academics and reviewers in relation to case study quality and the appropriateness of the inquiry process. Yin (2003) recommends that having a case study protocol and keeping a case study database helps reduce such suspicions. The case study protocol sets out the project objectives, field procedures, case study questions and report guide, while the database includes notes, documents used and interview transcripts. Drawing on these it would be possible to replicate the study or use it as a basis for another study. The credibility of a case is largely evidenced by the extent of triangulation, that is, multiple use of theories, data or methodologies. In this instance, by selecting interviewees from regional and local units and blending documentary and secondary sources, cross-checking was possible in relation to data accuracy and interpretation. The case study analysis approach used is descriptive rather than theoretical (Fisher et al., 2010) in that a series of themes were developed regarding sport NGB governance based on issues (in addition to theory) and used as main headings and subheadings. This approach was employed to illustrate tensions and contradictions within (not across) the organizations.

It is acknowledged by this author that focusing on three leading NGBs out of a total of over 60 provides a partial and possibly biased picture of sports governance in Ireland. Notwithstanding these limitations and bearing in mind organization variations in terms of culture, tradition, sporting ambitions and resources, valuable insights on governance principles and practice can be provided.

4   SPORTS NGB GOVERNANCE – DISCOVERIES

The dividing line between management and governance (particularly when management procedures are not fully developed) is thin, and this section briefly highlights three aspects of governance, focusing as appropriate on change and enhancement.

4.1   Governance Arrangements in Sports NGBs in Ireland

The FAI, the GAA and the IRFU each have a clearly articulated mission, which covers the coordination, promotion and management of their sport, and, in the case of the GAA, also includes a social and cultural remit, that is, the promotion of the Irish language, music and drama. Documentary evidence exists to support the contention that the approach to governance within the three bodies has changed, with a more long-term focus being taken. Interviewees from each organization outlined the changes which have occurred noting that FAI, GAA and IRFU governance structures are now broadly similar, which is possibly unsurprising as all three are essentially involved in the promotion and development of team field sports.

The main decision-making body for each NGB is the annual general meeting (AGM). Between AGMs, the council (membership of up to 60) oversees developments as required, and the body equivalent to the board of directors is the executive or management committee for which membership ranges between 11 and 15 members. The chief executive officer (CEO) in each organization is a full-time paid professional, supported by a team of full-time personnel. The president of each NGB is an elected position, normally for a three-year term. In the case of the GAA, the holder may complete just one term, and has an obvious leadership role while in office.

The internal organization structure of the NGBs consists of standing committees – these are broadly similar in the FAI and the IRFU. The GAA standing committee structure differs slightly in that it includes one standing committee which is dedicated to games development/research. The GAA is responsible for its playing rules, unlike the FAI and the IRFU which interpret and implement the playing rules on behalf of FIFA and the IRB, respectively. The role of standing committees can be equated to that of a functional area or department in a business entity, and they are supported in their work by a plethora of sub-committees in each NGB. The IRFU has approximately 20; the GAA 50, while the FAI has the number agreed as a result of the 2002 Genesis Review. This was a root-and-branch review of the FAI in the aftermath of the Republic of Ireland's team performance at the 2002 Football World Cup in Korea and Japan. According to two interviewees (R3 and R4) some GAA sub-committees were established for a particular purpose with specific objectives and might be labelled working groups or task forces in a different setting. An interviewee (R5) pointed out that IRFU sub-committee arrangements are relatively flexible – in some cases, sub-committees roles can be redefined depending on organizational needs.

The GAA Club is the 'bedrock of the Association' and is established using the local government boundary, that is, the parish. Each GAA club promotes Gaelic games; it also acts as a vital node of community socialization (O'Thuathaigh, 2009) with its own club premises, pitches and facilities. Club competitions are common in all sports codes, but the GAA has revitalized the local community involvement by its All-Ireland club championships for which the final is played each year in Dublin at Croke Park (over 80 000-seater stadium) on St Patrick's Day.

4.2 Individual/Team Roles

In 2003, the FAI implemented the recommendations of the 2002 Genesis Review which proposed a number of strategic changes be made to its internal organizational structure and governance. Specifications were formally adopted in relation to the following: the composition of the main board and standing committees; committee membership appointment criteria and terms of reference for each committee, and eligibility for appointment to committees and the duration of their term of office. The appointments of a chief executive and director of finance were specified, and further government funding was contingent upon these organizational changes being made. In 2011, the FAI organizational structure recommended by the Genesis Review remains in place.

The challenge of the growing importance of finance and commercial management expertise at leadership level has been embraced by these NGBs, as each have a finance standing committee and the GAA has a sub-committee, that is, the Financial Management Committee. Competition for players, spectators is intense in Ireland and the IRFU and the GAA engage in games promotion and marketing campaigns. The FAI no longer funds the appointment of a club promotions officer in each of the ten League of Ireland (Premier Division) clubs. This officer's role is to promote the club within the community, deepen its links with various stakeholders (schools and community organizations), coordinate such activities between clubs and increase attendances at league games. The GAA club representative (interviewee R11) affirmed that similar arrangements for community involvement are in place but added that there is a need for better relationship management of key stakeholders. He asserted that the strategy for GAA games development is to draw the elements of its mission, vision and ambition together, to emphasise the core message 'to stay and play with the GAA'.

A common feature of many NGBs is their reliance on voluntary personnel for input into and support with many activities (coaching, training, financial management and advice, medical support) and events. There are procedures (legal and otherwise) to be adhered to when employing voluntary personnel, such as training, security clearance, and health and safety aspects. The FAI has a volunteer education programme, in which courses on volunteer management, grounds-keeping and fund-raising are provided to club personnel. The number of full-time professional managers/administrators employed by many NGBs has grown in recent years, some of which are funded by external partners including the ISC. The increasing number stems from the strong emphasis on player development/coaching at all levels and ages. A government-funded Youth Participation Scheme was set up nine years ago and, since then, the FAI, the GAA and the IRFU have each received €3million per annum to develop more opportunities for young people to participate in field sports. This has led to a range of activities being offered to local communities, clubs, schools, referees and coaches, giving rise to an increased demand for competent personnel.

4.3   Main Governance Changes

A number of factors (political, legal, social and economic) have contributed to major changes in Sports NGB governance over the eight-year period, as outlined briefly below.

Regulation/codes
As occurs in many service entities, there are an increasing number of government regulations/codes to be adhered to and such stipulations apply to sports NGBs and affiliates. The examples cited by interviewees included financial reporting standards, auditing, health and safety requirements, child welfare, ethics, disability, employment policies (full-time, part-time, contract or voluntary), and the like. While all interviewees welcomed the introduction of such standards, a number of them emphasized the extra costs associated with compliance.

Planning
The practice of evaluating its organizational performance has been used by the GAA down through the years. Two organizational reviews are worth noting, the 'McNamee Review' (set up in 1969, reported in 1971) and the 'Strategic Review' (set up in 2000, reported in 2002). The earlier review provided a blueprint to take the GAA through the latter part of the century, while the 'Strategic Review' was more in-depth and strategic. Not all recommendations from the 'Strategic Review' were implemented, but were considered when preparing the more recent plan the 'Strategic Vision and Action Plan 2009–2015'. The essence and implementation of this plan centres on GAA core

values: community identity, amateur status, inclusiveness, respect, player welfare and teamwork. In 2004, the IRFU published its first strategic plan, while a second was published in 2008 which draws on the earlier plan. Details of the planning process used are described and key targets outlined. The FAI approach is more disjointed in that strategic plans for individual units within the association, such as *Universities and Colleges and Technical Development*, have been published. All interviewees agreed that sports NGBs, like multinational enterprises, need to engage in strategic planning which is efficient to ensure effective use of their capabilities and resources.

Functional areas
The Irish Sports Council aims to ensure that NGBs enhance their capabilities and competencies. To facilitate this, the Irish Sports Council provides support to assist with the organization, management, planning and provision of each NGB's core activities. During the financial year 2010, 59 NGBs shared €11.85 million in grants, to be used to enhance their administration procedures and processes, and expand participation programmes, coach development, hosting events, strategic planning and the employment of key professional staff.

Internationalization
For the FAI and the IRFU, the international dimension is embedded within each organization, as opportunities exist for players (national and club) to compete in international competition or to pursue a professional playing career oversees. As noted by Bourke (2011), opportunities for GAA players to play at an international level are confined to representative games such as All Star Competition and Compromise Rules fixtures against Australia. The GAA is increasing its presence overseas by setting up clubs in locations which have a large Irish diaspora, for example, New York, Sydney, London and other parts of the UK and continental European, and organizing regional competitions. This international dimension is now reflected in GAA governance with representatives from overseas clubs being members of Central Council. With the economic downturn in 2011 and increased emigration, GAA clubs overseas are considered vital for Irish emigrants; consequently, some GAA initiatives overseas are funded by the Irish Department of Foreign Affairs.

Games development
One of the largest units in the GAA is the Games Administration/Development which is not surprising as it has responsibility for developing its games, including the playing rules. The number of qualified coaches in all three codes is limited and Coaching Ireland in conjunction with the Irish Sports Council develops coaching programmes for all sports codes, designed for all levels up to elite professional.

5   REFLECTIONS ON THE PROJECT AND PROCESS

As noted earlier in this chapter, Hoye and Cuskelly (2007) assert that sport governance consists of *establishing a direction or overall strategy*, *controlling activities* of the organization and members and *regulating behaviour* which involves guidelines and policies. The case studies provided evidence of strategic developments and processes and procedures in place to regulate behaviour. While each NGB has its own unique strategy, the stage of development varies and is affected by the supports in place and evaluation procedures. Control mechanisms exist for both playing and non-playing activities with greater detail and coverage given to this by the GAA. Policy/guideline documents are available in relation to most regulations and policies, which need to be reviewed and updated regularly.

Ryan (2002) asserts there are three issues underpinning 'good governance': (1) how the organization develops strategic goals; (2) how the board monitors performance to ensure it achieves its goals, and (3) ensuring the board acts in the best interest of its members. These comparison case studies reveal governance enhancement has occurred particularly in the area of annual reporting and financial management, along with the use of central planning (GAA, IRFU) and external appointees to boards (GAA only). Some procedural issues need more attention, that is, the use of external/independent expertise to comment critically on and monitor key processes, web page management (FAI) and resource utilization and availability.

Completing a study such as this provides insights for sports NGB personnel and stakeholders in relation to governance theory and practice. Sekaran and Bougie (2010) assert that case study research is not often undertaken by organizations as a problem-solving technique. They suggest that this stems from the lack of cases for which the context and settings are similar, and reluctance by management as many organizations prefer to guard their proprietary data. While a problem-solving perspective was not employed for this study, discoveries here point to a number of governance gaps, such as communication processes, reporting mechanisms identified by several interviewees. Additionally, a rather static approach to NGB governance exists; in the current economic, social and political climate it would need to be considered a more dynamic process.

The focus of the study is on the governing body, but consideration needs to be given to ensure that subsidiary units' (clubs) governance operates using appropriate principles and processes. Governance guidelines for regional and county (provincial councils/ county board, clubs) entities are provided, but there is little assurance that arrangements in such entities are monitored and periodically reviewed. Sports NGBs (headquarters and local entities) are service enterprises, providing value for various stakeholders. Stakeholder interdependency ties and demands are complex and dynamic which makes devising a strategy, controlling activities and regulating behaviour (*the essence of governance*) a challenge, particularly for senior management and board members.

Using comparison cases to explore governance has advantages, as it forced this researcher to try and remain *detached* and throws up plenty of surprises on which to reflect. The resistance to making certain information available (confidentiality is always respected) was a surprise, but this author then tried other sources. The interviews 'degenerated' into conversations, at first the author was unhappy, but soon realized that to get insights on values, culture, processes, relationship management, power and hierarchy, a two-way discussion is more valuable, while difficult to write up. Following the discussions (interviews) contact was made with a number of interviewees to seek clarification and confirmation on certain matters. Individuals who work in sports organizations are generally passionate about their sport (not always the organization) which at times makes constructive discussion more testing.

What did this researcher learn from this exercise? First, it is challenging to retain an objective stance when completing qualitative case studies, as information obtained from interviewees or documents are likely to have a certain bias. Second, that the ownership structure (trustees) of sports NGBs complicates governance matters, as there is potential to retain an inward self-serving approach to governance matters. Third, stakeholders (commercial/voluntary) are difficult to manage, and NGB management needs to be skilled in that area. Fourth, the GAA's 'isolation' is somewhat reduced by its outward momentum targeting the Irish diaspora. Fifth, more effective use could be made of technology for internal and external communication and, sixthly, that there is a healthy respect between each of the leading NGBs in Ireland for the other.

Finally, what did you, the reader, learn? This author trusts that you will have gained a deeper understanding of the challenges associated with gathering and analysing qualitative data, and blending such data according to sources – primary and secondary. It is also expected that this chapter provides insights on completing case study research, noting the variations, particularly the service and value-added aspects, which arise in the sports setting.

Evidence from this study suggests that Irish sport NGBs now employ a corporate approach to governance matters. This shift has implications for organizational personnel as regulations and protocols need to be complied with which impose additional costs. Ireland is a relatively small country with a competitive sporting environment for spectators, participants and investors. This requires sports governing bodies to have clarity in relation to their strategic development and operations, which are clearly communicated, regularly reviewed and revised. Ultimately, it is the appeal of each NGB's *service concept* to its targeted market segment which confers on it a competitive edge.

So why have NGBs adopted a more corporate approach to governance? There are a number of possible reasons: it may be due to government demands, investment in sports events, facilities, programmes by various parties, or it might be the realization by certain NGB personnel that it is the 'right' thing to do.

REFERENCES

Amis, J., Slack, T. and Hinnings, C.R. (2004), Strategic change and the role of interests, power and organizational capacity, *Journal of Sport Management*, **18** (1), 158–98.

Blumberg, B., Cooper, D. and Schindler, P. (2008), *Business Research Methods*, 2nd European edn, Maidenhead: McGraw-Hill Education.

Bourke, A. (2011), International and professional dimensions of national governing bodies: insights from the Gaelic Athletic Association, in H. Dolles and S. Södermann (eds), *Sport as a Business: International, Professional and Commercial Aspects*, Basingstoke: Palgrave Macmillan, pp. 153–69.

Cadbury, A. (1992), *Report of the Committee on the Financial Aspects of Corporate Governance*, Cadbury Report London: Gee & Co.

Chait, R., Ryan, W. and Taylor, B. (2005), *Governance as Leadership: Reframing the Work of Non Profit Boards*, Hoboken, NJ: John Wiley & Sons.

Collis, J. and Hussey, R. (2009), *Business Research*, Basingstoke: Palgrave Macmillan.

Cronin, M. (1999), *Sport and Nationalization in Ireland*, Dublin: Four Courts Press.

Dibben, M. and Dolles, H. (2013), Participant observation in sport management research: collecting and interpreting data from a successful world landspeed record attempt, in S. Söderman and H. Dolles (eds),

Handbook of Research on Sport and Businzess, Cheltenham, UK and Northampton, MA, USA: Edward Elgar, pp. 477–94.

Dolles, H. and Söderman, S. (2013), The network of value captures in football club management: a framework to develop and analyze competitive advantage in professional team sports, in S. Söderman and H. Dolles (eds), *Handbook of Research on Sport and Business*, Cheltenham, UK and Northampton, MA, USA: Edward Elgar, pp. 367–95.

Fisher, C., Buglear, J., Lowry, D., Mutch, A. and Tansley, C. (2010), *Researching and Writing a Dissertation: An Essential Guide for Business Students*, Harlow: Financial Times/Prentice Hall.

Flyvbjerg, B. (2006), Five misunderstandings about case-study research, *Qualitative Inquiry*, **12** (2), 219–45.

Forster, J. (2006), Global sports organizations and their governance, *Corporate Governance – The International Journal of Business in Society*, **6** (1), 72–83.

Gammelsæter, H. and Senaux, B. (2013), The governance of the game: a review of the research on football's governance, in S. Söderman and H. Dolles (eds), *Handbook of Research on Sport and Business*, Cheltenham, UK and Northampton, MA, USA: Edward Elgar, pp. 142–60.

Grant, R.M. (2010), *Contemporary Strategy Analysis*, 7th edn, Chichester: John Wiley & Sons.

Gratton, C. and Solberg, H.A. (2013), The economics of listed sports events in a digital era of broadcasting: a case study of the UK, in S. Söderman and H. Dolles (eds), *Handbook of Research on Sport and Business*, Cheltenham, UK and Northampton, MA, USA: Edward Elgar, pp. 202–18.

Houlihan, B. (1997), *Sport, Policy and Politics: A Comprehensive Analysis*, London: Routledge.

Hoye, R. and Cuskelly, G. (2007), *Sport Governance*, Oxford: Elsevier.

Hums, M. and Maclean, J. (2009), *Governance and Policy in Sport Organizations*, 2nd edn, Scottsdale, AR: Holcomb Hathaway.

Jansson, H. and Söderman, S. (2013), Proposing a relationship marketing theory for sport clubs, in S. Söderman and H. Dolles (eds), *Handbook of Research on Sport and Business*, Cheltenham, UK and Northampton, MA, USA: Edward Elgar, pp. 350–66.

Johnston, R. and Clark, G. (2001), *Service Operations Management*, 3rd edn, Harlow: Financial Times/Prentice Hall.

Li, M., Pittsand, B.G. and Quarterman, J. (2008), *Research Methods in Sport Management*, Morgantown, WV: Fitness Information Technology.

Luthans, F. and Doh, J. (2009), *International Management: Culture, Strategy and Behavior*, 7th edn, New York: McGraw Hill/Irwin.

Mallin, C. (2004), *Corporate Governance*, Oxford: Oxford University Press.

McCarthy, D. and Puffer, S. (2002), Corporate governance in Russia: towards a European, US or Russian model, *European Management Journal*, **20** (6), 630–40.

Monks, R.A.G. and Minow, N. (2004), *Corporate Governance*, 2nd edn, Oxford: Blackwell.

Nadler, D. (2004), Building better boards, *Harvard Business Review*, **82** (5), 102–11.

O'Reilly, N. (2013), Portfolio theory and the management of professional sports clubs: the case of Maple Leaf Sports and Entertainment, in S. Söderman and H. Dolles (eds), *Handbook of Research on Sport and Business*, Cheltenham, UK and Northampton, MA, USA: Edward Elgar, pp. 333–49.

O'Thuathaugh, G. (2009), The GAA as a force in Irish society: an overview, in M. Cronin, W. Murphy and P. Rouse (eds), *The Gaelic Athletic Association, 1884–2009*, Dublin: Irish Academic Press, pp. 237–57.

Organisation for Economic Co-operation and Development (OECD) (eds) (2004), *Principles of Corporate Governance*, Paris: OECD.

Piekkari, R., Welch, C. and Paavilainen, E. (2009), The case study as disciplinary convention: evidence from international business journals, *Organizational Research Methods*, **12** (3), 567–89.

Remenyi, D., Williams, B., Money, A. and Swartz, E. (1998), *Doing Research in Business and Management*, London: Sage.

Ryan, C. (2002), *Sporting Bodies Urged to Practise Good Governance*, Australian Sports Commission, available at: http://fulltext.ausport.gov.au/fulltext/2002/ascpub/goodgovern.asp (accessed 25 January 2012).

Sarantakos, S. (2005), *Social Research*, 3rd edn, Basingstoke: Palgrave Macmillan.

Saunders, M., Lewis, P. and Thornhill, A. (2009), *Research Methods for Business Students*, Harlow: Financial Times/Prentice Hall.

Sekaran, U. and Bougie, R. (2010), *Research Methods for Business: A Skill Building Approach*, Chichester: John Wiley & Sons.

Skille, E.Å (2013), Case study research in sport management: a reflection upon the theory of science and an empirical example, in S. Söderman and H. Dolles (eds), *Handbook of Research on Sport and Business*, Cheltenham, UK and Northampton, MA, USA: Edward Elgar, pp. 161–75.

Stake, R.E. (2005), Qualitative case studies, in N.K. Denzin and Y.S. Lincoln (eds), *Sage Handbook of Qualitative Research*, 3rd edn, Thousand Oaks, CA: Sage, pp. 443–66.

Stiles, P. and Taylor, B. (2002), *Boards at Work*, Oxford: Oxford University Press.

Walters, G. and Hamil, S. (2013), Regulation and the search for a profitable business model: a case study of the English football industry, in S. Söderman and H. Dolles (eds), *Handbook of Research on Sport and Business*, Cheltenham, UK and Northampton, MA, USA: Edward Elgar, pp. 126–41.

Winand, M. and Zintz, T. (2013), Qualitative comparative analysis on sport governing bodies: a tool on ways towards high performance, in S. Söderman and H. Dolles (eds), *Handbook of Research on Sport and Business*, Cheltenham, UK and Northampton, MA, USA: Edward Elgar, pp. 76–93.

Yin, R.K. (2003), *Case Study Research. Design and Methods*, 3rd edn, London: Sage.

7 Regulation and the search for a profitable business model: a case study of the English football industry

Geoff Walters and Sean Hamil

1 INTRODUCTION

The fundamental reason why research is undertaken is to increase knowledge and understanding. When deciding upon a research project, there are a number of important choices that have to be made within the early stages of the research process. These include the nature of the data that will be collected, how it will be collected, the sources from where the data will be collected and how it will be analysed (Easterby-Smith et al., 2008: 82). These choices will influence the choice of research strategy that will act as a framework for the research process. One such research strategy that is popular in social science research is the case study.

The objective of this chapter is twofold. First, it aims to illustrate when, why and how the case study strategy can be a relevant approach for sport management research. It discusses how the case study strategy can be applied across competing epistemological positions (ibid.) and how a case study can also draw on multiple data collection methods. This will lead into the discussion of why the case study strategy is relevant to the study of sport management. This is particularly relevant given that the use of the case study strategy has become increasingly popular in sport management research (also in this volume, Dibben and Dolles, 2013; Gratton and Solberg, 2013; O'Reilly, 2013; Skille, 2013). For example, within the field of sport events there are numerous case studies that focus on economic impacts (Gratton et al., 2000; Wilson, 2006), environmental impacts (Collins et al., 2007), the role of government (Hill, 1994; Lee, 2002) and marketing (Chadwick and Holt, 2008; Taks et al., 2006). Second, the chapter illustrates the empirical use of the case study strategy in sport management by presenting a descriptive case study drawing on research that considers the need for sport governing bodies to impose effective regulation within their sport. The chosen case study is the English football industry, where, despite the highest financial revenues of any football industry in Europe, chronic loss-making and financial instability are widespread. The objective of the case study is to provide a descriptive account of the financial problems in the English football industry and the regulatory response by the football authorities. Although the case study is intrinsic in the sense that it aims to provide an understanding of regulation in the UK football industry it could also be argued to be instrumental (Stake, 1995) in that it will provide insights into financial regulation that may be relevant for other professional leagues within European and world football or, indeed, professional leagues within the wider sporting industry.

2   THE CASE STUDY STRATEGY

The use of the case study as a teaching strategy has a long history dating back to the 1920s during which Harvard Business School adopted the use of case studies as a way to prepare students for management roles by using case examples as a way to learn theories and principles relevant to business (Myers, 2009). The use of the case study as a research strategy differs in that the purpose is not to aid student learning but to contribute to knowledge and to demonstrate the relevance of a particular theory (ibid.). The commonly cited definition of a case study is that of Yin (2009: 18), who considers a case study as 'an empirical inquiry that investigates a contemporary phenomenon in depth and within its real-life context especially when the boundaries between phenomenon and context are not clearly evident'. This demonstrates the importance of context to the case study strategy. Indeed, the objective of a case study is to provide detailed contextual analysis of an individual organization, a group of organizations or even a particular industry. This focus means that the case study is particularly suited to answering explanatory research questions that begin with 'how' or 'why' that require a more in-depth understanding to help explain causal relationships. However, the case study strategy is also flexible – it can span competing epistemological positions (Easterby-Smith et al., 2008); it can be descriptive or exporatory as well as explanatory; it is appropriate to study a single case or multiple cases, and case studies can draw on multiple data collection methods. This flexibility is one reason to explain the growing popularity of the case study strategy.

2.1   Philosophical Implications of Case Study Research

The case study strategy can span different epistemological positions (Easterby-Smith et al., 2008). For example, a case study strategy can lean towards a positivist approach. The seminal work of Robert Yin (2009) in the field of case study research is often associated with this position. While positivist critics of the case study strategy have often pointed to the lack of scientific rigour and validity and the inability to generalize from the research findings (Easterby-Smith et al., 2008), Yin (2009) has long argued that a systematic and codified approach to case study research is needed to counteract these claims. Such an approach requires undertaking a methodical approach to case study research, beginning with the development of an overarching research question or set of questions that help to define the purpose of the case study, provide a framework for the case study design, and help to guide data collection, analysis and reporting (ibid.). The approach advocated by him requires the development of theory prior to the collection of case study data, illustrating that firstly, case studies can be deductive, and secondly, that there has been a movement towards theory-oriented case-study research in which the aim is to be able to make theoretical generalizations (analytical generalization).

   The nature of the research questions will underpin the case study selection and which organization(s) is chosen. It will also determine whether a single case or multiple cases are chosen as the unit of analysis. While Yin (2009) states that a single case-design is beneficial when the case is a critical case, a rare or unique case, a representative or typical case, a revelatory case or a case that was previously inaccessible, he advocates undertaking multiple-case or comparative-case studies. It is argued that direct replication with multiple cases can lead to cross-case comparisons that result in analytical generalizations whereby the results of the research are used to generalize to theory and the results are more powerful, valid and reliable (ibid.: 53). Again this shows the positivist influence underpinning Yin's work. Yin (2009: 79) also argues for the need to develop a case study protocol that is used as a framework to guide data collection and analysis and can be used to overcome issues of validity. Key issues that need to be considered prior to collecting the data are the objectives of the research, access to organizations and sources of information and the specific questions that will be asked (ibid.: 81). By considering these in advance of data collection it will help to ensure that issues of validity and reliability are considered.

The approach that Yin (2009) has taken to case study research is indicative of the recent trend towards structuring qualitative research in a more positivistic way that facilitates generalized conclusions, albeit analytical generalization (Schofield, 2000: 92). However, the case study strategy can be viewed differently from competing epistemological positions. From the constructivist position, there is far less attention paid to issues of validity and generalization. Indeed, many researchers reject generalizability as the objective of case study research and see it as irrelevant to their aims or low in their priorities (ibid.: 70). The work of Stake (1995), an ethnographer, is most commonly associated with this position that considers the search for generalizations to be flawed given that truth is a relative concept and generalizations can vary and change over time. The objective of the case study strategy can be intrinsic and within-case analysis can be used to provide a deeper, holistic understanding of a particular organization or issue. An additional epistemological position is that of relativism, in which it is argued the case study research strategy can be used to generate theory (Eisenhardt, 1989; Eisenhardt and Graebner, 2006). This approach demonstrates that the choice of one or more case studies can lead to the development of theoretical constructs that are generated from the case study data (Eisenhardt, 1989). There are similarities to both the positivist approach and constructivist approach to case study research in that a nine-stage process or research design is set out at the beginning of the case study research but there is also flexibility in data collection and analysis (Easterby-Smith et al., 2008). Table 7.1 outlines these three competing epistemological positions that demonstrate the flexibility of the case study strategy.

2.2 Data Collection Methods

The decision to use either quantitative or qualitative methods (or both) is influenced by the epistemological assumptions of the researcher, underlining that each approach

Table 7.1   Competing epistemological positions and case study research

	Realist	Relativist	Constructionist
Design	Prior	Flexible	Emergent
Sample	Up to 30	4–10	1 or more
Analysis	Across case	Both	Within case
Theory	Testing	Generation	Action

Source: Easterby-Smith et al. (2008: 99).

has different aims, generates different types of data and offers distinct forms of representation and interpretation (Denzin and Lincoln, 1994). Key elements of quantitative research methods include systematic, objective measurement, which aims to reduce error, increase validity and reliability, in addition to statistical and numerical analysis to reveal patterns and understand the relationships between variables. Qualitative research methods have a different emphasis and focus on interpretations, on eliciting meaning from social situations and developing a contextual appreciation.

The case study has been defined as an umbrella term for the use of many different types of data collection method (Remenyi et al., 2002). This demonstrates a high degree of flexibility on the part of the researcher who can draw on various types of data collection method such as interviews, questionnaires, observations and document analysis, and in the process combine both quantitative and qualitative techniques. This flexibility is both a positive and negative feature of case study research. For instance, the use of both quantitative and qualitative methods enables the collection of a large amount of varied data. The use of multiple data sources allows for triangulation in which multiple perceptions are drawn on to aid the intepretation of the data, reduce the potential for misinterpretation, and enhance the validity and reliability of research findings. However, the flexibility in the choice of research methods and the lack of a definitive method underpins the argument by research that takes a more positivist approach that the case study approach lacks scientific rigour, objectivity, and can be shaped by the researcher and as such, is value laden. These are reasons why the case study approach has been disparaged as a strategy of research. Moreover, it has been argued that unlike other research strategies, the skills for doing good case studies have not been defined and that there is no determined routine to conducting case study research. These criticisms underpin the need for a systematic approach to case study research (Yin, 2009).

2.3 Case Studies and Sport Management Research

There are two reasons to support the use of the case study strategy within sport management research. First, the case study is a broad research strategy that can be applied across many academic disciplines. That it has become increasingly popular, and more widely accepted, within social science and in business and management research, emphasizes that it too is an appropriate strategy for sport management researchers to use. Second, despite the fact that sport management is a relatively new discipline and a growing area of research, it can be argued that it has already undergone a period of self-examination. The special issue of the *Journal of Sport Management* in October 2005 discussed the need to broaden the range of theories and approaches used within sport management research in order to 'widen the space for thinking about critical and innovative approaches to the study of sport management' (Amis and Silk, 2005: 355). This call for a more critical approach to the discipline was intended to bring about a better understanding of the context in which research takes place, accounting for the broader cultural, economic, social and political contexts in which sport organizations exist (ibid.; Frisby, 2005). In advocating a critical approach to sport management, Frisby (2005: 6) argues that 'organizations are best viewed as operating in a wider cultural, economic, and political context characterized by asymmetrical power relations that are historically and deeply entrenched'. In this respect, it echoes the critique of organizational theory by Hinings and Greenwood (2002: 417) who stress that 'answering questions that focus on the role and effect of organizations in society requires long-term perspectives, a grasp of history, a focus on understanding, so that the complexities of political and social movements are not reduced to dummy variables in a regression equation, and an interest in specula-tion'. This argument provides support for the use of the case study as a research strategy in sport management. One of the key reasons for undertaking case study research is to understand better the context in which an organization operates and to take into account complex political, social, cultural and economic factors. It can therefore be argued that the case study strategy is particularly appropriate in order to gain an in-depth apprecia-tion of the context in which sport organizations exist.

3   A CASE STUDY OF THE ENGLISH FOOTBALL INDUSTRY

The increasing commercilization and professionalization of the sports industry within Europe has led to increasing concerns regarding issues of governance and regulation. These issues are particularly relevant for the European football industry during a period that has seen rapid commercial growth, the increasing power of the elite football clubs, and challenges to the traditional regulatory authorities. The implementation of free-market principles within the football industry is controversial as it undermines the peculiar economics of the sport industry (Neale, 1964). Sports leagues are joint products produced by groups of clubs and, hence, require an additional degree of co-ordination, governance and regulation (Noll, 2006) over and above what might be expected in more conventional business activities. In professional team sports, the product of sporting activity – match and the league competition – are reliant upon a degree of interde-pendence and cooperation between teams. The product is therefore an 'inverted joint product' (Neale, 1964: 2) in the sense that what is produced is not entirely the product of an individual team, illustrating the interdependence that exists within sporting com-petition (on this discussion, see also Dolles and Söderman, 2013 in this volume). In the football industry, the organizer of a league competition can be regarded as the 'firm', which occupies a position of monopoly power. For instance, there are a fixed number of league members; the league determines the games played; entry to a league is restricted, and often there are no other leagues that are in direct competition. The league is there-fore composed of competing interdependent teams and exerts a natural monopoly in the marketplace, illustrating the peculiarity of the structure. These features of the profes-sional sport industry demonstrate the need for an additional degree of coordination, governance and regulation over and above what might be expected in more conventional business activities.

3.1   Case Selection

The choice of case study is the English football industry. The English football industry provides an interesting insight into the issue of governance and regulation in professional sport. The Football Association (FA) is the governing body of the football industry in England with responsibility for the overall organization of professional football. However, the FA is not responsible for the organization of league competition; this has been the role of the Football League since its formation in 1888, combined with the Premier League after it was introduced in 1992. English league football is structured as a pyramid, with teams moving up and down its component leagues through the process of promotion and relegation based on sporting success or otherwise. The league below the Premier League is the Football League, consisting of the Championship, and Divisions 1 and 2.

The English football industry is an appropriate case study to illustrate issues of governance and regulation. The reason for this is that there has been an evolution in the regulatory role of the governing bodies since 2003, from an essentially laissez-faire approach with regulatory intervention seen as a last resort, to one where the FA, the Premier League and the Football League have increasingly found it necessary to undertake direct regulatory intervention to address a series of challenges. These challenges emanate, in one form or another, from the fundamental structural characteristic of English football; the inability to deliver a business model in which member clubs can be consistently profitable. The objective of this case study is to provide a descriptive account of the financial problems in the English football industry and the regulatory response by the football authorities. The case study is essentially intrinsic although it could also be argued to be instrumental (Stake, 1995) as it will provide insights into financial regulation that may be relevant for other professional leagues within European and world football or indeed professional leagues within the wider sporting industry.

3.2   Data Collection Methods

This case study draws on longitudinal case study research undertaken between 2006 and 2009. The case study was an appropriate strategy for this study as it allowed for a combination of data collection methods – both qualitative and quantitative data are used to provide rich and detailed evidence from a range of sources. The first phase of research was undertaken in 2006 and was used to develop an understanding of governance and regulation in the football industry between 1999 and 2006. During this first phase, 14 face-to-face semi-structured interviews provided the main source of data collection. A total of five interviews were conducted with representatives from the football authorities including the Football Association, the Football League, the now defunct Financial Advisory Committee of the Football Association, and the Football Conference (the league below the Football League, now branded as the Blue Square Premier). The Premier League was approached in relation to the research project, but declined to give an interview. A purposive sampling technique was used as the interviewees at the football authorities were senior members of staff who were purposely selected on the understanding that they would be able to provide relevant information relating to the regulatory structure in which football clubs operate and their role in relation to improving standards of corporate governance at club level.

A further nine interviews were conducted with senior representatives from a range of stakeholder organizations that have a strong interest in the governance and regulation of the football industry. These included a chief executive of a Premier League football club, a vice-chairman of a Football League club, representatives from the Independent Football Commission (an independent regulatory body that was created to examine the performance of the football authorities in England) and two national supporter organizations, Supporters Direct and the Football Supporters Federation. A prominent football journalist who writes on issues of governance was also interviewed. Each interview lasted between one and two hours and used an interview guide to structure the direction of questioning. In many cases new issues were brought to light during the interview and therefore opened up additional areas for questioning. Each interview was tape-recorded and transcribed. The interview transcriptions were read in full in order to provide a general understanding of the responses before they were coded to aid analysis and to identify key issues relating to club-level regulation and the regulatory role of the football authorities

The interview data was triangulated through the analysis of secondary data sources. The first phase of research drew on documents including FA, Premier League and Football League annual reports, annual reports of the Financial Advisory Committee, the *FA Guide of Governance*, Football League agent fees' reports, and press reports. This type of qualitative research has several benefits. It offers a richer understanding of cognition and discourse through analyses of text and respondent viewpoints; it can facilitate the understanding of the motivating rationales behind behaviours and actions, and secondary data of a textual nature, in particular, can offer access to longitudinal insights published by multiple agencies, helping to facilitate the understanding of processes (Hodder, 1998).

The second research phase began in 2009 with the objective to present an up-to-date analysis of developments in governance and regulation since 2006. The main method of data collection covering the period between 2006 and 2009 has been the use of secondary documents from the football authorities including the Premier League handbook, Football Association agent regulations and the Football League agent fees' reports, in addition to press reports and the Deloitte *Annual Review of Football Finance*. The article also draws on written evidence given to the All Party Parliamentary Report on English Football and its governance (Walters and Hamil, 2008). Secondary sources of information have been supplemented by interviews with three representatives from the Football Association, one from the Football League and a chief executive from a Football League club.

The two research phases, in addition to the analysis of documentary evidence have been one way in which this case study has attempted to overcome problems of validity. Indeed, as Yin (1984: 21) has pointed out, validity can be an issue with case study research: 'Too many times, the case study investigator has been sloppy, and has allowed unequivocal evidence or biased views to influence the direction of findings and conclusions.' The triangulation of data is one way to mitigate this concern. It also shows that despite the flexibility and the growing popularity of the case study strategy, it is not an easy option. When undertaking a case study there is a need to plan in advance and establish a clear design prior to data collection, particularly if you are concerned about issues of validity and reliability.

4   CASE STUDY DISCUSSION: FINANCIAL PERFORMANCE IN THE FOOTBALL INDUSTRY

After the formation of the Premier League in 1992, turnover in English football increased dramatically. Between 1992 and 2008 the aggregate growth in turnover of clubs in the

Table 7.2 English football – pre-tax profitability (£ sterling)

	2007/08		2006/07		2005/06	
	Pre-tax profit	Turnover	Pre-tax profit	Turnover	Pre-tax profit	Turnover
Premier League	−£240m	£1932m	−£285m	£1530m	−£200m	£1379m
Championship	−£80m	£336m	−£62m	£329m	−£36m	£318m
League One	−£18m	£125m	−£20m	£102m	−£17m	£102m
League Two	−£6m	£65m	−£4m	£63m	−£4m	£61m

Source: Deloitte (2008: 24; 2009: 24).

Premier League and the Championship (Football League) was, on average, 16 per cent and 12 per cent per annum respectively (Deloitte, 2009: 25). Revenue growth has been maintained largely due to a consistent rise in the value of broadcasting rights over the period (and with it associated sponsorship income), particularly in the Premier League. It is widely cited as Europe's most successful league in terms of revenue generation terms.

However, during this same period, the 92 clubs in the Premier League and Football League have, on aggregate, consistently failed to achieve pre-tax profits. There has not been a single year since the formation of the Premier League that the 20 member clubs in any one season have made a collective pre-tax profit. This is also the case for the Championship and Divisions 1 and 2 of the Football League. In 2007–08, the 20 clubs in the Premier League made a pre-tax loss of £240 million, while the 72 clubs in the Football League collectively lost £104 million (refer to Table 7.2). Although Premier League clubs are loss-making at the pre-tax level, owners have been willing to sustain these losses and as such, they are more stable than clubs in the Football League. For example Premier League clubs are at least profitable at the operating level (before transfers) making a cumulative operating profit of £1497 million in the 16 seasons to 2007/08 (Deloitte, 2009: 30). By contrast, the cumulative operating losses of the 72 clubs in the Football League in the 15 seasons up to 2007/08 were £1.067 million (ibid.: 30).

Sustained operating losses have also served to increase debt levels with the aggregate debt for the clubs in the Championship totalling £326 million in 2007/08, with total debt in the Premier League reaching £3.1 billion (ibid.: 59–65). In 2009 the combined Premier League clubs debt-to-turnover gearing was a very high 162 per cent. Unless football clubs are able to trade their way out of debt, which for the vast majority of clubs given the long history of loss-making in the Premier League and Football League is unlikely, the only way they will ultimately be able to address their debt issues is either by debt write-off, through new investment from existing or new investors, or through entering the financial administration process. Administration is the process whereby failed companies which are unable to meet their financial obligations are given protection from their creditors while being 'administered' by an insolvency practitioner until such time as they are restructured. Typically this involves the company writing off significant proportions of debt, hardly the symptom of a financially healthy industry.

While there has not been a case of administration in the Premier League, between 1992 and 2009 financial problems at Football League clubs have resulted in bankruptcy leading to 52 incidences of administration (ibid.: app. 13). The reason for this was because of overspending on player wages to achieve sporting success while some clubs in the Championship were committed to unaffordable player contracts upon relegation from the Premier League. For example, in 2007/08 the wages-to-turnover ratio for the Premier League was 62 per cent, while the comparative figures for the Championship, League 1 and League 2 were 87 per cent, 71 per cent and 69 per cent respectively (ibid.: 34–5). The wages-to-turnover ratio in the Championship in the 11 seasons from 1997/98 to 2007/08 has never been below 71 per cent, and was as high as 101 per cent in 2000/01. In effect, the reality is that the vast proportion of increased revenue that has been generated by the English football industry since its restructuring with the establishment of the Premier League in 1992 has been transferred to players in increased wages.

In England, if a club emerging from administration wishes to retain its place in the league then it must first pay all its football-related debt (player wages and transfer payment to other clubs) under a condition known as the Football Creditors' Rule. This is a football industry-specific rule which is designed to protect football clubs from the reckless financial behaviour of those peer clubs which fall into bankruptcy and financial administration. As a result, a particularly dubious scenario results whereby other creditors receive proportionately less from the reconstruction of the business. Often, significant losers are the UK tax authorities, who lost their preferential creditor status in the Enterprise Act 2002. So, in effect, a large part of the cost of failing English football clubs is being carried by the public purse, providing a public sector subsidy to a failing private business sector. Again this is a situation that would probably not be tolerated in any other industry, with the exception of the strategically critical UK financial services sector which was rescued by the British government over the 2008/09 period. Football trades on its status as among the most powerful cultural and social assets in England. For in reality, no state body, such as the tax authorities, up until now, has wanted to be the organization that ultimately liquidates a football club in the pursuit of unpaid taxes such is their iconic status in English popular culture. This, however, is changing as a number of football clubs have faced (and continue to face) winding-up orders from the tax authorities, including Southend United, Accrington Stanley, Notts County, Portsmouth, Cardiff City and Rochdale.

In a league which is not closed and where there is promotion and relegation there are clear incentives for all clubs, not just those seeking to win the league title, but those seeking to compete to qualify for European competition or to avoid relegation, to spend beyond their means to achieve their immediate sporting objectives. However, it can be argued that recent financial performance within the Premier League and Football League is unsustainable. While it is the responsibility of individual football clubs to decide on issues such as board structure, business planning or risk management, which in turn affect operational procedures at clubs, it can be argued that proper and appropriate regulation – including financial regulation – is also an issue that governing bodies and leagues have to address. The lack of external regulation has been recognized to have a negative impact on issues of transparency, accountability and, standards of club governance (FGRC, 2004: 7), and, as a result, there have been calls for governing bodies and leagues to ensure that 'appropriate regulatory controls are put into place to protect the principles of sound financial management and transparency in football clubs' (Independent European Sports Review, 2006: 69). It is against the context of a very high level of financial instability and bankruptcy in the Football League, and over-indebtedness and over-dependence on altruistic owners in the Premier League, that the gradual increase in regulatory assertiveness of the three UK football regulators – namely, the Football Association, the Premier League and the Football League – since 2003 needs to be seen.

5   THE REGULATORY RESPONSE OF THE FOOTBALL AUTHORITIES

In 2002 English football received a significant financial shock with the collapse of the ITV Digital pay-per-view broadcasting company. ITV Digital had just completed the first year of a three-year deal to broadcast live Football League matches. At the time that ITV Digital entered into administration, it owed the Football League £178.5 million. Although BSkyB subsequently agreed a four-year deal with the Football League, the value was less than that previously agreed with ITV Digital. The Football League pursued the outstanding monies through the courts but subsequently lost their case. The impact of the company's collapse and their inability to pay the remaining two years of the contract was immediate; ten Football League clubs went into administration in 2002 followed by six in 2003 (Deloitte, 2009: app. 13). While it is difficult to say with certainty whether this was the only catalyst for action, since 2003, the English football authorities have become more interventionist and have introduced a number of regulatory mechanisms designed to improve club-level corporate governance and to try to create an environment in which English clubs are managed in a more financially disciplined fashion. The following mechanisms are discussed: the fit and proper persons test; player agent regulations; monitoring transfer activity; third party ownership; sporting sanctions; salary cost management, and HMRC monitoring.

5.1   The Fit and Proper Persons Test

In 2003 the FA introduced the Financial Advisory Committee (FAC) that was created to promote the long-term financial health and stability of football clubs within their communities. The FAC, which included representatives from the Premier League and Football League, was originally responsible for the development of a fit and proper person test that would be a requisite for club directors. The reason underpinning the need for a fit and proper test was to prevent people with a criminal record from taking control of football clubs. This followed a series of fraud scandals at English football clubs. For example, at Chesterfield Football Club former owner Darren Brown was ultimately gaoled for fraud. Although the members of the FAC worked collectively on the development of the fit and proper person test in 2003, the Football League chose to introduce their own, very similar, version in 2004, with the Premier League soon following suit. The FA therefore has the responsibility to apply their fit and proper person test to clubs in the Football Conference, the Southern League, the Isthmian League and the Northern Premier Leagues. The three versions of the test are similar and currently forbid an individual from owning or being a director at a football club if they are subject to a number of criteria, such as having an unspent conviction relating to fraud or dishonesty or are disqualified from acting as a director of a UK registered company. Since the introduction of the fit and proper persons test in 2003, all three of the football authorities have made a number of additions. For example, in the Premier League, club shareholders that own a controlling stake in a club, defined as owning more than 30 per cent of the shares, also have to pass the fit and proper person test.

5.2   Player Agent Regulations

Increasing agent activity has led to concerns over the level of fees paid to agents, the effect that agent payments have had on clubs with financial difficulties, and whether agent involvement is undermining standards of governance in the industry. Agent behaviour is regulated on two levels: FIFA, the governing body for world football is responsible for developing agent regulations, while the FA is charged with monitoring and regulating agent activity by drawing on FIFA regulations to develop their own framework. An area of key concern has been dual representation and payment, where an agent is paid by both player and club for a particular transaction, which could potentially lead to a conflict of interest. The FIFA regulations forbid dual representation; however, agents and clubs across Europe have circumvented FIFA regulations by separating the representation of the player as one transaction and the payment for 'scouting' on behalf of the club as another transaction (Holt et al., 2006).

Although the revision of agent regulations by the FA in January 2006 resulted in the removal of regulations that forbid dual representation, allowing agents to be paid by a club for securing the services of the player and to also be paid by the player as a separate transaction, in September 2007 the FA introduced new agent regulations that tightened up the regulations governing dual representation. However, this was in large part a result of the Premier League decision to support legislation forbidding clubs from paying an agent when they were in the process of buying a player or renegotiating a contract; this payment had to come from the player. Nevertheless, in July 2009 FA regulations governing agent behaviour were revised and the rule banning dual representation was discarded, allowing the use of the same agent by the player and club in the same negotiation. However, as section C4 of the FA's agent regulations outlines, agents can only act for more than one party in a transaction or contract negotiation subject to the satisfaction of a number of requirements.

There have been moves made by the Premier League and Football League to increase the transparency of agent activity. The Football League has taken the lead on this by introducing legislation in 2004 that requires member clubs to disclose the total payments made for the services of an agent including new registrations and transfers, updated contracts, contract cancellations and loan transfers. The Football League publicly report the aggregate payments made by each member club every six months, the intention being to improve transparency in the industry and increase public confidence. The initial results demonstrated that overall spending on agents decreased from £7.8 million between July 2004 and June 2005 to £7.66 million between July 2005 and June 2006. However, between July 2006 and June 2007 spending on player agents increased to £8.58 million (Football League, various years). The Premier League has also implemented legislation that requires member clubs to complete an Annual Director's Report, part of which includes detailing financial transactions between the club and player agents that exceed

£25 000 (Premier League, 2007). Although the Premier League does not publicly report agent payments, it has led to increased transparency and has enabled the Premier League to monitor agent payments.

5.3   Monitoring Transfer Activity

Further evidence of a more interventionist regulatory climate includes the decision to investigate transfer activity. As has been discussed previously, whilst the FA introduced new regulations governing agent behaviour, in 2006 the Premier League commissioned Quest – a corporate intelligence consultancy – to undertake an inquiry into transfer deals within the Premier League owing to perceived breaches of transfer regulations. The investigation, led by former Metropolitan Police Commissioner Lord Stevens, examined 362 individual cases over a two-year period between 2004 and 2006. The final report in December 2006 found irregularities with 17 transfers, as well as citing failures by a number of clubs and the FA with respect to transfer regulations. It also made a number of recommendations, many of which the Premier League supported. The FA then further appointed Quest to audit a number of transfers that have taken place in the January 2008 transfer window.

5.4   Third Party Ownership

One of the key developments has been new legislation on third party ownership of player contracts. This situation arises when a contract exists in which a third party owns the economic rights to a particular player and where the third party is entitled to a percentage of any future transfer fee in return for financial support. This situation became prominent in the Premier League following the ownership of Carlos Tevez during the period in which he played for West Ham. The issue is that third party ownership can effectively undermine transparency and integrity, particularly if there is concern that the third party is able to influence club policy or where a third party is involved in one club but able to influence decisions taken by another club (Geey et al., 2007). The FA has introduced rules (in line with FIFA) that aim to protect club autonomy by stating that no third party can influence club policy. The Football League rules state that no entity (third party) can have an interest in more than one club. However, it is the Premier League that has introduced the most restrictive legislation following the 2008 Annual General Meeting (AGM) at which the club chairmen voted to prohibit third party ownership. However it has been stated that it is unlikely that third party ownership will be totally prohibited under the Premier League rules (Geey et al., 2007).

5.5   Sporting Sanctions

In 2004 the Football League introduced a sporting sanction whereby member clubs receive a ten-point penalty for entering into administration. The sporting sanction rule functions as a deterrent to administration following poor governance and financial management. It is also designed to ensure that clubs do not gain a competitive advantage by writing-off debt and to make directors more accountable for the way they run the club. Sporting sanctions were introduced because of a perceived abuse of the administration process. The case that prompted action was that of Leicester City who entered administration in October 2002, wrote of in excess of £30 million of debt, kept their best players and were promoted back to the Premier League at the end of the 2002/03 season; while promotion rival Nottingham Forest, who continued to meet the payments on their debt, did not go into administration, and narrowly avoided promotion, were perceived to have been disadvantaged as a result (Walters and Hamil, 2008). A number of football clubs have since incurred this penalty. Football League rules also place an 18-month limit on the period in which a club can remain in administration, requiring that clubs successfully negotiate a Company Voluntary Arrangement whereby creditors accept a percentage of the debts owed (Football League, 2004: 4). The penalty for failing to agree terms to exit administration is a further points' deduction as Luton Town, Bournemouth and Rotherham football clubs all faced for season 2008–09. Clubs in the Premier League that enter into administration also face a nine-point deduction. However, the Premier League has not yet had to apply this legislation.

5.6   Salary Cost Management

In 2003 the Football League introduced a salary cost scheme. The Salary Cost Management Protocol was designed to control aggregate wage expenditure and improve financial stability at clubs by limiting the amount that a club can spend on player wages to 60 per cent of turnover, while total spending on wages must not exceed 75 per cent. While restricting clubs to these spending parameters will not guarantee that an operating profit or pre-tax profit will be made, a club will be less likely to incur large deficits and debts will be more manageable. The Football League piloted the scheme on a voluntary basis with the clubs from League Two in season 2003/04, with the clubs voting to accept it as a formal mechanism for season 2004/05. The penalty for exceeding the 60 per cent wage to turnover ratio is that clubs are forbidden from signing new players. Member clubs from League One voted to implement the Salary Cost Management Protocol on a voluntary basis. This means that the clubs are still required to submit financial details of turnover and salary costs so that the Football League can calculate the wage/turnover ratio, but the League is unable to formally apply any sanctions on a club if the ratio exceeds 60 per cent. In the Championship, however, the Football League has been unable to persuade club chairmen to consider the implementation of the Salary Cost Management scheme, even on a voluntary basis. Restricting the ability of the clubs in the Championship to increase player wages is seen as excessive regulation by club chairmen who want to be able to determine their own wage budgets.

5.7   Her Majesty's Revenue and Customs Monitoring

A recent development has been the implementation of a monitoring system in order to ensure that clubs make their tax payments to Her Majesty's Revenue and Customs (HMRC) on time. In 2008 the FA introduced this mechanism in the Conference National Division, Conference North and South, whereby tax payments to HMRC are monitored. With the HMRC a major creditor at many football clubs, and therefore a potential barrier to overcome in the negotiation of a Company Voluntary Arrangement, the system was set up in order that the FA could monitor, and if necessary intervene in, any instances where a club in the Football Conference began to fall behind in their payments to the tax authorities. A similar mechanism has been passed by club chairmen at the Football League's AGM in June 2009 and ensured that from 1 July 2009, all clubs have to report to the Football League on a monthly basis whether they have paid their PAYE and National Insurance on time. The ruling also ensures that clubs must keep up payments on historic debt. If clubs fail to report to the Football League, the League has the authority to obtain the information from HMRC. If a club fails to report to the League that it has failed to pay HMRC on time, they are charged with misconduct and an immediate transfer embargo is placed on the club. This is a highly significant development as it represents a very serious attempt to address the impact of spiralling debt at clubs.

What the foregoing descriptive case study demonstrates is that, since 2003, there has been a gradual but nevertheless significant trend towards greater financial regulatory intervention by the three main English football bodies. This has been a direct response to a series of financial crises and controversies such as the ITV Digital collapse, abuse of the financial administration process by clubs, and player agent fees controversy. However, the effectiveness of these interventions has been hampered by the fragmented nature of their implementation. It is also the case that none of these interventions, except for the Salary Cost Management Protocol in League Two, either individually or collectively, addresses the fundamental structural problem in English football, which is the uncontrolled ability of leading clubs to debt finance player wages and transfer fees, and the impossibility of all but a handful of investors to make a pre-tax profit from the ownership of an English football club; with the inevitable consequence that chronic financial instability is the order of the day in English football. This reality poses a particular challenge for the football authorities – how do they implement regulation to create a framework for member clubs to maintain financial stability when the structure of the industry dictates that clubs can, will and do always overspend on player wages to achieve competitive success?

6   CONCLUSION

The objective of this chapter has been to illustrate when, why, and how the case study strategy can be a relevant approach for sport management research. The reason for undertaking a case study is to gain an in-depth contextual understanding of an individual sport's organization, a group of sports' organizations, or a particular sport industry. The empirical case study in this chapter focused on financial regulation in the English football industry, and provided detail on the measures that have been introduced by the football authorities in recent years. To begin with, however, it was important to set out the financial problems within English football; this helped to contextualize the increasing focus on financial regulation. The case study drew on interview data and documentary sources of evidence, therefore it is hoped that the triangulation of multiple data sources reduces the potential for misinterpretation. It also demonstrates the flexibility of the case study strategy in that multiple methods can be used. However, the fact that the Premier League declined to be interviewed shows that the inability to gain access to the relevant people/organizations can be a potential weakness of the case study strategy.

Case studies are also flexible in their objective. This flexibility is one of the positive aspects of undertaking case study research. However, if the aim of the case is to generalize in relation to theory (analytically generalize), then it is important to set out the theoretical approach at the beginning. This case study on English football is largely descriptive, rather than explanatory or exploratory, and is used to provide a deeper understanding of how the football industry has addressed the issue of financial regulation. Therefore, it was not the aim of this case study to generalize to theory. In this sense the case study is intrinsic. Nevertheless, given that regulation is an important aspect for all sports leagues, there is an argument that this case study also has instrumental value in that it could be of broader interest. Further case study research into regulation within other sports would be an interesting approach as this would clearly demonstrate instrumental value as part of a multiple, comparative case study approach. For example, while this case study has looked at the football industry in England, a multiple or comparative case study strategy identifying the range of regulatory measures that have been applied within different European countries would also be interesting and would help to broaden the debate to a pan-European level. Moreover, it can be argued that the topic underpinning this particular case study could be extended even further to focus on an examination of financial regulation across different sports leagues and the use of comparative case studies involving sports in the USA in particular (where regulation is more prevalent) would contribute to a greater understanding. Therefore, although this current case may be relevant for other professional leagues within European and world football or indeed professional leagues within the wider sporting industry, a comparative case study as described above would perhaps be of even greater value (both from a practitioners perspective and from a theoretical perspective), echoing the approach advocated by Yin (2009).

REFERENCES

Amis, J. and Silk, M. (2005), Rupture: promoting critical and innovative approaches to the study of sport management, *Journal of Sport Management*, **19** (1), 355–66.

Chadwick, S. and Holt, M. (2008), Releasing latent brand equity: the case of UEFA's Champions League, *Marketing Review*, **8** (2), 147–62.

Collins, A., Flynn, A., Munday, M. and Roberts, A. (2007), Assessing the environmental consequences of major sporting events: the 2003/04 FA Cup Final, *Urban Studies*, **44** (3), 457–76.

Deloitte (eds) (2008), *Annual Review of Football Finance*, Manchester: Deloitte Sports Business Group.

Deloitte (eds) (2009), *Annual Review of Football Finance*, Manchester: Deloitte Sports Business Group.

Denzin, N.K. and Lincoln, Y.S. (1994), *Handbook of Qualitative Research*, London: Sage.

Dibben, M. and Dolles, H. (2013), Participant observation in sport management research: collecting and interpreting data from a successful world landspeed record attempt, in S. Söderman and H. Dolles (eds), *Handbook of Research on Sport and Business*, Cheltenham, UK and Northampton, MA, USA: Edward Elgar, pp. 477–94.

Dolles, H. and Söderman, S. (2013), The network of value captures in football club management: a framework to develop and analyze competitive advantage in professional team sports, in S. Söderman and H. Dolles (eds), *Handbook of Research on Sport and Business*, Cheltenham, UK and Northampton, MA, USA: Edward Elgar, pp. 367–95.

Easterby-Smith, M., Thorpe, R. and Jackson, P.R. (2008), *Management Research*, 3rd edn, London: Sage.

Eisenhardt, K.M. (1989), Building theories from case study research, *Academy of Management Review*, **14** (4), 532–50.

Eisenhardt, K.M. and Graebner, M.E. (2006), Theory building from case studies: opportunities and challenges, *Academy of Management Journal*, **50** (1), 25–32.

Football Governance Research Centre FGRC (eds) (2004), The state of the game: the corporate governance of professional football 2004, *Football Governance Research Centre Research Paper*, no. 3, London: Birkbeck, University of London.

Football League (eds) (2004), *Annual Report and Financial Statements 2003–2004*, London: The Football League.

Football League (eds) (various years), *Agent Fees Reports*, London: The Football League.

Frisby, W. (2005), The good, the bad, and the ugly: critical sport management research, *Journal of Sport Management*, **19** (1), 1–12.

Geey, D., Ross, V. and Rotkvic, M. (2007), Integrity: player and club ownership in football, *World Sports Law Report*, **5** (12), 15–16.

Gratton, C. and Solberg, H.A. (2013), The economics of listed sports events in a digital era of broadcasting: a case study of the UK, in S. Söderman and H. Dolles (eds), *Handbook of Research on Sport and Business*, Cheltenham, UK and Northampton, MA, USA: Edward Elgar, pp. 202–18.

Gratton, C., Dobson, N. and Shibli, S. (2000), The economic importance of major sport events: a case-study of six events, *Managing Leisure*, **5** (1), 17–28.

Hill, C. (1994), The politics of Manchester's Olympic bid, *Parliamentary Affairs*, **47** (3), 338–54.

Hinings, C.R. and Greenwood, R. (2002), Disconnects and consequences in organization theory?, *Administrative Science Quarterly*, **47** (3), 411–21.

Hodder, I. (1998), The interpretation of documents and material culture, in N. Denzin and Y. Lincoln (eds), *Collecting and Interpreting Qualitative Materials*, London: Sage, pp. 110–29.

Holt, M., Michie, J. and Oughton, C. (2006), The role and regulation of agents in football, *Football Governance Research Centre Research Paper*, no. 1, London: Birkbeck, University of London.

Independent European Sport Review (2006), Final Version, October 2006, available at: http://www.independentfootballreview.com/doc/Full_Report_EN.pdf (accessed 10 January 2010).

Lee, P. (2002), The economic and social justification for publicly financed stadia: the case of Vancouver's BC Place Stadium, *European Planning Studies*, **10** (7), 861–73.

Myers, M. (2009), *Qualitative Research in Business and Management*, London: Sage.

Neale, W. (1964), The peculiar economics of professional sport, *Quarterly Journal of Economics*, **93**, 385–410.

Noll, R. (2006), Sport economics after fifty years, in P. Rodriquez, S. Kesenne and J. Garcia (eds), *Sports Economics after Fifty Years*, Asturias, Spain: University of Oviedo Press, pp. 17–49.

O'Reilly, N. (2012), Portfolio theory and the management of professional sports clubs: the case of Maple Leaf Sports and Entertainment, in S. Söderman and H. Dolles (eds), *Handbook of Research on Sport and Business*, Cheltenham, UK and Northampton, MA, USA: Edward Elgar, pp. 333–49.

Premier League (eds) (2007) *Premier League Handbook: Season 2007/2008*, London: The Premier League, available at: http://www.premierleague.com/staticFiles/2e/6d/0,,12306~93486,00.pdf (accessed 10 January 2010).

Remenyi, D., Money, A., Price, D. and Bannister, F. (2002), The creation of knowledge through case study research, *The Irish Journal of Management*, **23** (2), 1–18.

Schofield, J. (2000), Increasing the generalisability of qualitative research, in R. Gomm, M. Hammersley and P. Foster (eds), *Case Study Method: Key Issues, key Texts*, London: Sage, pp. 69–97.

Skille, E.Å. (2013), Case study research in sport management: a reflection upon the theory of science and an empirical example, in S. Söderman and H. Dolles (eds), *Handbook of Research on Sport and Business*, Cheltenham, UK and Northampton, MA, USA: Edward Elgar, pp. 161–75.

Stake, R. (1995), *The Art of Case Study Research*, Thousand Oaks, CA: Sage.

Taks, M., Girginov, V. and Boucher, R. (2006), The outcomes of coattail marketing: the case of Windsor, Ontario, and Super Bowl XL, *Sport Marketing Quarterly*, **15** (4), 232–42.

Walters, G. and Hamil, S. (2008), *All Party Parliamentary Football Group – Inquiry into English Football and its Governance: 'Memorandum of Evidence'*, Birkbeck Sports Business Centre, University of London, available at: http://www.sportbusinesscentre.com/images/APPFG%20Written%20EvidenceFinal20October2008_2_.pdf (accessed 10 January 2010).

Wilson, R. (2006), The economic impact of local sport events: significant, limited or otherwise? A case study of four swimming events, *Managing Leisure*, **11** (1), 57–70.

Yin, R. (1984), *Case Study Research: Design and Methods*, London: Sage.

Yin, R. (2009), *Case Study Research*, 4th edn, Thousand Oaks, CA: Sage.

8 The governance of the game: a review of the research on football's governance
Hallgeir Gammelsæter and Benoit Senaux

1 INTRODUCTION

Given that the membership of football's supreme international body Fédération Internationale de Football Association (FIFA) surpasses that of the International Olympic Committee (208 versus 205 member nations) and the United Nations (192 members), that allegations of corruption and mismanagement have followed FIFA for a long time (for example, Jennings, 2006), and that the sport has experienced soaring commercialization (for example, Giulianotti and Robertson, 2009), one should perhaps expect huge research interest about how 'the World's Game' (Murray, 1996) is structured and governed. This chapter takes stock of what has been published academically about the theme over the past decade or so, providing an overview of studies and research topics, and reflecting on further research.

In this chapter we confine our review to publications that address the governance of football (for other sports, see in this volume, for example, Bourke, 2013; Skille, 2013; Winand and Zintz, 2013). While this encompasses the regulation of clubs' organization and management by national and international governing bodies, and their interaction with a number of other organizations, for practical reasons we here exclude research on club management (research on club mangement is emphasized in this volume, for example, by Anagnostopoulos, 2013; Dolles and Söderman, 2013; Jansson and Söderman, 2013; O'Reilly, 2013). The examination is also primarily based on empirical and conceptual studies and with a wish to map and coarsely classify research areas, research questions and findings. In saying that, we have excluded writings that largely ignore *processes* of governance, typical for many studies in sport economics and marketing which often depart from the notion that industries and companies should make a profit, and from that position indulge in developing models of profitable business conduct. We also concentrate our treatment on studies appearing during roughly the past decade. We do not think this is a brutal limitation because this literature encompasses football's development in the past era and most of the academic material on the topic published in English also dates back to the past decade. Perhaps indicative, *Soccer and Society*, the only social scientific journal that dedicates itself entirely to football, appeared in 2000. Having said this, historical, sociological and economic studies appeared before this time that have a bearing on governance, organization and management issues. An example is the presentation of the theorem of uncertainty of outcome (for example, Neale, 1964; Rottenberg, 1956).

The remaining part of the chapter is structured as follows: in section 2 we outline the concept of governance and discuss how it applies to this text. In section 3 we review studies that address football's governance primarily from within its own ranks, first with an eye on the transnational level, then with a more national focus. Section 4 follows the structure of section 3, but its focus is on studies that see the governance of the game more from the outside in, as interactive processes within a web of stakeholders. Section 5 provides a brief discussion of political governance in football, before in the final section the state of the research field and the suggestions for further research is summarized.

2   THE STUDY OF GOVERNANCE IN TEAM SPORT

A defining characteristic of competition sport is the need to balance cooperation and competition. While the focus of contestants is to win competitions, competition is premised on the ability of contestants to cooperate in organizing the competition and to make sure that it is sustainable, that is, keeping a critical mass population of more or less equal competitors. The superior end to which governance is important is to ensure the popularity of the game, which, as long as a balance between competition and cooperation is maintained, possibly can happen in many ways encompassing different views of what the game should look like. In accepting these terms it follows that the issue of governance in sport particularly pertains to two levels: the organization and management of the competing unit (the club and national team); and the organization and management of the sport which aims to ensure continuous cooperation and competition between competing units (the football authorities). Albeit these two levels are obviously closely connected, here space allows us to address the latter only.

The concept of governance is often seen as the twin concept of government. *Government* entails the notion that a governing body can define and control its domain, while *governance* responds to the observation that this is frequently not the case; governing bodies have to compete, adjust and cooperate with other organizations and groups, and hence the structure and changes of a domain, including its borders, are subjected to contestation and negotiation. Henry and Lee (2004) assert that this is the case in sport where the traditional top-down hierarchies of governing sport bodies far from control their sport. On the contrary, sport changes through interaction in a complex web of stakeholders who make claims on it. Henry and Lee (ibid.), building on Leftwich (1994), label this *systemic* governance, of which they also identify two subsets: *organizational* and *political* governance.

Organizational governance refers to what is often labelled corporate governance, or 'good governance', that is 'the accepted norms or values for the just means of allocation of resources, and profits or losses (financial or other) and of the conduct of processes involved in the management and direction of organisations' (Henry and Lee, 2004: 26). This more normative branch of systemic governance is increasingly being associated with stakeholder theory (Freeman, 1984) and corporate social responsibility (CSR) (Lockett et al., 2006) as emerging fields of study.

Political governance relates to how political governing bodies seek to achieve goals by influencing other organizations through means such as licensing, regulation, financial incentives or moral pressure, rather than by using direct action and coercive control. While there is a mixture of profit, non-profit and public organizations in sport governance, this does not mean that governments – and the European Union (EU) at the European level – support sport without trying to steer it in particular directions. Since politics are generically related to issues of legitimacy, political governance is also an approach that in part is normative.

Henry and Lee's (2004) notions of sport governance capture efforts to understand the development of sport in part as the political economy of sport, in part as the legitimated intentional strategies, actions, structures and systems created by sports' mandated organizations and directors – which is often the case in sport management studies (compare Ferkins et al., 2005) – and partly as a matter of sport policy (for example, Bergsgaard et al., 2007; Houlihan, 2002). If we add to this typology that governance also has its ideational aspects, change can also be studied as the outcome of processes that designated managers do not always fully understand and steer, although, or perhaps because, they are deeply immersed in them (compare institutional organization theory; Greenwood et al., 2008). Arguably, conceiving even corporatized football as an economic activity that is managed by shareholders and their salaried managers, or politicians for that sake, falls short of capturing the complexities and dynamics of an activity which engages a multitude of logics and stakeholders whose engagement is perhaps more social or social-psychological than purely economic (Gammelsæter, 2010; Senaux, 2008; also Chadwick, 2013 in this volume). Accordingly, the question of governance should not be confined to 'who governs, and how?' but ask more broadly 'what governs, and how?'.

Having said this, describing properly the set-up, personalities and inner deliberations of the bodies and persons in football's own governance structure is a necessary prerequisite to understanding how football, and team sport more broadly, is governed and by what dynamics. If football is studied primarily from the vantage point of broader socio-political and economic processes, one runs the risk of depicting its development as a mere reflection of societal changes, ignoring or downgrading the agency and impact of football's own leadership and decision-making bodies. In a mature research field we would expect to see studies that profoundly address the internal arrangements and dynamics of the sport as well as studies that highlight the interaction and influence patterns between the sport's own governing bodies and external constituents.

3   FROM THE INSIDE OUT: HOW THE 'FOOTBALL FAMILY' GOVERNS THE GAME

In this section we look at studies that broadly can be labelled as organization governance oriented (note, however, our reservation in section 5). This does not mean that this literature is particularly normative or prescriptive, but it does have a bearing on discussions of how football authorities should organize themselves and behave in the future.

For those who expect to find a reader for football's basic organization principles and governing arrangements, titles in the academic literature do not abound. This possibly reflects a remaining dearth of governance studies in the sport field, and the lack of sport studies in organization theory (compare Henry and Theodoraki, 2002). Studies that provide some descriptive completeness of how football is set up and simultaneously account for the most frequently recurring issues that can be referred to its organizational principles and inward tensions are few. To learn about the set-up and challenges of the sport one has to reconstruct from a multitude of sources, often in the context of sport governance more broadly (for example, Foster and Pope, 2004; Hoehn, 2006).

3.1   Organizational Governance at Football's Transnational Level

Foster and Pope (2004) categorize FIFA as a team sport global sporting organization (GSO) which is composed of other organizations, pursues the mission to govern and promote the sport globally, and bases its decision-making on the one-member-one-vote principle. Sport historian Christiane Eisenberg (2006), co-author of the FIFA centennial book (Lanfranchi et al., 2004), concludes that FIFA has transformed itself into an international non-governmental organization (INGO) with powers not only in sport governance, but also in the field of development aid, alongside transnational organizations such as the International Red Cross and Amnesty International. This means that it operates independently of governments yet with the help of official elites, pursues cultural, humanitarian and developmental aims, and helps to spread universal ideas and activities globally. The synergy of this has been to help fulfil FIFA's original aims of regulating and promoting football and its competitions. While this has also been advanced by the commercialization of FIFA, Eisenberg repudiates the claim that FIFA has grown into a mere business enterprise. She acknowledges that the entrepreneurial success of FIFA erodes its democratic basis; when even the relatively wealthy national associations now receive more money from FIFA than they contribute, the power of FIFA's executive bodies which allocate the money is obviously enhanced. Nevertheless, FIFA's allocation of surpluses is conducted according to need or equality principles and not as dividends on invested capital which is the manner in shareholder companies.

In his essay on 'Decisive moments in UEFA' the previous chief executive of the Union of European Football Associations (UEFA) Lars-Christer Olsson addresses some key governance issues at the transnational level (Olsson, 2011). He sees it as a complication that the continental confederations, such as UEFA and CAF (Confédération Africaine de Football), are not fully integrated in FIFA. One consequence in Europe is that the EU has to keep relations with both UEFA and FIFA, which have not always coordinated their interests and agendas. In fact, the two organizations might compete for the patronage of such important authorities, thus the structure encourages politicking within the sport. Another deviation from the idealized model is harboured in the privileges still retained by the UK which on top of being admitted four associations, four national teams and four votes for the Congress, also maintains the right to elect one of FIFA's eight vice-presidents (the others being elected by the continental confederations) and cast half of the votes in the International Football Association Board (IFAB), the supreme authority for determining the laws of the game. Olsson asserts that IFAB can be used for political manipulation because it has a global impact that does not tally with its limited representation (Olsson, 2011).

Focusing more particularly on the interactions between UEFA and the EU, and relying on in-depth empirical research combining archival research and 43 semi-structured interviews, García (2008) concurred with Holt (2006, 2007) to say that football's traditional pyramid of government based on national associations, and in which UEFA had all authority to govern European football, has been challenged by emerging stakeholders. It is increasingly being replaced by a network structure in which new stakeholders – notably big clubs, leagues and the players associations – define the future alongside the traditional bodies. For instance, to counteract the actions of the powerful clubs previously associated as the G-14, UEFA created the European Club Forum (ECF) in 2002. As

UEFA's recognized partner and voice of the professional clubs, ECF was incorporated into UEFA's Professional Football Strategy Council. Thus, for the first time clubs could bypass the national football associations in making their voices heard in UEFA. While more recently the structural relations between the clubs and UEFA has changed again (García, 2011), the essential point here is that in Europe the confederation structure is under increasing pressure as a consequence of recent changes in the power relations between the professional clubs and national associations. Interestingly, Eisenberg (2006) reminds us that FIFA is not to the same extent as UEFA compelled to take account of the major clubs, hence it can continue to channel its funds to the national member associations while UEFA has adopted models where revenues have increasingly been skewed to gratify the major clubs in the major leagues in the major television markets (compare Guilianotti and Robertson, 2009: 118).

When jumping from structural issues to leadership the dearth of studies is only more noticeable. Fortunately, there are a few exceptions which show that added understanding can be reaped from studying the leaders of football's organizations. One of these is Tomlinson (2000) who employs the telling title 'FIFA and the men who made it' to build an argument that the way FIFA governs the game largely reflects the backgrounds and management styles of its presidents. In Tomlinson's account a particular shift in organization policies and power relations took place when the dynamic Havelange – the businessman who had promised not to be subjected to anyone, and 'a master of giving people the feeling that they are important without giving power away' (interviewee cited in Tomlinson, 2000: 64) – changed the atmosphere created by his predecessors Rimet and Rous who, with backgrounds in education and public service, led FIFA like 'idealist missionaries' (ibid.: 69). Havelange is depicted as the new type of international leader who takes advantage of the changes in world politics.

According to Sugden and Tomlinson (1997) it was the anxiety about Europe's persistent influence in world football that inspired European football associations to establish UEFA in 1954, and that speaking with one voice was decisive in keeping the presidency European until 1974 when Brazilian Havelange took over. Rous stood up for re-election but lost because Havelange, in contrast to Rous, canvassed energetically in post-colonial Africa and clearly supported the anti-Apartheid lobby in FIFA (ibid.; Darby, 2008). African votes were again pivotal when 82-year old Havelange stepped down in 1998 and his protégé Sepp Blatter stood against UEFA-president Lennart Johansson who, somewhat surprisingly, lost the election (Bairner and Darby, 2001). These studies highlight how the political clashes between FIFA and UEFA, epitomized in the battles over the election of presidents, were closely connected to changes in world politics. FIFA's aims of globalization, generous admission practice and the one-member-one-vote principle contributed to water down the European influence as new nations were taken on board. Simultaneously, more expansionist presidents were able to take advantage of the world political situation and the global strategies of corporations like Coca Cola and Adidas (Eisenberg, 2005, 2006).

Bairner and Darby (2001) spotlights the previous UEFA president Lennart Johansson and his philosophy and presidential campaign prior to the FIFA elections in 1998. According to these authors his campaign reflected his social-democratic background and Swedish international commitment. This background led Johansson to develop a working relationship with the African football confederation, CAF, based on a vision statement that included a transparent rotation system for FIFA Presidents and World Cup Finals around the continental confederations. We now know that Johansson's election manifesto based on democracy, solidarity and transparency did not appeal to the majority of the FIFA delegates, an issue that should attract our attention not merely to personalities but to the cultures of politics and friendship at the apex of football's hierarchy. Curiously, in contrast to the portrait of the last FIFA presidents as politically able and the rise of FIFA as an influential INGO, Eisenberg (2005) ascribes little to the analytical and political acumen of FIFA's leadership in her explanation of FIFA's transformation over the last century. She notes instead that thanks to the cause, the passionate involvement in the competition, and lifelong friendships among the sporting officials FIFA has been able to keep its direction and foster the development of football. More than anyone else, journalist Andrew Jennings (2006) has reminded us that these friendships and interactions may also have their darker sides.

The organization governance literature on the transnational structure and leadership of football is centred on FIFA and UEFA. It depicts UEFA as more subjected to systemic governance than FIFA, partly because of EU's growing intervention into professional football but also because UEFA is more of a front-line soldier having to battle directly with big European clubs and leagues backed by powerful sponsors and media corporations. In contrast, FIFA – and its presidents – is much described as operating independently of governments and powerful clubs due to its interaction with political, cultural and humanitarian elites and multinational corporations and its distance to club football. FIFA is in part seen as a reflection of the political leadership of its presidents which has been able to withstand allegations of corrupt practices exactly because of their support in global elites. Against the background of these diverse portraits of FIFA and UEFA, the interaction between these governing bodies as well as their relations to other continental confederations seems to be a much under-researched topic. This includes issues of formal structure and representation, but also issues relating to the asymmetry between Europe's central role in world football and its minority representation in FIFA's decision structure.

3.2 Organizational Governance at Football's National Level

Despite the recent professionalization and commercialization of football, analyses of football's national governance structures are far between. England to some extent represents an exception, but notwithstanding the many books, reports, essays and articles that have been produced on the effects of commercialization on English football, there are remarkably few that provide a complete outline of the governance changes that has taken place since the 1980s. For other countries, including leading nations such as France, Germany, Italy and Spain, what is available (in English) is often sketchy (for example, Desbordes, 2007; Hamil and Chadwick, 2010), and richer in descriptive numbers and graphs than in details about how the game is governed and by whom.

As with the inquiry into transnational governance structures there are exceptions to the broader pattern. Surely, the 'state of the game' reports on the corporate governance of English football, produced at Birkbeck University between 2001 and 2006 (for example, FGRC, 2002, 2003, 2004; Holt et al., 2005), provide detailed reviews and analyses of governance change based on surveys on attitudes and effects of policy measures. Notably, the Birkbeck analyses are policy oriented as they are produced by 'supporter activist' researchers which advocate measures to curb the corporatization of the clubs and the league, and what is seen as efforts to transform the fans into pure consumers (compare Hamil et al., 2000, 2001).

Another exception is a recent study of governance and regulation in Italian football provided by Hamil et al. (2010). Departing from observation of the series of misconduct and scandals in Italian football, these authors outline its structure while spotlighting the political and corporate governance culture in which Italian football is wreathed. While this study illuminates how organizational governance is confined by national culture, it concurs with Bairner (2004) who – reflecting on football governance in small countries – argues that local factors in the national football bodies can limit the capacity for change.

Gammelsæter and Jakobsen's (2008) exploration of the specific dual-structure of Norwegian top football clubs highlights how the structure of professional clubs largely reflects an institutionally derived national regulative system in which sport bodies are central stage. In comparing the governance of top football in the three quite homogeneous countries of Scandinavia, Gammelsæter (2009) found that despite great similarities in sport cultures and the set-up of elite football, there were marked differences in issues such as licensing, the way clubs are organized, and in the relations between the football authorities, top clubs and organized players. In an extension of the study, Gammelsæter et al. (2011) point out that, despite Sweden's much larger population and prouder traditions in international football, Swedish football economy is the smallest in Scandinavia. Since these countries largely share socio-political traditions and cultures, the differences are not convincingly explained as mere reflections of national regulative systems. Hay (2011) has claimed that structural issues, often set down by the sport's own authorities should play a more central role in explaining the development and position of soccer in Australia. Hay himself outlines how the structure of Australian soccer has changed over the past 50 years much as a result of decisions and non-decisions made by its own leaders.

One of the consequences of the low number of organization governance studies at football's national level – including comparative studies and studies of national bodies' relations with FIFA and their continental confederation – is little understanding of differences across countries and the extent to which football's own governing bodies influence different patterns of how football is organized and managed. We also observe the seeming oblivion of numerous national leaders that must have influenced their national football (notable exceptions are Hare, 2003, and Armstrong and Mitchell, 2008)). Where are the 'Havelanges', 'Blatters' or 'Johanssons' in national football? We assume that this picture is partly a false one in the sense that this domain of study has been the remit of sport historians writing in their national language. If we are correct this means that there is a reservoir of national studies that governance researchers can tap into. Another important source for organization governance studies could be public inquiries into football, for instance in many Anglo-Saxon countries.

In conclusion we think it is fair to say that despite the understanding that sport in general and perhaps football in particular are increasingly being transformed through processes of systemic governance, further research from an organization governance perspective should be encouraged. If it is true that the game is now governed through a wide web of interacting stakeholders (García, 2011; Henry and Lee, 2004), the need to outline and understand the impact of football's own governing bodies and leadership should be even more pressing. Disregarding research into the sport's own arrangements and personalities is of little help if we want to make sense of the dynamics that change football.

4 FROM THE OUTSIDE IN? A CHANGING GAME IN A CHANGING WORLD

Above we have reviewed literature that outlines how football has organized and managed itself transnationally and across nations. Now we turn to studies that to a much larger extent see developments in football as a reflection of broader dynamics that comprise sport as they do other sectors of society. These are studies that primarily see the governance of the game as systemic, that is, as moulded through interaction in a complex network of stakeholders.

4.1 Systemic Governance of Football at the Transnational Level

In borrowing from Castells' (1996) conceptualization of a 'network society', Sugden (2002) depicted the increasing influence of global business networks on the development and control of world football in an article titled 'Network football'. Holt (2007), finding that the big clubs and their sponsors increased their leverage in European football, maintains that the stepping stone for these empowered stakeholders is the recent commercialization of football, facilitated by simultaneous technological and political changes affecting the broadcasting industry, the autonomy of professional clubs and the interest of sponsors to develop football as an industry. Despite this increasing network character of football's governance, Holt argues that UEFA and national associations most likely will keep a strong position in European football in the future. He points out that even the biggest Europeans clubs depend on their domestic market, and given the fierce competition and the lack of trust and unanimity among them it is not likely that they will risk the consequences of breaking away from the system of governance that integrates all levels of football at the European level (ibid.).

Lee (2004) outlines the increasing corporate influence in football's governance and argues that only states and major political institutions possess the necessary power to impede the pursuit of private commercial interests to undermine the broader interests of sport. Noting the general reluctance of the British government to intervene in governance issues, Lee's hopes are directed towards the EU which, through the Bosman case, demonstrated willingness to involve itself in European sport. García (2007, 2011), analysing the EU–UEFA relationship after the Bosman ruling, finds that UEFA has changed its attitude towards the EU from seeing it as a threat to considering it a long-term strategic partner. UEFA has accepted that European law applies to the activities of football, and on this platform it has developed a policy dialogue with the EU which is now seen as an adequate vehicle in maintaining its own legitimacy in the governance of European football. According to García, the increasing demand for influence from the big clubs, the leagues' and players' associations as well as UEFA's partnership with the EU has transformed the governance structure into a 'stakeholder democracy' in which UEFA maintains its power through engaging in direct and regular contact with diverse players in the football field.

Another political economic contribution is provided by King in his two books on football's transformation in England (2002) and Europe (2003). In the first he is concerned with how the FA Premier League was established and how the new consumption of football came into existence in the 1990s. In the second he explores the emergence of new economic networks between football clubs and new solidarities among fans. King uses football to understand the transformation of society because 'once football is recognised as a social ritual rather than an escape from social reality, important new horizons are opened up' (King, 2003: 15). King's approach is to see football as a ritual which expresses the hegemonic framework of society; hence football and its governing structure provide an arena for the expression of identities, meanings and actions for society's dominant groups. Here governance becomes a matter of continuously 'controlling' the meaning of the ritual. In King's (2003) work the transformation of football was marked by the dissolution of Fordist economic regimes, deregulation of markets and free movement across borders, transformed nation-states menaced by the new region-cities and the European super-nation, and new identities rooted at different planes of social structure: the region, the nation and, less likely, the super-nation. The processes of changing the ritual – which in England produced the FA Premier League – is closely connected to changes in actors in the political economy, and in this sense it reflects changes outside the ritual itself. The transformations in European football came out of largely intended political, cultural and socio-economic transformation of the society.

In expanding the scope, Giulianotti and Robertson (2009) see the development of football as dynamics of pushes and pulls constituting the following four themes in the global field: individual selves, national societies, international relations and humankind. Associated with each of these themes they see political-economic strategies that relate to processes of globalization and the formation of football. Thus, *neo-liberalism* is associated with the idea of the individual free agent and the promotion of transnational corporations such as large clubs, media networks and key sponsors which benefit from deregulation of markets. *Neo-mercantilism* – epitomized as self-protecting and self-aggrandizing policies by nations, supra-state institutions and international governmental organizations – is promoted for example by nations hosting football mega-events and supporting their leagues in the international competition, such as the Russian state's channelling of money into Russian clubs and the expansionist televising of for example the English Premier League or the Spanish League. *International governance* is promoted by football's international government bodies such as FIFA and UEFA which, through their successful expansion, also have inherited competing interests and aspirations. Lastly, Giulianotti and Robertson (2009) see *global civil society* as harbouring ideas of a common world humanity and shared transnational fate, promoted for instance by INGOs and even transnational corporations which engage in football schemes to advance issues such as peace, development, democratization, reconciliation, and social responsibility. The governance of football is conceptualized as the temporary outcome of battles between the diverse actors that partly pursue, partly oppose these political-economic strategies within the field of football.

In these systemic governance contributions the organization of the game is largely seen as impacted by and reflecting, or – to concur with King (2003) – expressing, changes of the larger society: its changing cultural, political and economic ideologies and realities, and technologies. A pertinent question that arises out of this literature is whether football is merely a vehicle or medium that is malleable to all kinds of circumstances. Is it governed from the outside in, or has it a core identity of its own, a specificity that, given football's large outreach, may provide an autonomous force in transforming society? To get closer to an answer, it is not enough to assume that football's governance reflects societal changes and overlay this with selected examples. One needs instead to study empirically the micro-processes in which football's governing bodies and leaders interact with other powerful stakeholders in the network, be they media corporations, owners, sponsors, public authorities or fans. Thus, we encourage more studies like the ones undertaken by Holt (2007) and García (2008), at the transnational level as well as at the national to which we now turn.

4.2   Systemic Governance of Football at the National Level

Giulianotti and Robertson (2009) employ the concept of glocalization to describe effects caused by simultaneous global and local influences. While neo-liberalism, neo-mercantilism, international governance and global civil society are relevant strategies to understanding the shaping of football worldwide, local and national traditions, cultures and institutions will shape the local uptake of these influences. From this vantage point studying processes of football's governance at the national level is highly relevant, and while there are few studies that specifically revolve around the issue of national governance, the numbers of book titles and articles relating national football in its many aspects to national history, traditions and political-economic issues proliferate. Some are rather sketchy, as exemplified by the chapters on football in edited volumes in sport economics (Andreff and Szymanski, 2006), sport marketing (Desbordes, 2007) and sport management (Hamil and Chadwick, 2010). Others, reflecting the difference in disciplinary approaches as well, sweep more broadly without placing governance at the centre of the analysis, although it sometimes features as a sub-theme (for example, Horne and Manzenreiter, 2004; Miller and Crolley, 2007).

A study which – besides King (2002) – ploughs deep is Hare's (2003) historic-cultural examination of 'football in France'. Hare uses football as a window to study the revival of French national self-confidence, and identifies towns and cities, fans, coaches, player heroes, television and club chairmen as the major stakeholders in the development of French football. Nevertheless, in light of the study's pivotal question 'whether the values carried by football are simply the expression of identifiable collective cultures, or whether we are dealing with a process of top-down construction of values by the state or the media' (ibid.: 4), national football bodies are not fleshed out as major stakeholders in the analysis. Hare gives extensive attention to state influences in the coaching system and the regulation of club organization structures, but we learn little about the relationships between such stakeholders as the Ministry, the French FA and the League.

Another rich study, yet with a closer look at the personalities of the football leaders is Armstrong and Mitchell's (2008) anthropological exploration of football in the Maltese society on the fringes of Europe. This study's methodology and access to the political players (through interviews and observation) contrasts with the bulk of the literature on the governance of football in the centre, notably the UK. Much of the academic writing about transformations in professional football is produced by British authors and frequently uses English football as the 'natural' reference point even when other countries are treated (for example, Hamil et al., 2010; Hare, 2003), yet a comprehensive institutional analysis where football's governance is related to UK sport policies, the role of the state and the dealings of the football authorities are hard to find. Magee (2002: 223), for example, addresses the shifting balances of power in the new football economy through the 'examination of the combined issues of Premier League wealth, increased player salaries, increased labour rights through the Bosman case, the use of agents', but without an explicit framework that clearly situates the study in an institutional football system.

To alleviate the shortness of detailed description of football's governance and improve the basis for better understanding differences across countries, Gammelsæter and Senaux (2011) recently compiled contributions from 19 European countries. Relying on an institutionalist approach, these authors see football governance much as a mosaic of regional and national idiosyncrasies, and that prevailing differences are produced by different historical and evolving relationships between the state, sport associations, big clubs, sponsors and, increasingly, agents and media corporations. In Mediterranean Europe, for example, sport is frequently seen as the responsibility of the state and with the national association as its ally, while the clubs, with some exceptions in Italy, are historically rooted in non-profit traditions. Corporatization is therefore regulated or even induced by state laws that incorporate sporting ends into otherwise commercial companies. In Northern Europe, state involvement is more ad hoc, but non-governmental organizations rooted in traditions of voluntary sport in part play a similar role to the Southern European state in regulating the forms of football governance. Moreover, football in the British Isles has its own historical patterns with marked differences between Great Britain and Ireland. Similarly Eastern European countries share the legacy of football governance under communism, but – with the emancipation from ministries' funding and control – football seemingly has embraced a liberal market model with mixed success largely depending on the availability of private sponsors. Another trend across Europe is that leagues, sometimes set up as shareholder corporations owned by the clubs playing in the league, increasingly govern the national professional competition on behalf of the national football associations which concentrate their efforts on youth and amateur football.

A study which more strictly juxtaposes football's governance across nations is proposed by Amara et al. (2005) who compare such diverse countries as Algeria, China, England, France and Japan. These authors depict football governance as a systemic web of interactions between television broadcasters, players' associations (for example, FIFPro), sponsors, clubs' unions (for example, G-14), national or European governments who are now interacting with and influencing traditional football governing bodies. Drawing on the five case studies, they analyse how interactions between stakeholders shape the system in each country and compare the cases along variables such as: role of the central state, role of local governments, mode of resource allocation (market driven or apportionment by some authority), uncertainty of outcome, patterns of player movement and identification of dominant stakeholders in the web. Interestingly, they conclude that, despite the influence of global trends (such as the significance of merchandising, broadcasting deals and players' mobility), there is no teleological process at play that inevitably leads the systems towards a specific model of governance. The strength of the various stakeholders – and the network governance which results from it – differs from one country to another since local contexts have their own specific historical configurations.

In contrast to the conclusions in the previous studies, Meier (2008), in comparing the institutional dynamics in English and German football, shows that different national trajectories may lead to similar institutional outcomes. Meier sees the unstable governance in European football as the result of tensions between amateur and commercial logics. Amateurism, because of its initial hegemony and its emphasis on the educational and integrative value of team sport, has shaped the institutional preferences of political actors in Europe. This implies that 'professional sport is only regarded as an apex of a much larger and deeper grassroots movement' (ibid.: 105). It is this endogenous institutional tension that provided a fertile ground for governance changes when football confronted exogenous factors such as the deregulation of television-markets and the advance of satellite television. In England, the failure of football self-governance, illustrated by the crowd disasters of the 1980s, led the state to provide huge financial support to modernize stadiums, thus opening the way for a rapid commercialization. When the top clubs, which had been sharing their rights with lower professional divisions within the Football League, received a lucrative offer from BskyB, they were supported in their breakaway from the Football League by the Football Association which had been struggling with the Football League for institutional dominance and jumped on the opportunity to strengthen its position through the creation of the FA Premier League. In Germany, support for associational self-governance has been the dominant policy paradigm and, in the absence of any governance crisis, the political elites remained committed to the autonomy of sport despite an increased commercial context. Professional clubs were, however, able to use regulatory spill-over from the European level and pending antitrust suits to force the German football association to accept their adoption of corporate legal structures, to acknowledge their broadcasting rights and to increase their control of German football by gaining a blocking minority in the executive committee of the German football association. Rather than leading to homogenization, Meier (2008: 127) acknowledges that the endeavour to disentangle European football from the amateur logic has 'resulted in a further eclectic hybridization of practices and structures'.

Upon closing this section we should also mention that Niemann et al. (2011) released a book on the Europeanization of the national game. With its ten country studies on how a changing Europe influences the governance of the national game, the volume further adds to our understanding of systemic governance processes at the national and European level. Despite new releases, we reiterate the need for more empirically based studies into the micro-processes of systemic governance. We need to know more about similarities and differences across countries and what it is that causes them. Is football outside the pitch in a process of standardization, or are standardization efforts encountered by hybridization dynamics? An interesting question is also whether cross-country coalitions are being formed inspired by specific competition requirements, common interests or the pressure of sponsors and corporations. The idea of systemic governance entails the assumption that the powers of football's governing bodies are being diluted, but a pertinent question is also whether influence is transferred from the national to the transnational level and if some nations have more to gain than lose from such displacement.

5   POLITICAL GOVERNANCE IN FOOTBALL

If Henry and Lee's (2004) conceptual scheme of governance types should be criticized, it is perhaps because organizational and political governance seem to derive more from a distinction between private corporations and public government than from what characterizes governance dynamics in sport organizations. One might argue that these organizations are basically political, and if political governance relates to how governing bodies seek to achieve goals by influencing other organizations through means such as licensing, regulation, financial incentives or moral pressure, this is exactly what football associations do (Gammelsæter and Senaux, 2011). Accordingly, outlining governance in association football should be about political as much as organizational governance. Indeed, this reminds us of Meier's (2008) argument that the instability and hybridization of football's governance derives from the tension in the sport between amateur and commercial logics, and it also relates back to Eisenberg's (2006) repudiation of FIFA as a multinational corporation. This means, of course, that the question of football's identity and configuration is a political issue – and a research question – in its own right, and that King (2003) perhaps captures a key insight when he sees the configuration of football as the expression of political transformations. When we are inclined to see governance within football as corporate it is perhaps because we have come to see it through the lenses of the neo-liberalist political strategy (Giulianotti and Robertson, 2009).

Whereas the issue of how to conceptualize the governance of the game is immanent in several of the studies reviewed under the rubric of systemic governance, political governance as a specific type can also be reserved for strategies of intervention into football by public authorities. References to state intervention or intermediation abound in the literature (that is, Amara et al., 2005; Anagnostopoulos, 2011; García, 2008; Hare, 2003; Morrow, 2011; Relvas, 2011; Riordan, 2011; Senaux, 2011), but to our knowledge there are no systematic policy studies that focus particularly on the interface between football and public authorities. This is a domain ripe for academic research where empirical studies would help us to explain differences in governance across nations and, besides outlining diverse political strategies, possibly also highlight how and the extent to which public bodies mediate between various stakeholders in the systemic network.

6   SUGGESTIONS FOR FURTHER RESEARCH

Table 8.1 provides a summary of research topics and example studies sorted according to the types of governance suggested by Henry and Lee (2004). Whereas we hope this synopsis does right to the research that has been done in the field, Table 8.1 does not fully testify that research on this issue still has big leaps to take. To the extent that football governance constitutes a research field in its own right, it is fragmented and comprises as yet few studies which target football from a governance perspective. However, when many of the studies reviewed here suffer from not being situated in an explicit governance context, this does not mean that they are flawed. Rather, it reflects that many of them happen to fill a vacuum by providing descriptions and analyses that are relevant for conceptualizing how football changes. It also reflects a lack of engagement in studying football in more typical governance disciplines, such as management and organization

Table 8.1 Summary of research topics and example studies according to types of governance and geographic level

	Organizational governance		Systemic governance		Political governance	
	Topics	Example studies	Topics	Example studies	Topics	Example studies
Transnational level	Nature of governing bodies	Eisenberg (2005, 2006)	Network structure	Amara et al. (2005), Holt (2007), García (2008)	Nature of governing bodies	Meier (2008), Giulianotti and Robertson (2009) Gammelsæter and Senaux (2011)
	Relations between FIFA–UEFA governance structure	Holt (2007), García (2008), Olsson (2011)	Football as ritual of political-economic changes	King (2003)	Public sport policy for football	García (2008)
	Proliferation of powerful football associations	García (2008)	Globalization of network	Giulianotti and Robertson (2009)		
	Personalities and cultures	Tomlinson (2000), Bairner and Darby (2001)	Homogenization of governance structures	Meier (2008)		
National level	Good governance	Holt et al. (2005), Hamil et al. (2010)	Football as ritual of political-economic changes	King (2002)	Public sport policy for football	None
	Governance structure	Gammelsæter and Jakobsen (2008), Gammelsæter (2009)	Globalization effects, hybridization	Giulianotti and Robertson (2009), Gammelsæter and Senaux (2011), Niemann et al. (2011)		
			Football as identity network	Hare (2003)		

studies. Therefore the contribution to the understanding of governance often comes from disciplines that are dedicated to pursue other research questions than governance, such as ethnography, sociology, history and, in part, marketing.

We have identified several issues where we think our knowledge on football's governance is highly deficient. This includes straightforward outlines of how football is structured and has changed its structures, and research on the extent to which the still prevailing pyramid of membership-based associations defends the interests of the sport's members, whoever these are, or if football's superior bodies, notably FIFA and UEFA, now operate as commercial corporations, not to say conglomerates, in the disguise of voluntary non-profit organizations. This is a seasonable question in light of the skyrocketing revenues that the sport now generates (according to Deloitte, 2011: 8, the European football market amounted to €16.3 billion in 2009/10). Do the seemingly increased commercial orientation of the traditional governing bodies and the increased relative power of professional clubs undermine the 'one-member-one-vote' principle so entrenched in the governance of the game (Eisenberg 2005)?

Another similarly neglected research topic is the lateral and multilateral relations between national associations and how these connect to politics in regional confederations and FIFA. Olsson (2011) asserts that voting in the UEFA general assembly and representation in the executive committee before 1990 reflected the Cold War divide as well as a north–south split in Western Europe. This created an environment which slowed down the decision-making capacity of the associations. But what happened after 1990? Are there still powerful blocs in UEFA? How do they operate (and shift?) and what are the processes like? What issues have been (and are) at stake here, and what has been the upshot of such processes?

We have seen that some studies outline a context which is characterized by systemic governance; new interest groups short-cut the traditional bottom-up hierarchical process and become unavoidable interlocutors providing direct guidance to their members at national and international levels. European examples of such groups are the national players' unions, federated within the European division of FIFPro, the professional clubs' unions, gathered within the European Club Association (ECA) and the national professional leagues, associated in the European Professional Football League (EPFL). Although these organizations are increasingly important (Brand and Niemann, 2007), there is little research analysing their emergence and highlighting their role in the governance of the game. Studies are welcomed, therefore, on how actors, structures and processes evolve in this landscape and regarding the outcomes of the dealings between them.

When it comes to depicting the environments that football's governing bodies have had to deal with, there seem to be three favourite themes in the literature: the impact on world football (in particular on FIFA) in the aftermath of emancipation processes in Africa; the effect of technological developments and the liberalization of broadcasting, and the widespread influence of the Bosman case on player migration and its reverberation on the competition for players (and revenue) across the world. While these events undeniably have been very important, one wonders if there are not others that are much under-researched, such as the fall of communism in Eastern Europe and the liberalization and transformation of financial markets, an important part of what is often referred to as globalization. Giulianotti and Robertson (2009) have recently addressed the latter but, if football is the world's game, (Murray, 1996) there is obviously a multitude of events, among them national events, that should intrigue researchers. A case in point is the effects on football governance in Belgium coming out of the intensified language and culture divide in that country (Balduck and Lucidarme, 2011). An interesting question is also how football, through hosting World and European finals, affects the organization of football in the hosting countries as well as the wider society (compare Dolles and Söderman, 2011; Horne and Manzenreiter, 2002)?

The almost complete lack of analyses of individual leaders – and the cultures they create, sustain or change – is striking in a sport which is so focused on individual player and manager celebrities. As a consequence, we are not informed at all about the persons that manage football's governing bodies or the cultures that have developed in any of these organizations, not to mention if there are management issues related to the transition from hierarchical to systemic governance. Such studies would provide useful information for understanding the strategic actions of these organizations, whether it be the awarding of mega-events or the efforts to investigate (or ignore) practices that threaten to corrupt the game. Moreover, since most of these organizations are member based and their directors are trustees, knowledge about management in these organizations should not simply be inferred from management studies in other fields. While football is now frequently denoted a commercial industry, the organizations making up this industry deviate from those dominating other industries. It follows that questions about their specificity in terms of culture and management should be most adequate.

Finally, the modern game is encumbered with a lot of 'modern' problems and challenges that beg research, in part to learn more about their nature, but also to increase transparency. Economic unfair play through debt accumulation, doping (compare Malcolm and Waddington, 2008), corruption (Jennings, 2006), fixing (compare Hill, 2008), hooliganism (for example, Joern, 2009) trafficking and other migration-related issues belong to the dark side of the beautiful game. A pressing issue for the game's governing bodies is to fight these problems and design and employ effective measures. Being not merely a member-based pyramid but also, increasingly, a network of organizations, the development and governance of control measures do not come easily. Research into how football deals with these issues, such as the initiatives to license football clubs should be of utmost importance to football, but also to the research community which needs to address the pivotal question the game faces in our time.

REFERENCES

Amara, M., Henry, I., Liang, J. and Uchiumi, K. (2005), The governance of professional soccer: five case studies: Algeria, China, England, France and Japan, *European Journal of Sport Science*, **5** (4), 189–206.

Anagnostopoulos, C. (2011), The battlefield of Greek football. Organising top-tier football in Greece, in H. Gammelsæter and B. Senaux (eds), *The Organisation and Governance of Top Football across Europe: An Institutional Perspective*, New York: Routledge, pp. 209–23.

Anagnostopoulos, C. (2013), Examining corporate social responsibility in football: the application of grounded theory methodology, in S. Söderman and H. Dolles (eds), *Handbook of Research on Sport and Business*, Cheltenham, UK and Northampton, MA, USA: Edward Elgar, pp. 418–32.

Andreff, W. and Szymanski, S. (eds) (2006), *Handbook on the Economics of Sport*, Cheltenham, UK and Northampton, MA, USA: Edward Elgar.

Armstrong, G. and Mitchell, J.P. (2008), *Global and Local Football. Politics and Europeanisation on the Fringes of the EU*, London: Routledge.

Bairner, A. (2004), Creating a soccer strategy for Northern Ireland: reflections on football governance in small European countries, *Soccer and Society*, **5** (1), 27–42.

Bairner, A. and Darby, P. (2001), The Swedish model and international sport: Lennart Johansson and the governance of world football, *International Review for the Sociology of Sport*, **36** (3), 337–59.

Balduck, A-L. and Lucidarme, S. (2011), Belgian football. A uniting force in a two-track policy? in H. Gammelsæter and B. Senaux (eds), *The Organisation and Governance of Top Football across Europe: An Institutional Perspective*, New York: Routledge, pp. 107–22.

Bergsgaard, N.A., Houlihan, B., Mangset, P., Nødland, S.I. and Rommetvedt, H. (2007), *Sport Policy. A Comparative Analysis of Stability and Change*, Oxford: Butterworth-Heinemann.

Bourke, A. (2013), Sports governance in Ireland: insights on theory and practice, in S. Söderman and H. Dolles (eds), *Handbook of Research on Sport and Business*, Cheltenham, UK and Northampton, MA, USA: Edward Elgar, pp. 112–25.

Brand, A. and Niemann, A. (2007), Europeanisation in the societal/trans-national realm: what European integration studies can get out of analysing football, *Journal of Contemporary European Research*, **3** (3), 182–201.

Castells, M. (1996), *The Rise of Network Society*, Oxford: Blackwell.

Chadwick, S. (2013), From outside lane to inside track: sport management research in the twenty-first century, in S. Söderman and H. Dolles (eds), *Handbook of Research on Sport and Business*, Cheltenham, UK and Northampton, MA, USA: Edward Elgar, pp. 513–25.

Darby, P. (2008), Stanley Rous's 'own goal': football politics, South Africa and the contest for the FIFA presidency in 1974, *Soccer and Society*, **9** (2), 259–72.

Deloitte (2011), Annual review of football finance 2011, available at: http://www.deloitte.com/view/en_GB/uk/industries/sportsbusinessgroup/sports/football/annual-review-of-football-finance-2011/index.htm (accessed 25 January 2012).

Desbordes, M. (ed.) (2007), *Marketing & Football. An International Perspective*, Oxford: Butterworth-Heinemann.

Dolles, H. and Söderman, S. (2011), Learning from success: implementing a professional football league in Japan, in H. Dolles and S. Söderman (eds), *Sport as a Business: International, Professional and Commercial Aspects*, Basingstoke: Palgrave Macmillan, pp. 228–50.

Dolles, H. and Söderman, S. (2013), The network of value captures in football club management: a framework to develop and analyse competitive advantage in professional team sports, in S. Söderman and H. Dolles (eds), *Handbook of Research on Sport and Business*, Cheltenham, UK and Northampton, MA, USA: Edward Elgar, pp. 367–95.

Eisenberg, C. (2005), From political ignorance to global responsibility. The role of the World Soccer Association (FIFA) in international sport during the twentieth century, *Journal of Sport History*, **32** (3), 379–93.

Eisenberg, C. (2006), FIFA 1975–2000: the business of a football development organisation, *Historical Social Research*, **31** (1), 55–68.

Ferkins, L., Shilbury, D. and MacDonald, G. (2005), The role of the board in building strategic capability: towards an integrated model of sport governance research, *Sport Management Review*, **8** (3), 195–225.

Football Governance Research Centre (FGRC) (eds) (2002), The state of the game: the corporate governance of football clubs 2002, *Football Governance Research Centre Research Paper*, no. 3, London: Birkbeck, University of London.

Football Governance Research Centre (FGRC) (eds) (2003), The state of the game: the corporate governance of football clubs 2003, *Football Governance Research Centre Research Paper*, no. 4, London: Birkbeck, University of London.

Football Governance Research Centre (FGRC) (eds) (2004), The state of the game: the corporate governance of professional football 2004, *Football Governance Research Centre Research Paper*, no. 3, London: Birkbeck, University of London.

Foster, J. and Pope, N. (2004), *The Political Economy of Global Sporting Organisations*, Abingdon: Routledge.

Freeman, R.E. (1984), *Strategic Management: A Stakeholder Approach*, Boston, MA: Pitman Press.

Gammelsæter, H. (2009), The organization of professional football in Scandinavia, *Soccer and Society*, **10** (3–4), 305–23.

Gammelsæter, H. (2010), Institutional pluralism and governance in 'commercialized' sport clubs, *European Sport Management Quarterly*, **10** (5), 569–94.

Gammelsæter, H. and Jakobsen, S.-E. (2008), Models of organization in Norwegian professional soccer, *European Sport Management Quarterly*, **8** (1), 1–25.

Gammelsæter, H. and B. Senaux (eds) (2011), *The Organisation and Governance of Top Football across Europe: An Institutional Perspective*, New York: Routledge.

Gammelsæter, H., Storm, R. and Söderman, S. (2011), Diverging Scandinavian approaches to professional football, in H. Gammelsæter and B. Senaux (eds), *The Organisation and Governance of Top Football across Europe: An Institutional Perspective*, New York: Routledge, pp. 77–92.

García, B. (2007), UEFA and the European Union: from confrontation to cooperation, *Journal of Contemporary European Research*, **3** (3), 202–23.

García, B. (2008), The European Union and the governance of football: a game of levels and agendas, doctoral thesis, Loughborough University, Loughborough.

García, B. (2011), The influence of the EU on the governance of football, in H. Gammelsæter and B. Senaux (eds), *The Organisation and Governance of Top Football across Europe: An Institutional Perspective*, New York: Routledge, pp. 32–45.

Giulianotti, R. and Robertson, R. (2009), *Globalization & Football*, London: Sage.

Greenwood, R., Oliver, C., Sahlin-Andersson, K. and Suddaby, R. (eds) (2008), *The Handbook of Organizational Institutionalism*, Thousand Oaks, CA: Sage.

Hamil, S. and Chadwick, S. (2010), *Managing Football. An International Perspective*, Oxford: Butterworth-Heinemann.

Hamil, S., Michie, J., Oughton, C. and Warby, S. (eds) (2000), *Football in the Digital Age. Whose Game is it Anyway?* Edinburgh: Mainstream.

Hamil, S., Michie, J., Oughton, C. and Warby, S. (eds) (2001), *The Changing Face of the Football Business: Supporters Direct*, Abingdon: Frank Cass.

Hamil, S., Morrow, S., Idle, C., Rossi, G. and Faccendini, S. (2010), The governance and regulation of Italian football, *Soccer & Society*, **11** (4), 373–413.

Hare, G. (2003), *Football in France: A Cultural History*, Oxford: Berg.

Hay, R. (2011), Ethnicity, structure and globalization: an argument about association football in Australia, 1958–2010, *Sport in Society*, **14** (6), 833–50.

Henry I. and Lee, P.C. (2004), Governance and ethics, in S. Chadwick and J. Beech (eds), *The Business of Sport Management*, Harlow: Pearson, pp. 25–42.

Henry, I. and Theodoraki, E. (2002), Management, organizations and theory in the governance of sport, in J. Coakley and E. Dunning (eds), *Handbook of Sport Studies*, London: Sage, pp. 490–503.

Hill, D. (2008), *The Fix. Soccer and Organized Crime*, Toronto: McClelland & Stewart.

Hoehn, T. (2006), Governance and governing bodies in sport, in W. Andreff and S. Szymanski (eds), *Handbook on the Economics of Sport*, Cheltenham, UK and Northampton, MA, USA: Edward Elgar, pp. 227–40.

Holt, M. (2006), UEFA, governance and the control of club competition in European football, *Football Governance Research Centre Research Paper*, London: Birkbeck, University of London.

Holt, M. (2007), The ownership and control of elite club competition in European football, *Soccer & Society*, **8** (1), 50–67.

Holt, M., Michie, J., Oughton, C., Tacon, R. and Walters, G. (2005), The state of the game. The corporate governance of football clubs 2005, *Football Governance Research Centre Research Paper*, no. 3, London: Birkbeck, University of London.

Horne, J. and Manzenreiter, W. (eds) (2002), *Japan, Korea and the 2002 World Cup*, London: Routledge.

Horne, J. and Manzenreiter, W. (2004), *Football Goes East. Business, Culture and the People's Game in East Asia*, Abingdon: Routledge.

Houlihan, B. (2002), Politics and sport, in J. Coakley and E. Dunning (eds), *Handbook of Sport Studies*, London: Sage, pp. 213–27.

Jansson, H. and Söderman, S. (2013), Proposing a relationship marketing theory for sport clubs, in S. Söderman and H. Dolles (eds), *Handbook of Research on Sport and Business*, Cheltenham, UK and Northampton, MA, USA: Edward Elgar, pp. 350–66.

Jennings, A. (2006), *Foul! The Secret World of FIFA: Bribes, Vote Rigging and Ticket Scandal*, London: Harper Sport.

Joern, L. (2009), Nothing to hide, nothing to fear? Tackling violence on the terraces, *Sport in Society*, **12** (10), 1269–83.

King, A. (2002), *The End of the Terraces. The Transformation of English Football in the 1990s*, revd edn, London: Leicester University Press.

King, A. (2003), *The European Ritual. Football in the New Europe*, Aldershot: Ashgate.

Lanfranchi, P., Eisenberg, C., Mason, T. and Wahl, A. (2004), *100 Years of Football. The FIFA Centennial Book*, London: Weidenfeld & Nicolson.

Lee, S. (2004), Moving the goalposts: the governance and political economy of world football, in R. Levermore and A. Budd (eds), *Sport and International Relations: An Emerging Relationship*, London: Routledge, pp. 112–28.

Leftwich, A. (1994), Governance, the state and the politics of development, *Development and Change*, **25** (2), 363–86.

Lockett, A., Moon, J. and Visser, W. (2006), Corporate social responsibility in management research: focus, nature, salience and sources of influence, *Journal of Management Studies*, **43** (1), 115–36.

Magee, J. (2002), Shifting balances of power in the new football economy, in J. Sugden and A. Tomlinson (eds), *Power Games. A Critical Sociology of Sport*, Abingdon: Routledge, pp. 216–39.

Malcolm, D. and Waddington, I. (2008), 'No systematic doping in football'. A critical review, *Soccer & Society*, **9** (2), 198–214.

Meier, H.E. (2008), Institutional complementarities and institutional dynamics: exploring varieties in European football capitalism, *Socio-Economic Review*, **6** (1), 99–133.

Miller, R.M. and Crolley, L. (eds) (2007), *Football in the Americas: Fútbol, Futebol, Soccer*, London: Institute for the Study of the Americas.

Morrow, S. (2011), History, longevity and change: football in England and Scotland, in H. Gammelsæter and B. Senaux (eds), *The Organisation and Governance of Top Football across Europe: An Institutional Perspective*, New York: Routledge, pp. 46–61.

Murray, B. (1996), *The World's Game. A History of Soccer*, Urbana, IL: University of Illinois Press.

Neale W. (1964), The peculiar economics of professional sports, *The Quarterly Journal of Economics*, **78** (1), 1–14.

Niemann, A., García, B. and Grant, W. (eds) (2011), *The Transformation of European Football: Towards the Europeanisation of the National Game*, Manchester: Manchester University Press.

Olsson, L.-C. (2011), Decisive moment in UEFA, in H. Gammelsæter and B. Senaux (eds), *The Organisation and Governance of Top Football across Europe: An Institutional Perspective*, New York: Routledge, pp. 17–31.

O'Reilly, N. (2013), Portfolio theory and the management of professional sports clubs: the case of Maple Leaf Sports and Entertainment, in S. Söderman and H. Dolles (eds), *Handbook of Research on Sport and Business*, Cheltenham, UK and Northampton, MA, USA: Edward Elgar, pp. 333–49.

Relvas, H. (2011), The organization of football in Portugal, in H. Gammelsæter and B. Senaux (eds), *The Organisation and Governance of Top Football across Europe: An Institutional Perspective*, New York: Routledge, pp. 195–208.

Riordan, J. (2011), More serious than life and death. Russian and Soviet football, in H. Gammelsæter and B. Senaux (eds), *The Organisation and Governance of Top Football across Europe: An Institutional Perspective*, New York: Routledge, pp. 224–37.

Rottenberg, S. (1956), The baseball players' labor market, *Journal of Political Economy*, **64** (3), 242–58.

Senaux, B. (2008), A stakeholder approach to football club governance, *International Journal of Sport Management and Marketing*, **4** (1), 4–17.

Senaux, B. (2011), The regulated commercialisation of French football, in H. Gammelsæter and B. Senaux (eds), *The Organisation and Governance of Top Football across Europe: An Institutional Perspective*, New York: Routledge, pp. 123–37.

Skille, E.Å (2013), Case study research in sport management: a reflection upon the theory of science and an empirical example, in S. Söderman and H. Dolles (eds), *Handbook of Research on Sport and Business*, Cheltenham, UK and Northampton, MA, USA: Edward Elgar, pp. 161–75.

Sugden, J. (2002), Network football, in J. Sugden and A. Tomlinson (eds), *Power Games. A Critical Sociology of Sport*, Abingdon: Routledge, pp. 61–80.

Sugden, J. and Tomlinson, A. (1997), Global power struggles in world football: FIFA and UEFA, 1954–74, and their legacy, *International Journal of the History of Sport*, **14** (2), 1–25.

Tomlinson, A. (2000), FIFA and the men who made it, *Soccer & Society*, 1, 55–71.

Winand, M. and Zintz, T. (2013), Qualitative comparative analysis on sport governing bodies: a tool on ways towards high performance, in S. Söderman and H. Dolles (eds), *Handbook of Research on Sport and Business*, Cheltenham, UK and Northampton, MA, USA: Edward Elgar, pp. 76–93.

9   Case study research in sport management: a reflection upon the theory of science and an empirical example
Eivind Å. Skille

1   INTRODUCTION

Case study research is gaining popularity in sport management research (Slack and Parent, 2006). For example, *Understanding Sport Organizations* – an international textbook – contained not a single chapter on research methods in its first edition (Slack 1997). In the second edition (Slack and Parent, 2006) there is a separate chapter devoted to 'Doing research in sport management' (ibid.: 17–34), which includes several examples of case studies in sport management research. A similarity can be seen in terms of the content of the journal *European Sport Management Quarterly*. A review of three recent volumes (2007–09) reveals that about one out of four research articles use a case study approach. Thus, it is evident that case study research is worth some consideration by sport management researchers (also, in this volume, Dibben and Dolles, 2013; Gratton and Solberg, 2013; O'Reilly, 2013; Walters and Hamil, 2013). In this chapter I reflect upon the qualitative attributes of the case study – as an increasingly common approach used by sport management researchers – by considering notes from the theory of science.

Generally, case study research is considered appropriate when the research questions contain 'how' or 'why' formulations, and when the phenomenon being studied is in real-life contexts where there are often unclear boundaries with other real-life phenomena (Slack and Parent, 2006; Yin, 2003). The strength of the approach when it comes to descriptions and explanations of phenomena of reality and society (and the lack of possibilities for creating controlled experiments of such phenomena), makes case study research specifically apt for research into sport management (for example, investigating sport policy and sport organization). Common characteristics and advantages of the case study are underscored in many journal articles, such as its appropriateness for developing a holistic understanding of a phenomenon (high internal validity) and the possibility of expressing relatively general statements about other similar cases on the basis of relatively few observations (the degree of external validity) (for example, Leopkey and Parent, 2009). The latter requires a well-discussed and conscious selection of cases (for example Bayle and Robinson, 2007). A comparative case study of large-scale events in Canada (Leopkey and Parent, 2009) gives a comprehensive methodological description, and good arguments for each of the methodological choices are made. First, it provides a description of each of the cases. Second, procedures for data collections are well explained, as are the arguments for applying several methods. Third, the analysis is fully outlined.

The aim of this chapter is to consider how classic elements of the theory of science can contribute to a better understanding of the case study approach. This is, of course, not a reader in the philosophy of science. Neither is this a reader in case study research, as is, for example, Stake (2005) or Yin (2003) for general and much cited introductions, or Fitzgerald and Dopson (2009) for a reflection on the case study design's utility in organizational research. Nevertheless, it can be beneficial – both for researchers who are considering using a case study approach as well as when they read research where it has been used – to reflect theoretically upon the methodology used (McNamee, 2005). Such methodological reflections are generally missing in sport management literature. The results of a search in the Norwegian academic libraries' database, where it was searched for the combination of 'research methods' and 'sport management' only Li et al.'s (2008) *Research Methods in Sport Management*, appeared, where the case study approach is well defined and explained, regarding types, design, data collection and analysis. But there is not a word on theory of science mentioned supporting a case study approach. As a rare example in *Qualitative Research in Sport Management* (Edwards and Skinner, 2009), the chapter on case study research comprises one and a half pages on 'Epistemological and ontological dimensions of the case study' (ibid.: 204–5). I will come back to this later in the chapter.

The following two sections are short notes on the parts of the theory of science which are the roots of qualitative methods more generally and case studies in particular: phenomenology and hermeneutics. It needs to be mentioned, that case studies do not necessarily have to be qualitative (Yin, 2003). But as will be evident in the next section, the point of departure for this reflection was a qualitative study. Therefore, I searched those types of philosophical texts to shed light on the research design and methods used in the example. The next section gives a description of this specific empirical research project, which will be used as the focus for reflection. It is based on the fact that the need for reflection on the scientific theoretical underpinning of case study research occurred during an empirical investigation of Norwegian sport policy implementation. In the main section, simply called 'case study design', it is shown how the ideas presented in the sections on theories of science are utilized in the empirical research study. The final section contains a discussion of the quality of the exemplified research and case study research more generally (considering limitations of case study research, and assessing the strength of case study research by the classic criterion of validity).

2   PHENOMENOLOGY

Considering the research area of sport policy (see also the section 'Setting the scene for the empirical example', below), it is a premise that the impact of central policy must be investigated at the level where sport takes place. 'Sport' here refers to physical activity organized in local sport clubs. It should be noted that it is in sport clubs that sport activity takes place; all other sport organizations – at national and regional level – are considered as organizational environment (with various support or facilitating functions) for the sport club (Skille, 2008). Ideally, the outcome of policy must affect people in some respect. Therefore, since sport takes place in sport clubs, and since policy must affect people, the impact of sport policy on sport must be investigated by the revealing of the experience of people in sport clubs. People in sport clubs might be those playing sport or those providing sport. The latter comprises trainers and coaches on the field who are in direct contact with the athletes, as well as board members who make decisions which influence the athletes (regarding facilities, economy, and so on).

Phenomenology was originally a philosophical discipline, which also became a sociological discipline. Contemporary phenomenology comprises many branches, see *Stanford Encyclopedia of Philosophy, Phenomenology* (2003: 9–15) for an overview of history and variety, and *Stanford Encyclopedia of Philosophy, Phenomenology* (2003: 15–23) for a discussion about how phenomenology relates to other philosophical topics, that is, the philosophy of mind. In any case, speaking about phenomenology, we speak of a personal experience; thus phenomenology studies the appearance of a phenomenon, and the meaning attached to it, as it is perceived by individual persons. A more common understanding of phenomenology is that it is 'the study of *phenomena*: literally, appearances as opposed to reality' (*Stanford Encyclopedia of Philosophy*, 2003: 7). Phenomenology has changed, or developed, throughout history. Husserl (1970 [original 1936]) suggested that we should and could describe personal experiences. That implies, first, that in phenomenological reflection, it should not be necessary to consider whether or not the world exists in material terms, because it is human beings' experiences of the objects (whether they exist or not) that is of importance. The focus on personal experiences implies, second, that one should and could investigate the experiences of oneself or others, without being influenced by anything. That is what Husserl (1970) called (the method of) 'epoché'.

Another of Husserl's points which is of relevance for the exemplified case study discussed in this chapter is 'intentionality'. Husserl (1970) described intentionality as when a human being is conscious, she is always conscious about something. The point is that there is directedness in the thoughts and actions of individuals. In a study of local sport clubs with reference to central sport policy, the issue is that, the providers of sport activity either direct their consciousness towards central sport policy or towards something else (or both). Given the premise that the representatives of sport clubs focus their concentration on something (whatever it is), the researcher should observe it and analyse it with reference to the policy, the theory and other studies.

Later, and contrary to Husserl, Heidegger underscored that we must always consider all activities as being in the world (Heidegger, 1962). For Heidegger, activities and experiences cannot be studied only by investigating personal experiences, as Husserl suggested. For Heidegger, objects and activities emerge as more or less meaningful for us, through being interpreted. This process of interpretation is influenced by our contextual relations to other persons, objects and happenings around us. I follow Heidegger and lean on the branch of phenomenology that is called 'hermeneutical phenomenology'. In that branch the study of interpretative structures of experience is the focus, which means that researchers try to understand how people and things and events relate to each other in meaningful ways. For example, in my research, central sport policy relates to the phenomenon of sport as such, only if people in the sport clubs interpret the policy as meaningful.

Schutz (1972) brought phenomenology into the social sciences. He focused on getting behind the constituted meanings, because he wanted to understand the meanings that actors build up through their own actions. The point is that if central sport policy gives any meaning to the representatives of sport clubs, it does so through the practice of the representatives of sport clubs. This links to the theoretical perspective employed in the study that I use as an example, namely the translation perspective within neo-institutionalism (Skille, 2008, 2009). The translation perspective underscores that if a phenomenon (for example, elements of central sport policy) occurs in a focal context (for example, a sport club), it does so as the interpretation and implementation by actors in the latter (and not as the intention of the former).

3   HERMENEUTICS

As with phenomenology, hermeneutics has many versions, but what is agreed upon is that hermeneutics is about interpretation of meaning. In this respect, I follow Gadamer (2004 [original 1975]) and his emphasis on previous understanding, and Ricoeur's (1991) focus on the question of understanding and explanation. On the one hand, Gadamer (2004) refuses to see hermeneutics as some kind of methodology. For him, hermeneutics is about humans searching for meaning, rather than a scientific method. On the other hand, Ricoeur (1991) suggests, more or less explicitly, how the dialectic between understanding and explanation leads to validated interpretations, as is the aim of scientific methods. According to Gadamer (2004: 269):

> A person who is trying to understand a text is always projecting. He projects a meaning for the text as a whole as soon as some initial meaning emerges in the text. Again, the initial meaning emerges only because he is reading the text with particular expectations in regard to a certain meaning.

In short, expectations – partly at least – determine what people interpret, and people's expectations are based on their stock of knowledge, whether that knowledge is conscious or not. However, Gadamer does not see this prejudice or previous understanding only as a constraint, but asks: 'What distinguishes the legitimate prejudices from the countless others . . . ?' (2004: 278). The core point is that prejudice is always based on tradition, and for this apparently positive attitude towards tradition, Gadamer has received criticism, for example by Habermas (1987; see Skille, 2007). Gadamer (2004) also speaks of 'temporal distance' (to the object of study, I would assume, although he did not see hermeneutics as a method for a study as such). The 'temporal distance', from which we can interpret and understand something, varies with history and tradition. The principle of the history of effects (Gadamer, 2004) makes the interpretation process even more complicated and it becomes even more necessary to reflect upon the previous meaning and the phenomenon, and the relationship between them. In my case, the prejudices and previous understanding is made concise by reflections about how I lean on the existing research, as well as my own experience from the field of sport (as former athlete, former coach, voluntary father, and sport teacher and researcher). I start the analysis, based on this reflection.

According to Ricoeur (1991), action can be interpreted as text, thus what follows is considered valid for both classical hermeneutic text analysis and hermeneutic analysis of social phenomena, as sport policy and sport practice. For Ricoeur (1991), it is the relationship between the text and the reader which is our topic (and not the intentional meaning that the author tries to express with the text). Thus, 'a text is detached from its author, an action is detached from its agent and develops consequences of its own' (ibid.:

153), and '"objectivity" . . . proceeds from the "social fixation" of meaningful behaviour' (ibid.: 154). Further, the paradigm of text interpretation gives us a fresh approach to the never-ending question about the relation between explanation and understanding. Again, Ricoeur suggests that the answer lies in the dialectical character of the relation between explanation and understanding 'as it is displayed in reading' (ibid.: 156). In the same manner, a case under scrutiny can be 'read' through scientific methods, and 'explained' through scientific expression and subsequent debate (which in itself is dialectic), as will be seen in the empirical example in the next section.

Out of this dialectical relation a method for analysis is proposed: first a movement from understanding to explanation and then a movement from explanation to understanding. The first move is that from understanding to explanation, and it starts with 'guessing' the wholeness of the focal phenomenon. The text is not only a sequence of sentences, which are all separately understandable. Ricoeur sees a text is a whole, a totality. A problem is that there are no rules for guessing what the totality means. On the other hand, 'there are methods for validating guesses' (1991: 158) – I return to validation at the end of this chapter. The second move is from explanation to understanding, and it is about putting detailed words on the focal phenomenon. And the thicker and more detailed we are able to describe the phenomenon, the better we understand it. According to Alvesson and Sköldberg (2000), a 'thick description' (Geertz, 1973) is the first step in an interpretation process, which helps to grasp the whole in the analysis. With a 'thick description', the chances of discerning a coherence of meaning are increased. Thus there is a balance between 'the genius of guessing and the scientific character of validation' (Ricoeur 1991: 159); this balance is constituted in the dialectic between understanding ('*Verstehen*') and explanation ('*Erklären*'). 'At the same time, we are prepared to give an acceptable meaning to the famous concept of the *hermeneutic circle*. Guess and validation are in sense circularly related as subjective and objective approaches to text' (Ricoeur 1991: 159).

While the above are philosophical considerations, the perspective is conceived to have a number of applicatory areas, for example sport policy and sport organization at various levels. For a reflection on the interpretivism in organizational research in general, including notes on hermeneutics and phenomenology, see, for example, Yanow and Ybema (2009). In the following sections I will apply some of the aforementioned points to a case study research example. Before that, let me present the context in which the empirical research example took place.

4 SETTING THE SCENE FOR THE EMPIRICAL EXAMPLE

During the last decade, the conclusion from research into Norwegian sport policy is that it is a long and winding road from central sport policy-making to the implementation of that policy (Skille, 2005, 2006, 2007). Figure 9.1 summarizes this point. Central policy-making refers to policy-making which takes place at the national level, either in the public sector or in the voluntary sector.

Central policy in the public sector refers to state sport policy. The Norwegian state does, according to the White Paper on sport, base its subsidizing and support of the voluntary sector on two main sets of values (Stortingsmelding no. 14, 1999–2000). The

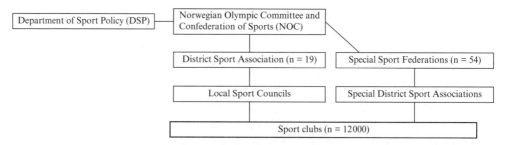

Source: Based on Skille (2008).

Figure 9.1   The Norwegian sport policy context

first set of core values defines sport as culture, in several respects: first, the intrinsic value ascribes qualities such as the experience of joy, mastery and achievement; second, sport activities create engagement, enthusiasm and belonging in that sport is considered an expression of values, references and symbols which unite people, and, third, the concept of culture relates to how sport organizations contribute to the creation of meaningful leisure experiences for their members. The latter relates to a belief in a strong and tight local community with a sport club at its core as being a good context for the upbringing and education of young people, and links to the second set of values for sport.

The second set of core values for sport, as expressed in the White Paper (Stortingsmelding no. 14, 1999–2000), are the societal or external values. Throughout history, the reason for the Norwegian national interest in sport has varied (Goksøyr, 1992; Olstad, 1987; Tønnesson, 1986). For example, while the Norwegian government first subsidized the voluntary sport organizations (late nineteenth and early twentieth century), it was for military reasons, and during the inter-war and early post-war period (1920s–1950s), the Norwegian government saw sport as a means to increase the production capacity of the workforce (Olstad, 1987; Tønnesson, 1986; Goksøyr et al., 1996). Today, the most visible instrumental values are sport as a vehicle for social policy, and sport as health promotion. Sport as social policy can be considered a continuation of the general belief in sport as an arena for the education (in the broadest sense of the term) of young people. 'It is valuable both for the individual and for society through the establishment of networks and organizations. Sport . . . is valuable for those who participate because there are established social bonds in the local communities'; sport as a means for social integration of immigrants is mentioned in particular' (Stortingsmelding no. 14, 1999–2000, p. 36, my translation).

Nevertheless, the most explicitly made instrumental value of sport, for public subsidies to sport, is that of health.

> The sport's instrumental value is, seen from the state, first and foremost related to the health perspective. The positive effect that physical activity has on the preventive health work, contributes to strengthen the legitimacy for state subsidies. Increased physical and mental surplus as a consequence of exercise is important, not only for the individual experience of joy and well being, but also as an accumulated health profit for the society. (Stortingsmelding no. 14, 1999–2000, p. 36, my translation)

In addition to state sport policy, central sport policy refers to policy in the voluntary sector, more precisely the policy of the Norwegian Olympic and Paralympic Committee and Confederation of Sports (NOC). The NOC is the umbrella organization for all conventional sport organizations in Norway. The sport policy document of the NOC is, as is the White Paper from the state, thematically widespread (NOC, 2007a). This sport policy document is the NOC system's guidelines for the next four years, from the general assembly which was held in May 2007 until the last general assembly in 2011. Many interests should be supported in one document of one umbrella organization, representing in Norway 54 special sport federations, 19 district sport federations, approximately 12 000 sport clubs and about 1.3 million individual members. One theme used as an example in this chapter is health. The goal of the NOC, with regard to health, is: 'To work for increased resources for sport, from the national budget, for health promotion' (NOC, 2007a: 13, my translation). In short, the NOC sees itself as a possible tool for health promotion. The impression was reinforced by a resolution from the last general assembly: 'Norwegian sport . . . has a unanimous request and offer to Norwegian society . . . Norwegian sport invites the authorities to cooperate for health promotion in the population. We suggest that . . . it should be allocated an amount equivalent to 1 per cent of today's health budget, to voluntary organizations working with health promotion' (NOC, 2007b, my translation). In any case, the implementation of sport policy – the provision of sport activity – takes place in sport clubs at the local level. Local sport clubs are part of the NOC system, and thus part of the voluntary sector. Research shows that in almost 90 per cent of Norwegian sports clubs, about 90 per cent of the work is conducted by volunteers (Enjolras and Seippel, 2001; Seippel, 2003). The remaining 10 per cent have higher levels of employed staff, especially due to professionalization in elite sport.

It could be speculated whether it is despite – or perhaps because of – its omnipresence in most western societies that sport clubs have predominantly been studied scientifically (see Heinemann, 1999). In Norway, the available research was one quantitative survey (Enjolras and Seippel, 2001; Seippel, 2003), which painted a broad picture of sports clubs' size, structure, funding, and so on. While this may be an important aspect of describing sport provision at a local level, a survey limits the opportunity to gain 'thicker' descriptions and understandings of the social processes going on in sport clubs that underpin implementation. In order to answer questions such as 'What does the board focus upon in their meetings?', 'How do, on the one hand, the internal processes in the sports clubs and, on the other hand, the external environment influence the debate and decisions that are made in the board of the sport clubs?' and 'Is the central sport policy considered at all by sport club representatives?', another approach was needed. Out of such queries the following major question emerged: 'What is the appropriate methodology to use to understand the impact of central sport policy on local sport provision?' When I wanted to find out as much as possible about how central policy impacts on local sport implementation, I had to deal within obvious limitations of research resources and time. A study's time span is often three years (here 1 August 2006 to 31 July 2009), owing to finding a balance between enough time for data collection, analysis, reflection and publishing. From this challenge, the methodology was developed. It built on two interrelated pillars of the theory of science treated above. Thus, the third pillar occurred; namely, a case study design and qualitative methods (Yin, 2003). The relevance of using a case study approach in order to understand the influence of sport policy on sport clubs was based on the following reflections. First, it was my intention to stay as close to the field of study as possible. With a phenomenological approach, I tried to understand the phenomenon of sport policy implementation by staying close to the real-life context of where sport is provided. Second, it was my intention to interpret the observations in the field with consciousness. With a hermeneutics approach, I reflected upon my prejudices and previous understanding (Gadamer, 2003), and then tried to find ways to understand *and* explain the phenomenon being studied (Ricoeur, 1991). The latter includes several validation procedures (Seale, 1999), including, in particular, the generation of 'thick descriptions' (Geertz, 1973).

5   CASE STUDY DESIGN

Based on the phenomenological hermeneutical approach, I demonstrate the perspective's applicability through a case study design where qualitative methods were applied in the study of Norwegian sport policy implementation. In addition to being grounded in phenomenology and hermeneutics, the exemplified research adhered to the 'pragmatist thesis'. Ontologically, it is believed that there exists a reality independent of humans' minds *and*, at the same time, there are acknowledged many socially constructed realities (Tashakkori and Teddlie, 1998). In addition, a case is conceived as a complexity comprising multiple and divergent elements that it is hard, if not impossible, to fully perceive the existence of (Edwards and Skinner, 2009). Epistemologically, the pragmatist thesis includes both inductive and deductive logics in the methodological approaches (Tashakkori and Teddlie, 1998); as a researcher I try to be open-minded *and* at the same time acknowledge, reflect upon, and be conscious about my prejudices. Moreover, a specific 'case epistemology' acknowledges – and takes advantage of – the necessary relationship between the inquirer and the inquired (the case) (Edwards and Skinner, 2009).

In other words, knowledge about the focal case is created in the interplay between the researcher and (representatives or elements of) the case. I here explain how the case study design was linked to the more philosophical outline above, with the utilization of two particular approaches. The first explicit link between the theory of science treated above (the hermeneutic phenomenological perspective) and the case study design is that previous research was used during the sampling procedure in order to select a few – some small – but purposive samples. The second link between the theory of science and case study design is methodological triangulation aimed at both understanding and explaining. This includes 'thick descriptions' and validation procedures. Both these approaches are often referred to as strengths of the case study design (Slack and Parent, 2006; Yin, 2003). Moreover, they overlap with commonly held advantages of qualitative methods, such as being exploratory and flexible with regard to both the sources of information and the access to informants. I start with the examples of how the cases were chosen. Based on former research into Norwegian as well as Danish sport clubs, it was possible to carry out strategic sampling based on the characteristics of sport clubs identified in that research. In that respect, it became possible to cover a broad part of the phenomenon with relatively few units, which made it possible to go into depth in each of them. Regarding the similarity across the Scandinavian countries, in terms of sport policy and sport organization, it was assessed as apt to adopt three ideal typologies of sports clubs developed in Denmark (Ibsen, 1992). The typologies were the small sports club, the ball club and '*den store mosjonsforening*' ['the large sport for all'; my translation] club. In addition, various structural characteristics were revealed in the quantitative research conducted in Norway (Enjolras and Seippel, 2001; Seippel, 2003). These attributes related to the number of sports, types of sports, the club's size, structure, economy and leadership.

Aiming at one sport club in each of Ibsen's (1992) typologies, in addition to identifying three sport clubs which varied with regard to other – structural – characteristics, the sample consisted of a football club, a cross-country ski club and a multi-sport club.

1. The football club represents the most popular sport in Norway. Football features in 23 per cent of all Norwegian sport clubs (Seippel, 2003). The football club has more than a thousand members, comprises 94 different teams, is organized into three departments, having a budget of about €500 000 (NOK4.5 million), and where the main board meets every month (in addition, regular board meetings are held in each department). This corresponds to Ibsen's (1992) 'ball club'.
2. The cross-country ski club represents the second largest (organized) sport. Cross-country skiing is represented in 14 per cent of all Norwegian sport clubs (Enjolras and Seippel, 2001; NSF, 2007). One needs to be aware, that the number of sports or disciplines which are governed by the special sport federations varies. For example, the football association only governs one (football), while the ski association governs six disciplines (cross-country skiing, ski jumping, biathlon, alpine skiing, freestyle and telemark). At least one of the six skiing sports takes place in 18 per cent of all sport clubs (Seippel, 2003). Cross-country skiing occurs in 1013 out of 1142 ski clubs (89 per cent; NSF, 2007). Cross-country skiing is an individual winter sport (compared with the team and summer sport football). The ski club has about 70 members who are not organized in teams or groups, and has a budget of about €2500 (NOK21 000). This matches Ibsen's (1992) 'small sport club'.
3. A multi-sport club represents 49 per cent of the sports clubs in Norway (Enjolras and Seippel, 2001), although 80 per cent of newly established sport clubs organize only one sport (Skirstad, 2002). Regarding structural characteristics, this third sport club represents a middle range as regards size and funding, but distinguishes itself by having multiple sports and six sub-units. This is similar to Ibsen's (1992) 'sport for all club'.

Of course, other sport clubs could have been chosen. At least, more sport clubs could be included in the sample, especially sport clubs which could be considered as fundamentally different from the three actually included. For example, smaller sports, or popular sport with low degree of organization would have been interesting for comparison.

When the sampling is done, data collection starts, as does the analysis. Data collection and analysis are simultaneous processes in qualitative case study research, or rather, it is one more or less intertwined process comprising two components. Gradually, the process moves on from data collection as the dominant part, to a process dominated by analysis. In both or any respects, triangulation is perhaps the most important tool for validating the data *and* the analysis in qualitative case study research. Nevertheless, I treat data collection first, and then analysis. It is also worth noting that there is a main phase of analysis, which takes place after the data collection is finished, and when the researcher sits down at the desk in the office, with a number of written sources.

Regarding triangulation of data-collecting methods, information was sought through documentary analysis, observation and interviews (Edwards and Skinner, 2009; Li et al., 2008; Stake, 2005; Yin, 2003). In addition, information was gathered through informal conversations, emails and telephone calls. It was all done in order to answer the research questions about how negotiations and decisions in sport clubs' boards were influenced by internal and external factors – such as central sport policy. The documents were meeting reports and strategy documents produced by the sports clubs (where they were available). Observation took place in board meetings in the football club, over the year 2007. Field notes were taken, as suggested by Dibben and Dolles (2013, in this volume). The documents and observations give the first impression of what the sports clubs are and do, and about how or if they relate to central sport policy. In addition, they serve as preparation for the interviews through a process during which the researcher becomes aware of the issues that might be important and worth exploring in the field. From each of the sport clubs, the board members were interviewed, which comprised a total of 18 leaders of three different sport clubs. The study was reported formally to, and accepted by, the Norwegian Social Science Data Services, which is the privacy ombudsman for social research in Norway and the intermediate link between research institutions and the data inspectorate.

An interview guide was developed to ensure that each of the main topics of the study was covered in every interview. These were: (1) the sports club in general (history, aim and organization); (2) what constitutes the work of the sports club (elite versus mass focus, intrinsic versus external values, the leaders' interests and competence, and so on); (3) what influences the work of the sports club (authorities, market, other sport organizations, local context and members), and (4) the informants' background and sport involvement. The interviews with the sport club representatives were recorded and transcribed shortly after each interview. The analysis was done manually, in a herme-neutic procedure, based on Ricoeur (1991), sketched above, split into four phases with gradual transitions. First, each piece of text (documents, field notes and interview tran-scripts) were read, to get an impression of its meaning. Second, the texts were searched particularly for passages related to the object of study, namely, the central sport policy and its impact on the sport clubs policy and practice. Together, these are the phases where the 'thick description' is valuable, to get a good 'first guess' (ibid.), that is, getting an understanding of the wholeness of each case. In the third phase, themes or codes were identified in order to analyse the first guess, in terms of dividing the overall phe-nomenon into smaller pieces for investigation. These analytic codes paved the way for a presentation of the case study, for example, in manuscripts, which are often divided into chapters, sections and paragraphs based on the analytic codes. Fourth, quotes were found to use as citations in the various manuscripts which came out of the study. Thus, the citations are found to support the explanation that the researcher gives, in his or her own words, trying to explain what he or she (thinks he or she has) understood of the focal phenomenon.

Somewhere between phase one and two, the writing process starts. The 'validation test' on whether I had understood the research phenomenon, the cases of sport clubs, occurred through an exchange of understanding and explanation (ibid.). Imagine that you are supposed to tell something about a specific phenomenon to a friend. In order to be able to tell someone else about a phenomenon, you must feel that you have an understanding of it yourself. Understanding here refers to an idea of the phenomenon as a totality. But when you are about to tell your friend about it, you have to describe the phenomenon piece by piece. In other words, you explain it in an analytic way (analysis is 'the process of separating something into its constituent elements' and comes from Greek 'analusis'/'analuein' which means 'unloose' (*Oxford Dictionary of English*, 2005)). In that respect, the very presentation of the results (based on data), contributes to validate the interpretation of the research phenomenon.

6 AN EVALUATION OF THE QUALITY OF THE CASE STUDY

Limitations of case study research are, for the exemplified study as for case study more generally (Stake, 2005; Yin, 2003), related to the lack of possibilities of statistical generalization and – especially as long as it is used in a qualitative approach – the lack of opportunities for replication of the study. Nevertheless, in this chapter, I have focused on the positive sides of case study research, and used philosophical background information to support my argument. A more middle range approach in the assessment of case study research is, however, to use established concepts of evaluating a study's quality. Hence, in order to evaluate the design and the methods applied in the sketched example, I take as a starting point a classic division (for example, Yin, 2003: 33–9) of concepts summarized in the term of trustworthiness (Henderson, 1991: 134–9). Moreover, the traditional terms used to evaluate research quality relate to the above-presented elements of philosophy of science. 'Classic text books on methodology distinguish between three main kinds of validity: construct, internal and external. The former asks whether the instruments are accurate measures of reality; the second asks whether research design is capable of eliminating bias and the effect of extraneous variables, and the third involves defining the domains to which the results of the study may be generalized' (Easterby-Smith et al., 2002: 53). For other solutions on labeling assessments of a study's quality, see for example Creswell (2003: 171–5, 195–7, 220–22), Kvale (1996: 13, 236–52), Tashakkori and Teddlie (1998: 83), Thomas and Nelson (2001: 181, 338–9) and Utwin (1995: 3). Kvale (1996) is close to the qualitative end (on a scale with qualitative and quantitative as dichotomies) and focuses on interview skills as the point of departure, when he speaks about the validity of craftsmanship, communicative validity and pragmatic validity. Thomas and Nelson (2001), on the other hand, are close to the quantitative end when speaking about logical validity (equals face validity), content validity, criterion validity, construct validity and reliability (focusing on preventing measurement errors).

Construct validity, or measurement validity, is about how the terms used describe the reality in which we are conducting research. Internal validity, or credibility, may have slightly different meanings in qualitative research (about interpreting meanings and presenting different perspectives) compared with quantitative research (about causality), but overall it is about how to describe, explain and understand the object of study. External validity, or transferability, is about how the findings could be generalized to populations outside the sample from which the data is taken. This is particularly important to discuss in relation to case study research, because the logic of transferability differs from a classical notion of generalization.

With regard to construct and internal validity, it is considered high in qualitative research in general, for two interrelated reasons. First, there is little reason to disbelieve the informants' expressions of their understanding of their own sports club. Second, the constructs applied – such as sport policy and sport club – relate as much to the researcher's approach to the analysis through a conscious use of prejudice. In addition, three specific efforts were made to increase the internal validity: first, previous research was utilized for making a purposive sampling (Gadamer, 2004; Yin, 2003), and as a basis for a systematic search for differences and similarities during the analysis; second, triangulation of methods was applied as is suggested by most case study literature (for example, Edwards and Skinner, 2009; Li et al., 2008; Stake, 2005; Yin, 2003), and third, the 'double approach' of analysis was used, combining understanding and explanation in order to interpret the case as one unit which is built up by separate, identifiable and constitutive elements. In sum, these three approaches all contribute to create 'thick descriptions' (Alvesson and Sköldberg, 2000; Geertz, 1973) of the phenomenon under scrutiny – the case. I claim that 'thick descriptions' are the basis for strong internal validity and a significant attribute for good case study research.

External validity, the extent to which the knowledge generated in a study can be transferred to and considered as relevant for other contexts, based on a special logic in case study research. First, it could be claimed that case study research is more about particularity and contextualization than about generalization (Yin, 2003). Second, Yin (2003) underscores that case study research adheres to analytical generalization (and not statistical generalization such as in survey studies). In that respect, the prejudice comes into play again, in terms of the theoretical approach applied. The theory must be tested by replicating the findings from one case, on other cases. Thus, one method of increasing external validity is to conduct a multiple case study (see also Dopson, 2003). In that respect, the sampling procedure – or more precisely the specific cases chosen – also increases external validity; the ideal types together probably represent a significant proportion of Norwegian sport clubs. To be more precise, while 49 per cent of sports clubs in Norway comprise several sports, and many football and ski clubs are special sport clubs, it is safe to claim, although impossible to find the accurate numbers, that the three ideal types sampled here, represent more than half of Norwegian sports clubs.

The main point is that it is argued that the design and methods applied, give the opportunity to generate as many 'thick descriptions' and validated interpretations as possible about the focal phenomenon. Thus, what is not yet underscored is that the hermeneutic explanation, as for example Ricoeur's (1991), is not identical with, nor even similar to, explanation in natural scientific terms. Explanation is here a necessity to express the interpretation, which is part of the understanding process that the researcher goes through during research and particularly during analysis. Let me elaborate the arguments by taking up again some ideas from the theory of science as well as the empirical example sketched above.

The relationship between health rhetoric in the central policy papers and sport policy and practice at the grass-roots level is a more complicated relationship than a top-down policy being implemented. There is probably something – or many things – out there, which are more or less shared between central policy-makers and grass roots-level implementers of policy. One of these is the health focus, and part of the health focus is that of physical activity. Following Husserl (1970), who held that every first-person experience has to be directed towards something, the sport club representatives' intentionality has to be directed towards central sport policy in order to establish a causal relationship between central policy-making and local policy implementation.

As long as the sport club representatives direct their consciousness towards aspects other than central policy, such as competitiveness (Skille, 2010, 2011), there is no causal relationship. In that respect, this conclusion from the empirical example indicates the main argument I have tried to put forward throughout this chapter, namely, the answer to questions such as 'Why bother using the case study framework including its "theory of science" in Sport Management research?' or 'What did I find that I could not have found using other approaches?' A purposive sampling (based on hermeneutics) and a close relationship with the phenomenon (based on phenomenology), coupled with a tri-angulation of methods which led to 'thick descriptions', have allowed me to discover the 'reality' of sport club board decisions better than would have been possible with altern-ative approaches.

REFERENCES

Alvesson, M. and Sköldberg, K. (2000), *Reflexive Methodology: New Vistas for Qualitative Research*, London: Sage.
Bayle, E. and Robinson, L. (2007), A framework for understanding the performance of national governing bodies of sport, *European Sport Management Quarterly*, 7 (3), 249–68.
Creswell, J.W. (2003), *Research Design. Qualitative and Quantitative and Mixed Methods Approaches*, 2nd edn, London: Sage.
Dibben, M. and Dolles, H. (2013), Participant observation in sport management research: collecting and interpreting data from a successful world landspeed record attempt, in S. Söderman and H. Dolles (eds), *Handbook of Research on Sport and Business*, Cheltenham, UK and Northampton, MA, USA: Edward Elgar, pp. 477–94.
Dopson, S. (2003), The potential for the case study method in organizational analysis, *Policy and Politics*, 31 (2), 217–26.
Easterby-Smith, M., Thorpe, R. and Lowe, A. (2002), *Management Research: An Introduction*, London: Sage.
Edwards, A. and Skinner, J. (2009), *Qualitative Research in Sport Management*, Oxford: Elsevier.
Enjolras, E. and Seippel, Ø. (2001), *Norske idrettslag 2000: struktur, økonomi og frivillig innsats* [*Norwegian Sport Clubs 2000: Structure, Economy and Voluntary Work*], Oslo: Institute for Social Research.
Fitzgerald, L. and Dopson, S. (2009), Comparative case study designs: their utility and development in organi-zational research, in D.A. Buchanan and A. Bryman (eds), *The Sage Handbook of Organizational Research Methods*, London: Sage, pp. 465–83.
Gadamer, H.G. (2003), *Forståelsens filosofi* [*The Philosophy of Understanding, Norwegian Selections*], Oslo: Cappelen.
Gadamer, H.G. (2004), *Truth and Method*, 2nd edn, London: Continuum. First published 1975.
Geertz, C. (1973), *The Interpretation of Cultures*, New York: Basic Books.
Goksøyr, M. (1992), *Staten og idretten 1861–1991* [*The State and Sport 1861–1991*], Oslo: Kulturdepartementet [Ministry of Cultural Affairs].
Goksøyr, M., Andersen, E. and Asdal, K. (eds), (1996), *Kropp, kultur og tippekamp* [*Body, Culture and TV Football: The History of the Department of Sport Policy*], Oslo: Universitetsforlaget.
Gratton, C. and Solberg, H.A. (2013), The economics of listed sports events in a digital era of broadcasting: a case study of the UK, in S. Söderman and H. Dolles (eds), *Handbook of Research on Sport and Business*, Cheltenham, UK and Northampton, MA, USA: Edward Elgar, pp. 202–18.
Habermas, J. (1987), *Knowledge and Human Interests*, Cambridge: Polity Press.
Heidegger, M. (1962), *Being and Time*, New York: Harper and Row.
Heinemann, K. (ed.) (1999), *Sport Clubs in Various European Countries*, Schorndorf, Stuttgart and New York: Karl Hofmann and F.K. Schattauer.

Henderson, K.A. (1991), *Dimensions of Choice: A Qualitative Approach to Research in Recreation, Parks, and Leisure*, College Park, PA: Venture.

Husserl, E. (1970), *The Crisis of European Sciences and Transcendental Phenomenology: An Introduction to Phenomenological Philosophy*, Evanston, IL: Northwestern University Press. First published 1936.

Ibsen, B. (1992), *Frivilligt arbejde i idrætsforeninger [Voluntary Work in Sport Clubs]*, Herning: DHL/Systime.

Kvale, S. (1996), *Interviews: An Introduction to Qualitative Research Interviewing*, Thousand Oaks, CA: Sage.

Leopkey, B. and Parent, M.M. (2009), Risk management issues in large-scale sporting events: a stakeholder perspective, *European Sport Management Quarterly*, **9** (2), 187–208.

Li, M., Pittsand, B.G. and Quarterman, J. (2008), *Research Methods in Sport Management*, Morgantown, WV: Fitness Information Technology.

McNamee, M. (ed.) (2005), *Philosophy and the Sciences of Exercise, Health and Sport: Critical Perspectives on Research Methods*, London: Routledge.

Norwegian Olympic Committee and Confederation of Sports (NOC) (2007a), *Idrettspolitisk dokument 2007–2011 [Sport Policy Document 2007–2011]*, Oslo: Norges idrettsforbund og olympiske komité [Norwegian Olympic Committee and Confederation of Sports].

Norwegian Olympic Committee and Confederation of Sports (NOC) (2007b), *Resolusjon fra idrettstinget [Resolution from the General Assembly]*, Skien: Norges idrettsforbund og olympiske komité [Norwegian Olympic Committee and Confederation of Sports].

Norges skiforbund [Norwegian Ski Association] (NSF) (2007), *Beretning 2006–2007 [Report 2006–2007]*, Oslo: Norges skiforbund [Norwegian Ski Association].

Olstad, F. (1987), *Norsk idretts historie [Norwegian Sport's History]*, vol. I, Oslo: Aschehoug.

O'Reilly, N. (2013), Portfolio theory and the management of professional sports clubs: the case of Maple Leaf Sports and Entertainment, in S. Söderman and H. Dolles (eds), *Handbook of Research on Sport and Business*, Cheltenham, UK and Northampton, MA, USA: Edward Elgar, pp. 333–49.

Oxford Dictionary of English (2005), Oxford: Oxford University Press.

Ricoeur, P. (1991), *From Text to Action: Essays in Hermeneutics II*, Evanston, IL: Northwestern University Press.

Schutz, A. (1972), *The Phenomenology of the Social World*, London: Heinemann Educational Books.

Seale, C. (1999), *The Quality of Qualitative Research*, London: Sage.

Seippel, Ø. (2003), *Norske idrettslag 2002 [Norwegian Sport Clubs 2002]*, Oslo: Institute for Social Research.

Skille, E.Å. (2005), *Sport Policy and Adolescent Sport. The Sports City Program (Storbyprosjektet)*, Oslo: Norwegian School of Sport Sciences.

Skille, E.Å. (2006), *Idrettslaget som helseprodusent. Introduksjon, teori og metodologi i studiet av idrettslag og sentral idrettspolitikk med fokus på helse [Sport Clubs as Health Producers. Introduction, Theory and Methodology in the Study of Sport Clubs and Central Sport Policy with Focus upon Health]*, Elverum: Hedmark University College.

Skille, E.Å. (2007), *Idrettslaget som helseprodusent – andre refleksjon om perspektiver – første tanker om presentasjon av empiri [Sport Clubs as Health Producers – Second Reflection on Perspectives – First Reflection on Empirical Presentation]*, Elverum: Hedmark University College.

Skille, E.Å. (2008), Understanding sport clubs as sport policy implementers, *International Review for the Sociology of Sport*, **43** (2), 181–200.

Skille, E.Å. (2009), State sport policy and the voluntary sport clubs: the case of the Norwegian Sports City Program as social policy, *European Sport Management Quarterly*, **9** (1), 63–79.

Skille, E.Å. (2010), Competitiveness and health – the work of sport clubs seen from the perspectives of Norwegian sport club representatives, *International Review for the Sociology of Sport*, **45** (1), 1–13.

Skille, E.Å. (2011), The conventions of sport clubs: enabling and constraining the implementation of social goods through sport, *Sport, Education and Society*, **16** (2), 253–65.

Skirstad, B. (2002), 'Norske idrettslag: Oversikt og utfordringer' [Norwegian sport clubs: overview and challenges], in Ø. Seippel (ed.), *Idrettens bevegelser [Sport's Movements]*, Oslo: Novus, pp. 229–54.

Slack, T. (1997), *Understanding Sport Organizations: The Application of Organization Theory*, Champaign, IL: Human Kinetics.

Slack, T. and Parent, M.M. (2006), *Understanding Sport Organizations: The Application of Organization Theory*, 2nd edn, Champaign, IL: Human Kinetics.

Stake, R.E. (2005), Qualitative case studies, in N.K. Denzin and Y.S. Lincoln (eds), *Sage Handbook of Qualitative Research*, 3rd edn, Thousand Oaks, CA: Sage, pp. 443–66.

Stanford Encyclopedia of Philosophy (2002), *Alfred Schutz*, available at: http://plato.stanford.edu/entries/schutz (accessed 11 September 2007).

Stanford Encyclopedia of Philosophy (2003), *Phenomenology*, available at: www.plato.stanford.edu/entries/phenomenology (accessed 11 September 2007).

Stortingsmelding no. 14 (1999–2000), *Idrettslivet i endrng [White Paper on Sport: Sport Life a Change]*, Oslo: Kulturdepartementet [Ministry of Cultural Affairs].

Tashakkori, A. and Teddlie, C. (1998), *Mixed Methodology. Combining Qualitative and Quantitative Approaches*, London, Sage.

Thomas, J.R. and Nelson, J.K. (2001), *Research Methods in Physical Activity*, 4th edn, Champaign, IL: Human Kinetics.

Tønnesson, S. (1986), *Norsk idretts historie* [*Norwegian Sport's History*], (vol. II), Oslo: Aschehoug.

Utwin, M.S. (1995), *How to Measure Survey Reliability and Validity*, London: Sage.

Walters, G. and Hamil, S. (2013), Regulation and the search for a profitable business model: a case study of the English football industry, in S. Söderman and H. Dolles (eds), *Handbook of Research on Sport and Business*, Cheltenham, UK and Northampton, MA, USA: Edward Elgar, pp. 126–41.

Yanow, D. and Ybema, S. (2009), Interpretivism in organizational research: on elephants and blind researchers, in D.A. Buchanan and A. Bryman (eds), *The Sage Handbook of Organizational Research Methods*, London: Sage, pp. 39–60.

Yin, R.K. (2003), *Case Study Research. Design and Methods*, 3rd edn, London: Sage.

PART III

MEDIA AND TECHNOLOGY

10 Social media and prosumerism: implications for sport marketing research

James Santomier and Patricia Hogan

1 INTRODUCTION

The future envisioned by Alvin Toffler in his trilogy *Future Shock* (1970), *The Third Wave* (1980) and *Powershift* (1990) is a testament to Toffler's prescience. His predictions of monumental social, cultural and economic change wrought by new information technologies and a shift to a prosumer economy have become reality (Siegel, 2008). Toffler foretold that an increase in knowledge (owing to new, more effective ways to communicate information) will lead to de-massification, where mass marketing gives way to niche and micro-marketing, where mass production is replaced by increasingly customized production and where knowledge (that is, the ability to apply information to the solving of problems or to the creation of opportunity) is power.

The pressure to de-massify, Toffler suggested, is being driven by the increasing awareness of better-informed and empowered individuals and is becoming practiced through the unstoppable development of information technology (Chartered Management Institute, 2001). These better-informed and empowered individuals were termed 'prosumers' (Toffler, 1980), networked individuals who simultaneously can *pro*duce, distribute and con*sume* their own goods or services, usually outside the monetary economy (Ferguson, 2009). The unstoppable information technology is social media, including mobile media, made possible due to Web 2.0. Ritzer and Jurgenson (2010) indicate that the emergence of the Internet followed by the materialization of Web 2.0 (that is, interactive or social web) technologies and the social media (such as Facebook, Twitter and YouTube) it spawned have provided a showcase and launch pad for the prosumer economy. 'Prosumption was clearly not invented on Web 2.0, but given the massive involvement in, and popularity of, many of these developments (for example, social networking sites), it can be argued that it is currently both the most prevalent location of prosumption and its most important facilitator as a "means of prosumption"' (ibid.: 13).

Web 2.0 and social media are making it possible for millions of sport fans to become prosumers. Fans, along with athletes and sport organizations worldwide, can directly correspond and interact using social media. For example, fans are empowered to participate on sport-specific organization or team wikis, homepages, blogs, micro-blogs, pictures, podcasts, video sites, Twitter, Facebook, iTunes, and so on. Soon it may be possible for fans to use tele-immersion technologies to insert themselves into sporting events on their HD/3D televisions or mobile devices, and, given empathetic social media now being developed, to actually feel the impacts in football or other sports (Kelly, 2009). In addition, many sport enterprises such as Nike, Adidas and Prince are using content-based social media in efforts to directly engage customers, build brand communities, build long-term customer relationships and market products. Definitely, as

Dolles and Söderman (2011: 4) point out: 'The proliferation of information technology has made it possible to serve the needs of fans all over the world. They can consume [prosume] an event either real-time or recorded from virtually anywhere. As a result of this, the opportunities for the promotion of sport, and the benefits for sport and its partners, are significant.'

Yet, despite the rapid development and integration of social media into the marketing strategies of many sport and sport-related brands worldwide, many organizations have neither developed an efficacious social media measurement strategy nor determined how well social media compares with other digital marketing initiatives relative to the important metrics of business (Linnell, 2010). And, many are still trying to understand the phenomenon that is social media. Social media marketing in general and social media sport marketing in particular, therefore, represent fruitful areas for research and for developing new research methodologies.

Social media is changing the way businesses, including sport businesses, communicate in the pursuit of brand building and commerce, and is compelling these businesses to create new and innovative ways to capitalize on the prosumer economy (MarketingSherpa, 2010). As such, there is a call for the rethinking of marketing and its metrics for social media (Light, 2010; Rust et al., 2010). And, there will definitely need to be a rethinking of sport marketing and its metrics, now that the fans (prosumers) are in charge (Sports Marketing2.0, 2010; also Dolles and Söderman, 2013 in this volume). Such new territory represents a rich opportunity for new research. Given (1) the call for rethinking marketing efforts and metrics (or, e-metrics) for the social Web due to the roles social media and prosumerism are playing in this economy; (2) the quickly expanding use and potential of social media in sport and sport related industries, especially in sport marketing, and (3) the bountiful opportunities for research and for inventing research methodologies in the realm of social media marketing, we explore the following question in this chapter: what are the implications of social media and the prosumer economy for research in sport marketing?

More specifically, we discuss the need to rethink marketing in light of social media and the prosumer economy in this chapter, explore the current frontier of theory and practice in marketing using social media (where, for research concerning practice we mainly use www sources owing to the fact there is no systematic research in this rapidly emerging area), and address the implications of the aforementioned for research in sport marketing for scholars, organizations and/or marketing professionals. Finally, research idea-matrices based on major concepts, definitions, theoretical foundations, metric models and tools, and research models are included as a quick reference to generate variables or ideas for research.

2   SOCIAL MEDIA AND THE NEED TO RETHINK MARKETING AND ITS METRICS

Social media supports the democratization of knowledge and information, transforming people from content consumers into content *producers* and con*sumers* – or 'prosumers' (Davis, 2009). Kaplan and Haenlein (2010: 59) define social media as 'a group of Internet-based applications that build on the ideological and technological foundations of Web 2.0, and that allow the creation and exchange of user-generated content (UGC) or consumer-generated media (CGM)'. Lietsala and Sirkkunen (2008: 3–4) categorized social media into six areas (which may serve as useful delineations for research in social media): (1) content creation and publishing (for example, blogs, v-blogs or video-blogs, podcasts); (2) content sharing (for example, Flickr, YouTube, del.icio.us, Digg.com); (3) social networking websites (for example, Facebook, LinkedIn, MySpace); (4) collaborative productions (for example, Wikipedia/Wikis, OhmyNews); (5) virtual worlds (for example, Second Life, WOW) and (6) add-ons (for example, RockYou, Slide, Friends for Sale). However, given the rapidly changing nature and growth of social media, new categories may be added – for example, immersion or empathetic social media (Kelly, 2009).

Figures from the 2009 Nielsen Report on social media indicate that the amount of time spent surfing social networking and blogging websites has almost tripled (that is, time spent on social networking and blogging websites accounted for 17 per cent of the total time spent online) from 2008 to 2009, 'suggesting a wholesale change in the way the Internet is used' (Perez, 2009: 1). Facebook, YouTube, Twitter, Blogger. com, and Wikipedia all were ranked in the top 15 on Alexa (which posts the top 500 websites) in April 2010 (Alexa, 2010). Similarly, Viralblog reported (in July 2010) that YouTube receives over 200 million views per day (with 24 hours of video uploaded every minute) where over 70 per cent of activity is from outside the United States. Also, it is estimated that over 50 million tweets are sent per day on Twitter. These numbers are astounding; more and more it appears the Internet is being used to stay connected and to communicate and share in social networks, and advertisers/marketers have taken notice of this social media phenomenon: where before, advertisers were somewhat wary of social media properties, they are now spending more than ever buying prominent spots on social networking sites. Even as companies decreased their overall advertising expenditures, they increased their spending on top social networks and blogs – up 119 per cent (that is, US$108 million in August 2009 up from US$49 million in August 2008) (Perez, 2009: 1). When broken down by category, the increases are even more dramatic. The entertainment industry, for example, has increased spending by 812 per cent year-over-year on social network sites, and the travel industry increased spending by 364 per cent (ibid.: 1).

Vitrue's Social Media Index (SMI), which assigns brands and products a score based on overall buzz from status updates, videos, photographs and blog posts, has tallied its 2010 results and has released its top 100 social brands based on index scoring (Vitrue, 2011). The iPhone was once again ranked number one. Many sport or sport-related brands, however, were in the list as well (for example, NBA rank 18; Nike 24; Adidas 34; NFL 36; Converse 51; ESPN 55; NHL 65; Major League Baseball 68; Puma 70; NASCAR 73). Visa moved up 45 spots (from Vitrue's 2009 tally) to rank 42 on the list, probably because it was a title sponsor of the 2010 FIFA World Cup in South Africa where it placed significant resources into Facebook and YouTube – such as the campaigns 'Go Fans' and 'VISA Match Planner' – in multiple languages to generate tremendous buzz worldwide. Even though the Vitrue SMI 'focuses on consumer mentions and reactions – as opposed to indexing brand engagement via social media – the list is still a veritable powerhouse of information in terms of consumer buzz and word-of-mouth recommendations' (Van Grove, 2010: 1). However, solid research data related to brand engagement via social media represents a needed, potential area for research in sport marketing.

Although for some professionals in the advertising industry, social networks may still seem like an emerging medium, if an advertising medium at all, the 2010 Media Planning Intelligence Study Report by the Center for Media Research on the media buying plans of advertisers and agencies indicated that having a presence on social networks is one of the top priorities of their media plans for next year. The report specified that 57.7 per cent of respondents ideally plan, and 56.3 per cent realistically plan to include social media in their media plans next year. 'That finding is significant because it shows the rapid speed with which social media, including social networks like Facebook, micro-blogging services such as Twitter, and other new and emerging formats connecting people to each other online have taken a precedent with both consumers and marketing industry professionals' (Mandese, 2009: 1).

As indicated earlier, however, social media is not concerned with consumers, but with prosumers – yet traditional marketing and marketing research assumes a consumer. For example, Morgan and Summers (2005: 106) define marketing research as 'the function that links the *consumer* [emphasis added], customer, or public to the marketer through information – information used to identify and define marketing opportunities and problems; generate, refine and evaluate marketing actions; monitor marketing performance; and improve marketing performance'. And, Mullin et al. (2008: 2) define sport marketing as consisting of 'all activities designed to meet the needs and wants of sports *consumers* [emphases added] through exchange processes. Sport marketing has developed two major thrusts: the marketing of sport products and services directly to *consumers* of sport, and marketing of other *consumer* and industrial products or service through the use of sport promotions'. Sport promotion, part of the traditional marketing mix, represents 'the deployment of a fully integrated set of communication activities intended to persuade *consumers* [emphasis added] toward a favorable belief or action as a tactical component of the overall marketing campaign' (Irwin et al., 2008: 3). Another area for research, therefore, could consider the role of sport marketing, especially social media sport marketing, in the age of the prosumer versus the consumer.

Definitions for social media marketing focus on 'reader customers' who will share their experiences, attitudes and information about the brand with their social networks through, for example, blogging, Facebook, Twitter, or specialized wikis. Braithwaite (2010: 1) identifies a common definition for social media marketing:

> social media marketing usually centers around efforts to create content that attracts attention, generates online conversations, and encourages readers to share it within their social networks. The message spreads between users and resonates because it is coming from a trusted source, as opposed to the company or brand. Through social media marketing, organizations increase their brand awareness and facilitate conversations with the customer. Social media marketing is therefore, basically an effort to humanize a company or brand by encouraging customers and prospective customers to engage, thus driving loyalty and preference.

Getting the attention of the customer is an important component of the marketing effort, and traditional sport promotion efforts (for example, sponsorships, athlete appearances, informercials, endorsements, sales presentations, websites, speeches, demonstrations, ticket brochures, advertisements, autograph sessions, community projects,

DVDs and videos, press conferences, media guides, interactive analog exhibits, exhibitions, hospitality areas, national-anthem singers, contests, video games, stadium tours, museums, fantasy leagues and competitions) are not as effective in the current marketing environment (Irwin et al., 2008), and need to be adapted to the prosumer economy through social media via digital marketing. Digital marketing is 'marketing that leverages the interactive connections between seekers and providers enabled by digital media and devices' (Walsh, 2009: 1). The efficacy of using digital marketing in sport marketing also represents a promising area for sport marketing research.

Although a recent report from Knowledge Networks indicated that 83 per cent of the Internet population (ages 13 to 54) participates in social media (47 per cent do so on a weekly basis), less than 5 per cent of social media users reported that they regularly turn to these sites for guidance on purchase decisions in any of nine product/service categories. Also, currently, only 16 per cent of social media users say they are more likely to buy from companies that advertise on social sites (Loechner, 2009). Basically, the report finds that social media is having a profound impact on the way people connect with each other, but that it does not seem to be a very meaningful way for people to connect with brands, or advertising that is promoting brands. This kind of research could be applied to sport marketing as well to determine if conclusions are consistent.

As mentioned previously in reference to Visa as a product marketed through sport, the social media phenomenon and attempts at digital marketing were particularly pronounced in the marketing of the 2010 Football World Cup, where participants engaged in a global conversation. Fans used Twitter's hashtag #WorldCup, and practically every game hit Twitter's trending topics list. Facebook offered The Facebook Guide to the World Cup, which explained worldwide live streaming partnerships (including one in the US for ESPN), as well as Facebook's Support Your Team Leaderboard that tracked elements such as fan 'intensity'. In the mobile location world, Foursquare partnered with CNN to offer specific badges for users that check-in to over 100 viewing venues in 32 countries around the world. Similarly, Gowalla partnered with Major League Soccer to create trips in local areas that highlight soccer. And, the *New York Times* tracked athlete Facebook mentions in the World Cup and compiled the data for fans. Finally, and contrary to the Knowledge Networks report regarding brand connection, social media appeared to have provided a platform for ambush marketing and usurping perceptions of official sponsorship status for the World Cup. Although Nike was not an official sponsor of the World Cup (Adidas was an official sponsor), its three-minute 'Write the Future' YouTube soccer video went viral and garnered the record for the largest audience in the first week of its campaign with 7.8 million views (Learmouth, 2010). Given the aforementioned, new ideas for research include looking at effective social media marketing models in sport and the role of ambush marketing in sport through social media.

Even though many sport teams, sport product representatives, athletes, and so on currently use social media (especially websites, Facebook, Twitter, Blogs, YouTube) in their marketing plans, the metrics touting the efficacy of those efforts relative to return on investment (ROI) including measures related to return on objectives (ROO) or on customer relationship management (CRM), currently seem to be in their infancy and only measured in terms of number of clicks or click-throughs (Emarketer, 2009; KLM, 2010). For the most part, the data focused on by marketing professionals to evaluate social media include: (1) internal sales and distribution data; (2) consumer behavior studies for target identification; (3) media channel data for media consumption information and (4) buzz data related to buzz or viral marketing. However, many are still struggling to fully understand social media and to measure the efficacy of social media marketing initiatives (given the time and effort they take) relative to ROI and ROO (Emarketer, 2009). Yet, as Gummesson (2008: xii) admonishes, we must remember that 'marketing deals with the generation of revenue and revenue must exceed costs. Don't ever forget it! The cry for marketing accountability and metrics is currently loud – again'. Indeed, however, some claim that social media marketing will not lend itself to ROI (Mandese, 2009). Research that could document the role of social media in sport relative to ROI and/or ROO would be most welcome.

Currently most sport enterprises and sport-related industries seem to be only monitoring visits to their social media websites. For example, the backend of the National Hockey League (NHL) website, which was constructed by a third party firm, contains analytics features that enable the NHL to monitor hits, clicks and session length (Sherman, 2009). Social media websites related to brands or events typically allow participants to interact by describing, rating/evaluating and discussing the product or services or content (Lefer, 2008). Others use coupons: measuring the success of social media marketing can be difficult, but using a variety of hard and soft ROI metrics is one solution. For example, distributing a coupon via a social network and monitoring its redemption can put a concrete number on social success. Marketers can also assign a dollar value to soft metrics, such as number of fans or followers, to measure ROI (Emarketer, 2009).

Ultimately, then, in light of the social media networked, prosumer economy, the new purpose of a business may be to *Serve* a customer who creates other customers (Stern, 2010). The sheer volume of potential customers in social media and the continuing exponential growth of social network platforms demand marketers' attention. It appears necessary for companies and/or brands to integrate social media into their overall marketing strategies. Customer service aspects of social media in general is a viable topic for research, and proposed integration models that have been researched and provide evidence-based information represent another area for proposed research.

3   SOCIAL MEDIA USE FOR MARKETING IN SPORT BUSINESS

In spite of the current ROI/ROO limitations related to social media marketing, there have been many predictions about increased and enhanced social media use in the sport industry. Rose (2009) identifies the following predictions (which could be measured and researched) for what the future holds for athletes using social media platforms:

1. Athletes will embrace new and creative outlets and platforms, such as Ustream (live broadcast site), to connect with fans. [In essence, the athlete can now become a media platform by creating and atomizing exclusive multi-media content, having a broad social footprint, and owning relationships with fans (Marobella, 2009).]
2. Social media numbers may become a part of contract negotiations with athletes.
3. Teams and management will increase content restrictions for athletes.

4. Social media will become an integral part in the philanthropic endeavors of athletes.
5. There will be more involvement from retired athletes.

Also, Peck (2009) presents his 'Sports and social media predictions 2010' – containing predictions from a number of sport marketing experts and thought-leaders – concerning the use of social media in sport. Major predictions include the use of social media for 'glocalization' (simultaneous local and global) of brands, teams and leagues attempting to build communities using their own proprietary networks, properties redefining and creating new rules concerning tweeting in order to reduce image problems, sport blogging personalities (athletes) becoming even more popular, experts being hired to manage sport social media campaigns, sport businesses figuring out ways to make money on social media (perhaps resulting in social media websites becoming more public relations oriented), fans wanting even deeper and more meaningful interaction with sport teams and athletes, the move to video, mobile and virtual games with consumer involvement in co-creation, and brands fine-tuning their measurement efforts past just counting hits. In addition, the rise of 'social business' in sport is predicted where the need for measurement efforts focused on ROI often come up as a theme in social media use for marketing and promotion. Any of the aforementioned areas represent new avenues for potential research.

Social media has changed the dynamics of marketing. According to Gillin (2007: i), the 'real influencers are no longer marketing experts, nor the traditional media that has always controlled and filtered marketing messages, but millions of ordinary people who are determining in direct and powerful ways what people hear, say, and believe'. Consumers increasingly turn away from print media, skip television commercials and ignore 1990s-style cost-per-thousand banner advertisements (ibid.). But customers or fans are still seeking information, and many are embracing social media, a media that empowers consumers and facilitates their metamorphosis into prosumers. A comparison of prosumer attitudes towards traditional versus new media marketing in sport may be an area of research interest for some.

Underhill and Kurit (2009) emphasize that since Google has over 200 million look-ups per day and there are over 600 million people on Facebook, social media is an important marketing area. They contend social media marketing is about content, not commercials, about relationships, not selling. The focus should be on developing authentic relationships (people prefer to buy from people they know, like and trust) since, ultimately, it is difficult to make money directly through social media. However, Alvin Toffler states that we have so far not adequately recognized the extent and power of the interactions between the non-money, or 'prosumer', economy and the money economy (Fisher, 2006: 1). He contends that although prosumer activities are very different from the money economy, they have a powerful aggregate impact on the money economy since the cyber structure allows prosumers to create value and rapidly disseminate it across the globe, where others can commercialize it: 'Recognize that it [prosumer economy] can take activities out of the market, the way Napster took music out of the money economy and transferred it into the non-money economy. Then iTunes used the Web to move music downloading back into the money economy, creating a very viable business that did not exist before' (ibid.: 2). The rapid rise of prosumerism on the social Web has major implications for both the global economy and for humanity in general – implications that have been largely unmeasured and underestimated according to Toffler and Toffler

(2006). It appears that businesses, including sport businesses, have a need to rethink marketing and its metrics in the realm of social media, and that there is a plethora of research that could be done around the areas of social media, prosumerism and sport business.

4   RETHINKING MARKETING: THEORETICAL FOUNDATIONS

A number of business thought leaders have proposed a rethinking of marketing due to new media and to prosumerism, and any of their models could be applied to research in sport marketing. Tables 10.1 to 10.5 found in the final section of this chapter provide a quick reference summary for research topics and ideas and include a summary of the following thought leaders and their proposed models for potential research.

Vargo and Lusch's (2004: 1) talk of businesses evolving to 'a new dominant logic for marketing'. They indicate a need to move from the logic of the exchange of goods (which focused on tangible resources, embedded value, and transactions) to a logic focused on intangible resources, the co-creation of value, and relationships – a 'service-centered logic'. They define service as 'the application of specialized competences (knowledge and skills) through deeds, processes, and performances for the benefit of another entity or the entity itself' (ibid.: 1). From their perspective, primary marketing activities should now include the Tofflerian focus on 'interactivity, integration, customization, and coproduction' (ibid.: 11). In their customer-focused and relational model, where value 'is defined and co-created' with the customer 'rather than embedded in output' (ibid.: 6), the goals of marketing are 'to customize offerings, to recognize that the "consumer" is always a co-producer, and to strive to maximize consumer involvement in the customization' (ibid.: 12). The stated goals reflect the conceptual shift of the consumer to a co-producer – prosumer.

Gummesson (2002: 587) called for marketing practitioners and scholars to change their theoretical approach to marketing, and recommended a reduction in the distinction between producer and consumer, conceptualizing the consumer as an 'active co-producer, user, and value creator'. He (Gummesson, 2007) proposed, based on Vargo and Lusch's (2004) service-dominant logic, that marketers abandon services marketing (as in goods and services) and embrace service marketing (relationships) as defined by Vargo and Lusch. Gummesson (2008) recommends marketing strategy moves from the 4Ps (product, price, promotion, place) of traditional marketing to the 30Rs (30 relationships identified in his text), a new marketing paradigm. These 30Rs are distributed thusly: 3Rs in classic market relationships; 14Rs in special market relationships; 6Rs in mega relationships and 7Rs in nano relationships.

Another proposed model for successful social marketing in the networked era involves a play on the 4Ps of marketing. Clark (2009) introduced the 5Fs of social media which he contends should increase the likelihood of ROI in social media brand promotion. Clark's 5Fs are familiarity, fortune, fame, fun and forwardability.

The advent of social media is a contributing factor in naming this era the 'attention age' or 'attention economy'. This age began with the emergence of social media in the first years of the twenty-first century (Sullivan, 2009), and is marked by the ability of individuals to become prosumers, to create and consume information instantly and freely as well as share it on the Internet using social media – most wikis and blogs are developed and maintained by prosumers. However, Toffler and Toffler (2006) contend those who call it the attention economy assume attention means intention (of social media participants to purchase products or services), but, owing to the nature of prosumers, they claim that attention does not mean intention and that marketers need to change their ways to embrace social media and the prosumer economy it ushers in. Esther Dyson concurs in the interview by Kleiner (2009: 3):

> The online and media worlds are dealing with a crumbling economy across almost all sectors. Advertising revenue is going down; venture capitalists are getting nervous. And separately, there is a change in the way people spend their time and buy things, as a result of being online, that has begun to affect all marketing and media enterprises. A lot of marketers call the Internet an 'attention economy'. They are looking for consumers who will pay attention to their product, and they try to calculate consumers' propensity to purchase. They think that *attention* means *intention*. But it doesn't. The reality is, people don't go online to *give* attention, but to *get* it. They don't want to be part of the audience. They want to perform and to be heard, to be present. That's why digital media are replacing old media so rapidly – and why this new era is so difficult for marketers. They need to learn to join the conversation rather than interrupt it.

Similarly, Kunz (2008) argues that marketers need to be aware of the three modes or mindsets (that is, receiving, hunting and doing) people engage when using interactive communications, and match business marketing strategies accordingly. 'The entire mindset of a person engaged on MySpace or LinkedIn is different from that of a hunter on a search engine. A Google user is walking into a store. A Facebook user is walking into a bar' (Kunz, 2008: 1).

Deighton and Kornfeld (2007) assert that the anticipated new model of marketing, in which digital media facilitates the delivery of marketing messages, has not developed and consider the word 'consumer' to be of limited value in understanding the current new media marketing context. Rather than the consumer, there exists a model of consumer collaboration or prosumerism, where consumers communicate among themselves 'responding to marketing's intrusions by disseminating counterargument, information sharing, rebuttal, parody, reproach and, though more rarely, fandom' (ibid.: 2). They identified five discrete roles for interactive technology (ibid.: 8): thought-tracing (search), ever-present connectivity, property exchange, social exchange and cultural exchange. They claim these roles are actually 'responses to the diminution of marketing's power relative to the consumer in the new media environment' (ibid.: 13), and if the 'marketer wants to survive it has to be by becoming an ally, someone who is welcomed into social or cultural life and is, perhaps, even sought out as someone with cultural capital' (ibid.: 13).

Prahalad (2009) argues, as do Vargo and Lusch (2004) and Gummesson (2002, 2007, 2008), that companies have not made enough use of the opportunities provided by globalization and prosumerism, and calls for value co-creation of companies with prosumers: the move from a product-centric view of value creation to an experience-centric view of value co-creation. He argues that the rules of the game and the role of the players have changed, thanks to the Internet, and that companies need to adapt to the new rules, rules that involve the co-creation of value with customers. Steps in the co-creation of value process include (Ramaswamy and Prahalad, 2006):

1. Defining clear objectives for the project (for example, social media marketing plan).
2. Figuring out who are the right customers to involve in the process (who to involve in the network).
3. Working with customers to find out what they really want to include in a product or service.
4. Designing products/services or systems jointly to meet those customers' needs.
5. Deciding how to share the value.
6. Overcoming internal resistance to change – within seller, buyer and partner organizations. This is a critical step to ensuring that you control the channel.

According to Kelly (2009) companies are going to have to be more agile, more collaborative, and transition from traditional models of competition to shared webs of innovation. Dyson elaborates (Kleiner, 2009: 1): marketers will use the new media to interact with consumers directly, leaving the traditional content providers in the lurch. Increasingly, consumers are interested in talking to one another, rather than reading the precious words of the experts. That does not mean the death of professional content, but it does mean a dramatic change in the content providers' business models. Meanwhile, marketers will have to integrate themselves into conversations already taking place on the Web. The really good marketers will become much more clever about what they do, and engage with people more effectively (ibid.).

Rust et al. (2010), given the cyber structure and the prosumer economy, also call for a rethinking of marketing and its metrics in the direction of relationships. They recommend that companies shift their focus from marketing products to cultivating customers in order to maximize customer lifetime value, replace the chief marketing officer with the chief customer officer, and adopt a new set of metrics (that is, customer profitability versus product profitability, customer lifetime value versus current sales, customer equity versus brand equity and customer equity share versus market share) for measuring success. 'Never before have companies had such powerful technologies for interacting directly with customers, collecting and mining information about them, and tailoring their offerings accordingly' (ibid.: 96).

The social media-prosumer movement and relationship economy requires that marketers change their focus from that of pushing products or services on consumers to building long-term customer (fan) relationships (Light, 2010; Rust et al., 2010). Such a customer-focused business involves leading customer-driven innovation based on customer needs and desires (Light, 2010) through seeing customers as prosumers. Social media allows sport 'consumers' or fans to directly participate and relate to sport teams and players in real ways never before possible: social media allows the public to interact with sport organizations and high-profile personnel who may have otherwise been inaccessible because of time and security constraints. Thus, targeted use of social media, especially when used consistently with other marketing and publicity activities, may exponentially expand fan involvement and loyalty for sports programs. Sports organizations and players who are actively engaging fans via social media are generally finding that use to be a net positive, and the most progressive among them realize that social media will be a vital part of fan outreach in the future (Sideman, 2009).

However, many others (Emarketer, 2009; Peck, 2009; Prahalad, 2009) argue that the marketing and promotion game has changed and that businesses need to learn how to use social media marketing even though 'online social network applications are mainly used for explaining and maintaining personal networks, and most adults, like teens, are using them to connect with people they already know' (Lenhart, 2009: 3). They argue that it is a matter of time before these websites are used to generate ROI. Any of the aforementioned models could be used as a theoretical framework for social media marketing research in sport business.

5 CURRENT MODELS AND METRICS FOR SOCIAL MEDIA MARKETING

Models for developing social media marketing plans that account for the prosumer phenomenon abound online, many in multi-media forms. For example, Dailey (2009) presents a comprehensive online guide for a social media marketing strategy that focuses on insuring authenticity (where real people communicate with real people in unfiltered, genuine ways), transparency, immediacy and a trusted community. He contends that the social media department (comprised of marketing, communications and public relations personnel) of any company or agency will deal with social media strategy and functional alignment, channel selection, compliance, metrics, managing blog operations, reputation and brand managing, crisis management support, bringing social media innovation and best practices to the company, and external outreach. Using social media for research and development (instead of focus groups) will, according to him, save much money. Research concerning the relative costs of traditional versus social media marketing in sport business represents a potential endeavor.

Social media monitoring tools are potential starting points for gaining a better understanding of how effective brand marketing is within the social media space. Internet searches will result in a significant number of free and paid tools to choose from. Companies such as Spredfast.com and Radian6 have developed comprehensive Web-based software and e-guides that help companies manage their social media marketing efforts. This software not only measures audience size and engagement, but also allows coordinated planning and automated posting across multiple social media platforms, where the goal is to inform companies as to whether or not the time put into social media is helping build brand awareness and why. Generally,

> Web-based software counts how many people view a company's Twitter, LinkedIn, Facebook, YouTube, and Flickr updates, as well as posts managed by several popular blogging platforms, such as Moveable Type, WordPress, Blogger, Lotus Live, and Drupal. It also measures how the audience is interacting with all this content – for instance, how much they are commenting on posts, clicking on links, or retweeting updates. (Jonietz, 2009: 1)

However, how all that data relates to ROI is a question businesses will have to address and is ripe for research.

Braithwaite (2010) states that the essential steps to a successful social media marketing plan involve: (1) listening (to determine what is being discussed and how you can contribute before launching your company or brand into the social media world); (2) positioning your brand around an ethos; (3) clarifying and determining an overall objective and outlining a social media plan to fit it; (4) setting trackable goals (defining specific measurable goals to provide a benchmark against which to evaluate performance); (5) developing a content strategy in order to attract and engage your target; (6) choosing appropriate social media tools (such as Facebook and Twitter) to maximize your social media bang; (7) implementing and engaging the plan by joining the conversation and participating as a genuine member of the community and (8) monitoring and evaluating progress through appropriate measurement and monitoring systems.

Maynard (2009) explains the need for social media marketing campaigns and indicates that since the brand is the company's face to the world, how it is perceived and what people say about it are measures of success. She recommends that companies, first, make their website the hub of all social media activity and, second, use social media for buzz, customer service, brand loyalty, search engine optimization (SEO), networking, thought leadership, promotion and sales, driving traffic, deepening relationships and getting feedback. She provides a general framework for a social media marketing strategy (objectives, target audience, perceptions, desired response, tone/personality, and brand values) and gives guidance in applying this general framework to Twitter and Facebook.

Many sport organizations, and marketing professionals may approach social media simply as a list of technologies (blogs, podcasts, and so on) that can be deployed as required, depending on the marketing goal. However, this may not be the best method of deploying social media initiatives. Rather, a more coherent approach is to start with the target audience and then determine the type of relationship that the organization wants to build with them (Radian6, 2010). Happe (2010) warns that metrics should be selected based on relevance to the company or brand goals and objectives, and lists potential social media marketing metrics: (1) activity metrics (page views, unique visitors, members, posts – ideas/threads, number of groups – networks or forums, comments and trackbacks, tags/ratings/rankings, time spent on the website, contributors, word count, referrals, completed profiles, connections between members, relationship ratios, periods – day, week, month, year and frequency of visits, posts and comments); (2) survey metrics (satisfaction, affinity, quality and speed of issue resolution, referral likelihood and relevance of content and connections) and (3) ROI measurements (marketing/sales, cost per number of engaged prospects – community versus other initiatives), number of leads/period, number of qualified leads/period, ratio of qualified to non-qualified leads, cost of lead, time to qualified lead, lead conversion, number of pre-sales reference calls – to other customers, average new revenue per customer, lifetime value of customers, customer support, customer satisfaction, number of initiated support tickets per customer per period, and support cost per customer in community). Similarly, and as identified earlier, Rust et al. (2010) identify customer (fan-) profitability, customer lifetime value, customer equity, customer equity share as important metrics in a customer-centric (versus product/service-centric) marketing campaign, whereas Gummesson (2008) recommends the 30Rs.

Hanna and Donnelley Interactive (2009) reported in their business social media benchmarking study that companies typically judge social media success based on metrics of engagement (with prospects and customers), brand impact (awareness and reputation) and leads (quantity and quality). Actually, a number of digital social media marketing e-handbooks concerning the how-tos of social media measurement and analyses are also available online. Specific examples include Radian6 (*Practical Social Media Measurement and Analysis*), Freeman (*Social Media: Extending and Growing*

Your Brand) and *Social Media for Small Business* guides on Facebook. In addition, many Web analytics companies such as Click Tale Limited, Coremetrics, Omniture, WebTrends and One Stat have emerged to help organizations collect, measure, analyse and report social media data to optimize social media usage in the service of organizational objectives. Web analytics can help organizations measure traffic and do business and market research. According to Wikipedia (2011) there are two categories of web analytics: off-site (measurement of brand's potential audience – opportunity, share of voice – visibility and buzz), and on-site (measurement of what landing pages encourage people to make a purchase, of social media performance fit with key performance indicators, and so on).

Lake (in Social Media Optimization, 2009) identified the following metrics as appropriate for measuring the efficacy of a social media marketing venture: traffic, interaction, sales, leads, search marketing, brand metrics, PR, customer engagement, retention and profits. MarketingSherpa (2009: 14) identifies the following metrics for social media marketing: increase brand or product awareness; improve brand or product reputation; improve public relations; increase website traffic; increase lead generation; increase offline sales revenue; and increase online sales revenue. According to the MarketingSherpa search media report (2010: 14) social media is believed to be a more effective tactic (than search engine optimization) for marketing for objectives that are new to measurement (for example, improved brand or product reputation and public relations). Even though many marketers think these objectives are difficult to measure, the growth of social monitoring tools (for example, Trackur, Spiral16, Radian6, search. twitter.com, Facebook Business Page) makes it possible to define brand reputation and reach.

The annual e-metrics optimization summit (see Emetrics 2010) may be a resource for learning about website optimization, search analytics, campaign optimization, behavioral targeting, competitive analysis, customer experience, public sector metrics, statistical analysis, business implementation and multi-channel marketing metrics. The Sports Social Media Index (SSMI) was developed by Sports Geek (2010) to rate the performance of social media used by sport franchises. The SSMI covers the key platforms of social media, how each platform is used and how each team engages its fan base. The SSMI also rates teams on their execution on social media platforms relative to the teams' fit with best practices engaged in by teams (such as the Dallas Mavericks, LA Kings and New York Knicks) in the vanguard of digital sport marketing.

Researchers interested in sport social media may consider joining a sport marketing social networking group such as Sport Marketing 2.0 (www.sportsmarketing20.com), which provides up-to-date insights regarding best practices in sport media marketing, how to utilize available platforms, who uses sport media well, and the latest technologies. In addition, the Social Media and Sport Summits and BeyondSport.org provide information relevant to social media marketing and research in sport. Sideman (2009) contends digital marketing through social media can address the following media goals of most sport enterprises, goals that could also be used as metrics: generate fan participation and discussion; establish control over team messages and news; announce signings, injury updates or other breaking news; create relationships among fans, athletes and coaches; provide fans with 'inside' information and product promotions; boost traffic to the official team website, and sell more tickets.

Overall, however, the landscape regarding why, what and how to implement effective marketing strategies through social media seems to be changing almost daily, given the exponential growth and use of social media outlets and the trial and error nature of the research into this burgeoning field. The current status of sport social media, the changing nature of marketing, causal complexity and the dynamic nature of social media marketing provide unlimited opportunity for those interested in research focused on social media and sport marketing. Relative to research related to social media marketing in sport business, however, any of the aforementioned models or guides could form the basis for evaluating sport business social media marketing efforts.

6   OVERALL IMPLICATIONS FOR RESEARCH IN SOCIAL MEDIA SPORT MARKETING

'Research is the systematic activity directed towards objectively investigating specific problems in order to discover the relationships between and among variables. It seeks to answer specific questions' (Nyanjui, 2010). Fundamentally, therefore, research is about asking questions and then answering them through observation, survey or experiment in an organized fashion in order to describe, explain and/or predict phenomenon or control events. According to the Web Center for Social Research Methods (2006) there are three basic types of research questions (descriptive, correlational, or causal) that can be applied (usually in combination) to research in social media sport marketing:

1. *Descriptive*: when a study is designed primarily to describe what is going on or what exists. For example, 'How are sport enterprises using social media in their marketing efforts?'
2. *Correlational*: when a study is designed to look at the relationships between two or more variables. For example, 'What is the relationship between the level of social media used in a marketing campaign and team (or athlete) brand awareness or brand recognition?'
3. *Causal*: when a study is designed to determine whether one or more variables (for example, a social media campaign) causes or affects one or more outcome variables (for example, ticket sales). For example, 'What is the effect of a new pre-season social media campaign on the number of season tickets sold?'

The basic research process may still be able to function as the fundamental framework for any research study related to social media and sport marketing, whether from the perspective of a scholar or a marketing professional. Researchers in academe, whether engaging in qualitative or quantitative forms of research, typically employ some version of the following: first, identify the research problem or question, review the literature, choose a research design, identify the data collection method, design the data collection forms, select the sample, collect, analyse and interpret the data relative to the research problem or question, and do the research report (Morgan and Summers, 2005). Whereas, although such methods have been criticized as inadequate

(Ehrenberg and Barnard, 2000), those in sport marketing research may choose the DECIDE method: Define the marketing problem; Enumerate the controllable and uncontrollable decision factors; Collect relevant information; Identify the best alternative; Develop and implement a marketing plan, and Evaluate the decision and the decision process.

It is clear that the fast-paced, constantly changing, networked, integrated and relentlessly competitive (but simultaneously cooperative) business environment of today has changed the world and appears to demand a change in thinking in order to more successfully navigate through the current milieu in order to collect data, address problems and capitalize on opportunities. Martin (2009) contends that deductive and/or inductive thinking are necessary but not sufficient for this rapidly changing world and suggests the addition of abductive thinking – integrative or design thinking that builds its own way of understanding what's going on and then goes on to develop ways to address the problem. The abductive thinking stance involves merging models or creating new models to creatively develop new options for solving problems, addressing issues or creating opportunity. This thinking has four components (salience, causality, sequencing and resolution) and involves the logic of 'what might be' – it is critical to the creative process according to Martin (2005).

The webifying of the world ushers in the need for changes in the way that research is conducted. As an example, the Inspired Research Wiki (2010) which was designed for sharing creative research methods used by planners, researchers and the design community, is replete with innovative ideas for collecting data using interactive media and for sparking new ideas for 'what might be'. Abductive-thinking researchers may want to visit that wiki to obtain or adapt ideas and methods for their planned research. Similarly, Taylor and Coffee (2008: 13) identify categories and examples for different forms of innovation in research. The following represents an expansion of these three categories. These categories could be adapted and applied to any of the social media platforms (Twitter, Facebook, YouTube, and so on) using specific digital technologies (Internet, mobile, and so on) for sport business research in social media.

1. *New designs or methods*:
   – new ways of collecting or generating quantitative or qualitative data (for example, on-line interviews or observations, enhanced use of photography and other audio/visual methods, sensory ethnography, soundscapes, eliciting creative writings from respondents);
   – new analytical techniques (for example, the development of new software packages, undertaking critical discourse analysis);
   – new representations of qualitative research (for example, visual 'texts', using hypermedia, ethnographic fiction, multilayered and multi-vocal texts).
2. *New concepts*:
   – generating new ways of thinking about research (for example, drawing on autobiographical practices, practitioner-led research, multi-modal research practices);
   – developing new methodological concepts (for example, hypermedia ethnography, qualitative longitudinal research).
3. *New ways of doing research*:
   – working with new participants or new groups;

– combining methods and methodologies (for example, textual with visual, qualitative with quantitative);
– cross-disciplinary research;
– responding to changing research landscapes (for example, enhanced information and communication technology (ICT) capacities, new ethical challenges and guidelines).

In addition, the Research Information Network (2011) provides an extremely helpful guide (replete with links and resources) to assist researchers to use social media in their research. Academic and research blogs, research and writing collaboration tools and project management tools are also presented in this guide. Those interested in applying social media research to sport business would find it a very worthwhile reference that could stimulate a number of ideas for research. An example of innovative research methodology (for scholars and marketing practitioners) using social media and an integrative, cross-organizational (that is, university business schools, sport business, research companies, and so on) format involves the ESPN XP project. ESPN XP provides a vehicle to introduce new techniques and innovative methodologies (cross-media measurement) to sport industry research:

in March 2010 ESPN Research+Analytics revealed plans for ESPN XP, an encompassing research initiative, to study consumer behavior around major sporting events beginning with the 2010 FIFA World Cup South Africa. Using one of the largest collections of research companies ever assembled, plus a top-tier business school, ESPN XP attempted to measure media usage and advertiser effects for the World Cup across all media platforms – television, radio, Internet, mobile and print – in order to advance knowledge about multi-media use and the total and incremental impact it has on their clients' media campaigns. Initial research companies joining ESPN in this initiative included the Keller Fay Group, Knowledge Networks, the Media Behavior Institute, the Nielsen Company and the Wharton Interactive Media Initiative (WIMI) [of the Wharton Business School]. ESPN will take the best of what is learned from the World Cup and apply it to football in the fall and other sports during 2011. The goal is to create a scalable research plan to measure cross-media audiences 12 months out of the year by 2012. Wharton's focus on online behavior using ESPN.com, ESPN Mobile, ESPN3 and ESPN Deportes (the Spanish-language portal) is to build a state-of-the-art predictive model to understand and project 'multichannel' behaviors of its audience across digital properties (Internet and mobile). The academic involvement means opportunities for graduate students as well. From this project they hope to develop a rich database and predictive models for academic researchers as well as for professional marketers. (ESPN Media Zone, 2010)

The commercial goal of most sport enterprises regarding their digital initiatives is to leverage as much of their sport content across as many multi-media platforms as possible in order to aggregate as many consumers as possible. Therefore, researchers may want to focus on any one or more of these dimensions at any point in the digital media value chain, which includes: (1) various types of sport content and digital rights ownership; (2) technical aspects of digital production; (3) distribution channels including sport specific portals, websites, and so on; (4) delivery technologies such as broadband, satellite, cable, and so on, and (5) reception by consumers via specific digital devices. In addition, there may soon be synergistic mergers of different social media to build partnerhips (for example, iTunes + Facebook + ?) to accomplish business or social

Table 10.1   Major concepts matrix

Author/s and year	Toffler (1980)	Ritzer and Jurgenson (2010)	Sullivan (2009), Toffler and Toffler (2006), Kleiner (2009)	Deighton and Kornfeld (2007), Rust et al. (2010), Kleiner (2009)	Prahalad (2009)	Kelly (2009)
Concept/s	Prosumer vs consumer or producer	Prosumer capitalism	Attention economy vs intention economy	Diminution of marketing	Co-creation of value	Competition vs shared web of value

Table 10.2   Relevant definitions for marketing and social media

Author/s	Morgan and Summers (2005)	Mullin et al. (2008)	Braithwaite (2010)	Walsh (2009)	Kaplan and Haenlein (2010), Lietsala and Sirkkunen (2008)
Idea/concept	Marketing research	Sport marketing	Social media marketing	Digital marketing	Social media, content areas and platforms

responsibility goals, and the impact of such synergy on sport marketing would be an interesting study.

For the purposes of flexibility and creativity, especially given the colossal pace of change in information technology, a number of research idea-matrices (Tables 10.1 to 10.5) are presented that can be used by scholars and/or marketing practitioners to generate research ideas. These, of course, should be considered flexible for additions or deletions given the time-dependent nature of the work and the quickly changing social media environment, but could represent a quick reference for identifying variables or generating ideas for (descriptive, correlational or causal) research or evaluation related to social media and the marketing of sport or of the marketing or products/services through sport. These matrices include: major concepts, relevant definitions, theoretical foundations, other metric models and tools, and models for social media application for research.

In conclusion, it must be recognized that social media and the techniques and processes related to marketing using social media are changing at an incredible rate and will require continual monitoring for those involved in social media research. As such, we identified the need for sport marketing researchers who are abductive thinkers who can design, combine and use innovative research methodologies as stimulated by the continually evolving technology. Ultimately, however, research prospects related to social media and sport marketing are vast for scholars and marketing professionals alike, and are replete with opportunities for designing new research methodologies.

Table 10.3   Theoretical foundations: rethinking marketing and metrics – beyond the 4Ps

Author/s and year	Proposed model or concept
Vargo and Lusch (2004)	Service-centered logic vs services centered logic
Gummesson (2002, 2007, 2008)	Relationship or R marketing
Clark (2009)	Social media brand promotion
Kunz (2008)	Mindsets of modes marketing model
Deighton and Kornfeld (2007)	Discrete roles for social media
Rust et al. (2010)	Move from marketing products to cultivating customers
Ramaswamy and Prahalad (2006)	Customer co-creation of value, new form of strategic capital vs product-centric view of value creation
Dailey (2009)	Comprehensive guide to social media marketing
Meerman Scott (2010)	New rules for marketing and PR
Braithwaite (2010)	Essential steps to a social media marketing plan

Table 10.4 Other metric models and tools for social media research

Author/s (company) and year	Chris (in Social Media Optimization, 2009)	Marketing Sherpa (2010)	Sideman (2009)	Sports Geek (2010)	Spredfast.com, Radian6, and so on	ClickTale, Coremetrics, Omniture, WebTrends, One Stat
Proposed model or concept	Metrics for social media campaigns	Goals for social media	Goals for social media in sport	Sport Social Media Index (SSMI)	Web-based companies that set up and manage social media marketing plans and strategies	Web analytics models
Content areas and metrics	Traffic Interaction Sales Leads Search marketing Brand metrics PR Customer engagement Retention Profits	Increase brand or product awareness Improve brand or product reputation Improve PR Increase website traffic Increase lead generation Increase offline sales revenue Increase online sales revenue	Generate fan participation and discussion Establish control over team messages Announce signings, injury updates, or other breaking news Create relationships among fans, athletes, and coaches Provide fans with 'inside' information and product promotions Boost traffic to the official team website Sell more tickets	Rates the performance of sports franchise using social media. SSMI covers key platforms of sports social media, how each platform is used and how fan base is engaged	Social media planning and monitoring tools	Helps organizations collect, measure, analyse, and report social media data to optimize social media usage in the service of organizational objectives

Table 10.5   Models for social media applications and research innovation around descriptive, correlational or causal research questions

Author/s and year	Morgan and Summers (2005) and Wikipedia	Martin (2005, 2009)	Inspired Research Wiki (2010), Taylor and Coffee (2008)	Wharton School with ESPN research model	Kelly (2009), Rose (2009), Peck (2010)
Model	Traditional research model, DECIDE model for marketing	Abductive thinking (or integrative or design thinking)	New research designs and methodology driven by social media	ESPN XP project	Predictions for social media use in sport

REFERENCES

Alexa (eds) (2010), Top sites: the top 500 sites on the web, available at: http://www.alexa.com/topsites (accessed 22 June 2010).

Braithwaite, D. (2010), Social media strategy, *PXLD DESIGN, WEB & SOCIAL MEDIA BLOGS*, 10 May, available at: http://pixldinc.com/blog/social-media/social-media-strategy-steps-to-successful-implementation/ (accessed 20 May 2011).

Chartered Management Institute (eds) (2001), Alvin Toffler: the futurologist's futurologist, available at: http://www.thefreelibrary.com/Alvin+Toffler+:+The+Futurologist%27s+Futurologist.-a085608629 (accessed 10 November 2010).

Clark, R. (2009), The 5 F's of social media, *Richard Clark's Marketing Blog*, 2 November, available at: http://richclark.wordpress.com/2009/11/02/5-fs-of-social-media/ (accessed 30 November 2010).

Dailey, P. (2009), Social media: finding its way into your business strategy and culture, available at: http://www.linkageinc.com/thinking/linkageleader/Documents/Patrick_Dailey_Social_Media_Finding_Its_Way.pdf (accessed 21 January 2011).

Davis, A. (2009), Three keys to social media success, available at: http://prezi.com/wj_hkk6_wreo/ (accessed 23 December 2010).

Deighton, J. and Kornfeld, L. (2007), Digital interactivity: unanticipated consequences for markets, marketing, and consumers, *Harvard Business School Working Paper*, 08–017, available at: http://www.hbs.edu/research/pdf/08–017.pdf (accessed 10 May 2010).

Dolles, H. and Söderman, S. (2011), Sport as a business: introduction, in H. Dolles and S. Söderman (eds), *Sport as a Business: International, Professional and Commercial Aspects*, Basingstoke: Palgrave Macmillan, pp. 1–12.

Dolles, H. and Söderman, S. (2013), The network of value captures in football club management: a framework to develop and analyse competitive advantage in professional team sports, in S. Söderman and H. Dolles (eds), *Handbook of Research on Sport and Business*, Cheltenham, UK and Northampton, MA, USA: Edward Elgar, pp. 367–95.

Ehrenberg, A. and Barnard, N. (2000), Problems with marketing decision models, available at: http://members.byronsharp.com/6896.pdf (accessed 2 July 2010).

Emarketer (eds) (2009), Social media measurement lags adoption, *Emarketer Daily Newsletter*, 22 September, available at: www.emarketer.com/Article.aspx?R=1007286 (accessed 12 November 2010).

Emetrics (eds) (2010), Marketing optimization summit, available at: www.emetrics.org (accessed 22 April 2010).

ESPN Media Zone3 (eds) (2010), ESPN launches unprecedented cross-media research initiative: ESPN XP, *ESPN Media Zone*, available at: www.espnmediazone3.com/us/2010/03/espn-launches-unprecedented-cross-media-research-initiative-espn-xp/ (accessed 10 June 2010).

Ferguson, T. (2009), The rise of the medical prosumer, *HealthyWorld Online*, available at: http://www.healthy.net/scr/Article.asp?Id=1039 (accessed 12 November 2010).

Fisher, L. (2006), The thought leader interview: Alvin Toeffler, *strategy + business*, (45), available at: www.strategy-business.com/article/06408?gko=decb3 (accessed 5 April 2010).

Gillin, P. (2007), *The New Influencers: A Marketers Guide to Social Marketing*, Sanger, CA: Quill Driver Books/Word Dancer Press.

Gummesson, E. (2002), *Total Relationship Marketing*, Oxford: Butterworth-Heinemann.

Gummesson, E. (2007), Exit services marketing – enter service marketing, *Journal of Customer Behaviour*, **6** (2), 113–14.

Gummesson, E. (2008), *Total Relationship Marketing*, 3rd edn, Oxford: Butterworth-Heinemann.

Hanna, B. and R.H. Donnelley Interactive (2010), 2009 B2B Social Media Benchmarking Study, available at: http://www.business.com/info/b2b-social-media-benchmark-study (accessed 1 June 2010).

Happe, R. (2010), Social media metrics, available at: www.thesocialorganization.com/social-media-metrics.html (accessed 5 April 2010).

KLM (eds) (2010), Cashing in the clicks, *Holland Herald – Inflight Magazine of KLM*, May, available at: http://holland-herald.com/2010/05/add-it-up/ (accessed 1 June 2010).

Inspired Research Wiki (2010), Inspired research, available at: http://inspiredresearch.pbworks.com/Inspired%20Research#Links (accessed 10 June 2010).

Irwin, R., Sutton, W. and McCarthy, L. (2008), *Sport Promotion and Sales Management*, 2nd edn, Champaign, IL: Human Kinetics.

Jonietz, E. (2009), Making money with social media, *Technology Review*, 29 December, available at: www.technologyreview.com/news/416939/making-money-with-social-media/ (accessed 19 November 2012).

Kaplan, A. and Haenlein, M. (2010), Users of the world, unite! The challenges and opportunities of social media, *Business Horizons*, **53** (1), 59–68.

Kelly, C. (2009), How pro sports will dramatically change: stadiums will shrink. Players may be robotic duplicates. Fans? Not necessary, *thestar.com*, 16 August, available at: www.thestar.com/news/insight/article/681818 (accessed 1 December 2009).

Kleiner, A. (2009), The thought leader interview: Esther Dyson, *strategy+business*, (55), available at: http://www.strategy-business.com/media/file/sb55_09209.pdf (accessed 14 December 2009).

Kunz, B. (2008), Why widgets won't work, *Bloomberg Business Week*, 3 March, available at: www.business-week.com/technology/content/feb2008/tc20080229_131531.htm (accessed 2 April 2010).

Learmonth, M. (2010), Nike breaks own viral record with World Cup ad, *Ad Age DIGITAL*, 27 May, available at: http://adage.com/digital/article?article_id=144083 (accessed 28 May 2010).

Lefer, L. (2008), Social media in plain English, available at: www.youtube.com/watch?v=MpIOClX1jPE (accessed 1 May 2010).

Lenhart, A. (2009), Social networks grow: friending mom and dad, *Pew Research Center Publications*, 14 January, available at: http://pewresearch.org/pubs/1079/social-networks-grow (accessed 8 December 2009).

Lietsala, K. and Sirkkunen, E. (2008), *Social Media: Introduction to the Tools and Processes of Participatory Economy*, Hypermedia Laboratory Net Series 17, Tampere: University of Tampere Press.

Light, L. (2010), Marketing is being devalued, *Forbes.com*, 24 March, available at: www.forbes.com/2010/03/23/devalued-marketing-consumers-cmo-network-larry-light.html (accessed 2 April 2010).

Linnell, N. (2010), Measuring social media with web analytics: part 2, *Search Engine Watch*, 5 April, available at: http://searchenginewatch.com/3639988 (accessed 16 June 2010).

Loechner, J. (2009), Social media for commercial decisions, *Media Post Blogs*, 28 May, available at: www.mediapost.com/publications/?fa=Articles.showArticle&art_aid=106676 (accessed 2 April 2010).

Mandese, J. (2009), Study finds social nets 'realistically' near top of 2010 media buying plans, *Online Media Daily*, 10 September, available at: www.mediapost.com/publications/?fa=Articles.showArticle&art_aid=113269 (accessed 12 November 2009).

MarketingSherpa (eds) (2009), *2010 Social Media Marketing Benchmark Report*, Warren, RI: MarketingSherpa, available at: www.marketingsherpa.com/SocialMediaMarketing2010EXE.pdf (accessed 2 December 2011).

MarketingSherpa (eds) (2010), *2011 Search Marketing Benchmark Report – SEO Edition*, Warren, RI: MarketingSherpa, available at: http://www.marketingsherpa.com/Search2011seoExcerpt.pdf (accessed 2 December 2011).

Marobella, P. (2009), Social media in sports: the athlete, *Slideshare – Present Yourself*, 16 March, available at: www.slideshare.net/marobella/social-media-in-sports-the-athlete-1151579 (accessed 20 December 2009).

Martin, R. (2005), Creativity that goes deep, *Bloomberg Businessweek*, 3 August, available at: www.business-week.com/innovate/content/aug2005/di20050803_823317.htm (accessed 10 June 2010).

Martin, R. (2009), *The Design of Business: Why Design Thinking is the Next Competitive Advantage*, Boston, MA: Harvard Business School Press.

Maynard, W. (2009), Social media bootcamp, *Slideshare – Present Yourself*, 13 October, available at: www.slide-share.net/wendymaynard/social-media-bootcamp-by-wendy-maynard?src=related_normal&rel=3611267 (accessed 6 June 2010).

Meermoan Scott, D. (2010), *The New Rules of Marketing and PR: How to Use Social Media*, Hoboken, NJ: John Wiley & Sons.

Morgan, M.J. and Summers, J. (2005), *Sports Marketing*, Southbank, Victoria: Thomson Press.

Mullin, B., Hardy, S. and Sutton, W. (2008), *Sport Marketing*, 4th edn, Champaign, IL: Human Kinetics.

Nielsen Report on Social Media (eds) (2009), The global online media landscape: identifying opportunities in a challenging market, available at: http://blog.nielsen.com/nielsenwire/wp-content/uploads/2009/04/nielsen-online-global-lanscapefinal1.pdf (accessed 1 January 2010).

Nyanjui, P.J. (2010), Research portal, available at: http://wikieducator.org/Research (accessed 4 May 2010).

Peck, J. (2009), Sports and social media predictions 2010, available at: http://www.scribd.com/doc/24084005/Sports-Social-Media-Predictions-2010 (accessed 1 January 2010).

Perez, S. (2009), Social networking use triples from only a year go, *New York Times*, 25 September, available at: www.nytimes.com/external/readwriteweb/2009/09/25/25readwriteweb-social-networking-use-triples-from-only-a-y-72670.html (accessed 2 December 2009).

Prahalad, C.K. (2009), Interview for thinkers50, available at: www.thinkers50.com/interviews/1/2009 (accessed 20 November 2009).

Radian6 (2010), New media, new metrics, *Video & Presentations Radian6*, 5 March, available at: http://www.radian6.com/resources/library/new-media-new-metrics/ (accessed 18 June 2011).

Ramaswamy, V. and Prahalad, C.K. (2006), *The Future of Competition: Co-creating Unique Value with Customers*, Boston, MA: Harvard Business School Press.

Research Information Network (eds) (2011), *Social Media: A Guide for Researchers*, International Center for Guidance Studies at the University of Derby, available at: http://tech.groups.yahoo.com/group/libtech/message/4707?var=1 (accessed 31 December 2011).

Ritzer, G. and Jurgenson, N. (2010), Production, consumption, prosumption: the nature of capitalism in the age of the digital 'prosumer', *Journal of Consumer Culture*, **10** (1), 13–36.

Rose, J. (2009), 5 predictions for athletes on social media in 2010, *Mashable Social Media*, 17 December, available at: http://mashable.com/2009/12/17/athletes-predictions-social-media/ (accessed 28 December 2009).

Rust, R., Moorman, C. and Bhalla, G. (2010), Rethinking marketing, *Harvard Business Review*, **88** (1), 94–110.

Sherman, C. (2009), NHL Facebook page to debut with virtual gifts, *Virtual Goods News*, 26 October, available at: www.virtualgoodsnews.com/2009/10/nhl-facebook-page-to-debut-with-virtual-gifts.html (accessed 6 December 2009).

Sideman, G. (2009), How the NBA is using social media, *Mashable Social Media*, 9 June, available at: http://mashable.com/2009/06/09/social-media-nba/ (accessed 16 November 2009).

Siegel, L. (2008), *Against the Machine: Being Human in the Age of the Electronic Mob*, New York: Random House.

Social Media Optimization (eds) (2009), 10 ways to measure a social media campaign, available at: http://social-media-optimization.com/2009/03/10-ways-to-measure-a-social-media-campaign/ (accessed 10 June 2010).

Sports Geek (eds) (2010), Sport social media index, *Slideshare – Present Yourself*, 27 June, available at: www.slideshare.net/SportsGeek/sports-social-media-index-nrl-2010-4631799 (accessed 2 July 2010).

Sports Marketing2.0 (eds) (2010), Re-thinking sports marketing now that fans are in charge: a digital think-tank for sports marketers in the Web 2.0 world, available at: www.sportsmarketing20.com (accessed 8 January 2010).

Stern, A. (2010), The best social media definition today, *Center Networks Posts*, 21 January, available at: http://www.centernetworks.com/social-media-definition (accessed 10 June 2010).

Sullivan, L. (2009), 2010: the year social marketing gets serious, *Online Media Daily*, 21 December, available at: www.mediapost.com/publications/article/2010-the-year/-social-marketing-gets-serious/119493 (accessed 19 November 2012).

Taylor, C. and Coffee, A. (2008), Innovation in qualitative research methods: opportunities and challenges, *Cardiff School of Social Sciences Working Paper Series*, no. 121, available at: http://www.cardiff.ac.uk/socsi/resources/wp121.pdf (accessed 10 June 2010).

Toffler, A. (1970), *Future Shock*, New York: Bantam.

Toffler, A. (1980), *The Third Wave*, New York: Bantam.

Toffler, A. (1990), *Powershift*, New York: Bantam.

Toffler, A. and Toffler, H. (2006), *Revolutionary Wealth*, New York: Random House.

Underhill, J. and Kurit, E. (2009), Upsidedown iceberg, available at: http://www.youtube.com/watch?v=gza8dvN8Hkc&feature=related (accessed 5 June 2010).

Van Grove, J. (2010), Revealed: the 100 most social brands of 2009, *Mashable Social Media*, 4 January, available at: http://mashable.com/2010/01/04/most-buzzed-about-brand/ (accessed 10 January 2010).

Vargo, S. and Lusch, R. (2004), Evolving to a new dominant logic for marketing, *Journal of Marketing*, **68** (1), 1–7.

Vitrue (eds) (2011), The Vitrue 100: Consumer electronics reigned supreme in 2010, available at: http://vitrue.com/blog/the-vitrue-100-consumer-electronics-reigned-supreme-in-2010/ (accessed 7 January 2011).

Walsh, M. (2009), Digital and social influence marketing, *Slideshare – Present Yourself*, 23 July, available at: www.slideshare.net/martinwalsh/monologue-to-dialogue-social-media-and-digital-marketing-mwalsh-1759244 (accessed 5 April 2010).

Web Center for Social Research Methods (2006), Research Methods Knowledge Base, available at: www.socialresearchmethods.net/kb/resques.php (accessed 5 April 2010).

Wikipedia (2011), Web analytics, available at: http://en.wikipedia.org/wiki/Web_analytics (accessed 31 December 2011).

11 The economics of listed sports events in a digital era of broadcasting: a case study of the UK

Chris Gratton and Harry Arne Solberg

1 INTRODUCTION

This chapter focuses on direct regulations in sports broadcasting that regulate which channels are allowed to broadcast specific sports events. Examples of such regulations are the European Listed Events legislation and the Australian Anti-Siphoning List, which prevent pay-television (TV) channels from broadcasting events that are of special value for society. It specifically concentrates on the UK since, in 2009, an independent review of the UK listed events legislation was carried out by an Independent Advisory Panel (IAP) of experts appointed by the then Minister for Culture Media and Sport, Andy Burnham. This IAP received evidence from broadcasters, national and international governing bodies of sport, and media experts over a four-month period.

The aim of this chapter is to use that evidence (at least, the part of it that is in the public domain) to examine the question of whether or not in the coming digital age of broadcasting it is still necessary for governments to intervene in broadcasting markets to ensure that major sports events are shown on channels available to the whole nation or, at least, a high percentage of it. The methodology used to achieve this aim is outlined below. Although the case study is of the UK situation, the research evidence and approach is of more general validity. As the chapter indicates, many European countries have similar listed events. Most of these lists overlap in that all refer to the Summer and Winter Olympics (with the exception of Ireland which excludes the Winter Olympics), and the World Cup and European Championships in football, although some countries do not include all the matches in the finals of these tournaments as the UK does. The evidence provided by the international governing bodies which own the broadcasting rights for these sports (the International Olympic Committee (IOC), the Fédération Internationale de Football Association (FIFA), and the Union of European Football Associations (UEFA)) is relevant to all these countries, not just the UK. The principle of listing and the arguments for and against again are also relevant for all countries. They are particularly relevant at the present time since many of these countries are also looking at these lists closely and reviewing the legislative situation particularly because of the new digital broadcasting environment that is emerging. As well as the UK, Ireland and Australia were also carrying out a review of their listed events over the same time period as the UK review reported on here.

Before coming to the new UK evidence, however, it is first necessary to look at the background to this type of government intervention in sport broadcasting markets.

2 HISTORY OF LISTED EVENTS LEGISLATION

Throughout the 1990s, the growth of pay-TV channels raised concerns regarding the general public's ability to watch popular sport. European politicians were alarmed in 1996, when News Corporation almost bid the Olympic Rights away from the European Broadcasting Union (EBU). Their fear received more fuel when FIFA, the same year, sold the 2002 and 2006 World Cup Soccer finals to the German Kirch corporation and the Swiss ISL marketing agency, instead of to the EBU as they had done in the past. As consequence of this, viewers in many nations would not be able to watch the entire tournament on free-to-air broadcasters as in the past. In 2005, the EBU lost the rights for Euro 2008 to Sportfive, a media agency, for a fee of more than €600 million. Live matches in European premier soccer leagues have mainly been broadcast exclusively on pay-TV channels since the late 1990s. In general, free-to-air channels have been restricted to showing highlight programmes. In Australia the growth of pay-TV channels in the 1990s caused a fear of a similar development, so that people in general would not be able to watch their favourite sports on free-to-air television.

A consequence of this development is that governments on the two continents have invented regulations that define sports programmes as a part of the public domain. Late in the 1990s so-called Listed Events Regulations were established in several European countries, while the Australian Anti-siphoning List was launched in the mid-1990s.

2.1 The European Listed Events Regulations

Listed Events was first introduced as a national regulation in the UK in 1984. It prevented certain sporting events from being shown exclusively on a pay-per-view basis, whilst allowing the events to be shown on non-terrestrial subscription channels. Later the regulation was tightened in the Broadcasting Act 1996, which extended the prohibition from pay-per-view to subscription channels, but without changing the list of events (Cowie and Williams, 1997). The idea was later adopted by the European Commission in the 'Television Without Frontiers' directive (EU, 1989). The principle in the directive is that each member state can draw up a list of events, national or non-national, that it considers being of major importance for the society. These events should only be allowed to be broadcast on channels with a minimum penetration decided in the respective nations. Among the nations that had passed their own list by 2005 were Austria, France, Germany, Ireland, Italy and the UK, while regulations were on their way in other countries. Denmark was among the first nations to draw up a list, but withdrew it in 2002. The minimum penetration that is required to be allowed to broadcast events that are on the list varies. The UK requires that channels that can broadcast listed events have a minimum penetration of 95 per cent, Ireland and Italy 90 per cent, France 85 per cent, Austria 70 per cent and Germany 67 per cent (European Commission, 2008).

2.2 The Australian Anti-siphoning List

The Australian Anti-siphoning List, which is contained in section 115 of the Broadcasting Services Act 1992, empower the Minister for Communications, Information Technology and the Arts to list in a formal notice events that should be available on free-to-air television for viewing by the general public. The first list was gazetted in the Broadcasting Services (Events) Notice No. 1 of 1994 (Australian Government, 2010). According to the guidelines its purpose is to protect the access of Australian viewers to events of national importance and cultural significance on free-to-air television by preventing pay-TV operators from siphoning off television coverage of those events before free-to-air broadcasters have had an opportunity to obtain the broadcasting rights. Free-to-air television providers include national broadcasters such as the Australian Broadcasting Corporation (ABC) or Special Broadcasting Services (SBS), as well as the commercial channels, Channel Seven, Channel Nine and Channel Ten, which all can be watched by the majority of viewers.

The channels that are allowed to broadcast events on the Anti-siphoning List must have a minimum penetration of 50 per cent of Australian television households. Less than one in four Australian households had access to subscription television in 2004. This regulation also allows events to be de-listed if no free-to-air broadcaster is interested in acquiring the broadcast rights, which would allow pay-TV broadcasters to broadcast the event. However, the Anti-siphoning List is not a list of sporting events reserved solely for free-to-air channels. It does not guarantee them exclusive rights to such events. Pay-TV channels are allowed to acquire such rights, but not exclusively as they also must be held by free-to-air channels that meet the 50 per cent requirement. Furthermore, the regulation does not compel free-to-air broadcasters to acquire the rights to listed events. Neither does it compel them to broadcast events to which they hold rights.

The anti-siphoning provisions were amended in 2001 to allow the automatic de-listing of specified events 1008 hours (six weeks) before the start of the event. Later, the period has been extended to 2016 hours (or 12 weeks). The reason for this amendment was to provide adequate time for free-to-air broadcasters to negotiate broadcast rights, while at the same time providing a timely window prior to the event, for pay-TV licensees to acquire and promote an event, if a free-to-air broadcaster does not acquire the broadcasting rights.

2.3   A Comparison between European and Australian Regulation

A comparison between the European and Australian regulation reveal similarities as well as differences. First, the Australian regulation is the most comprehensive of the two. The threshold for being listed is lower than in Europe. As an example, all matches in Australian Rules Football and Rugby League Football are listed. The equivalence of this would be that the UK Listed Event covered the entire matches in the English Premier League and Rugby Super League; the German list covering all Bundesliga matches as well as domestic leagues in handball; the Italian list covering all Seria A matches and all matches in the domestic leagues in basketball. However, such a pattern is not found in Europe. Indeed, no nation has listed matches in domestic premier leagues, in soccer or in any other team sports. This partly explains why European pay-TV channels have acquired a dominating position in soccer.

As another example, the Anti-siphoning List includes the Commonwealth Games while the UK regulation has them only on the B-list. This allows a pay-TV channel to broadcast live programmes as long as free-to-air channels broadcast delayed highlights. Furthermore, the Anti-siphoning List covers the entire FIFA's Football World Cup finals, despite the fact that soccer has a significantly weaker position relative to other sports in Australia than in Europe. With the exception of the UK, the European lists only cover the matches of the respective nations and the final, while Germany and Austria also include the opening match and the semi-finals. The Anti-siphoning List also includes the English FA Cup Final, while neither of the European lists covers any foreign cup finals.

The comprehensiveness of the Australian list leaves the impression that the major concerns have been the entertainment aspect and inefficiency in charging for public goods. This is underpinned by the following statement of the Minister for Communications, Information Technology and the Arts: 'For many Australians, knowing that they can switch on their free-to-air television and watch a football grand final or a Test match is as important as having free access to Australian-made drama or a daily news bulletin' (Australian Government, 2004).

This is different in the European television 'Without Frontiers Directive' where the guidelines concentrate more on market failures related to *externalities* and *merit goods*, and not the efficiency loss from charging for public goods. The legitimizing of the Austrian list uses the phrase, 'event that is an expression of Austria's cultural, artistic or social identity' (The Commission of the European Communities, 2007a). Likewise, the Italian list uses the phrase, 'events that have a particular cultural significance and strengthen the Italian cultural identity' (The Commission of the European Communities, 2007b). Furthermore, the UK regulation declares that: 'the event must have a special national resonance, not simply of significance to those who ordinarily follow the sport concerned, and is an event that serves to unite the nation; a shared point in the national calendar' (The Commission of the European Communities, 2007c). These formulations indicate that the main purpose was not to protect sports fans from being charged when watching their favourite soccer club on television.

3   THE UK LIST

The 1984 Cable and Broadcasting Act was the first time a list of events of national importance that could not be broadcast live exclusively on pay-per-view television was acknowledged in statute. However, the Act did not set the criteria for what constituted 'national interest' according to the Department for Culture, Media and Sport (DCMS, 2009). The list was reviewed in 1989, 1991 and 1998. It was only in 1998, however, that transparent and published criteria were established as to what constituted 'national interest' or an event of 'national importance'. The result of the 1998 review is in Box 11.1, which was the starting point for the 2009 Review Committee. The list contains Group A events which are protected for live coverage and Group B events which are protected for delayed or highlights coverage. Events on the A-list must be screened live on a channel with 95 per cent penetration. Events on the B-list are allowed to be screened exclusively on channels that do not meet the 95 per cent penetration, assuming edited highlights or delayed coverage are broadcast on a channel with 95 per cent penetration.

BOX 11.1   UK LISTED EVENTS

The UK list contains both an A list and a B list. The A list includes the following events:

- The Olympic Games
- The FIFA World Cup Finals tournament
- The FA Cup Final
- The Scottish FA Cup Final (in Scotland)
- The Grand National
- The Derby
- The Wimbledon tennis finals
- The European Football Championship Finals tournament
- The Rugby League Challenge Cup Final
- The Rugby World Cup Final

The B list includes the following events:

- Cricket Test Matches played in England
- Non-finals play in the Wimbledon Tournament
- All other matches in the Rugby World Cup Finals tournament
- Five Nations Rugby Tournament matches involving Home Countries
- The Commonwealth Games
- The World Athletics Championship
- The Cricket World Cup – the final, semi-finals and matches involving Home Nations' teams
- The Ryder Cup
- The Open Golf Championship

3.1   The Independent Advisory Panel's Role and the Criteria for Listing

The terms of reference for the 2009 IAP were that the panel should review:

- the principle of listing;
- the criteria against which events were currently, or might in the future be listed;
- the events which make up the current list, and those which should do so in the future (DCMS, 2009).

The main criterion for listing in the previous review in 1998 was that the event has a special national resonance, not just a significance to those who ordinarily follow the sport concerned; it is an event which serves to unite the nation, a shared point on the national calendar.

For a sporting event, it would also fall into one or both of the following categories:

- it is a pre-eminent national or international event in the sport;
- it involves the national team or national representatives in the sport concerned.

Obviously it was part of the panel's remit to consider the suitability of this criterion.

3.2   The Arguments for Listing

The theoretical rationale behind government interventions in sport broadcasting are based on market failures in the sport broadcasting market caused by public good issues or externalities. *Externalities* are usually referred to as the result of an activity that causes incidental benefits or costs to others with no corresponding compensation provided or paid by those who generate the externality. The costs or benefits are not included in the supply price or the demand price and hence not in the market price.

Celebrating the achievements of national competitors in international championships can generate externalities. People in general will regard it to be a value of its own to be able to share the pleasure with someone else. Indeed, the 'common sharing' element is usually a part of the celebration and the atmosphere that exists under such circumstances. Having a party completely alone is not much value. A state of national celebration will require that a large number of people follow the event on television. The possibility will be reduced if only a minority of people have the ability to watch the channels that broadcast it. Furthermore, a state of national celebration also requires that the sport and the event really enjoy a widespread recognition by the general public. Hence, guaranteeing that everybody has access to television programmes from the event represents a prerequisite for such effects to occur. Such impacts also have a momentum dimension. The fact that people enjoy the experience at the same time, for example watching it live on television, will strengthen the impacts compared to if people only could read about it in newspapers the day after. There is no doubt that the effects can be stronger if each one of us is able to watch it live on television.

These kinds of impacts also fall into the category of *pure public goods*. It has long been recognized that international sporting success for a national team or national athletes is a public good (Gratton and Taylor, 2000). It is impossible to exclude someone from feeling pride and enjoy the successes of national participants in international competitions (that is, the benefit is non-excludable). Moreover, the fact that one person is enjoying this success does not prevent others from enjoying the same feeling (that is, the benefit is non-rival). There is a problem, then, if restricted access to television coverage of that success prevents the public enjoying that success. Television is the normal mechanism by which this success is transmitted to the public. Thus we see that the biggest television audiences, particularly in Europe, for terrestrial channels are achieved for major international sporting competitions such as the Olympic Games or football's World Cup.

Boardman and Hargreaves-Heap (1999) identify a different category of externalities, which they refer to as network externalities, when the broadcasting of popular events stimulates conversation about those events, so that people have a broader platform for initiating conversations with strangers. These are sometimes referred to as 'water-cooler moments' that bring people together to discuss events all have seen on the television the previous evening.

The migration of popular sporting events to pay-TV channels represents a disadvantage for those who cannot afford to subscribe to these channels. Thus, a concern with equity also provides a reason for government intervention. However, the equity argument is insufficient as a single argument for a governmental intervention, since unequal income distribution influences people's ability to purchase all sorts of goods. The sport programmes themselves really must be so important, that they should be provided for people who cannot afford to subscribe on channels with restricted penetration.

It will be difficult or impossible to achieve the optimal production level of sport programmes that generate externalities without any market regulation. Profit maximizing advertising channels will always prioritize sports and events that attract the interest from mass audience. Pay-TV channels will base their activity on programmes that a sufficient number of viewers are willing to pay for watching. Hence, commercial channels always have a motive to undermine the impacts we have discussed above, that relate to externalities and public good aspects.

3.3   The Arguments against Listing

The objective of regulations such as the Listed Events is to move sporting events back to the public domain. On the other hand, any regulations that regulate the ability to keep sporting events out of the public domain reduce the rights owner's ability to make a profit. As a rule of thumb, the higher degree of the public domain, the lower the commercial value of the ownership will be. A high degree of public domain reduces sellers' freedom to exploit the commercial value of the product. The negative relationship is illustrated in Figure 11.1. A regime of strict legislative protection of the owner's broadcasting rights to the event improves the owner's ability to make a profit from the product. This means that the governing body can sell it to the highest bidder in the case of an auction.

The listed events legislation removes the channels who are likely to pay most for the event (for example, in the UK, Sky) from the auction for the rights. This reduces the competition substantially and lower competition means a lower price for the rights. The governing body that owns the rights itself has a dilemma. By selling to a broadcaster with limited penetration they maximize revenue but reduce the exposure of the event to the public. At the same time this reduces the attractiveness of the event to sponsors who want maximum exposure. Ideally, governing bodies want maximum exposure of their sport and the highest revenue but Figure 11.1 shows that this is not possible. In general in the UK, the highest revenue from the sale of the broadcasting rights for a specific event is achieved by selling the rights to a pay-TV channel, normally Sky, which means a more restricted audience than would be achieved from a terrestrial channel. If the event is listed, the choice is no longer with the governing body. It is the government that decides to give the event maximum exposure. The cost is reduced revenue to the governing body. If the event is not listed (or is on the B-list), then the governing body must decide where it wants to be on the curve in Figure 11.1. The main case against listing is that governing bodies argue that they know more about their own sport than anybody else and that they are in the best position to make the decision as to whom to sell the broadcasting rights. Different governing bodies make different decisions.

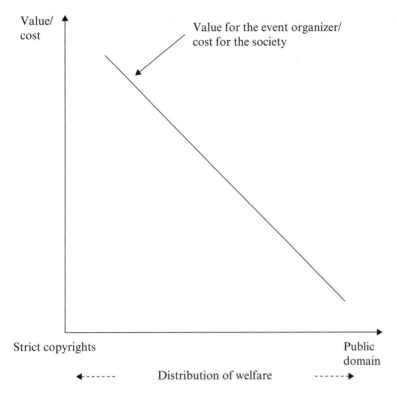

Source: Gratton and Solberg (2007).

Figure 11.1 Public domain versus private ownership

Rugby union has decided to keep the Six Nations Championship on the BBC even though it is not on the A list. England autumn internationals on the other hand are on Sky. Both the Open Golf Championship (which is on List B) and Wimbledon (where only the two finals days are on List A) are shown in total on the BBC since the governing bodies involved have chosen this route to obtain maximum exposure for the events. Cricket controversially since 2005 has only been shown live on Sky. This is controversial because in 2005 England won the Ashes series against Australia generating more interest in cricket than had been seen for decades. Once the series finished no more Test Match cricket has been seen live on terrestrial television in the UK. In 2009, England again won the home Ashes series. Television audiences for the series dropped form 8 million in 2005 to 1.5 million in 2009. There was considerable discussion in the media as to whether the removal of the Ashes series from terrestrial television had substantially reduced the national euphoria for the success that had been clearly visible in 2005 but much less so in 2009. This 2009 series was being played at the time the Independent Advisory Panel was making its deliberations.

Another argument against listing is that the changing broadcasting landscape has made listing an anomaly from a previous non-digital era. The previous UK review of the listed events legislation took place in 1998. This was prior to Sky launching Sky Digital, changing radically the nature of broadcasting. In October 2002, the BBC, BSkyB and others launched Freeview, a package of 30 free digital channels through an aerial. As a result, by 2009, 87 per cent of UK homes were watching digital services, with Freeview the leading television platform. In 2003 the number of channels broadcasting in the UK was 204; in 2010, it was over 500 (DCMS, 2009). As a result of this dramatic change in the media landscape the share of the total television audience captured by the terrestrial channels is falling year by year. In 1998, a decade after the beginning of satellite and cable television in the UK, the five main terrestrial channels still captured 97 per cent of the total viewing audience. By 2007, this was down to 64 per cent. In addition to this, the Internet is competing with television as the main source of viewing for younger audiences in particular (DCMS, 2009).

Some argue that, in this dramatic new digital era the listing of events is no longer appropriate since the market is becoming so fragmented, it is no longer relevant to protect certain events for five terrestrial channels. In addition, given the fragmentation, it is increasingly the case that instead of five channels, the listing is reducing the market to two and one broadcaster, the BBC. The reason is that commercial terrestrial channels, have had huge drops in advertising revenue during this expansion in the number of channels as the advertising budget gets spread increasingly thinly. These channels find it harder and harder to bid for expensive sports broadcasting rights. This is evidenced by the recent switch of Formula 1 racing from ITV to the BBC. Despite these changes in the broadcasting landscape, however, terrestrially televised football matches at the European Championships of 2008 and the World Cup of 2010 attracted some of the largest television audiences of the past decade, peaking at over 20 million, suggesting that sport still has the potential to unite the nation and suggest some legitimacy to the idea of listing.

4   METHODOLOGY APPLIED BY THE PANEL TO REACH A RECOMMENDATION

The panel fist met in early February 2009 and had its final meeting in October 2009. The final report with the panel's recommendations was submitted to the Minister in November 2009. The methodology of conducting the review was as follows (DCMS, 2009):

- the panel launched a formal consultation from 8 April to 20 July 2009 and issued a consultation document;
- 187 sporting, media, broadcasting, viewer and other organizations were written to informing them of the existence of the review seeking their views on the existing list and possible changes to it;
- reviewed listing regimes in other countries in Europe and in Australia;
- commissioned the British Market Research Bureau to conduct 12 focus group discussions throughout the UK and undertake a UK wide social survey to provide evidence on the opinions of the viewing public.

The evidence submitted is discussed below under the following groupings:

- UK Sporting Organizations (concentrating on the evidence provided by those responsible for the sports of cricket and horse racing). Evidence was submitted by 28 UK sporting organizations.
- International sporting organizations (concentrating on the evidence provided by the IOC and FIFA). Evidence was submitted by six international sporting organizations.
- Terrestrial broadcasters (including the BBC, ITV, Channel 4 and Channel 5). Altogether, seven terrestrial broadcasters submitted evidence.
- Satellite broadcasters (concentrating on the evidence provided by Sky, the only satellite broadcaster to submit evidence).
- The public (evidence on the public's attitude to the listing of events was collected by the British Market Research Bureau (BMRB) in 12 focus group discussions across the country and in a survey based on a representative sample of 2072 adults aged 15+).

In addition to the above evidence, the panel were provided with forecasts of the major changes likely to take place in the broadcast market over the next ten years in particular after the UK switches over to digital only transmission in 2012 and an expert report on the analysis of viewing patterns for sports events and on developments in the market for broadcasting rights for sports events.

5   THE EVIDENCE

5.1   UK Sporting Organizations

The evidence from two UK governing bodies will be looked at here: a governing body with two events currently on the A list, the Jockey Club who own the rights to the Grand National and the Derby; and a governing body on the B list, the England and Wales Cricket Board (ECB), who own the England team cricket rights.

The Jockey Club indicated that the A-listing of both the Derby and the Grand National in the current climate was seriously affecting the revenue from the sale of broadcasting rights to these events. The rights to these events have declined in value by 70 per cent over the past five years. They argued that the decline in revenues for the three commercial terrestrial broadcasters, ITV, Channel 4 and Channel 5 has effectively left the BBC in a monopoly position in bidding for acquiring the rights to these events. They blamed the loss in revenue on the List A status of these events and the lack of serious competition from the other qualifying broadcasters.

The ECB indicated how increasing revenues from the sales of broadcasting rights had radically changed the financial situation of cricket since cricket was removed from the A list in 1998. UK revenues from the sale of broadcasting rights accounted for 57 per cent of ECB revenues in 2008 compared to just 34 per cent in 1997 (DCMS, 2009). These revenues were £15 million per year during 1995–98, just before the last review of listed events, and £53million a year in the 2006–09 period, just before this review. The contract with Sky for 2010–13 gives the ECB £65 million per year for that period, with a further £1 million from the sale of highlights package to Channel 5. The written evidence from the ECB claimed that 80 per cent of its revenues now came from the sale of broadcasting rights. The ECB argued that this increased level of revenues was used to invest in both first-class cricket (that is, the counties) and recreational cricket, in particular for women and young people. They claimed huge increases in participation for these two groups as a direct result of the new investments made possible by the increased revenues. If cricket were listed, they argued, these investments would be severely affected and participation in cricket as well as performance at the elite level would suffer as a result.

Similar arguments were repeated time and time again by other governing bodies submitting evidence to the panel. Rugby union referred to listing as the 'nationalization' of their sport and the Welsh Rugby Union argued that listing Welsh rugby union matches would decimate the sport in Wales. Six Nations Rugby Union also argued strongly against listing even though they choose to broadcast all these matches on the BBC. There was a consistent argument from all governing bodies that the best organization to make decisions on what was best for their sport was them and that they should be allowed to do it without interference from government (DCMS, 2009).

5.2 International Sporting Organizations

Here we look at the evidence of the owners of the rights to the two biggest global events on the planet, the Olympic Games and the football World Cup, the IOC and FIFA.

The IOC argued that it had always tried to achieve the widest possible dissemination of images of the Olympic Games in line with the Olympic Charter, which requires that the IOC take 'all necessary steps in order to ensure the fullest coverage by the different media and the widest possible audience in the world for the Olympic Games' (IOC written evidence to panel, June 2009). In general then, this requires the IOC to sell the broadcasting rights to free-to-air broadcasters. However, although the IOC is happy for all those parts of the Olympics that are of significant importance to the UK viewing public to be shown on terrestrial television and even be listed, it objects to the whole of the Olympic Games being listed. The argument is quite straightforward. At the Beijing Olympics live Olympic Games content amounted to 5000 hours covering 28 sports. To broadcast all 5000 hours live would require at least 26 channels broadcasting 12 hours a day for the 16 days of the Olympics. In fact the BBC broadcast 240 hours of live content from Beijing or just 4.8 per cent of the total. That is, 95 per cent of the Olympic Games content was not broadcast to the UK viewing public. The IOC argues that the current UK listing arrangements, where the whole of the Olympic Games is listed, is detrimental to Olympic sports, some of which get no coverage at all by the BBC, and to the host cities and National Olympic Committees, who receive 92 per cent of all the Olympic Games marketing revenues. Quite simply, the IOC would like a form of listing which allows the BBC, or any other terrestrial broadcaster, to broadcast the content most demanded by the UK viewers, but preserves the right of the IOC to market the remaining live content to other broadcasters.

FIFA's argument in relation to the World Cup was similar in that they were happy for part of the tournament to be listed (for example, the opening match, matches of home nations, semi-finals and final) but they preferred a model operated in some other European countries (for example, France) where a partnership between free-to-air and pay-TV broadcasters shared the tournament. The IOC argument focused on the lack of coverage of live Olympic content. This is not the case with the World Cup, however, as all matches are currently shown live. It was the loss of broadcast revenue that was FIFA's main concern. In 2007, event income accounted for 89 per cent of FIFA revenue, with the bulk of this coming from the sale of broadcasting rights to the 2010 World Cup (DCMS, 2009).

5.3   Terrestrial Broadcasters

The BBC, ITV, Channel 4 and Channel 5, the only channels currently satisfying the 95 per cent penetration rule, all confirmed their continued support for the listed event regime. The three commercial terrestrial channels indicated that the sharp drop in advertising revenue (down as much as 20 per cent in the first quarter of 2009) limited their ability to bid for expensive broadcasting rights in the current climate. It is not surprising then the majority of events on the current List A are broadcast by the BBC.

5.4   Satellite Broadcasters

Sky is by far the dominant satellite broadcaster in sport in the UK. There was one smaller competitor, Setanta, when the panel's deliberations began, but their UK operation went into receivership during the consultation phase of the committee. Sky's evidence will be the focus of this sub-section. The arguments put forward by Sky were essentially the same as those put forward by the governing bodies:

> It is the responsibility of sports bodies to decide what is in the best interests of their sport. They have the experience and the expertise to make these decisions, and should be free to do so. This is particularly important in the case of selecting the appropriate broadcast partner(s), given the complexity of the issues and the trade-offs involved. It is a decision made on the basis of multiple factors which include: generating sufficient income from the sale of rights; delivering the appropriate audience; supporting grassroots participation, coaching and facilities; impact on the experience of fans watching at grounds or stadiums; and securing the best quality TV coverage. (Sky written evidence to panel, May 2009)

Listing an event against the wishes of a sport body means that it becomes a forced seller of its rights and denies it the ability to get a fair deal from its chosen broadcast partners. This amounts to a tax on sport to subsidize terrestrial broadcasters, at a time when sports are in need of greater levels of funding in order to invest in facilities and their grassroots, and face pressure from the government to increase levels of participation (Sky written evidence to panel, May 2009). The written submission concluded that sports governing bodies should be left free of government interference to make decisions about their sport which they consider to be best for the sport, its participants and its fans.

5.5   The Public

Evidence on the public's attitude to the listing of events was collected by the British Market Research Bureau in 12 focus groups discussions across the country and in a survey based on a representative sample of 2072 adults aged 15+ (DCMS, 2009). In general, people thought they had an entitlement to watch sport on free-to-air television because they paid a television licence fee and some sports events received public funding. Eighty-two per cent of all respondents agreed that they deserved to watch certain sporting events on free-to-air television. Sixty-six per cent of those with no interest in sport and 72 per cent of those who thought there was too much sport on television also agreed. There was wide support for the concept of listed events and the current criteria for listing were thought to be fair. Eighty-four per cent thought sport was an important way of bringing people together in society. This sentiment is even acknowledged by those with no interest in sport (70 per cent agreed). The listed events were regarded as important as many consider sport to play a vital role in society.

6   DISCUSSION

It is clear from the evidence submitted that the organizations that own the broadcasting rights to their sports events feel that they know their sport better than any other organization including government. They have three main priorities: first, to promote the sport so that participation in their sport increases; second, to achieve international sporting success in their sport which satisfies the public demand for such international success and at the same time contributes to the first objective of increasing participation, and third, to make the sport financially viable both in the short and long term by having sufficient income to meet the first and second objectives. They believe that listing of their sports events is an unwelcome intrusion to their expert decision-making in meeting these three objectives.

In the current media environment, sport is the main target for pay-per-view broadcasters to attract subscriptions from an audience willing to pay a premium price to have exclusive coverage of the most popular sports events. Only sport is capable of attracting the highest premium prices for exclusive live coverage. Sky has proved remarkably successful in using exclusive live coverage of football and cricket in particular to expand its subscriber base and generate substantial profits from this. It is interesting that none of Sky's broadcasting competitors had any criticism of the way that Sky delivered its sporting coverage. On the contrary, virtually all of them had nothing but praise for the quality of their coverage. There is therefore no issue of the removal of sporting events form terrestrial television leading to a reduced quality product. There is also the issue of whether the restriction of viewing of the event to only those who subscribe provides a serious welfare loss to the public.

Terrestrial broadcasters increasingly cannot match the prices that satellite broadcasters are willing to pay. Listing of events is one way they can continue to provide a menu of top-class sports events that have the potential to generate the public good benefits of international sporting success that can be enjoyed by the whole nation. In the UK, it is increasingly only the BBC that can do this because of the decreasing revenue of commercial terrestrial broadcasters brought about by the digital era of broadcasting and the spreading of advertising income across an increasingly large number of channels. Thus the battle for sports events broadcasting is more and more between Sky and the BBC.

The government has to make perhaps one of the most complicated decisions in any area of government policy:

- Do we still need a list in the modern digital broadcasting environment?
- If so, what events should be on the list?
- How does government deal with the issue that listing an event potentially loses a large part of the governing body's income. This restricts it in its ability to promote participation in the sport with the associated health benefits. At the same time, it reduces the governing body's ability to generate international sporting success. It is precisely this international sporting success that is the main argument for listing in the first place, because the impact of this success is maximized by it being watched by the biggest television audience.

7 THE PANEL'S RECOMMENDATIONS

The panel decided that despite these complicated problems, in the end the strong views of the public in favour of a list and the large television audiences that many of these events attract provide strong evidence that a list is still necessary. The panel also concluded that in the modern environment it was no longer appropriate to list highlights packages as the main interest was in live broadcasts. Consequently, the panel recommended abolishing List B (DCMS, 2009).

Although the panel recognized the right of governing bodies to make decisions about their own sport, these organizations had no responsibility for the viewing public which the list was designed to protect. All the evidence suggested that sport clearly has the ability to generate the public good and externality benefits discussed earlier as justification for having a list.

In deciding which events to include on the list the criterion of national resonance was used. The panel had no remit to assess the economic cost to the governing body of listing, or even to take this into consideration, although the Secretary of State in considering the recommendations may do so. The panel's remit, once the case for listing was accepted, was simply to identify those events that had clear national resonance. Many events such as the Open Golf and Wimbledon were included even though they currently are broadcast on free-to-air by the choice of the governing body. Qualifying matches for the World Cup and European Championships were included for the first time. Most controversially, the home Ashes Series in cricket was included. The Derby, the Winter Olympics and the Rugby League Cup Final were considered not to have national resonance and were not included on the recommendations for the new list (DCMS, 2009).

The panel concluded that listed events do not necessarily have a long-term future. The changing media landscape may one day render them obsolete, but not yet. The recommended list is in Box 11.2.

The recommendation was to the Minister of Culture, Media and Sport. He then took further consultation on these recommendations which lasted until March 2010. However, the Labour government called a general election in May 2010, which they lost, and a new coalition government of the Conservative Party and the Liberal Democrats came into power as a result. The new government, in July 2010, announced that any decision to amend the Listed Events legislation would be deferred to 2013 after the completion of the digital switchover. Up until that time the list would remain as it was prior to the panel being set up.

BOX 11.2   RECOMMENDATIONS FOR THE NEW LIST OF UK LISTED EVENTS

- The Summer Olympic Games
- The FIFA World Cup Finals tournament
- The EUFA European Football Championships
- The FA Cup Final
- The Scottish FA Cup Final (in Scotland)
- The Grand National
- The Wimbledon tennis tournament (whole tournament)
- The European Football Championship Finals tournament
- Home and away qualification matches in the FIFA World Cup and the UEFA European Football Championships (in the Home Nation to which they relate)
- The Open Golf Championship
- Home Ashes Series in cricket
- Ruby Union World Cup tournament
- Wales matches in the Six Nations Rugby Championship

---

8   CONCLUSIONS

Despite the fact that the UK government has decided not to implement the recommendations of the panel immediately, the review process carried in 2009 in the UK has revealed several clear issues related to government intervention in the sports broadcasting market.

There is overwhelming evidence there are sporting events that still have special national resonance and that the viewing public still wants the government to intervene to guarantee that such events are seen by the largest television audience by preventing exclusive coverage on pay-per-view television. It is relatively easy to identify which events have this special national resonance. Some of them (Six Nations rugby, Wimbledon, the Open Golf Championship) are already shown on terrestrial television even though they are not on the list, because the governing bodies of these sports choose to have the largest television audience possible, even though this may result in a reduced fee for the broadcasting rights.

There was a very important issue, though, that was excluded from the panel's deliberations because it was not included within the terms of reference: is it fair to reduce the income of a sport governing body by including them on the list? When the list was first introduced in 1984 this issue was almost irrelevant. Since the early 1990s the price of sports broadcasting rights for major sports events has increased tremendously. In 1984, whether an event was on the list or not made little difference to the income of the governing body. Now for many governing bodies the majority of their income comes from the sale of broadcasting rights. If listing their events substantially reduces this income, they lose a lot of the ability to promote increased participation in their sport and to generate international sporting success. By intervening in the market for broadcasting rights to enhance the welfare of the viewing public the government may be preventing the achievement of two other public objectives in sport: increased participation and increased international sporting success.

The broadcasting landscape may be changing, affecting the way we view these major sporting events. More important, though, is the way the market for broadcasting rights has changed over recent years, escalating the price of these rights substantially. If government wants to continue to see certain events remain on terrestrial television in the future, it may have to compensate the sports affected in order to meet other public objectives in sport. This issue is equally relevant to other countries with listed events legislation and it is an issue likely to become more important with the escalation in the price of broadcasting rights for sports events.

One final development in relation to the listed events legislation emerged in late 2010 and the first part of 2011. During FIFA's deliberations over the choice of host countries for the World Cup in 2018 and 2022, there was much comment as to the governance procedures in FIFA amid accusations of corruption. These claims were exacerbated in early 2011 when FIFA moved on to elect its president. Again, many commentators were asking the question of the governance procedures adopted by international sports organizations such as FIFA and pointing out the fact that such organizations were responsible to no overall authority other than themselves. The listed events legislation, particularly in the European Union where it is backed up by an EU Directive, provides one of the few opportunities for governments to have some control over such organizations. In February 2011, EUFA and FIFA lost an appeal in the EU Court to prevent all of the football World Cup and European Championship football to be shown on free-to-air television in both the UK and Belgium. In the end, perhaps the strongest argument for the listed events legislation is that it allows government control of international sports organizations that seem to lack any other form of control mechanisms.

REFERENCES

Australian Government (2004), Speech by the Minister for Communications, Information Technology and the Arts given at the annual conference of the Australian Subscription Television and Radio Association on 8 April, available at: http://www.aph.gov.au/library/pubs/bd/2004–05/05bd004.htm (accessed 25 January 2012).

Australian Government (eds) (2010), Broadcasting services (events) notice, available at: http://www.comlaw.gov.au/Details/F2010L03383 (accessed 2 February 2012).

Boardman, A.E. and Hargreaves-Heap, S.P. (1999), Network externalities and government restrictions on satellite broadcasting of key sporting events, *Journal of Cultural Economics*, **23** (3), 167–81.

Cowie, C. and Williams, M. (1997), The economics of sports rights, *Telecommunication Policy*, **21** (7), 619–34.

Department for Culture, Media and Sport (DCMS) (eds) (2009), *Review of Free-to-air Listed Events: Report by the Independent Advisory Panel to the Secretary of State for Culture, Media and Sport*, London: Department for Culture, Media and Sport.

European Commission (eds) (2008), AVMS Directive/TVwF – application and implementation, available at: http://ec.europa.eu/avpolicy/reg/tvwf/implementation/events_list/index_en.htm (accessed 2 February 2012).

European Union (EU) (1989), Television broadcasting activities: 'Television without Frontiers' (TVWF) Directive, available at: http://europa.eu/legislation_summaries/audiovisual_and_media/l24101_en.htm (accessed 25 January 2012).

Gratton, C. and Solberg, H.A. (2007), *The Economics of Sport Broadcasting*, London: Routledge.

Gratton, C. and Taylor, P. (2000), *Economics of Sport and Recreation*, London: E&FN Spon.

The Commission of the European Communities (eds) (2007a), Commission decision of 25 June 2007 on the compatibility with Community law of measures taken by Austria pursuant to Article 3a(1) of Council

Directive 89/552/EEC on the coordination of certain provisions laid down by law, regulation or administrative action in Member States concerning the pursuit of television broadcasting activities, available at: http://eur-lex.europa.eu/LexUriServ/site/en/oj/2007/l_180/l_18020070710en00110016.pdf (accessed 2 February 2012).

The Commission of the European Communities (eds) (2007b), Commission decision of 25 June 2007 on the compatibility with Community law of measures taken by Italy pursuant to Article 3a(1) of Council Directive 89/552/EEC on the coordination of certain provisions laid down by law, regulation or administrative action in Member States concerning the pursuit of television broadcasting activities, available at: http://eur-lex.europa.eu/LexUriServ/site/en/oj/2007/l_180/l_18020070710en00050007.pdf (accessed 2 February 2012).

The Commission of the European Communities (eds) (2007c), Commission decision of 16 October 2007 on the compatibility with Community law of measures taken by the United Kingdom pursuant to Article 3a(1) of Council Directive 89/552/EEC on the coordination of certain provisions laid down by law, regulation or administrative action in Member States concerning the pursuit of television broadcasting activities, available at:http://eurlex.europa.eu/LexUriServ/site/en/oj/2007/l_295/l_29520071114en00120027.pdf (accessed 2 February 2012).

12 The sale of media sports rights: a game theoretic approach

Harry Arne Solberg and Kjetil Kåre Haugen

1 INTRODUCTION AND BACKGROUND

Many stakeholders involved in sport have experienced that miscalculations of the revenues and costs can cause severe consequences. In recent years, a number of European sports clubs have been on the brink of bankruptcy. In addition, several sport governing bodies and organizers of sporting events have also had financial problems. One reason for this has been unforeseen negative shifts in demand. Such incidents can cause problems, particularly for non-profit producers and organizations. Different from profit maximizing companies, these agents do not have any 'safety margin' if the revenues are being reduced. For them, the ability to accurately predict the costs and revenues will be of importance. This particularly applies to production processes involving a high proportion of fixed costs.

The objectives of the stakeholders involved in sport and sporting activities have been thoroughly discussed in the sports economic literature. As for team sports, there has been a consensus that North American teams behave like profit maximizers, whereas in Europe and other continents, some kind of utility maximization seems to be the objective (Fort, 2003; Késenne, 1996; Rottenberg, 1956; Sloane, 1971; Vrooman, 1997). Sloane (1971) considers European football clubs as utility maximizers where the utility function of club owners also includes sporting performance. According to Vrooman (1997), European football club owners are willing to sacrifice some financial return in order to achieve better sporting performance. It would probably be more correct, however, to regard these two regimes as polar cases where the behaviour of North American teams is closer to profit maximization, whereas the behaviour of European teams is closer to win maximization, but that teams on both continents emphazise both objectives (Gratton and Solberg, 2007). There are many indications that financial problems have been more common in European professional team sports than in North America (Haugen and Solberg, 2010). Similar objectives can also apply to stakeholders in other sports, including individual sports. In general, we do not believe that profit maximization is the major objective of sport governing bodies and hosts of sporting events, as an example.

In recent years, many clubs, event organizers and sport governing bodies have earned substantial revenues from the sale of media rights (Gratton and Solberg, 2007; Hoehn and Lancefield 2003). These revenues can be affected by many factors, where the strategy of rivalling buyers is one example. The major reason behind the strong inflation of sports rights has been the fierce competition between commercial broadcasters. However, in recent years, we have also seen incidents where the rights fees have declined instead of continuing to grow. In football, the rights fees of the English Premier League were reduced in 2004 compared with the previous deal. Also in football, the sale of international rights for Italy's Serie A brought in less for the 2009 and 2010 seasons than the previous deals did. The sale of the highlights for Serie A on the domestic market, commencing from 2009 also brought in less revenue than the former deal. High entry costs reduce the number of broadcasters that can operate successfully in these markets. Hence, any forms of horizontal integration, for example merger or collusion can bring the market closer to a monopoly on the demand side, that is, a monopsony.

Game theory, originally introduced by mathematicians von Neuman and Morgenstern (von Neuman and Morgenstern, 1944), has grown into a mature scientific toolbox to explore such situations. Central to game theory are concepts like players, preferences, pay-offs, strategies and information. Through careful definition of such concepts, best reply functions or correspondences can be derived as optimizing behaviour for each player as functions of all other players' possible strategies. The central solution concept, the 'Nash equilibrium', can then be defined as 'intersecting points' on such best replies. In addition to the pioneers von Neuman and Morgenstern – Nobel laureates in 1994 – Nash (1951), Harsanyi (1967) and Selten (1975) have contributed significantly to game theory's widespread applicability today.

Game theory can help both the sellers and buyers to gain insight into the processes affecting the terms of trade. It can improve the ability to foresee the strategies of the rivals, and also the consequences of these strategies. In some cases, it can help the owners of sports rights to better analyse the alternative strategies of the television channel(s) as well as their consequences, and vice versa. Additionally, it can also help consumers (which in this case are television viewers) to understand when the sellers and/or buyers are bluffing as a part of the negotiations. As an example, we sometimes get the impression that there is a risk that mega events such as the Olympic Games or World Cup football finals may not be broadcast on television because the sellers have put a too expensive price tag on the rights.

This is of course a bluff. Such events are extremely popular, and therefore they generate enormous revenues for both the seller (for example, the International Olympic Committee (IOC) and the Fédération Internationale de Football Association (FIFA)) and the buyers (commercial television broadcasters). First, if the events are not broadcast, the sellers will not receive any media rights. Second, the value of sponsorship deals will also drop dramatically in case the event is not on television. Similar circumstances apply to the buyers. There are hardly any television programmes that can attract the same audiences, and thus generate the same advertising revenues, as the most popular sports contests. Since both the sellers and the buyers are aware of the enormous revenues such programmes will generate, they also wish to maximize their own proportion of it.

However, signalling to 'the outside world' that there is a risk of blank television screens can be used as instruments during the sales processes. Television broadcasters may hope it will put pressure on the seller to lower the price, and vice versa. Non-commercial and semi-commercial public service broadcasters may use the uncertainty whether the sports events will be broadcast or not, to persuade politicians to give them more favourable conditions, for example more funding. Indeed, such strategies have been observed on several occasions in Europe over the past decade.

We will look at two different situations. In the first, we imagine a situation where two rival television channels are interested in broadcasting live sports events. The analyses present in this chapter of course also applies to cases when sports programmes are shown on other alternatives than traditional television, such as, for example, touch pad and mobile telephone. One of the sports is more popular, and the events in this sport will attract higher television audiences and more revenues than the other sport. In the second situation, there is only one upcoming event. Furthermore, we assume that one of the television channels has disappeared from the market. Here we analyse the variables that will influence the strategies of the event organizer and the remaining television channel, and, in turn, how this will affect the distribution of the profit that the broadcasting of the event can generate. This involves variables such as sponsorship support, gate receipts as well as the profit the channel can make from alternative programmes. This section also illustrates under which circumstances the event will not be broadcast.

2   SITUATION ONE: THE COMPETITION BETWEEN TELEVISION CHANNELS

This section analyses the competition between television channels. To do this we imagine a situation where there are two sport broadcasters, which we call Channel A and Channel B. Both are involved in broadcasting two particular sports events, which we call Sport P and Sport U. Four events are coming up, two in each sports. This could, for example, be two different matches in different team sports, say football and handball. However, since all events will take place simultaneously, only two of them can be broadcast live. Sport P is the most popular. Hence, its live sports programmes attract higher audiences and generate more revenues than events in sport U. We also assume that the popularity of the two events within the same sport is equal. If, say the events are football matches and handball matches, the two football matches attract the same audiences while the two handball matches attract the same audiences.

The revenues can come from the sale of advertising in connection with the programmes or from charging the viewers, that is, the pay-television (TV) principle. The channels make their choices on which sport they will broadcast simultaneously. Hence, they do not know which sport the rival will prioritize when making their own decision. Sport P denotes the choice of an event in the most popular sport, while Sport U denotes the choice of an event in the less popular sport. If both channels choose an event in the same sport, they will attract the same number of viewers (that is, an underlying assumption of equal channel size) and hence earn identical revenues. This pattern applies when both broadcast the most popular sport as well as when both broadcast the less popular sport.

The pattern described above, where the popularity of sports is varying is common all over the world. In Europe, football has acquired the leading position in terms of rights fees values. Next follows a few sports fighting for second position. In the United States, the National Football League (NFL) has been in the leading position, with the professional leagues in basketball (NBA) and baseball (MLB) following next among the professional team sports tournaments. Similar patterns are found in other countries. Cricket is the number one sport in India, ice hockey in Canada, rugby in New Zealand, Australian football in Australia, and so on. These patterns have also been reflected in the values of the rights fees. On the basis of these experiences, our model corresponds with reality in most countries.

Equation (12.1) denotes the profit (Π) of the channels, with R being the revenues and

		Channel B	
		Sport P	**Sport U**
Channel A	**Sport P**	$R_3 - C_2$ $R_3 - C_2$	$R_2 - C_1$ $R_4 - C_2$
	Sport U	$R_4 - C_2$ $R_2 - C_1$	$R_1 - C_1$ $R_1 - C_1$

Figure 12.1 Pay-off matrix

C the costs. Since both channels have the same penetration, their revenues will be identical if they make the same decision.

$$\Pi_i = R_i - C_i, \quad i = A, B, \tag{12.1}$$

R can take four levels, while C can take two levels. The ranking order is assumed as follows:

$$R_4 > R_3 > R_2 > R_1 \tag{12.2}$$

$$C_2 > C_1 \tag{12.3}$$

In the following, we will only take into account the rights fees and not the programming costs. Owing to the differences in popularity, the rights of the events in Sport P are more expensive than the rights of events in Sport U, hence $C_2 > C_1$. Figure 12.1 defines the pay-offs (profit) of the two channels in four alternatives. The bottom-left triangles of the rectangle denote the pay-off of Channel A, while the top-right triangles denote the pay-off of Channels B. We assume some cannibalism when both channels broadcast the same sport, compared with when they televise different sports. If, say, both channels broadcast football, then football fans will be spread over two channels instead of one. Since the events take place simultaneously, the viewers can only watch one of the matches live. This explains why $R_4 > R_3$, and $R_2 > R_1$.

In the north-west window, the channels broadcast separate events in sport P. In the

Table 12.1   Conditions for Nash equilibria

North-west	If $R_3 - C_2 > R_2 - C_1 => R_3 - R_2 > C_2 - C_1$, then a unique (P,P) Nash equilibrium emerges
North-east/ South-west	If $R_4 - C_2 > R_1 - C_1$ and $R_2 - C_1 > R_3 - C_2$, then the unique (P,U) or (U,P) solutions are Nash equilibria
South-east	If $R_1 - C_1 > R_4 - C_2$, then a unique (U,U) Nash equilibrium emerges

south-west window, Channel A broadcasts an event in Sport P and Channel B an event in Sport U. This is turned around in the north-east window with Channel B broadcasting from Sport P and Channel A from Sport U. In the south-east window, they broadcast separate events in the least popular sport. Channel A will attract the highest attendance/revenues in the north-east window and the lowest attendance/revenues in the south-west window. Vice versa, Channel B will attract the highest attendances/revenues in the south-west window, and the lowest attendance/revenues in the north-east window.

We start the analysis of the pay-off matrix in Figure 12.1 by identifying the best reply functions. Let us now put ourselves in the position of Channel A. If Channel B acquires an event in Sport U, Channel A will acquire an event in sport P if $R_4 - C_2 > R_1 - C_1$. In other words, if $R_4 - R_1 > C_2 - C_1$. This means that the wider the gap in revenues and the narrower that gap in costs, the more likely Channel A is to prioritize an event in Sport P.

If Channel B chooses an event in Sport P, then Channel A will do the same if $R_3 - C_2 > R_2 - C_1$, that is, if $R_3 - R_2 > C_2 - C_1$. If so, the former condition, namely that $R_4 - R_1 > C_2 - C_1$ will also be satisfied. Since the situation is symmetric, Channel B will react identically if the conditions are turn around.

Table 12.1 shows under which circumstances the alternative windows are Nash equilibria. That means that neither of the two will regret their decision as long as the rival upholds his or her strategy. Both channels prefer an event in Sport P, that is, the north-west window, if $R_3 - R_2 > C_2 - C_1$. The revenues will be lower than if the channels choose different sports, which is due to the cannibalism effect ($R_3 < R_4$).

The north-west window is a *prisoner's dilemma* if $R_3 - C_2 < R_1 - C_1$, that is, if $R_3 - R_1 < C_2 - C_1$. In other words, if the aggregate profit in the north-west window is lower than in the south-east window. Prisoner's dilemma refers to a situation where the channels could have been better off by agreeing to collude instead of competing. The more expensive the rights fees of the events in Sport P, the more likely it is that a Nash equilibrium where both prioritize Sport P events represents a prisoner's dilemma.

The north-east and the south-west window represent the 'chicken solution'. The *chicken game* is well known in game theory literature. The most famous example is a game that was supposedly played by American teenagers in the 1950s. Two teenagers take their cars to opposite ends of a street and then start to drive towards each other. The one who swerves to avoid a collision is the chicken, and the one who keeps going straight is the winner (Dixit and Skeath, 1999). As one can imagine, the outcome is catastrophic for both drivers when neither of them swerved. A slight variant was made famous by the 1955 Nicholas Ray movie 'Rebel without a Cause'. In that game two cars are driving towards a cliff and the winner of the game is the last driver to jump out of his car.

Table 12.2   Three numerical illustrations

Situation 1	Situation 2	Situation 3
$R_4 = 8, R_3 = 6, R_2 = 4, R_1 = 2$	$R_4 = 8, R_3 = 6, R_2 = 4, R_1 = 2$	$R_4 = 8, R_3 = 6, R_2 = 4, R_1 = 3$
$C_2 = 2, C_1 = 1$	$C_2 = 5, C_1 = 1$	$C_2 = 6, C_1 = 0$

The north-east and south-west windows represent Nash equilibria if $R_4 - R_1 > C_2 - C_1$ and $R_3 - R_2 < C_2 - C_1$. Both channels will be better off by maintaining this strategy, assuming the rival channel does the same. However, the figures cannot explain which of these two solutions will be chosen, that is, who will broadcast an event in Sport P and who will broadcast an event in Sport U.

The south-east window presents the profit when both channels prefer events in Sport U. This represents a Nash-equilibrium if $R_1 - C_1 > R_4 - C_2$, which is equivalent with $R_4 - R_1 < C_2 - C_1$. In other words: The gap between the highest and the lowest revenue the channels can make must be narrower than the gap between the rights fees of the two events.

These illustrations show that all the four windows are possible. We also see that the gaps between the alternative scenarios of the revenues and the costs decide the optimal strategy.

The figures show that a 'stag-hunt' (or coordination game) solution is impossible. A *stag-hunt* equilibrium occurs when both the north-west window and the south-east window are Nash equilibria. In our case, this would require $R_4 - R_1 < C_2 - C_1$ and $R_3 - R_2 > C_2 - C_1$, which we easily see is impossible, as this would require $R_3 - R_2 > R_4 - R_1$ which violates equation (12.2).

In the next section, the parameters are given values to illustrate under which circumstances the alternative solutions can occur. Table 12.2 presents three alternative situations that give different Nash equilibria, and which correspond with the scenarios presented in Figure 12.1.

The white rectangles denote the optimal choices of Channel A in Figure 12.2, given the respective choice of Channel B, while the shaded rectangles denote the optimal choices of Channel B, given the respective choices of Channel A. In Figure 12.2, both channels will prioritize the popular sport, no matter what strategy the rivalling broadcaster prefers. The best reply will always be to prefer an event in Sport P as $6 > 1$ and $4 > 2$. Thus, Channel A will always prefer an event in Sport P, no matter what strategy Channel B adopts. Channel B will adopt the same strategy since the channels are identical. This means that we have a dominant strategy. We see that the rights fees are moderate, also for the more popular sport. Since the revenues from broadcasting an event in Sport P are significantly higher than the costs, Sport P will generate the highest profit. The aggregate profit is higher in the north-west window than in the south-east window. Thus, the north-west solution, which is the only Nash equilibrium, is not a prisoner's dilemma situation.

In Figure 12.3 'chicken solution' the rights fees of the unpopular sport have increased from 2 to 5, while the other variables remain unchanged. We can imagine that the stakeholders hosting events in Sport P have become more aware of the commercial value of the sport. As a consequence of this, they now charge higher fees when selling the rights. This reduces the profit that is left to the channels. However, this makes it more tempting

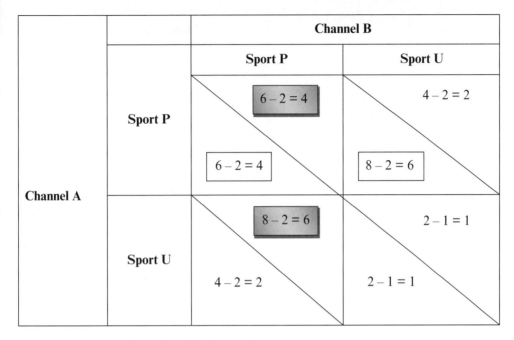

Figure 12.2   Both channels prefer the popular sport

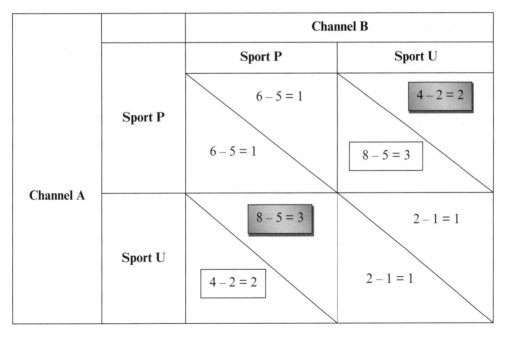

Figure 12.3   Chicken solution

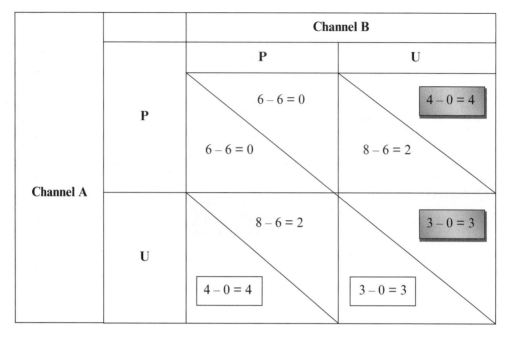

Figure 12.4   Both channels prefer the least popular sport

to broadcast events in Sport U. The two Nash equilibria in pure strategies (the south-west window and the north-east windows) now indicate that one event in Sport P and one event in Sport U will be broadcast. Neither of the channels will regret any of these solutions, once they have been established. However, the figures do not tell us who will broadcast a Sport P event and who will broadcast a Sport U event, only that both sports will be broadcast. The south-west window and the north-east window (and the invisible mixed strategy Nash equilibrium) represent a 'chicken solution'.

In Figure 12.4, the gap between the rights fees has further widened. Acquiring an event in Sport P now costs 6, while an event in Sport U is free of charge. In addition, the revenues from broadcasting an event in Sport U have increased in the case that both channels are doing it. The owners of Sport P events now charge so expensive fees that neither of the channels will make a profit if both channels broadcast events in this sport. The most popular sport will only be profitable if the rival channel broadcasts an event in Sport U.

At first sight, the policy of not charging any rights fees may look like a stupid strategy. However, as we see, this can motivate both broadcasters to prefer events in this sport, while the most popular sport is not being broadcast. Additionally, we can also imagine that other revenues, for example, support from sponsors, will increase if the event is shown on television. Such impacts, however, are not indicated in Figure 12.4.

Figures 12.4 also illustrates some interesting (and obvious) points. If the owner of the popular sport becomes too greedy and charges a very high price, there is a risk that both channels will prioritize the least popular sport. This also assumes that the owner of the least popular sport lowers the rights fees, which in our example are zero.

So far we have assumed the production costs of the two sports to be identical, that is, zero. This, of course, does not always correspond with reality. Events that take place outside stadiums may require considerably higher programming costs than those inside stadiums. Broadcasting the Tour de France (the most prestigious cycling race in the world, with a duration of three weeks), is of course more expensive than to broadcast a 100 metre race in athletics. Such differences can change the outcome in the alternative windows and, therefore, the strategies of the television channels. The same applies if the channels are of different size, for example have different penetration. Alternatively, we can also imagine that they earn revenues from different sources, for example, one is a pay-TV channel while the other is selling advertising. This may also alter the outcome presented in the pay-off matrix, for example, create 'chicken solutions' where the optimal strategy is to prefer different sports.

3   SITUATION TWO: BILATERAL MONOPOLY

The fact that broadcasting is characterized by high entry costs reduces the number of producers that can successfully operate in the same markets. The high degree of fixed costs can make television channels vulnerable if unforeseen negative shifts in demand occur. If competition becomes very fierce, with the viewers spread over too many channels, this will reduce the profitability of the separate programmes. Such problems can motivate television channels to integrate horizontally in order to reduce competition. We have seen several such examples in Europe in recent years. In 2002, the competitive authorities in Italy allowed Telepiu and Stream (the two leading pay-TV broadcasters at that time) to merge into Sky Italy (see Giomi, 2010). A similar merger, between rivalling pay-TV broadcasters took place in Spain the same year (Europa Press Releases, 2003). Another merger took place in 2007 when the French pay-TV platforms, Canal Sat and TPS, merged into Canal Plus France.

Horizontal integration can also include various forms of collaboration. Channels that normally would have competed fiercely may agree which events and sports they will bid on to prevent sport governing bodies from orchestrating bidding wars. Additionally, we also have seen joint purchases of sports rights. The European Broadcasting Union (EBU) has a long history with acquiring television rights for mega events on behalf of their member channels, that is, public service broadcasters. If the market initially has very few television channels, any retraction will bring it closer to monopoly. At the extreme, it can turn into a monopsony, that is, with only one buyer operating at the demand side.

To analyse the consequences of such a development, we revise the conditions in the former section. Now there is (only) one upcoming event. The revenues of the event organizer come from the sale of media rights and sponsorship deals. Sponsors get involved in such events mainly to promote themselves and their products. Hence, the higher the television rating, the more they are willing to support. For the same reason, they are likely to reduce their support if the event is not on television.

We now assume that there is only one channel left in the market. Hence, it will be impossible to stage an auction. Broadcasting the event can generate substantial revenues (and profit). Therefore, the channel is interested in acquiring the media rights, but not at any price. The higher the rights fees, the lower the profit. While the former section analysed the competition between the channels, this section will focus on the interaction between the event organizer and the remaining channel. Both want to maximize their own proportion of the 'broadcasting profit'. We define the profit as the difference between the revenues (advertising revenues and/or pay-per-view fees) and the programming costs. In this context, the rights fees should not be regarded as costs, but as a transfer of (a proportion of) the broadcasting profit from the television channel to the event organizer. The higher the fees, the higher the proportion that goes to the event organizer, and vice versa.

The situation can now turn into a negotiation process between the two, where both try to agree on terms as favourable to themselves as possible. Before going into the details, it is important to remind us about some characteristics of live sports programmes. First, such programmes cannot be stored without losing most of their commercial value. Few spectators, if any, are willing to spend time and money watching yesterday's contests on television. Second, since the event takes place during a specific period of time, the television programme has to be produced during this period. After the event is over, it is too late. In reality, the deal has to be completed some time prior to the event, owing to the time required for preparations. This puts a pressure on the event organizer and the television channel to agree on a deal some time before the event takes place.

In the negotiations, we assume that the event organizer and the television channel can (only) adopt one of two strategies; a *tough strategy* or a *soft strategy*. An event organizer who adopts a tough strategy will demand a high price and be unwilling to reduce it. A television channel that adopts a tough strategy will bid moderately and be unwilling to increase this bid. If both adopt a tough strategy, we assume that the event will not be televised.

The other alternative is to adopt a soft strategy. An event organizer who adopts a soft strategy will be willing to reduce the price (significantly) if the first bid is rejected. A television channel that adopts this strategy may submit a moderate bid, but will be willing to increase this bid significantly if it is rejected. We assume the event will be broadcast if at least one of the agents adopts a soft strategy.

Π_{TV} in equation (12.4) denotes the profit the television channel can make from broadcasting the event, with R representing the revenues and C the costs. For the case of simplicity, we assume that C only covers the rights fees. Hence programming costs are omitted. Z represents the profit the channel can earn from alternative programmes if it does not broadcast the sports programme.

Equation (12.5) shows the revenues of the event organizer, Π_{EO}, come from the sale of sports rights, C, and sponsorship revenues, S. Hence, C represents costs for the television channel and revenues for the event organizer. In this case, we will not take into account any other costs the event organizer may have to incur.

$$\Pi_{TV} = R - C + Z \tag{12.4}$$

$$\Pi_{EO} = C + S \tag{12.5}$$

$$\beta_1 > 1 > \beta_0 \tag{12.6}$$

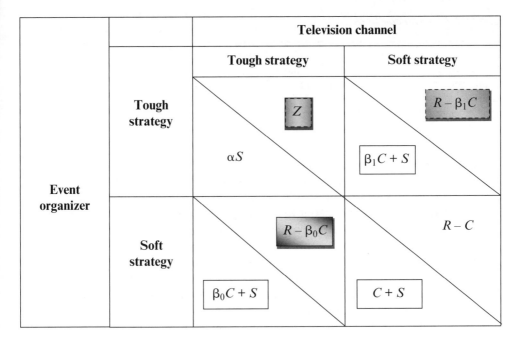

Figure 12.5 The event organizer versus the television channel

Figure 12.5 presents the pay-off matrix of the event organizer and the television channel. In the north-west window, both have adopted a tough strategy. As a result of this, the event will not be televised. This means that the revenues of the television channel only come from the alternative programme, that is, Z, while the revenues of the event organizer only come from sponsorship support. However, since the event is not on television, the support from sponsors will be reduced. α reflects the reduction compared to the situation where the event is broadcast $(0 < \alpha < 1)$. The more sponsorship support is reduced, the lower is α.

In the north-east window, the event organizer adopts the tough strategy, while the television channel adopts the soft strategy. This is turned around in the south-west window, where the event organizer adopts the soft strategy and the television channel the tough strategy. In the south-east window, both agents adopt a soft strategy. This means that the event will be televised under any circumstances, except from in the north-west window.

The parameter β indicates how much, and in which direction the rights fees are affected by the alternative strategies. If $\beta = 1$, the profit of the programme is equally distributed, as in the south-east window. When $\beta > 1$ (as β_1 is) the rights fees are higher with the result that the event organizer absorbs the lion's share of the profit. When $\beta < 1$ (as β_0 is) the rights fees are reduced so that the television channel absorbs the lion's share of the broadcasting profit.

The dotted rectangles represent the scenarios when the optimal solutions depend on the values of the variables. The unbroken rectangles refer to solutions where this alternative always will be the optimal choice, given that the rival upholds this choice.

Table 12.3   Nash equilibria

North-west	$\alpha S > \beta_0 C + S$ and $Z > R - \beta_1 C$	Impossible
North-east	$\beta_1 C + S > C + S$ and $R - \beta_1 C > Z$	
South-west	$\beta_0 C + S > \alpha S$ and $R - \beta_0 C > R - C$	
South-east	$C + S > \beta_1 C + S$ and $R - C > R - \beta_0 C$	Impossible

To illustrate the 'best reply' function, let us first put ourselves in the position of the event organiser. When the television channel adopts a soft strategy, the event organizer will always adopt a tough strategy. Since $\beta_1 > 1$, we will also have $\beta_1 C + S > C + S$. When the TV Channel adopts a tough strategy, the event organizer will always adopt a soft strategy ($\beta_0 C + S > \alpha S$). It is better to accept a reduction in the rights fees so that the event is being broadcast, instead of requiring so much that it not is being broadcast.

We now investigate the best reply function of the television channel. If the event organizer adopts the soft strategy, the television channel will always adopt the tough strategy, since $R - \beta_0 C > R - C$. If the event organizer adopts the tough strategy, the television channel will compare Z (the profit from alternative programmes) and $R - \beta_1 C$. The higher the income from alternative programmes and the lower the revenues of the sport programme, the more likely the television channel is to adopt the tough strategy, that is, offering a moderate C and not being willing to increase it. However, as mentioned above, if the television channel adopts the tough strategy, the event organizer will adopt a soft strategy since $\beta_0 C + S > \alpha S$. We see that when $Z < R - \beta_1 C$, the event organizer will always adopt the soft strategy.

Table 12.3 clarifies which windows are Nash equilibria. We see that the north-west solution and the south-east window are both impossible, since we will always have $\alpha S < \beta_0 C + S$, and $C + S < \beta_1 C + S$. The north-east and the south-west windows, however, are both possible. These are known as 'chicken solutions'. Both agents will benefit if the event is broadcast. However, since we are unable to predict who will play tough who will play soft, it is impossible to predict how the profit will be distributed.

The results are not surprising. If the event is not broadcast, the event organizer loses the rights fees, and sponsorship support will be reduced too. Hence, if the television channel adopts a tough strategy, the event organizer is likely to give in and significantly reduce the rights fees so that the television channel finds the programme profitable, particularly when sponsorship support is greatly affected. Whether it will be broadcast, however, also depends on the profit the channel can make from alternative programmes (Z). The higher the profit from these programmes, the more the event organizer will have to lower the rights fees to motivate the television channel to prefer the sports event.

4   GATE RECEIPTS AFFECTED BY TELEVISION BROADCASTING

We will now extend the model presented in the former section by also taking into account that live sport programmes can affect gate receipts. Fears that too much sport on tele-

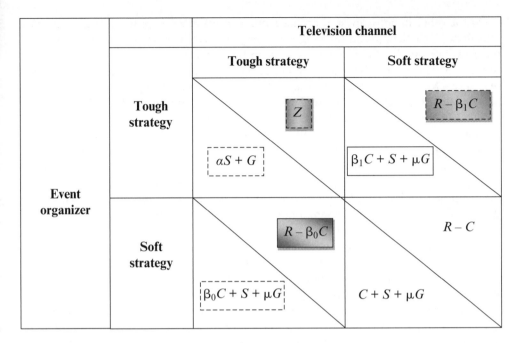

Figure 12.6   Television broadcasting reduces gate receipts

vision can reduce the attendance at the event are widespread in the sport business industry. For many years, clubs in the English Premier League were sceptical towards live broadcasting. When BSkyB first acquired the live rights in 1992, they were only allowed to broadcast 60 of 360 matches, that is, 20 per cent. Since then the number has increased, first to 110 (31 per cent) in 2001 and from the 2004 season to 138 (38 per cent) (Harris, 2009). By 2010, the English Premier League still did not allow live broadcasting from the main round, which is at 3 p.m. on Saturdays.

Similar concerns have influenced sports rights deals in North America. Since 1973, games in the National Football League (NFL) that do not sell out at least 72 hours prior to kick-off are subject to a local blackout. This means that these matches cannot be aired in the primary market. If the blacked-out home game is a nationally televised game on a broadcast network, all local stations inside a 75-mile radius must broadcast alternative programming (NFL on Television, 2011).

Figure 12.6 illustrates to what degree gate receipts can affect the strategies of the event organizer and the television channel. Theoretically, the effects on gate receipts can be both positive and negative. Some (potential) spectators may stay at home instead of going to the game if the event is on television. This will also be affected by the price policy of the event organizer and the television channel. If the event is broadcast on a free-to-air channel, the substitution effect will be stronger than if it is broadcast on a pay-TV channel. Such effects represent a double-edged sword for the television channel, since the quality of a live sport programme usually is better the larger and livelier the audience is. Hence, the television rating may decrease if attendance in the arena is significantly reduced.

On the other hand, television broadcasting can promote a sport and hence increase attendances, particularly in the long run. The net effect will depend on the strength of these two effects. In this context, we assume the substitution effect to be the stronger of the two. This means the gate receipts will be reduced if the event is on television. We regard this to be the most realistic scenario in the short run. The parameter μ illustrates how strong this effect is. The more the gate receipts are reduced, the lower is μ.

The introduction of gate receipts can only affect the strategy of the event organizer, not the television channel. There will not be any consequences if the television channel adopts a soft strategy. We will always have $\beta_1 C + S + \mu G > C + S + \mu G$. However, if the television channel adopts a tough strategy, the event organizer may adopt the same strategy if μ is very moderate. Hence, if gate receipts are significantly reduced when the event is on television, the event organizer will demand higher fees to compensate this reduction. On the other hand, a reduction in gate receipts can be compensated by increased sponsorship support since sponsors are willing to pay more when the event is televised. Additionally, the nominal value of the various revenues will also influence the decision. If gate receipts are moderate compared with media rights fees and sponsorship support, this can motivate the event organizer to accept a reduction of spectators at the arena. In that respect, it is worth keeping in mind the rapid growth in media rights we have observed in recent years. For many football clubs in the big-five European leagues (England, Spain, Italy, France and Germany) it has become the major revenue source (see also, Dolles and Söderman, 2013; Solberg and Gratton, 2013 in this volume).

Which strategy the event organizers will adopt can also be influenced by the residence of the spectators (see also Guala and Turco, 2013 in this volume). Many of those who reside a long distance from the arena may stay at home, no matter if the event is broadcast live on television or not. This particularly applies to supporters of the away team. For many of them, watching the match on television might be the only option. Travel costs, as well as the time the match is staged can also affect whether they will come to the arena. Matches during the weekend can attract more away supporters than those in the middle of the week. Such effects will be different for supporters of the home team, whose choices are unaffected by which day the match takes place. For them, attending the arena will always be an alternative to watching the match on television.

Table 12.4 illustrates that we now can have three Nash equilibria in pure strategies; the north-west window, the north-east window and the south-west window. The north-west window is a prisoners' dilemma situation if $\alpha S + G + Z < C + S + \mu G + R - C$, in other words if $\alpha S + G + Z < S + \mu G + R$.

Table 12.4   Nash equilibria

North-west	$\alpha S + G > \beta_0 C + S + \mu G$ and $Z > R - \beta_1 C$	
North-east	$\beta_1 C + S + \mu G > C + S + \mu G$ and $R - \beta_1 C > Z$	
South-west	$\beta_0 C + S + \mu G > \alpha S + G$ and $R - \beta_0 C > R - C$	
South-east	$C + S + \mu G > \beta_1 C + S + \mu G$ and $R - C > R - \beta_0 C$	(Impossible)

5   SUMMARY AND CONCLUSIONS

This chapter has illustrated how game theory can help stakeholders involved in the trade of sports rights to better predict the consequences of alternative strategies. We have focused on two alternative situations. We have analysed the situation where two rival television channels could broadcast one event each from two alternative sports where the popularity of the sports varied. We saw that three situations are possible. First, both preferred an event in the most popular sport. Second, one channel broadcast an event in the most popular sport while the other broadcast an event in the other sport. Third, both channels broadcast an event in the least popular sport. The latter alternative can occur if the rights fees in the most popular sport become extremely expensive, while the rights fees in the less popular sports become very cheap (in our case rights fees were zero). In the long run, however, this alternative is unlikely. Owners of popular sports events will be better off by having their events broadcast. Therefore, they are likely to reduce the rights fees, at least enough to have the event televised.

The second situation focused on a case with only one television channel and one event organizer. If gate receipts are small and not being reduced if the event is broadcast on television, the event organizer is more likely to accept moderate rights fees. The profit from alternative programmes will influence the television channel's strategy when negotiating with the event organizers. The more profit it can make from alternative programmes, the less it will be willing to pay for sports rights. Similarly, the event organizer will also consider if television programmes can affect other revenues. If gate receipts are substantial, and likely to be significantly reduced if the event is on television, then rights fees will have to increase to compensate the reduction.

In addition, to analyse some situations that are common in the market for television sports rights, we also aimed to illustrate how game theory can help stakeholders involved in sport management to better analyse the consequences of alternative strategies. We believe that sport governing bodies, event organizers, sports clubs and other stakeholders involved in sport activities are often involved in situations where game theoretic approaches can help them to better understand how market forces can affect the outcome of their own decisions. It can also help them to better analyse the strategies of their rivals as well as their counterparts, for example in sale processes.

So far, the methodology has been used in related issues, for example analyses of doping (Haugen, 2004), competitive balance (Haugen, 2006), football regulation (Haugen, 2007, 2008) and match analysis (Haugen, 2010), the financial problems in European club football (Solberg and Haugen, 2010) and other sport broadcasting issues related to the analyses presented in this chapter (Gratton and Solberg, 2007; Solberg, 2006).

Hopefully, we have been able to demonstrate the power of game theory as a tool to analyse relevant sport management problems. The complexity of mathematics may surely limit our possibilities in analysing 'real-world' game situations, but we still believe that relevant simplifications, as demonstrated in this chapter, may provide valuable managerial information. The most significant conclusion to draw is perhaps that the simple games we have analysed indicate a great complexity in seemingly simple television-rights gaming situations. As such, we predict a promising future for game theoretic applications in sport management.

REFERENCES

Dixit, A. and Skeath, S. (1999), *Games of Strategy*, New York: W.W. Norton & Company.
Dolles, H. and Söderman, S.C. (2013), The network of value captures in football club management: a framework to develop and analyse competitive advantage in professional team sports, in S. Söderman and H. Dolles (eds), *Handbook of Research on Sport and Business*, Cheltenham, UK and Northampton, MA, USA: Edward Elgar, pp. 367–95.
Europa Press Releases (2003), Commission closes its probe of Audiovisual Sport after Sogecable/Vía Digital merger, available at: http://europa.eu/rapid/pressReleasesAction.do?reference=IP/03/655&format=HTML&aged=0&language=EN&guiLanguage=en (accessed 19 December 2011).
Fort, R. (2003), *Sports Economics*, Upper Saddle River, NJ: Prentice Hall/Pearson Education.
Giomi, E. (2010), Media landscape: Italy, available at: http://www.ejc.net/media_landscape/article/italy/ (accessed 19 December 2011).
Gratton, C. and Solberg, H.A. (2007), *The Economics of Sport Broadcasting*, London: Routledge.
Gratton, C. and Solberg, H.A. (2013), The economics of listed sports events in a digital era of broadcasting: a case study of the UK, in S. Söderman and H. Dolles (eds), *Handbook of Research on Sport and Business*, Cheltenham, UK and Northampton, MA, USA: Edward Elgar, pp. 202–18.
Guala, A.C. and Turco, D.M. (2013), What do they really think? Researching residents' perception of megasport events, in S. Söderman and H. Dolles (eds), *Handbook of Research on Sport and Business*, Cheltenham, UK and Northampton, MA, USA: Edward Elgar, pp. 295–311.
Harris, N. (2009), £1.78bn: record Premier League TV deal defies economic slump, *Independent*, 7 February, available at: http://www.independent.co.uk/sport/football/premier-league/163178bn-record-premier-league-tv-deal-defies-economic-slump-1569576.html (accessed 14 July 2011).
Harsanyi, J. (1967), Games with incomplete information played by 'Bayesian' players, I–III, Part I: the basic model, *Management Science*, **14** (3), 159–82.
Haugen, K.K. (2004), The performance enhancing drug game, *Journal of Sports Economics*, (5) 1, 55–66.
Haugen, K.K. (2006), Research note: an economic model of player trade in professional sports – a game theoretic approach, *Journal of Sports Economics*, **7** (3), 309–18.
Haugen, K.K. (2007), An improved award system for soccer: a (game theoretic) comment, *CHANCE Magazine*, **20**, 22–4.
Haugen, K.K. (2008), Point score systems and competitive balance in professional soccer, *Journal of Sports Economics*, **9** (2), 191–210.
Haugen, K.K. (2010), The Norwegian soccer wonder – a game theoretic approach, *Scandinavian Sports Studies Forum*, **1**, 1–26.
Haugen, K.K. and Solberg, H.A. (2010), The soccer globalization game, *European Sport Management Quarterly*, **10** (3), 307–20.
Hoehn, T. and Lancefield, D. (2003), Broadcasting and sport, *Oxford Review of Economic Policy*, **19** (4), 552–68.
Késenne, S. (1996), League management in professional team sport with win maximizing clubs, *European Journal for Sport Management*, **2** (2), 14–22.
Nash, J. (1951), Non-cooperative games, *Annals of Mathematics*, **54**, 286–95.
NFL on Television (2011), Wikipedia, available at: http://en.wikipedia.org/wiki/NFL_on_television#Blackout_policies (accessed 14 July 2011).
Rottenberg, S. (1956), The baseball players' labour market, *Journal of Political Economy*, **64**, 243–58.
Selten, R. (1975), Reexamination of the perfectness concept for equilibrium points in extensive games, *International Journal of Game Theory*, **4** (1), 25–55.
Sloane, P.J. (1971), The economics of professional football: the football club as a utility maximiser, *Scottish Journal of Political Economy*, **17** (June), 121–45.
Solberg, H.A. (2006), The auctioning of TV sports rights, *International Journal of Sports Finance*, **1** (1), 33–45.
Solberg, H.A. and Haugen, K.K. (2010), European club football – why enormous revenues are not enough, *Sport in Society*, **13** (2), 329–43.
Von Neuman, J. and Morgenstern, O. (1944), *Theory of Games and Economic Behaviour*, Princeton, NJ: Princeton University Press.
Vrooman, J. (1997), A unified theory of capital and labour markets in major league baseball, *Southern Economic Journal*, **63**, 594–619.

PART IV

PLACE, TIME AND SPECTATORS

13 Triple impact assessments of sport events
Tommy D. Andersson

1 IMPACTS OF SPORT EVENTS

Sport events have impacts on individuals, social life and society at large in many different ways. Tangible impacts such as improvement of local infrastructure, urban regeneration or 'architectural pollution' are common for sport mega events. But intangible effects may be at least as important. Sport events are manifestations and often celebrations of sports values such as competitiveness, fairness and loyalty. Such values are important for the social fabric and have an impact on social life not only in the short run but also on the accumulated social capital of the community.

The purpose of this chapter is to discuss how impacts of sports events can be assessed from a wide social science perspective with a focus on sustainability. The major objectives are, first, to examine analytical frameworks related to sustainability of sport events, second to discuss analyses related to the triple bottom line framework, that is, economic, sociocultural and environmental impacts, and, third, to review implications and challenges for future research.

Most sport competitions such as everyday soccer league matches, junior regional athletics competitions as well as mega events such as Olympic Games and Fédération Internationale de Football Association (FIFA) World Cups are examples of sport events that in this chapter are defined as 'temporary occurrences with a predetermined beginning and end. Every such event is unique, stemming from the blend of management, programme, setting and people' (Getz, 2005: 16).

Although the focus in this chapter will be on sport events, a triple impact perspective is applicable to a wide range of sports and business activities. 'Triple bottom line' was originally suggested by Elkington (1997) as a way of analysing impacts of industrial business activities but has also been applied to an analysis of charter tourism to peripheral areas (Lundberg, 2011). Sports club activities for youth certainly have economic, environmental, cultural and social impacts that can be described by triple impact assessments.

In social science research there is a tradition of describing how people are affected by arts, events and sports. At the individual level, positive effect on health (Haley and Andel, 2010), education (Deasy, 2002) and measurable impacts on attitudes and behaviour (Eisner, 2002) have been reported. On an aggregated social level, the impacts by sports and sport events, affect social capital (for example, Putnam, 2001) through social interaction related to sports, the economy, as well as the cultural capital of the society.

A broad overview of impacts is illustrated in Figure 13.1 where 'extrinsic impacts' describe effects coming from individuals or society to manifest themselves in often quite measurable impacts, whereas 'intrinsic impacts' become internalized as part of the personal or social value system and typically are more challenging to measure.

The horizontal axis from 'individual' to 'society' is to a large extent a reflection of how impacts on the individual level are aggregated into concepts on a social level, such as

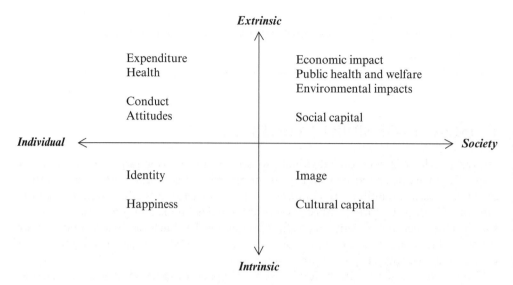

Figure 13.1   *A two dimensional illustration of major sport event impacts (cf. Armbrecht, 2009; McCarthy et al., 2004)*

when health, identity, attitudes and conduct on the individual level are reflected in social concepts such as public welfare, cultural capital and social capital. This axis also points to the need for a clearly defined 'subject of analysis', meaning: from whose perspective is an analysis being made, for instance is the focus on impacts on the individual, the company, the region, the state or society.

Sport events provide an arena for individuals to form and test certain behaviours often based on acquired attitudes. Sports ethics as manifested at sport events include some of society's most cherished social values, such as fair play and sportsmanship, but also highly disapproved of attitudes and conduct, such as hooliganism, misdirected team identity and nationalism.

The vertical axis in Figure 13.1 from 'extrinsic' to 'intrinsic' indicates to what extent the impacts lend themselves to measurement and observation, and that an impact assessment requires a clearly defined 'object of analysis', for instance: what aspects are being analysed.

1.1   Aggregated Impacts

Impact assessments are in most cases being aggregated to describe total effects on society. On this aggregated level, the concept of social welfare may be all inclusive especially in an analysis following the tradition of cost–benefit analysis. A similar all-inclusive approach is represented by the concept of sustainability: 'Sustainable development is development that meets the needs of the present without compromising the ability of future generations to meet their own needs' (World Commission on Environment and Development, 1987: 43).

More detailed approaches have been suggested in terms of economic, social, cultural, environmental, physical, experiential and political/administrative impacts (Getz, 1983; McCool and Lime, 2001), and Mykletun (2009) suggests seven types of capital that are impacted by events: social, human, cultural, natural, physical, financial and administrative capital.

An analysis based on several types of capital assets is attractive (cf. Bourdieu, 1973) and indicates how certain types of capital, such as physical or financial capital, are being used and reduced in value when a sport event is produced and used. But there are other types of capital, such as social and human capital, that are used for an event but nevertheless increase in value from being used in the event. When volunteers help out they not only contribute as human capital, but also get training and, possibly, new skills that enhance their human capital. The amount of volunteerism in a society is also an indicator of social capital.

Compared with the general definition of sustainability by the World Commission on Environment and Development (1987), sustainable tourism has been given more detailed criteria by a partnership (Global Sustainable Tourism Council (GSTC), available 1 August 2010 at: http://www.sustainabletourismcriteria.org/) uniting large tourism organizations such as the United Nations World Tourism Organization (UNWTO) and the United Nations Environment Programme (UNEP). The criteria stipulate that sustainable tourism should maximize benefits and minimize negative impacts regarding:

- Economic impacts on the local community;
- Social impacts on the local community;
- Cultural heritage;
- The environment.

Triple bottom line (Elkington, 1997; Getz, 2009; Sherwood, 2007; Vanclay, 2004) has a split focus on three types of impacts – economic, sociocultural and environmental – which is similar to the four criteria used for the GSTC definition. Triple bottom line is a tool under development for general business activities that also provides a suitable framework for analyses of the sustainability of sport events. One advantage is that it brings three perspectives together under one catchy phrase. The three bottom lines will not be measured in comparable units and therefore political judgement is still required to assess the overall impact of an event by weighing, for example, positive economic impacts against negative environmental impacts. The following impacts may be included (cf. Lundberg, 2011; Sherwood, 2007):

Economic impacts	Direct expenditure related to the event
	Leakage out of the local community
	Value added (wages, salaries, taxes and gross profit)
	Indirect and induced economic impact
	Opportunity cost.
Sociocultural impacts	Impact on social capital
	Impact on cultural capital
	Impact on public health and welfare
	Impact on community pride
	Impact on quality of life.

Environmental impacts   Emissions from transport to and from event
Energy and gas use
Solid waste – percentage of recycled waste
Water use.

1.2   Who Will Be Impacted?

Sport events are interesting organizational phenomena in the sense that the organization is typically hibernating during long periods to wake up to a very intensive and active period of limited time. To be able to do this, an event organization is depending on a large number of partners or stakeholders and all stakeholders involved in an event will not only affect the event, but will also be affected by the impacts of the event. A stakeholder is defined as 'any group or individual who can affect or is affected by the achievement of the firm's objectives' Freeman (1984: 25).

Impact analysis of a sport event needs to recognize that a large number of stakeholders will be affected and that impacts will differ depending on from whose perspective they are assessed. To have a rough understanding of what total effects could include, a stakeholder analysis presents a way to disentangle and clarify various subjects that are affected. Stakeholders to a sport event are illustrated in Figure 13.2.

Although simplified, the stakeholder model illustrates the stakeholders that affect and are affected by a typical sport event. Three major 'spheres' of stakeholders are suggested:

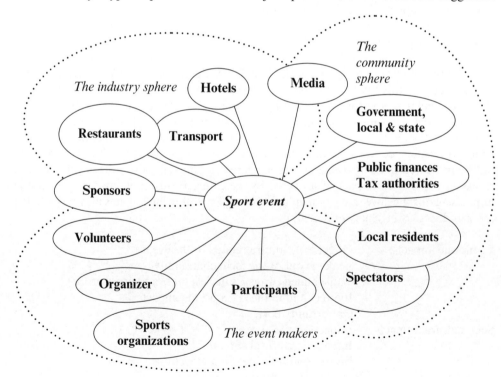

Figure 13.2   A typical stakeholder model of an assumed sport event

1. *The industry sphere* is dominated by the tourism industry comprising hotels, restaurants, transport, shopping and other commercial attractions. Mega events typically also generate activity in the construction industry. The industry sphere is normally positively affected by events economically and is the focus of most economic impact studies. Sponsors participate mainly for commercial/industrial reasons, but may also become an important partner for the event and play a positive role in creating an event.
2. *The event makers* centre around the event organization. Volunteer work is of great importance for the organizer and it would not be possible to organize many sport events without the support from volunteers. But volunteers are also affected socially, and social impacts affecting the social capital are generated among participants, volunteers, spectators and organizers. Sponsors are important for the sport event budget and sometimes also for the quality, image and marketing of the event, but are also concerned about their own interests in terms of, for example, branding and creating image effects.
3. *The community sphere* affects the event through the political process. Media plays a role in setting an agenda and providing a channel for communication and discussion between local residents, and local as well as national politicians. Pressure groups may be formed to voice community interests. Various local social and cultural associations may play a political role supporting and legitimizing political processes. One argument often raised concerns the impacts an event has on public finances. For most sport events, the local community is the dominating segment of the spectators and most of the positive impacts experienced by spectators remain within the community sphere.

Analyses of events from a stakeholder perspective have been developed (Andersson and Getz, 2008) and an impact analysis of a sport event should preferably start with a stakeholder analysis which is not only illustrative of all affected, but also of a discussion around what impacts will be included in an impact analysis and what impacts will not be included.

1.3 Objects and Subjects of Event Impacts

The complexity of an assessment of the impacts of sport events may be described in terms of the *objects of analysis*, that is, what type of impacts should be taken into consideration. But it is equally important to be clear about the *subject of analysis*, that is, from what stakeholder perspective should an analysis be made (Table13.1).

At the community level, economic impacts are preferably described by a cost–benefit analysis including tangible as well as intangible costs and benefits, whereas the financial effects are more relevant to the industry and the event organization. Sociocultural impacts of sport events normally include positive as well as negative effects at the community level and may be framed by the social exchange theory (Ap, 1992). The event makers are able to control and enhance sociocultural impacts and are therefore important stakeholders for the management of these impacts Environmental impacts are similarly experienced mainly by the local and global community but managed by the industry and the event makers.

Table 13.1   Subjects and objects of an impact analysis

Objects Subjects	Economic impacts	Sociocultural impacts	Environmental impacts
The community			
The regional economy			
The industry			
The event			

2   ECONOMIC IMPACTS

There is a comparatively long tradition of economic impact analysis. Archer (1989) introduced econometric methods to the study of tourism. The discernible financial inflow from tourism represents a marginal economic effect that lends itself to economic analyses based on theories by Keynes (1933) and Leontief (1936). There are, however, a number of fundamental issues that need to be clarified in order to interpret correctly the results of an economic impact analysis of sport events. A good review of economic impacts of sport events is provided by Preuss (2004).

2.1   Gross Economic Impact or Net Economic Efficiency

A large number of economic impact analyses describe the inflow of money in terms of 'direct economic effect'. This is sometimes further elaborated with the help of multipliers to include indirect and induced effects. Such an analysis describes the positive economic effects but does not identify negative economic effects, so the gross effect is therefore always positive. To turn a gross economic effect into a net economic effect, a discussion about opportunity cost is necessary.

2.2   The Opportunity Costs

This is an assessment of the value a resource would have generated in the best alternative use and this value represents the cost of using that resource for a sport event. A hotel room occupied by a visitor to a sport event may serve as an illustration. If the sport event is scheduled during a weekend when the occupancy rates at local hotels are low, then the opportunity cost is low and the difference between gross and net economic effect for the hotel industry is negligible. But if the sport event takes place during a busy period, the hotel room might alternatively be let out to a business person who now has to cancel a visit. The opportunity cost will then be based on the financial effects foregone and it is quite possible that a business person would have spent more in the local economy than the sports tourist would. The net efficiency in that case would be negative, although the gross effect from the visiting sports tourist is large and positive.

   This effect is referred to as displacement and should be considered in economic impact analysis, particularly for large sport events that are not carefully scheduled in periods with low seasonal demand. Similarly, attention should be paid to whether tourists that attend the event come specifically for the event or whether they go to the event as they are already in town visiting for other reasons, in which case they are referred to as casuals. Another type of visitor is known as a time-switcher if the visitor reschedules an already planned visit to coincide with the event. The economic impact from both time-switchers and casuals should be excluded in a correct economic impact analysis, and the displacement effects must be deducted as an opportunity cost. The opportunity cost has a strong logical appeal but may in certain cases seem rather impractical to apply to an impact evaluation.

2.3 Economic Impact Measured in Terms of Value Added or in Terms of Sales Value

The direct economic impact, which is a basic approach to economic impact analysis, typically measures the economic inflow into a region in terms of, for example, visitors' expenditure. For local industry this is equivalent to a measure of increased sales (or turnover). The economic indicators used politically and by economists, such as gross domestic product (GDP), however are based on econometric measures that use value added as the basic measure, and there is a large difference between the two measures of sales value and value added. Value added is often around half as much as sales value since it is calculated as sales value less the cost of input goods and services.

Use of multipliers is relevant when calculations are made in terms of value added and it is then important to know that multipliers applied to direct value added can never come to a higher value than direct sales value. This is quite logical since the final effect can never be more than the inflow of money. It is normally less, since money leaks out of the economy owing to necessary imports related to the sport event.

The three issues discussed above are all relevant irrespective of which of the three dominant methodologies that is applied. Cost–benefit analysis covers a wide area and is particularly suitable when the community is the subject of analysis (Mules and Dwyer, 2005). Cost–benefit analysis attempts to include not only financial impacts, but all impacts that create value (both negative and positive) in a society. Measurements of value are therefore often based on assessments of willingness-to-pay.

The second major methodology is input–output analysis which is based on the work of outstanding economists such as John M. Keynes and Wassily W. Leontief. Input–output analysis elaborates measurements of direct economic effects, such as visitor expenditure, in terms of direct value added as well as indirect and induced value added, and not only for total effects on the economy but also specified by industry. A weak point in most input–output analyses made of sport events is the lack of cost assessments, so these incomplete input–output analyses come out very rosy and always demonstrate large positive gross economic effects. A correct input–output analysis must also calculate the direct, indirect and induced economic impact of the opportunity cost and deduct this from the gross economic effect to arrive at the net economic efficiency of a sport event.

The third major methodology for economic assessments is known as computed general equilibrium (CGE) and includes a consideration of alternative uses of all the resources that are used for a sport event directly or indirectly (Dwyer, Forsyth and Spurr, 2004, 2006). The methodology is also dynamic in the sense that the cost of resources may be affected by the demand created by an event. This is relevant for mega events but less relevant for smaller sport events.

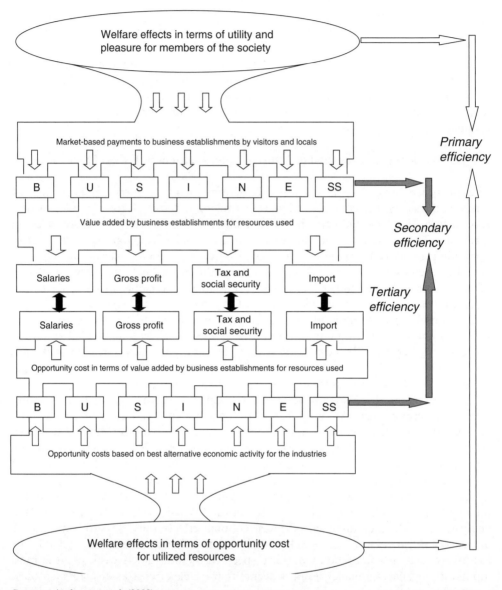

Source: Andersson et al. (2008).

Figure 13.3   A synthesis of cost–benefit analysis and input output analysis

A synthesis of various methodologies with a particular emphasis on the opportunity cost (Andersson et al., 2008) is described in Figure 13.3. The model is based on three levels that correspond to the three subjects of analysis: the community, the local industry and the regional economy.

The *primary efficiency* is calculated through an assessment of all values created in a community by a particular sport event and by comparing these to the values that would have been created if that sport event had not taken place (the opportunity cost). Examples of values created may be expenditure in town by sports tourists and a more exciting ambience. Examples of opportunity costs may be lost business from regular (business) tourists and the loss of a normal peaceful day without traffic congestions.

The *secondary efficiency* is financial in nature and compares the financial impact of a sport event to the financial impact of the opportunity cost. This is an analysis of expenditure generated by the event in terms of sales figures, which is a relevant measure for the industry. Likewise the opportunity cost is assessed in terms of revenue foregone owing to the sport event. The secondary efficiency is assessed for each industry and it is therefore possible to indicate industries that benefit from a sport event as well as industries that lose business opportunities due to the event.

The *tertiary efficiency* has a focus on value added, including direct and indirect effects, and is computed using inverted matrices according to the input–output methodology. It furthermore differentiates between the four major types of value added, that is: salaries and wages; gross profit to be used for investments, rent and net profit; taxes and social security income, and import. Import represents what is normally labelled as 'leakage' not only direct leakage but also indirect leakage. Since import (leakage) is included as a value added, the sum of the four types of value added equals the total direct economic effect. In congruence with primary and secondary efficiency, the opportunity cost in terms of value added is deducted from the computed value added from the sport event in order to assess the tertiary efficiency. Apart from an assessment of the total net value added, the model also describes how this total value is distributed among the four types of value added, that is, salaries and wages, gross profit, tax revenue and import.

This model spells out the logic but also illustrates the complexity of a correct economic assessment if complete accuracy is the aim. Complete accuracy however, is an unrealistic aim for any type of economic impact analysis and, if the synthesis model uses a few assumptions, this will make a computation of the opportunity cost fairly straightforward:

1. If it is assumed that the sport event will not significantly change local residents' expenditure pattern in the regional economy, then local residents can be excluded from the assessments of secondary and tertiary efficiency.
2. If it is assumed that a small sport event only uses otherwise free capacity in the regional economy (hotel rooms, restaurant seats, and so on) which is the case if the event takes place during off season, then it can be assumed that the opportunity cost is nil.
3. If it is assumed that a mega event has considerable displacement effects, then the opportunity cost can be calculated based on economic tourism statistics from a corresponding period during a previous year. It then implicitly assumes that all normal tourism during the mega event period is displaced owing to, for example, lack of lodging.

Secondary and tertiary efficiency can also be computed using the computed general equilibrium model, briefly described above, which implicitly assumes opportunity costs for all economic activities based on econometric statistics for the region. The advantage of using a CGE method is that the net efficiency is computed directly and without any specific assumptions about whether the disadvantage is the linear view that does not allow a specific discussion and assumptions about how various sectors of the economy are affected by a sport event. An ambitious attempt to model the effects of the Olympic Games 2000 in Sydney using CGE was made by Madden (2006).

3   SOCIOCULTURAL IMPACTS

Sociocultural impacts comprise social as well as cultural impacts but have only rarely and only recently (for example, Dolles and Söderman, 2008) been measured in sport event impact studies. Reviews of literature on social impact studies are provided by Armbrecht (2009), Deery and Jago (2010), Lundberg (2011), Reid (2007) as well as Robertson et al. (2009).

Social impacts can be positive, such as increased recreation opportunities, but also negative, such as increased crime risks and social stress, just as cultural impacts may be positive, such as meeting more visitors and having more cultural exchange, or negative, such as a risk of developing a superficial popular culture based on team identification and narrow-minded nationalism.

Social exchange theory as developed by Ap (1992) and Zhou and Ap (2009) is the dominating theoretical framework for discussing sociocultural impacts from tourism and events. This theory is economic in nature and states that local residents weigh positive impacts against negative impacts to arrive at an overall attitude towards the event. This is congruent with a cost–benefit approach, discussed above, and several social impacts are also normally included in a cost–benefit analysis. Attitudes regarding social impacts can be assessed in terms of a value, using willingness-to-pay measures. Such a value-attitude study will then be able to integrate social impact analysis with cost–benefit analysis as in a study by Lindberg et al. (2001). Reviews of literature on social exchange theory are provided by Andereck et al. (2005), Deery and Jago (2010), Easterling (2004), Harril (2004) as well as by Ryan and Gu (2008).

Sociocultural impacts may also relate to the concepts social capital and cultural capital (for example, Bourdieu, 1973) with an accumulative view that sport events contribute to an existing social fabric just as cultural impacts from a sport event will be integrated in the accumulated cultural capital. These aggregated concepts present opportunities to measure sociocultural impacts objectively in terms of, for example, number of volunteers involved in the sport event, although measurements of social and cultural capital is still a debated and not yet resolved issue.

3.1   Objective Measures or Perceptions of Sociocultural Impacts?

The measurement of sociocultural impacts related to events have so far mainly focused on individual attitudes and subjective assessments (cf. Figure 13.1) surveyed from a sample of the local community. The advancement of methods for measuring social capital (for example, Narayan and Cassidy, 2001), however holds a promise of a more objective approach in the near future to measure the marginal effect on social and cultural capital that a sport event may have. Measures such as increased volunteer activity, formation of sports clubs and increased sports club activity may be some examples of relevant objective measures of the effects a sport event may have on social capital. Studies using this approach are still predominantly qualitative in nature. Moscardo (2007) suggested after a content analysis of 36 events that the key themes for affecting social and cultural capital include level of community involvement, building networks, fun, family socialization, and maintaining culture.

The social impact evaluation framework (SIE) developed by Small et al. (2005) is partly objective in the sense that it is based on an assessment of sociocultural impacts likely to occur. This assessment *ex ante* is then followed up by an *ex post* social impact perception (SIP) study. This approach follows closely expectancy-value (EV) and value-attitude (VA) models suggested by Lindberg and Johnson (1997) and developed into assessments of economic value in terms of willingness-to-pay for various social impacts of tourism (Lindberg et al., 2001).

However, the most frequently used approach is to assess perceptions and attitudes. Based on a multiple item tourism impact attitude scale (TIAS) by Lankford and Howard (1994), a festival social impact attitude scale (FSIAS) was developed by Delamere (2001) and Delamere et al. (2001). Further developments of instruments to measure sociocultural impacts of events have been made by, for example, Fredline et al. (2003). These scales are based on answers in ordinal scales to a large number of items, and cluster analyses as well as factor analyses are frequently used statistical techniques.

An important study related to expectations versus perceptions of sociocultural impacts of events is reported by Balduck et al. (2013, in this volume) showing significant differences and a general change towards 'milder', lower post-event values both for positive and negative impacts related to social impacts of a Tour de France cycling event in 2007.

A cluster analysis of local residents during Gold Coast Indy (Fredline and Faulkner, 2001) identified five clusters: ambivalent supporters, haters, realists, lovers and concerned for a reason. Another cluster analysis related to the Beijing 2008 Olympics (Zhou and Ap, 2009) found two clusters: embracers and tolerators.

In a study of the Australian Grand Prix, factor analysis was used to reduce the number of concepts explaining attitudes, and Fredline et al. (2003) identified six factors describing local residents' concerns about social impacts: social/economic developments, injustice/inconvenience, facilities, bad behaviour, environmental long-term impacts, and price of goods and services. Kim et al. (2006) identified six factors of concern to local residents in relation to the World Cup of Soccer 2002: economic benefits, benefits of cultural exchanges, construction costs, price increases, social problems, traffic congestion and pollution.

The latter study clearly underlines the overlap between economic impacts and social impacts. Local identity is closely related to social capital, and a sports mega event can change and reinforce local identity, which may be beneficial for the local development process. The economy is a social phenomenon integrated with other social phenomena (Getz and Andersson, 2008). Local residents who gain economically from tourism also are more positive towards tourism than local residents who do not benefit economically from tourism activities in the region (Ap, 1992; Preuss and Solberg, 2006). This overlap should be borne in mind if an impact study of a sport event takes the three perspectives of economic, sociocultural and environmental impacts.

4   ENVIRONMENTAL IMPACTS

Environmental impact analyses of sport events are not common, although a number of mega events such as the Olympic Games have declared a strong commitment to environmental care:

> Caring for the environment is an important part of the work of the Olympic Movement. If sport events and activities are not planned and managed carefully, they can cause degradation of the natural environment. Equally important is the collective responsibility of those involved in sport to ensure that athletes and sport participants are able to train and compete in clean and healthy conditions. We also recognise there are many opportunities for sport, including sport events like the Olympic Games, to provide sustainable environmental legacies. (International Olympic Committee, 2009 quoted in Schlenker et al., 2010)

This powerful statement is a strong incentive to measure environmental impacts as a part of an impact analysis of sport events. The FIFA Football World Cup 2006 in Germany had an ambitious 'Green Goal' for the event (Dolles and Söderman, 2010). Researchers from the German Öko-Institut and the World Wildlife Fund suggested measurable environmental objectives for waste, water, energy and transport, according to Dolles and Söderman (2010). Environmental impacts have in general been measured by rather technical 'engineering-like' methods and the two dominating measures are known as ecological footprint and carbon calculation.

The ecological footprint gives a measure in a single unit of land that is required to support consumption and subsequent waste discharge. Empirical studies suggest, for example, that the average Londoner has an ecological footprint of 5.8 'global hectares' (gha) whereas the average world citizen has an ecological footprint of 2.2 gha. The world's bio-capacity is calculated as 1.8 gha per world citizen indicating that the world citizen is at present consuming above the world's bio-capacity (WWF, 2006).

Ecological footprint analysis is a concept developed at the University of British Columbia (Rees, 1997; Wackernagel and Rees, 1996) that works well as a catchphrase with an interesting conceptual history. A Swedish geographer, Georg Borgström, calculated the acreage that a country would require as a supplement to its present acreage in order to be able to feed itself and called this acreage 'Ghost acres' (Borgström, 1965). A similar concept was called 'Phantom land' and suggested by Catton (1980) whereas the United Nations Conference on Environment and Development (UNCED) at Rio de Janeiro used the concept 'Shadow land'. Footprint analysis is congenial with impact analysis since footprint is a perfect metaphor for an impact.

Carbon calculations are specifically focused on the greenhouse effect and produce one single measure similar to a footprint analysis, although not in terms of global hectares but rather in terms of the weight of greenhouse gas emissions.

Both of these methods are fairly easy to administer since there are several tools or 'calculators' specifically developed for event impact analysis. Many are also available for free and provided by public bodies or non-profit organizations. At the time of writing, there is an Australian Carbon and Ecological Footprint Events Calculator http://www.epa.vic.gov.au/ecologicalfootprint/calculators/event/introduction.asp, accessed 16 June 2001). The strong back-up for empirical assessments, as well as the fact that both of these concepts have been successfully established in the public debate, explains the popularity among planners and politicians. There is also a growing market for consultancy firms in this area. A study of nine event organizers revealed that the environmental impacts identified as the most important were transport, waste management and noise (Jones et al., 2008).

The strong focus on one measure 'global hectares' is probably one factor explaining the success of the concept ecological footprint. From a political and business point of view gha represents a global measure that all can measure their environmental ambitions against and, although the details behind the measurement may be impenetrable, it is still obvious that positive environmental efforts have a positive impact on gha, by reducing it. This is also closely related to the 'management mantra' that in order to manage something effectively you need to be able to measure it (McManus and Haughton, 2006).

While most academics probably are enthusiastic about the attention to environmental impacts that the concept of ecological footprint has created, this does not mean that academic scrutiny and reflection should be ignored and the universality of the measure is an issue that raises academic concern. Different areas have different absorptive capacities and waste that is extremely harmful in one area may be easily absorbed in another area. Water is one resource that carries little weight on the ecological footprint which may be acceptable in Finland or Sweden but not in a country like Australia. Substitution in one and the same area is also possible and may be counter-productive, although it reduces global hectares in that area with its own specific biodiversity.

Substitution between areas with different productive and absorptive capacities has no 'global' effect. There is a lack of incentives to allocate gha to areas where a it has a large marginal utility as long as the focus is solely on minimizing gha for an area. Cost–benefit analysis based on gha is not possible as long as 'benefits' are not part of the methodology (McManus and Haughton, 2006).

The market for trade of emission rights may present an opportunity to overcome many of these setbacks. A sport event may take responsibility for emissions related to the event and, by using prices from the emission rights market, the sport event will be able to monitor environmental impacts in a way that creates most welfare per unit of emission rights. Ideally, the emission rights market will help to allocate environmental impacts not only between areas, but also between industries and it is thus theoretically possible that, for example, a petroleum refinery will reduce production and emissions to allow for an exciting soccer cup final to take place simply because the cup final creates more pleasure and utility than a day's production at the refinery. In practice, however, it seems difficult to create a well-functioning emission rights market (Grubb and Neuhoff, 2006) and it is realistic to assume that it will take many years before emissions and gha are used in the most effective way.

If environmental impacts could be valued with the help of a well-functioning emission rights market, this would also present exciting opportunities to integrate an economic impact analysis with an environmental impact analysis.

5   CONCLUSIONS AND IMPLICATIONS FOR RESEARCH

The discussion in this chapter about impact analysis of sport events has been pursued within the framework of a triple bottom line approach. Three types of event impacts have been discussed in detail, that is, economic, sociocultural as well as environmental, and particular focus has been on measurement issues. The triple bottom line approach is not a strict final methodology but a framework under development, and in this concluding section a number of issues related to a triple bottom line approach will be discussed.

5.1   Scope of Assessment

The concept of triple bottom line may owe part of its success to the magic number three and to the fact that three perspectives provide an acceptable complexity. There have been unsuccessful suggestions of 'quadruple bottom line', adding climate as a fourth bottom line. Multiple bottom lines as a concept has also been suggested (Vanclay, 2004). An important issue is, of course, whether important perspectives are missing in a triple bottom line approach.

Two concepts similar to the idea of 'bottom line' are 'carrying capacity' and 'capitals'. Lundberg (2011) suggests six types of carrying capacity – physical, visitors' perception, social, cultural, economic and political – and an analysis of impacts from sport events could be structured according to an assessment of to what extent the carrying capacity of the destination, according to these six aspects, is large enough to accommodate the sport event. The seven capitals suggested by Mykletun (2009), that is, social, human, cultural, natural, physical, financial and administrative capital, provide another approach to assess how a destination is affected by a sport event.

Triple bottom line has a focus on economic, sociocultural and environmental aspects which cover a great deal of perspectives suggested by other researchers but it is not a complete coverage, which is important to keep in mind when the scope of a triple bottom line approach is discussed. A cost–benefit analysis is all inclusive but only implicitly so. A cost–benefit analysis should include all aspects and 'externalities' that are affected by the sport event, but for practical reasons all cost–benefit studies are limited and, unfortunately, in different ways. Thus cost–benefit analyses, although in theory more inclusive, lack the clarity of presentation that a triple bottom line approach has. The scope of a cost–benefit analysis is also related to the time horizon. An analysis of the complete life cycle of a sport event is desirable in order to describe not only cash flows over the life cycle, but also how other tangible as well as intangible impacts are distributed over time (I owe this point to an anonymous referee).

Another issue related to scope is to what extent an impact assessment should describe not only direct but also indirect effects. This is explicitly discussed in economic assessments and, if calculated, there are theoretically well-developed methods to do so. Sociocultural impacts, if measured by instruments using attitude scales, can be considered as direct impacts. The next question may be how these attitudes affect local residents' peace of mind and happiness, which may later on also influence local residents' desire to continue living in the area, and so on. Although these chains of sociocultural impacts should be relevant for an impact assessment, it may be too difficult theoretically to describe them with any certainty. It is, however, worth pointing out this difference in scope between an economic and a sociocultural impact assessment.

An analysis of indirect impacts of sport events must also consider that, apart from spending time on participation in sport events, active sports persons spend a lot of time training and preparing themselves for competitions, whereas passive spectators spend time and effort gathering information and preparing to watch a game or a race. The indirect impact of the time spent in preparation for a sport event by participants, as well as spectators, also has considerable effects socially, culturally and economically.

It has been recommended (Jago and Dwyer, 2006) that an economic impact assessment should be limited to a description of direct expenditure (which they call 'inscope expenditure') and they put forward three good reasons for this: first, by using a simple generally accepted method comparisons over time and across events and regions will be facilitated. Second, one will avoid being sidetracked by debating how multipliers should be used. Third, since more advanced methods, such as input output analysis and computed general equilibrium models, use direct expenditure as input, the opportunity to use more advanced models is still there. Limiting an assessment to direct expenditure would also eliminate the difference in scope between economic and sociocultural impact analyses discussed above.

5.2 Opportunity Cost

The need to consider opportunity cost, that is, the impact from the best alternative action, has been strongly argued. This is relevant not only for the economic analysis but equally important for a sociocultural and environmental analysis. Not discussing the opportunity cost is equal to assuming that participants, spectators and others involved in a sport event would be living in a vacuum with nil economic expenditure, nil sociocultural activity and nil environmental impact if they did not participate in the sport event. This is, of course, an incorrect assumption and may severely distort the result. It is closely related to whether the aim of the impact assessment is to describe gross impacts or net impacts.

Taking the tram to the city centre to watch a sport event may in fact have a large positive net environmental impact if the alternative was to go on a weekend trip to London. It would also have a large positive net regional economic impact, although less money is spent at the sport event than for the London trip. But it is spent in the region rather than being leaked out of the regional economy. It is also interesting to discuss the net sociocultural impact by comparing the sport event to a weekend in London. The point is that the issue of alternative activity cannot be ignored in a sport event impact assessment. In an empirical study this can be achieved by the use of statistics over average environmental impact and economic activity.

5.3 Commensurability

By producing results of a triple bottom line assessment in three non-comparable units, that is, monetary value, a 1–7 ordinal scale value and global hectares, the researcher avoids giving a final total measure of the impact of a sport event. An argument for doing so is that it must be a political decision to weigh cultural and social impacts against economics and against the environment. Many political scientists would be very sceptical about this romantic view of politics (for example, Caplan, 2007) and would rather argue that if researchers leave too much room for flexible interpretations of the impact assessment, other political issues will determine the final decision.

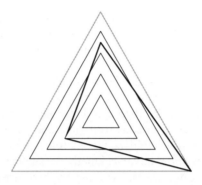

Source: Fredline et al. (2005).

Figure 13.4   An illustration of a transformation of TBL into a uniform measure of event impact

One way to achieve commensurability has been suggested by George (2003) for triple bottom line assessment of business firms where a maximum of 100 points were allocated to ten aspects of a firm's achievements in each of financial performance, social performance as well as environmental performance. Thus the ideal firm would score 300 points.

A similar idea applied to event impact analysis has been put forward by Fredline et al. (2005) where the ideal 30-point event can also be represented in a diagram as in Figure 13.4. Assume, for example, that a hypothetical sport event illustrated in Figure 13.4 scores 7 out of 10 in economic impact since the event is estimated to have 70 per cent of the indirect economic effects compared to the best benchmarking event in the region. The hypothetical sport event also scores 4 out of 10 in sociocultural impact since the event has considerably less favourable social impacts than the benchmarking event. Finally it scores 10 out of 10 in environmental impact since it is considered just as environmentally friendly as the benchmarking event.

Both the approach suggested by George (2003) and the approach suggested by Fredline et al. (2005) are based on a transformation from a measure in monetary value, a 1–7 ordinal scale value, and global hectares into a value on a scale from 1 to 10. In a benchmarking exercise the score could be set for a specific sport event in relation to its performance compared to the average, or the best of the other events taking part in the benchmarking.

Cost–benefit analysis provides another way of assessing a sport event in one uniform monetary measurement unit. Proponents of the contingent valuation method (Mitchell and Carson, 1989) and similar methods such as choice modelling (Garrod and Willis, 2001) to measure willingness-to-pay are optimistic about the feasibility of measuring the value of social and cultural impacts in monetary value (Armbrecht, 2009; Noonan, 2003). Environmental impacts may have a correct opportunity cost expressed as a monetary value, provided there exists a well-functioning emission rights market. Economic impacts are already in monetary values, although some adjustments will be needed to transform financial values into a correct economic value.

5.4   Managerial Implications

Organizers of sport events are typically closely connected to the 'community sphere' (cf. Figure 13.2) and affected by a political agenda. Organizers depend on public acceptance in order to get permissions to arrange an event, to rent publicly owned arenas and sometimes also to get public financial support. Sustainability is high on the political agenda and will probably continue to be so for the foreseeable future. Organizers can therefore expect to be challenged on issues such as environmental, social and economic impacts on the society of a sport event they wish to organize.

By shifting focus from a traditional economic impact analysis normally based on inflated multipliers to a more balanced approach, organizers will be more in tune with public opinion. A more balanced approach includes a straightforward description of direct economic impacts which is complemented by an equal importance given to environmental and social impacts of an event. Triple impact assessments provide an attempted framework for such a more balanced impact analysis of the sustainability of a sport event.

5.5   Future Research

Economic impact analysis has been tested through *ex post* analyses (Baade et al., 2008) where the impacts have been studied some years after a sport event by an analysis of regional economic statistics for the year a particular sport event took place. In most of these studies economic impacts turn out to leave much smaller traces in the regional economic statistics (regional domestic product) than was predicted by the use of expenditure data and input–output analyses. A development of this approach to comprise *ex post* analyses also of sociocultural and environmental impacts would be a fruitful approach to learn more about both how correct and how stable over time triple bottom line results are (cf. Balduck et al., 2013, in this volume).

The theory of various forms of capital (Mykletun, 2009) needed for a sport event holds a promise of a consistent framework where a particular event leaves an impact on all types of capital. Such an approach should also clarify the difference between capital and flow. Another issue is the fact that in triple bottom line certain impacts are described by perceptions of impacts, especially so sociocultural impacts, whereas other impacts are described in concrete technical (environmental) or financial (economic) units. A theoretical development of social capital and measurements of social and cultural capital can in the future hopefully be integrated in a triple bottom line approach.

Theoretical developments in the field of measuring willingness-to-pay may also influence the development of economic impact assessments of sport events. When sociocultural impacts can be given an economic value this will certainly increase the relevance of analytical results not only for the community and politicians, but also for the event managers in their strategic decisions. Similarly, a well-functioning emission rights market is hopefully not too far away in the future (Grubb and Neuhoff, 2006). Sport events will then be able, just like other industries, to work with market prices for environmental emissions and integrate an environmental strategy with an overall economic and sociocultural strategy. A fully fledged cost–benefit analysis will then be feasible and impact assessments of sport events can be integrated not only in the long tradition of cost–benefit analyses from a wide range of industries, but also in the well-established theoretical framework of welfare economics.

REFERENCES

Andereck, K.L., Valentine, K.M., Knopf, R.C. and Vogt, C.A. (2005), Residents' perceptions of community tourism impacts, *Annals of Tourism Research*, **32** (4), 1056–76.
Andersson, T.D. and Getz, D. (2008), Stakeholder management strategies of festivals, *Journal of Convention and Event Tourism*, **9** (3), 199–220.
Andersson, T.D., Armbrecht, J. and Lundberg, E. (2008), Impact of mega-events on the economy, *Asian Business and Management*, **7** (2), 163–79.
Ap, J. (1992), Residents' perceptions on tourism impacts, *Annals of Tourism Research*, **19** (4), 665–90.
Archer, B. (1989), *Progress in Tourism, Recreation and Hospitality Management*, London: Belhaven Press.
Armbrecht, J. (2009), Att värdera det ovärderliga [Valuing the invaluable], Licentiate thesis, University of Gothenburg, School of Business, Economics and Law.
Baade, R.A., Baumann, R. and Matheson, V.A. (2008), Slippery slope? Assessing the economic impact of the 2002 Winter Olympic Games in Salt Lake City, College of the Holy Cross, Department of Economics Faculty Research Series, Paper No. 08–15, Worcester, USA.
Balduck, A-L., Maes, M. and Buelens, M. (2013), Social impacts of hosting major sport events: the impact of the 2007 arrival of a stage of the Tour de France on the city of Ghent, in S. Söderman and H. Dolles (eds), *Handbook of Research on Sport and Business*, Cheltenham, UK and Northampton, MA, USA: Edward Elgar, pp. 274–94.
Borgström, G. (1965), *The Hungry Planet*, New York: Macmillan.
Bourdieu, P. (1973), Cultural reproduction and social reproduction, in R. Brown (ed.), *Knowledge, Education and Cultural Change*, London: Kegan Paul, pp. 71–112.
Caplan, B. (2007), *The Myth of the Rational Voter; Why Democracies Choose Bad Policies*, Oxford: Princeton University Press.
Catton, W. (1980), *Overshoot: The Ecological Basis of Revolutionary Change*, Urbana, IL: University of Illinois Press.
Deasy, R. (2002), *Critical Links: Learning in the Arts and Student Academic and Social Development*, Washington, DC: Arts Education Partnership.
Deery, M. and Jago, L. (2010), Social impacts of events and the role of anti-social behavior, *International Journal of Event and Festival Management*, **1** (1), 8–28.
Delamere, T.A. (2001), Development of a scale to measure resident attitudes toward the social impacts of community festivals. Part II: verification of the scale, *Event Management: An International Journal*, **7** (1), 25–38.
Delamere, T.A., Wankel, L.M. and Hinch, T.D. (2001), Development of a scale to measure resident attitudes toward the social impacts of community festivals. Part I: item generation and purification of the measure, *Event Management*, **7** (1), 11–24.
Dolles H. and Söderman, S. (2008), Mega-sporting events in Asia. Impacts on society, business and management: an introduction, *Asian Business and Management*, **7** (2), 147–62.
Dolles H. and Söderman, S. (2010), Addressing ecology and sustainability in mega-sporting events: the 2006 Football World Cup in Germany, *Journal of Management and Organisation*, **16** (4), 587–600.
Dwyer, L., Forsyth, P. and Spurr, R. (2004), Evaluating tourism's economic effects: new and old approaches, *Tourism Management*, **25** (3), 307–17.
Dwyer, L., Forsyth, P. and Spurr, R. (2006), Assessing the economic impacts of events: a computable general equilibrium approach, *Journal of Travel Research*, **45**, 59–66.
Easterling, D. (2004), The residents' perspective in tourist research: a review and synthesis, *Journal of Travel and Tourism Marketing*, **17** (4), 45–62.
Eisner, E.W. (2002), *The Arts and the Creation of Mind*, New Haven, CT: Yale University Press.
Elkington, J. (1997), *Cannibals with Forks: The Triple Bottom Line of 21st Century Business*, Oxford: Capstone.
Fredline, E. and Faulkner, B. (2001), Residents' reactions to the staging of major motorsport events within their communities: a cluster analysis, *Event Management*, **7** (2), 103–14.
Fredline, E., Raybould, M., Jago, L. and Deery, M. (2005), Triple bottom line event evaluation: a proposed framework for holistic event evaluation, in A. John (ed.), *The Third International Event Management Research Conference*, Sydney, University of Technology Sydney.
Fredline, L., Jago, L. and Deery, M. (2003), The development of a generic scale to measure the social impacts of events, *Event Management*, **8** (1), 23–37.
Freeman, R.E. (1984), *Strategic Management: A Stakeholder Approach*, Boston, MA: Pitman.

Garrod, G. and Willis, K.G. (2001), *Economic Valuation of the Environment: Methods and Case Studies*, Cheltenham, UK and Northampton, MA, USA: Edward Elgar.

George, G. (2003), A theoretical examination of triple-bottom-line reporting, Victoria University Working Paper Series, 25/2003, Melbourne, Victoria University of Technology, School of Management.

Getz, D. (1983), Capacity to absorb tourism: concepts and implications for strategic planning, *Annals of Tourism Research*, **10** (2), 239–63.

Getz, D. (2005), *Event Management and Event Tourism*, 2nd edn., Elmsford, NY: Cognizant Communication.

Getz, D. (2009), Policy for sustainable and responsible festivals and events: institutionalization of a new paradigm, *Journal of Policy Research in Tourism, Leisure and Events*, **1** (1), 61–78.

Getz, D. and Andersson, T.D. (2008), Sustainable festivals: on becoming an institution, *Event Management*, **12** (1), 1–17.

Grubb, M. and Neuhoff, K. (2006), Allocation and competitiveness in the EU emissions trading scheme: policy overview, *Climate Policy*, **6** (1), 7–30.

Haley, C. and Andel, R. (2010), Correlates of physical activity participation in community-dwelling older adults, *Journal of Aging and Physical Activity*, **18** (4), 375–89.

Harril, R. (2004), Residents' attitudes toward tourism development: a literature review with implications for tourism planning, *Journal of Planning Literature*, **18** (3), 251–66.

International Olympic Committee (2009), 'Innovation and inspiration' in sport for a better environment, 23 March, available at: http://www.olympic.org/news?articleid=72314 (accessed 17 December 2011).

Jago, L. and Dwyer, L. (2006), *Economic Evaluation of Special Events: A Practitioner's Guide*, Gold Coast, Queensland: Sustainable Tourism Cooperative Research Centre.

Jones, R., Pilgrim, A., Thompson, G. and Macgregor, C. (2008), *Assessing the Environmental Impacts of Special Events: Examination of Nine Special Events in Western Australia*, Gold Coast, Queensland: Sustainable Tourism Cooperative Research Centre.

Keynes, J.M. (1933), The multiplier, *The New Statesman and Nation*, 1 April, 405–7.

Kim, H.J., Gursoy, D. and Lee, S. (2006), The impact of the 2002 World Cup on South Korea: comparisons of pre- and post-games, *Tourism Management*, **27** (1), 86–96.

Lankford, S.V. and Howard, D.R. (1994), Developing a tourism impact attitude scale, *Annals of Tourism Research*, **21** (1), 121–39.

Leontief, W. (1936), Quantitative input-output relations in the economic system of United States, *The Review of Economics and Statistics*, **18** (3), 105–25.

Lindberg, K. and Johnson, R.L. (1997), Modeling resident attitudes toward tourism, *Annals of Tourism Research*, **24** (2), 402–24.

Lindberg, K., Andersson, T.D. and Dellaert, B. (2001), Tourism development: assessing social gains and losses, *Annals of Tourism Research*, **28** (4), 1010–1030.

Lundberg, E. (2011), Evaluation of tourism impacts. A sustainable development perspective, Licentiate thesis, University of Gothenburg, School of Business, Economics and Law.

Madden, J.R. (2006), Economic and fiscal impacts of mega sporting events: a general equilibrium assessment, *Public Finance Management*, **6** (3), 346–94.

McCarthy, K.F., Ondaatje, E.H., Laura, Z. and Brooks, A.C. (2004), *Gifts of the Muse: Reframing the Debate about the Benefits of the Arts*, Santa Monica, CA: RAND Corporation.

McCool, S.F. and Lime, D.W. (2001), Tourism carrying capacity: tempting fantasy or useful reality?, *Journal of Sustainable Tourism*, **9** (5), 372–88.

McManus, P. and Haughton, G. (2006), Planning with ecological footprints: a sympathetic critique of theory and practice, *Environment and Urbanization*, **18** (1), 113–27.

Mitchell, R.C. and Carson, R.T. (1989), *Using Surveys to Value Public Goods: The Contingent Valuation Method*, Washington: Resources for the Future; Baltimore, MD: Johns Hopkins University Press.

Moscardo, G. (2007), Analysing the role of festivals and events in regional development, *Event Management*, **11** (1–2), 23–32.

Mules, T. and Dwyer, L. (2005), Public sector support for sport tourism events: the role of cost-benefit analysis, *Sport in Society*, **8** (2), 338–55.

Mykletun, R. (2009), Celebration of extreme playfulness: Ekstremsportveko at Voss, *Scandinavian Journal of Hospitality and Tourism*, **9** (2), 146–76.

Narayan, D. and Cassidy, M.F. (2001), A dimensional approach to measuring social capital: development and validation of a social capital inventory, *Current Sociology*, **49** (2), 59–102.

Noonan, D.S. (2003), Contingent valuation and cultural resources: a meta-analytic review of the literature, *Journal of Cultural Economics*, **27** (3), 159–76.

Preuss, H. (2004), *The Economics of Staging the Olympics. A Comparison of the Games 1972–2008*, Cheltenham, UK and Northampton, MA, USA: Edward Elgar.

Preuss, H. and Solberg, H.A. (2006), Attracting major sporting events: the role of local residents, *European Sport Management Quarterly*, **6** (4), 391–411.

Putnam, R.D. (2001), *Bowling Alone: The Collapse and Revival of American Community*, London: Simon & Schuster.

Rees, W. (1997), Is a sustainable city an oxymoron?, *Local Environment*, **2** (3), 303–10.

Reid, S. (2007), Identifying social consequences of rural events, *Event Management*, **11** (1–2), 89–98.

Robertson, M., Rogers, P. and Leask, A. (2009), Progressing socio-cultural impact evaluation for festivals, *Journal of Policy Research in Tourism, Leisure and Events*, **1** (2), 156–69.

Ryan, C. and Gu, H. (2008), Constructionism and culture in research: understandings of the fourth Buddhist festival, Wutaishan, China, *Tourism Management*, **31** (2), 167–78.

Schlenker, K., Foley, C., Getz, D. and Schweinsberg, S. (2010), STCRC ENCORE: Festival and event evaluation kit, available at: http://www.sustainabletourismonline.com/1005/events/encore-festival-and-event-evaluation-kit-review-and-redevelopment (accessed 17 December 2011).

Sherwood, P. (2007), A triple bottom line evaluation of the impact of special events: the development of indicators, PhD thesis, Victoria University, Melbourne, available at: http://wallaby.vu.edu.au/adt-VVUT/uploads/approved/adt-VVUT20070917.123458/public/01front.pdf (accessd 17 December 2011).

Small, K., Edwards, D. and Sheridan, L. (2005), A flexible framework for evaluating the socio-cultural impacts of a small festival, *International Journal of Event Management Research*, **1** (1), 66–77.

Vanclay, F. (2004), The triple bottom line and impact assessment: How do TBL, EIA, SIA, SEA and EMS relate to each other?, *Journal of Environmental Assessment Policy and Management*, **6** (3), 265–88.

Wackernagel, M. and Rees, W.E. (1996), *Our Ecological Footprint: Reducing Human Impact on the Earth*, Philadelphia, PA: New Society Publishers.

World Commission on Environment and Development (1987), *Our Common Future*, Oxford: Oxford University Press.

World Wildlife Fund (WWF) (2006), *Living Planet Report 2006*, Gland: WWF International.

Zhou, Y. and Ap, J. (2009), Residents' perceptions towards the impacts of the Beijing 2008 Olympic Games, *Journal of Travel Research*, **48** (1), 78–91.

14 Sacrés Français! Why they don't have great football stadia; how they will: political, economic and marketing implications of the UEFA EURO 2016

Boris Helleu and Michel Desbordes

1 INTRODUCTION

In May 2010, France was awarded the right to host the final round of the Union of European Football Associations (UEFA) European Championship in 2016 (hereafter EURO 2016). The French bid rested mainly on the quality of both its private and public infrastructures, with the exception of its stadia. The French bid has pledged to guarantee the 1.7 billion euro cost of building and renovating ten stadia.

In fact, no French stadium, not even the Stade de France (capacity 80 000; opened in 1998 to host the football World Cup), matches these standards. It begins to look as if France is failing to keep up with developments in the area of sporting facilities. It should be noted that since the early 2000s one line of thought, admittedly a controversial and minority one, has sparked a debate on the future of France: those who foresee its decline point to the country's diminished international influence, expressed in its inability to meet economic challenges or to maintain the cachet it earned during the age of enlightenment. Without being as pessimistic, one may observe that gloominess has affected the field of sport, battered by a number of setbacks. We may look at the field of organization of international events to illustrate this point and see how the French last four bids for the Olympic Games have failed (Lille 2004, Paris 2008 and 2012, Annecy 2018); as regards sporting competition, French football clubs have not done well in continental contests, with only two titles since the creation of the European Cup (Olympique de Marseille in 1993 and Paris Saint-Germain in 1996), they now rank fifth in the UEFA ranking (UEFA, 2012), behind England, Spain, Germany and Italy, and as concerns facilities, its stadia are an average of 66 years old.

Yet as we enter the twenty-first century, the stadium has become a center of urban living, incorporating spaces for leisure activities, movie theaters, stores, hotels and restaurants, and offices. These multi-purpose sporting venues also host shows, and football shares the space with other sports. The match itself is the center of a 'package event' and can no longer be the only item of fan experience: the pre-match, half-time and post-match periods are occasions for a variety of attractions, intended not only to appeal to the whole family, but also to encourage the spectators to arrive earlier, leave later, and to eat and drink more (the match and the arena as a matter of concern for football management is also adressed in Dolles and Södermann, 2008, 2013 in this volume). The multi-purpose stadium is equipped with a retractable roof, a removable playing field and a central video screen, offering an optimal level of comfort for the public.

If we then accept that the stadium is the basic tool for the economic (and thus sporting) success of the clubs, France became a candidate for the final round of the EURO 2016, seen as an opportunity to fill the gaps in its current facilities. In January 2010, Frédéric Thiriez, the President of the Professional Football League (LFP), described the situation as follows:

> The future of football depends on the renovation of our stadia. . . . As regards stadia, we are 15 years behind, and need to catch up. . . . Our stadia are now dilapidated. There is not a single club stadium in France capable of hosting a Champions League final: it's a disgrace to French football. . . . France should also be a candidate for the Euro 2016 Championship. This would be the way to speed up our stadium-construction programs. (Thiriez, 2007; translated by the authors)

This chapter presents how stadia development might be researched by providing a detailed analysis of the status of French stadia. The aim of this contribution is to describe how a country negotiates its transition to stadia designed as true recreational spaces and profit centers. The marketing, economic and political issues are identified and evaluated by using both second-hand quantitative data, and qualitative data obtained via discussions with the following experts: Xavier Daniel, former Manager of the Stadium Department of LFP now Director of Stadia for Euro 2016; François Hilbrandt, a consultant with INEUM, and Guillaume Gouze, a former stadium consultant with Sportfive now with Lagardère Unlimited Stadium Solutions. The exercise involves two stages. We first compile an overall inventory, by considering what is needed to place the clubs in a competitive position (section 2.1), which then partly controls what sporting events are to be offered (2.2) in the stadia (2.3). It thus becomes a matter of understanding the development of attendance and occupancy rates, and the motivations and purchasing behavior of the French public. We then see that the 1998 Football World Cup opportunity was poorly handled in terms of upgrading the quality of sporting venues. Second, we see how the actors in French football propose to correct the shortcomings of the stadia. Particular attention is given to the political aspects, by showing how the need to renovate French stadium facilities is justified, and describing the legislative provisions (3.1) and the financing arrangements (3.2). A case study involving the new Lille stadium illustrates all aspects of this demonstration (3.3).

2   FEW FANS IN SMALL CITIES AND OLD STADIA

We first attempt to highlight the shortcomings of French football's economic model, in particular the deficiencies in its stadia operations. To do this, we start with a simple observation: the clubs are operating in a competitive market and have stadia that host a varied public. These three aspects, which incidentally have been extensively discussed in the academic literature, need to be fully understood.

2.1   The Clubs: The Competitive Market in French Professional Sports

The ability of a sporting event to become a permanent feature of a town's character depends in part on the town's size and functionality. This is supported by geographic studies of both the European model (Bale, 1993; Helleu and Durand, 2007) and the North American model (Danielson, 2001; Jozsa and Guthrie, 1999). Similarly, the French market for professional sports is conditioned by its particular urban pattern, based, on the one hand, on the disproportionate size of Paris (the capital is seven times larger than Lyons, the second city) and, on the other, by the lack of urban areas with more than 2 million inhabitants (apart from Paris). Consideration of this structural deficit suggests optimal location strategies for the supply of sporting events. Taking our inspiration from the sporting venue model developed by the sports geographer John Bale (1989: 78–79), our approach is to consider a professional team as if it were an urban facility, like a university, a hospital or an opera house. According to Bale, the higher the urban level, the more numerous and better the clubs (ibid.). We therefore accept that the presence of a team and the stadium in which it operates is related to the demographic weight of the host city. In the marketing area, Westerbeek and Shilbury (1999) emphasize the importance of the 'place' variable in the marketing mix. According to them, 'the "place" variable becomes the most important element of the marketing mix when marketing facility-dependent sport services' (ibid.: 2).

During the 2007–08 season, 166 clubs operated at the top level of the major sports (football: 20 clubs in League 1 and 20 clubs League 2; basketball: 16 clubs in Pro A, 18 clubs in Pro B; rugby: 14 clubs in Top 14, 16 clubs in Pro D2; 14 clubs in D1 Handball, Volleyball Pro A and Magnus League Ice Hockey). They were distributed among 104 towns, totaling 34.5 million inhabitants. Thus 54 per cent of the French population had direct access to at least one major-league sporting event. Further, it becomes apparent that a town cannot support more teams than its market will allow. In fact, not every town is capable of providing the quality and quantity of supporters and sponsors needed to ensure a varied range of attractions. Valid strategies for promoting one discipline rather than another will develop according to the size of the towns. Some 30 towns with more than 250 000 inhabitants thus account for 40 per cent of all French sporting attractions. At this level, the existence of a major-league club is seen as a required service, guaranteeing the true legitimacy of the town and national (even European) renown. Thus the French League 1 (hereafter L1) or League 2 (hereafter L2) football teams prefer to be located in towns that are still in a position to handle additional attractions in a minor sport. Below the 250 000-inhabitant threshold, a single activity becomes the rule. When L1 or L2 level football is present, it blocks the emergence of a new discipline. Football, especially at the L1 level, is seen as a demanding sport that corners the local resources: in nine towns it is the only sporting event. Thus although the promotion/relegation system might theoretically enable small towns to be included among the elite at the most prestigious championships, we see an obvious link between sporting hierarchy and urban hierarchy. The largest urban areas are in a position to support a variety of sporting attractions, thereby responding to the diversity of their social demand.

The shortcomings of the French urban framework thus encourage the location of L1 and L2 clubs in the biggest markets, while discouraging diversity. No French town has more than one L1 or L2 football club; this has the immediate effect of considerably reducing local competition, which is exercised only against other minor sports or other leisure attractions. If we add up the number of inhabitants of towns that have one club, we find that professional football has a potential direct public of about 28 million consumers. Put another way, almost one out of every two French persons is able to get to a football stadium a short distance from their homes.

2.2   Do French Fans Really Love Football?

There is not much marketing literature concerning French fans. Monnin and Licina (2007) have outlined the profile of a typical FC Sochaux Montbéliard spectator: a man 35 to 45 years old, with a season ticket to the cheap stand; he comes to the stadium with friends an hour before kickoff, but will not eat or drink much while there. The spectator's satisfaction is mainly based on the modest price of the ticket but also on the quality of the facility (little waiting at the entrance, comfortable seats, safety, cleanliness, access to refreshment stands, toilets and parking) (ibid.). Blumrodt and Bodin (2009) have described the marketing strategy of the Stade Rennais FC, which is aimed at building a brand image that matches the aspirations of its public. The club manages to convey an image that reconciles tradition (the region's roots and culture) with modernity (a renovated stadium that is welcoming and comfortable) (ibid.). Concerning rugby, Bodet (2009) shows how Stade Français, by applying an innovative and audacious marketing strategy, has built a strong brand image for itself. This enables the club to use the Stade de France for its most important matches, attracting a broad family audience without much understanding of rugby (ibid.). For our part, in order to define the motivations and behavior of the French public, we will rely on the latest studies available now. But we will first consider football's power of attraction, by looking at attendances.

During the 2007–08 seasons, the 380 matches in the League 1 championship drew 8.2 million spectators. This represents an average of 21 811 spectators (including 12 267 season ticket holders) per match, for an occupancy rate of 75 per cent. At the junior level, 2.8 million spectators went to the stadium, for an average of 7354 spectators per match, including 3139 season ticket holders. Thus in 2007–08, 11 million spectators attended the L1 and L2 stadia, making football the live event with the greatest number of direct customers. For comparison, Top 14 rugby attracts about 2 million spectators per year (La Ligue 1, 2010; Ligue Nationale de Rugby, 2012). Table 14.1 reveals that the average attendances for L1 are raised up by the three largest French towns, which record more than 35 000 persons per match. Twelve clubs are unable to attract more than 20 000 persons and the number of season ticket holders ranges from 1 to 16, depending on the club. At the junior level, although the largest towns do succeed in attracting spectators, on average the stadia are half empty. At this level of competition the number of season-ticket holders is small, consumers preferring to select their events rather than commit to a full season. Records of more recent seasons are available but without the season ticket holders. For example during the 2010–11 season, the average L1 percentage of capacity fell to 68.5 per cent.

Viewed from a historical perspective, French attendances seem to have reached an impassable threshold. From the 2000–01 to the 2007–08 season the average attendance for L1 were around 21 000 spectators per match without recording any significant improvement. Over the same period, attendances have grown by 9 per cent in England (34 300 spectators per match), by 16 per cent in Spain (25 500), and by 26 per cent in Germany (39 900). Italy, in spite of a 26 per cent decline in attendance since 2001

Table 14.1   Stadium capacity, attendances, and occupancy rates in Leagues 1 and 2 (2007–08 season)

	Teams	Stadium capacity	Average attendance	Occupancy rate (%)	Season tickets holders	Season tickets holders (%)
Ligue 1	Marseille	60 013	52 600	87.6	42 050	70.1
	Lyon	41 044	37 297	90.9	25 110	61.2
	PSG	47 428	36 946	77.9	21 059	44.4
	Lens	41 233	34 654	84.0	21 395	51.9
	Saint-Etienne	35 616	29 248	82.1	16 422	46.1
	Rennes	31 127	25 640	82.4	14 273	45.9
	Bordeaux	34 694	25 489	73.5	10 236	29.5
	Toulouse	36 508	20 180	55.3	9 237	25.3
	Caen	22 864	19 658	86.0	13 404	58.6
	Strasbourg	29 000	19 401	66.9	10 456	36.1
	Nancy	20 087	18 741	93.3	11 851	59.0
	Lille	17 963	17 238	96.0	5 913	32.9
	Sochaux	20 005	15 930	79.6	8 104	40.5
	Valenciennes	16 547	13 799	83.4	9 028	54.6
	Metz	26 661	13 183	49.4	4 949	18.6
	Lorient	15 870	12 304	77.5	6 259	39.4
	Nice	18 696	11 282	60.3	4 469	23.9
	Le Mans	16 600	11 066	66.7	5 650	34.0
	Monaco	18 521	10 832	58.5	3 261	17.6
	Auxerre	23 508	10 591	45.1	2 558	10.9
	Average	28 699	21 804	74.8	12 284	40.0
Ligue 2	Nantes	38 004	22 771	59.9	10 836	28.5
	Le Havre	16 382	11 632	71.0	5 454	33.3
	Troyes	20 340	10 110	49.7	4 769	23.4
	Grenoble	20 068	9 999	49.8	4 130	20.6
	Sedan	23 189	9 590	41.4	5 024	21.7
	Amiens	11 932	9 427	79.0	5 926	49.7
	Guingamp	18 036	9 043	50.1	3 642	20.2
	Montpellier	32 950	7 247	22.0	2 042	6.2
	Angers	14 808	6 973	47.1	1 629	11.0
	Reims	9 236	6 861	74.3	4 025	43.6
	Châteauroux	17 072	6 520	38.2	2 872	16.8
	Brest	10 228	5 730	56.0	2 036	19.9
	Clermont	11 980	5 368	44.8	1 673	14.0
	Niort	10 898	5 358	49.2	1 382	12.7
	Boulogne	8 726	5 180	59.4	2 482	28.4
	Dijon	7 729	4 890	63.3	1 683	21.8
	Gueugnon	13 148	2 830	21.5	487	3.7
	Bastia	11 460	2 685	23.4	1 161	10.1
	Libourne	6 002	2 608	43.5	672	11.2
	Ajaccio	8 219	2 218	27.0	752	9.1
	Average	15 520	7 352	48.5	3 134	20.3

owing to problems with violence in stadiums, is still ahead of L1 with 23 400 spectators per match (La Ligue 1, 2010; Ligue Nationale de Rugby, 2012). In the second level of competition, L2 is catching up with the Italian and Spanish championships but still remains far behind the League Championship and the German second division ('Zweite Bundesliga').

The French fans demonstrate a lesser infatuation with football than its European neighbors, even though during World Cup and European Championship years the French national team's matches account for almost all of the year's ten best audiences. But this interest is event related and is not successfully carried over into the French L1 championship. In fact, according to a study by TNS (2008), 40 per cent of the French population voluntarily declare that they are interested in football, whereas this figure is always greater than 55 per cent in Germany, Spain, Italy and England.

Moreover, a survey carried out in 2008 by IPSOS, a market research company, shows that this interest is not necessarily expressed by going to the stadiums (the survey results are summarized in Belaygue, 2009). In fact, 71 per cent of those indicating a positive interest in these events did not go to the stadiums. So although an unexploited potential does exist, current spectators are distinguished by fragile consumption habits, showing that French stadiums are not recreational spaces, still less centers of consumption. Yet, these rather young spectators (half of the audience is under 35) have comfortable incomes: 34 per cent of them belong to households earning more than 3000 euro per month and 32 per cent to households earning between 2000 and 3000 euro. Their relationship with football remains essentially affective and not strictly commercial: only 15 per cent of those questioned defined themselves as 'customers', the others considering themselves to be spectators (38 per cent), supporters (35 per cent) or fans (11 per cent) (ibid.). As a result, it is as if the sporting event was limited to the 90 minutes of playing time. Typical spectators get to the stadium 30 minutes before the start of the match. When they consume food or drink there, they prefer to do it in the vicinity of the stadium rather than inside it. But, three-quarters of the spectators questioned are willing to devote a maximum budget of 10 euros to the purchase of food and drink (ibid.).

Although in the IPSOS survey 40 per cent of those who come to a stadium say they are very satisfied with the quality of the facilities, this does imply overall approval. As much as the spectators are reassured by the security measures deployed in the stadium and its surroundings, they are equally critical of its standards of comfort and convenience: the accessibility and cleanliness of the toilets, the accessibility of the club's shop, the comfort of the seats, protection from the weather, and the quality/price ratio at the refreshment stands are all given low marks by the consumer (ibid.).

The stagnating attendances are expressed in smaller revenues from ticketing: the average income per club is 6.6 million euro in France, or one-third of the average for the other four championships (18.7 million euro, Germany, England, Italy and Spain). The club's average income per spectator is 16 euro in France, versus 32.5 euro in the other four championships. As a result, while England, Germany and Spain are managing to diversify their sources of income, France – like Italy – is suffering from a dependency on television rights. As shown in Figure 14.1, the poor earnings from stadium resources partly explain why the L1 championship is the only championship unable to break through the billion-euro sales mark.

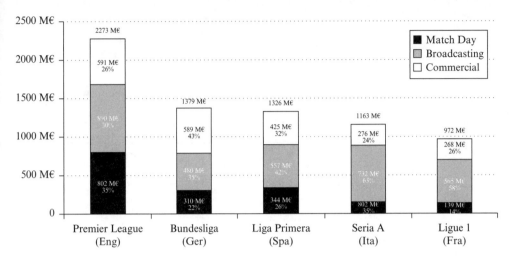

Source: Deloitte.

Figure 14.1 Economic model of the five major European championships, 2006–07

2.3 The Stadiums: Why so Old and so Poorly Run?

It thus appears obvious that French football must develop its ticketing resources in order to free itself from dependency on television rights. Noting that the average price of a ticket in France, 26 euro, is less than in England (43 euro) or in Spain (40 euro), the consultants Simon, Kucher and Partners (SKP) recommend an increase in prices (Chamoret, 2008). This policy would enable the creation of new income and involve the clubs in a virtuous circle: incomes increase and diversify; the clubs invest in talented players, thereby attracting the interest of a greater number of spectators and generating victories. This strategy seems dangerous, to say the least, since the average stadium occupancy rates do not suggest such a pressing need. That being the case, we have to wonder about the public's willingness to suffer a significant price increase when at the same time the stands are not full. For example, Marseilles and Paris, which have the highest ticket prices, play their home games in a stadium having an average of 10 000 empty seats. Figure 14.2 reveals that of the 14 clubs with prices below the national average, six still have occupancy rates below the average figure of 75 per cent.

This price strategy would correct the effects without tackling the root causes of the problem, such as economic, structural and managerial issues. The economic causes may be found in the 1998 World Cup opportunity, which was poorly handled. Of the ten stadiums involved in the event, only one was built (the Stade de France at a cost of 407 million euros, with no resident club) while the other nine were partially renovated, for 205 million euro. In comparison, when Germany organized the final round of the Football World Cup in 2006, Germany invested 1.4 billion euro (including 50 per cent from private financing) to build five new stadiums and renovate seven others (Daniel, 2008). Having said this, in the early 1990s safety concerns far outweighed standards of comfort. The Taylor Report on the 1989 Hillsborough disaster prompted all the

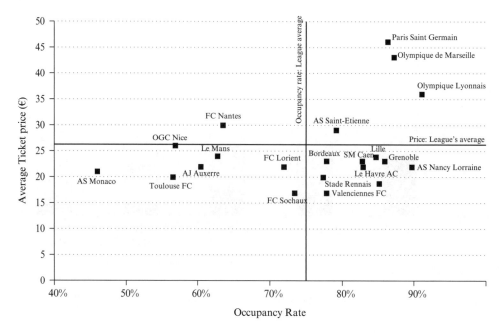

Source: LFP- SKP.

Figure 14.2   Average ticket price and occupancy rate in L1, 2008–09

European countries to engage in a wide-ranging discussion on the elimination of violence in their stadiums (Williams, 1995). In France this led to the adoption, in 1993, of a law concerning the safety of sporting events, driving hospitality, catering and multifunctionality in general from the forefront of the discussion. These concepts only really emerged with the inauguration of the Amsterdam ArenA in 1996, becoming a priority in the early 2000s. Thus more than a decade after the 1998 World Cup, France's stadiums have received no more than cosmetic attention and remain an aging resource (see Figure 14.3).

But from now on most of the income related to ticketing will come from seats that offer services. For example, Manchester United, the leading European club in terms of match-day revenues, creates 43 per cent of its ticket-sale income from the 9 per cent of top-price seats. In comparison with countries that have renewed their facilities (the new Wembley stadium includes 20 per cent VIP seating), French clubs have an insufficient number of premium (serviced) seats. This can be read in a study conducted by the Stadia Consulting Group (Hugues, 2008), covering 13 stadiums worldwide (including four in France). On average, a luxury seat brings in sales of 4000 euro per year in a French stadium, compared with 4600 euro in a foreign stadium. But the gap is made wider because of a deficiency in facilities. In fact, whereas a foreign stadium has an average of 4460 premium seats, a French stadium has only 1305 premium seats to work with. French stadiums are thus architecturally incapable of accommodating profitable customers, since they do not have premium services to sell. However, the development of hospitality services, even if it were made possible by major renovations, remains inconceivable because of the way in which the stadiums are operated.

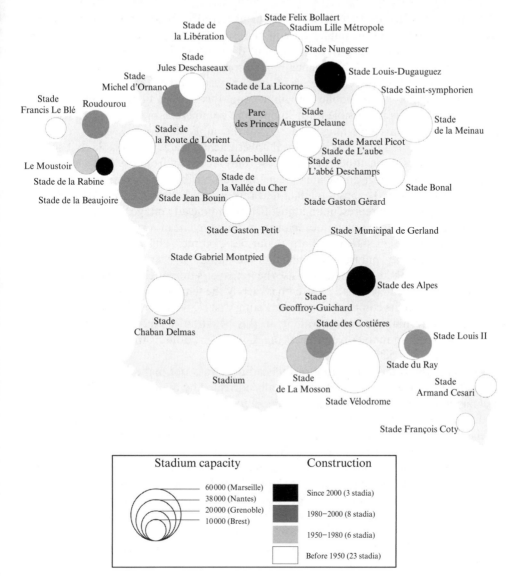

Figure 14.3   Inventory of League 1 and League 2 stadiums, 2008–09 season

The unusual nature of the French model (Gouguet and Primault, 2006) arises from the interdependence of amateur and professional sport written into the law. In fact, the federations and the professional leagues are deemed to be carrying out activities in the public interest. Accordingly, the Professional Football League organizes and manages its championships by delegation of public service. In this context, the link between the political sphere and professional football has always been close. This link endures in the management of stadiums, which belong to local government. Of the 20 clubs taking part in League 1 during the 2007–08 season, 17 are tenants of the public domain, in the form of a state lease. This contract allows the licensing authority to authorize a user to occupy temporarily a parcel of the public domain, in return for the payment of a fee, for a specific purpose and on a long-term basis – but the contract is precarious and revocable. This system exempts the club from bearing the construction cost of a stadium and allows it to have exclusive or preferential use of the facilities. On the other hand, the club pays a fee for occupancy of the public domain; it cannot use the stadium but only rents it for its matches and it is impossible for it to optimize commercial operations because of the restrictive regulations governing private use of the public domain.

It should be noted that making a local government's stadium available to a sporting company obviously constitutes an indirect subsidy. A report from the Auditor General's Department (the French financial court mainly responsible for checking on the legality of the public accounts) exposes the fact that this provision 'is still mainly carried out on irregular terms, which represent an unjustified economic advantage for the beneficiaries; the absence of a fee for private occupancy or the payment of a symbolic fee very often constitutes the current state of affairs' (Cour des Comptes, 2009: 58, translation by the authors). In this way, public management of the stadium acts as a brake on renovations, since the public sphere is reluctant to use the taxpayer's money to fund activities focused on profits for the clubs. Finally, the club is merely the tenant of a building that it cannot mold according to its commercial and marketing wishes, while the municipal owners lack the expertise to manage and operate it. In this situation the incentive to modernize is weak, and when an innovative project comes along, the administrative hurdles are both numerous and restrictive.

Although the run-down nature of the stadiums does not make for facilities that are attractive at first sight, this could be partially corrected by the systematic introduction of a commercial and marketing policy designed to retain the loyalty of existing customers and attract new ones. But this is where we encounter the managerial shortcomings of the French clubs, which are disinclined to adopt aggressive marketing policies. According to Xavier Daniel, the LFP's Stadiums Manager, while access-control systems are found in all the major championships, and are sometimes imposed by law (in Spain and Italy), only eight French stadiums (including the Stade de France, which lacks a resident club) are equiped with them (Daniel, 2008). Such access-control systems, over and above promoting security, is a prerequisite for the implementation of a direct-marketing strategy. In fact, it enables a detailed understanding of the purchasing habits and behaviors of the spectators, facilitates dialog and allows multiple formats for entry documents (e-tickets, mobile tickets and smart cards).

Indeed, customer relationship management (CRM) strategies, aimed at collecting and capitalizing on a set of data that will optimize customer understanding and satisfaction, are faltering. A study by INEUM Consulting shows that only seven clubs in the L1 use CRM software, whereas all the clubs in the English Premier League and 13 clubs in the German Bundesliga do so. As regards distribution systems, physical points of sale remain the preferred option. On the night of a match, 74 per cent of sales are made at the points of sale of clubs, of partners or at the ticket office. Only 18 per cent of sales are made on the Internet, whereas this rate reaches 47 per cent in England. In total, 76 per cent of all tickets in the German Bundesliga are sold ahead of the event, compared with 98 per cent in the English Premier League (personal interview with INEUM Consulting).

3   JUSTIFYING THE NEED TO BUILD NEW STADIUMS

French football now realizes how far behind it has fallen, so some 30 football-related construction or renovation projects have been launched independently of the French bid to host the final round of EURO 2016. The French EURO 2016 bid had a double interest: first, to submit an application requires that the country meets UEFA's requirements. These naturally concern the capacities of the selected stadiums (two stadiums with a capacity above 50000, three with 40000 and four with 30000), but they also involve technical standards, and stipulations concerning the stands, media accommodation and security. Meeting these requirements will mean executing a qualitative jump to reposition French stadiums closer to international standards. UEFA then recommends that the stadiums be delivered two years before the start of competition. Overcoming this time constraint requires the administrative and legal procedures to be made easier. In fact, there are so many of these procedures that it can take 10 years to complete a project. On occasion, the procedures may even suspend a worksite. For example, in July 2009, when the worksite had already been in operation for a year and the stadium was more than half built, the Lille Administrative Court ordered the cancellation of the construction permit for the new Valenciennes stadium because its impact studies were inadequate.

3.1   The Stadium as a Public-interest Facility

The political sphere undertook a detailed study leading to the publication of two reports at the end of 2008. The first, entitled 'Increasing the competitiveness of French professional football clubs' (Besson, 2008), highlights the clubs' lack of sporting success, attributable to economic backwardness. The report recommends reforming the French model by making the modernization of its stadia the principal lever for the development and diversification of its income. The second report was conducted by the Commission Grands Stades Euro 2016 (Séguin and Valentin, 2008). Philippe Séguin (2008, translation by the authors) states: 'In comparison to 1998, we are recommending a system where we may perhaps be able to do without a penny of public money. As long as the clubs do not own their stadiums and as long as they can't turn them into profit centers, they will continue to be economic dwarfs. The first thing to do is to fix the legal problem.' Therefore, the Commission recommends a new sharing of responsibilities between the public authorities and the private actors, and the provision of legal protection for major stadium projects by recognizing the public interest of these facilities, whether they were originally public or private. Finally, the unusual French approach (public management of stadia) is an obstacle for owners unwilling to invest without a guarantee that they will be the sole user of the stadium over a long period.

In line with the reports by Besson (2008) as well as Séguin and Valentin (2008), in July 2009 an article devoted to stadiums was included in a law for the modernization and development of services for the tourist industry (Chapitre V 'Grands Stades et équipements Sportifs' du projet de Loi de développement et de modernisation des services touristiques, 2009 [Chapter V 'Stadia and Sports Facilities' of the bill of development and modernization of the tourist services; translation by the authors]. It might appear surprising that the French government would show a concern for major stadiums in the context of a law on tourism, rather than in the context of a law on sport. Anxious to act as quickly as possible to strengthen France's chances of securing the organization of the final round of the EURO 2016 tournament, the legislators chose this approach, arguing that major stadiums contribute to France's sporting reputation. Furthermore, during the debate on this article of the Act, Bernard Laporte, at that time the Secretary of State for Sport, asked:

> Why this urgency? Because we have to meet a schedule: if the French Football Federation has to decide which towns the matches will be played in, the file containing the list of towns has to be completed by December 2009 in order to be submitted in February 2010; UEFA is to announce its decision in May 2010. . . . Today, we have to compile an application for the Euro, taking into account private stadia, and this is a matter that goes beyond political divisions. . . . The question that is being raised is whether or not we want to regain France's sporting prestige! (Assemblée Nationale, 2009)

According to this law, stadiums are declared to be of public interest whether they are public or private. The object is to facilitate their construction or renovation, and to provide a legal basis for the participation of public and private actors. The declaration of public interest applies to the sporting venues but also to the associated facilities that enable their operation. This is to remove any uncertainty concerning the execution of certain stadium projects. Thus, by way of illustration, the Olympique Lyonnais club wished to build a new complex including a stadium, a large supermarket, two hotels, an area for leisure activities, several office buildings, the new team training center, the club's head office, a store and a museum. If this 450 million euro project were taken on in its entirety by the club, the cost of access infrastructure (about 180 million euros) would be paid by the state and local governments. This last item is holding up the realization of the project; many local deputies are indignant about seeing taxpayers made to pay for the benefit of a private sporting-event company which could be listed on the stock exchange. As an example, Olympique Lyonnais became the first French club to be listed on the exchange in 2007. The capital raised was intended to finance the new stadium. Thus recognition of the public-interest aspect raises this type of opposition.

Lastly, these measures are likely to encourage the creation or modernization of stadia used by professional clubs, by diversifying the methods and sources of their funding: the sources of financing for these venues would no longer be limited to local governments. It should be noted that the concept of a public-interest facility is not defined in any legal text. Of course, it obviously seeks to portray the stadium as a public good, but it is really a matter of a label that removes the administrative constraints.

3.2   Financing: From Public to Private

The private financing and operation of stadiums by the clubs is thus seen as an ideal, without necessarily being generally applied at this time. In fact, the transfer of ownership of infrastructure from a local government to a club would probably not be welcomed by public opinion. Consequently, the role of local government remains essential, for several reasons. First, French clubs do not have the property holdings required for the construction of new stadia. Thus, making a site available requires the intervention of local governments, which also have the power to issue the administrative documents necessary for the construction or renovation of the stadium.

Table 14.2   The ten stadiums of Euro 2016

City	Stadium names	Under construction/ renovation	Capacity (for EURO 2016)	Cost (million €)	State subvention (million €)
Lyon	OL Land	Construction	58 200	450	20
Lille	Grand Stade	Construction	50 200	324	28
Marseille	Stade Vélodrome	Renovation	65 000	267	28
Nice	Grand Stade	Construction	33 500	184	20
Bordeaux	Grand Stade	Construction	42 600	165	28
Lens	Stade Bollaert	Renovation	45 000	111	12
Paris	Parc des Princes	Renovation	51 000	100	
Saint-Etienne	Stade Geoffroy Guichard	Renovation	39 300	75	8
Toulouse	Stadium	Renovation	37 100	56	6
Paris, Saint-Denis	Stade de France	Ready	81 300		

Between the 'all public' and 'all private' approaches, a partnership contract is seen as an alternative. This enables a public authority to entrust a company with the task of financing, designing in whole or in part, building, maintaining, and managing the public structures or facilities and the services contributing to the administration's public-service mission, under a long-term arrangement and against payment to be made by the public entity and staggered over time. Its objective is to optimize the respective performances of the public and private sectors so as to complete projects of an urgent or complex nature, such as hospitals, schools, prisons, on behalf of local government and as quickly and as effectively as possible. Used for the first time in the middle of the 2000s, the public–private partnership is the equivalent of the British Private Finance Initiative, a contract that has existed since the mid-1990s. This public–private partnership enables private operators to design and manage public facilities. They supply the investment while the local government partner provides reimbursement in the form of regular payments. It thus consists of a complex tripartite arrangement involving regional governments, the operator and the club, who will share both the costs and the income generated by the facility and its operation. As a consequence, up to 60 per cent of the 1.7 billion euro needed for the facilities will be financed for by the private sector. The French state undertakes to provide a subsidy of 158 million euro (see Table 14.2).

In order to strengthen the legitimacy of public assistance, the Sportfive agency conducted a study of the impact on the economics of football clubs, and the additional fiscal and social revenues for the state, which could be produced by the renovation of 20 French stadiums by 2014–15 (Bolotny and Debreyer, 2009). The 13 L1 and seven L2 clubs forming the sample would benefit from an average gain in 'match day' income of 118 per cent, or 182.6 million euro per season. This increase consists of two components. First, assuming an increase in stadium capacity at constant occupancy rate (75 per cent for L1, 42 per cent for L2) and given a reasonable increase in the average ticket price, the ticketing income would go from a total of 95.4 to 181.1 million euro for the 20 stadiums considered. Second, by making up the deficiency in VIP seats, the income from hospitality services would go from 59.7 to 156.6 million euro for these 20 stadiums. This would have the mechanical effect of rebalancing the business model, by reducing its dependence on media rights.

3.3 Case Study: The Grand Stade de Lille

The Lille Olympique Sporting Club (LOSC) is a football club founded in 1944, playing in L1. Since the beginning of the 2000s, the club has had success in the French championship, enabling it to play in the Champions League. However, in spite of these good results and a considerable local potential (Lille is the fourth largest French town, with more than 1 million inhabitants), the club attracted an average of only 17000 spectators (including 6000 season ticket holders) during the 2007–08 season.

Since 1974, LOSC has played in the Grimonprez-Jooris stadium. An ambitious renovation of the aging stadium was to increase its capacity to 33000 spectators. But, the proximity of the Vauban Citadel, a classified national monument, is preventing the start of construction and, since 2004, the club has been forced to play in the Stadium Nord at Villeneuve-d'Ascq, a community adjacent to Lille. Opened in 1976 with a capacity of 18000, this stadium is primarily devoted to athletics. As a consequence, the facilities are more basic and the club is unable to develop its hospitality services since the stadium has no box seats. In addition, this facility lacks UEFA approval, obliging the club to move its Champions League matches to the Stade Félix-Bollaert (in Lens) and then to the Stade de France (Paris).

To remedy this situation the Lille Urban Community has launched the Grand Stade Lille Métropole project, to build a multi-use stadium with a capacity of 50000 spectators. With a retractable roof and a removable playing field, the stadium can be converted into an indoor arena with a capacity of 16000, which can be increased to 30000 (Grand Stade Lille Métropole, 2012). In line with the Green Goal program promoted by the football's supreme international body, Fédération Internationale de Football Association (FIFA) (see Dolles and Söderman, 2010), the stadium will be equipped with two wind generators and a photovoltaic solar facility, to produce energy. The need to develop the luxury option is included. One hundred boxes will provide 1842 seats; there will also be 4950 business seats and 4950 square meters of display space. A total of 3500 parking places are planned. Three annexes will house two hotels, a sports/health center, leisure businesses and restaurants. Apart from LOSC matches, the facility will also be used for many other sporting, cultural and festive events (basketball, volleyball, tennis, boxing, opera, concerts, and so on).

The construction cost is estimated at 282 million euro for the stadium and 42 million euro for the associated facilities. The arrangement selected for the execution of the project is that of a public–private partnership covering the construction and operation of the stadium over a 31-year period. Following a request for proposals, the Eiffage company was selected. It will be responsible for the construction, financing, maintenance and operation of the stadium and the surrounding areas for the duration of the contract. Project financing of 324 million euro is being arranged by Eiffage, which is contributing 60 million euro of its own money. The balance of 264 million euro comprises debt, obtained from a syndicate of banks, and subsidies, in particular one from the Regional Council for 45 million euro. For the duration of the public–private partnership, the Lille Urban Community will pay an annual rent of 9.7 to 19.5 million euro. In this way the private sector assumes 56 per cent of the project cost compared with 44 per cent for the public sector. The multi-use stadium opened in August of 2012. It took four years from the decision to inauguration.

4 CONCLUSION

Sports economists have produced a significant literature questioning the supposed economic impact of a new facility (Baade, 1996; Baade and Dye, 1988; Bast, 1998; Irani, 1997; Noll and Zimbalist, 1997) and the lasting effects of the facility in terms of attendance (Clapp and Hakes, 2005; Howard and Crompton, 2003; Leadley and Zygmont, 2005). Not only because of the costs associated with, but also environmental and social impacts of mega-sports events, impact studies are of major concern for research (see, for example, Andersson, 2013 in this volume; Balduck et al., 2013 in this volume; Dolles and Söderman, 2010) The French case embodies the problem of 'public cost for private gain' showing how a discourse that legitimizes public support is constructed. For example, a strong argument is that sport is a response to the crisis as told to UEFA's ruling executive by French President Nicolas Sarkozy during the French presentation to host the EURO 2016 (BBC, 2010).

Finally, the legitimacy of such support is becoming clear, since this concept of the stadium as a public good already exists in Europe and in North America. More broadly, it is perhaps the organizational model of sport in France that should be questioned. It should be remembered that the state is involved in sport through economic and legal regulation, and stands as the guarantor of the interdependence between amateur and professional sport. Thus, research on govenance in sports is also of importance (see, for example, Gammelsæter and Senaux, 2013 in this volume) in order to fully understand processes of hosting mega events. In France, currently, a 5 per cent tax is levied on total television rights and turned over to amateur sport. In fact, now that they are authorized, if they choose, to finance the facilities associated with stadiums, local governments whose budgets are not inexhaustible will be forced to make a choice. As long as they provide 76 per cent of the financing in France, should we not fear that choices will be made in favor of facilities intended for professional sport, to the detriment of sport for all?

REFERENCES

Andersson, T. (2013), Triple impact assessments of sports events, in S. Söderman and H. Dolles (eds), *Handbook of Research on Sport and Business*, Cheltenham, UK and Northampton, MA, USA: Edward Elgar, pp. 237–56.

Assemblée Nationale (2009), *Full Proceedings of the 2nd Session*, 17 June, available at: http://www.assemblee-nationale.fr/13/cri/2008–2009/20090274.asp (accessed 20 January).

Baade, R.A. (1996), Stadium subsidies make little economic sense for cities: a rejoinder, *Journal of Urban Affairs*, **18** (1), 33–7.

Baade, R.A. and Dye, R.F. (1988), Sports stadia and area development: a critical review, *Economic Development Quarterly*, **2** (3), 265–75.

Balduck, A., Maes, M. and Buelens, M. (2013), Social impacts of hosting major sport events: the impact of the 2007 arrival of a stage of the Tour de France on the city of Ghent, in S. Söderman and H. Dolles (eds), *Handbook of Research on Sport and Business*, Cheltenham, UK and Northampton, MA, USA: Edward Elgar, pp. 274–94.

Bale, J. (1989), *Sports Geography*, London: E. & F.N. Spon.
Bale, J. (1993), *Sport, Space and the City*, New York: Routledge.
Bast, J.L. (1998), Sports stadium madness. Why it started – how to stop it, *Heartland Policy Study*, (85), 1 February.
BBC (2010), France beat Turkey and Italy to stage Euro 2016, available at: http://news.bbc.co.uk/sport2/hi/football/europe/8711016.stm (accessed 20 February).
Belaygue, J. (2009), Cap sur l'EURO 2016 [Head for EURO 2016], *footpro magazine*, (42), 42–4, available at: http://www.lfp.fr/footpro/pages42/footpro42.pdf (accessed 8 January 2012).
Besson, E. (2008), *Accroître la compétitivité des clubs de football professionnel français [Increasing the Competitiveness of French Professional Football Clubs]*, Paris: La documentation Française, available at: http://www.ladocumentationfrancaise.fr/rapports-publics/084000693/index.shtml (accessed 25 February).
Blumrodt, J. and Bodin, D. (2009), La communication marketing et son impact sur la perception des publics. Un exemple de l'industrie du sport spectacle [Marketing communication and its impact on the audiences perception. An example of the sports spectacle industry], *Revue européenne de management du sport*, (24), 17–31.
Bodet, G. (2009), 'Give me a stadium and I will fill it'. An analysis of the marketing management of Stade Français Paris Rugby Club, *International Journal of Sports Marketing and Sponsorship*, **10** (3), 252–62.
Bolotny, F. and Debreyer, D. (2009), Les Stades, un investissement indispensable et rentable pour la France [Stadiums, an indispensable and profitable investment for France], Etude de l'agence Sportfive.
Chamoret Alexandre (2008), Faut-il payer le billet plus cher? [Is it necessary to pay a higher ticket price?], *L'Equipe*, 25 October, 10.
Clapp, C.M. and Hakes, J.K. (2005), How long a honeymoon? The effect of new stadiums on attendance in Major League Baseball, *Journal of Sports Economics*, **6** (3), 237–63.
Cour des Comptes (eds) (2009), *Les collectivités territoriales et les clubs sportifs professionnels [Local Authorities and Professional Sports Clubs]*, Paris: La documentation Française, available at: http://www.ladocumenta-tionfrancaise.fr/rapports-publics/094000597/index.shtml (accessed 25 February 2011.
Daniel, X. (2008), Le contrôle d'accès en question [Access control in question], in J.-P. Hugues (ed.), *Nouveaux Stades: top depart [New Stadia: Top Departures]*, Ligue de Football Professionnel Report, February, Paris: Ligue de Football Professionnel, 71–3, available at: http://www.lfp.fr/dossiers_presse/2008_2009/stade.pdf (accessed 12 July 2011).
Danielson, M.N. (2001), *Home Team, Professional Sports and the American Metropolis*, Princeton, NJ: Princeton University Press.
Dolles, H. and Söderman, S. (2008), The network of value captures: creating competitive advantage in football management, *Wirtschaftspolitische Blätter Österreich [Austrian Economic Policy Papers]*, **55** (1), 39–58.
Dolles H. and Söderman, S. (2010), Addressing ecology and sustainability in mega-sporting events: the 2006 Football World Cup in Germany, *Journal of Management and Organisation*, **16** (4), 587–600.
Gammelsæter H. and Senaux, B. (2012), The governance of the game. a review of the research on football's governance, in S. Söderman and H. Dolles (eds), *Handbook of Research on Sport and Business*, Cheltenham, UK and Northampton, MA, USA: Edward Elgar, pp. 142–60.
Gouguet, J.-J. and Primault, D. (2006), The French exception, *Journal of Sports Economics*, **7** (1), 47–59.
Grand Stade Lille Métropole (eds) (2012), available at: http://www.grandstade-lillemetropole.com/ (accessed 20 February 2012).
Helleu, B. and Durand, C. (2007), La métropolisation du sport professionnel en Europe et en Amérique du Nord: une approche comparative [The metropolization of professional sport in Europe and North America: a comparative approach], *Mappemonde*, **88** (4–2007), available at: http://mappemonde.mgm.fr/num16/articles/art07402.html (accessed 12 July 2011.
Howard, D.R. and Crompton, J.L. (2003), An empirical review of the stadium novelty effect, *Sport Marketing Quarterly*, **12** (2), 111–16.
Hugues, J.-P. (ed.) (2008), *Nouveaux Stades: top depart [New Stadiums: Top Departures]*, Ligue de Football Professionnel Report, February, Paris: Ligue de Football Professionnel, available at: http://www.lfp.fr/dossiers_presse/2008_2009/stade.pdf (accessed 12 July 2011).
Irani, D. (1997), Public subsidies to stadiums: do the costs outweigh the benefits?, *Public Finance Review*, **25** (2), 238–53.
Jozsa, F.P. and Guthrie, J.J. (1999), *Relocating Teams and Expanding Leagues in Professional Sports: How the Major Leagues Respond to Market Conditions*, Westport, CT: Quorum Books.
La Ligue 1 (eds) (2010), Le Fantasy officiel de la Ligue 1. Inscrivez-vous pour gagner les nombreux lots mis en jeu, available at: http://new.lfp.fr/ligue1/affluences/journee (accessed 20 February 2012).
Leadley, J.C. and Zygmont, Z.X. (2005), When is the honeymoon over? National basketball association attendance 1971–2000', *Journal of Sports Economics*, **6** (2), 203–221.
Ligue Nationale de Rugby (eds) (2012) Les meilleures attaques à ce jour, available at: http://www.lnr.fr/statistiques-generales.html (accessed 20 February 2012).

Monnin, E. and Licina, J. (2007), Les spectateurs du Football Club Sochaux-Montbéliard' [The spectators of Sochaux-Montbéliard football club], *Revue européenne de management du sport* (20), December.

Noll, R.G. and Zimbalist, A. (1997), *Sports, Jobs and Taxes*, Washington, DC: Brookings Institution Press.

Séguin, P. (2008), Philippe Séguin souhaite un financement privé des stades [Philippe Séguin recomments private financing for stadia], *Le Monde*, 26 November, available at: http://www.(emonde.fr/cgi-bin/ACHATS/acheter.cgi?offre=ARCHIVES&type_item=ART_ARCH_30J&object_id=1060830&xtmc=philippe_seegu in&xtcr=28 (accessed 4 December 2012).

Séguin, P. and Valentin, J.-L. (2008), *Grands stades – Rapport de la Commission Euro 2016* [*Big Stadiums – Report of the Euro Commission 2016*], Paris: La documentation Française, available at: http://www.ladocu mentationfrancaise.fr/ (accessed 12 July 2011).

Thiriez, F. (2007), Les stades, un chantier bien entamé [The stadia, a job well begun], 26 November, available at: http://new.lfp.fr/corporate/article/frederic-thiriez-les-stades-un-chantier-bien-entame.htm (accessed 20 February 2012).

TNS (2008), TNSSPORT Euro SoccerScope, Results Summary Wave 9, internal company document.

UEFA (eds) (2012) UEFA rankings country coefficients 2011/12, available at: http://www.uefa.com/mem berassociations/uefarankings/country/index.html (accessed 17 February 2012).

Westerbeek, H.M. and Shilbury, D. (1999), Increasing the focus on 'Place' in the marketing mix for facility dependent sport services, *Sport Management Review*, **2** (1), 1–23.

Williams, J. (1995), English football stadia after Hillsborough, in J. Bale and O. Moen (eds), *The Stadium and the City*, Keele: Keele University Press, pp. 219–53.

15 Social impacts of hosting major sport events: the impact of the 2007 arrival of a stage of the Tour de France on the city of Ghent

Anne-line Balduck, Marc Maes and Marc Buelens

1 INTRODUCTION

In this chapter, we examine the social impact of the arrival of the Tour de France in Ghent. More specifically, residents' perceptions towards the impact of the arrival of the Tour de France in Ghent are studied before and after the arrival of the event. There is strong competition between cities and communities to host major sport events. The main reason why cities compete against each other to host major sport events is that it is expected that hosting major sport events will generate benefits for the community (Dolles and Söderman, 2008a, 2008b, 2011; Gratton et al., 2005; Kim et al., 2006; Maenning and Du Plessis, 2007). In contrast to the Olympic Games and the Football World Cup which take place every four years, the Tour de France (TDF) is an annual cycling event. The majority of the stages starts in one city and ends in another hosting city. A stage of the TDF lasts only one day, whereas most other sporting events last for several days at the same location. Although cities hosting a stage of the TDF have very limited time to realize their objectives, there is a high level of competition among cities and towns to host a stage of the TDF. The prestige of hosting the TDF, the perceived beneficial impacts and the intense media attention are the main drivers to bid for a stage (Bull and Lovell, 2007).

Local authorities especially use the economic impact as a rationale to promote and justify the bidding and hosting of a major sport event (Bull and Lovell, 2007). Public opinion is very susceptible to expected economic returns. Other impacts such as social and cultural impacts are often ignored as a result when hosting the event. The reason for this inattention is that social and cultural impacts are rather intangible impacts that are difficult to measure (Getz, 1997; Kim and Petrick, 2005). Social and cultural impacts are often linked to negative outcomes, which is detrimental for gaining public support. Similarly, there has been a predominant focus in literature on economic impact studies of hosting major sport events (Fredline and Faulkner, 2000; Getz, 2008; Waitt, 2003). More recently, researchers have been focusing on dimensions beyond the traditionally economic ones, such as environmental aspects (Dolles and Söderman, 2010) or the social impact of hosting events (Andersson, 2013, in this volume; Andersson et al., 2008; Dolles and Söderman, 2008a; Getz, 2008; Gursoy and Kendall, 2006). Studying these impacts is important to reduce undesirable outcomes from hosting major sport events such as disruption to community life that may be caused by the event (Delamere, 2001). Moreover, the enthusiasm of the local community towards hosting major sport events is an important factor for the success and the sustainability of those events (Getz, 1993; Gursoy et al., 2004). Support of residents is likely to convert a major sport event into an urban festival, whereas opposition to host the event may lead to delays to, and even abandonment of, the event (Gursoy and Kendall, 2006).

In this chapter, we explain what we mean by social impact, we outline the most important results of previous studies, we describe our methods used and we discuss the results and the lessons learned.

2 THE ROLE AND MEANING OF IMPACT STUDIES IN THE LEVERAGING OF MAJOR SPORT EVENTS

Similar to the exploration of impacts other than merely the expected economic benefits, there is a growing body of literature that explores the leveraging of major sport events (for example, Chalip, 2004; Chalip and Leyns, 2002; O'Brien, 2006). Chalip (2004: 228) defined leverage as 'those activities which need to be undertaken around the event itself . . . which seek to maximize the long-term benefits from events'. Chalip (2001) stated that a traditionally short-term focus on sport events fails to legitimize the public investments necessary to stage them. The goal of event leverage is to identify strategies and tactics to optimize desired event outcomes and that can be implemented prior to and during the event. The purpose of event leverage is not only to evaluate what has been done, but to learn from the event in order to enhance future leveraging of sport events. Impact studies are indispensable as they provide useful information about which strategies and tactics are effective (see the chapter by Andersson, 2013, in this volume). Preuss (2007) distinguished between impacts and legacies. He defined impacts as short-term outcomes, such as the economic boost directly related to the event, whereas legacies are the additional events due to changes in the host cities location factors, such as post-event tourism owing to hosting the event. The measurement of legacies, however, is difficult since measurement of legacies involves all changes caused by a major sport event over time (ibid.).

Social impact definitions are often drawn from the field of tourism studies since events are often perceived as touristic activities (Ohmann et al., 2006). 'The social impact of tourism refers to the manner in which tourism and travel effect changes in the collective and individual value systems, behaviour patterns, community structures, lifestyle and quality of life' (Hall, 1994: 136; also Hall, 1992). In the literature, there is often misunderstanding about the difference between social and cultural impacts. In general, social impacts have an immediate effect on the quality of life of residents and must be seen as short-term consequences. Cultural impacts, on the other hand, are long-term in nature and include changes in social relationships, norms and standards (Brunt and Courtney, 1999; Teo, 1994).

There is a small but growing number of studies that focus on social impacts of hosting major sport events. Waitt (2003) studied the temporal dynamics of the social impact of the 2000 Sydney Olympics. The respondents were Sydney residents who were surveyed 24 months before and during the games by using telephone surveys. Feelings of enthusiasm before the event were positive. The level of enthusiasm during the games, however, increased as expressed in feelings of patriotism, community spirit and the desire to participate as a volunteer. When differentiating for education, occupation or income, there was no significant difference in levels of enthusiasm. The level of enthusiasm was also related to residents' willingness to make personal economic sacrifices. If residents evaluated the public costs as excessive, they expressed lower levels of enthusiasm towards the Olympics. Overall, the number of respondents who perceived increased taxation and living costs declined over time. Perceptions of positive economic impacts of hosting the Olympics also declined over time.

Kim and Petrick (2005) investigated residents' perceptions and opinions of impacts of the FIFA 2002 World Cup Korea/Japan in Seoul. The most positive perceived impact was image enhancement and consolidation, while the most negative impacts of hosting the World Cup were negative economic perspective and traffic problem and congestion. Younger respondents experienced more negative impacts than older respondents. Female residents perceived both positive and negative impacts more highly than male residents. Over time, results showed that residents' levels of enthusiasm were less three months after hosting the event compared with the fervent feelings during the event. A comparison of residents' opinions revealed that the youngest age group showed the highest level of desire to travel to the host country of the next football World Cup. Positive opinions of female residents were higher compared with male residents. Over time, positive opinions about feeling patriotism and unity and the desire to participate in future mega-events declined. Waitt (2003) found similar conclusions that attitudes towards events are likely to change over time as the exchange relationship is a dynamic process. Kim et al. (2006) focused on residents' perceptions of the 2002 World Cup. They used a pre- and post-design. The results supported previous studies (for example, Kim and Petrick, 2005; Waitt, 2003) that perceptions of impacts change significantly over time. Before the event, residents indicated that they expected economic and cultural benefits but also acknowledged that the event would come at a cost. After the event, residents perceived benefits as lower than they had expected. In particular, the perceived economic benefits were lower after the event than before the event. Residents also perceived negative impacts such as social problems and price increases less after the event than before. The highest perceived negative impact factor was traffic problems, even though this factor declined over time. Ohmann and colleagues (2006) measured perceived social impacts of the 2006 football World Cup. The methodology used was face-to-face structured interviews with Munich residents. The interviews were carried out shortly after the World Cup. Overall, Munich residents encountered largely positive experiences of hosting the Word Cup. Sense of community, the collective sharing of the event experience and sense of security were judged as positive social impacts. Urban regeneration, which was seen as improvements in infrastructure, was also perceived as a positive result of hosting the event. Negative impacts such as crime increase, prostitution, bad fan behaviour or displacement of local residents were not experienced. The highest negative perceived impact of hosting the World Cup was increase in noise during the event.

Bull and Lovell (2007) examined the views and perceptions of Canterbury residents in relation to the arrival of the Tour de France. The overall perception of the event was very positive, although almost 40 per cent of the respondents were aware, through negative media attention, of the road closures and disruption. The majority of the respondents indicated that they had plans to participate in the various Tour de France events. Residents also indicated that the key benefits from hosting the event were the promotion of Canterbury, increased tourism and an incentive for the local economy.

Residents indicated that they perceived social goals, such as promoting community spirit, promoting sport and health, and developing cross-cultural experiences, as far less important as an outcome of hosting the Tour de France. This study supported the view that residents are willing to accept negative outcomes such as disruption and inconveniences to a certain degree in exchange for positive outcomes (Bowdin, et al., 2006).

This literature review shows that major sport events have the potential to create a number of positive and negative impacts. The studies used different methods, different time frames and different approaches to the content of social impacts. It is clear that social impacts should not be perceived as a generic set of outcomes of any sport event. Social impacts may be apparent at certain events while absent at others. There is a need for a variety of impact studies in order to identify patterns and trends so that these impacts can be managed before, during and after the event (Ohmann et al., 2006). However, researchers should be critical about the implications of their methodological choices.

3 THE TOUR DE FRANCE: A UNIQUE CYCLING EVENT

The Tour de France (http://www.letour.fr, accessed 18 August 2011) is a unique cycling event that takes place every year. The contest consists of 20 separate stages covering approximately 3500 km on closed public roads. Spectators do not have to pay to watch the contest. Twenty-one teams and 189 riders are allowed to participate. Peculiar to this major cycling event is that the event moves from city to city over a period of three weeks. The majority of the stages start in one city and end in another hosting city. This implies that cities hosting a stage have very limited time to realize their objectives. More than 4500 people are involved in the organization of the event, together with 2000 accredited journalists and 1800 technicians or drivers. Ninety-two television channels broadcast the TDF, with 51 of them broadcasting the event live on television. The contest is televised in 180 countries and more than 3200 hours of television are devoted to the event. A peculiarity of the event is the publicity caravan, a 45-minute rolling entertainment of 200 decorated vehicles representing 43 brands and distributing 15 million gifts to spectators. The caravan has become part of the TDF and adds to the spectacle as the brands try to outdo each other.

Although cities have very limited time to realize their objectives, there is a high level of competition among cities and towns to host a stage of the TDF. The prestige of hosting the TDF, the perceived beneficial impacts and the intense media attention are the main drivers to bid for a stage (Bull and Lovell, 2007). While the majority of the stages of the TDF take place in France, a few stages may take place in neighbouring countries such as Belgium, the Netherlands, the UK, Spain and Switzerland. The city of Ghent succeeded in hosting the arrival of the second stage of the TDF in 2007. At the time of the arrival of the cyclists in Ghent, 13 million people watched the TDF on television. The city, with its fabulous monuments, was on television for more than five minutes. Local authorities took the opportunity to organize a lot of other events that were geared to the TDF. It is estimated that 150 000 people watched the cyclists along the route upon their arrival in Ghent.

4   THEORETICAL FRAMEWORK FOR RESEARCH

This study focuses on the social impact of the Tour de France as measured by residents' perceptions of positive and negative impacts of the arrival of the TDF in Ghent. Social exchange theory is often used as theoretical framework to explain residents' reactions to host events. It is a behavioural theory that aims to understand and predict individuals' reactions in an interactive process (Ap, 1990). Social exchange theory states that people evaluate an exchange in terms of expected costs and benefits incurred as a result of that exchange. Individuals engage in an exchange whereby they seek something of value, be it material, social or psychological. Thus, residents who perceive benefits from the exchange are likely to express positive attitudes towards the event; residents who perceive costs are likely to evaluate the event negatively (Gursoy et al., 2002).

Social exchange relations are not temporally static. Residents continuously re-evaluate the exchange transaction (Waitt, 2003). Before the actual exchange occurs, initial perceptions prior to the event serve as a reference point for future re-evaluations of the value of exchange. After the event, residents are likely to re-evaluate the exchange transaction. Perceived outcomes which are below the reference point will be evaluated as disadvantages, thus, generating negative perceptions. Perceived outcomes above the reference point will be seen as wins, thus, resulting in positive perceptions towards the event. Based on the re-evaluation of the exchange, residents establish a new reference point that helps them to determine whether or not they will support the event in the future. If residents believe that the expected benefits are realized, it is more likely that they will support the hosting of the event in the future. If there is a disparity between pre- and post-event perceptions, it is more likely that residents will modify their perceptions towards hosting the event and that they will abandon future support towards hosting the event. There are a lot of factors that might affect the evaluation of exchange of residents towards hosting the event (Kim et al., 2006). For example, media, government agencies and the organizing committee generally create a hype around the event. It is possible that residents' perceptions are influenced by this positive message and that they are thus more likely to believe that the benefits of hosting the event will outperform the costs. So the external information provided by media and government agencies interacts with individual factors such as residents' own knowledge, values and past experiences with similar events. This interaction influences the perceptions of residents towards the event.

5   METHOD

5.1   Sampling Technique

Several methods have been used to measure social impacts of hosting major sport events, but there is a preference for using a quantitative research design. A quantitative research design allows for collecting a lot of data from the population being studied. Waitt (2003) used telephone surveys with Sydney residents to study the social impact of the 2000 Sydney Olympics. Other researchers (for example, Kim and Petrick, 2005; Kim et al., 2006) applied a questionnaire to measure the impact of a major sport event. Ohmann and colleagues (2006) used face-to-face structured interviews with Munich residents to measure perceived social impacts of the 2006 football World Cup in Germany. Bull and Lovell (2007) used both surveys and face-to-face structured interviews.

A number of criteria should be considered in order to choose the most appropriate sampling technique: time available to collect data, time period that the study considers, cost of data collection, sample respondents and the research team. A questionnaire was used for the purpose of this study. This sampling technique was chosen because a substantial number of respondents could be reached very quickly. In addition, since the purpose was to obtain perceptions of respondents one week prior and one week after the arrival of the TDF in Ghent, the sampling technique would allow the collection of data in a limited time period.

5.2   Data Collection

Ghent is a city with 25 districts and it has a surface of 156 km². With 240 000 residents, Ghent is Belgium's second largest municipality by number of residents. The population of interest to this study were residents of Ghent who lived along or near to the route of the TDF. Researchers drew a plan of the route and they identified the streets along or near to the route. The on-site survey was carried out in this area. Only residents of Ghent who lived in the selected area were allowed to participate in the study. This strategy was chosen because the purpose was to obtain perceptions of residents who experienced a clear effect of the arrival of the TDF. The data were collected randomly from door to door. Most respondents willingly answered the questionnaire. Respondents were asked to fill in the questionnaire immediately. The surveys were carried out at two time periods: one week prior and one week after the arrival of the TDF in Ghent. Respondents were asked to participate in the follow-up study and the interviewers noted their name and address. They were assured that this information was only used to be able to collect data for the post-test and to be able to link the data of the pre-test with the data of the post-test. The survey team consisted of Master's students who were well instructed in the purpose and method of the study.

5.3   Sample Size

A total of 421 questionnaires were obtained from the pre-test. All respondents indicated that they were willing to participate in the post-test. One week after the arrival of the TDF, the survey team visited the respondents again and they used the same method as in the pre-test. When the respondent of the pre-test was not at home, a questionnaire with a covering letter were left. As a result, 259 questionnaires were collected from the post-event survey.

After data collection, the questionnaires were screened for their usefulness. Questionnaires with more than 10 per cent missing values on the impact scale items were excluded from further data analyses. As a result, a total of 396 valid questionnaires from the pre-test were used for further analyses. For the data of the post-test, nine questionnaires were excluded because essential data was missing so the questionnaire from the post-test could not be linked to the questionnaire from the pre-test. Fifteen questionnaires did not meet the 10 per cent missing values criterion. As a result, the database of the post-test consisted of 235 valid questionnaires that were matched with the questionnaires of the pre-test.

5.4   Measurement

Socio-demographic variables, such as age, gender and occupation, were included in the questionnaire. A total of 33 Likert items were adopted from previous studies on the impacts of events (for example, Delamere, 2001; Kim and Petrick, 2005; Turco, 1998). These items were chosen because of their relevance to this study. The items were adjusted to residents' perceptions on the impact of the 2007 arrival of a stage of the TDF in Ghent and referred to economic, social/cultural, environmental and tourism infrastructure development impacts. The 33 items included 12 negative and 21 positive impact items. Respondents were asked to evaluate the statements on a 7-point Likert scale ranging from 1 = absolutely disagree, 4 = neutral, to 7 = absolutely agree. A 7-point Likert scale allows for more detailed answers than a 5-point Likert scale. Surveys collected before the arrival of the TDF aimed to measure expected benefits and costs, whereas surveys collected after the arrival of the TDF aimed to measure perceived benefits and costs.

5.5   Data Analysis

The statistical software SPSS was used. Exploratory factor analysis was used to delineate the underlying factors. The purpose of factor analysis is to reduce the set of observed variables into a much smaller and more simple structure by discovering the pattern of relationships among the variables. Factor analysis was performed by using the data of the pre-test. Principal component analysis with varimax rotation was used to reveal the underlying dimensions. The cut-off criterion to determine the factors was the Kaiser criterion (1974) or 'eigenvalue greater than 1 criterion'. Only items with communalities higher than .40 and factor loadings higher than .40 were retained and were included in the final factor structure. Our sample size was adequate as a minimum of five, preferable ten observations per variable is recommended for factor analysis (Hair et al., 1995). Reliability analysis using Cronbach's alpha was used to confirm the internal consistency of the resulting factors.

The purpose of this study was to compare resident's perceptions of impacts before and after the arrival of a stage of the TDF in Ghent. All respondents who participated in the pre-test were invited to participate in the post-test. We obtained a valid post-response rate from 235 residents. This resulted in a dropout of 40 per cent. Before we compare pre- and post-data, it is recommended to do a dropout analysis. This analysis tests whether there are differences between the dropout group and the group of respondents who also participated in the post-test and reveals whether there might be a selection bias that might influence our results and conclusions.

Repeated measures MANOVA was performed to examine significant changes in residents' perceptions of impacts before and after the arrival of a stage of the TDF in Ghent. The dependent variables were the impact factor dimensions, and the within-subjects factor time represented the time period before and after the arrival of the stage of the TDF in Ghent. Logistic regression was used to assess the relationship between residents' willingness to host the TDF next year and the impact factor dimensions. Odds ratios

(EXP(B)) were calculated, as well as 95 per cent confidence intervals (CIs) and *p*-values. The goodness-of-fit of the final model was determined by using the Hosmer-Lemeshow test.

6   RESULTS

6.1   Demographic Profile and Additional Information of the Sample

A total of 396 respondents participated in the pre-test of who we obtained 235 valid questionnaires in the post-test. Table 15.1 presents detailed information of the socio-demographic profile of the respondents. At both time periods (pre- and post-test), just over one-half of the respondents were female. The mean age of the respondents was 42.64 years (*SD* = 17.53) in the pre-test and was 42.19 (*SD* = 17.18) in the post-test. There was an equal distribution of respondents in the three age categories (± 32.00–35.00

Table 15.1   Socio-demographic profile of the sample

Pre-test (N = 396)		Post-test (N = 235)	
Socio-demographic variables	(%)	Socio-demographic variables	(%)
Gender		Gender	
Male	49.24	Male	49.15
Female	50.76	Female	50.85
Age		Age	
0–30	34.52	0–30	34.89
31–50	31.73	31–50	33.19
51 and above	33.76	51 and above	31.91
Occupation		Occupation	
Blue-collar worker	7.34	Blue-collar worker	7.69
Employee	34.18	Employee	33.76
Shopkeeper	19.49	Shopkeeper	20.51
Top/senior management	4.30	Top/senior management	4.70
Housewife/husband	3.04	Housewife/husband	4.70
Student	4.05	Student	4.70
Unemployed	13.42	Unemployed	13.25
Others	14.18	Others	10.68
Educational level		Educational level	
None	2.79	None	2.16
Primary school	6.35	Primary school	3.02
Secondary school		Secondary school	
Lower secondary school	10.91	Lower secondary school	11.64
Higher secondary school	27.66	Higher secondary school	28.02
Higher education		Higher education	
Bachelor	24.11	Bachelor	23.28
Master	23.10	Master	25.00
Postgraduate/doctorate	3.55	Postgraduate/doctorate	4.31
Others	1.52	Others	2.59

per cent per category). Employees and shopkeepers amounted for approximately 50 per cent of the occupations. There was also a high percentage of respondents who indicated being unemployed ($\pm$ 13.00 per cent), and who classified themselves in the category 'others' ($\pm$ 11.00–14.00 per cent). Almost 40 per cent of the respondents had a degree of secondary school, and approximately 47 per cent of the respondents had a degree of higher education.

6.2   Factor Analysis

A principal component factor analysis with varimax rotation was carried out to examine the underlying dimensions. The 33 impact items yielded eight factors with eigenvalues greater than 1.0. These factors explained 58.81 per cent of the variance. However, two items did not meet the factor loading criteria and one item did not load highly on any one factor. Therefore, these items were excluded for further analysis. After these adjustments, factor analysis revealed seven factors representing 30 items that explained 58.42 per cent of the variance. Results of the exploratory factor analysis and reliability analysis are presented in Table 15.2. The final seven factors were labelled: 'economic and tourism development' (eight items), 'cultural interest and consolidation' (five items), 'external image enhancement' (three items), 'disorder and conflicts' (five items), 'price increase' (three items), 'excessive spending and mobility problems' (three items) and 'interest in foreign cultures' (three items). Cronbach's alpha's ranged from α = .61 to α = .84 and were considered to be satisfactory (Mueller, 1986; Nunnally, 1970).

6.3   Dropout Analysis

Of the 396 respondents who participated in the pre-test, 235 residents participated in the post-test. Chi-square statistics were performed to reveal whether there are differences between the dropout group (161 residents) and the group of respondents who also participated in the post-test (235 residents). Chi-square statistics revealed no significant differences between both groups for age [χ^2 (2, N = 394) = 1.39, p = .50], for gender [χ^2 (1, N = 396) = 0.003, p = .95], for occupation [χ^2 (7, N = 395) = 7.08, p = .42] and for educational level [χ^2 (7, N = 394) = 13.32 p = .07]. Independent sample *t*-tests revealed no significant differences between both groups on the seven impact dimensions. Therefore, we concluded that the dropout group and the group of respondents who also participated in the post-test have a similar socio-demographic profile. Moreover, as we found no significant differences between both groups on the seven impact dimensions, we concluded that there is no selection bias that might influence our conclusions.

6.4   Residents' Expected and Perceived Impacts of Hosting the Arrival of the TDF

Table 15.3 presents the means and standard deviations of the seven impact factors before and after hosting the arrival of the TDF. Overall, the means of the impact factors of the pre-test are slightly higher compared to the means of the impact factors of the post-test. The most highly expected benefit prior to the TDF was 'external image enhancement' (M = 5.31, SD = 1.11), and the most highly expected problem

Table 15.2 Principal component factor analysis with varimax rotation and reliability analysis (N = 396)

Factors	Factor loadings	Communalities	Eigenvalues	% of variance	Cronbach's alpha
1. Economic and tourism development			4.35	14.51	.84
Improved the economic conditions	.72	.61			
Increased investment in Ghent	.70	.60			
Enhancement of cycling road in and around Ghent	.69	.53			
Enhancement of tourism infrastructure	.67	.60			
Accelerated the economic growth of Ghent	.60	.54			
Increased employment	.60	.47			
Enhancement of preserving heritage tourism resources	.55	.58			
Increased leisure facilities with accentuation of Ghent as a cycling city	.45	.41			
2. Cultural interest and consolidation			2.59	8.62	.77
Increased number of cultural events	.72	.64			
Enhanced pride of Ghent residents due to being hosts	.62	.65			
Increased interest in international cycling events	.60	.61			
Reinforced community spirit	.53	.53			
Enhanced embellishment of Ghent	.50	.57			
3. External image enhancement			2.42	8.06	.80
Improved image of Ghent internationally	.82	.76			
Increased opportunity to inform Ghent to the world	.81	.71			
Enhanced recognition of Ghent internationally	.66	.66			
4. Disorder and conflicts			2.39	7.98	.72
Increased noise	.80	.67			
Brought disturbance and disorder by visitors	.73	.60			
Increased garbage on the streets	.68	.61			
Lack of parking places	.46	.54			
Brought conflicts and antagonism between visitors and residents	.46	.42			

Table 15.2 (continued)

Factors	Factor loadings	Communalities	Eigenvalues	% of variance	Cronbach's alpha
5. Price increase			2.32	7.72	.71
Increased speculation of real estate	.84	.71			
Increased price of houses	.75	.67			
Increased price of daily products	.66	.45			
6. Excessive spending and mobility problems			1.83	6.11	.61
Excessive spending of government of Ghent for hosting the TDF	.73	.64			
Increased inaccessibility of houses	.66	.51			
Increased congestion	.54	.46			
7. Interest in foreign cultures			1.63	5.43	.67
Increased interest in foreign languages	.65	.59			
Increased tourist information facilities	.55	.56			
Increased interest in foreign cultures	.55	.63			

Table 15.3   Repeated measures MANOVA for comparison of residents' perceptions on the impact dimensions before and after the TDF (N = 235)

Factors	Mean ± SD		F-test	p-value
	Before (pre-test)	After (post-test)		
Positive impact factors (benefits)				
1. Economic and tourism development	4.05 ± 1.02	3.89 ± 1.04	9.65**	< .01
2. Cultural interest and consolidation	4.55 ± 1.15	4.58 ± 1.07	0.31	.58
3. External image enhancement	5.31 ± 1.11	5.12 ± 1.27	5.80*	.02
4. Interest in foreign cultures	3.53 ± 1.06	3.57 ± 1.14	0.29	.59
Negative impact factors (problems)				
1. Disorder and conflicts	4.90 ± 0.97	4.11 ± 1.12	105.68**	< .01
2. Price increase	2.75 ± 1.12	2.83 ± 1.17	1.57	.21
3. Excessive spending and mobility problems	5.64 ± 0.99	5.12 ± 1.10	53.22**	< .01

Note: * $p < .05$, ** $p < .01$.

was 'excessive spending and mobility problems' ($M = 5.64$, $SD = 0.99$). Prior to the arrival of the TDF, residents did not perceive 'interest in foreign culture' as an expected benefit as the mean was below average ($M = 3.53$, $SD = 1.06$). Conversely, residents also rated the factor 'price increase' below average ($M = 2.75$, $SD = 1.12$), indicating that they did not perceive this factor as an expected problem of hosting the arrival of the TDF. From the post-test, we observed that residents perceived 'external image enhancement' ($M = 5.12$, $SD = 1.27$) as the highest positive impact of hosting the arrival of the TDF, whereas they perceived 'excessive spending and mobility problems' ($M = 5.12$, $SD = 1.10$) as the highest negative impact. After the TDF, residents did not perceive 'economic and tourism development' ($M = 3.89$, $SD = 1.04$), and 'interest in foreign cultures' ($M = 3.57$, $SD = 1.14$) as benefits, and they agreed that 'price increase' ($M = 2.83$, $SD = 1.17$) was not a cost.

Repeated measures MANOVA revealed a significant change in residents' perceptions over time (Wilks' Lambda = 0.62, $F(7, 235) = 19.74$, $p < .01$). Follow-up univariate tests were performed to analyse which dimensions were significantly different over time. There was a significant difference ($p < .01$) between the mean of the pre-test ($M = 4.05$, $SD = 1.02$) and the post-test ($M = 3.89$, $SD = 1.04$) for the dimension 'economic and tourism development'. There was also a significant difference ($p < .05$) between the mean before ($M = 5.31$, $SD = 1.11$) and after ($M = 5.12$, $SD = 1.27$) hosting the TDF for the positive impact dimension 'external image enhancement'. Moreover, there were also significant differences for two negative impact dimensions. There was a significant difference ($p < .01$) for 'disorder and conflicts' before ($M = 4.90$, $SD = 0.97$) and after ($M = 4.11$, $SD = 1.12$) hosting the TDF, and for 'excessive spending and mobility problems' ($p < .01$) before ($M = 5.64$, $SD = 0.99$) and after ($M = 5.12$, $SD = 1.10$) the TDF.

6.5   Residents' Expected and Perceived Impacts of Hosting the Arrival of the TDF by Gender and Age Groups

Repeated measures MANOVA, with time as within-subjects factor and gender as between-subjects factor, was carried out. There was a significant time effect (Wilks' Lambda = 0.62, $F(7, 235) = 19.96$, $p < .01$) and a significant time $\times$ gender interaction (Wilks' Lambda = 0.93, $F(7, 235) = 2.53$, $p < .05$). Follow-up univariate tests (Table 15.4) were performed to analyse which dimensions had significant time $\times$ gender interactions. ANOVA indicated a significant time $\times$ gender interaction ($p < .05$) for the dimension 'cultural interest and consolidation'. Men were less positive over time, whereas women's perceptions increased over time. There was a significant time $\times$ gender interaction ($p < .05$) for the dimension 'external image enhancement'. Female respondents had similar perceptions over time, while male respondents' perceptions decreased over time. Considering the negative impact factors, there was a significant time $\times$ gender interaction ($p < .05$) for the dimension 'disorder and conflicts'. While women before the arrival of the TDF were more negative than men, their perceptions of this impact after the TDF were less negative than men's perceptions.

Repeated measures MANOVA, with time as within-subjects factor and age as between-subjects factor, was performed (Table 15.5). There was a significant time effect (Wilks' Lambda = 0.62, $F(7, 235) = 20.09$, $p < .01$), and a non-significant time $\times$ age interaction (Wilks' Lambda = 0.93, $F(7, 235) = 1.21$, $p = .27$).

Table 15.4   Repeated measures MANOVA for comparison of residents' perceptions on the impact dimensions before and after the TDF by gender

Factors	Mean ± SD				F-test	p-value
	Before (pre-test)		After (post-test)			
	Male (N = 116)	Female (N = 119)	Male (N = 116)	Female (N = 119)		
Positive impact factors (benefits)						
1. Economic and tourism development	3.90 ± 1.03	4.20 ± 0.99	3.67 ± 1.01	4.11 ± 1.03	1.78	.18
2. Cultural interest and consolidation	4.51 ± 1.16	4.59 ± 1.13	4.40 ± 1.03	4.76 ± 1.08	6.18*	.01
3. External image enhancement	5.35 ± 1.09	5.27 ± 1.14	4.99 ± 1.27	5.24 ± 1.27	4.64*	.03
4. Interest in foreign cultures	4.84 ± 0.96	4.97 ± 0.98	4.23 ± 1.09	4.00 ± 1.14	2.03	.16
Negative impact factors (problems)						
1. Disorder and conflicts	4.84 ± 0.96	4.97 ± 0.98	4.23 ± 1.09	4.00 ± 1.14	5.47*	.02
2. Price increase	2.78 ± 1.11	2.71 ± 1.15	2.79 ± 1.21	2.87 ± 1.14	1.20	.27
3. Excessive spending and mobility problems	5.58 ± 0.93	5.70 ± 1.04	5.10 ± 1.10	5.13 ± 1.11	0.40	.53

Note: * $p < .05$, ** $p < .01$.

Table 15.5   Repeated measures MANOVA for comparison of residents' perceptions on the impact dimensions before and after the TDF by age

Factors	Mean ± SD						F-test	p-value
	Before (pre-test)			After (post-test)				
	Age 0–30 (N = 83)	Age 31–50 (N = 78)	Age +51 (N = 74)	Age 0–30 (N = 83)	Age 31–50 (N = 78)	Age +51 (N = 74)		
Positive impact factors (benefits)								
1. Economic and tourism development	4.32 ± 0.79	3.87 ± 1.04	3.94 ± 1.16	4.05 ± 0.78	3.73 ± 1.12	3.89 ± 1.19	1.50	.23
2. Cultural interest and consolidation	4.74 ± 0.95	4.41 ± 1.23	4.48 ± 1.25	4.65 ± 0.96	4.49 ± 1.12	4.60 ± 1.15	1.34	.27
3. External image enhancement	5.35 ± 0.95	5.15 ± 1.23	5.43 ± 1.15	5.07 ± 1.14	5.18 ± 1.36	5.11 ± 1.31	1.92	.15
4. Interest in foreign cultures	3.58 ± 1.01	3.31 ± 1.02	3.70 ± 1.14	3.63 ± 1.00	3.40 ± 1.25	3.68 ± 1.18	2.52	.08
Negative impact factors (problems)								
1. Disorder and conflicts	4.92 ± 0.85	4.93 ± 1.01	4.86 ± 1.06	4.31 ± 0.93	4.18 ± 1.19	3.83 ± 1.20	0.07	.93
2. Price increase	3.00 ± 1.06	2.59 ± 1.11	2.62 ± 1.17	3.12 ± 1.12	2.64 ± 1.10	2.71 ± 1.26	2.07	.13
3. Excessive spending and mobility problems	5.55 ± 0.86	5.61 ± 1.00	5.76 ± 1.10	5.21 ± 0.98	5.09 ± 1.13	5.05 ± 1.20	0.21	.81

Note: * $p < .05$, ** $p < .01$.

6.6 Residents' Expected and Perceived Impacts of Hosting the Arrival of the TDF as Predictors of Residents' Willingness to Host the TDF Next Year

Two logistic regression models were performed to assess the relationship between residents' willingness to host the TDF next year and the seven expected and perceived impacts of hosting the arrival of the TDF. The seven impact factors were the predictors and residents' willingness to host the TDF next year was the criterion variable. The Hosmer-Lemeshow statistic for goodness-of-fit showed that the data fitted the model well for both the pre-test ($\chi^2 = 11.24, p = .19$) and the post-test ($\chi^2 = 8.54, p = .38$). As shown in Table 15.6, the dimension 'cultural interest and consolidation' and the dimension 'excessive spending and mobility problems' were significantly associated with the willingness to host the TDF in the future. For every one-unit increase in the dimension 'cultural interest and consolidation', the odds of willingness to host the TDF (versus non-willingness) increased with a factor 2.62 in the pre-test and with a factor 2.26 in the post-test. However, for every one-unit increase in the dimension 'excessive spending and mobility problems', the odds of willingness to host the TDF decreased with a factor 0.60 and 0.50 in respectively the pre-test and the post-test.

7   DISCUSSION

This study analysed residents' perceptions of impacts of hosting a stage of the TDF 2007 in Ghent. The results indicated that residents' perceptions of the impact of hosting the TDF had changed over time. Before the arrival of the TDF, residents expected that the event was an excellent vehicle for city marketing and for obtaining cultural benefits. On the other hand, residents recognized that hosting the event would come at a cost. After the TDF, residents still perceived positive cultural and image benefits but they indicated that the negative impacts were less severe than they had expected. Overall, women perceived the positive and negative impacts higher than men did. There were no significant differences between age groups. Our results corresponded only to some extent with the results of the study of Bull and Lovell (2007). Bull and Lovell found that Canterbury residents perceived that the arrival of the TDF would result in an increase of tourism and in a boost of the local economy. Ghent residents did not perceive that the TDF would positively affect economic and tourism development. Ghent residents perceived far more cultural benefits than Canterbury residents. Both Canterbury and Ghent residents, however, perceived that the TDF is an excellent means to promote the city. The positive impact factor 'cultural interest and consolidation' and the negative impact factor 'excessive spending and mobility problems' were significant predictors of residents' willingness to host the TDF in the future. Thus, if the cultural benefits do not outperform costs of hosting the TDF and traffic problems, the social exchange will be perceived as negative. In this situation, it is more likely that residents become unwilling to host the event in the future. This result suggested that residents adopt an attitude of 'what's in it for me?'. Moreover, it seemed that residents perceive that a short-term event such as the TDF allows cultural benefits rather than economic benefits to be realized. Residents are, however, only to some extent willing to accept the costs related to the hosting of the event. As mobility is a daily concern in cities, additional traffic problems are only

Table 15.6 Logistic regression results relating residents' willingness to host the TDF next year and the seven expected (pre-test) and perceived (post-test) impacts of hosting the arrival of the TDF

Impact factors	Before (pre-test, $N = 396$)				After (post-test, $N = 235$)			
	B	SE B	EXP(B) (CI)	p-value	B	SE B	EXP(B) (CI)	p-value
Positive impact factors								
1. Economic and tourism development	0.15	0.19	1.17 (0.80 – 1.69)	.42	−0.46	0.28	0.63 (0.36 – 1.10)	.10
2. Cultural interest and consolidation	0.96	0.18	2.62 (1.85 – 3.70)**	< .01	0.82	0.27	2.26 (1.32 – 3.86)**	< .01
3. External image enhancement	0.13	0.14	1.13 (0.86 – 1.49)	.37	−0.01	0.18	0.99 (0.69 – 1.42)	.97
4. Interest in foreign cultures	−0.15	0.16	0.87 (0.63 – 1.19)	.37	0.33	0.23	1.39 (0.89 – 2.17)	.15
Negative impact factors								
1. Disorder and conflicts	−0.27	0.16	0.76 (0.56 – 1.04)	.09	0.05	0.20	1.05 (0.72 – 1.54)	.79
2. Price increase	−0.22	0.13	0.81 (0.63 – 1.03)	.09	−0.14	0.18	0.87 (0.61 – 1.23)	.42
3. Excessive spending and mobility problems	−0.50	0.16	0.60 (0.44 – 0.82)**	< .01	−0.70	0.22	0.50 (0.32 – 0.76)**	< .01

Notes:
78.80 per cent of the cases were successfully categorized in the sample of the pre-test and 81.90 per cent of the cases were successfully categorized in the sample of the post-test.
* $p < .05$, ** $p < .01$.

accepted to some extent. Overall, three-quarters of the residents answered positively on the question whether the arrival of the TDF may return next year. This suggested that most residents evaluated the social exchange as beneficial.

The implications of this study need to be examined particularly with regard to the methodology used, the strengths and the limitations. The strength of this study is the method applied. Most studies focus on impacts before or after an event. This study continues by considering a before-and-after analysis associated with the event. The advantages of doing so is that perceptions of residents can be evaluated over time. However, most studies that used a before-and-after analysis, randomly collected data from respondents for the pre-test and the post-test. Thus, respondents of the pre-test were different persons than respondents of the post-test. Although these studies draw conclusions over time, before and after the event, results should be interpreted with caution since there is no control variable on any selection bias of the sample. Our study controlled for a selection bias of the research sample. We were able to match the data of 235 respondents of the pre-test and the post-test since we obtained the names and addresses of our respondents. Questionnaires that could not be matched were excluded from further analyses. By doing so, this method allowed us to take conclusions over time, since data were obtained before and after the event from the same sample of respondents. In addition, this study performed a dropout analysis to indicate whether a selection bias for the sample of the post-test might affect our results and, thus, our conclusions. It might be that a specific group of respondents participated in the pre-test but did not participate in the post-test. If this is the case, then results should be interpreted with caution. It might be, for example, that residents especially less satisfied with the event did not participate in the post-test and that residents especially satisfied with the event participated in the post-test. If this were to be the case, conclusions might be erroneous. A dropout analysis might indicate whether there is a selection bias for the sample of respondents. Our study controlled for demographic variables such as age, occupation and education level. No significant differences were found, suggesting that the dropout group and the post-test group had a similar socio-demographic profile. The study also controlled whether there were significant differences between both groups on the seven impact dimensions. No significant differences were found, suggesting that a selection bias was less likely in our study.

Besides the strengths of the study, we have to recognize a number of limitations or concerns. First, although the sample strategy has a number of strengths, the nature of the sample limits generalization of the findings. Since only residents of Ghent who lived in the selected survey area were allowed to participate, we may not generalize the findings to all residents of Ghent. The findings can only be attributed to residents who lived in the selected survey area. It might be that there is a difference in perceptions between residents living along the route and residents living in Ghent but not directly being confronted with the negative impacts of the event (such as traffic problems). In addition, it might be that Ghent residents living near the route but not immediately abutting the race could have more of less favourable perceptions of the event. Second, the city of Ghent hosted the stage of the TDF for the first time. Researchers should be aware of a possible novelty effect when hosting a major sport event for the first time. Therefore, follow-up studies are important to understand the long-term effect of hosting similar major sport events. Third, since we used a quantitative approach, we were not able to obtain a richer and in-depth dataset that could be obtained by using a qualitative approach. A qualitative approach might allow us to reveal other perceived benefits and costs that were not taken up into our survey. Fourth, our time period was one week prior to and one week after the arrival of the TDF in Ghent. Therefore, our results give indications of the effect of the event in the short term. We have no insight of a possible long-term effect. Fifth, it might be that perceptions of residents are influenced by the popularity of the sport. There is a long cycling tradition in Belgium which may influence the positive social impact of that kind of event. In addition, it might be that residents who cycle may be more likely to accept the event than non-cyclists. Therefore, researchers should deal with following questions when doing research on the social impact of events:

- Is the time period a significant determinant when studying sport events with different stages? For example, is there a difference in perceptions of residents when hosting the first, the fifth or the final stage of such a major sport event? Also, would residents have different perceptions about the event when hosting a departure or an arrival? If so, why is there a difference and which kind of stage would have the biggest social impact?
- What is the popularity of the sport hosted by the sport event and what impact might the popularity of the sport have on perceptions of residents?
- What is the impact of local sport stars participating in the event on the perceptions of residents?
- How do perceptions of residents change over time? What can be learned from it?

Chalip (2006) stated that the social value of major sport events should earn more attention. Sport events are more than just entertainment, they are social events that add a social value to the event. Other researchers support this (for example, Deccio and Baloglu, 2002; Kim et al., 2006), arguing that social impacts are a core source of potential significance or a core source of potential troubles. The social impact of sport events should not be left to coincidence and should be managed. The expected outcomes of major sport events depend merely on the preparation and planning process. In our study, half of the residents indicated that the TDF was like a social event to them. The importance of the cultural interest and consolidation factor also indicated that the social aspect of hosting the TDF was the surplus value for residents. Residents did not perceive any economic benefits. Residents of Ghent especially perceived the social value of the TDF along with the enhanced image of the city. Important practical implications result from this conclusion.

Besides diminishing the negative impacts for residents when hosting major sport events, it is time to leverage major sport events. Cities should take up the hosting of major sport events into the overall strategy of the city in order to maximize the long-term benefits. The event is an opportunity to foster and nurture long-term outcomes (O'Brien, 2006). The importance of social value of hosting major sport events is a central outcome of our study. Although there are studies that focused on the leveraging of events (for example, Kellett et al., 2008; O'Brien, 2006; Sparvero and Chalip, 2007), social leveraging of major sport events is only in its preliminary phase (Chalip, 2006). Further research should focus on the most effective ways to implement, create and maintain the leverage of major sport events. Impact studies provide useful information about the outcomes of hosting major sport events, including environmental concerns as investigated by Dolles and Söderman (2010).

Considering a methodology that uses a before-and-after analysis provides rich information about the impact of the event. This kind of methodology allows us to measure changes of the measurement items over time. As a result, more detailed conclusions about the impact of the event can be drawn. Before-and-after analyses can be done by using questionnaires, personal or telephone interviews, and can easily be monitored by researchers. Therefore, this methodology should be given more attention by researchers in addressing research questions.

REFERENCES

Andersson, T. (2013), Triple impact assessments of sport events, in S. Söderman and H. Dolles (eds), *Handbook of Research on Sport and Business*, Cheltenham, UK and Northampton, MA, USA: Edward Elgar, pp. 237–56.

Andersson, T.D., Armbrecht, J. and E. Lundberg (2008), Impact of mega-events on the economy, *Asian Business and Management*, 7 (1), 163–79.

Ap, J. (1990), Residents' perceptions research on the social impacts of tourism, *Annals of Tourism Research*, 17 (4), 610–16.

Bowdin, G.A.J., Allen, J., O'Toole, W. and Harris, R. (2006), *Events Management*, 2nd edn, Oxford: Elsevier.

Brunt, P. and Courtney, P. (1999), Host perceptions of sociocultural impacts, *Annals of Tourism Research*, 26 (3), 493–545.

Bull, C. and Lovell, J. (2007), The impact of hosting major sporting events on local residents: an analysis of the views and perceptions of Canterbury residents in relation to the Tour de France 2007, *Journal of Sport and Tourism*, 12 (3–4), 229–48.

Chalip, L. (2001), Sport and tourism: capitalising on the linkage, in D. Kluka and G. Schilling (eds), *The Business of Sport*, Oxford: Meyer and Meyer, pp. 77–89.

Chalip, L. (2004), Beyond impact: a general model for sport event leverage, in B.W. Ritchie and D. Adair (eds), *Sport Tourism: Interrelationships, Impacts and Issues*, Clevedon: Channel View, pp. 226–52.

Chalip, L. (2006), Towards social leverage of sport events, *Journal of Sport and Tourism*, 11 (2), 109–27.

Chalip, L. and Leyns, A. (2002), Local business leveraging of a sport event: managing an event for economic benefit, *Journal of Sport Management*, 16 (2), 132–58.

Deccio, C. and Baloglu, S. (2002), Nonhost community resident reactions to the 2002 Winter Olympics: the spillover impacts, *Journal of Travel Research*, 41 (1), 46–56.

Delamere, T.A. (2001), Development of a scale to measure resident attitudes toward the social impacts of community festivals, Part II: verification of the scale, *Event Management*, 7 (1), 25–38.

Dolles, H. and Söderman, S. (2008a), Formula One in the US. Interview with Joie Chitwood III President and Chief Operating Officer Indianapolis Motor Speedway LLC, *International Journal of Sports Marketing and Sponsorship*, 10 (1), 11–14.

Dolles, H. and Söderman, S. (2008b), Mega-sporting events in Asia: impacts on society, business and management – an introduction, *Asian Business and Management*, 7 (1), 1–16.

Dolles, H. and Söderman, S. (2010), Addressing ecology and sustainability in mega-sporting events: the 2006 football World Cup in Germany, *Journal of Management and Organisation*, 16 (4), 587–600.

Dolles, H. and Söderman, S. (2011), Sport as a business: introduction, in H. Dolles and S. Södermann (eds), *Sport as Business: International, Professional and Commercial Aspects*, Basingstoke: Palgrave Macmillan, pp. 1–12.

Fredline, E. and Faulkner, B. (2000), Host community reactions: a cluster analysis, *Annals of Tourism Research*, 27 (3), 763–84.

Getz, D. (1993), Festivals and special events, in M.A. Khan, M.D. Olsen and T. Var (eds), *Encyclopedia of Hospitality and Tourism*, New York: Van Nostrand Reinhold, pp. 789–810.

Getz, D. (1997), *Event Management and Event Tourism*, New York: Cognizant Communication.

Getz, D. (2008), Event tourism: definition, evolution, and research, *Tourism Management*, 29 (3), 403–28.

Gratton, C., Shibli, S. and Coleman, R. (2005), The economics of sport tourism at major sports events, in J. Higham (ed.), *Sport Tourism Destinations: Issues, Opportunities and Analysis*, Oxford: Elsevier, pp. 233–47.

Gursoy, D. and Kendall, K.W. (2006), Hosting mega events. Modeling local's support, *Annals of Tourism Research*, **33** (3), 603–23.

Gursoy, D., Jurowski, C. and Uysal, M. (2002), Resident attitudes: a structural modeling approach, *Annals of Tourism Research*, **29** (1), 79–105.

Gursoy, D., Kim, K. and Uysal, M. (2004), Perceived impacts of festivals and special events by organizers: an extension and validation, *Tourism Management*, **25** (2), 171–81.

Hair, J.F., Anderson, R.E., Tatham, R.L. and Black, W.C. (1995), *Multivariate Data Analysis*, 4th edn, Upper Saddle River, NJ: Prentice-Hall.

Hall, C.M. (1992), Adventure, sport and health tourism, in B. Weiler and C.M. Hall (eds), *Special Interest Tourism*, London: Belhaven, pp. 141–58.

Hall, C.M. (1994), *Tourism and Politics: Policy, Power and Place*, Chichester: John Wiley & Sons.

Kaiser, H.F. (1974), An index of factorial simplicity, *Psychometrica*, **39** (1), 31–6.

Kellett, P., Hede, A.-M. and Chalip, L. (2008), Social policy for sport events: leveraging (relationships with) teams from other nations for community benefit, *European Sport Management Quarterly*, **8** (2), 101–21.

Kim, H.J., Gursoy, D. and Lee, S.-B. (2006), The impact of the 2002 World Cup on South Korea: comparisons of pre- and post-games, *Tourism Management*, **27** (1), 86–96.

Kim, S.S. and Petrick, J.F. (2005), Residents' perceptions on impacts of the FIFA 2002 World Cup: the case of Seoul as a host city, *Tourism Management*, **26** (1), 25–38.

Maenning, W. and Du Plessis, S. (2007), World Cup 2010: South African economic perspectives and policy challenges informed by the experience of Germany 2006, *Contemporary Economic Policy*, **25** (4), 578–90.

Mueller, D.J. (1986), *Measuring Social Attitudes: A Handbook for Researchers and Practitioners*, Columbia University, New York: Teacher's College Press.

Nunnally, J.C. (1970), *Introduction to Psychological Measurement*, New York: McGraw-Hill.

O'Brien, D. (2006), Event business leveraging the Sydney 2000 Olympic Games, *Annals of Tourism Research*, **33** (1), 240–61.

Ohmann, S., Jones, I. and Wilkes, K. (2006), The perceived social impacts of the 2006 Football World Cup on Munich residents, *Journal of Sport and Tourism*, **11** (2), 129–52.

Preuss, H. (2007), The conceptualisation and measurement of mega sport event legacies, *Journal of Sport and Tourism*, **12** (3–4), 207–27.

Sparvero, E. and Chalip, L. (2007), Professional teams as leverageable assets: strategic creation of community value, *Sport Management Review*, **10** (1), 1–30.

Teo, P. (1994), Assessing socio-cultural impacts: the case of Singapore, *Tourism Management*, **15** (2), 126–36.

Turco, D.M. (1998), Host resident's perceived social costs and benefits toward a staged tourist attraction, *Journal of Travel and Tourism Marketing*, **7** (1), 21–30.

Waitt, G. (2003), Social impacts of the Sydney Olympics, *Annals of Tourism Research*, **30** (1), 194–215.

16 What do they really think? Researching residents' perception of mega-sport events
Alessandro 'Chito' Guala and Douglas Michele Turco

1 INTRODUCTION

Sport mega-events including the Olympic Games and Fédération Internationale de Football Association (FIFA) World Cup are intrusive by their very nature, bringing large numbers of visitors and media in contact with local residents for a relatively short period of time, impacting the host's culture, economy and environment. At the pre-bid stage, an Olympic Games is 'sold' to residents on the basis of anticipated economic benefits (that is, employment, visitor spending, direct foreign investments, and so on), improved infrastructure and quality of life, and enhanced city image. Residents' perceptions of major sport events should be assessed due to these impacts, yet residents are often overlooked as event stakeholders. Residents experience at first hand the impacts of an Olympic Games and are in a unique position to evaluate an event's legacy as taxpayers, daily consumers of infrastructure and leisure consumers of Olympic sport venues. From a strategic management standpoint, it behoves a local organizing committee to communicate with residents, particularly if investments of up to $US50 billion (the cost to produce the 2008 Beijing Olympic Games) are at stake!

Other than Ritchie and Aitken's (1984, 1985) landmark study of the Calgary Winter Olympic Games, relatively few studies on the Winter Olympic Games have been published and fewer still across the lifecycle of an event from bidding, preparation, operation and legacy stages. This chapter reviews the literature of prior studies pertaining to residents' perceptions of hosting an Olympic Games. What can be concluded from the review is that such studies are few and far between. The chapter describes a recent longitudinal study carried out by scholars from the Omero Centre (University of Torino), for example, Guala and Turco (2009) examined Torino residents' perceptions of their city as host of the 2006 Torino Winter Olympic Games from 2002 to 2007. They analysed annual survey data (attitudes, expectations, fears and concerns) at city (Torino) and regional (Alps Valleys) levels in the context of social exchange and stakeholder theories. These theories remain in the background of the research, but founded the selection of the main questions, the majority of which dealt with the evaluation of the expected positive impacts against negative ones: their ultimate balance let interviewed people define an overall attitude toward the event, the forthcoming Winter Olympics Torino 2006 (see Apt, 1992, for social exchange theory applied), at the same time research faced problems that were affecting the local population in terms of different stakeholders – individuals and groups – who were involved in different ways by the Olympiad (see Andersson and Getz, 2008, for the stakeholders theory applied).

The research procedures for the telephone interviews with randomly selected subjects (n = 900 subjects annually over six years) are detailed later in the chapter. In addition, main questions of a telephone questionnaire used in the first poll in Torino (November 2002) are in the appendix at the end of this chapter in order to provide the reader with examples of questions used in a resident perception study in sport.

2   RESIDENTS' PERCEPTIONS OF OLYMPIC GAMES: PREVIOUS STUDIES

Research on residents and the Olympic Games throughout the history of the modern Olympiad, and particularly during the past 20 years, have investigated the attitudes of the host population with respect to the Games and their impacts. In general we find many concerns before the Games, but few problems after the event; but the degree of favour is not always the same, it changes in the different editions of the Games.

In 1977, the City of Los Angeles initiated a survey of the population in light of the decision to bid for the 1984 Olympic Games. The response was relatively positive but revealed certain worries. In particular, respondents were concerned about the burden placed on the local community to finance the Games. The percentage of agreement among polled population varied considering the necessity to raise funds from different institutional levels: people in favour of hosting the Games were 70 per cent unless public funds were needed, but dipped to 60 per cent if federal funds were requested, to 45 per cent if state funds were required, and to 35 per cent if city or county monies were needed (Burbank et al., 2001: 59). To date, the 1984 Games are the only Games to turn a profit, owing to the decision of the Los Angeles Olympic Organizing Committee (LAOOC) to sell the television broadcasting rights to ABC Sports; it was the first time this had happened in the history of the Games (ibid.: 66).

An investigation during the Lillehammer Winter Games of 1994 relied on two samples of the population, one national (Norway) and one local (Lillehammer), both of which were longitudinal surveys that were repeated between 1991 and 1994 (Spilling, 1996). Responses that preceded the Olympic event were not favorable (positive responses totaled 55 per cent and 50 per cent, respectively). Post-event research in 1994 resulted in the attainment of a significant increase in the level of support: positive evaluations totaled 80 per cent at the national level and 88 per cent at the local level. In contrast with Torino (where those opposed were very few ever since the beginning), Lillehammer reported significant quotas of people that were opposed to the bid, reaching a peak of 30 per cent. The surveys implemented after the Olympic Games reported a drastic reduction in negative responses with respect to the fears that were exhibited before the Games (ibid.).

Concerning the 1996 Atlanta Summer Olympic Games, a systematic survey of the population was implemented between 1992 and 1996. Two annual polls were conducted at both the state (Georgia) and local (Atlanta) levels. The questionnaire consisted of 12 questions using a Likert scale, and a total of 9000 subjects were interviewed (Mihalik, 2000, 2003). The research design was based on Ritchie's study on the 1988 Olympic Winter Games in Calgary (Ritchie and Aitken, 1984). In Atlanta before the Olympic Games, the interviewed parties expressed many concerns which decreased significantly after the event. This trend confirmed that which was previously noted in Lillehammer: there were many concerns before the Games but few problems after the event. The survey revealed residents' concerns over traffic, inflation and excessive costs. Residents' attitudes became more positive after the Games with the sole exception of 'security', given that the event was marred by an attempted attack in the Centennial Olympic Park.

Other Olympic Games surveys have focused on marketing, both for the promotion of the Games and of the host territory, and forecasts of tourist flows, although it is known that the Olympics do not bring large net 'inflows' during the event but mainly qualified guests, that is, the 'Olympic family', journalists, hosts of the main sponsors, and so on (De Moragas et al., 2003: 179–204; Preuss, 2004: 46–52). In the study of Torino, the main focus was not only on the population's attitudes toward the 2006 Olympic Games but also their perceptions of local tourism development. A similar study was conducted for the Winter Olympics of Nagano in 1998. In the spring of 1997, the Roper Poll Center implemented a survey of the Japanese population in order to forecast the number of visitors that could affect the city of Nagano. One year before the Winter Games, the national sample revealed a low propensity for travel while some degree of interest was expressed in 30 per cent of the sample; negative responses totaled 65 per cent. Half of the interviewed parties, however, showed a generic interest in attending the Olympic Games in Sydney 2000 (for Olympic tourism research see, for example, Cashman, 2006; Preuss, 2004; Weed, 2008).

In the study by Ritchie and Aitken (1984, 1985) residents were asked before the 1988 Winter Olympic Games whether they felt in general it was a good idea for Calgary to host the event. Nearly 85 per cent responded positively and this figure increased to 97.8 per cent after the event: first figures of the post-event survey were reported by the XV Olympic Winter Games Organizing Committee (Olympiques Calgary Olympics '88 (OCO'88), 1988) and related to the survey 'Olympulse', commissioned by OCO'88, carried out by Ritchie and others (Ritchie, 2000; Ritchie and Aitken, 1984, 1985; Ritchie and Lyons, 1990; Ritchie and Smith, 1991). Residents are often concerned by an influx of tourists to their city during and after the Olympic Games. Surveys by the State of Utah (2001) and Jedwab (2002) conducted on Salt Lake City's population before and after the Winter Games 2002 confirmed the same trend already verified in earlier research by Spilling (1996) on the Lillehammer Games: happiness and trust at the nomination, some concerns two or three years before the event (public works, queues, confusion, sometimes scandals), then trust and being proud when approaching the Games and shortly after they ended. Following the 2002 Winter Olympic Games, tourism increased dramatically in Utah; the 2004–05 ski season was the best on record based on skier visits, surpassing the record established the year before, and Utah's 13 ski resorts hosted 4.1 million skier days during the 2005–06 season. Utah registered 3.0 million skier days in 2000. Increasing tourism was related to the availability of new facilities, the positive image of the venues and a good marketing strategy (Burbank et al., 2001), but it is very difficult to distinguish exactly the reasons for positive economic and tourist development (Cashman, 2003, 2006; Cashman and Hughes, 1999; Dolles and Söderman, 2008; Preuss, 2004; Turco, 1998).

During the bid phase, city officials promise to make Olympic facilities available to residents for sport for all, but greater emphasis is usually placed on job creation and staging other sport events to attract more tourist spending. The lack of resident perception studies associated with previous Winter Olympic Games may be due to a lack of regard for residents as stakeholders by organizing committees. In short, residents do not really count, especially at the beginning, when the city decides to bid, or when the nomination is obtained. Shortly after, the population must be involved: participation works as a retroaction tool, that helps to release some more information, to legitimize (or not) the municipality and the organizing committee. The position of government and business stakeholders concerning mega events is political and financial. If the event works, it will bring more tourists and more money to the host economy, while residents are concerned that more tourists will lead to higher consumer prices, traffic congestion, sometimes crime, and so on. A general hypothesis tested in Torino was that the attitudes of the local community, looking forward to host the Olympic Games, could be divided into four main steps, considering the lifecycle of the event. The steps are the following:

1. At the very beginning, surprise, optimism and pride for the nomination are very high.
2. While preparing for the Games, worries and concerns increase a little; at the same time trust and pride continue to be largely diffused, coexisting with strong concerns.
3. During the Games, and shortly thereafter, happiness for the overall success emerges.
4. A more realistic evaluation is shared over time, confirmed one and two years later.

3   TORINO OLYMPIC GAMES: THE ROLE OF SURVEY IN MONITORING PUBLIC OPINION

Torino (Turin) is located in the Piedmont region of northern Italy and has a population of 900 000. The province hosts 2 300 000 inhabitants, and the larger region 4.5 million. The region accommodated 2500 athletes, 10 000 media representatives, officials, 20 000 volunteers and 1 million spectators (tickets sold) during the 2006 Olympic Games (Bondonio and Campaniello, 2006a, 2006b; Bondonio et al., 2008). The competitions were hosted in two main venues, Torino (and its metropolitan area) and the Alp Valleys. The metropolitan area of Torino hosted the ice competitions (hockey and skating sports) and the Alp Valleys hosted all other sport events: Alpine skiing, cross country, ski jumping, bobsleighing, snowboarding, and so on. The city of Pinerolo (40 km away from Torino) hosted the curling competitions. Prior to the Olympic Games, tourism accounted for 5–6 per cent of Italy's gross domestic product (GDP), but only 2 per cent in the Piedmont region owing to its reliance on winter tourism (Bondonio and Campaniello, 2006b).

The complex task of monitoring public opinion concerning the 2006 Torino Olympic Games started in 2002 and was completed in 2007. It included a series of studies that were conducted in the two primary areas that hosted the 2006 Olympic Games: Torino and the Alp Valleys. The monitoring of public opinion involved information, recommendations and expectations which were acquired from the population by means of various surveys which were generally implemented as polls. People were questioned about positive effects (urban regeneration, new infrastructures, sport facilities, public transportation system, new image and visibility, and tourism) and negative effects (heavy expenditures for new buildings, high costs for maintaining the ice facilities, political corruption and inflation): the questions were balanced between a new local development, based on sport, tourism and culture, and the scenario of rusting monuments and white elephants, considering the Games only an 'intermezzo', as Spilling (1996) concluded about the Games in Lillehammer.

The general principle of social research – that the subject's perceptions are a 'moving target' – also applies to research on public opinion that may change over time and must be captured through the use of new measurement tools, new questions and new response modalities. This is exactly what occurred during the four years which preceded the Torino 2006 Olympic Games as well as during other post-event research studies. Monitoring of public opinion can assume a variety of forms, timing sequences and sample sizes, but certain effects of the surveys (and of referenda, despite their differences on the political and institutional level) are, in the end, similar:

- Surveys basically monitor the attitudes and intents of the population (at a different level also the referenda serve the same goal).
- Surveys provide information to public decision-makers but also provide feedback on current projects or the approaches being following by local or national administrations.
- They facilitate participation processes that in turn can serve to define new forms of governance and the effective utilization of social capital.
- They can legitimate or delegitimize political choices as well as guide the public decision-making process.

Surveys are, of course, not the only tool available to understand a population; other modalities for verifying the intentions of citizens, such as referenda and public forums, may be used. A referendum serves an institutional role with specific legal-administrative consequences. From a strictly methodological viewpoint, the referendum may not retain the same 'representative' nature that a random sample investigation has – for the referendum, only motivated individuals will vote. Surveys may analyse specific or more general themes and may have different degrees of actual impact, that is, the implication that the results may have for the social, cultural and political environment.

There are different techniques for collecting survey information from residents. They are implemented through interviews or questionnaires (telephone interviews are currently used, in particular) with respect to a representative sample of the population; in some cases, the samples may be 'designed' or 'by quota'. In certain cases, surveys are conducted for specific purposes that are not connected to other studies; in other cases, longitudinal surveys are implemented in order to periodically gauge the moods of the population: this is generally the best solution. Surveys may be implemented with respect to the same population sample, monitored over time (a panel) or different samples may be selected each time so long as they are created on the basis of the same criteria. The latter solution – which is simpler from an organization aspect – is a real longitudinal study and allows the changing attitudes of the population to be verified over time. It is true that in this manner the file is composed of several samples, but the latter are, in any case, always comparable given that they are stratified samples, that is, created from the same variables that are typically age, gender and residency; the sample may subsequently be modified by controlling variables such as employment, professional title or level of education.

4   RESEARCH METHODS

Results of a longitudinal study of Torino residents are presented here to reflect the attitudes of the population toward the 2006 Winter Olympic Games over time. From 2002 to 2007 six polls were conducted, with 900 telephone interviews per year, for a total amount of 5400 cases. The sample size (900 interviews each year) was defined considering a sampling error of plus or minus 3.2, at a confidence level of 95 per cent. The sampling error is a measure of the reliability of the estimates, and is affected by the sample size and the variability in the population. In the Torino survey, for example, if the 80 per cent of interviewed people are in favour of the 2006 Winter Games, the precision of the estimates lies in the range within 83.2 and 76.8 per cent. In other words, we can be 95 per cent confident that the range 80 + or − 3.2 is correct, that is, the chances are 1 in 20 that it is incorrect (Moser Sir and Kalton, 1971: 70–72). The samples were reliable, and the data sufficient for further analysis.

Four polls were conducted before the 2006 Winter Olympic Games, in November in each of 2002, 2003, 2004 and 2005; two more polls were performed after the Games in March 2006 and in January 2007. So we dealt with data from four surveys before the Games, and two surveys after the Games; in the two last surveys the sampling error, at a confidence level of 95 per cent, was plus or minus 3.7 (a little higher, owing to the sample dimension, n = 700). We must add that in the Alp Valleys three polls were performed before the Olympic Games in November 2003, 2004 and 2005; one survey was carried out in March 2007, after the Games, and each poll involved 400 subjects (sampling error of plus or minus 4.9). All polls were conducted by trained interviewers over the telephone with a randomly drawn sample of residents. This chapter does not include the results from the Alp Valleys surveys, which were published in several reports and papers (for example, Bondonio and Campaniello, 2006a, 2006b; Bondonio et al., 2008; Guala, 2006).

We must underline that sampling residents for telephone surveys is more difficult now than in the 1980s. Many residents have unlisted or unpublished telephone numbers making random sample selection from a directory incomplete. Further, many people now use mobile phones more than their landline phones, if they have landline phones at all. One approach that permits random sample selection from the total population of residents is random telephone number dialing with a weighted, stratified sample based on the area code of known telephones in the designated community. An example is offered to clarify this approach. Suppose 30 per cent of residents of Philadelphia in the USA reside in the 484 area code, and have 895 as the prefix for their telephones. The remaining four numbers or suffix for a valid telephone number in Philadelphia are then generated at random to produce the sample of numbers for calling (for example, 484+895+XXXX). It may well be that when using the random dial technique some of the numbers generated are unlisted, not connected to a telephone or are institutional rather than personal telephone numbers. If not connected or are institutional, the numbers are excluded from the sample and new numbers are generated. Three attempts to reach residents by telephone are recommended before excluding the number from the sample. Attempts to reach residents should be at different times of the day and on different days of the week. After three attempts, new numbers are generated for the sample.

With regard to the Italian region Piemonte, it should also be noted that the Institute for Economic and Social Research (IRES Piemonte) had, as of 2001, included certain questions for the population within the annual economic and social surveys of the region and noted differences between the region and province of Torino in terms of knowledge and interest with respect to the Games. The first survey revealed worries that the 2006 event would end up being localized. This was actually what occurred despite the media success just before the Games and during the course of the latter (Ferlaino and Rubbi, 2002: 191–204; Scamuzzi, 2002).

The questionnaire used in the first telephone survey in November 2002 had been designed in several versions due to four pre-tests before the final version. The pre-tests were conducted on a small sample of the reference population and in small focus groups. The questions were working, but with exceptions: too many people had precise ideas about the venues that should host the competitions; many interviewed gave uncertain answers about the places and the different locations (Torino versus Alp Valleys). The final version of the questionnaire (see the Appendix for a sample of the questions) included 31 questions, generally close ended; several in the form of a Likert scale; some questions were structured as response set; a few questions requested a score (from 1 to 10). Some questions were open ended, and the answers were classified *ex post*, following the rules of the content analysis, that is, creating categories and considering key word distribution. The telephone interview (900 cases per survey in Torino) took between 20 and 30 minutes to be completed. A very low degree of refusals were encountered (10 to 15 per cent of the people contacted). A probability sample was extracted using gender, age and territorial distribution of the population. The data were then checked and weighted considering the official distribution of main educational levels. The questionnaire was divided into two main parts, with a conclusive appendix dedicated to socio-demographic variables. The first part dealt with the Games, the bidding, the pride to have received the nomination, the expectations and the fears linked to the organizational problems, and concerns about the impact of the work for the Games on the everyday life of the population. For this part previous research about cities hosting the Games was consulted; in particular, questionnaires used during the preparation of the three previous Olympic experiences were examined. The first source was the questionnaire used for the survey on the Winter Games in Calgary and the data published was useful in preparing some questions; other figures and data on Calgary, presented by Ritchie and Aitken (1984), were utilized. A second source was the survey used for the Games in Lillehammer 1994 (Spilling, 1996). A third source was the survey carried out in occasion of Salt Lake City 2002. The polls were conducted by Dan Jones and Associates for KSL/Deseret News, and a table with main longitudinal data (1989–99), provided by Dan Jones, was published by Burbank et al. (2001: 136).

The second part of the questionnaire was related to the future of Torino, its international image, its hopes and preparations for a new town devoted to culture and tourism. The questions were derived from previous investigations and polls about the quality of urban life in Torino and other Italian cities, such as Rome, Venice, Florence, Bologna, Milan, Naples and Genoa; an example is Ezio Marra (1989), who carried out research on the 'cultural components of the urban quality'.

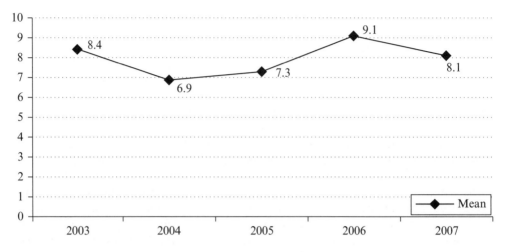

Note: Evaluate the overall experience of the 2006 Torino Winter Olympic Games; 1 equals poor and 10 equals excellent (N = 900 to 915).

Figure 16.1   Residents' perceptions of 2006 Torino Winter Olympic Games

5   RESULTS AND DISCUSSION

Torino residents were asked to evaluate the overall experience hosting the 2006 Winter Olympic Games. As revealed in Figure 16.1, residents assigned highly favorable ratings to the Olympic Games at the outset followed by a downswing in 2004 and 2005. After the Olympic Games evaluations were most favorable and remained high one year later. As was the case with previous resident studies of the Olympic Games, the same trend of early worries followed by strong approval emerged within the research studies of Torino 2006. From the data, four main stages emerge in the evolution of residents' expectations with respect to the Olympic Games fostering the cultural and tourist development of the city. As mentioned above, the stages are as follows:

1. Initial surprise, optimism and pride for having won the bid to host the Games;
2. While preparing for the Games, worry and trust at the same time, and some concerns;
3. Happiness for the success during the Games and shortly thereafter;
4. A more rational evaluation over time, confirmed one and two years later.

5.1   Initial Phase: Surprise, Optimism and Pride

At the end of 2002, when the first poll was carried out, research followed an exploratory course, aiming to verify whether the population of Torino knew that the city would host the Games and which areas of the city and the Alps would be involved. At the same time, the survey investigated the general attitudes of the population. In particular, the aim was to understand whether the organization of the Games would retain the support of the local community and if the Olympic Games would create a cultural shock within a city

Table 16.1 *'Are you in favor of holding the Winter Olympic Games in Torino in 2006?'*

In favor	79.0%
Moderately in favor	13.4%
Moderately against	1.1%
Against	2.7%
Don't know	3.8%

Note: Torino Olympic Survey 2002, N = 900.

Table 16.2 *'Do you believe the city should be proud of having won the international competition to become the site of the Olympic Games?'*

Very	66.7%
Fairly	24.6%
Not much	4.4%
Not at all	3.1%
Don't know	1.2%

Note: Torino Olympic Survey 2002, N = 900.

worried about the negative economic situation of its primary employer in town, the auto-motive manufacturer Fiat, that was involved in a difficult period of economic conver-sion, and whose future was far from certain. The first survey showed that all interviewees were proud of the nomination and considered the 2006 event to be an opportunity for transforming the development model of the city. Negative responses were in a minority. This can be illustrated by reporting a few of the questions (Segre and Scamuzzi, 2004).

In the two questions reported in Tables 16.1 and 16.2, a clearly favorable atti-tude emerged with respect to the Games. Those 'in favor' totaled almost 80 per cent of responses, while the net 'participation' in the feeling of 'pride' was 66.7 per cent. Contrary opinions were very marginal in weight. Other survey questions dealt with the opportunities linked to the Games. Interest with respect to tourist development was clearly evident in the responses. The analytical distribution of the responses is reported below. Trends in the data remained very similar during all subsequent surveys, including those of the surveys carried out after the Games ended. The general impression from the data is that the population of Torino was considering the future of their city as not only an industrial city but also a tourist and cultural capital.

On the one hand, interviewees recognized the importance of infrastructures and serv-ices (the acceleration of public works and the upgrading of sports facilities) and, on the other, they emphasized objectives such as the visibility of the city at the national and international level and the strengthening of cultural and tourism services. These items refer to urban renewal processes: tourism is a significant component of local economic growth and the Olympics serve as a tool for urban renewal (Essex and Chalkley, 1998). Public trust in investments by the private sector (new companies and employment) appeared to be lesser in degree. A mega event such as an Olympic Games is recognized as an accelerator of public works which otherwise would never have been started or would have been initiated with long delays and probable downsizing: this is exactly the case of Torino's subway line. Initially there was strong agreement with respect to the '2006 operation' while at the same time there were serious concerns about corruption, a common issue in public opinion with respect to political and administrative life in Italy. Two real problems were found in Torino, as experienced in all the cities hosting major events: inconveniences linked to the realization of public works and the probable disruption associated with traffic, parking, confusion and queues. During the course of the interviews conducted in Torino, other problems were less felt, such as pollution and environmental damage. This worry took on a different hue among the population of Alpine valleys, the other important area involved in the 2006 Games and located about 80 km from Torino; another study, conducted simultaneously with Torino's, highlighted the fact that in the Alp Valleys residents were more sensitive to environmental risks (Segre and Scamuzzi, 2004). In our first poll in 2002, however, no specific worries emerged with regards to sports facilities, which are expensive and not easy to manage once the Games are over. This is a significant problem for cities hosting the Olympic Games; organizers tend to overlook this point during the preparation phases of the event. It is not only a question of the 'gigantic entity' of the Games (many facilities for some sports without any guarantee of adequate demand in the future) but also of reliability once the Olympics are over, as well as the careful planning of future destinations of buildings and main facilities.

5.2   Second Phase: Awaiting the Event with Worries, Confidence and Some Concerns

During subsequent investigations (November 2003 and 2004), there was still a high level of support for the Games among Torino's population, although with a slight fall as a result of two factors. First, the city was affected by many public works directly or indirectly linked to the Games; second, public opinion reflected certain political and managerial difficulties (problems of decision-making within the Organizational Committee, controversies on the contracting system, and actual or presumed disputes between local authorities, the Piedmont Region and central government). These difficulties were partly real, partly 'political'; the media did not hesitate to report them, and contributed to create more realistic responses, that is, the Olympics could not be the solution to the economic crisis, and that of the automotive sector, given the car producer Fiat and its main manufacturing plant located in the area, but might provide an opportunity for urban renewal if suitably planned. These findings are remarkably similar to those involved in previous studies with regard to the implications of the Games in the medium to long-term (Cashman 2003; Cashman and Hughes, 1999; Chappelet, 2003; Preuss, 2004). During this phase, attention gradually shifted the focus from the Olympic event to its legacy, as illustrated in Table 16.3.

The data are positive for all surveys, although in the later surveys the 'very positive' answers tended to decrease, as some worries and concerns emerged. Confidence also varied over time, as noted in Tables 16.4 and 16.5. Table 16.4 offers a summary 'score' assigned to Torino (2004 and 2005 surveys) and Table 16.5 a projection of the 'score' the city should have earned at the end (maximum score was 10).

It is clear that the critical year for the 2006 Torino Olympic Games was 2004 (many public works and some political controversies) while the score became more favorable in the months preceding the beginning of the Games (November 2005) when the tests of

Table 16.3   An evaluation of the positive or negative effects of the Games on the territory

'Do you think that the effects of the Olympics on the territories will be:'

Year	2002		2003		2004		2005	
	N	%	N	%	N	%	N	%
Very positive	130	14.4	145	16.0	85	9.3	104	11.4
Slightly positive	668	74.2	687	75.9	675	73.8	653	72.0
Slightly negative	37	4.1	44	4.9	92	10.0	55	6.1
Very negative	9	1.0	70	0.8	11	1.2	10	1.1
Don't know	57	6.3	22	2.5	52	5.7	80	8.8
TOTAL	900	100.0	905	100.0	915	100.0	907	100.0

Note: Torino Olympic Survey 2002, 2003, 2004 and 2005; N = 900 to 915.

Table 16.4   'What score has the city of Torino earned so far?'

2004: Average score 5.97
2005: Average score 6.48

Note: Torino Olympic Survey 2004 and 2005; N = 900 to 915.

Table 16.5   'What score will the city of Torino earn in the end?'

2002: Average score 7.50
2003: Average score 7.39
2004: Average score 7.29
2005: Average score 7.67

Note: Torino Olympic Survey 2002, 2003, 2004 and 2005; N = 900 to 915.

the facilities had been successful and the majority of the public works projects had been completed. The same trend can be seen in another question with an initially higher score, then lower scores in 2003 and 2004, and finally growing confidence as the Games were about to begin. The data is illustrated in Table 16.5. The data show a growing confidence among residents that the bidding process for winning the nomination had 'liberated' energies and expectations for a new Torino, thereby no longer making it a 'one company town'. The fading of the traditional image of Torino as 'automotive city' was accepted, or was in the process of being accepted, also because the car manufacturer Fiat showed signs of recovery in the mean time. This process supported the idea that the city might focus on tourism and culture, thereby favoring the birth of a new identity for the city.

5.3   Third and Fourth Phases: After the Games, a Long Way to a Diversified Economy

After the Games ended, two more surveys were carried out in Torino. The results are very positive, with some small differences between the first one (March–April 2006), totally enthusiastic about the Olympic experience, and the second one (January 2007), when more realistic answers recognized that the carnival was over and the city had to come back to 'normal' everyday life.

During the Games people experienced high rates of participation, caused by the unique Olympic atmosphere, and unusual in the tradition of the city. Some behavior, as testified by the following behaviors, can be considered expression of pride, consent and participation: 65.9 per cent of people went downtown and joined bars and restaurants during the Olympics, 42.6 per cent visited the sport facilities and the Nation's Houses, 58 per cent joined theatres and exhibitions, and visited the museums during the 'White Nights'. Data show a high degree of participation of the population to main events during the Olympics in Torino, and that the Olympics were a cultural shock for the local identity, and the attitude toward the future of the city. When we consider that 88.6 per cent of the population interviewed would like Torino to continue to organize special events and open the culture and leisure facilities as happened for the Games, this is a turning point for the collective mind, something new in comparison with the traditional attitude of Torino's society.

This new spirit of participation draws an optimistic view of the future: in the post-event survey (2006) people are confident that the 'positive effects of the Games' will be long lasting after they ended, with increasing values in comparison with all the previous survey on the same issue; this confidence rises to 53 per cent (2006), after swinging from 40 per cent (in 2002 and 2003) to 30 per cent (in 2004 and 2005) in our surveys. And these expectations, registered by the 2006 survey (carried out just one month after the Games ended), are confirmed by answers given to a question about the foreseen tourism inflows in the future, which are predicted as growing. This means that people are confident that Torino is facing a diversification of its economy, obviously without losing the traditional industrial roots (mainly but not only, in the automotive industry): the future appears to be more complex, and supported by culture, tourism and a 'qualified' leisure.

It is interesting to underline that the positive attitude about Torino and its future is related to expectations of increased tourism; but people think that tourism arrivals will continue to increase in Torino after the Games, even if the same people do not have any specific information about the tourism market. This is exactly a cultural symptom of changing values and optimism (Bobbio and Guala, 2002; Bondonio and Guala, 2009; Guala, 2009: 25–6).

6   CONCLUSIONS AND FUTURE RESEARCH

Throughout the lifecycle of an Olympic Games the perceptions of residents toward hosting the Olympic Games can affect community planning decisions and tourism. Positive perceptions may stimulate support for increased tourism development, while negative sentiments might create a backlash against future tourism growth and subsequent event bids. Further, direct encounters with tourists and negative or positive word of mouth will influence tourists' perceptions of the host community at large (and their willingness to return).

The post-Games slogan for Torino's Olympic Park (TOP) was 'Experience the passion'. As Torino residents experienced the Olympic Games during preparation, implementation and legacy stages, their perceptions changed. Torino residents experienced euphoria when the IOC announced the city had won the rights to host the Olympic Games. They took a 'wait and see' approach in assessing the Winter Olympics during the preparation stage, in large part because of the Italian central government's issues in financing the Games. When development projects were completed, public confidence and support generally increased (Guala and Turco, 2009).

There is a general perception among residents that the Olympic legacy in Torino has been more favorable than in the Alp Valleys. This is attributed to the more visible and pronounced changes in the city centre, including new stores and façades, roads and accommodation. Future analysis within this dataset will compare residents' evaluations of the Olympic Games in Torino and the Alps Valleys. Interpreting survey findings is not always entirely clear for the researcher. Responses may appear to be obvious but their deeper meaning is only understood in light of other data, other sources and more analysis. In certain cases, the data serve as social indicators in the sense that they aid in more effectively understanding a given phenomenon. For example, the high level of pride exhibited by the interviewed parties in Torino – ever since the first survey in November 2002 – served as an indicator of a new mentality, a turning point and moment of increased trust for the future of the city, overcoming the stereotype of a grey 'one company town' (the automotive manufacturer Fiat) which had always been associated with the image of Torino. It should also be noted that research in itself – other than its analytical results – provides an opportunity for communications, discussions and envisioning projects; it may also weaken or legitimatize certain political choices, and open new scenarios for the future of the city and region. The present studies were noted at press conferences and in the media as well as in congresses and during the many opportunities for discussing the outcomes of the research. Describing the post-Olympic condition of Calgary and the importance of regularly assessing residents' perceptions, Ritchie observed (1999), 'each Olympic Games, while drawing on the legacy of its forerunners, reflects a unique set of circumstances. The characteristics of the host region and its people, the prevailing international situation, and the evolving nature of the event itself . . . produce a set of impacts which can be anticipated but which are difficult to predict accurately' (Ritchie, 1999, quoted in State of Utah, 2001: 13).

The global financial crisis of 2008–09 prompted cities to more carefully consider the views of residents toward hosting mega events, particularly since residents will be the likely ones to cover event costs. Organizers of London 2012 have experienced significant cost overruns during the current economic downturn. We should therefore expect less favorable public opinion regarding the event until conditions improve. Host residents are important event stakeholders who must deal with the pre-Games, Games and post-Games conditions. Event organizing committees and host governments should seek the voices of residents before during and after a sport mega event as their perceptions will change over time. Periodic resident perception research should be featured in event legacy planning as residents will encounter the legacy on a daily basis and can therefore offer intimate perspective on the event. This research could be useful for upcoming editions of the Olympic Games, particularly for developing nations (that is, India, United Arab Emirates, South Africa, and so on) keen to bid on the Games. These surveys not only serve the purpose of data collection and information, but are also an opportunity for knowledge transfer to initiate discussion on the future of the Olympics and impacts on host countries.

In summary, the phases or stages of the sport mega-event lifecycle vary considerable in length of time. For a football world cup, the bidding alone takes one to two years, seven years for preparation, 40 days of competition, and potentially decades for the legacy stage. For hosting the Olympic Games, the cycle is similar though the event takes place over 17 days. Public perceptions of the event shift across the lifecycle, from elation and euphoria at the bid stage; concerns over readiness, costs, anxiety and 'wait-and-see' in the preparation stage; relief and joy during operations; and pride, appreciation and satisfaction following the Games. This 'rollercoaster' pattern of resident perceptions is illustrated in Figure 16.1.

Torino residents were asked between 2003 and 2007 to evaluate the overall experience hosting the Olympic Games. Residents assigned highly favorable ratings at the outset followed by a downswing in 2005 and 2006. After the Olympic Games, evaluations were most favorable and remained high one year later. The ups-and-downs of a mega event, as perceived by residents of the host city over the event's lifecycle, are consistent across several Winter and Summer Olympic Games, spanning continents, cultures and time. As the sport event evolves so too do the opinions of host residents toward the event. Therefore it behoves the host city and sport event organizing committee to conduct periodic assessments of both tourists and residents across the event lifecycle.

REFERENCES

Andersson, T.D. and Getz, D. (2008), Stakeholder management strategies of festivals, *Journal of Conventions and Event Tourism*, **9** (3), 199–220.

Apt, J. (1992), Residents' perceptions on tourism impacts, *Annals of Tourism Research*, **19** (4), 665–90.

Bobbio, L. and Guala, A.C. (eds) (2002), *Olimpiadi e grandi eventi* [*Olympiads and Great Events*], Rome: Carocci.

Bondonio, P. and Campaniello, N. (2006a), Torino 2006: an organisational and economic overview, OMERO Working paper, no. 2/2006, Torino: OMERO.

Bondonio, P. and Campaniello, N. (2006b), Torino 2006: what kind of Winter Olympic Games were they? A preliminary account from an organizational and economic perspective, *Olympika. The International Journal of Olympic Studies*, **15**, 1–33.

Bondonio, P. and Guala, A.C. (2009), Torino 2006 Winter Olympic Games. An 'Intangible to Tangible' legacy case study, *IOC OGKM Service*, Lausanne: IOC, pp. 1–51.

Bondonio, P., Guala, A.C. and Mela, A. (2008), Torino 2006 OWG. Any legacy for the IOC and the Olympic territories?, in R.K. Barney, M.K Heine, K.B. Wamsley and G.H. MacDonald (eds), *Pathways. Critiques and Discourse in Olympic Research*, London, ON: ICOS, pp. 151–65.

Burbank, M.J., Andranovich, G.D. and Heying, C.H. (2001), *Olympic Dreams. The Impact of Mega-events on Local Politics*, Boulder, CO: Lynne Rienner.

Cashman, R. (2003), *Impact of the Games on Olympic Host Cities*, Barcelona: Centre d' Estudis Olympics.

Cashman, R. (2006), *The Bitter-sweet Awakening: The Legacy of the Sydney 2000 Olympic Games*, Sydney: Walla Walla Press/Australian Centre for Olympic Studies.

Cashman, R. and Hughes, A. (eds) (1999), *Staging the Olympics: The Event and Its Impact*, Sydney: University of New South Wales Press.

Chappelet, J.L. (2003), The legacy of the Winter Olympic Games – an overview, in M. De Moragas, C. Kennett and N. Puig (eds), *The Legacy of the Olympic Games, 1984–2000*, Lausanne: International Olympic Committee, pp. 54–66.

De Moragas, M., Kennett, C. and Puig, N. (eds) (2003), *The Legacy of the Olympic Games: 1984–2000*, Lausanne: International Olympic Committee.

Dolles, H. and Söderman, S. (2008), Mega-sporting events in Asia. Impacts on society, business and management: an introduction, *Asian Business and Management*, **7** (2), 147–62.

Essex, S.J. and Chalkley, B.S. (1998), The Olympics as a catalyst of urban renewal: a review, *Leisure Studies*, **17** (3), 187–206.

Ferlaino, F. and Rubbi, E. (2002), Da Zurigo a Torino: informazione, consenso e opinione pubblica [From Zurich to Turin: information, consent and public opinion], in L. Bobbio and A.C. Guala (eds), *Olimpiadi e mega eventi* [*Olympics and Mega Events*], Roma: Carocci, pp.191–204.

Guala, A.C. (2006), Guardare avanti. Problemi, fiducia e attese nella popolazione di Torino [Looking forward. Problems, trust and expectations of the population], in P. Bondonio, E. Dansero and A. Mela (eds), *Olimpiadi. Oltre il 2006* [*Olympics. Beyond 2006*], Roma: Carocci, pp.235–57.

Guala, A.C. (2009), To bid or not to bid: public opinion before and after the Games. The case of the Turin 2006 Olympic Winter Games, in J. Kennell, C. Bladen and E. Booth (eds), *The Olympic Legacy: People, Place, Enterprise. Proceedings of the First Annual Conference on Olympic Legacy*, 8–9 May 2008, Greenwich: University of Greenwich, pp.21–30.

Guala, A.C. and Turco, D.M. (2009), Resident perceptions of the 2006 Torino Olympic Games, 2002–2007, *Choregia. Sport Management International Journal*, **5** (2): 21–42.

Jedwab, J. (2002), Beyond Salt Lake City: analysis of a national opinion poll, Association of Canadian Studies, available at: www.acs-aec.ca/pdf/polls/pd16.pdf (accessed 23 November 2012).

Marra, E. (ed.) (1989), *Componenti culturali della qualità urbana* [*Cultural Components of Urban Quality*], Milano: Etas Libri.

Mihalik, B.J. (2000), Host population perception of the 1996 Atlanta Olympics: support, benefits, and liabilities, *Tourism Analysis*, **5** (1), 49–53.

Mihalik, B.J. (2003), Host population perceptions towards the 1996 Atlanta Olympics: Benefits and liabilities, in M. De Moragas, C. Kennett and N. Puig (eds), *The Legacy of the Olympic Games, 1984–2000*, Lausanne: International Olympic Committee, pp.339–45.

Moser, C.A. and Kalton, G. (1971), *Survey Methods in Social Investigation*, 2nd edn, London: Heinemann Educational Books.

Olympiques Calgary Olympics '88 (OCO'88) (1988), Calgarians 98% satisfied. A poll on post-games reaction, *Olympic Review*, (247), 228–31.

Preuss, H. (2004), *Economics of Staging the Olympic Games: A Comparison of the Games 1972–2008*, Cheltenham, UK and Northampton, MA, USA: Edward Elgar.

Ritchie, J.R.B. (2000), Turning 16 days into 16 years through Olympic legacies, *Event Management*, **6** (2), 155–65.

Ritchie, J.R.B. and Aitken, C. (1984), Olympulse I: the research program and initial results, *Journal of Travel Research*, **22** (1), 17–25.

Ritchie, J.R.B. and Aitken, C.E. (1985), Olympulse II: evolving resident attitudes toward the 1988 Olympic Winter Games, *Journal of Travel Research*, **23** (3), 28–33.

Ritchie, J.R.B. and Lyons, M. (1990), Olympulse VI: a post-event assessment of resident reaction to the XVth Olympic Winter Games, *Journal of Travel Research*, **28** (3), 14–23.

Ritchie, J.R.B. and Smith, B.H. (1991), The impact of a mega-event on host region awareness: a longitudinal study, *Journal of Travel Research*, **30** (1), 3–10.

Scamuzzi, S. (2002), Perché le città hanno bisogno di marketing ma solo alcune lo fanno con successo? [Why do cities need marketing, but only some of them do it successfully?], in L. Bobbio and A.C. Guala (eds), *Olimpiadi e mega eventi* [*Olympics and Mega Events*], Roma: Carocci, pp.87–93.

Segre, A. and Scamuzzi, S. (eds) (2004), *Aspettando le Olimpiadi. Primo Rapporto sui territori olimpici Torino 2006* [*Waiting for the Olympics. First Report on the Olympic Territory Torino 2006*], Roma: Carocci.

Spilling, O. (1996), Mega-event as strategy for regional development: the case of the 1994 Lillehammer Winter Olympics, *Entrepreneurship & Regional Development*, **8** (4), 321–43.

State of Utah (eds) (2001), 2002 Winter Olympic Games – impact, images and legacies, State of Utah Governor's Office of Planning and Budget, available at: http//travel.utah.gov/ research and planning/2002_ olympics/documents/OlympicTTRA (accessed February 2 2012).

Turco, D.M. (1998), Host residents' perceived social costs and benefits towards a staged tourist attraction, *Journal of Travel and Tourism Marketing*, **7** (1), 21–30.

Weed, M. (2008), *Olympic Tourism*, Oxford: Elsevier.

APPENDIX

OMERO (Olympics and Mega Events Research Observatory)
Interdepartmental Centre, University of Torino
Sample First Questionnaire (translated from Italian)
Used for the Telephone Survey (November 2002)

Interview identification number (XXXXXX)

(Q1)   Do you agree with the project of hosting the Games?
(Q2)   Do you feel proud thinking that Torino won this nomination?
(Q3)   Do you know where main facilities and buildings will be built?
(Q4)   Do you know exactly which kind of facilities and buildings will be built?
(Q5)   Some people think that the Olympic Games could be useful to the city also after 2006. How much do you agree with the following statements? *Answers in Likert scale: agree, slightly agree, slightly disagree, disagree.*
Olympics are useful . . .
– for the improvement of the infrastructures and public transportation system
– for the improvement of sport facilities
– for the visibility and the image of the place, the city
– for a broader cultural and tourism development
– for new jobs and entrepreneurships (or firms)
– the Games are an occasion of investments for the private sector
– for accelerating public works as the underground, new trains, highways, etc.
– for the recovery of abandoned areas and other public works and services
(Q5)   Some people think that the Olympics can create many problems. What do you think about the following statements? *Answers in Likert scale: agree, slightly agree, slightly disagree, disagree.*
Olympics create . . .
– heavy works before the Olympics
– traffic and parking problems during the Games
– confusion, queues, crowding during the Games
– excess of expenditure for the local Municipality
– risk investments for the private sector
– facilities too expensive, difficult to be managed or maintained after
– heavy damages to the environment, pollution
– corruption, illecit wages
(Q6)   Do you think there could be other (important) problems, above not mentioned?
(Q7)   In your opinion, in the region/area where you live, the Games will have effects positive or negative?
(Q8)   In your opinion, the positive effects of the Games will be long or briefly lasting? And the negative effects will be long or briefly lasting?
(Q9)   Do you think that the information about the Games and about the way they are planned can be considered sufficient?
(Q10)   Do you think that the Games will be an occasion of promoting and improving Torino and Piedmont?

(Q11)   Do you remember any cities that hosted the Olympic Games? *(Please, list the cities that you remember)*

(Q12)   Do you know how many gold medals Italy won at the last Olympics in Athens 2004?

(Q13)   Are you confident that Italy will gain a good success at the Winter Games 2006?

(Q14)   Torino, in the last years, organized many great events: Can you list some of them, considering culture, theatre, music, sport, etc.?

(Q15)   Do you think you can get new job opportunities from the Torino 2006 Olympic Games?

(Q16)   Are you confident that the Olympic Games will create some advantages or disadvantages to a person as you are?

(Q17)   In general, do you watch on TV the sports events? Do you follow on TV some sport in particular?

(Q18)   Do you practice some sports? Or did you do sports in the past?

(Q19)   Which of the following statements are closer to your opinion, considering the general meaning and the issues of the Olympic Games?
 – the Games are overall a sport event
 – the Games are an educational event
 – the Games are an economic business
 – the Games are a media event
 – the Games are a cultural event

(Q19)   In a ranking from 1 (the least) to 10 (the top), which score will Torino achieve in the organization of the Winter Games 2006?

(Q20)   Focusing socio-demographic information on the interviewees, like birth year, gender, educational degree, employment position, etc.

Addendum

During the years, in the new polls, the structure of the questionnaire remained approximately the same. Only some questions were eliminated after the first polls. In the post-event surveys (March 2006 and January 2007) the survey paid more attention to the future of the city, the tourism expected trend, the changing identity and image of the city, and the possible repositioning of Torino in the national and international arena.

17 Lessons from the field: spectator research for sport businesses
Douglas Michele Turco

1 INTRODUCTION

There are a number of reasons why sport businesses conduct market research. Sport spectator market profiles, economic impact studies and sponsorship effectiveness research allow organizations to understand consumer behaviors, quantify sport benefits and determine the value of their operations. For example, Brandon Igdalsky, President of the Pocono 500 Raceway, queried his NASCAR race fans in Pennsylvania during the 2009 economic recession to determine their spending patterns, brand loyalty and trip characteristics. He then compared 2009 research findings with previous race research as well as national NASCAR fan data to gain further market insights (Turco, 2009).

The body of knowledge in sport business research is diverse and considerable. Organizational theory and human resource management, coaching, finance and economics, law, marketing and sponsorship, and sport tourism are among the general research areas covered in sport business. Sport business research is presented in several publication outlets focused on these specialty areas, including the *Journal of Sport Management, International Journal of Sport Finance, Journal of Sports Economics, Journal of Sport and Tourism, International Journal of Sports Marketing and Sponsorship, Sport Marketing Quarterly* and the *Journal of Sport and Social Issues*.

The goal of this chapter is to familiarize the reader with sport business field research topics, common research procedures, research issues and proper ways to address them. Field research is the most direct approach to gather data from sport consumers, and is conducted where the action is – at the sport setting (this perspective is further supported in this volume, for example, by Balduck et al., 2013; Dibben and Dolles, 2013; Jansson and Söderman, 2013; Skille, 2013). The research procedures presented in this chapter are based on several theoretical approaches including input–output and cost–benefit analyses, transaction-cost analysis, balance scorecard and diamond framework (in this volume also see Andersson, 2013).

There are numerous examples of field research and many lessons from the field that can be gleaned: spectator profiles of U.S. Open Women's Golf Championship attendees revealed a significant presence of golf moms – mothers of the professional golfers. A study of fans at the Little League Baseball World Series found that those with a relative competing in the tournament attended more games and spent as much as three times more money than other fans. My chosen methodology is based on a thorough review of literature, extensive experience and spectator research practice. The methods described may be applied to a range of sport contests where primary data from participants and spectators is needed. Analyses can be performed to aid sport business leaders in decision-making with respect to sponsorship, marketing and promotional campaigns (see in this volume, for example, Schlesinger, 2013).

An array of sampling techniques for qualitative and quantitative research studies in sport business is described. Appropriate subject sizes for a single case study, and small and large probability and non-probability samples are addressed. Several mini-cases in sport business research are interspersed throughout the chapter to demonstrate the application of key steps in the research process. Further, two vignettes are presented to illustrate field research steps and practices in sport business. The first involves the use of advanced spectator research technologies at the 2009 Pocono 500 NASCAR race. The second concerns the 2007 Cricket World Cup Super Eight matches in Guyana that required two sampling locations, one at Providence Stadium and the other at the international departure lounge at the airport in Georgetown.

2   STEPS TO SPORT BUSINESS RESEARCH SUCCESS

There are five key steps to field survey research for sport businesses: (1) developing the problem (defining and delimiting it); (2) formulating hypotheses or research questions; (3) research design; (4) data gathering, treatment and analysis; and (5) reporting. Each step is described in the following sections.

2.1   Step One – Developing the Problem

At the outset, there must be something problematic for the firm to address. *What is the problem? Why must it be resolved?* Perhaps the firm needs to profile its spectators because potential sponsors demand this information before signing on. A professional sport team may wonder: *Why are fans not renewing their season tickets? Are they (dis) satisfied with our service? Why?* The answers may allow the firm to take corrective action and satisfy and retain customers. Another firm may have a sponsor who wants to know if their sponsorship 'works' before agreeing to a long-term contract. Once the research problem is identified it can be refined, and research questions or hypotheses formed and addressed to ultimately resolve the problem.

2.2   Step Two – Formulating Research Questions

Research questions drive a field study. As a scholar and sport business manager, *what do you want to know?* For example, the Albuquerque International Balloon Fiesta Inc. wanted to know balloon pilots' satisfaction with event operations, facilities and safety. The purpose of the 2007 and 2009 World Summer Universiade Games research was to compare the spending of participants across two events and continents (Turco et al., 2011). Among other things, Pocono 500 NASCAR race officials also wanted to know the radio music preferences of spectators, so as to leverage a media rights deal with appropriate company (Turco, 2009).

Research hypotheses are anticipated outcomes for a study. They can be posed directionally or in the null. For example, a null hypothesis for a sport tourism study is: there will be no significant difference in the per capita per day spend by spectators with or without relatives or friends competing in the event. In many cases, the direction of an anticipated outcome may be surmised from previous research. In the previous example, research has shown that sport event tourists with direct association to competitors do spend more money than other event tourists (Scott and Turco, 2007). Therefore, a directional hypothesis is more appropriate: visitors with relatives or friends competing in the event will spend significantly more money in the host economy per capita per day than other event visitors.

Certain terms or conditions must be defined for field research. For a sport event economic impact study, one of the first parameters to be defined is the economy. Economic costs and benefits from sport events may occur at the national, regional/provincial, state, county, metropolitan, district, city, and/or neighborhood levels. Often, geopolitical boundaries are used to define economies for impact studies since governments maintain tax records and multiplier coefficients are computed for various jurisdictions. Likewise, a 'sport tourist' study must operationalize who is and who is not a sport tourist. A definition for 'tourist' may seem to be a fairly simple definition to come up with but that is not the case. Place of visitor origin, length of stay, distance traveled, and mode of transport are variables that influence the tourist definition. Add 'sport' to the mix (for example, sport tourist) and the tourist definition becomes further complicated. There is still considerable disagreement about what is or is not sport! Is ballroom dance a sport? Synchronized swimming? Snooker? Curling? Rodeo? Horseracing?

Another consideration may be the definition of large-scale, mega and/or hallmark events. What constitutes are large-scale event? Mega event? Over 1 million spectators? An international television audience? See Dolles and Söderman (2008) for a classification of sports events. Hallmark events are defined, for example by Ritchie (1984: 2) as: 'Major one-time or recurring events of limited duration, developed primarily to enhance the awareness, appeal and profitability of a tourism destination in the short and/or long term. Such events rely for their success on uniqueness, status, or timely significance to create interest and attract attention'.

2.3   Step Three – Research Design

Once the purpose and research questions for a study are confirmed, it must be determined how the data will be obtained, where, when and by whom – key questions in research design. Decisions concerning instrumentation, logistics, scheduling, research methods and resources are to be made during this stage. Most field studies using primary data gather information from a sample of subjects, unless a total population can be queried. Subject sampling, procedures and protocols for data gathering and treatment must be prepared and practiced in advance of the event to ensure reliability.

2.3.1   Field survey data collection approaches
There are several methods to collect participant and spectator data at sport events: on-site interview, mail-back survey, self-administered diary, two-stage approach, and e-mail survey, each with relative advantages and disadvantages as briefly described below. Also see the chapter in this Handbook on participant observation (Dibben and Dolles, 2013, in this volume).

On-site approaches   Gathering data at the sport venue permits immediate data acquisition as opposed to traditional or electronic mail surveys that may take several weeks for responses to be received. In addition, the on-site survey allows the interviewer to reinterpret a question for a subject if necessary. With mail surveys, if a subject does not understand a question she may be more likely to skip it and/or discontinue the survey altogether. A disadvantage of the on-site data collection approach is that it may intrude on participant's leisure experience, particularly if subjects are approached during a sport contest. On-site interviews are labor intensive and for international events, multilingual interviewers may be required and difficult and/or costly to obtain.

For participant studies, it may be possible to gather data from surveys distributed by other means at the sport venue. For marathons and triathlons, participants receive race gift bags filled with 'goodies' including a T-shirt, race number and instructions. Placing a survey in each racer's bag is an easy method of distribution. The problem is getting a high percentage of the racers to complete and return the questionnaires. An incentive to complete the survey, for example, free registration for next year's event, cash, and so on, may elicit a higher rate of return.

A self-administered visitor log or diary requires subjects to record their transactions and other consumer behaviours on and away from the event venue. Subjects are intercepted at or around the event site early on and asked to participate in the study. Often an incentive to complete the survey is used to encourage and maintain participation. While this approach has the potential to generate accurate information, diaries or logs have the highest mortality or dropout rate (Yu and Turco, 2000). It has also been found that by recording their transactions, subjects have a heightened awareness of their spending and may alter subsequent purchase decisions. Most often they cut back on spending for the remainder of the visit.

'Knock-knock': going door-to-door   In an era of instantaneous drive-through windows and electronic communication, that is, Facebook, Twitter, texting and electronic mail, the old-fashioned approach to field survey research – going door-to-door is making a comeback! Some people still appreciate direct face-to-face communication over new media forms. Door-to-door surveys of residents with homes adjacent to a sport event venue have been employed in several studies including the Ice Climbing World Cup, the Tour de France and the Winter Olympic Games (Bull and Lovell, 2007; Ritchie and Lyons, 1990; Turco and Dinu, 2009). In the case of the Tour de France study, a cluster sample of homes along the racecourse was drawn. Field researchers conducted the surveys before and after the event and compared the results pre- to post-event. See the chapter by Balduck et al., 2013, in this volume. Going door-to-door may involve interviews or simply leaving a questionnaire with the head of household to complete and return either in a return addressed, postage paid envelope or to be collected by field researchers at a designated day/time.

Skier lift technique   A field survey data collection approach that is used at ski resorts is the skier lift technique. Here, subjects in chair lift lines are asked to participate in the study by trained interviewers on skis. Upon consent, the interview is performed while they ride the lift to the top of the ski run. The interviewer poses the questions and records the responses. At the end of the lift, the interviewer skis down the hill and returns to the

BOX 17.1   RESEARCH VIGNETTE: THE NEED FOR SPEED

Speed was of the essence for researchers at the 2009 Pocono 500 NASCAR race at Pocono Raceway, Long Pond, Pennsylvania (Turco, 2009). With only a few hours before the race to interview spectators, researchers used high-tech, handheld devices for data collection and analysis. The researchers performed the interviews on the Raceway grounds at the Sponsors' Village prior to race start using the i-Pod touch and surveyor application. Questions posed were to ascertain spectators' geographic and socio-demographic characteristics, and spending in the Pocono Mountain area. Spectator data were entered and immediately uploaded in WiFi zones for analysis. At the conclusion of the data-gathering phase, preliminary findings were sent to the race organizers via electronic mail before the green flag was waved for the race to begin. The entire process was paperless.

Among the key findings of the study were:

Small groups: Spectator groups to the 2009 Pocono 500 averaged 3.87 persons in size. Groups were comprised primarily of family (46.7 per cent), family and friends (24.5 per cent) and friends (22.3 per cent).

Short stays: Among visitors staying overnight in the Poconos, the average length of stay was one night. Accommodations used by visitors included hotel/ motel (22.3 per cent), camping (14.1 per cent), private residence of friends/ relatives (11.4 per cent), and other (18.5 per cent).

Local spending: Visitor groups spent a total of US$462.12 in the Poconos (off-site). Visitors spent US$141.70 for lodging, US$149.79 for food and beverage, US$117.35 for shopping, and US$53.28 for other expenses. Per person spending off-site averaged US$119.41.

Experience counts: Spectators had attended an average of 6.5 Pocono Raceway races prior to the 2009 Pocono 500. Repeat visitation is a significant indicator of customer satisfaction.

Radio: Spectators favored country music (37 per cent), and classic rock (32.6 per cent) for radio entertainment. Other favored radio entertainment included pop/contemporary (7.6 per cent), news (4.9 per cent), talk (4.3 per cent), and other (9.2 per cent).

Race information: Spectators primarily relied on the official NASCAR website for information on the Pocono 500 (41.3 per cent), the official Pocono 500 website (22.8 per cent), Speed Channel (13 per cent), NASCAR radio (3.8 per cent), and other sources (13 per cent).

Profile: Spectators ranged in age from 16 to 72 years with a mean age of 39.4 years. Sixty one per cent of subjects were male and 39 per cent were female. Nationwide, NASCAR fans aged 18–44 years comprised 49 per cent of the spectator market. In general, NASCAR fans at raceways mirror the Pocono gender profile: 60 per cent are male and 40 per cent are female. Approximately 28 per cent of spectators interviewed had children under the age of 18 years.

Nationally, 43 per cent of NASCAR fans have children under the age of 18 years. Approximately 36 per cent of Pocono 500 spectators had 2008 household incomes over US$50 000; 21.5 per cent has incomes below US$50 00. 48 per cent of NASCAR fans across the country US$50 000+ per year.

lift line to select another subject. To enhance external validity, the sample is drawn in proportion to the volume of skiers who typically ride lifts to hills that are designated for beginner, intermediate and advanced. Of course, the approach works equally as well for snowboarders. Advantages of the skier lift technique are (1) subjects are a 'captive' audience since they cannot escape the interviewer, leading to high response rate; (2) there is no intrusion on the leisure time of subjects; and (3) it is easy to recruit volunteer interviews since they get to ski as part of their assignment.

Traditional mail-back surveys The traditional mail survey is useful when a relatively large population or subject group(s) is geographically dispersed and post-event evaluation is desired. Mail-back surveys are low labor-intensive but the costs for photocopying and postage can add up, particularly with large sample sizes and follow-up mailings that may be necessary to gain an appropriate response rate. The time lag between a subject's behavior and survey response may be considerable, contributing to inaccuracies (recall bias). Low response rates have plagued mail-back surveys.

A combination of the on-site and mail-back approaches could be employed whereby subjects are systematically sampled at the sport venue and asked a brief set of qualifying questions. For example, 'Are you a visitor to this city?' 'Would you be willing to respond to a mail survey about the event upon your return home?' If so, the subject's name, physical and electronic mail addresses and telephone numbers are recorded. The survey questionnaire and cover letter are sent at once to the subjects, with a postage paid, return address envelope. The two-stage approach permits reliability checks for variables asked on-site and post-event. Further, higher response rates are achieved as subjects have given their word that they would respond to the mail-back survey. Most people, once reminded of their commitment, are true to their word and respond. Of course, this approach is time-consuming and costly but the question is 'How much are you willing to spend on your survey to achieve a high response rate?'

E-surveys Electronic mail surveys can lead to fast and low-cost survey distribution. With corresponding software for analyses, survey responses can be uploaded immediately, permitting real-time results. However, acquiring the e-addresses of a population may not be possible, as some subjects may not have access to e-mail. Further, those with e-addresses may possess characteristics that differ from other members of the population, that is, computer knowledgeable, younger, more education, income, and so on, thereby limiting the external validity of the study.

Unobtrusive measures We can learn a great deal about people simply by observing them, capturing their actions rather than their stated views. What one *says* they will do may not always be what they *actually do*. Watching people as the proverbial 'fly on the

---

BOX 17.2   GO FISH! THE 2005 BASSMASTER ELITE 50
SERIES SPECTATOR STUDY

What could be more exciting than watching people fish? Fifty of the world's best BASS pros visited the Chippewa Valley to participate in the 2005 Bassmaster Elite 50 Series. Practice days began on 12 June through to 14 June with competition days held 15–18 June on Lake Wissota in Chippewa Falls, Wisconsin. In addition to the fishing tournament, there was an outdoor expo featuring numerous fishing vendors and displays. Total attendance was estimated to be 14 000 spectators. In an attempt to gather more information about sport event spectators in Wisconsin, the Department of Tourism, Chippewa Valley Convention and Visitors Bureau, Department of Natural Resources, and the University of Wisconsin's Department of Urban and Regional Planning partnered to gather marketing and economic impact information. A stratified random sample of spectators was drawn during the final four days of competitive fishing. Field interviewers randomly selected/intercepted spectators at nightly weigh-ins, as they toured the Outdoor Expo or waited in line for transportation shuttles. A survey instrument jointly developed by the participating agencies was administered on site. A drawing for free tickets to Eau Claire's Country Jam USA was used to entice visitors to fill out a survey. A total of 238 visitor parties were intercepted; there were 39 refusals and 18 parties had previously been surveyed. A total of 181 completed surveys were obtained. Spectators were classified into two categories: local and non-local. Local spectators accounted for 67.6 per cent of the sample. Non-locals lived outside Eau Claire and Chippewa Counties and accounted for 32.4 per cent of the respondents. Non-local spectators spent on average US$290.56 per person, primarily on lodging, food/beverage, and gasoline. In total, all non-local spectators spent US$1 317 425 in the Chippewa Valley.

Source: Wisconsin Department of Tourism (2005).

---

wall' allows subjects to behave naturally and without inhibition. Unobtrusive measures include video and audio recording, photography and personal observation. These approaches are time-consuming and costly. A disadvantage of unobtrusive measure is interpreting the data, invasion of privacy and confidentiality.

2.3.2   Instrumentation: writing the survey
Survey questions should be posed to generate data necessary to respond directly to the key research questions asked at the beginning of the research process (see Appendix for a sample questionnaire). Additional questions may be posed to further examine the responses given by different types of people. For example, responses to a spectator survey on the effects of sponsorship on purchase intentions can be cross-tabulated with data from the survey's socio-demographic questions, for instance, gender, age, occupation and highest level of education attained, to shed light on the extent to which there are differences in how males and females, young and older adults, and so on may be

---

BOX 17.3   LITTLE LEAGUE BASEBALL WORLD SERIES

The Little League World Series is one of the most popular youth sporting events in the world, attracting 325 000 spectators and media coverage spanning the globe (Scott and Turco, 2007). Thirty-two games were televised by ESPN or ESPN2 and the final was nationally televised by ABC Sports. The Little League World Series features the top teams from the United States and abroad by virtue of local and regional playoffs. In all eight divisions more than 30 000 games are played in less than two months to determine eight world champions (Little League). Playoffs are held in late July for the international teams and early August for the domestic teams. Domestic teams competing in the Little League World Series were from Pennsylvania, Hawaii, Iowa, Florida, Maine, California, Kentucky and Louisiana. The international teams were from Mangialo-Barrigada, Guam, Mexicali, Mexico, Surrey, Canada, Moscow, Russia, Valencia, Venezuela, Chiba City, Japan, Willemstad, Curaçao and Saudi Arabia.

Scott and Turco (2007) conducted a visitor survey during each of the eight days on which games were played during the 2005 Little League World Series. Researchers approached adult spectators on the Little League grounds between Lanade and Volunteer Stadiums, and asked them to participate in the study. Every tenth spectator was selected for the sample as they passed a designated area on site. Upon the subject's consent, a clipboard, questionnaire and pen were handed to the subject, and verbal instructions to complete the survey were given. Visitors were asked to return the completed questionnaires clipboards and pens to a designated collection bin nearby. The visitor questionnaire was developed by the research team to determine the following visitor characteristics: location of primary residence: city, state, country, postal code; visitor group size; relationship to player(s); length of stay in Williamsport; spending in Williamsport by category: lodging, meals, shopping, souvenirs, other, and so on; prior attendance, and plans to return.

---

induced to purchase an event sponsor's products. For an event economic impact study, at a minimum, the following survey information should be obtained to calculate visitor spending: (1) residency; (2) primary reason for visiting designated economy, and (3) local spending by visitors. Box 17.3, 'Little League World Series', is offered to illustrate the aforementioned stages of field research.

2.3.3   Survey Sampling

Sample size   A common question concerning field research is 'How many sport event spectators should be surveyed?' The standard answer is 'As many as possible', since the accuracy of survey data is linked to the number of respondents. Hallmark or large-scale sport events usually have spectator populations over 100 000 and are considered infinitely large, thereby requiring parametric sampling for enhanced external validity. Minimum

Table 17.1   Spectator survey sample sizes and precisions levels

Attendance	Precision levels and sample sizes			
	+3%	+4%	+5%	+10%
Under 10000	1000	588	385	99
20000	1053	606	392	100
50000	1087	617	397	100
100000	1099	621	398	100
Over 100000	1111	625	400	100

Source: Yamane (1967).

sampling sizes of 38 persons will produce results accurate to within ± 5 per cent of the actual reported figure; a sample of 588 yields results ± 4 per cent and a sample of 1000 generates a ± 3 per cent ranges at the 95 per cent confidence level. Since greater sample sizes often lead to additional time and financial costs, the researcher must decide how much variability he or she is willing to accept in the study. It is recommended that sample sizes for economic impact studies be large enough for a ± 4 per cent to ± 5 per cent tolerated error level (see Table 17.1). For participant surveys it may be practical to query all athletes or their coaches/managers unless the field is unusually large or difficult to access. Often, coaches or managers are capable of accurately providing spending information for an athlete or team since they act as fiscal agents during travel competitions.

Sample subjects: who to survey?   For visitor expenditure studies, field researchers should seek an adult decision-maker or head of household to provide the requested information. Subjects should be instructed to divulge their own expenditures if traveling unaccompanied or those of their immediate travel group if traveling with others. If at all possible, subjects should be selected at random to avoid sample bias and ensure generalizability (external validity). True random sampling grants everyone in the designated population an equal chance to be selected. Most field studies do not include professional or elite athletes because they are limited for time and organizers do not want them distracted from their sport focus or exploited. Some recreational athletes may feel the same way, though they generally are willing to comply with purposeful research if it is not too intrusive.

2.3.4   Logistics: where to survey?
Distinct spectator markets may attend events at different days and/or times, and congregate in certain areas of an event venue. For example, spectators in luxury skybox suites and those in general admission seating typically possess different socio-demographic characteristics and spending behaviors. Samples drawn exclusively from an event location frequented by a distinct market segment diminishes the study's external validity and its termed sample location bias.

2.3.5   Scheduling: when to survey
It is not practical or necessary to sample participants or event spectators during every hour of operation. Determining the proper times to survey is important for the same

reasons as where to survey. The days and hours of operation to sample event spectators must control for sampling bias and assure generalization of results to the total population. For example, young adults are more likely to attend late night events than older adults or families with young children. If event spectators were surveyed only during late evening hours, the sample would likely be skewed younger than the true spectator population. For multiple day events with at least eight hours of operation per day, a recommended survey schedule is to establish time blocks to conduct the survey. These periods should be weighted by projected attendance and randomly selected from all possible hours of the event. Another survey scheduling technique is to stratify survey distribution based upon anticipated or past event attendance. For example approximately 20 per cent of the total attendance at the Albuquerque International Balloon Fiesta occurred during the first day, whereas 14 per cent occurred during the eighth day. Therefore, approximately 20 per cent of all the surveys were administered during the first day and 14 per cent during the eighth day. Therefore, caution must be taken when scheduling times for field data collection to avoid sample bias.

Sport events that last a day, for example, the Kentucky Derby, or a month, for example, the FIFA World Cup, may have a production lifecycle extending for months or years. For sport event impacts studies, it must be remembered that impacts occur prior to the event during bid preparation and planning, during the event, and post-event as part of the event legacy. Therefore, it must be decided *when* direct spending occurs and *when* it will be measured. Most sport event economic impact studies include only the spending that occurs *during* the event, although recent emphasis has been placed on measuring longer-term post-event impacts or legacies.

Gathering participant or spectator data in the field is dynamic and invasive. Weather-dependent events may be altered owing to climatic conditions, and field research may need to be altered accordingly. For example, if a match was rained out during the time surveys were to be conducted, the data collection schedule must be revised.

Field surveys should not be conducted during active periods of a match or contest. After all, spectators and participants are involved in a particular sport for a reason and should not be distracted by field researchers during competition. Few would want to be interrupted from a critical point in a match by a field researcher. Before or after matches and/or during intermissions when there is 'down time' are the best times to query subjects at sport events.

2.4 Step Four – Data Treatment and Analysis

The fourth step in the field research process is treating and analysing the data collected. Data may be coded into numeric values and entered into a computerized statistical package or software spreadsheet for analysis. Programs including Microsoft Excel, SPSS and SAS are commonly used for data computation. Internet surveys may immediate upload responses and provide immediate analysis in real time.

For economic impact studies involving multi-day events and relying on survey data from visitors, it is necessary to adjust event attendance records to reflect the true number of distinct individuals attending rather than the total event attendance. Repeat attendance by visitors must be factored as the amount visitors spend in the host economy multiplied by the number of actual visitors. Failure to account for repeat visitors would obviously overinflate the total direct economic impact figures. To calculate the number

BOX 17.4   RESEARCH VIGNETTE: 2007 ICC CRICKET
WORLD CUP

The International Cricket Council (ICC) Cricket World Cup (CWC) tournament
is one of the world's largest sporting events. As indicators of its worldwide
appeal, 2007 CWC matches were televised in 200 countries to over 2.2 billion
television viewers. Television rights for the 2011 and 2015 World Cup were
recently sold for over US$1.1 billion, and sponsorship rights were sold for a
further US$500 million (cricinfo.com, 2007). The 2007 CWC sold more than
672000 tickets and recorded the highest ticketing revenue for a CWC
(IndiaNews.com, 2007). Attendance for the entire 2007 Cricket World Cup averaged 11176 per match (www.icc-cricket.com, accessed 26 January 2012). The
West Indies hosted the 2007 CWC with 16 teams – Australia, Bangladesh,
Bermuda, Canada, England, India, Kenya, Ireland, Netherlands, New Zealand,
Pakistan, Scotland, South Africa, Sri Lanka, West Indies and Zimbabwe –
selected to play 51 one-day matches, between 13 March to 28 April 2007.
Territories (Antigua and Barbuda, Barbados, Grenada, Guyana, Jamaica, St
Kitts and Nevis, St Lucia, and Trinidad and Tobago) were selected to host the
main matches, with each country hosting six matches, with the exception of
Barbados, Jamaica and St Lucia, which each hosted seven matches and
Barbados hosting the final. Guyana built a new 16000-seat stadium at a cost of
US$25 million to host the Super Eight matches of the 2007 CWC. Matches and
attendance in Guyana for the tournament were as follows:

2007 Cricket World Cup matches, Guyana National Stadium at Providence

Date	Teams	Official attendance
28 March	Sri Lanka v South Africa	5220
29 March	England v Ireland	4800
1 April	Sri Lanka v West Indies	12208
3 April	Ireland v South Africa	5673
7 April	Bangladesh v South Africa	9460
9 April	New Zealand v Ireland	6500

Note: Average attendance at Guyana National Stadium was 7310.

Source: International Cricket Council (www.icc-cricket.com, accessed 26 January 2012).

A study was commissioned to measure the tourist impacts of the Super Eight
on Guyana. Visitor interviews were arranged at the Guyana National Stadium
at Providence during selected days on which matches were played in Guyana
during the Super Eight stage of the 2007 CWC (1, 3 and 7 April) and in the
departure lounge of the Cheddi Jagan International Airport on 2, 7, 8 and 10
April. Trained field researchers approached adult spectators and invited them

to participate in the study. Upon consent, questions were posed to determine the following spectator characteristics. Survey data were entered and analysed using the Statistical Package for Social Sciences (SPSS) computer software. Key findings are presented in the following section.

Results and discussion

A total of 394 spectators were interviewed for the study. Spectators resided in the United States (n = 201), Trinidad (n = 68), Canada (n = 33), the United Kingdom (n = 30) and Barbados (n = 10). Other countries represented in the spectator sample included Antigua, Australia, Bahamas, India, South Africa, Spain and Sri Lanka. Visitors from the United States accounted for 50 per cent of the total spectator sample, while those from the Caribbean formed 25 per cent, followed by Canada with 13 per cent. Visitor spending for the 2007 and 2003 Cricket World Cups were compared. The 2003 Cricket World Cup took place in South Africa, Zimbabwe and Kenya. Fifty-eight per cent of the net benefit to South Africa arose from spending by foreigners, who spent an average of R1400 per day (approximately US$190) for an average of 16 days. However, per day visitor spending figures for 2003 and 2007 CWC were nearly identical (US$190 for 2003 and US$191 in 2007). The 2003 CWC matches in South Africa were attended by 626 845 people while the 2007 CWC sold more than 672 000 tickets and recorded the highest ticketing revenue for a CWC. The average length of stay of a foreign visitor in CWC 2003 was 16 days, which was slightly longer than for the average non-CWC foreign visitor (12 days). Visitors that came specifically for the CWC 2003 stayed the shortest, while those that had timed their holiday to coincide with the event ended up staying over 22 days – this trend was also evident in the Guyana edition of CWC 2007.

of direct visitors at a sport event, several data points are required, including event attendance, number of days/sessions visitors attended, whether or not attending the event was the primary reason for visiting and average visitor group size. Accurate event attendance records are critical to the validity of any sport event field study. Some events tally individual visits by scanning barcodes on ticket passes but many do not. For multiple day or session events, total attendance must be adjusted to reflect the total number of primary visitors or visitor groups. To do so requires the following data:

- total event attendance;
- average days/sessions attended;
- primary reason for visiting host economy – sport event;
- Average visitor group size.

Data collected from visitor surveys may be applied to the template below to adjust attendance totals taking into account repeat visitation and primary reason for visiting the host community. For a four-day event with an attendance of 100 000 and visitors attending

---

BOX 17.5   TOUR DE GEORGIA

A field study revealed that the 2005 Tour de Georgia generated US$36.2 million in economic impact for the state of Georgia and local communities (www.tour-degeorgia.com). Conducted by the Community Policy and Research Services division at Georgia Tech's Economic Development and Technology Ventures, the study featured 1386 visitor surveys. The number of respondents saying the cycling race was their primary purpose for visiting was 905. The percentage of those at the race sites from out of state that were there just for the race was about 43.4 per cent (of the 905). The other visitors (those visiting for other reasons or who were Georgians) were not considered as part of the impact.

2005 Tour de Georgia Survey visitor statistics

	Number	**Percentage**
Number of surveys completed	1386	100.0
TDG respondents	905	65.3
In-state TDG respondents	512	56.6
Out-of-state TDG respondents	393	43.4

Attendance:	All specific sites	380 000
	Along the route	422 250
	Total: all visitors	802 250

Spending patterns of out-of-state visitors:

Per person days spent on TDG activities:	3.87 days

Average daily spending on:

Local transportation	US$61.71
Lodging	US$85.05
Restaurants	US$13.07
Retail	US$26.92
Total daily spending	US$186.75

2.5 days, the total number of visitors would be 40 000. Primary visitors represented 50 per cent of the sample and once applied to the total number of visitors (40 000) reveals a total of 20 000 primary visitors. The average visitor group size (four persons) applied to the primary visitor total (20 000) produces a total of 5000 primary visitor groups.

Worksheet – Sport event visitor attendance

Total event attendance	_____
Average days/sessions attended by visitors	÷_____
Total individuals attending event	=_____
Per cent primary visitors	×_____
Total primary visitors attending event	=_____
Average primary visitor group size	÷_____
Total primary visitor groups	=_____

2.5 Step Five: Reporting

Once the field data are analysed and research questions addressed, the study findings may be reported internally and/or externally. Typically, a written report is prepared containing an executive summary, introduction, purpose statement, review of related research, methods, analysis, discussion, conclusions and recommendations. Findings may be illustrated in tables, graphs and narrative statements. A list of references cited and appendices that may contain maps and diagrams, sampling schedules, event information, questionnaires, and so on are contained in the final section of the report. Oral reports often follow the same sequential order as the written report with presentation slides containing key findings, tables, graphs and photographs from the event.

3 DISCUSSION

3.1 Research Issues in the Field

At times, research may be conducted for political purposes and to a self-serving point. Crompton (2006) contends that many sport event economic impact studies are commissioned to justify a political position rather than to search for economic accuracy, resulting in the use of questionable procedures that produce bloated numbers. Among the questionable research procedures: including local resident spending; appropriate aggregation; inclusion of time-switchers and casuals; abuse of multipliers; ignoring costs borne by the local community; ignoring opportunity costs; ignoring displacement costs; expanding the project scope; exaggerating visitation numbers and inclusion of consumer surplus (see also in this volume, for example, Andersson, 2013; Balduck et al., 2013; Helleu and Desbordes, 2013; Guala and Turco, 2013). Regardless of the motives for conducting research, what is most important is that sound, systematic and ethical procedures are followed for data gathering and analysis. Internal validity or the extent to which an instrument accurately measures what it purports to measure, is critical to any field study. Estimates or projections of sport tourist activity generally come from attendance figures, room occupancy rates or some other system to measure tourism demand. Internal validity is threatened from poorly constructed and formatted questionnaires that produce responses of little worth. In short, a study will only be as accurate as the data collected – as the saying goes, 'Garbage in, garbage out'.

3.2 Threats to Validity

A threat to external validity (how true what one found is of the general population) can occur when a survey reaches a high level of non-response bias, also contaminating its reliability. Non-respondents may differ from survey respondents in certain ways. For example, they may have spent less money, stayed fewer days and/or been less satisfied with their experiences. Non-response bias may be unintentionally encouraged by researchers in a number of ways. For international events, the language used for field surveys may lead to non-response among those who are not fluent. Mail-back surveys without accompanying postage-paid, return addressed envelopes will also yield high non-response rates. The proliferation of junk mail and spam has made it very difficult for researchers conducting postal and electronic mail surveys to obtain high response rates.

'At what point (or response rate) does subject non-response compromise the generalizability of a study's findings?' As a general rule, surveys with less than a 50 per cent response rate are at risk of non-response bias. A common practice for addressing the issue is to randomly select a sub-sample of non-respondents and survey them by another method. If responses are statistically similar for this sub-sample as for the original respondents, it may be assumed that the response group is representative of the population and, therefore, the results may be generalized with greater confidence in their accuracy. If the responses differ significantly, such differences as well as resulting limitations to the study's generalizability should be described in the final research report. In the field, subjects are more likely to respond to polite, well-trained, well-groomed surveyors who are dressed in uniforms and possess official photograph identification.

The accuracy of spectator studies may be limited by the amount of time that transpires between a subject's event attendance and the survey, inducing what is termed, recall bias. Recall bias is particularly acute in economic impact studies with mail-back surveys when a lengthy time lag between the event and survey has occurred. Visitors tend to underestimate their expenditures when asked for information after a considerable time has elapsed from their visit. They also tend to perceive their travel experiences more positively as time transpires. To address the issue of recall bias, visitors should be queried as soon after their experiences as possible; at least within one to two weeks of their visit. The flipside of recall bias is projection bias, which can occur when subjects are asked to estimate their spending early in their trip or visit. To address projection bias, visitor samples should be drawn near the end of, or immediately after, the event. A split-method research approach may also be employed, that is, on-site interview and post-event e-mail survey, permitting comparisons based on when the surveys were conducted.

3.3   Future of Sport Business Research

Technology will play an increasingly important role in sport business research in this decade. Smart phones and other small portable electronic devices will permit sport consumer research that is less intrusive and can collect data immediately. Some researchers are accessing sport consumer data from large mines gathered by credit card companies. For example, Simon Chadwick has published research on fans' spending behaviors and economic impacts at the Rugby World Cup 2011 in New Zealand based on data accessed from MasterCard (Chadwick et al., 2011). This direct, 'top-down' approach to research offers advantages to the labor-intensive field research. The research topics or problems in sport business are enduring and will be facing scholars and managers in the future. Research will become more central to the strategic planning process as a new wave of well-educated managers enters the sport business area, armed with research skills and an appreciation for data-driven decision-making.

4 CONCLUSION

This chapter was intended to familiarize the reader with sport business field research by describing the key steps to research success: (1) developing the problem, (2) formulating hypotheses or research questions, (3) research design, (4) data gathering, treatment and analysis, and (5) reporting. Several data collection approaches for field research in sport business were described including on-site interviews, door-to-door, e-surveys and the skier lift technique. Five cases were presented to illustrate the field research steps and applications in sport business. In addition, an example of the questionnaire used for the Little League Baseball World Series research is appended to the chapter.

It must be remembered that research in the field is fluid and dynamic, and requires, at times, flexibility by the researchers. This lesson came across loud and clear for field researchers at the 2010 FIFA World Cup in South Africa. Fans blaring the vuvuzelas made match-day interviews at the stadium precincts extremely difficult. The survey schedules were altered and additional surveys were gathered at the FIFA Fan Fests where the decibel levels were not as high.

REFERENCES

Andersson, T. (2013), Triple impact assessments of sports events, in S. Söderman and H. Dolles (eds), *Handbook of Research on Sport and Business*, Cheltenham, UK and Northampton, MA, USA: Edward Elgar, pp. 237–56.

Balduck, A., Maes, M. and Buelens, M. (2013), Social impacts of hosting major sport events: the impact of the 2007 arrival of a stage of the Tour de France of the city of Ghent, in S. Söderman and H. Dolles (eds), *Handbook of Research on Sport and Business*, Cheltenham, UK and Northampton, MA, USA: Edward Elgar, pp. 274–94.

Bull, C. and Lovell, J. (2007), The impact of hosting major sporting events on local residents: an analysis of the views and perceptions of Canterbury residents in relation to the Tour de France 2007, *Journal of Sport & Tourism*, **12** (3/4), 229–48.

Chadwick, S., Semens, A. and Arthur, D. (2011), Economic impact report on global rugby: Part IV: Rugby World Cup 2011, available at: http://media.nzherald.co.nz/webcontent/document/pdf/201138/MasterCard%20Economic%20Impact1.pdf (accessed 1 February 2012).

Crompton, J.L. (2006), Economic impact studies: instruments for political shenanigans?, *Journal of Travel Research*, **45** (1), 67–82.

Dibben, M. and Dolles, H. (2013), Participant observation in sport management research: collecting and interpreting data from a successful world land speed record attempt, in S. Söderman and H. Dolles (eds), *Handbook of Research on Sport and Business*, Cheltenham, UK and Northampton, MA, USA: Edward Elgar, pp. 477–94.

Dolles, H. and Söderman, S. (2008), Mega-sporting events in Asia. Impacts on society, business and management: an introduction, *Asian Business and Management*, **7** (2), 147–62.

Guala, A.C. and Turco, D.M. (2013), What do they really think? Researching residents' perception of mega-sport events, in S. Söderman and H. Dolles (eds), *Handbook of Research on Sport and Business*, Cheltenham, UK and Northampton, MA, USA: Edward Elgar, pp. 295–311.

Helleu, B. and Desbordes, M. (2013), Sacrés Français! Why they don't have great football stadia; how they will: political, economic and marketing implications of the UEFA EURO 2016, in S. Söderman and H. Dolles (eds), *Handbook of Research on Sport and Business*, Cheltenham, UK and Northampton, MA, USA: Edward Elgar, pp. 257–73.

Jansson, H. and Söderman, S. (2013), Proposing a relationship marketing theory for sport clubs, in S. Söderman and H. Dolles (eds), *Handbook of Research on Sport and Business*, Cheltenham, UK and Northampton, MA, USA: Edward Elgar, pp. 350–66.

Ritchie, J.R.B. (1984), Assessing the impact of hallmark events: conceptual and research issues, *Journal of Travel Research*, **23** (1), 2–11.

Ritchie, J.R.B. and Lyons, M. (1990), Olympulse VI: A post-event assessment of resident reaction to the XVth Olympic Winter Games, *Journal of Travel Research*, **28** (3), 14–23.

Schlesinger, T. (2013), A review of fan identity and its influence on sport sponsorship effectiveness, in S. Söderman and H. Dolles (eds), *Handbook of Research on Sport and Business*, Cheltenham, UK and Northampton, MA, USA: Edward Elgar, pp. 435–55.

Scott, A.K.S. and Turco, D.M. (2007), VFRs as a segment of the sport event tourist market, *Journal of Sport and Tourism*, **12** (1), 41–52.

Skille, E.Å (2013), Case study research in sport management: a reflection upon the theory of science and an empirical example, in S. Söderman and H. Dolles (eds), *Handbook of Research on Sport and Business*, Cheltenham, UK and Northampton, MA, USA: Edward Elgar, pp. 161–75.

Turco, D.M. (2009), A need for speed: 2009 Pocono 500 NASCAR spectator profile, technical report prepared for Pocono Raceway, Inc., Long Pond, PA.

Turco, D.M. and Dinu, M.S. (2009), The economic significance of a mountain tourism event: the case of the 2009 Ice Climbing World Cup in Busteni, Romania, *Journal of Tourism Challenges and Trends*, **2** (2), 11–21.

Turco, D.M., Papapdimitriou, D. and Berber, S. (2011), Athletes as tourists: consumer behaviours of participants at the 2007 and 2009 World Universiade Games, *Physical Culture and Sport Studies and Research*, **51**, 72–9.

Wisconsin Department of Tourism (2005), *Profile of the Bassmaster Elite 50 Series Fishing Tournament: Economic and Demographic Assessment of Those Involved in the June 15–18 Event*, Madison, WI: University of Wisconsin Cooperative Research Program.

Yamane, T. (1967), *Elementary Sampling Theory*, Englewood Cliffs, NJ: Prentice-Hall.

Yu, Y. and Turco, D.M. (2000), Issues in tourism event economic impact studies: the case of the 1995 Kodak Albuquerque International Balloon Fiesta, *Current Issues in Tourism*, **3** (2), 138–49.

APPENDIX: 2005 LITTLE LEAGUE WORLD SERIES VISITOR SURVEY

Welcome to Williamsport! We would like to learn more about your visit to our community. Please take a few moments to answer the following questions and promptly return the completed questionnaire to the Williamsport Chamber of Commerce kiosk. Thank you.

Q1. Where are you from?

City_____

State/Prov._____ Zip/mail code_____

Country_____

Q2. How many people, including yourself, are in your immediate travel party?
_____

Q3. Do you have a relative or friend associated with one of the teams participating in the 2005 Little League World Series?   Yes   No

Q4. How many times will you attend the 2005 Little League World Series during your stay in Williamsport?

Q5. Have you attended the Little League World Series prior to 2005?
Yes   No

Q6. How many nights will you stay in the Williamsport area for the 2005 Little League World Series? _____

Q7. How much were your travel costs to the Williamsport area? US$_____

Q8. How much do you plan to spend for your immediate travel party while in Williamsport on:
Food and beverages? US$_____Retail Shopping? US$_____
Lodging? US$_____ Other goods/services? US$_____
Items at the Little League World Series complex? US$_____

Q9. What changes if any could be made to the Williamsport area to improve your visit?
_____

Q10. Do you think you will visit the Williamsport area again?
Yes   No   Not sure

Q11. Once you return home, may we ask you a few additional questions about your visit to Williamsport?

If so, please provide your e-mail address:

_____

and/or telephone numbers: _____

PART V

CLUB MANAGEMENT
AND TEAMS

18 Portfolio theory and the management of professional sports clubs: the case of Maple Leaf Sports and Entertainment
Norm O'Reilly

1 INTRODUCTION

Models of management are known to render decision-making less complex and more certain when implemented properly and in a timely fashion by experienced managers, and have therefore been the topic of frequent discussion (Mintzberg, 1987). In fact, one group of researchers (ten Have et al., 2003) have produced a compilation of more than 50 of the most used and cited management models, noting the importance of the manager's active role and the necessity of research into new models. Practitioners of professional sport support this argument: Richard Peddie, President of Maple Leaf Sports and Entertainment, assures that his organization is 'batting much better' than Henry Mintzberg's claim that organizations follow only 10 per cent of their strategic plans (personal communication, 7 April 2008). Examples of widely accepted management models include Kaplan and Norton's (2007) balanced scorecard, Mintzberg's (1983, 1990) configurations of organizational structures and Porter's (1998) five forces model.

This chapter focuses on the development of a management model specific to professional sport clubs. Although there have been calls for improved decision-making (Gerrard, 2005), and theoretical models for certain aspects of club management have been proposed (Kedar-Levy and Bar-Eli, 2008), a comprehensive management model remains absent from the sport management literature. In response to that void, the purpose of this research is to develop a management model for professional sports clubs, guided by portfolio theory, and based on the input of senior practitioners via an extensive case study that assesses a specific professional sport conglomerate as a portfolio of assets.

2 BACKGROUND INFORMATION AND LITERATURE

2.1 Management Models and Related Sport Management Research

Those who have spent time reviewing the existing management models report that many are simply guiding tools that help management remember what is important when they make decisions (Ten Have et al., 2003). For example, the management model known as 'scenario planning' typically involves the development of three to five scenarios of potential outcome (Wack, 1985) that are combined with the organization's vision and planning to illuminate future decisions. Similarly, Mintzberg (1990) provides managers with six configurations for management, noting a seventh when a management approach is absent. Other models include Porter's (1998) management model, which is based on the idea that the attractiveness of an industry is defined by its competitive forces, and Nolan's (1979) six phases in the growth and development of information technology (IT) products, which is based on a specific industry.

Within the sport management literature, the presentation of management models for professional sport organizations is rare, although a few frameworks or implied models can be found (for example, Cousens and Slack, 2005; Richelieu and Boulaire, 2005; Slack and Parent, 2006). Others have modelled professional sport management from sport finance perspectives such as profitability (Nadeau and O'Reilly, 2006), a network of value captures (Dolles and Söderman, 2008, 2011, 2013 in this volume), revenue (O'Reilly and Nadeau, 2006), value of team ownership (Fort, 2006) and brands as assets (Richelieu and Pons, 2006).

2.2   Professional Sport

Prior to 1970, professional sport as an industry was much less developed corporately than in 2011; three decades ago it had lower player wages and locally focused fan bases. However, a variety of transformations since then have driven drastic change in professional sport (Cousens and Slack, 2005). Today, it is a major, high-profile global industry, comprised of leagues and clubs of all sizes, that continues its rapid growth and expansion (Foster et al., 2006) using a resource-based approach to achieve competitive advantage and long-term stability (Mauws et al., 2003).

There are a variety of constructs, issues and factors that influence the management of a professional sport club. For example, with profit maximization now a priority for some team owners, the threat of expansion and relocation can influence important decisions with regard to club profitability (Nadeau and O'Reilly, 2006). Club management must also be aware of fan loyalty to its brand, since brand loyal fans are psychologically committed to the club's brand and, in turn, attend games, purchase merchandise, support sponsors and, ultimately, drive the club's business success (Bauer et al., 2005).

2.3   Portfolio Theory

Most often applied in accounting, investment banking, finance and strategy (Elton and Gruber, 1997), portfolio theory uses the perspective of an investor and seeks to optimize investment benefits through the diversification and risk management of the investor's portfolio. It considers the portfolio problem, where the risk of a given investment is determined based on each investor's preferred portfolio. The level of risk is based on his or her own risk aversion, the overall composition of his or her portfolio and sought return objectives (Markowitz, 1952). Over time, changes to a portfolio that maintain the same level of expected return, but with reduced risk, are sought (Sharpe, 1963). The separation theorem is an important aspect of portfolio theory that considers the implications of a riskless asset and how it compares to the risk/return outcomes of alternate investment options (Ross, 1978), noting (1) that an investor can obtain his or her desired portfolio with a mix of high risk and riskless assets, and (2) more effective evaluation by comparing alternatives to the riskless option (Elton and Gruber, 1997).

Optimization, or finding the optimal mix of high and low risk assets, is a common aspect of portfolio theory (Andrikopoulos and Koronis, 2007). In practice, portfolio theory typically guides investment portfolio decisions by considering the expected return and the unique risk of a given asset as part of a larger portfolio of assets. Defining a professional sport club as a series of assets forms the basis for applying portfolio theory as a foundation for a model for professional sport club management, which is the objective of this research.

3   METHODOLOGY

This research involved a three-phase methodology. First, based on the literature and secondary data, a portfolio theory-inspired categorization of professional sport assets was developed to guide the case study. Second, an in-depth case study on a major professional sport conglomerate was carried out to assess the categorization. Finally, building on the case study, a management model was drafted.

3.1   Unit of Analysis

Two primary types of organizations typically operate in professional sport: leagues and clubs (or teams). The league is the entity that governs a group of clubs by carrying out tasks such as marketing the league and enforcing the rules of the game (for example, Major League Baseball). A club is a group of players who compete as a team against other clubs in their league, with elite clubs being among the most recognized brands in the world (Richelieu and Pons, 2006). Although leagues act as the power brokers, it is the clubs who win, garner fan attention, become community assets and create, with some exceptions (for example, league-wide television contracts), a significant portion of the profit (Foster et al., 2006). Clubs are therefore the focus of this research, which has precedent in the literature (Gladden and Funk, 2002; Hill and Vincent, 2006).

3.2   Case Study Method

A case study of a sport entertainment conglomerate (owner of four professional sport clubs) is adopted to provide quality content to analyse and categorize assets into an evocative management model. Owing to the extensive time requirements, permissions and costs involved in the case study method, the sample is limited to one organization (Yin, 2003). The case study identified and assessed the risk of all assets of the organization of interest using both primary (interviews) and secondary data. Specific criteria to grade and evaluate player and facility assets were developed with the organization.

Player risk was calculated using four measures: performance (based on offensive and defensive statistics), financial risk (determined qualitatively by considering players' age, and the size of and remaining years on their contracts), brand value (based on tenure with team, popularity with fans, and overall performance) and opportunity cost (determined based on the previous year's performance, age and the length of time with the team, where players who perform at a high level and have been with the team for a number of years are assessed as low risk in terms of opportunity cost). Specific to opportunity cost, it needs to be revisited for each player as time goes by as the determining factors may change over time.

Facility risk is also determined based on a variety of criteria, including facility operations, use, tenant structure, ownership and age. Each criterion for both player and facility risk was estimated using a 10-point scale, from 1 (no risk to the club) to 10 (very high
risk to the club). The figures presented later in the chapter are the resulting averages of
these risk assessments.

For the corporate partnership assets, a senior official at the organization provided an
assessment of the importance and length of each partnership with the organization or
any of its clubs or facilities based on their importance. Corporate partners were graded
as A, B, C or D. An A-grade partnership is viewed by the organization as imperative and
not easily replaceable. In contrast, a D-grade partnership has little impact on the team
and is easily replaceable. In addition to the evaluation of importance, corporate partners
were also graded on contract length, where an A-graded contract is for five years or
more, a B-graded contract is between one and five years and a C-graded contract is less
than one year.

3.3 Categorization of Assets

Hill and Vincent (2006) support including marketing assets (brand, sponsors) along with
players (contracts) and facilities as club assets. Specific to building a successful global
sport team brand (or brands in the case of a multi-club conglomerate), they note the
importance of team composition, player development systems, partnerships with corporate sponsors, and the scheduling of world tours (Hill and Vincent, 2006). A sport club's
contracts between players, facilities and corporate sponsors are all highly beneficial
assets, where player performance contributes to team success, facilities may be attractions in themselves and provide other sources of revenue (parking, concessions, promotions, and so on) and sponsorships provide associations that can be highly beneficial
for both parties (Seguin et al., 2005). Similarly, a strong brand, or set of brands, may
provide for increased revenue from a number of areas, including increases in ticket sales,
television rights and merchandising. A strong player development system and effective
management group (chief executive officer, general manager, coach, and so on) are also
important. The resulting six categories of assets are presented in Figure 18.1.

4   CASE STUDY: MAPLE LEAF SPORTS AND
ENTERTAINMENT IN 2008

The subject of this case is the largest sport entertainment organization in Canada, Maple
Leaf Sports and Entertainment (MLSE). The foundation for MLSE was laid when
Toronto businessman Conn Smythe purchased a professional ice hockey franchise in
1927 (which he renamed the Toronto Maple Leafs) and built a new arena (Maple Leaf
Gardens) in downtown Toronto in 1931. In 1996, new owner Steve Stavro purchased
the Toronto Raptors NBA franchise and named the new conglomerate MLSE. In 1999,
MLSE opened the Air Canada Centre (ACC), a state-of-the-art arena in the heart of
downtown Toronto. Reportedly now worth upwards of CDN$1.75 billion (Westhead,
2008), MLSE today has an ownership stake in a variety of assets, including four professional sport clubs: Toronto Maple Leafs of the National Hockey League (NHL), Toronto

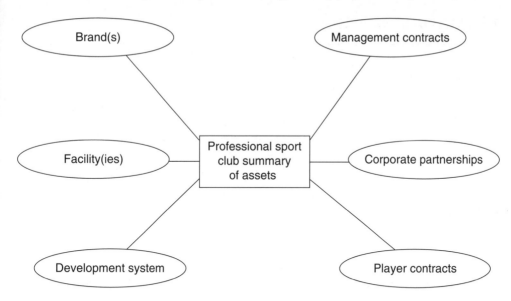

Figure 18.1   Asset categories

Raptors of the National Basketball Association (NBA), Toronto FC of Major League Soccer (MLS) and Toronto Marlies of the American Hockey League (AHL). Maple Leaf Sports and Entertainment is the second largest sports conglomerate in North America, trailing only New York-based Madison Square Gardens (MSG) Enterprise LP (a subsidiary of Cablevision Systems) (Forbes, 2007a). It holds property management contracts for two additional facilities in the Greater Toronto Area, which has a population in excess of 5 million people: BMO Field and Ricoh Coliseum. Prior to 2008, MLSE also operated the General Motors Centre, an arena east of Toronto. Detailed information about these MLSE assets is outlined in Table 18.1, including an estimate of risk for each asset.

A private, for-profit corporation, MLSE is managed by a nine-member board of directors and a management team of 14 employees. Full-time staff are organized by its major clubs: Raptors (31 staff), Leafs (45 staff) and FC (30 staff).

4.1   Maple Leaf Sports and Entertainment Professional Sport Club Assets: Toronto Maple Leafs

The Toronto Maple Leafs, MLSE's NHL franchise, is estimated to be the most valuable professional ice hockey franchise in the world, at approximately US$413 million, an estimated 350 per cent increase over the past decade (Forbes, 2007a). Forbes estimates, although controversial, can be considered for descriptive analysis (see Nadeau and O'Reilly, 2006). The Forbes estimate is based on four components: (1) club revenues (US$138 million), (2) operating income (US$53 million), (3) total player expenses (US$49 million), and (4) gate receipts (US$62 million). The most important asset that a professional hockey club owns is its player contracts (Cousens and Slack, 2005). Table 18.2 outlines the Maple Leafs's player roster (contract and risk assessment) as of 15 March 2008.

Table 18.1   MLSE asset chart

Asset	Type of asset	Features
Air Canada Centre	Facility	– Home to Maples Leafs (NHL), Raptors (NBA), Rock (NLL) – 1020 Club Seats, 40 Platinum Lounges, 65 Executive Suites, 24 Theatre Suites, 24 Loge Suites – 3 restaurants, Raptors practice court, 15-storey office tower, Bell Media Centre Capacity: 18 800 (Hockey), 19 800 (Basketball), 5800 (Theatre), 20 000+ (Concerts) Ticket price: $70 Hockey, $54 Basketball
BMO Field	Facility	– Home to Toronto FC (MLS), Soccer/Ultimate Frisbee/Flag Football Community Programs – 30 executive suites, 200 P.O.S. for food and beverage Capacity: 20 000 (Soccer), 28 000 (Concerts) Ticket price: $21.85 Soccer
Ricoh Coliseum	Facility	– Home to Marlies (AHL), Toronto Boat Show, Royal Winter Fair – Available for Rent for Hockey and Skating Parties Capacity: 8140 (Hockey), 9250 (Concerts) Ticket price: $10.38 Hockey
Leafs TV/Leafs TV HD	Specialty television networks	– Exclusive Maple Leaf and Marlies games – Recent and classic re-airings, pre-, post-game coverage – Player biographies, etc. Broadcast Region: Ontario excluding Ottawa Valley Availability: Rogers, Bell, Star Choice, Cogeco, Mountain Cablevision, Source Cable Limited
Raptors NBA TV/Raptors NBA TV HD	Specialty television networks	– Exclusive Raptors games plus live games from NBA, WNBA, D-League and NCAA NIT tournament games – Classic NBA games and other NBA related programmes Broadcast Region: National Availability: Rogers, Bell, Star Choice, Cogeco, Mountain Cablevision
NBA Marketing Rights	Contractual asset	– NBA Broadcasting Relationships in Canada – National Raptors Marketing Rights – Exclusive programming for Raptors NBA TV/HD
Maple Leaf Square	Property asset	– Two 54-storey condo towers – 9000 sq ft Maple Leafs, Raptors and TFC store – HD Broadcast Studio – Public Square

Note: Based on assessments and data collection in 2008.

The rationale for calculating and presenting the risk assessments is to support the decisions of club management. Each asset (or player) has a risk value based on what his performance both on and off the ice means to the team determined by its performance, opportunity cost, contract length, contract size and off-ice marketing contributions. As noted in Table 18.2, player risk ranges from 6.3 (Mats Sundin) to 3.3 (Jeremy Williams).

Table 18.2   Toronto Maple Leafs and Raptors player contracts and risk assessment

Player	Age	Years remaining	Salary (CDN$)	Risk
Toronto Maple Leafs				
Mats Sundin	37	0	5 500 000	6.3
Nik Antropov	28	1	1 950 000	5.7
Mark Bell	27	1	2 000 000	4.3
Jason Blake	34	4	5 000 000	6.2
Darryl Boyce	23	1	475 000	4.0
Boyd Devereaux	29	1	550 000	4.4
Robert Earl	22	2	575 000	3.8
Alex Foster	23	0	660 000	3.7
Dominic Moore	27	0	700 000	4.1
Kris Newbury	26	1	475 000	3.9
John Pohl	28	0	475 000	3.8
Alexei Ponikarovsky	27	2	1 575 000	5.3
Matt Stajan	24	0	950 000	4.4
Alex Steen	24	3	870 200	5.1
Jiri Tlusty	20	1	850 000	4.0
Darcy Tucker	33	3	3 000 000	5.7
Kyle Wellwood	24	0	950 000	4.1
Jeremy Williams	24	1	475 000	3.3
Carlo Colaiacovo	25	2	1 050 000	3.9
Tomas Kaberle	30	3	4 250 000	6.2
Pavel Kubina	30	2	5 000 000	6.0
Bryan McCabe	32	3	7 150 000	5.9
Anton Stralman	21	2	565 000	3.9
Ian White	23	2	750 000	4.8
Andrew Raycroft	27	1	2 000 000	4.3
Vesa Toskala	30	1	4 000 000	5.4
Staffan Kronwall	25	1	475 000	3.5
Toronto Raptors				
Andrea Bargnani	22	1	4 838 880	6.4
Chris Bosh	24	2	13 041 250	8.0
Primoz Brezec	28	0	2 750 000	3.0
Jose Calderon	25	0	2 471 604	6.2
T.J. Ford	25	2	8 000 000	6.4
Jose Garbajosa	30	1	4 050 000	3.7
Joey Graham	25	1	1 596 600	3.3
Kris Humphries	23	3	2 522 913	3.9
Jason Kapono	27	3	5 356 000	5.5
Rasho Nesterovic	31	1	7 840 000	6.2
Anthony Parker	32	1	4 350 000	6.8
Maceo Baston	22	1	1 830 000	3.3

Notes:
1.   Similar risk assessment tables were also created for the Raptors, FC and Marlies.
2.   Based on assessments and data collection in 2008.

The high scores (Mats Sundin, and Jason Blake and Tomas Kaberle, both 6.2) are attributable to the factors noted above. In the case of Sundin, he is high risk because (1) he is in the final year of his contract, (2) he commands a large salary, (3) he is the team captain and is very popular with the fans, and (4) he is a top on-ice performer and off-ice presence. The lower-risk players are generally those who are performing well or are prospects who have been developed through the Leafs' development system. In addition to its current roster, the Leafs also hold the rights to a number of its draft picks from recent years. The risk assessment for each player-prospect is 7 (high) for the club, regardless of potential or draft order. This is due to the opportunity cost of allocating resources to these risky assets, and not others.

With a classic logo that is widely known to sports fans, the Maple Leafs brand is a valuable asset. According to Forbes (2007a), 14 per cent of the Leafs' franchise value is attributed to its brand and its many loyal fans. Corporate partnerships, or sponsorship contracts, are also important assets. Overall, MLSE has approximately 50 sponsors: an optimal number (Tom Pistore, personal communication, 20 June 2008) that includes an impressive list of blue chip partners such as Ford, Coca-Cola and Air Canada. Given that MLSE packages the majority of its sponsorships to include the ACC, Toronto Maple Leafs and Toronto Raptors, it is difficult to attribute these assets specifically to the Leafs. As a result, all corporate partners of the ACC, Leafs and Raptors grouping (Table 18.3) and each of the four individual clubs (Table 18.4) are presented, including some key details about each and MLSE's Director of Corporate Partnership's assessment of risk for each (Tom Pistore, personal communication, 20 June 2008).

The Leafs are also engaged in profitable television rights deals with CBC, TSN and Sportsnet, and the radio station AM640. The Leafs recently invested in its practice facility in west Toronto, known as Leafs Hockey Nation Headquarters, which has four ice surfaces, seating for 4000, a large training and exercise space, a medical room, a physiotherapy room, is used by both the Marlies and the Leafs, and houses Hockey Canada's Ontario Regional Office and a Hockey Hall of Fame Resource Centre (OHF, 2006). The club also has contracts with a number of key technical hockey experts, including Coach, Ron Wilson, and interim General Manager, Cliff Fletcher.

4.2   Maple Leaf Sports and Entertainment Professional Sport Club Assets: Toronto Raptors

The Toronto Raptors's inaugural season was 1995–96. For the first three seasons, the Raptors played home games in the SkyDome, Toronto's baseball stadium. In 1999, the Raptors began to play in the ACC. In its short history, the club has had limited success highlighted by its stars Vince Carter (past) and Chris Bosh (present). The team won the Atlantic Division title in 2007 and hired respected basketball mind Brian Colangelo as Team President and General Manager in 2006. Forbes reports that the Toronto Raptors are the fourteenth most valuable NBA franchise, with an estimated franchise value of US$373 million, a 300 per cent increase over the past decade (Forbes, 2007b). The Forbes (2007b) estimate is comprised of club revenues at US$124 million, operating income of US$29 million, total player expenses of US$57 million, and gate receipts of US$37 million.

Table 18.3   Air Canada Centre, Leafs and Raptors corporate partners

Arena dashboard sponsors			Media Partners for TML and TR		
Name	Importance	Length	Name	Importance	Length
AMJ Campbell	B	A	AM640 Toronto	A	A
Canon	A	A	FAN 590	B	A
Casino Rama	B	A	Sportsnet	A	A
Discount Car & Truck	D	A	Toronto Sun	A	A
Rentals			TSN	C	C
Effem Inc.	C	B			
ESQ	C	B	**Food and beverage providers**		
Ford	A	A	Coca-Cola	A	A
Frito Lay	D	B	Diageo	B	B
Gatorade	C	A	Molson Canadian	A	A
Home Depot	A	A	Pizza Pizza	A	A
IBM	B	B	Tim Horton's	A	A
Imperial Oil	B	A			
Vale Inco	C	B	**Other partners**		
Loblaws	A	B			
MasterCard	B	B	Air Canada	B	A
McDonald's	B	B	Adidas	C	B
Mr. Sub	A	A	Bank of Montreal	A	A
Ogilvy Renault	B	B	Colgate	C	C
OLGC	C	B	Danone	C	C
Pfizer-Viagra	C	B	Direct Energy	A	A
Poker Stars	C	C	Good Humour Breyers	C	A
Purolator	C	B	MBNA Canada	B	A
ReMax	C	B	NBC Universal	D	B
Rogers Communications	A	A	Sony of Canada	B	A
Sony Playstation	B	A	TD Waterhouse	B	A
SportChek	C	B	Westin Harbour Castle	C	B
The Keg	C	B			

Note: Based on assessments and data collection in 2008.

A risk assessment table was also created for the Raptors's players assets (presented in Table 18.2). Chris Bosh is a very high-risk asset (8.0) due to his contributions to the team's performance and brand, and his large contract. Although he is paid much less, Jose Calderon is also high risk (6.2) as his contract is about to expire (Richard Peddie, personal communication, 7 April 2008). Other high-risk assets include Andrea Bargnani (6.4), the former first overall draft selection, whom the club has identified as a key to the future. The bench players are lower risk to the club owing to their limited playing time and the fact that they are easily replaceable. The Raptors, unlike the Leafs, have limited rights to draft picks, since the NBA only allows a maximum of three players under contract who are not on the club's active roster. The Raptors (as of May 2008) have no such player contract.

Table 18.4   Club-specific corporate partners

Toronto Maple Leafs corporate partners			Toronto FC/BMO Field corporate partners		
Name	Importance	Length	Name	Importance	Length
AM 640 Toronto	A	A	Bank of Montreal	A	A
Bank of Montreal	A	A	Adidas	C	B
Coca-Cola	A	A	Cadbury Adams	C	C
Effem Inc.	C	B	Canon	A	A
Ford	A	A	Carlsberg	A	A
Home Depot	A	A	Coca-Cola	A	A
MBNA Canada	B	A	ESQ	C	B
McDonald's	B	B	Good Humour Breyers	C	A
Mr. Sub	A	A	Kia Motors	B	B
OLGC	C	B	Frito Lay	D	B
Rogers Communications	A	A	Longos	C	C
Tim Horton's	A	A	McDonald's	B	B
			Purolator	C	B
			Rogers Communications	A	A
			Rona	B	B
			Sony of Canada	B	A
			Sony Playstation	B	A
			Toronto Sun	B	B
			Unico	D	C
			Woodbine	C	C

Toronto Raptors corporate partners			Toronto Marlies corporate partners		
Name	Importance	Length	Name	Importance	Length
Bank of Montreal	A	A	AM640 Toronto	A	A
Diageo	B	B	Home Depot	A	A
Effem Inc.	C	B	MBNA Canada	B	A
ESQ	C	B	McDonald's	B	B
FAN 590	B	A	Pizza Pizza	A	A
Ford	A	A	Purolator	C	B
MasterCard	B	B	Ricoh	A	A
MBNA Canada	B	A	Rogers Communications	A	A
Molson Canadian	A	A	Subway	C	B
Mr. Sub	A	A	Tim Horton's	A	A
OLGC	C	B	Toronto Sun	B	B
Rogers Communications	A	A			
Sirius Satellite Radio	B	B			
Sony Playstation	B	A			
Sportsnet	A	A			
TD Waterhouse	B	A			

Note: Based on assessments and data collection in 2008.

The Raptors's management team is considered one of its strongest assets. General Manager Brian Colangelo was named the NBA's executive of the year in 2005 when he was with the Phoenix Suns. The Raptors coach since 2004, Sam Mitchell, who was the NBA's Coach of the Year in 2007, signed a four-year contract in 2007, reportedly worth US$12 million plus bonuses.

Although a relatively new brand, the Raptors, as Canada's only NBA team, have developed significant brand equity as estimated by Forbes (2007b), who reported the brand contribution to the overall Raptors team value at US$36 million. Over the past two years, since Colangelo became General Manager, the Raptors have worked to re-brand as a 'high energy' club. Sponsorship contracts or corporate partnerships for the Toronto Raptors are structured as per the Leafs with the ACC/Leafs/Raptors package (Table 18.3). However, the Raptors also have specific promotions with partners as noted in Table 18.4. The lone partner that is exclusive to the Raptors is Sirius Satellite Radio. The Raptors also have television deals with TSN, CBC, the Score and Raptors NBA TV. The FAN 590 does radio coverage of Raptors games.

4.3 Maple Leaf Sports and Entertainment Professional Sport Club Assets: Toronto FC

Toronto FC is MLSE's MLS franchise. They play at MLSE-owned BMO Field in down-town Toronto. The club began play in 2007 and has been successful from a marketing point of view, well beyond expectations (Tom Pistore, personal communication, 20 June 2008). This success has been attributed, in part, to the success of the team's marketing tactics, David Beckham coming to the MLS and the diverse demographics of Toronto. All FC player assets are new to MLSE and their salaries are low (relative to the Leafs and Raptors), ranging from CDN$12 900 to CDN$315 000. Given this reality, all players are considered to be of moderate risk or less.

As a new organization in a new league, the Toronto FC has low but growing brand equity. In fact, MLSE management believes that the FC is one of the most successful young brands they have ever seen or read about (Tom Pistore, personal communication, 20 June 2008). However, on-field performance to date has been poor, which may detract from the brand. The analysis of FC's corporate and media partnerships was completed based on expert input from Tom Pistore, Director of Corporate Partnerships for MLSE, and is included in Table 18.4.

Since the FC plays at a different venue (BMO Field) than the Leafs or Raptors, in most cases their sponsorships are sold separately from other MLSE properties. The FC and BMO Field have 25 corporate partners with a variety of contractual lengths, of which seven partners are exclusive to the team and the facility: Carlsberg, Kia Motors, Rona, Woodbine, Longo's, Unico and Cadbury Adams (Tom Pistore, personal communication, 20 June 2008).

4.4 Maple Leaf Sports and Entertainment Professional Sport Club Assets: Toronto Marlies

The Toronto Marlies are the Maple Leafs's development team. No risk assessment table is provided for these players, owing to the fact that the chances of these players making the NHL are very low, and the cost of investment in each player and opportunity costs

Table 18.5   Ricoh Coliseum corporate partners

Arena dashboard sponsors

Name	Importance	Length
Auto Trader	D	B
Bank of Montreal	A	A
Canpages	D	C
Direct Energy	A	A
ESQ	C	B
Freemyteam.com	D	C
Holiday Inn	B	C
Home Depot	A	A
JB Goodhue Boot Co	C	C
Longo's	C	C
McDonald's	B	B
Molson Canadian	A	A
Pizza Pizza	A	A
ReMax	C	B
Rogers Communications	A	A
Sony of Canada	B	A
Sony Playstation	B	A
Subway	C	B
The Keg	C	B
Turtle Island Recycling	C	C
Woodbine	D	C
X Copper	D	C
Yamaha	D	C

Media partners for Toronto Marlies

Name	Importance	Length
AM640 Toronto	A	A
Sportsnet	A	A
Toronto Sun	B	B

Note: Based on assessments and data collection in 2008.

if they are not successful are high (Richard Peddie, personal communication, 7 April 2008). The Marlies's brand equity is limited at best. The club has some name equity as it was used previously for another hockey franchise in Toronto and through its link as the Maple Leafs's farm team. Rendon (2005) described the situation when MLSE brought the Marlies to Toronto from St. John's: 'add to that list MLSE's newest offerings like the recently located Toronto Marlies and the city-owned 10,000-seat Ricoh Coliseum at Toronto's Exhibition Place . . . and it's clear MLSE is at the top of its game'. Sponsorship of the club and arena is good (see Table 18.5), while media coverage is limited, although a number of the ACC/Leafs/Raptors partners are also partners of the Marlies.

5   CONCEPTUAL DEVELOPMENT: DRAFT MODEL FOR PROFESSIONAL SPORT MANAGEMENT

Portfolio theory was originally developed to help investors find the optimum portfolio of assets (Markowitz, 1952). Here, it is applied to support the decisions of professional sport club management. As illustrated by the MLSE case, a portfolio theory approach views the club as a portfolio of assets, namely, the commoditization of players, sponsorships, coaches, management, facilities, brands and other club properties as assets. For players, coaches, management and sponsorships, the asset is measured by the club risk associated with the relevant contract. For facilities and brands, it is the value of those assets to the club. Upon articulation of all of its assets, club management should be able to better make decisions, where the diversification of assets will reduce an organization's overall risk exposure (Lubatkin and Chatterjee, 1994).

Building upon the index models of previous portfolio theory writers (Elton and Gruber, 1997; Ingersoll, 1987; Markowitz, 1952; Ross 1978; Sharpe, 1963) and the learning provided by the MLSE case, a professional sport club management model is proposed. The proposed model is based on the multi-antecedent business success (or profitability) of the club where on-field performance is but one of many factors to consider (Nadeau and O'Reilly, 2006). In this regard, the contribution of each category of asset is included. Although the issue of time or periods of returns is a challenge emphasized in the portfolio theory literature (see Fama and French, 1989), it is mitigated in the context of professional sport, which is typically organized in annual seasons with off-seasons between each. This reality renders the time issue clear and provides for facilitated articulation in the management model. The concept of hedging, or investing in high-risk assets against market trends, is also part of the portfolio theory literature (Merton, 1990) that is easily adapted to professional sport. Specifically, the high-risk (both financial and performance) investment in older or injury-prone players with impressive past successes or high draft picks with vast potential could be considered hedging. Examples from the case include Mark Bell (injury-prone player) and Andrea Bargnani (high potential). Further, the inclusion of liabilities in a portfolio model has been noted as an important future direction in portfolio theory where 'the idea of simply treating liabilities as assets with negative cash flows' (Elton and Gruber, 1997: 1751) was put forward. An example from the case would be Leafs's goaltender, Andrew Raycroft, who signed a large, long-term contract and has under-performed.

Figure 18.2 outlines a two-stage model of management for professional sport clubs. The first index (P_{ct}) calculates the overall portfolio return for the club based on all of its assets. In carrying out the calculation, N includes each asset identified in each category. In the case of MLSE, this would include four brands, 50 or more corporate partnerships, over 100 player contracts, one player development system, four facilities and a few dozen management contracts. Thus, N is approximately equal to 200 MLSE assets. For each of the 200 or more assets, R (return) mitigated by risk (gamma) would be calculated to provide a total expected return +/− the range due to risk associated with the totality of assets. In order to calculate the first index, the second index (R_{jt}) that involves the calculation of the return (liability if negative) of each specific asset of the club, must be run. The calculation of the second index requires further calculations of the other variables noted in Figure 18.2.

$$P_{ct} = \sum_{j=1}^{N} R_{jt} + \gamma_{ct}, \text{ where } j = 1,2,...N$$

Where, P_t = the total (expected) portfolio return of all club c assets for season of interest t

    t = refers to the complete league session of interest (e.g., 2006–07)

    N = total number of club assets (player/coach contracts, brand(s), facility(ies), etc.)

    R_{jt} = the (expected) return of asset j in period t (*as calculated by equation below*)

    γ_{ct} = the total risk associated with the club (all of its assets combined) in season t

$$R_{it} = \alpha_i + \beta_i R_{ct} + \gamma_{it}$$

Where, R_{it} = the (expected) return of asset i for the season of interest t

    i = reference number of each club asset

    R_{ct} = the (expected) return generated by club performance in season t

    β_{it} = the sensitivity of asset i to club performance R_{ct} in season t

    γ_{it} = the unique risk associated with each asset i: its variance in season t

    α_{it} = the unique expected return of asset i in season t

Figure 18.2   Proposed management model for professional sport clubs

First, alpha, or the unique expected return for each asset, could include metrics such as (1) points, goals, trophies, awards or championships for players, (2) wins, playoffs made or club improvement for management, or (3) ticket sales, sponsorships sold, or fan satisfaction for facilities. Second, for overall club performance in the season of interest, R_{ct}, would involve a combination of on-ice and off-ice performance as determined by the ownership objective(s) for the club (Nadeau and O'Reilly, 2006). Finally, beta, or the sensitivity of the specific asset to R_{ct}, would be determined based on the asset. For example, a long-term sponsorship with an established partnership would be less sensitive to R_{ct} than the management contract of the coach. The list of all assets with their expected return and risk assessments would also provide valuable information to club decision-makers. If increased sensitivity is required and the relevant information is available, an additional term could be added to the model. This term, R_{Ft}, or the riskless rate for season t for each asset i, provides an assessment where this value would be subtracted from each R_{it} calculation to achieve an improved assessment of the contribution or detraction to club revenues/profits made by each asset (Jensen, 1969). It is important to note, however, that the nature of professional sport club management makes the determination of R_{Ft} very challenging (that is, does a riskless player contract exist?), thereby rendering the equations in Figure 18.2 more appropriate.

6 DISCUSSION

Despite its exponential growth, professional sport is often characterized as being corporately inferior to other industries, with examples of sophisticated practice found only in isolated cases of effective management (Richelieu and Boulaire, 2005). This characterization is potentially due to the lack of an effective management model for professional sport clubs (Alexander and Kern, 2004; Dolles and Söderman, 2008; Fort 2006; Nadeau and O'Reilly, 2006). In response, the current research adopts portfolio theory as the basis for an approach to develop a professional sport club management model that considers the club to be a portfolio of assets. The numerous assets of MLSE were articulated in a detailed case study to support theory development. The portfolio theory approach is echoed by the President of MLSE who noted that 'we [MLSE] understand this approach ... we do have a diversification of assets and we do think that we have a good portfolio ... but I can tell you that no one in sport is thinking like a portfolio manager in stocks' (Richard Peddie, personal communication, 7 April 2008).

This research sets the stage for considerable future research. First, specific to this model, work in partnership with professional sport clubs needs to be carried out to both (1) determine metrics for the specific variables in Figure 18.2, and (2) implement, test and improve the draft model. Second, the MLSE case brought forth the vast volume and complexity of assets under the direction of professional sport club management. Indeed, research supporting an 'asset-based' management philosophy is required, as it works to develop tools to aid decisions vis-à-vis club assets. Third, because of the varied nature and objectives of any corporate partnership or sponsorship, future research specific to these relationships is important. Consideration of the fact that some relationships are more important than others should be taken into account as noted in the MLSE case study where certain corporate and media partners are considered to be exceptional partners (Tom Pistore, personal communication, 20 June 2008). Fourth, based on the fact that one of the important tenants of portfolio theory is related to the management of risk and reward through an efficient portfolio of assets, the conceptualization of risk adopted for this chapter requires further clarification. Specifically, questions such as 'what is the relative risk of high versus low return?', 'what is the specific relationship between time left on a player's contract and the club's risk?', 'what are the variables that determine management's determination of a player's risk?' and 'what is the impact of industry (sport) and geographical setting (one city) on the club's investment strategy?' Finally, an adaptation of the model with player as the unit of analysis (as opposed to club) should also be developed.

The establishment of a portfolio theory management model by which to manage professional sport clubs has practitioner implications. Managers of professional sports clubs could adopt (or enhance their use of) such an approach to be able to better view their organizations based on their assets, with improved business performance possible. Team management personnel can use these risk assessments in order to optimize the team's performance, structure their team around the salary cap and build a strong brand image or market individual players. In the case of MLSE, general managers can use the assessments in order to compare players with one another, assess their impact on the team's statistical performance, and better understand their contributions to team revenue (Elton and Gruber, 1997). It also allows for player comparisons to be drawn in order to make decisions like signing free agents, trading players, and the promotion and demotion of players, through the development system. Finally, the proper combination of high risk and risk-free assets will obtain the correct diversified portfolio or team (Elton and Gruber, 1997), which should result in successful performance.

There are a few important limitations to this research. First, there is the limited related literature to build upon. Second, although MLSE management provided input, the research is largely based on publicly available information. Third, the greatest challenge imposed on a developmental study such as this will be the implementation and the study of the management model's effectiveness in the future. In this regard, the support of a corporate partner may be a challenge, as noted by Richard Peddie: 'I wouldn't know where to begin' (personal communication, 7 April 2008). This view speaks to the fast-paced nature of the business of sports and the high volatility of coaches, players and facilities as assets.

In conclusion, this research sets an important agenda for future research and provides a management model for consideration by practitioners in professional sport. Most importantly, an asset-based approach to management that is posited to have considerable potential for improved organizational performance is developed further.

ACKNOWLEDGEMENTS

The author would like to thank George Foster, Tyler Aird and Jeremy Rody for their support of this study. He also recognizes, and is indebted for, the important contributions provided by Richard Peddie, President of Maple Leaf Sports and Entertainment (MLSE), and Tom Pistore, Director of Corporate Partnerships at MLSE.

REFERENCES

Alexander, D.L. and Kern, W. (2004), The economic determinants of professional sport franchise values, *Journal of Sports Economics*, **5** (1), 51–66.
Andrikopoulos, A. and Koronis, E. (2007), Reputation performance: a portfolio selection approach, *International Journal of Business Performance Management*, **9** (4), 406.
Bauer, H., Sauer, N.E. and Exler, S. (2005), The loyalty of German soccer fans: does a team's brand image matter?, *International Journal of Sports Marketing & Sponsorship*, **7** (1), 14–23.
Cousens, L. and Slack, T. (2005), Field-level change: the case of North American major league professional sport, *Journal of Sport Management*, **19** (1), 13–42.
Dolles, H. and Söderman, S. (2013), The network of value captures in football club management: a framework to develop and analyse competitive advantage in professional team sports, in S. Söderman and H. Dolles (eds), *Handbook of Research on Sport and Business*, Cheltenham, UK and Northampton, MA, USA: Edward Elgar, pp. 367–95.
Dolles, H. and Söderman, S. (2008), The network of value captures: creating competitive advantage in football management, in *Wirtschaftspolitische Blätter Österreich* [*Austrian Economic Policy Papers*], **55** (1), 39–58.
Dolles, H. and Söderman, S. (2011), Learning from success: implementing a professional football league in Japan, in H. Dolles and S. Söderman (eds), *Sport as a Business: International, Professional and Commercial Aspects*, Basingstoke: Palgrave Macmillan, pp. 228–50.
Elton, E.J. and Gruber, M.J. (1997), Modern portfolio theory, 1950 to date, *Journal of Banking & Finance*, **21** (11/12), 1743–59.
Fama, E.F. and French, K.R. (1989), Business conditions and expected returns on stocks and bonds, *Journal of Financial Economics*, **25** (1), 23–49.

Forbes (2007a), NHL team valuations: Toronto Maple Leafs, available at: www.forbes.com/lists/2007/31/biz_07nhl_Toronto-Maple-Leafs_312012.html (accessed 19 July 2008).
Forbes (2007b), NBA team valuations: Toronto Raptors, available at: www.forbes.com/lists/2007/32/biz_07nba_Toronto-Raptors_321933.html (accessed 19 July 2008).
Fort, R. (2006), The value of Major League Baseball ownership, *International Journal of Sport Finance*, **1** (1), 9–20.
Foster, G., Greyser, S.A. and Walsh, B. (2006), *The Business of Sports: Cases and Text on Strategy and Management*, Scarborough, Canada: Nelson Education.
Gerrard, B. (2005), A resource-utilization model of organizational efficiency in professional sports teams, *Journal of Sport Management*, **19** (2), 143–69.
Gladden, J.M. and Funk, D.C. (2002), Developing an understanding of brand associations in team sport: empirical evidence from consumers of professional sport, *Journal of Sport Management*, **16** (1), 54–81.
Hill, J. and Vincent, J. (2006), Globalization and sport branding: the case of Manchester United, *International Journal of Sports Marketing & Sponsorship*, **7** (3), 213–30.
Ingersoll, J. (1987), *Theory of Financial Decision Making*, New York: Rowman and Littlefield.
Jensen, M. (1969), Risk, the pricing of capital assets, and the evaluation of investment portfolios, *Journal of Business*, **42** (2), 167–247.
Kaplan, R.S. and Norton, D.P. (2007), Using the balanced scorecard as a strategic management system, *Harvard Business Review*, **85** (7/8), 150–61.
Kedar-Levy, H. and Bar-Eli, M. (2008), The valuation of athletes as risky investments: a theoretical model, *Journal of Sport Management*, **22** (1), 50–81.
Lubatkin, M. and Chatterjee, S. (1994), Extending modern portfolio theory into the domain of corporate diversification: does it apply?, *The Academy of Management Journal*, **37** (1), 109–36.
Markowitz, H. (1952), Portfolio selection, *Journal of Finance*, **7** (1), 77–91.
Mauws, M., Mason, D.S. and Foster, W.M. (2003), Thinking strategically about professional sports, *European Sport Management Quarterly*, **3** (3), 145–64.
Merton, R.C. (1990), *Continuous Time Finance*, Oxford: Basil Blackwell.
Mintzberg, H. (1983), *Structure in Fives: Designing Effective Organizations*, Englewood Cliffs, NJ: Prentice Hall.
Mintzberg, H. (1987), The strategy concept I: five P's for strategy, *California Management Review*, **3** (1), 11–23.
Mintzberg, H. (1990), *Mintzberg on Management: Inside our Strange World of Organizations*, New York: The Free Press.
Nadeau, J. and O'Reilly, N. (2006), Developing a profitability model for professional sport leagues: the case of the National Hockey League, *International Journal of Sport Finance*, **1** (1), 46–52.
Nolan, R.L. (1979), Managing the crises in data processing, *Harvard Business Review*, **57** (2), 115–26.
Ontario Hockey Federation (OHF) (2006), Leafs make $2 million dollar commitment to Hockey Canada, internal document, 16 November.
O'Reilly, N. and Nadeau, J. (2006), Revenue generation in professional sport: a diagnostic analysis, *International Journal of Sport Management and Marketing*, **1** (4), 311–30.
Porter, M.E. (1998), *Competitive Strategy: Techniques for Analyzing Industries and Competitors*, New York: Free Press.
Rendon, P.M. (2005), Hot properties, *Marketing Magazine*, **110** (23), 11.
Richelieu, A. and Boulaire, C. (2005), A post modern conception of the product and its application to professional sports, *International Journal of Sports Marketing and Sponsorship*, **7** (1), 23–34.
Richelieu, A. and Pons, F. (2006), Toronto Maple Leafs vs Football Club Barcelona: how two legendary sports teams built their brand equity, *International Journal of Sport Marketing & Sponsorship*, **7** (3), 231–51.
Ross, S.A. (1978), Mutual fund separation in financial theory – the separation distributions, *Journal of Economic Theory*, **17** (2), 254–86.
Seguin, B., Teed, K. and O'Reilly, N. (2005), National sport organizations and sponsorship: an identification of best practices, *International Journal of Sport Management and Marketing*, **1** (1/2), 69–92.
Sharpe, W. (1963), A simplified model for portfolio analysis, *Management Science*, **9** (2), 277–93.
Slack, T. and Parent, M. (2006), *Understanding Sport Organizations: The Application of Organization Theory*, 2nd edn, Windsor, Canada: Human Kinetics.
Ten Have, S., Ten Have, W. and Stevens, F. (2003), *Key Management Models*, London: Prentice Hall.
Wack, P. (1985), Scenarios: unchartered waters ahead, *Harvard Business Review*, **63** (5), 73–89.
Westhead, R. (2008), MLSE explores notion of buying into top league, *Toronto Star*, 24 April 2008, p. A1.
Yin, R.K. (2003), *Applications of Case Study Research*, 2nd edn, Thousand Oaks, CA: Sage.

19 Proposing a relationship marketing theory for sport clubs

Hans Jansson and Sten Söderman

1 INTRODUCTION

The attendance at Wembley was approximately 87 000 people for the Champions League final 28 May 2011 between FC Barcelona and Manchester United while the television viewers were approximately 300 million (UEFA, 2011). Sports clubs must now market to fans attending a match as well as a television audience. Originally, the consumer was a live spectator but now sporting events are watched by fans across the globe. Aspects that are becoming more and more important are sponsors and advertisers (Beech and Chadwick, 2007). Concomitantly, clubs become outlets for commercial messages and through sponsorship they also get involved in the marketing systems of firms (Beech and Chadwick, 2007; Mullin et al., 2007; Shank, 2005). A major purpose of a professional elite club is, therefore, to be profitable as well as to be instrumental in sponsor and advertising firms to be profitable, otherwise the club might not survive because of the relegation principle in Europe and elsewhere when teams are transferred between divisions based on their performance that season. This chapter, though, is not focusing on the role of sponsors and fans (refer to Schlesinger, 2013 and Cornwell, 2013, both this volume) nor branding (see Ströbel and Woratschek, 2013 in this volume).

Franchising in the United States is a different way of league organization and not a consequence of performance leading to relegation. In addition to earning a profit, clubs must also satisfy non-profit needs of the audience, whether it is a member's ideals in general or more specific needs of certain member groups like supporter associations. Clubs are also involved with other stakeholders such as the local community, and joining associations at local, national and international levels. For non-profit organizations, it is a question of creating values for their members by living up to various expectations which aid the club in creating a legitimate image in the eyes of these stakeholders (Anagnostopoulos, 2013, in this volume). The key issue is how to relate such profit and non-profit approaches to each other, that is, to solve the dilemma between being profitable and being legitimate. This type of 'double-faced' problem is overlooked in extant marketing research. To accomplish this, clubs need to understand the major differences between these two major different decisions and how to align them.

The forum where marketing occurs is defined as the 'social arena'. It is a more general term than a stadium, for example, and it takes a broader view on what is happening in the stadium and outside it. Social arenas are embedded in society, meaning that they cannot be understood without considering their context, for example, the legal system, other public systems and values/belief systems. Thus, marketing becomes both an economic and a social issue.

2   THE RESEARCH ISSUES

The overall purpose of this chapter is to identify and describe relevant marketing theories for sports clubs, which differ from those normally found for typical commercial organizations and firms. Armstrong and Kotler (2007: 199) define regular products as 'anything that can be offered to a market for attention, acquisition, use, or consumption that might satisfy a want or a need. Products include more than just tangible goods. Broadly defined, products include physical objects, services, events, persons, places, organizations, ideas, or mixes of these entities'. According to Mullin et al., sport marketing consists of all activities designed to meet the needs and wants of sport consumers through exchange processes (2007: 11): 'Sport marketing has developed two major thrusts; the marketing of sport products and services directly to consumers of sport, and the marketing of other consumer and industrial products or services through the use of sport promotions.'

This chapter takes stock of what has been published in general marketing literature academically over the past two decades, providing an overview of studies and research topics, and reflecting on further research. We confine our review to publications that address marketing. The application of theories and how they can assist in deepening sport problem analysis is illustrated and partly explained in this chapter, mainly by presenting a preliminary framework. More specifically, we develop a network marketing theory for football clubs, which we also believe is relevant for other sports, sports clubs and commercial firms facing social and economic pressures. The marketing decisions are therefore affected by how successful the clubs are in the social environment, implying that marketing needs to be practised in an ethical and legitimate way. The following partnership illustrates this aspect (Unicef, 2011).

FC Barcelona and the United Nations Children's Fund (Unicef) signed a five-year partnership in 2006 to raise awareness and generate funds for children affected by HIV and AIDS. Every year for a five-year period, FC Barcelona donated 1.5 million euros to Unicef to fund projects to combat HIV and AIDS in Africa and Latin America. Furthermore, FC Barcelona also spent an additional 500 000 euros to publicize the partnership and to remind the importance of combating children diseases on a priority basis. Through this partnership the football club was not only promoting a worthwhile cause, but also strengthening its corporate social responsibility image in comparison to other football clubs.

However, social issues are missing from mainstream marketing theory (Hunt, 2002). We therefore must take a socio-economic approach, in which we establish an institutional base and a network foundation for analysing the factors in the external context of the clubs that influence marketing decisions. We examine how the 'logic of appropriateness' (March, 1994) can be applied to marketing decisions. When social issues are included, the market as an arena for exchange, transactions or relationships becomes unclear. Despite the fact that the market is the foundation of marketing, its boundaries are rarely problematized. The focus is on the action of marketing, with little consideration for the marketplace. We, on the other hand, find it necessary to develop the relation between markets and marketing in order to develop a suitable marketing theory for sports clubs, where social issues are critical. Our starting point is constituted by marketing theories which have such a broad approach, mainly the specific relationship marketing perspective defined as the inter-organizational approach by Jansson (1994, 2006), and to some extent the practice-based approach to markets and marketing (Araujo, 2007; Araujo et al., 2008; Kjellberg and Helgesson, 2006, 2007).

We use institutional theory to define the market as a social arena. The starting point is the markets-as-networks perspective (Johanson and Mattsson, 1987a), since it is based on social and political aspects originating from social exchange theory, social network theory and power/dependency theory. Through its broad view on relationships, this approach constitutes a relevant basis for developing a network marketing framework. This is valid for sports clubs focusing on establishing relationships with various types of stakeholders, market and non-market actors.

Our socio-economic perspective to marketing is defined as the institutional network marketing (INM) theory, which is based on Jansson (2007a; 2007b). It is interdisciplinary since it combines economic and social theories. The markets-as-networks approach is developed further by using institutional theory, implying that the market as an insti-tution is developed along similar lines as found in Araujo (2007). The INM shares many basic characteristics with the more recently developed practice-based approaches (Kjellberg and Helgesson, 2006, 2007), the main one being the interest is in the interplay between the market as a social arena and marketing activities. However, while the INM concentrates on how marketing activities are influenced by the market, the practice-based approach is more interested in the opposite relation, how markets are constructed through the marketing practice.

To give a background to the socio-economic approach to marketing developed in this chapter, other major marketing theories are analysed. The treatise starts from the early dawn of the establishment of the modern formal market and the theory behind it, namely, in economics with the mother of all markets, the neoclassical perfect market. In this market, the behaviour does not include any marketing practice at all. Such behaviour is introduced in monopolistic competition, which is one of the cornerstones of the markets-as-networks approach. The relation between market form and market-ing theory is then developed further in a section on the market imperfections approach. Finally, another perspective to markets is represented by the market as an economic institution, which is behind the network marketing theory.

3   METHODOLOGY

Market form and marketing practice are both built on the epistemology of scientific realism (Hunt, 1991). When Kjellberg and Helgesson (2006) combine this perspective with ontological relativism, they characterize their methodological stance as pract-ical constructivism, implying that the ongoing construction of social reality is studied, excluding the physical reality. This is also a suitable perspective for the sports marketing theory developed in this chapter. Marketing practice is assumed to be constructed differ-ently depending upon the marketing situation encountered, in this case, for sports organ-izations, not firms. While firms operate in markets, sports clubs operate in arenas, where they capture values (Dolles and Söderman, 2005, 2008, 2011a, 2013 in this volume). This implies that sports marketing is different from the ordinary marketing of firms. Therefore, one cannot take for granted that business-oriented marketing theories can be used directly by sports organizations. Rather, the marketing theory must be developed based on the specific marketing situation faced by such organizations, which is applied in this chapter. Beech and Chadwick (2007: 129) state that in order to market a sport product, a marketer has to consider several influencing factors that are unique for sport marketing: 'The fundamental aim of the sport marketing activity is to satisfy the right sport customer needs with sport products or services that offer benefits in excess of all other competitors offerings whilst making the maximum sustainable profit.'

To understand the distinctive features of the sports business, especially football, Dolles and Söderman (2013 in this volume, and based on earlier work 2005, 2008, 2011a, 2011b) explore the unique management challenges of the game and thereby develop a 'football package' consisting of the following eight 'products' or offerings provided to six groups of customers.

(1) *Team*: Football is a team sport, however 11 skilled players do not necessarily comprise a winning team.
(2) *Sporting competition*: Football as a team sport requires coordination among the contesting teams, because the game involves at least two distinct teams, which must agree on the rules of the game, how to schedule matches or tournaments, and so on.
(3) *Club*: Not only must the players in the sporting team be able to give their utmost to the cause of winning, but the financial and organizational structure behind it must work closely to ensure that its business goals will be achieved.
(4) *Players*: Football clubs are sending out scouts to discover young players in the region and to sign contracts with them, as some of them might later find their way to a professional team. Some of them become stars.
(5) *Football services*: A rather new development in the commercial activities of a club which includes an offering of service to help other clubs to sell tickets, to collaborate with sponsors and establishing of youth academies.
(6) *Event and arena*: A sporting event is intangible, short-lived, unpredictable and subjective in nature. It is produced and consumed by the spectators in the arena at the same time, mostly with a strong emotional commitment from the fans.
(7) *Merchandise*: This is the supporting products attached to the club like scarves and symbols.
(8) *Other commercial activities* (ibid.).

This framework by Dolles and Söderman might be applied by sport clubs to analyse their scope of competitive advantage(s) (thus applying a strategic management perspective) and how to link this advantage with the various customer groups (thus applying a marketing perspective). The purpose in this chapter, however is to elaborate on social and institutional factors the eight offerings are embedded in, which requires a broader view of marketing. We base our theoretical development on general overviews of marketing theory, mainly Easton (1992), Hunt (1991, 2002), Jansson (2006) and Sheth et al. (1988), to which we add other theories not covered by these works. Through this process, the marketing theory for sports clubs including their underlying social factors is primarily developed as an institutional network (Jansson, 2007a), being based on the market-as-networks approach (Johanson and Mattsson, 1987b; Mattsson and Johanson, 2006).

The methodology for the theoretical framework developed in this chapter is based on an abductive approach, which is signified by the evolvement of the theoretical frame-work and the empirical fieldwork as being both parallel and interrelated (Alvesson and Sköldberg, 2008; Dubois and Gadde, 2002; Jansson and Söderman, 2012). Extant marketing theories are compared, integrated and changed by being continuously confronted with the empirical world of football based on previous knowledge and experience, thereby making a preliminary assessment of the empirical support for the theories. This is illustrated through the examples given in the text in connection with the presentation of the theories and constructs.

4   THE MARKETING MANAGEMENT THEORY

Mainstream marketing theory emphasizes marketing management and the marketing mix according to the managerial school (Sheth et al., 1988). The major theoretical bases are micro-economic theory and economic psychology theory (Mattsson, 1997). This micro-marketing theory differs from macro-marketing theory, a theory of consumer behaviour, and with different theories concerning, for example, distribution channels.

Even if marketing has no place in the neoclassical perfect product market, it has strongly influenced mainstream marketing theory by focusing on marketing management. This market is characterized by perfect information, fully rational decision-makers, atomistic competition, homogeneous resources and no entry/exit barriers. This 'economic man' is also an ideal in marketing management theory. In accordance with March and Olsen (1989), this praxis of decision-making follows an efficiency based logic and is defined as the 'logic of consequence' (ibid.). In economics, this means that decision-making is done according to some formal rational logic based on individual utilities. More realistic market forms have been developed by economists over the years by taking away some of the strict premises of the perfect market, for example, monopolistic competition, which is based on heterogeneous resources. This means that information is imperfect and that more decision parameters are introduced into the economy; consequently creating more room for marketing. There are even more realistic theories on industrial organization and market imperfections, for example, Bain (1956), Caves (1979), Scherer (1980). In these imperfect markets, the decision-maker has a more limited cognitive capacity and the rationality is bounded, pertaining to a 'rule of thumb' character. Instead of maximizing the potential, the decision-maker is satisfying the needs by searching for and evaluating a limited number of alternatives (Cyert and March, 1963). Even if imperfect and more realistic 'logics-in-use' prevail, the praxis of decision-making still follows the logic of consequence (Hunt, 2002).

5   CUSTOMER-FOCUSED RELATIONSHIP MARKETING THEORY

Relationship marketing theories, including marketing to consumers (Parvatiyar and Sheth, 2000; Sheth and Parvatiyar, 1995, 2001) and marketing of services (for example, Grönroos, 1995, 2000, 2011), mostly deal with practices in imperfect markets (Jansson,

2006), applying traditional marketing concepts and tools according to the managerial school as described by Sheth et al. (1988). Even if the focus gradually changes to the buyer–seller relationship from the marketing mix, the basis of the marketing theory does not change, including being based on the logic of consequence (March, 1994; Zey, 1992). It is more a shift of approach, looking at marketing from another angle. The traditional focus of the marketing management theory on the customer is still kept, but has been refocused and altered to fit with the new relationship orientation. The emerging service-oriented dominant marketing logic developed in Vargo and Lusch (2004, 2008) and Gummesson et al. (2010) also belongs to this mainstream marketing theory base.

As illustrated below, it is more fruitful to see the marketing of sports clubs as relationship marketing; some sponsoring agreements are typically relationship oriented. Major football clubs have accepted, for example telecommunication firms named on their shirts. The members of the club are offered favoured services leading to new relations. A prominent example was Manchester United and Vodafone and, later, the partnership between Bayern Munich and Deutsche Telecom (T-Mobile); T-Mobile in 2011 was the lead sponsor for Bayern Munich. The benefits of the sponsorship deal are dual as Bayern Munich gets paid by T-Mobile in the form of sponsorship fees and T-Mobile gets access to the huge fan base of Bayern Munich fans for the promotion of its products and services. Ströbel and Woratschek (2012) analyse various brand equity models in relation to sports. Relationship marketing is not limited to geographical boundaries. At the beginning of 2011, Real Madrid signed a deal to open a soccer school in Saudi Arabia, which is an example of extended outreach and brand awareness in markets where football is considered to be extremely popular (Dorsey, 2011)

Customer-focused relationship marketing theory belongs to the narrow stream of relationship marketing research as defined by Mattsson (1997). It is distinguished from the broad stream of research catering to a wider set of relationships. The 'multiple markets' perspective belongs to the broad stream, since it includes relationship marketing in six markets: customer and intermediary markets, supplier and alliance markets, referral markets and influence markets, and also internal markets and recruitment markets (Payne, 2000; Peck et al., 1997). A similar approach is also taken by Gummesson (1995), who identifies and analyses 30 different types of business relationships. For the co-creation of value in team-sports management Dolles and Söderman (2013 in this volume) distinguish eight types of football offerings in various exchange relations with six groups of customers. These customer types include: supporters, club members, media, corporate partners (sponsors), local communities and other clubs. It is obvious and, as illustrated below, sports clubs operate in multiple markets.

Football clubs are engaged in multiple markets and carry out a wide spectrum of activities. We consider the example of Real Madrid which frequently buys new players and sells players simultaneously. It is also one of the most popular football clubs in the world and therefore has marketing/promotional activities that are also extremely fast paced. Real Madrid has bought famous players like Ronaldo, Kaka, Benzema and Di Maria. It also pushes the sales of apparel (team T-shirts and match-day kits) and pulls its customers towards the wide range of products and services it offers in collaboration with its partners. Today, football clubs are like conglomerates, with football being the nucleus around which other supporting activities revolve. In conjunction with football, clubs are also pursuing other revenue generation avenues, for example, Real Madrid also has a basketball team, a full-fledged television channel, a chain of retail outlets selling branded merchandize and it is engaged in a broad set of activities (Kase et al., 2006).

6   THE NETWORK MARKETING THEORY

The network marketing theory or the inter-organizational approach to marketing (Jansson, 2006) is based on the market-as-networks approach. Marketing takes place through relationships, which are embedded in an economic and social structure in the form of networks (Easton, 1992; Hägg and Johanson, 1982; Håkansson and Johanson, 1992; Håkansson and Snehota, 1995; Johanson and Mattsson, 1987a, 1987b; Mattsson and Johanson, 2006). The market structure consists of strong interdependencies between firms organized in networks, where marketing both influences the market structure and is influenced by it. Owing to bonds created, relationships are continuous and stable. The strong social content of the relationships makes the market more a social arena rather than an economic arena. Sociology theory is used to describe and explain marketing behaviour, for example, Granovetter (1973, 1985).

The Stockholm football club, Brommapojkarna (BP), focuses on youth development as a networker. They have identified and attracted a number of volunteering coaches who have found talented youngsters during many years and developed a huge network with other clubs. The club is only the fifth largest club in Stockholm and the other four have often recruited talents from BP to their junior clubs. Häcken in Göteborg has a similar networking approach, but with an international development perspective. Every summer a youth tournament including 35000 young players from the whole world are invited to Göteborg. The profit from this event creates a surplus for the club which then can finance purchase of top players when needed.

These industrial networks consist of differing individual firms that match heterogeneous resources to heterogeneous demands. The network is also viewed as a specific market form of its own that is found in between the neoclassical market and the hierarchy (Powell, 1990). The main concepts describing and explaining marketing practice according to the inter-organizational approach are mainly found in Ford et al. (1998), Håkansson (1982), Håkansson and Snehota (1995), Johanson and Mattsson (1987a, 1987b), Mattsson and Johanson (2006) and Snehota (1990). The more intense the processes of exchange become, the stronger the reasons are for making adaptations and not replacing the other party. Change takes place within the relationship, rather than the relationships with other parties. A mutual orientation is created, which results in a preparedness to interact in a dyad, leading to cooperation and solution of conflicts. An example of this would be BP selling a young player to any one of the bigger Stockholm clubs. This reciprocity is largely shaped by social exchange processes, but also by business and information exchange. Different forms of investment in relationships shape the future behaviour of the parties involved, since they affect the parties' access to heterogeneous resources. These dyads are influenced by indirect linkages within the network or networks to which the seller has access. Within a given network, macro and micro competitive positions are taken. Networks subject an organization to the manipulations and influence of other organizations outside its sphere of control, which creates uncertainty. Management of this uncertainty without losing organizational autonomy is a chief concern for individual units within a network.

7   THE INSTITUTIONAL NETWORK MARKETING THEORY

Institutional theory makes it possible to develop further the market as a social arena, and resolve the contradictions of the network marketing theory between social and economic perspectives. Such a socio-economic perspective means that the market as an economic institution is integrated within the social frame, making the latter the overriding point of departure. This means that the market is viewed as an efficiently oriented social order. Marketing activities taking place in market networks are now determined by the institutional set-up of this market and the market environment. The markets as a social structure involves relationships developed, for example, by French football national team 'Les Bleus', and are described by using terms such as roles, groups, values, status and trust. The under-socialized economic man and contractual man are replaced by the 'relationship man', who has both a brain and social relations.

'A risk management company approached Zidane and offered the player to arrange a transfer package to Real Madrid. They then offered to Real Madrid a package of sponsor contracts and Zidane played several years for the club. Zidane was not only an outstanding footballer but also the role model in the French national team' (Philippe, 2002: 65). Thus, the world of sports has a social side, such as that of ethics, that is, institutionalized principles, norms and standards of conduct that govern individuals and groups but which are relative and therefore vary. Thus, there is a 'social foundation' for marketing decisions in sports clubs. This means that if the major strategic orientation in the arena revolves around being efficient and competitive with regard to marketing, distribution and serving, then in a social environment this orientation of the sports club is about adhering to a number of rules, regulations, values and norms in order to gain, or maintain, extend environmental support, that is, to be a legitimate actor in the society.

The practice of decision-making in a social context follows a different logic than in an economic context. Rather than an efficiency based logic of consequence approach, decisions in social environments defined as institutions concern the following rules. These rules are based on the logic of appropriateness, where decision-makers ask three questions, according to March (1994): what kind of situation is this (recognition)? What kind of organization is this (identity)? What does an organization such as this do in a situation like this (rules)? This process is complicated and characterized by systematic reasoning of establishing identities and matching rules to recognized situations (March and Olsen, 1989). This matching is viewed as a marketing decision custom based on legitimacy seeking. In summary, there are rules related to negotiations regarding players' conduct on and off the field, dressing-room conduct, social/promotional interaction, collaboration with sponsors and, ultimately, rules related to achieving long- and short-term goals.

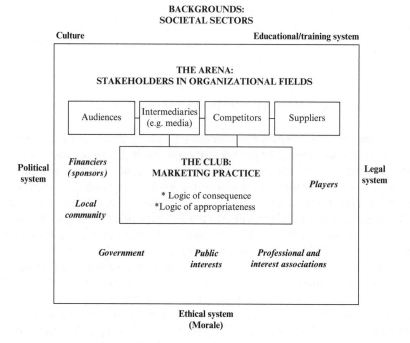

Figure 19.1   The institutional network model (INM)

7.1   The Institutional Network Model

The institutional network approach is developed in this section by specifying in more detail the interplay between institutions on one side, and between institutions and network marketing practice on the other. This is illustrated in Figure 19.1. The external environment is seen in terms of an institutional set up, within which relationships take place. The club, which has the best ability to design its internal institutional set-up in such a way that it permits the club to respond effectively to its external institutional set-up through the relationship marketing practice, will be the most competitive club in its arena and thus, in the best position to take advantage of arena opportunities.

The stadium, for example, is looked upon as a social arena, where the club produces the experience. A few years ago Arsenal abandoned their old stadium, Highbury (38 419 seats), to move to a new venue, the Emirates Stadium, (60 355 seats) after partnering with a new shirt sponsor, Emirates. This relationship was mutually beneficial since the new stadium was named after the sponsor and expanded seating capacity almost twofold. Furthermore, through this arrangement, Arsenal also ensured a valuable long-term sponsorship deal (Tong, 2006). Arsenal uses the Emirates Stadium to effectively create, build, and manage valuable relationships in and around the arena. In addition to the revenue from tickets, Arsenal has produced revenue through its apparel shop, Armoury, located within the stadium, built a highly profitable relationship with Emirates airlines, which enables its fan base to access numerous promotions, and has a museum within the stadium, offering banqueting and conferencing services.

7.2   The World of Institutions

To describe institutions words like codes, rules, habits, routines and procedures are often used, which all imply that human behaviour is regular and stable (Jansson, 2007a). By institution we also mean the social unit that houses this behaviour, for example, a game, ceremony, organization, family, nation or market. Institutions are therefore defined as programmes, routines and codes typical of a legitimized social grouping. Members behave according to the codes of the organization and its network. Institutions provide individuals with normative rules and codes of conduct which guide actions. New members will imitate this practice, many times even being unaware of the rules behind it. A first main characteristic of institutions is the rule-like or organizing nature (Nabli and Nugent, 1989). Every football club follows a certain hierarchy through which it controls its day-to-day activities. A locus of control is exercised, reporting lines are followed and activities are carried out in accordance with their timelines. The level of control, centralization or decentralization may vary depending on the size, performance or popularity of the club.

A second characteristic is the ability to facilitate and constrain the relations among individuals and firms. Third, institutions are signified by predictability. Institutions standardize marketing activities and transfer rules between individuals such as norms and ideas. Behaviour following from them is repeated over time, meaning that the practice is also valid for future situations. Uncertainty is reduced and marketing activities can be anticipated because of repetition. Football clubs revolve around the axis of their results. Manchester United, Real Madrid, Barcelona and Inter Milan are all top football clubs because of their capability to deliver results which are obviously predictable and consistent owing to their high level of performances (Edmans et al., 2007)

Since institutions are characterized by established patterns of behaviour, they are also stable. These traits make institutions excellent instruments for describing, explaining and predicting actual marketing behaviour, thereby reducing uncertainty and risks. Networks in social arenas are organized according to institutional principles. Sets of rules and regulations govern marketing practices, which are executed collectively by the individual members of the social groups. Society is divided into different social groups characterized by different rules and practices, forming a multi-layered system of institutions. The organization of one part of society is influenced by how other parts of society are organized. This institutional world is divided into three levels of societal rules: micro institutions (for example, the club), meso institutions (for example, an organizational field) and macro institutions or societal sectors. The macro rules are defined as societal sectors, for example, the legal system, political system, ethical system and culture. Government is defined as both a stakeholder and an arena structure or an organizational field, which are separated from the political system and is defined as an overall structure influencing the arena. The arena consists of organizational fields, for example, groups of audiences such as members and non-members, financiers such as sponsors and 'employees' such as players. There are also non-market fields, for example, local community, and public interests. Organizational fields are therefore described at two levels. At the micro-institutions level, specific institutions defined as stakeholders within organizational fields are taken up, for example, specific member groups, sports authorities within government and television within public interests. At the meso level, organizational fields are viewed as an entity, where stakeholder groups share common norms and rules. The meso and macro institutions link to each other in a certain way, constituting an institutional framework that influences marketing practice in networks.

Every institution at these three levels is assumed to consist of four basic rules: thought styles that come from the ideational part, and three rules belonging to the social structure – values, norms and enforcement mechanisms. Those members sharing thoughts and making classifications have a unified thought style. Their common frame of reference works as guidelines for sense making and practice. These established patterns of thinking therefore work as cognitive recipes for how people behave. Norms and values also influence how members think and act. Values are the root of cultures and behaviour, defined as 'conceptions of the preferred' (Scott, 1995: 37) and as standards for comparison. They set the priorities and function as guiding principles. Norms, on the other hand, specify how things should be done. They work as guiding principles for how to act, a kind of decree about how one should act or how something should be constituted or organized. Sports fans are unlikely to purchase products from a rival sport organization, as indicated below.

Marketing practice is also controlled by incentives and sanctions. Such enforcement mechanisms concern how to construct the sanction and incentive system in order to reward or punish individuals and groups within the club together by establishing surveillance and an assessment system to control the enforcement of marketing practice.

7.3   Marketing in Stakeholder Networks

Relationship marketing in stakeholder networks varies with the mix of rules of the institutional set-ups faced by the club. Some key stakeholders in the marketing of football clubs are illustrated in the following.

The Swedish elite football clubs during the 1990s and 2000s were in a volatile situation. They were on losing grounds and their FIFA rankings were also plummeting The reason behind this downfall was the loss of good Swedish players to foreign clubs. Swedish clubs simply cannot afford to retain quality players. There is an institutional norm not allowing capital to be deployed in Sweden (Gammelsæter et al., 2011: 87–9).

Football clubs that are owned by their members, like Real Madrid and Barcelona, are heavily influenced by those members (Forbes, 2010). Each and every performance is measured through a microscope; membership-based clubs failing to meet the expectations consequently undergo tremendous changes. A rather recent case was the change in the Barcelona board of directors during 2003 when Joan Laporta took over. The club was losing games and was not winning enough titles or tournaments for many seasons, which prompted the board members to elect a new club governing structure. English Premier League clubs Bolton Wanderers and Everton work together with the community, constituting another stakeholder focus. The players from Bolton Wanderers regularly visit different schools in their vicinity to promote football as a sport in order to encourage the younger generation to pursue healthy activities. Although these activities have no monetary impact, they prove to be beneficial in spreading good 'word of mouth' about these clubs (Bolton Wanderers Community Trust, 2011; Everton Football Club, 2011).

Since there are no pure economic environments for sports clubs, audiences and suppliers are also stakeholders, who have social goals. Clubs then act to match the internal and external institutional frameworks to each other. A practice is developed to match the norms and values of the stakeholders, and relationship marketing is focused on how to establish and maintain relationships with audiences and suppliers. Relationship marketing done correctly will create value for the different stakeholders. Thus, the mix of marketing decisions taking place according to the logic of consequence and the logic of appropriateness varies. Satisfying social needs brings in other stakeholders such as the media and local community with goals of increasing audience value. Relationships might therefore also need to be established with other stakeholders rather than audiences, intermediaries or sponsors. Here, it is a question of matching the external regulations, values and norms of these stakeholders in order to gain or maintain their support, to achieve legitimacy.

The network strategy (Jansson, 2007b) concerns marketing practice related to the whole network of the sports club. This includes all actors in the arena, such as audiences, competitors, financiers and the local community. The network strategy is how the club deals with this whole network of groupings from a relationship marketing point of view. Big football clubs have specific relationship management departments that are responsible for managing relationships with sponsors, fans/members, suppliers and the media. In order to create a strong negotiation position with sponsors and the media, some clubs initiate partnerships with other clubs, or get the whole league to work together like the British Premiership League. It is therefore legitimate to develop a clear focus on why a network-based relationship marketing theory should be applied in sport management research, and what other researchers should do, when having this approach in mind.

8   CONCLUSIONS AND FUTURE RESEARCH

Manchester United's members have a loyal member base which can be evaluated using this logic (Manchester United, 2011). The consequences of various legitimacy acts can be looked into for profitability, competitive advantage or audience value. The matching strategy can also be evaluated regarding the consequences of various legitimacy acts on social values of the stakeholders, and what it means for competitiveness.

A coherent link exists between the market as a social arena and marketing activities. The INM focuses on factors which influence what happens within a specific market, while the practice-based approach focuses on creating the market and its opportunities through marketing practices. It is important to note that there is no hard and fast rule about adopting a specific approach. In fact, the adoption of approaches varies with the task/activity at hand and considering a hybrid approach might be the most beneficial. Rational decision-making is then aligned with the mainstream marketing theories, and fits into the logic of consequence. It is valid for all three of the relationship marketing theories discussed above to work in imperfect market situations, ranging from the marketing management theory to the network marketing theory.

The 'customer focused relationship marketing' theory caters to a narrow range of stakeholders and activities. Pivotal attention is only aimed at relationships and making profits through them. Access to 'multiple markets' enables an enterprise to cover a broader spectrum of stakeholders and activities as it includes relationship marketing in 'six different types of markets'. These are supporters, club members, media, corporate partners (sponsors), local communities and other clubs (Dolles and Söderman, 2013, in this volume).

The 'networking marketing' theory is another broad relationship marketing theory, where marketing takes place through a set of network relationships. Since it is based on the markets as networks approach and sociology, the market is viewed as a social arena. The decisions are made on the basis of actual happenings in the market and outside it.

In the 'institutional-network theory' the logic of appropriateness and logic of consequence go hand in hand. The logic of appropriateness is used to find alternatives to a problem as the word 'appropriate' suggests. Conversely, the logic of consequence plays a critical role in solving the problems outlined and maximizing the social values from an economic point of view. This logic therefore goes a step further by translating social values into economic consequences, for example, the competitiveness of the club. It can therefore be concluded that the logic of consequence is valid for all four marketing theories, while the logic of appropriateness is only included in the institutions network marketing theory.

As stated by Beech and Chadwick (2007), in order to market a sport product, a marketer has to consider several influencing factors that are unique for sport marketing. The most distinctive and challenging factors are that sport is product led. Sport is dominated by an uncertainty of outcome and a customer who helps to produce the product itself, while at the same time those customers who help create the product usually refrain from purchasing products of rival sports organizations.

The four groups of marketing theories mentioned in this chapter therefore correspond with different products depending upon the marketing situation in modern day football. In a nutshell, the earlier indicated football package consists of eight products, that is, team, sporting competition, club, players, football services, event arena, merchandise and other commercial activities (Dolles and Söderman, 2013 in this volume). In the case of some products, there are two theories simultaneously corresponding with the products. Football services, merchandising and other commercial activities mostly take place according to the marketing management theory. In football, 'the team' plays a focal role; being the pedestal around which the majority of the marketing activities converge. In this situation, customer focused relationship marketing and network marketing play major roles. In terms of 'the players', the marketing management and network marketing theories are most prevalent. In terms of the 'sporting competition', the institutional network marketing theory comes into play. As argued for in the chapter, this theory is also the most suitable for the 'club' in order to broaden its horizon. The network marketing theory is also suitable. For the 'event arena' the marketing management and the customer focused relationship marketing theories are most prevalent.

Continued research based on the preliminary framework of this chapter needs to be done by studying a few clubs in depth, since detailed, insider information about football clubs' marketing is needed. At the same time, the clubs cannot be too few, since this would jeopardize the purpose to develop propositions. The next step in accordance with the abductive approach would then be to develop the preliminary theoretical framework further by the research strategy of case studies (Dubois and Gadde, 2002; Merriam, 1998; Yin, 2009). This strategy allows a variety of evidence to be included such as interviews, documentation and observations. To ensure variation in the case database and allow analytical generalization to find the propositions, multiple and embedded cases are recommended, approximately ten clubs (Yin, 2009). To reach an appropriate match between the theoretical constructs and reality, a purposeful sampling procedure should be continuous, and undertaken by a theory led sampling logic (Dubois and Gadde, 2002; Glaser, 1978). Based on the preliminary theory, a semi-structured questionnaire would be developed, being flexible enough to continuously match reality and theory by adding new questions (Merriam, 1998). Thus, the external validity of the study would be achieved through analytical generalization, where the findings would be related to the broader preliminary theoretical framework of this chapter (Yin, 2009). This will require an acceptable internal validity by establishing proper relationships between the constructs, mainly through pattern matching.

The main limitation of the methodology used is that it does not allow theory testing. The final aim would therefore be to develop a well-structured theory with strong empirical support to make it possible to formulate propositions as a basis for further research. To validate this procedure would require more than using refined marketing theory, rather, the propositions developed would need to be specified more as hypotheses and operationalized before being tested on a larger sample for statistical inference.

REFERENCES

Alvesson, M. and Sköldberg, K. (2008), *Tolkning och Reflektion* [*Interpretation and Reflection*], Lund: Studentlitteratur.
Anagnostopoulos, C. (2013), Examining corporate responsibility in football: the application of grounded theory methodology, in S. Söderman and H. Dolles (eds), *Handbook of Research on Sport and Business*, Cheltenham, UK and Northampton, MA, USA: Edward Elgar, pp. 418–32.
Araujo, L. (2007), Markets, market-making and marketing, *Marketing Theory*, **7** (3), 211–26.
Araujo, L., Kjellberg, H. and Spencer, R. (2008), Market practices and forms: introduction to the special issue, *Marketing Theory*, **8** (1), 5–14.
Armstrong, G. and Kotler, P. (2007), *Marketing: An Introduction*, international edn, Upper Saddle River, NJ: Pearson Education.
Bain, J.S. (1956), *Barriers to New Competition*, Cambridge, MA: Harvard University Press.
Beech, J. and Chadwick, S. (2007), *The Marketing of Sport*, Harlow: Prentice Hall & Pearson Education.
Bolton Wanderers Community Trust (eds) (2011), Community cohesion and education, available at: http://www.bwct.org.uk/community-cohension/ (accessed 21 March 2011).
Caves, R.E. (1979), Industrial organization, corporate strategy and structure, *Journal of Economic Literature*, **18** (1), 64–92.
Cornwell, T.B. (2013), State of the art and science in sponsorship-linked marketing, in S. Söderman and H. Dolles (eds), *Handbook of Research on Sport and Business*, Cheltenham, UK and Northampton, MA, USA: Edward Elgar, pp. 456–76.
Cyert, R.M. and March, J.G. (1963), *A Behavioural Theory of the Firm*, Englewood Cliffs, NJ: Prentice Hall.
Dolles, H. and Söderman, S. (2005), Ahead of the game – the network of value captures in professional football, *DIJ Working Paper*, no. 05/5, Tokyo: German Institute for Japanese Studies.
Dolles, H. and Söderman, S. (2008), The network of value captures: creating competitive advantage in football management, *Wirtschaftspolitische Blätter Österreich* [*Austrian Economic Policy Papers*], **55** (1), 39–58.
Dolles, H. and Söderman, S. (2011a), Learning from success: implementing a professional football league in Japan, in H. Dolles and S. Söderman (eds), *Sport as a Business: International, Professional and Commercial Aspects*, Basingstoke: Palgrave Macmillan, pp. 228–50.
Dolles, H. and Söderman, S. (2011b), プロ・サッカーのマネジメントにおける経済価値獲得のネットワーク―日本プロ・サッカー・リーグ発展の分析― [The network of economic value captures in professional football management: analyzing the development of the Japanese professional soccer league], *Shōgaku Ronsan, The Journal of Commerce*, **40** (1–2), 195–232.
Dolles, H. and Söderman, S. (2013), The network of value captures in football club management: a framework to develop and analyse competitive advantage in professional team sports, in S. Söderman and H. Dolles

(eds), *Handbook of Research on Sport and Business*, Cheltenham, UK and Northampton, MA, USA: Edward Elgar, pp. 367–95.

Dorsey, J.M. (2011), Real Madrid to open sports academy in Saudi Arabia, *Bleacher Report*, 6 February 2011, available at: http://bleacherreport.com/articles/599355-real-madrid-to-open-sports-academy-in-saudi-arabia (accessed 13 February 2011.

Dubois, A. and Gadde, L.-E. (2002), Systematic combining: an abductive approach to case research, *Journal of Business Research*, **55** (7) 553–60.

Easton, G. (1992), Industrial networks: a review, in B. Axelsson and G. Easton (eds), *Industrial Networks. A New Reality*, London: Routledge, pp. 3–27.

Edmans, A., Garcia, D. and Norli, O. (2007), Sports sentiment and stock returns, *Journal of Finance*, **62** (4), 1967–98.

Everton Football Club (eds) (2011), Everton's charitable work, available at: http://www.evertonfc.com/club/everton-s-charitable-work.html (accessed 21 March 2011).

Forbes (2010), Soccer team valuations, available at: http://www.forbes.com/lists/2010/34/soccer-10_Barcelona_340011.html (accessed 22 March 2011).

Ford, D., Gadde, L.-E., Hakansson, H., Lundgren, A., Snehota, I., Turnball, P. and Wilson, D. (1998), *Managing Business Relationships*, Chichester: John Wiley.

Gammelsæter, H., Storm, R.K. and Söderman, S. (2011), Diverging Scandinavian approaches to professional football, in H. Gammelsæter and B. Senaux (eds), *The Organisation and Goverance of Top Football across Europe*, London: Routledge, pp. 77–92.

Glaser, B.G. (1978), *Theoretical Sensitivity: Advances in the Methodology of Grounded Theory*, Mill Valley, CA: Sociology Press.

Granovetter, M. (1973), The strength of weak ties, *The American Journal of Sociology*, **78** (6), 1360–80.

Granovetter, M. (1985), Economic action and social structure: the problem of embeddedness, *The American Journal of Sociology*, **91** (3), 481–510.

Grönroos, C. (1995), Relationship marketing: strategic and tactical implications, *Management Decision*, **34** (3), 5–14.

Grönroos, C. (2000), *Service Management and Marketing: A Customer Relationship Management Approach*, Chichester: John Wiley & Sons.

Grönroos, C. (2011), A service perspective on business relationships: the value creation, interaction and marketing interface, *Industrial Marketing Management*, **40** (2), 240–7.

Gummesson, E. (1995), *Relationship Marketing: From 4P to 35 Rs*, Malmö: Liber Hermods.

Gummesson, E., Lusch, R. and Vargo, S. (2010), Transitioning from service management to service-dominant logic observations and recommendations, *International Journal of Quality and Service Sciences*, **2** (1), 8–22.

Hägg, I. and Johanson, J. (1982), *Företag i Nätverk – Ny Syn på Konkurrenskraft [Business in Networks – A New View of Competition]*, Stockholm: SNS.

Håkansson, H. (ed.) (1982), *International Marketing and Purchasing of Industrial Goods – an Interaction Approach*, Chichester: Wiley.

Håkansson, H. and Johanson, J. (1992), A model of industrial networks, in B. Axelsson and G. Easton (eds), *Industrial Networks. A New Reality*, London: Routledge, pp. 28–34

Håkansson, H. and Snehota, I. (1995), *Developing Relationships in Business Networks*, London: Routledge.

Hunt, S.D. (1991), *Modern Marketing Theory. Critical Issues in the Philosophy of Marketing Science*, Cincinnati, OH: South-Western.

Hunt, S.D. (2002), *Foundations of Marketing Theory: Toward a General Theory of Marketing*, Armonk, NY: M.E. Sharpe.

Jansson, H. (1994), *Industrial Products. A Guide to the International Marketing Economics Model*, New York: International Business Press.

Jansson, H. (2006), From industrial marketing to business-to-business marketing and relationship marketing, in S. Lagrosen and G. Svensson (eds), *Marketing: Broadening the Horizons*, Lund: Studentlitteratur, pp. 115–36.

Jansson, H. (2007a), *International Business Strategy in Emerging Country Markets. The Institutional Network Approach*, Cheltenham, UK and Northampton, MA, USA: Edward Elgar.

Jansson, H. (2007b), *International Business Marketing in Emerging Country Markets. The Third Wave of Internationalization of Firms*, Cheltenham, UK and Northampton, MA, USA: Edward Elgar.

Jansson, H. and Söderman, S. (2012), Initial internationalization of Chinese privately-owned enterprises – the take-off process, *Thunderbird International Business Review*, **54** (2), 183–94.

Johanson, J. and Mattsson, L.G. (1987a), Interorganizational relations in industrial systems. A network approach, in N. Hood and J.E. Vahlne (eds), *Strategies in Global Competition*, New York: Croom Helm, pp. 287–314.

Johanson, J. and Mattsson, L.G. (1987b), Interorganizational relations in industrial systems. A network approach compared with the transaction-cost approach, *International Studies of Management and Organization*, **17** (1), 33–48.

Kase, K., Gomez, S., Urrutia, I., Opazo, M. and Marti, C. (2006), Real Madrid – Barcelona, business strategy vs. sport strategy, IESE Business School, University of Navarra, *IESE Occasional Papers*, June available at: http://www.iese.edu/research/pdfs/op-06–12-e.pdf, accessed 7 January 2011.

Kjellberg, H. and Helgesson, C.-H. (2006), Multiple versions of markets: multiplicity and performativity in market practice, *Industrial Marketing Management*, **35** (7), 839–55.

Kjellberg, H. and Helgesson, C.-H. (2007), On the nature of markets and their practices, *Marketing Theory*, **7** (2), pp. 137–62.

Manchester United (eds) (2011), Manchester United Finance, available at: www.manutd.com/en/MAN-UTD-Finance.aspx (accessed 7 January 2011).

March, J.G. (1994), *A Primer on Decision Making. How Decisions Happen*, New York: Free Press.

March, J.G. and Olsen, J.P. (1989), *Rediscovering Institutions: The Organizational Basis of Politics*, New York: Free Press and Macmillan.

Mattsson, L.G. (1997), Relationship marketing and the markets-as-networks approach – a comparative analysis of two evolving streams of research, *Journal of Marketing Management*, **13** (5), 447–61.

Mattsson, L.G. and Johanson, J. (2006), Discovering market networks, *European Journal of Marketing*, **40** (3–4), 259–74.

Merriam, S.B. (1998), *Qualitative Research and Case Study Applications in Education*, San Francisco, CA: Jossey-Bass.

Mullin, B.J., Hardy, S. and Sutton, W.A. (2007), *Sport Marketing*, 3rd edn, Champaign, IL: Human Kinetics.

Nabli, M.K. and Nugent, J.B. (1989), *The New Institutional Economics and Development: Theory and Applications to Tunisia*, Amsterdam: North-Holland.

Parvatiyar, A. and Sheth, J.N. (2000), The domain and conceptual foundations of relationship marketing, in J.N. Sheth and A. Parvatiyar (eds), *Handbook of Relationship Marketing*, Thousand Oaks, CA: Sage, pp. 3–38.

Payne, A. (2000), Relationship marketing. The U.K. perspective, in J.N. Sheth and A. Parvatiyar (eds), *Handbook of Relationship Marketing*, Thousand Oaks, CA: Sage, pp. 39–67.

Peck, H., Payne, A., Christopher, M.G. and Clark, M.K. (1997), *Relationship Marketing: Strategy and Implementation*, Oxford: Butterworth-Heinemann.

Philippe, C. (2002), L'Equipe de France du monde: sport and national identity, *French Cultural Studies*, **13** (37), 65, available at: http://sites.duke.edu/wcwp/research-projects/players-and-migration/french-players-and-migration/#fn-1200–2 (accessed 14 January 2011).

Powell, W.W. (1990), Neither market nor hierarchy: network forms of organization, *Research in Organizational Behaviour*, **12**, 295–336.

Scherer, F.M. (1980), *Industrial Market Structure and Economic Performance*, 2nd edn, Chicago, IL: Rand McNally College.

Schlesinger, T. (2013), A review of fan identity and its influence on sport sponsorship effectiveness, in S. Söderman and H. Dolles (eds), *Handbook of Research on Sport and Business*, Cheltenham, UK and Northampton, MA, USA: Edward Elgar, pp. 435–55.

Scott, R.W. (1995), *Institutions and Organizations*, Thousand Oaks, CA: Sage.

Shank, M.D. (2005), *Sports Marketing: A Strategic Perspective*, 3rd edn, Upper Saddle River, NJ: Pearson Education.

Sheth, J.N., Gardner, D.M. and Garrett, D.E. (1988), *Marketing Theory: Evolution and Evaluation*, London: Wiley.

Sheth, J.N. and Parvatiyar, A. (1995), The evolution of relationship marketing, *Journal of Academy of Marketing Science*, **23** (4), 255–71.

Sheth, J.N. and Parvatiyar, A. (2001), Customer relationship management: emerging practice, process and discipline, *Journal of Economic and Social Research*, **3** (2), 1–34.

Snehota, I. (1990), Notes on a theory of business enterprise, unpublished dissertation, Uppsala University, Department of Business Administration.

Ströbel, T. and Woratschek, H. (2013), Brand equity models in the spotlight of sport business, in S. Söderman and H. Dolles (eds), *Handbook of Research on Sport and Business*, Cheltenham, UK and Northampton, MA, USA: Edward Elgar, pp. 495–510.

Tong, A. (2006), Emirates Stadium: new goal for the Gunners, *Independent*, 4 December available at: http://www.independent.co.uk/student/magazines/emirates-stadium-new-goal-for-the-gunners-427035.html (accessed 21 March 2011).

Union of European Football Associations (UEFA) (eds) (2011), Behind the scenes: a Wembley final in the making, available at: http://www.uefa.com/uefachampionsleague/news/newsid=1637590.html (accessed 30 May 2011).

United Nations Children's Fund (Unicef) (eds) (2011), Sport for development, available at: www.unicef.org/sports/index_40934.html (accessed 14 January 2011).

Vargo, S. and Lusch, R. (2004), Evolving to a new dominant logic for marketing, *Journal of Marketing*, **68** (January), 1–17.

Vargo, S. and Lusch, R. (2008), Reconfiguration of the conceptual landscape: a tribute to the service logic of Richard Normann, *Journal of the Academy of Marketing Science*, **36** (1), 152–5.

Yin, R.K. (2009), *Case Study Research: Designs and Methods*, 4th edn, London: Sage.

Zey, M. (1992), *Decision Making. Alternatives to Rational Choice Models*, London: Sage.

20 The network of value captures in football club management: a framework to develop and analyse competitive advantage in professional team sports
Harald Dolles and Sten Söderman

1 THE MANAGEMENT CHALLENGES OF FOOTBALL

The reasons why football clubs win or lose, make profits or losses, are perhaps the central questions in football management research. The causes of a club's success or failure are inextricably tied to questions about why clubs differ, how they act on and off the pitch, how they choose strategies for performance on the pitch and within the club on different levels, and how they are managed. While much of research on football has a more national focus, it also has become increasingly apparent that any quest for the causes of a club's success must also confront the reality of international competition, the difference in governance structures of the game and the striking differences in the performance of clubs in different nations (Gammelsæter and Senaux, 2011; Hamil and Chadwick, 2010; Söderman et al., 2010). Yet, the question of why clubs win or lose raises a still broader question. Any effort to understand 'success' in a broader sense of a football club must rest on an underlying economic and managerial theory of the industry, where the clubs are the actors. In recent years, the world of football has been referred to more and more as an industry in its own right. Its characteristics have been getting closer to those of services or the entertainment business, as people worldwide may choose whether to go to the cinema, an amusement park or to the stadium to watch a match. The ranking of football as a business activity has risen in the economies of those countries where football is promoted as a national sport. In many of these countries, it represents today a large percentage of a nation's gross domestic product (GDP), because football events also drive a considerable number of other sectors, such as media and different services like catering and transportation.

Competitive advantage in the football business cannot be examined independently from each actor's (each club's) competitive scope. The purpose of this chapter is therefore to develop and introduce a 'network of value captures' encompassing a football club's competitive scope, defined as a number of value captures (the array of product offerings and different customer groups served), the strategic vision and the extent of coordinated strategy. Competitive advantage of a football club is attained within some scope, and the choice of value-capturing activities, defined as the relationship between value captures, is therefore an important decision-making and a decisive task for professional football club management.

The complexity, the specifics and the changing nature of the football business and its environment strain conventional approaches to theory building in management sciences and hypothesis testing. Early sport management research offered no theory for examining the professional football club and its business environment. Streams of research in strategic management on how to create and maintain competitive advantage as well as research in marketing on value and its co-creation are used as a basis to develop the network of value captures in football club management (section 2). To advance both knowledge and practice, we emphasize in this chapter a framework approach to theory building rather than developing a model of the football business (section 3). The framework and its three components, comprising seven value offerings, six customer categories, and management's strategy intent and strategies, is introduced in detail in the following section 4. We end this chapter by providing some conclusions as well as ideas for how the network of value captures could be applied in future research and used in practice (section 5).

The network of value captures for professional football club management, as introduced in section 4 of this chapter, benefited very much from the discussion succeeding its initial presentation at the Academy of International Business 2005 annual meeting and the circulation of the subsequent working papers printed at Stockholm University (Stockholm, Sweden) and the German Institute for Japanese Studies (Tokyo, Japan) afterwards (Dolles and Söderman, 2005b, 2006). All the comments received have led to a revised version of the initial working paper, first to be published with the *Austrian Economic Policy Papers* in 2008 as 'The network of value captures: creating competitive advantage in football management' (Dolles and Söderman, 2008).[1] This framework was presented and discussed at various conferences and workshops, thus involving practitioners from the football industry as well as academics in the field. The network of value captures in football club management presented in this chapter is an extension and revision of the earlier 2008 version and reflects the development in the football industry. It also incorporates the changes suggested by Dolles and Schweizer (2010) in regard to football services and the relationship between clubs. An application of the initial framework on the development of the Japanese professional football league is made by Dolles and Söderman (2005a, 2011a, 2011b) and was discussed at research seminars at Chuo University and Waseda University in Tokyo.

2 THE CONCEPTUAL BACKGROUND IN MARKETING AND STRATEGIC MANAGEMENT

The service society requires a tangible product combined with a certain set of services to be successful (Normann, 2001). Expected by consumers, this service stage has nowadays become so rooted and so prevalent that in many industries it is becoming commoditized. In order to differentiate themselves on the market many companies need to move beyond services into 'experiences' or 'entertainments' (Holbrook, 1996; Levitt, 1983; Wolf, 1999). The concept of entertainment is closely related to experienced value, which can be defined as 'an interactive relativistic preference experience' (Holbrook, 1996: 138). A myriad of research has recently been conducted in the area of value and perceived value as described in the preceding section, however, little has been done in regard to describing entertainment value or experience value.

Value and the notion of value as co-created are fundamental concepts within contemporary marketing research and practice and according to some, marketing research is now experiencing a 'co-creation paradigm' (Pongsakornungsilp and Schroeder, 2009).

Although, existing literature has predominantly focused on conceptualizations of value and value creating processes (for example, Grönroos, 2011; Normann and Ramírez, 1993; Prahalad and Ramaswamy, 2004; Vargo and Lusch, 2004) and on how consumers integrate resources to create value in their consumption practices (for example, Arnould et al., 2006; Schau et al., 2009), little attention has been devoted to how firms and other stakeholders interact and how they capture value – each stakeholder group by itself or as co-creation in-between.

Because of a proliferation of products and competitors, many companies are being forced to innovate beyond tangible products and commoditized services to create more value for their customers. To differentiate their offers they are creating and managing customer experiences (Kotler and Amstrong, 2010). Pine II and Gilmore (1999) believe that those experiences are an offering distinct from ordinary services. In their view, customer experience matters more than the economic experience. If people are able to buy goods and services at the lowest possible prices, then they seek to take their hard-earned time – and harder earned money – to spend it on more engaging, more memorable, and more highly valued experiences (Pine II, 2011). As a consequence, experiences must provide a memorable offering that will remain with the consumer for a long time, but in order to achieve this, he or she must be drawn into the offering such that a sensation is felt. And to feel that sensation, the consumer must participate actively. This requires highly skilled actors who can dynamically personalize each event according to the needs, the response and the behavioural traits of the consumer. This is labelled by Vargo and Lusch (2004), as a new service-dominant logic supporting the customers' role as co-creators of our economies.

But the nature of football, or professional team sport in general, and its dependency on uncertainty complicates the analysis. Every individual sports consumer has his or her own thoughts, experiences and expectations of the game or events around the match – a 'something else' associated with the football experience. There are even two more layers to consider. First, sports consumers might want different product offerings at different times under different circumstances. Second, it is not one single product, service or entertainment that is offered in professional team sports, what could be termed the competitive scope of a football club, and this will become obvious later in section 4. It is therefore the managerial task to evaluate, change, bundle and utilize the club's resources (value captures), or as Hansen et al. (2004: 1280) conclude: 'What a firm does with its resources is at least as important as which resources it possesses'.

Our understanding of value captures is based on Barney's (1991) conceptualization of resources and sustained competitive advantage. A football club's resources can only be a source of competitive advantage when they are valuable and recognized by the customer, as stated by Dolles and Söderman (2011a: 233):

> Resources are considered to be value captures when they enable a football club to implement strategies (value-capturing activities) that improve its efficiency and effectiveness. Valuable football club resources possessed by a large number of competing clubs cannot be sources of sustained competitive advantage, if a club is not differentiating upon them. A football club only enjoys a competitive advantage when it is implementing a unique value-creating strategy combining bundles of valuable club resources (value captures) recognized and accepted by the customer (by the customer's groups).

3   METHODOLOGY

Gummesson (2007: 233) questioned: 'Why cannot we learn from its practice? Is it still that business schools only go to sociology and ethnography to learn about research and science? It certainly seems so when looking at the references to articles. How then are we going to establish methodology in business and management?' The ambition of this chapter is to construct a tool that enables a more profound analysis of the tasks associated with professional football club management – or more generally, associated with professional team sport management. In order to construct such a tool, two options are discussed in the literature (for example, Porter, 1991): the model-based economic approach or the framework approach.

If we implement the model-based approach, we would abstract the complexity of the football business to isolate a few key variables based on certain selection criteria of the researcher whose interactions are examined in depth in research. This implies the creation of a wide range of situation-specific scenarios or, in other terms, several mathematical models of limited complexity. The normative significance of each model then would depend on the fit between its assumptions and reality. Porter (1991: 97) concludes, 'no one model embodies or even approaches embodying all the variables of interest, and hence the applicability of any model's findings is almost inevitably restricted to a small subgroup of firms or industries whose characteristics fit the model's assumptions'. The model-based approach to theory building has been characteristic of economics research in the last few decades and has spawned a wide array of interesting models in both industrial organization and trade theory. As Porter (1991) points out, these models provide clear conclusions, but it is well known that they are highly sensitive to the assumptions underlying them and to the concept of equilibrium that is employed. Another problem with the model-based approach is that it is hard to integrate the many models into a general framework for approaching any situation, or even to make the findings of the various models consistent. 'While few economists would assert that this body of research in and of itself provides detailed advice for companies, these models, at their best, provide insights into complex situations that are hard to understand without them, which can inform the analysis of a particular company's situation' (ibid.: 98).

Instead of developing a management model of a football club and in order to make progress in research, it was necessary to go beyond those limiting principles. Based on a mere wholistic understanding of a club's competitive environment and its relative position in the market, our approach was to construct a framework for team sport management based on the football industry. A framework is particularly valuable, as it encompasses many variables and seeks to capture much of the complexity. According to Porter (1991: 98), 'frameworks identify the relevant variables and the questions which the user must answer in order to develop conclusions tailored to a particular industry and company. In this sense they can be seen as almost expert systems'. The approach to theory embodied in the framework is contained in our choice of included variables, the way we organized the network of value captures, the proposed interrelation among the value captures, and the way alternative patterns of value captures and club management choices might affect outcomes.

We need to be aware that, when taken, the framework approach to the equilibrium concept is not precise. The development of frameworks embodies the notion of optimization, but not equilibrium in the normal sense of the word. Instead, and emphasized by Porter (1991), there is a continually evolving environment in which a perpetual competitive interaction between rivals takes place. It also needs to be mentioned that all relations among the variables incorporated in the framework cannot be rigorously drawn. A framework, however, seeks to help both – the practitioner as well as the researcher – to better analyse the problem by understanding the sport club and its environment, and by defining and selecting among the strategic alternatives available, regardless of what kind of team-sport industry (for example, football, ice hockey, handball) the club is going to compete in.

These two approaches to theory building are not mutually exclusive. Indeed, they should create a constructive tension with each other as easily can be understood. The model-based approach is particularly valuable in ensuring logical consistency and exploring the subtle interactions involving a limited number of variables. Porter (1991: 98) writes: 'Models should challenge the variables included in frameworks and assertions about their link to outcomes. Frameworks, in turn, should challenge models by highlighting omitted variables, the diversity of competitive situations, the range of actual strategy choices, and the extent to which important parameters are not fixed but continually in flux.' The need to inform practice as proclaimed by Gummesson (2007) from the start, has deemed it necessary to pursue the development of a framework for professional team-sport club management, rather than restrict our research on club management only to theories that can be formally modelled. In line with Porter (1991), we conclude that as long as the building of frameworks is based on in-depth empirical research, it has the potential to not only inform practice but also to push the development of more rigorous theory.

The development of our network of value captures therefore utilizes existing ways of value offerings by football clubs and empirical investigations of customer groups' behaviour. To a large extent empirical literature on stories of success or failure of professional football clubs are used to build the network. In addition, to confirm our findings we requested comments from football club managers, football associations' officials and sport management experts during about 20 narrative interviews. Some comments were very general in nature or related to fundamental concerns about the cases and models we used or the assumptions we made. Other comments were more specific and very detailed in nature. We responded to the more general, broad-based comments, concerns and issues in order to develop a general framework that can be applied by the management in professional team sports, for example, football. What becomes obvious during the interviews are that the management challenges of professional clubs seem ever to increase.

4 THE NETWORK OF VALUE CAPTURES IN FOOTBALL CLUB MANAGEMENT

To advance understanding of the distinctive features of the football business, we need to explore the unique management challenges of the game and to search for various ways in which football is organized and managed. We therefore developed a framework on

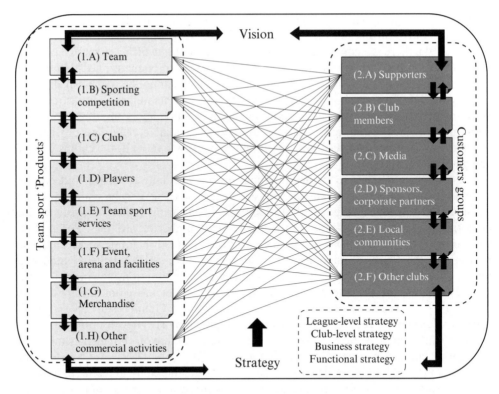

Figure 20.1   The network of value captures in professional team sports

football management by examining the following dimensions: (1) the product and its features, (2) the customers and (3) the business process, strategic vision and intent.

4.1   The Football Package – What is the Product?

Football does not offer a single product, service or entertainment. We can consider the following possible 'offerings', termed 'value captures': (1.A) team; (1.B) sporting competitions; (1.C) club; (1.D) players; (1.E) team sport services; (1.F) event, facilities and arena; (1.G) merchandise and (1.H) other commercial activities. The arrows in Figure 20.1 indicate that all value offerings are interlinked and might also be considered as bundles of a club's value captures.

Value capture 1.A: Team
Football is a team sport, however 11 skilled players do not necessarily comprise a winning team. A team with superior physical ability alone cannot beat an opponent that has good technique and a carefully planned strategy. Furthermore, without adequate training and performance techniques, even the most well-intentioned teams fail to win the match. Top players sometimes serve as a guiding light for the team, but their character, which stresses individuality, often does not gel with the role of a team leader.

A variety of models have been proposed and explored in the literature on organizational behaviour and personnel psychology to understand work team effectiveness in various industry settings (that is, Campion et al., 1993; Gladstein, 1984; Hackman, 1987; Hackman and Morris, 1975; McGrath, 1964) and their findings might be transferred to a team sport setting. LaFasto and Larson (2001) based their model for team effectiveness upon the insights they gained from investigating 600 teams in a variety of industries. On the basis of four necessary behaviours for members in a team setting – openness, supportiveness, action orientation and positive personal behaviour – they theorize that there are five fundamental questions which must be understood and actively managed to increase the likelihood of team effectiveness: (1) what constitutes a good team member – the abilities and behaviours that really matter? (2) What actions in a group foster effective team member relationships? (3) What behaviour of teams – as perceived by their members and leaders – causes some teams to be more successful than others at problem solving? (4) What behaviour of team leaders – as viewed by members of the team – foster team success or failure? (5) What organizational processes and practices promote clarity, confidence, and commitment in a team?

In addition, Hackman (2002) declared that a team is most likely to be effective when the following conditions are provided at a satisfactory level: (1) it is a real team rather than a team in name only (clear boundaries, clearly assigned authority, membership stability); (2) the team has a compelling direction for its work, with clear, challenging and consequential goals; (3) it has an enabling internal structure that facilitates team efforts and a code of conduct to be agreed upon; (4) the team operates within a supportive institutional context, in regard to adequate resources, rewards, information, education, intergroup organization; and (5) it has ample expert coaching in teamwork available to help team members to deal with potential issues or existing problems. Lencioni (2002) took a different approach, when hypothesizing that all teams have the potential to be dysfunctional. According to him it is critical to understand the different types and levels of dysfunction to improve the functioning of a team. In hierarchical order he developed five levels in his 'dysfunction model': dysfunction 1 (the basis) – absence of trust; dysfunction 2 – fear of conflict; dysfunction 3 – lack of commitment; dysfunction 4 – avoidance of accountability; and dysfunction 5 – inattention to results.

Despite the approaches mentioned above, still several gaps remain in transferring those theories to professional football, as many researchers have argued that their findings may be very context sensitive (for example, Campion et al., 1996; Janz et al., 1997; McGrath, 1984) and related to the configuration of the team (for example, Hackman and Oldham, 1980). According to Gréhaigne et al. (2001) when it comes to configuration of teams in sports, elements relating to its perception and interpretation and the ensuing anticipation and decision-making are of the most importance. In connection with teaching-learning settings, observation and verbalization are presented as key strategies for eliciting critical thinking and the development of strategic and tactical knowledge (Gréhaigne et al., 2005; Griffin et al., 1997). There is also emprical evidence that the atmosphere within the team might be much more important in team sports than in an industry setting. We might conclude, that 'fail factors' of football teams might also be related to the nature of the football game and the dynamic of the team in regards to the design (for example, independence from the club owners), process (for example, cooperation between the players, between players and coach) and contextual variables (for example, adequate resources like players in reserve).

Value capture 1.B: Sporting competitions
Football as a team sport also requires coordination among the contesting teams, because the game involves at least two distinct teams, which must agree on the rules of the game. Theoretically those decisions could be made by the contesting teams on a game-by-game basis. However, if several teams play against each other, clubs as hosts for teams and a league need to be organized in order to be efficient, and rules must be adopted to determine the champion (Késenne, 1996). Revising the arguments for the necessary institutional features of a league (see Kipker and Parensen, 1999; Noll, 2003a, 2003b; Smith and Westerbeek, 2004), we prefer to change perspective and to focus on the following elements of sporting competitions, which club managers should keep in mind for successfully promoting their club:

1. Distribution: how to schedule matches or tournaments to determine the champion and how to bring the game to the market.
2. Hierarchy: what are structural pathways for players and teams to progress and regress between different leagues of lesser and greater quality.
3. Multiplicity: how many leagues should be at the same level of hierarchy (that is, unified league structures or geographically distinct divisions).
4. Membership: what are the conditions under which a team enters and exits a league (performance-linked open leagues or closed leagues, which offer no opportunity for additional teams to join).
5. Governance: how are league rules decided and enforced as well as controlling of the economic behaviour of its members handled;
6. Labour: what is the structure of the transfer market and how to determine the level of compensation to players, coaches and managers.

Value capture 1.C: Club
Hosting a winning team has a dual meaning for professional sports organizations. Not only must the players on the sporting team be able to give their utmost to the cause of winning, but the financial and organizational structure behind it must also work closely to ensure that its business goals will be achieved (thus referring to the contextual factors of team effectiveness, see 1.A). European football clubs were largely owned and run as a hobby, until the 1980s, by each club's president, who were very wealthy men who held other large business interests. Those presidents did invest money in 'their club' for such psychological reasons as 'the urge for power, the desire for prestige, the propensity to group identification and the related feeling of group loyalty' (Hamil, 1999: 24). By adhering to such a 'vision', it is not surprising that the management techniques employed by many football clubs had remained virtually unchanged for decades. Cheffins (1997a: 75) adds that the marketing strategies of the football clubs surveyed were 'unsophisticated', their internal cost controls had been 'slack' and their accountancy practices had been 'archaic, village hall stuff'.

However, old prejudices against professionalism continued to give way in the 1990s by the advent of television in sports, free market arguments and governing regulatory interventions (Gratton and Solberg, 2013, in this volume; King, 1998; Walters and Hamil, 2013, in this volume). Television contracts involved millions of euros and the medium's requirements affected the following factors:

1. Increasing broadcasting revenues and competition for available resources leads to growing power of professional football clubs vis-á-vis the amateur game (refer also to value capture 2.C). In total, the big five European football leagues (England's Premier League, Germany's Bundesliga, Italy's Serie A, Spain's La Liga and France's Ligue 1) generated revenues of €7900 million in 2008/09 (€6300 million in 2004/05 (Jones et al., 2006)). The combined revenue of the top 20 European football clubs broke the €3 billion barrier after growing by 6 per cent annually in recent years (Dolles and Söderman, 2011c).

2. By being subject to the force of the market and adopting management practices of successful contemporary business, some football clubs in the major European leagues turned into public limited companies quoted on the stock exchange (Andreff, 2006; Baur and McKeating, 2009; Berument et al., 2006; Conn, 1999; FGRC, 2004; Hamil et al., 2000; Michie, 1999; Michie and Ramalingham, 1999; Samagaio et al., 2009). This development is not exclusively visible in the big five European football leagues, as some football clubs throughout Europe have transformed into profit-generating entities, for example in Portugal the two major football clubs – Sporting and Porto – changed into publicly listed companies in 1997 (Duque and Ferreira, 2007).

3. The relationship with the clubs' fans needs to reflect increasing diversity and geographic and psychic spread (refer to the discussion value capture 2.A and 2.B). By moving towards a public limited company, clubs also need to (re-)consider their governance structure (Margalit, 2009) by conceptualizing the role of different groups of fans and integrating their formal voice in the decision-making power of the club.

4. Players (also value capture 1.D) benefited from this state of affairs, although they had little control over how leagues or teams were run, their salaries came close to those of chief executive officers of large corporations. Sport agencies and the players' agents they employ occupy a controversial position in this development. At the micro-level, criticism is directed by the FGRC (2003) towards certain individual agents with regard to the amount that they negotiate from brokering deals. At the macro-level, if a player's agent is looking to achieve maximum returns, they may encourage a player to move clubs frequently (ibid.).

Value capture 1.D: Players
Players and their development are of prime concern to football managers. Football clubs send out their scouts to discover young players in the region and to sign contracts with them, as some of them might later find their way to a professional team. For example, David Beckham first signed a trainee's contract with Manchester United in 1991 and made his League debut in 1995, aged 19. In 2003, he signed a four-year contract with Real Madrid, potentially worth up to €35 million. Beckham's contract with the Los Angeles Galaxy, effective 1 July 2007, gave him the highest salary in Major League Soccer (MLS) (Francis, 2011). Player migrations such as this were further exacerbated by the Bosman Ruling in 1995 which increased the movement of professional football players from one club to another when their contract term ended with their present team (for example, Büch, 1998; Campell and Sloane, 1997; Stopper, 2004). Haan et al. (2002) as well as Binder and Findlay (2009) conclude that at club level, there is little evidence that the competitive balance of the domestic leagues in Europe was harmed by the Bosman Ruling, however international quality differences did increase as a result.

Driven by the Bosman Ruling, the rise in transfer fees of players, and the increase in value of young players, professional football clubs in European leagues started to operate Youth Academies (refer also to value capture 1.F). British players, such as Wayne Rooney and James Vaughan, are just examples of former students that have graduated through the Premier League club's academy system. Football youth academies are considered as a move toward more professional structures for coaching, recruitment, medical and sports science support, administration, education and welfare. The following statement of England's Everton Football Club – one of the forerunners in this development – underlines the commitment of the club towards the youth academy:

> As Manager of Everton Football Club I am aware of the strong tradition of youth development and I will play my part in providing the opportunity for the young players to progress into the first team. Our supporters appreciate the attitude and commitment shown by home produced players and their enthusiasm often rubs off on their team-mates. (Moyes, 2011)

The overall benefits of establishing a youth academy for a football club are summarized by Dolles and Schweizer (2010) as follows: (1) To identify and develop players for the first team squad and to train them to make professional football their first career; (2) to develop players in order to save the club expenditure otherwise spent on transfer fees; (3) to develop players who can earn the club revenue through transfer fees; (4) to prepare players also to make a career outside football, and (5) to offer all players of all youth ages and nationalities an opportunity to experience the best development programme possible.

Value capture 1.E: Team sport services
Football services are considered a rather new development in the commercial activities of a club (Dolles and Schweizer, 2010) and cover three different areas. First, the idea of a one-stop shop for all club related services and merchandizing products, that is, anything from ticketing, organized fan tours to discount offers in collaboration with sponsoring partners (refer also to value capture 1.G). Second, the establishment of football youth academies as a service to recruit and retain talented young players (refer also to value capture 1.D and 1.F). Third, specialized tailored services offered as a development programme for other football clubs, coaches and players all over the world.

The latter is best explained by taking the English Premier League club Everton FC and its 'Everton Way' (ibid.; Everton FC, 2011). The online football services are a spin-off of Everton's youth academy and its Elite Player Development Programme. They are developed as an online training tool that supports coaches at all levels on how one can get the best from individual players, and how players can learn how to develop on their own. The programme includes: recruitment techniques, technical football coaching and fitness tips, physiotherapy, sports psychology, as well as education and welfare. The services include various presentation forms, such as video clips, audio commentary, editorial walkthroughs and diagrams, and are recommended as tactical advice and soccer coaching tips to comprehensively reveal the club's proven techniques, transforming schoolboys to professional football players. Furthermore, audio commentary and editorials are continuously updated to reveal more coaching sessions, exercises and physiotherapy treatment sessions. Regarding the latter, the site for example offers advice on how Everton diagnoses, treats and rehabilitates their players through common injuries in the game. The programme is promoted and sold on the club's website for an annual subscription.

In conclusion, team sport services are a strategic option to support scouting and recruiting activities of the club and a way to spread the club's coaching and training practice internationally. On the basis of subscription agreements, international partnerships could be initiated aiming to further promote the club on the international level. Supporting subscribing partner club's activities in specific regions might also be beneficial to attract international sponsorship and international fans. Conversely, using a subscription model runs the risk of connecting the success of a club on the pitch to performance of the team, and thus a club might face difficulties in maintaining subscriber membership if its performance fails.

Value capture 1.F: Event, arena and facilities
A sporting event (football match) is intangible, short-lived, unpredictable and subjective in nature (Couvelaere and Richelieu, 2005; Gladden et al., 1998; Holbrook and Hirschman, 1982; Levitt, 1981). It is produced and consumed by the spectators in the arena at the same time, mostly with a strong emotional commitment from the fans. In recent years those football games have been transformed into media events for the benefits of millions of spectators, few of whom were in attendance at the live event. The growth of 'second-hand', or vicarious experiences, is huge. Television recordings also serve as permanent library records. Such mediatized events affect even the stadium or arena they are attached to, attaining the power to transform ordinary places into special sites. Today, forced by media and regulations by the football governing bodies, arenas of most of the top clubs represent the state of the art in sports-leisure multiplex architecture (Dietl and Pauli, 2002; see also Helleu and Desbordes, 2013, in this volume).

As a consequence, facility management has become a major part in the clubs managerial tasks and adds on the expenditures (Crompton, 1995; Noll and Zimbalist, 1997; Pauli, 2002; Schwarz et al., 2010; Zimmermann, 1997). In recent years, club management has also become increasingly concerned with the environmental impact of sporting events, the arena and training facilities in regard to water treatment, waste avoidance and recycling, energy consumption and transportation issues. Energy costs are the largest expenditure in arena operations (heating of the building and the football pitch, air-conditioning, light management), followed by the costs of potable water (water fit for drinking, sprinkling pitches and external areas, for flushing toilets and for cleaning purposes), the costs of wastewater and the costs of waste disposal (Dolles and Söderman, 2010). Costs of potable water, energy and waste treatment increased continually over many years around the globe. Capital expenditure on energy and water saving investments as well as into waste avoidance and recycling practices is soon to be recouped through reduced operating costs. Moreover, capital expenditures will be recouped sooner the more expensive water and energy consumption as well as waste treatment will become in the future. Currently, the idea of environmentally friendly sporting events, arenas and training facilities has become the predominant issue in sports facility management (ibid., also Andersson, 2013, on measuring impact, in this volume). Therefore, environmental management competence in arena management needs to be strengthened, as it was only a few years ago when the arenas in Nuremberg and Munich (both

Germany) became the first football stadiums in Europe adopting the eco-management and audit scheme (Environment Management System, 2010), while at the same time the German football arenas in Hamburg and Gelsenkirchen introduced the ÖKOPROFIT environmental management system (ECOlogical PROject For Integrated Environmental Technology, 2010).

By taking English football as an example, the majority of arenas and training facilities are still owned by the football clubs (53 per cent; see FGRC, 2002: 19). Creating revenues from selling those assets to investors leaves the football club with a position in the league, but no home in the community where the club was established. The story about Wimbledon FC might be a warning example of too strong commercialization (FGRC, 2002: 19; Woodman, 2011). Sam Hammam, the previous owner of Wimbledon FC, sold the Plough Lane home ground of the club to the supermarket chain Safeway for €12.7 million in 2001, leaving the club without a home and forced to relocate to Milton Keynes. The club was then sold to Norwegian businessmen and the previous owner bought another club in Cardiff, without any investment in a new facility in Milton Keynes. Rather than cultivate its own team from grass roots, the Milton Keynes Council saw an opportunity to buy one ready-made franchise. A multimillion pound consortium representing the town as well as IKEA and ASDA-Walmart, proposed a new retail park complete with football stadium for the franchised club. The sale of the ground and the club, followed by the move to Milton Keynes, removed Wimbledon FC from the community it had traditionally served, which subsequently led to the first big business football franchise created in English football: the renamed Milton Keynes Dons FC. The fans of Wimbledon FC however did not accept the move and did not start commuting 100 miles every Saturday to watch 'their' team. Instead, they founded a new community-owned football club, AFC Wimbledon, starting from the very bottom league again. Woodman (2011) emphasizes that during their re-building process AFC Wimbledon has been watched by average crowds of nearly 5000 supporters, and the Wimbledon community has engaged in continuous fundraising that culminated in buying a new home ground for 'their' football club. By acting together, the fans and the community have demonstrated, in this case, that football at its best can still be an expression of community spirit (see value capture 2.E).

The leasing of the ground by a football club from a third party is also becoming increasingly common, according to the FGRC (2002: 20) as an alternative to mortgaging the property in order to alleviate long-term debt. The value of the arena and the ground in a sale and leaseback is likely to be considerably less than the total cost of buying the freehold and arena construction. The arena itself is of value only for the football club; its value for commercial institutions is the land on which the arena is built, and the commercial value for redevelopment (see value capture 1.H.). The FGRC (2002: 21) concludes, that in the case of football clubs, ownership and security of the ground is essential to long-term health, which can be jeopardized by selling the ground.

Value capture 1.G: Merchandise
The Penrosian tradition (Penrose, 1959; Prahalad and Hamel, 1990) reflects the traditional marketing focus on the firm's core competences combined with opportunities in the external environment. When considering the implication of product positioning, it is important to realize that positioning can vary from market to market because the

target customers for the product may differ from country to country. In confirming the positioning of a product or a service in a specific market or region, it is therefore necessary to establish from the consumer's perception exactly what the product stands for and how it differs from existing and potential competition. In developing a market specific product positioning, the firm can focus upon one or more elements of the total product offer so that the differentiation might be based upon price and quality, on one or more attributes, on a specific application, on a target consumer or on direct comparison with one competitor. Building and properly managing brand equity has therefore become a priority for companies of all sizes, in all types of industries in all types of markets. After all, from strong brand equity flows customer loyalty and profits (Aaker, 1996; Keller, 2000). The rewards of having a strong brand are clear and the football business seems to be no exception (refer, for example, to Couvelaere and Richelieu, 2005; Mohr and Bohl, 2001; Mohr and Merget, 2004; Woratschek and Popp, 2010).

However, we see the parameters in football are singularly different from those in manufacturing or other services, as the very nature of the game enhances the risks. A main factor in uncertainty is also found in the definition of the market; football is a series of markets as developed in our framework. One of the key ingredients of the business of football is its local character, yet one that participates in a global football market; this presents special challenges to marketing the brand. Simply put, the brand is standing for everything about a football club, from the team to its players, which is communicated by the name and related identifiers (football merchandise). Football merchandise, means goods held for resale but not manufactured by the football club, such as flags and banners, scarves and caps, training gear, jerseys and fleeces, footballs, videos and DVDs, blankets and pillows, watches, lamps, tables, clocks and signs.

Value capture 1.H: Other commercial activities

Chadwick and Clowes (1998) explored brand extension strategies by Premier League football clubs, by examining factors which have led clubs to consider extending their product lines and their brands further. They concluded as the key consideration for both clubs and their supporters that there is a clear and obvious link between the club's brand and the extension. Consistency between the clubs' core brand and the extension or a high degree of similarity between the core brand and the extended product/service is of importance. For further extensions, beyond the core product, they emphasize the effects that this might have on the credibility of the club brand. For example, both club supporters and general consumers may not make the connection between the core product 'football' and property investment or other experience industries. Many football clubs around the world are embedded in different service and product structures for various reasons. Take the Danish club Brøndby IF as example. The club invested in the early 1990s heavily in the stock market, in property, and in banking. The case study by Madsen (1993) explains, that after initially being very successful, Brøndby IF failed and was salvaged from bankruptcy in 1992 by benevolent creditors.

Another Danish club, FC Copenhagen, and its charismatic leader and businessman Flemming Østergaard, however embarked on a similar brand extension strategy at the end of the 1990s with more success. FC Copenhagen bought Parken, the Danish national stadium, took up property investments, and bought a chain of fitness centres (www.fitness.dk), along with two large vacation resorts, one of them close to the Legoland Theme Park in Billung (Storm, 2009). Besides hosting football events, the renovated Parken arena has been developed as a prime location for concerts, boxing events and speedway competitions, thus generating additional revenue streams, even larger than the initial football business. Gammelsæter et al. (2011) add that FC Copenhagen's business success increased the enthusiasm in Danish football for brand extensions. For example, in 2007 Odense Boldklub merged with a local congress centre to expand its domain of business to concerts, conferences and other experience-based activities. They believed that this would enhance Odense's economic potential. The strategic decision was reinforced by its sporting success in the following season. It seems that the transfer of revenues from other business areas into the core 'football' business increased the likelihood of acceptance by supporters. It is therefore a matter for clubs that the introduction and exploitation of extensions should retain a degree of focus and familiarity for the benefit of the club and consumers. However it needs to be mentioned that the development of brand extensions also depends on the national governance structures of the game, seeing the commercial model adopted in Danish sport as just one example with only a few restrictions on external shareholding and floating (ibid.; Storm, 2010, 2011).

4.2 Who 'Buys' Football – How to Define the Customers?

Why do supporters choose one team over another? Cost is certainly not the sole argument in the football business for fans, whereas fun, excitement, skilled players and regional embeddedness might be all good reasons for supporting a team. The bottom line may be the corporate culture of the football club as the underlying culture helps to determine the value that consumers place on the football club; however, we need to recognize that every customer integrates multiple markets. Consumers want different offerings at different times under different circumstances. Consequently, the variety of offerings creates a broader consumer approach in football by addressing (2.A) spectators and supporters (fan base), (2.B) club members (club membership), (2.C) media, (2.D) sponsors and corporate partners, (2.E) local communities and (2.F.) other clubs. Arrows in Figure 20.1 indicate that all customer groups are interlinked and can also be considered as bundles of a club's value captures.

This classification, its development and shift towards increased media and commercial revenues during recent years is illustrated through examination of the main figures, in the revenues of professional football clubs. If we compare Manchester United's 2002 and 2010 figures, as an example, (2.A and 2.B) match day revenues (gate receipts, season tickets and OneUnited memberships) accounts for €76.3 million (2002) and €117.7 million (2010); (2.C) media revenue (broadcasting domestic and international competitions) for €70.4 million (2002) and €123.1 million (2010); (2.D) commercial revenues (sponsorship and merchandising) for €40 million (2002) and €95.2 million (2010); (2.F) profit player sales to other clubs €3.6 million (2001), €26.6 million (2002), €94 million (2009) and €14.8 million (2010) give a total group turnover of €198 million (2002) and €350.8 million (2010) (BBC, 2011; CNN, 2002; Dolles and Söderman, 2008; Stone, 2011). We also added (2.E) local communities as those are the home base of a football club and often serve as a lender of last resort in times of financial trouble.

Value capture 2.A: Supporters

When it comes to 'sales' in the football business, the supporters, with regard to ticket sales and merchandising, create the main attention. According to Fisher and Wakefield (1998) fan motivation and subsequent behaviour goes beyond the record of the team and, at times, seems unrelated to performance. Football without fans with a shared emotional investment in their team's performance, and an emotional investment in the failure of their competitors, does not work – either as a human experience or as a commercial venture (Hamil, 1999; Ozawa et al., 2004). This makes the football business different from conventional marketplaces. Cheffins (1997b: 109) quotes a Newcastle United fan saying after the club's managing director had drawn parallels between shopping at Safeway and following Newcastle United: 'I don't go around wearing Safeway replica shirts. I don't wait for hours to get on a coach to go and see Safeway in other parts of the country. I don't pay GBP340 for a season ticket to go to Safeway.'

Fan motivation and behaviour vary depending upon the type of fan. Therefore Hunt et al. (1999) propose five different types of fans: the temporary fan, the local fan, the devoted fan, the fanatical fan and the dysfunctional fan. There is also an extensive literature on gender differences investigating different motives for becoming a fan and consumer behaviour (Dietz-Uhler et al., 2000a, 2000b; James and Ridinger, 2002). For our purposes, we adopt a slightly different classification by introducing the 'psychic distance' dimension, defined as factors that make it difficult to understand the local embeddednes of a club and the 'geographic distance': local fans and international fans. 'Local fans' exhibit their behaviour because of identification with a geographic area, and either born, living or staying in the home region of the club. We further distinguish three groups among the local fans: 'core fans', attending home and away matches; 'regular fans', attending most home matches but less likely away matches; and 'occasional supporters', attending some matches each season. The commitment to the club is total in the first group and they regard themselves as the only real fans. The second group is an aged offshoot of the first group and most season ticket holders are to be found among them. The irregularity of match attendance of the third group is due to moving away from the home town, working commitments, financial reasons or disappointment about the team's performance. Fans abroad are 'international fans' who do not get many opportunities to see the team play live. Their attendance is mainly virtual, via the radio, television or Internet, and for this group of fans – if they do not have local roots – it is quite difficult to understand the local context and contextual regional decision-making (for example, when deciding on board room positions).

To reach the group of international fans and to raise the international profile of the club's brand, a different strategy compared to approaching local fans is needed. Exposure of football clubs playing friendlies, for example, in the Far East or recruitment of foreign players, enable the emergence of 'brand communities' abroad (Muniz and O'Guinn, 2001) in the football business. Expatriates might have a special role as 'boundary spanning agents' between both groups, as confirmed by Kerr et al. (2011) in their survey on foreign Ajax FC supporters. There is, however, a clear line of distinction between linking clubs' activities to a largely accepted broader process of globalization versus the progressive Americanization of sports. The American model of sports is characterized by Duke (2002) as more commercially oriented, with key roles for advertising, sponsorship and television. The primary function of sports team franchises is profit-making, which results in a different relationship between spectators and the team, whereby 'the discerning consumer replaces the committed fan' (ibid.: 5).

Value capture 2.B: Club members

The football club, as host of their teams, wants to have a sustainable stock of members, which requires an iterative approach between the product and the customer. Such approaches are covered in the vast literature on 'interactive marketing' and on 'customer driven product development' (Adler et al., 1996) and more and more in 'interactive marketing' or 'relationship marketing' (Bühler and Nufer, 2010; Gummesson, 2002; Lovelock et al., 2005; Nicole, 2000), meaning that marketing by a service firm that recognizes that perceived service quality depends heavily on the quality of buyer–seller interaction during the service encounter (Gummesson et al., 2010; Kotler and Armstrong, 2010). However, we see the parameters in football are singularly different from those in manufacturing or other services, as the very nature of the game enhances the risks. A main factor in uncertainty is also found in the definition of the market; football is a series of different markets presenting special challenges to marketing the brands. By focusing on club members which 'buy football' through its membership, we identify at least two distinct groups:

1. Football by nature is fun; it involves exercise and is competitive. For this reason, the football clubs facilitate opportunities for its *active members* to engage in exercise and to play football in a team. The Bayern Munich club, besides its professional team, hosts 20 other football teams: one semi-professional amateur team, three women's teams, five senior teams, and 165 players in 11 youth teams. Bayern Munich incorporates six other divisions besides football, whereby basketball is also played at professional level in Germany's top league.
2. Others may join the football club as *passive members* to support their favourite team. Bayern Munich has the largest club membership in the German Bundesliga of 162 187 (Bayern Munich, 2011). It is said that Manchester United has 333 million followers around the world (Anderson, 2008; Cass, 2007), including 193 million in Asia and 9.5 million Facebook followers. The club's worldwide fan base includes more than 200 officially recognized branches of the Manchester United Supporters Club in at least 24 countries. Manchester United's membership scheme, called 'OneUnited', is the club's preferred customer approach and, with 139 million subscribers, OneUnited is the largest membership scheme in English football.

Value capture 2.C: Media

With regard to income in professional football, the media is the other main customer – or the main sales channel. The importance of football for the media business can be seen in the increasing amounts of money paid for broadcast rights to the national league or for events such as the FIFA World Cup, as well as the growth in the number of sports-oriented radio talk shows and sports oriented television networks (Gratton and Solberg, 2007). These revenues can be positively affected by the competition between commercial broadcasters, but may result in strange outcomes, as in the Italian league, where there are often empty stands in the stadium, but the media is still willing to pay a lot for broadcasting. We also have seen cases, like in the English Premier League, where the fees for broadcasting rights declined instead of continuing to grow (Solberg and Haugen, 2013, in this volume). Rowe (1996, 2000) notes that sport and television have become mutually and internationally indispensable (similar Andreff, 2000). As mediatized events, football matches 'are privileged means of communication for businesses wishing to conquer new markets, improve their image, and enhance brand recognition' (Manzenreiter, 2004: 289).

However, football marketers also need to look ahead to the new 'attention age', or 'attention economy'. This age began with the emergence of social media in the first years of the twenty-first century (Sullivan, 2009), and is marked by the ability of individuals to become 'prosumers', to *produce*, con*sume* and distribute information instantly and freely as well as share it on the Internet using social media (Santomier and Hogan, 2013, in this volume). This changes the perspective as social media 'people don't go online to *give* attention, but to *get* it. They don't want to be part of the audience. They want to perform and to be heard, to be present.' (Kleiner, 2009: 3, original emphasis) Marketers will increasingly use the new media to interact with consumers directly, however, as explained by Santomier and Hogan (2013), conventional marketing efforts do not appear to be working (or are inappropriate) on the social Web and many businesses are still struggling to determine how to capitalize on digital marketing in the prosumer economy, in particular on what research to engage in and on what metrics (or e-metrics) to use. Kunz (2008) argues that marketers need to be savvy about the three modes or mindsets (that is, receiving, hunting and doing) people engage with when using interactive communications, and match business marketing strategies accordingly. He concludes 'the entire mindset of a person engaged on MySpace or LinkedIn is different from that of a hunter on a search engine. A Google user is walking into a store. A Facebook user is walking into a bar' (ibid.: 1).

Value capture 2.D: Sponsors and corporate partners

Football is a natural area for sponsorship as it carries very strong images, has a mass international audience and appeals to all classes (Ferrand and Pages, 1996). Each sponsored event is capable of reaching differently defined audiences (Javalgi et al., 1994; Meenaghan and Shipley, 1999; Söderman and Dolles, 2008, 2010; Thwaites, 1995). According to Chajet (1997), sponsorship has an increasing role to play in gaining entry to overseas markets. It can be a powerful means of enabling an organization to raise both its club brand and corporate brand, across new frontiers (Dolphin, 2003; Lund, 2010; McCosker, 2004). Commercial sponsorship represents one of the most rapidly growing sectors of marketing communications activity. In fact, with the exception of movie stars and singers, sports teams generate a stronger emotional response from fans than in any other industry (Meenaghan, 2001; Richelieu, 2003).

Sponsorship may therefore be selected as a strategic tool to shape and promote the image of football, the club and its sponsor partners in markets needing to be developed. Top European clubs aim to create global sponsorship alliances by seeking to encourage and reward investment in the club to the mutual advantage of both parties worldwide. A large number of club members with some similar traits constitute a good opportunity and a resource base for the management when they identify and negotiate new sponsorships. Club managers seem to develop a clear idea of the ideal composition of their cluster of sponsors. They need to identify and describe the optimal fit between existing market segments (club members) and the potential rewards of existing and potential sponsors. This business strategy is based on aligning with companies that could contribute to the club's fan base with added-value products and services which were previously unavailable to them, such as a WAP service to provide all the latest club news.

Value capture 2.E: Local communities
The relationship between football clubs and their communities has been subject of debate and discussion in political circles and in academic research (for example, Bale, 2000; Coalter, 2000; Dolles and Söderman, 2005a, 2011c; Jaquiss, 2001, 2003; Morrow and Hamil, 2003; Oughton et al., 2003; Williams et al., 2001). The case of Wimbledon FC introduced earlier in value capture 1.F serves as a good example of the converging interests of the different parties involved. Morrow (1999) argues that a football club's community is made up of two interrelated and often overlapping dimensions: 'first, a direct community of supporters and, second, a wider notion encompassing people and groups who can be affected either directly or indirectly by the existence and operation of a football club within a particular space, usually geographical, but also potentially religious or social' (Morrow and Hamil, 2003: 1–2). Both dimensions can be found in the Wimbledon FC case.

The focus on the relationship between football clubs and their local communities is also to some extent debt driven, when communities serve as a lender of last resort in times of financial trouble for football clubs. This can been seen in the case of the German club Karlsruher SC. In 1997 the club was sixth in Germany's top division and qualified for the UEFA Cup, but then the team fell apart the next season and dropped into the second division. Two years later it dropped another level to the Regional League. 'Cut off from TV revenue and deserted by many fans, the team reached the brink of insolvency in 2002 and had to be rescued by the city of Karlsruhe and local banks' (Ewing, 2004: 20). Shortly after the club returned to Germany's second division and back up to Germany's top division in 2007. Another example was demonstrated by Shimizu S-Pulse from the Japanese professional J-League, as reported in Manzenreiter (2004) and Moffett (2002). S-Pulse's holding company S-Rap, which made the same mistake of overspending and brought in top foreign players, as well as built a new training ground, thought this strategy would help to attract fans and turn S-Pulse into one of the top teams. Average arena attendance, however, fell during the latter half of the 1990s. By 1997 it had lost a cumulative total of US$23 million and S-Rap had to announce that the main shareholder TV Shizuoka would invest no new money. S-Pulse faced collapse and was only saved after fans collected 300 000 signatures and persuaded a local industry group to take over. Both cases show how football is firmly rooted in the local setting and a vital part of the cultural and social make-up of local communities, and as a result, community funds or pooled resources can be justifiably spent to keep clubs in business. In this sense football clubs remain largely untouchable by economic forces that determine the fate of other companies.

Value capture 2.F: Other football clubs
Other football clubs are of prime importance when it comes to player transfers as well as lending players as mentioned in the discussion of value capture (1.D). Additionally, by introducing team sport services as a value capture (1.E), we might consider other football

clubs – amateur as well as professional clubs and national as well as international – also as potential recipients of football services. And at the regional level, clubs are collaborating in player development in youth teams by providing football services in exchange.

On the international market we also see various ways toward collaborative agreements, for example, between the Japanese J-League 1 club Urawa Reds and Germany's Bayern Munich. This partnership was signed in January 2006 with the aim of (Urawa Reds, 2006): (1) playing team friendlies against each other in both countries and training camp cooperation for each team category (value captures 1.A, 1.D, 1.E, 1.F); (2) sharing scouting information (value capture 1.A, 1.D); (3) accepting each other's players for training and the development of exchange systems for youth players (1.D); (4) mutual merchandising support (1.G) and (5) cooperation for promotional activities (value captures 1.G, 2.A, 2.C, 2.D). Bayern Munich and Urawa Reds played friendlies in 2006 and 2008 and the Reds U-15 team visited Germany. Red Voltage, the official Urawa Reds shop, now has a corner dedicated to Bayern goods and the official Urawa Reds website is linked to Bayern's Japanese language page. Bayern Munich celebrated Urawa Reds' J-League championship victory in 2006 with a large-screen congratulatory message at their own home match at the Allianz Arena. The invitation for Urawa Reds to play in Austria was also orchestrated by Bayern Munich. Indications are that the further strengthening of exchange and meetings between club officials is set to make the partnership even closer.

4.3   Business Framework of Football – Vision and Strategy

A business framework is the entire system for delivering value to customers and earning a profit on that activity. It incorporates a set of assumptions about customers and economics, giving insight into how the firm/club expects to compete (Slywotzky et al., 1997). It must fit external reality and be internally consistent. For our purpose we will focus on the overall direction and ambition of a club (vision) as well as the strategy (where and how to compete).

3.A: Vision

The highest and broadest level business objective is the vision of the football club. This is a statement of broad aspiration, as it deals with where the club hopes to be in the future. The vision is concerned with the strategic intent of the club, by applying Hamel and Prahalad (1989, 1994) to the football business. This is not about winning the next game, it is the attempt by the club manager and/or the trainer to define where they expect the club to be in the future: to win the championship, to stay in the league, to make profit or to go international. With the exception of merchandising (value capture 1.G), the arena and training facilities (value capture 1.F), football services (value capture 1.E) and other commercial activities (to some extent, value capture 1.H), the football business lacks in its core business the option of producing and storing inventory for future sale, as the main characteristic of football is its ambiguity and the uncertainty of the outcome of a game.

3.B: Strategy

In order to reach the goals attached to the vision of where the club should be in the future, what kind of strategies should be applied? Strategies can be made for different activities within the club, where the lowest level of aggregation is one specific task, while the highest level of aggregation encompasses all activities within the club. The most common distinction between those levels of aggregation made in the strategic management literature is between the functional level (in regard to specific functions, such as marketing and financing), business level (in respect of a specific group of customers) and corporate level (aligning the various business level strategies, if an organization is involved in two or more businesses) (refer to De Wit and Meyer, 2004; Thompson, 2001). A logical extension of this distinction is to explicitly recognize the level of aggregation higher than that of the individual organization, as companies often cluster together into groups of collaborating organizations. This level is referred to by De Wit and Meyer (2004) as the network level of strategy.

By applying these level distinctions to the football business, we recognize that a few years ago the key success factor was the sport's performance, reducing all strategy levels to two questions: first, how to create a good player and, second, how to create a good team? Philippe Troussier states in his book on the relationship between those two objectives as a trainer: 'Sixty percent of my football is based on team play; the rest relies on individual talent' (Troussier, 2002: 56). However, owing to the nature of a game, even if the players have the physical ability and technique and form a strong team together, they will not necessarily win the match. The changing nature of the football business adds a third question to the two prevailing questions: how to manage the whole set of possible products and offerings?

1.   *'Create a good player.'* To develop a skilled player clubs needs to scout, recruit and train. The principle human resource question for the club is, to buy or to train and develop a player? To develop an in-house organization or to buy an accomplished 'ready-made' player from a different club at home or abroad, he should be physically checked and examined before the purchase.
2.   *'Create a team.'* Eleven skilled players constitute a team, but a team should be more than 11 good players. The trainer's competence, evaluation of the situation and relation with the players, and the players attitude to each other and the ability to get them to play for each other – all these elements contribute to a skilled team. All is open information to the public, and all steps are observed by the fans and the media. This makes (the transparent character of) football distinct from other branches and industries: trainer and players are always monitored, and the training methods applied are evaluated by the public. 'The fans in the stadium see themselves as actors. In one way or another, the fans relate to the team – as a spectator, newspaper reporter, TV analyst, coach, player or the club president. They all have their own idea about who should be in the team and what tactics should be used. They think they have the right to complain if a coach or a player fails to meet their standards' (Troussier, 2002: 115)
3.   *'Manage the whole set of possible products and offerings.'* The commercialiazation of the game requires management structures and techniques to manage the whole set of possible products and offerings on a corporate level with the current and potential financial resources. Presently, the football industry contrasts with the fundamental economic principle: success is in obtaining the biggest possible result with minimal financial effort. We may say that sport successes help to sell their own products and,

if they are valued, high revenues help to reach sport successes, but one condition is not enough to reach the other. At the network level of strategy, all clubs must necessarily interact with other clubs as football is a team sport. Clubs form leagues with a clear strategic intent and current lower-level squads are forced either to spend more on players and coaches, or to have no hope of being in contention for the championship. In our view, we might therefore conclude that the practice of football management is largely eclectic, as football managers need to be able to work across economic, technical, cultural and functional boundaries.

5   TEAM SPORT MANAGEMENT: THE NETWORK OF VALUE CAPTURES AS A MANAGEMENT TOOL AND A FRAMEWORK FOR FUTURE RESEARCH

Having combined the eight 'offerings' with the six groups of 'customers' 48 relations appear, showing the competitive scope of a football club. Each of these relations constitutes a value capturing activity through which a football club can create value and competitive advantage. Value capture 1.G meets value capture 2.A when 'merchandise products' are sold to 'supporters'. The 'players' (1.D) are of interest to 'sponsors and corporate partners' (2.D), to the 'media' (2.C), to 'local communities' (2.E) or to 'other clubs' (2.F). Thus, a mixture of such relations does constitute a network of value captures for the football industry, observing that not all value-capturing activities are equally important in every given situation. We also emphasize that the eight 'offerings' and the six 'customer groups' are interconnected among themselves. This broadens the choice of strategic options and allows strategies of bundling value captures (for example, when 'Players' (1.D), the 'team' (1.A) and the 'club' (1.C) are presented to the 'media' (2.C) or to 'sponsors and corporate partners' (2.E). The network of value captures framework can be applied at the level of the football industry, the level of strategic groups (for example, clubs in the first division compared to lower divisions, professional clubs against semi-professional institutions) or the individual club. Its ultimate function is to explore and explain the sustainability of competitive advantage in the management of professional football.

Drawing on recent research, some parts of our framework can be filled in, as for example in Schlesinger (2013, in this volume) investigating the relationships between 'fan identity' (2.A and B), a 'club' (1.C) and sponsorship effectiveness (2.E) or O'Reilly (2013 in this volume) concepualizing 'player risks' (1.D), 'facility risks' (1.C and 1.F) and their value as 'corporate partnership assets' (2.D). Many unanswered questions remain, however, we will highlight in the following some of the most important of them. The challenge for future research in this field will be both conceptual – where recent approaches into marketing and networks (for example, Gummesson, 2007; Grönroos, 2011) will be used to align our approach – but also empirical. The research tasks in the latter might resist into developing measurements, creating scores and describing exchange standards to further analyse the relationships between the value captures. There is thus a need to further operationalize each of the 14 value captures (eight 'offerings' with the six groups of 'customers'), the basic 48 dual value-capturing activities and combined strategies using bundles of value-captures. It is also important to further investigate how to measure the size of these value captures (in monetary and non-monetary terms), the importance of value-capturing activities and their growth potential. We thus suggest research on perceived value for each customer group and how specific value can be created. What might be a value for one customer group might not be perceived as valuable for another customer group, see, for example, acceptance of jersey sponsors, selling the naming rights of the stadium, and so on. There also might be tensions between the different value captures, for example, individual players versus the team spirit or the development of VIP lounges versus standing rows. It also needs to be explored how value is to be co-created between sets of value captures. Is there empirical evidence – exemplified in single and multiple case studies or by large-scale quantitative surveys – whether certain combinations of value captures are more successful than others, measured on a clubs' success during one season or longitudinal. Are we able to define 'minimum standards' to each value capture or to each value capturing activity of our framework, thus enabling the club management to benchmark with other clubs (developing an expert system) – nationally or internationally? The speed of commercialization as well as internationalization also needs to be elaborated for each value capture and value capturing activity.

By adding the strategy dimension to our framework of value captures, we introduce the vision and imagination of the future of the game, which influences the football package. The multiple dimensions of the football package are central to the level of strategy aggregation. The network level of strategy is, for example, closely connected with the league's procedures of promotion and relegation (1.B), the costs of scheduling games (1.C), requirements to develop their arenas (1.F) or a regulated labour market for player movements (1.D). Research questions in this regard might focus on the execution of different strategies, including relevant combination of value captures in regard to the standing of a club during a season or the level of competition (international, first league, lower leagues). Clubs also might be equally successful in the long run but focusing on different combinations of value captures, for example, a young talent development strategy versus a highly selective buying strategy of ready-made players.

Furthermore, the framework draws on the condition that professional football is embedded in the socio-cultural environment in which football has evolved, is performed, is sold and is consumed. Research questions in this regard might be focusing on international comparisons, as such, are all value captures equally important in different football cultures? Do we find differences between the big five European football leagues (England's Premier League, Germany's Bundesliga, Italy's Serie A, Spain's La Liga and France's Ligue 1) and smaller leagues, like the Scandinavian ones or the Dutch league? Does the network of value captures also apply to clubs and/or leagues in Asia, Southern America, North America or Australia/New Zealand?

Although developed in the football industry, our framework is purposely named 'a network of value captures in professional team sports'. The question remains on the industry level or the level of broader generalization. We thereby encourage studies to compare the business of football with other professional team sports, such as ice hockey, basketball, field hockey, handball or cricket, by applying our framework. In this sense, our network of value captures aims to link context, practices and institutions of the business of sports, and at the same time responds to the call for building theoretical models in sports management.

NOTE

1. This chapter is a completely revised and largely updated version of our article 'The network of value captures: creating competitive advantage in football management', first published in *Wirtschaftspolitische Blätter Österreich* [*Austrian Economic Policy Papers*, ISSN 1605–8704], vol. 55 (2008), no.1 (April), pp. 39–58. We are grateful for receiving the permission to use parts of this article by MANZ'sche Verlags- und Universitätsbuchhandlung GmbH (Vienna), Verlagsredaktion ZVB & WPBl.

REFERENCES

Aaker, D. (1996), *Building Strong Brands*, New York: Free Press.

Adler, P.S., Mandelbaum, A., Nguyen, U. and Schwerer, E. (1996), Getting the most out of your product development process, *Harvard Business Review*, **74** (2), 134–52.

Anderson, D. (2008), Man Utd's 333M fans, *Daily Mirror*, 8 January, available at: http://www.mirror.co.uk/sport-old/football/2008/01/08/man-utd-s-333m-fans-115875-20278453/ (accessed 14 December 2011).

Andersson,T. (2013), Triple impact assessments of sport events, in S. Söderman and H. Dolles (eds), *Handbook of Research on Sport and Business*, Cheltenham, UK and Northampton, MA, USA: Edward Elgar, pp. 237–56.

Andreff, W. (2000), Financing modern sport in the face of a sporting ethic, *European Journal for Sport Management*, **7** (1), 5–30.

Andreff, W. (2006), New perspectives in sports economics: a European view, International Association of Sports Economists working paper series, no. 06–05, available at: http://college.holycross.edu/RePEc/spe/Andreff_NewPerspectives.pdf (accessed 6 August 2011).

Arnould, E.J., Price, L.L. and Malshe, A. (2006), Toward a cultural resource-based theory of the customer, in S. Vargo and R. Lusch (eds), *The Service-dominant Logic of Marketing: Dialog, Debate and Directions*, Armonk, NY: ME Sharpe, pp. 320–33.

Bale, J. (2000), The changing face of football: stadiums and communities, in J. Garland, D. Malcolm and M. Rowe (eds), *The Future of Football: Challenges for the Twenty-first Century*, London: Frank Cass, pp. 91–101.

Barney, J. (1991), Firm resources and sustained competitive advantage, *Journal of Management*, **17** (1), 99–120.

Baur, D. and McKeating, C. (2009), The benefits of financial markets: a case study of European football clubs, DCU Business School Research Paper Series, no. 45 (May), Dublin: Dublin City University, available at: http://doras.dcu.ie/4586/1/DCUBS_Research_Paper_Series_45.pdf (accessed 14 December 2011).

Bayern Munich (2011), FCB posts profit for 18th year in a row, available at: http://www.fcbayern.telekom.de/en/news/news/2010/26911.php (accessed 14 December 2011).

BBC (2011), Glazers deny Man United sale as strong figures revealed, *BBC News*, 25 February, available at: http://www.bbc.co.uk/news/business-12578645 (accessed 13 December 2011).

Berument, H., Ceylan, N.B. and Gozpinar, E. (2006), Performance of soccer on the stock market: evidence from Turkey, *Social Sciences Journal*, **43** (4), 695–99.

Binder, J. and Findlay, M. (2009), The effects of the Bosman Ruling on national and club teams in Europe, *Social Science Research Network*, 29 May, available at: http://ssrn.com/abstract=1317204 (accessed 6 August 2011).

Büch, M.P. (1998), Das 'Bosman-Urteil' – Transferentschädigungen, Ablösesummen, Eigentumsrechte, Freizügigkeit [The 'Bosman Ruling' – transfer payments, property rights, freedom of movement], *Sportwissenschaft*, **28** (3–4), 283–96.

Bühler, A. and Nufer, G. (2010), *Relationship Marketing in Sports*, Oxford: Butterworth-Heinemann.

Campbell, A. and Sloane, P.J. (1997), The implications of the Bosman Case of professional football, Discussion Paper 97–02, Aberdeen: University of Aberdeen.

Campion, M.A., Medsker, G.J. and Higgs, A.C. (1993), Relations between work team characteristics and effectiveness: implications for designing effective work groups, *Personnel Psychology*, **46** (4), 823–50.

Campion, M.A., Papper, E.M. and Medsker, G.J. (1996), Relations between work team characteristics and effectiveness: a replication and extension, *Personnel Psychology*, **49** (2), 429–52.

Cass, B. (2007), United moving down south as fanbase reaches 333 million, *Daily Mail Online*, 15 December 2007, available at: http://www.dailymail.co.uk/sport/football/article-502574/United-moving-south-fanbase-reaches-333-million.html#ixzz1gWEp5jmK (accessed 15 July 2011).

Chadwick, S. and Clowes, J. (1998), The use of extension strategies by clubs in the English Football Premier League, *Managing Leisure*, **3** (4), 194–203.

Chajet, C. (1997), Corporate reputation and the bottom line, *Corporate Reputation Review*, **1** (1–2), 19–23.
Cheffins, B. (1997a), UK football clubs and the stock market: past developments and future prospects (Part 1), *The Company Lawyer*, **18** (3), 66–76.
Cheffins, B. (1997b), UK football clubs and the stock market: past developments and future prospects (Part 2), *The Company Lawyer*, **18** (4), 104–11.
CNN (2002), Player sales boost Man Utd, *CNN.com Business*, 30 September, available at: http://edition.cnn.com/2002/BUSINESS/09/30/manutd (accessed 13 December 2011).
Coalter, F. (2000), *The Role of Sport in Regenerating Deprived Urban Areas*, Edinburgh: Scottish Executive Central Research Unit.
Conn, D. (1999), The new commercialism, in S. Hamil, J. Michie and C. Oughton (eds), *A Game of Two Halves: The Business of Football*, Edinburgh: Mainstream, pp. 40–55.
Couvelaere, V. and Richelieu, A. (2005), Brand strategy in professional sports: the case of French soccer teams, *European Sport Management Quarterly*, **5** (1), 23–46.
Crompton, J.L. (1995), Economic impact analysis of sports facilities and events: eleven sources of misapplication, *Journal of Sport Management*, **9** (1), 14–35.
De Witt, B. and Meyer, R. (2004), *Strategy – Process, Content, Context*, 3rd edn, London: Thomson.
Dietl, H. and Pauli, M. (2002), Die Finanzierung von Fußballstadien – Überlegungen am Beispiel des deutschen Profifußballs [Financing football stadia – reflections by taking the German professional football as an example], *Zeitschrift für Betriebswirtschaft*, special issue 4, 239–62.
Dietz-Uhler, B., End, C., Jacquemotte, L., Bentley, M. and Hurlbut, V. (2000a), Perceptions of male and female sport fans, *International Sport Journal*, **4**, 88–97.
Dietz-Uhler, B., Harrick, E.A., End, C. and Jacquemotte, L. (2000b), Sex differences in sport fan behavior and reasons for being a sport fan, *Journal of Sport Behaviour*, **8** (3), 219–31.
Dolles, H. and Schweizer, R. (2010), Advancing the network of value captures in the football business: the Everton Football Club case, *European Academy of Management 10th Annual Meeting*, Rome: Tor Vergata University, available at: http://www.euram2010.org (accessed 20 June 2010).
Dolles, H. and Söderman, S. (2005a), Implementing a professional football league in Japan – challenges to research in international business, *DIJ Working Paper*, no. 05/6, Tokyo: German Institute for Japanese Studies.
Dolles, H. and Söderman, S. (2005b), Ahead of the game – the network of value captures in professional football, *DIJ Working Paper*, no. 05/5, Tokyo: German Institute for Japanese Studies.
Dolles, H. and Söderman, S. (2006), Ahead of the game – the network of value captures in professional football, working paper, Stockholm University, Business School.
Dolles, H. and Söderman, S. (2008), The network of value captures: creating competitive advantage in football management, *Wirtschaftspolitische Blätter Österreich* [*Austrian Economic Policy Papers*], **55** (1), 39–58.
Dolles, H. and Söderman, S. (2010), Addressing ecology and sustainability in mega-sporting events: the 2006 Football World Cup in Germany, *Journal of Management and Organisation*, **16** (4), 587–600.
Dolles, H. and Söderman, S. (2011a), Learning from success: implementing a professional football league in Japan, in H. Dolles and S. Söderman (eds), *Sport as a Business: International, Professional and Commercial Aspects*, Basingstoke: Palgrave Macmillan, pp. 228–50.
Dolles, H. and Söderman, S. (2011b), プロ・サッカーのマネジメントにおける経済価値獲得のネットワーク一日本プロ・サッカー・リーグ発展の分析一 [The network of economic value captures in professional football management: analyzing the development of the Japanese professional soccer league], *Shōgaku Ronsan, The Journal of Commerce*, **40** (1–2), 195–232.
Dolles, H. and Söderman, S. (2011c), Sport as a business: introduction, in H. Dolles and S. Söderman (eds), *Sport as a Business: International, Professional and Commercial Aspects*, Basingstoke: Palgrave Macmillan, pp. 1–12.
Dolphin, R. (2003), Sponsorship: perspectives on its strategic role, *Corporate Communications: An International Journal*, **8** (3), 173–86.
Duke, V. (2002), Local tradition versus globalisation: resistance to the McDonaldisation and Disneyisation of professional football in England, *Football Studies*, **5** (1), 5–23.
Duque, J. and Ferreira, N.A. (2007), Explaining share price performance of football clubs listed on the Euronext Lisbon, *Working Paper Series*, Lisbon: Technical University of Lisbon.
ECOlogical PROject For Integrated Environmental Technology (2010), ECOPROFIT. The idea, available at: http://www.oekoprofit.com/about/ (accessed 16 October 2010).
Environment Management System (2010), EMAS – the credible environmental management system, available at: http://www.emas.de/fileadmin/user_upload/06_service/PDF-Dateien/UGA_Infoblatt-EMAS_June2010.pdf (accessed 16 October 2010).
Everton FC (2011), The aim of the academy, available at: http://www.evertonfc.com/academy/the-aim-of-the-academy.html (accessed 13 December 2011).
Ewing, J. (2004), Can football be saved?, *Business Week*, European edition, 19 July, 16–20.

Ferrand, A. and Pages, M. (1996), Image sponsoring: a methodology to match event and sponsor, *Journal of Sports Management*, **10** (3), 278–91.

Fisher, R.J. and Wakefield, K. (1998), Factors leading to group identification: a field study of winners and losers, *Psychology and Marketing*, **15** (1), 23–40.

Football Governance Research Centre (FGRC) (eds) (2002), The state of the game: the corporate governance of football clubs 2002, *Football Governance Research Centre Research Paper*, no. 3, London: Birkbeck, University of London.

Football Governance Research Centre (FGRC) (eds) (2003), The state of the game: the corporate governance of football clubs 2003, *Football Governance Research Centre Research Paper*, no. 4, London: Birkbeck, University of London.

Football Governance Research Centre (FGRC) (eds) (2004), The state of the game: the corporate governance of professional football 2004, *Football Governance Research Centre Research Paper*, no. 3, London: Birkbeck, University of London.

Francis, J.D. (2011), Learning from failure: is Major League Soccer repeating the mistakes of the North American Soccer League, in H. Dolles and S. Söderman (eds), *Sport as a Business: International, Professional and Commercial Aspects*, Basingstoke: Palgrave Macmillan, pp. 213–27.

Gammelsæter, H. and Senaux, B. (eds) (2011), *The Organisation and Governance of Top Football across Europe*, London: Routledge.

Gammelsæter, H., Storm, R.K. and Söderman, S. (2011), Diverging Scandinavian approaches to professional football, in H. Gammelsæter and B. Senaux (eds), *The Organisation and Governance of Top Football across Europe*, London: Routledge, pp. 77–92.

Gladden, J.M., Milne, G.R. and Sutton, W.A. (1998), A conceptual framework for evaluating brand equity in Division I College Athletics, *Journal of Sport Management*, **12** (1), 1–19.

Gladstein, D.L. (1984), Groups in context: a model of task group effectiveness, *Administrative Science Quarterly*, **29** (4), 499–517.

Gratton, C. and Solberg, H.A. (2013), The economics of listed sports events in a digital era of broadcasting: a case study of the UK, in S. Söderman and H. Dolles (eds), *Handbook of Research on Sport and Business*, Cheltenham, UK and Northampton, MA, USA: Edward Elgar, pp. 202–18.

Gratton, C. and Solberg, H.A. (2007), *The Economics of Sport Broadcasting*, London: Routledge.

Gréhaigne, J.F., Godbout, P. and Bouthier, D. (2001), The teaching and learning of decision making in team sports, *QUEST*, **53** (1), 59–76.

Gréhaigne, J.F., Richard, J.F. and Griffin, L.L. (2005), *Teaching and Learning of Decision Making in Team Sports and Games*, New York: Routledge Falmer.

Griffin, L.L., Mitchell, S.A. and Oslin, J.L. (1997), *Teaching Sport Concepts and Skills: A Tactical Games Approach*, Champaign, IL: Human Kinetics.

Grönroos, C. (2011), Value co-creation in service logic – a critical analysis, *Marketing Theory*, **11** (3), 279–301.

Gummesson, E. (2002), *Total Relationship Marketing: Rethinking Marketing Management*, Oxford: Butterworth-Heinemann.

Gummesson, E. (2007), Case study research and network theory: birds of a feather, *Qualitative Research in Organizations and Management: An International Journal*, **2** (3), 226–48.

Gummesson, E., Lusch, R.F. and Vargo, S.L. (2010), Transitioning from service management to service-dominant logic: observations and recommendations, *International Journal of Quality and Service Science*, **2** (1), 8–22.

Haan, M., Koning, R. and Witteloostuijn, A. (2002), Market forces in European soccer, University of Groningen, Department of International Economics and Business, Groningen, available at: http://www.eco.rug.nl/~haanma/soccer.pdf (accessed 6 August 2011).

Hackman, J.R. (1987), The design of work teams, in J.W. Lorsch (ed.), *Handbook of Organizational Behaviour*, Englewood Cliffs, NJ: Prentice Hall, pp. 315–42.

Hackman, J.R. (2002), *Leading Teams: Setting the Stage for Great Performance*, Boston, MA: Harvard Business School Press.

Hackman, J.R. and Morris, C.G. (1975), Group tasks, group interaction process, and group performance effectiveness: a review and proposed integration, in L. Berkowitz (ed.), *Advances in Experimental Social Psychology*, New York: Academic Press, pp. 45–99.

Hackman, J.R. and Oldham, G.R. (1980), *Work Redesign*, Reading, MA: Addison-Wesley.

Hamel, G. and Prahalad, C.K. (1989), Strategic intent, *Harvard Business Review*, **67** (3), 63–76.

Hamel, G. and Prahalad, C.K. (1994), *Competing for the Future*, Boston, MA: Harvard Business School Press.

Hamil, S. (1999), A whole new ball game? Why football needs a regulator, in S. Hamil, J. Michie and C. Oughton (eds), *A Game of Two Halves: The Business of Football*, Edinburgh: Mainstream, pp. 23–39.

Hamil, S. and Chadwick, S. (eds) (2010), *Managing Football: An International Perspective*, Amsterdam: Butterworth-Heinemann

Hamil, S., Michie, J., Oughton, C. and Warby, S. (2000), Recent developments in football ownership, *Soccer & Society*, **1** (3), 1–10.

Hansen, M.H., Perry, L.T. and Reese, C.S. (2004), A Bayesian operationalization of the resource-based view, *Strategic Management Journal*, **25** (13), 1279–95.

Helleu, B. and Desbordes, M. (2013), Sacrés Français! Why they don't have great football stadia; how they will: political, economic and marketing implications of the UEFA EURO 2016, in S. Söderman and H. Dolles (eds), *Handbook of Research on Sport and Business*, Cheltenham, UK and Northampton, MA, USA: Edward Elgar, pp. 257–73.

Holbrook, M.B. (1996), Customer value – a framework for analysis and research, *Advances in Consumer Research*, **23** (1), 138–42.

Holbrook, M.B.and Hirschman, E.C. (1982), The experiential aspects of consumption: consumer fantasies, feelings, fun, *Journal of Consumer Research*, **9** (2), 132–40.

Hunt, K.A., Bristol, T and Bashaw, R.E. (1999), A conceptual approach to classifying sports fans, *Journal of Service Marketing*, **13** (6), 439–52.

James, J.D. and Ridinger, L.L. (2002), Female and male sport fans: a comparison of sport consumption motives, *Journal of Sport Behavior*, **25** (3), 260–78.

Janz, B.D., Colquitt, J. and Noe, R.A. (1997), Knowledge worker team effectiveness: the role of autonomy, interdependence, team development, and contextual support variables, *Personnel Psychology*, **50** (4), 877–904.

Jaquiss, K. (2001), Mutualism rules: the community in football. Introduction to model rules for a football community trust, in S. Hamil, J. Michie, C. Oughton and S. Warby (eds), *The Changing Face of the Football Business: Supporters Direct*, London: Frank Cass, pp. 51–6.

Jaquiss, K. (2003), Introduction to model rules for a football community trust, *Football Governance Research Centre Research Paper*, no. 2, London: Birkbeck, University of London.

Javalgi, R.G., Traylor, M.B., Gross, A.C. and Lampman, E. (1994), Awareness of sponsorship and corporate image: an empirical investigation, *Journal of Advertising*, **23** (4), 47–58.

Jones, D., Parkes, R. and Houlihan, A. (2006), *Football Money League: Changing of the Guard*, Manchester: Deloitte Sports Business Group, available at: http://www.deloitte.com/assets/DcomUnitedKingdom/Local%20Assets/Documents/UK_SBG_DeloitteFootballMoneyLeague2006.pdf (accessed 9 September 2010).

Keller, K.L. (2000), The brand report card, *Harvard Business Review*, **78** (1), 147–57.

Kerr, A., Smith, N.F. and Anderson, A. (2011), 'As American as mom, apple pie and Dutch soccer?': the team identification of foreign Ajax FC supporters, in H. Dolles and S. Söderman (eds), *Sport as a Business: International, Professional and Commercial Aspects*, Basingstoke: Palgrave Macmillan, pp. 15–34.

Késenne, S. (1996), League management in professional team sports with win maximizing clubs, *European Journal of Sports Management*, **2** (2), 14–22.

King, A. (1998), *The End of the Terraces. The Transformation of English Football in the 1990s*, Leicester: Leicester University Press.

Kipker, I. and Parensen, A. (1999), Strukturierungsprobleme europäischer Fußballwettbewerbe am Beispiel der Champions League und der European Super League [Problems of structuring in European Football leagues. The case of the Champions League and the European Super League], *Betriebswirtschaftliche Forschung und Praxis*, **51** (2), 136–50.

Kleiner, A. (2009), The thought leader interview: Esther Dyson, *strategy+business*, no. 55 (Summer), available at: http://www.strategy-business.com/media/file/sb55_09209.pdf (accessed 14 December 2009).

Kotler, P. and Armstrong, G. (2010), *Principles of Marketing*, 13th revd edn, International edn, Harlow: Pearson Education.

Kunz, B. (2008), Why widgets won't work, *Bloomberg Business Week*, 3 March, available at: www.businessweek.com/technology/content/feb2008/tc20080229_131531.htm (accessed 2 April 2010).

LaFasto, F. and Larson, C. (2001), *When Teams Work Best: 6000 Team Members and Leaders Tell What It Takes to Succeed*, Thousand Oaks, CA: Sage.

Lencioni, P. (2002), *The Five Dysfunctions of a Team: A Leadership Fable*, San Francisco, CA: Jossey-Bass.

Levitt, T. (1981), Marketing intangible products and product intangibles, *Harvard Business Review*, **59** (3), 94–102.

Levitt, T. (1983), *The Marketing Imagination*, New York: The Free Press.

Lovelock, C., Wirtz, J., Tat Keh, H. and Lu, X. (2005), *Services Marketing in Asia*, 2nd edn, Singapore: Prentice Hall.

Lund, R. (2010), Leveraging cooperative strategy – cases of sports and arts sponsorship, doctoral thesis in Economics, Stockholm University, School of Business.

Madsen, H. (1993), *Brøndbys bagmænd. Per Bjerregaard og Leif Jensen spil om penge, fodbold og magt* [*Stringpullers at Brøndby. Per Bjerregaard and Leif Jensens Gambling over Money, Football and Power*], København: Børsen Bøger.

Manzenreiter, W. (2004), Japanese football and world sports: raising the global game in a local setting, *Japan Forum*, **16** (2), 289–313.

Margalit, A. (2009), You'll never walk alone: on property, community and football fans, *Theoretical Inquiries in Law*, **10** (1), 217–40.

McCosker, P. (2004), Manchester United: the transformation of a football club into a global brand, ECCH Collection, case no. 304–178–1, Worcester Business School, Worcester University College.

McGrath, J.E. (1964), *Social Psychology: A Brief Introduction*, New York: Holt.

McGrath, J.E. (1984), *Groups: Interaction and Performance*, Englewood Cliff, NJ: Prentice-Hall.

Meenaghan, T. (2001), Understanding sponsorship effects, *Psychology and Marketing*, **18** (2), 95–122.

Meenaghan, T. and Shipley, D. (1999), Media effect in commercial sponsorship, *European Journal of Marketing*, **33** (3/4), 328–47.

Michie, J. (1999), *New Mutualism: A Golden Goal? Uniting Supporters and their Clubs*, London: The Co-operative Party.

Michie, J. and Ramalingham, S. (1999), Whose game is it anyway? Stakeholders, mutuals and trusts, in S. Hamil, J. Michie and C. Oughton (eds), *A Game of Two Halves: The Business of Football*, Edinburgh: Mainstream, pp. 139–58.

Moffett, S. (2002), *Japanese Rules. Why the Japanese Needed Football and How They Got It*, London: Yellow Jersey Press.

Mohr, S. and Bohl, M. (2001), Markenstrategie: Die Königsdisziplin im Profisport [Brand strategy. The pinnacle in professional sports], *Absatzwirtschaft*, special issue (October), 142–9.

Mohr, S. and Merget, J. (2004), Die Marke als Meistermacher [The brand as a champion maker], in K. Zieschang and C. Klimmer (eds), *Unternehmensführung im Profifussball. Symbiose von Sport, Wirtschaft und Recht* [*Management in Professional Football. Symbiosis of Sports, Business and Law*], Berlin: Erich Schmidt, pp. 103–20.

Morrow, S. (1999), *The New Business of Football: Accountability and Finance in Football*, Basingstoke: Palgrave Macmillan.

Morrow, S. and Hamil, S. (2003), Corporate community involvement by football clubs: business strategy or social obligation?, *Stirling Research Papers in Sports Studies*, no. 1, Stirling: University of Stirling.

Moyes, D. (2011), *FC Everton Youth Academy – manager – testimonial*, available at: http://www.evertonfc.com/academy/testimonials (accessed 11 December 2011).

Muniz, Jr, A.M. and O'Guinn, T.C. (2001), Brand community, *Journal of Consumer Research*, **27** (1), 412–32.

Nicole, A. (2000), Team web sites and relationship marketing for sports fans, *Integrated Marketing Communication Research Journal*, **6** (Spring), 29–35.

Noll, R. (2003a), The organization of sports leagues, *Oxford Review of Economic Policy*, **19** (4), 530–51.

Noll, R. (2003b), The organization of sports leagues, *SIEPR Discussion Paper*, no 02–43, Stanford: Stanford University, Stanford Institute for Economic Policy Research.

Noll, R.G. and Zimbalist, A. (eds) (1997), *Sports, Jobs and Taxes. The Economic Impact of Sports Teams and Stadiums*, Washington, DC: Brookings Institution Press.

Normann, R. (2001), *Reframing Business: When the Map Changes the Landscape*, New York: John Wiley & Sons.

Normann, R. and Ramírez, R. (1993), From value chain to value constellation: designing interactive strategy, *Harvard Business Review*, **71** (4), 65–77.

O'Reilly, N. (2013), Portfolio theory and the management of professional sports clubs: the case of Maple Leaf Sports and Entertainment, in S. Söderman and H. Dolles (eds), *Handbook of Research on Sport and Business*, Cheltenham, UK and Northampton, MA, USA: Edward Elgar, pp. 333–49.

Oughton, C., Hunt, P., Mills, C. and McClean, M. (2003), *Back Home: Returning Clubs to their Communities*, London: Mutuo.

Ozawa, T., Cross, J. and Henderson, S. (2004), Market orientation and financial performance of English professional football clubs, *Journal of Targeting, Measurement and Analysis for Marketing*, **13** (1), 78–90.

Pauli, M. (2002), *Kooperationsformen der Stadionfinanzierung im deutschen Profifussball* [*Forms of Co-financing Arenas in German Professional Football*], Tübingen: Mohr Siebeck.

Penrose, E.T. (1959), *The Theory of the Growth of the Firm*, reprinted 1968, Oxford: Basil Blackwell.

Pine II, B.J. (2011), Memorable events are the most valuable experiences, *Harvard Business Review Online*, available at: http://blogs.hbr.org/cs/2011/04/memorable_events_are_the_most.html (accessed 20 July 2011).

Pine II, B.J. and Gilmore, J.H. (1999), *The Experience Economy. Work Is Theater & Every Business a Stage*, Boston, MA: Harvard Business School Press.

Pongsakornrungsilp, S. and Schroeder, J. (2009), Understanding value co-creation in a co-consuming group, Management Paper, University of Exeter, Business School, available at: http://business-school.exeter.ac.uk/documents/discussion_papers/management/2009/0904.pdf (accessed 16 December 2011).

Porter, M.E. (1991), Towards a dynamic theory of strategy, *Strategic Management Journal*, **12** (special issue), 95–117.

Prahalad, C.K. and Hamel, G. (1990), The core competence of the corporation, *Harvard Business Review*, **68** (3), 79–91.
Prahalad, C.K. and Ramaswamy, V. (2004), Co-creating unique value with customers, *Strategy & Leadership*, **32** (3), 4–9.
Richelieu, A. (2003), A new brand world for sports teams, in B.G. Pitts (ed.), *Sharing Best Practices in Sport Marketing: The Sport Marketing Association's Inaugural Book of Papers*, Morgantown, WV: West Virginia University Press, pp. 3–21.
Rowe, D. (1996), The global love-match: sport and television, *Media, Culture and Society*, **18** (4), 565–82.
Rowe, D. (2000), No gain, no game? Media and sport, in J. Curran and M. Gurevitch (eds), *Mass Media and Society*, 3rd edn, London: Edward Arnold, pp. 346–61.
Samagaio, A., Couto, E. and Caiado, J. (2009), Sporting, financial and stock market performance in English football: an empirical analysis of structural relationships, *CEMAPRE Working Paper*, no. 06, Lisbon: Technical University of Lisbon, available at: http://cemapre.iseg.utl.pt/archive/preprints/395.pdf (accessed 5 August 2011).
Santomier, J. and Hogan, P. (2013), Social media and prosumerism: implications for sport marketing research, in S. Söderman and H. Dolles (eds), *Handbook of Research on Sport and Business*, Cheltenham, UK and Northampton, MA, USA: Edward Elgar, pp. 179–201.
Schau, H., Muniz Jr, A. and Arnould, E. (2009), How brand community practices create value, *Journal of Marketing*, **73** (5), 30–51.
Schlesinger, T. (2013), A review of fan identity and its influence on sport sponsorship effectiveness, in S. Söderman and H. Dolles (eds), *Handbook of Research on Sport and Business*, Cheltenham, UK and Northampton, MA, USA: Edward Elgar, pp. 435–55.
Schwarz, E., Hall, S. and Shibli, S. (2010), *Sport Facility Operations Management: A Global Perspective*, Amsterdam: Butterworth-Heinemann.
Slywotzky, A.J., Morrison, D.J. and Andelman, B. (1997), *The Profit Zone: How Strategic Business Design Will Lead You to Tomorrow's Profits*, St Leonard, NSW: Allen & Unwin.
Smith, A. and Westerbeek, H. (2004), *The Sport Business Future*, Basingstoke: Palgrave Macmillan.
Söderman, S. and Dolles, H. (2008), Strategic fit in international sponsorship. The case of the Olympic Games in Beijing 2008, *International Journal of Sports Marketing & Sponsorship*, **9** (2), 95–108.
Söderman, S. and Dolles, H. (2010), Sponsoring the Bejing Olympic Games – patterns of sponsor advertising, *Asia Pacific Journal of Marketing and Logistics*, **22** (1), 8–24.
Söderman, S., Dolles, H. and Dum, T. (2010), Managing football. International and global developments, in S. Hamil and S. Chadwick (eds), *Managing Football: An International Perspective*, Amsterdam: Butterworth-Heinemann, pp. 85–101.
Solberg, H.A. and Haugen, K.K. (2013), The sale of media sports rights: game theoretic approach, in S. Söderman and H. Dolles (eds), *Handbook of Research on Sport and Business*, Cheltenham, UK and Northampton, MA, USA: Edward Elgar, pp. 219–34.
Stone, S. (2011), Manchester United deny drop in merchandising revenue, *Independent*, 25 February 2011, available at: http://www.independent.co.uk/sport/football/premier-league/manchester-united-deny-drop-in-merchandising-revenue-2225518.html# (accessed 13 December 2011).
Stopper, M. (2004), Mehr sportlicher Wettbewerb durch begrenzte Umverteilung [More competition in sports by limited redistribution], in K. Zieschang and C. Klimmer (eds), *Unternehmensführung im Profifussball. Symbiose von Sport, Wirtschaft und Recht* [*Management in Professional Football. Symbiosis of Sports, Business and Law*], Berlin: Erich Schmidt, pp. 141–62.
Storm, R.K. (2009), The rational emotions of FC København: a lesson on generating profit in professional soccer, *Soccer & Society*, **10** (3), 459–79.
Storm, R.K. (2010), Professional team sports clubs and profits: an irreconcilable combination?, in U. Wagner, R.K. Storm and J. Hoberman (eds), *Observing Sport: Modern System Theoretical Approaches*, Schorndorf: Hofmann Verlag, pp. 103–30.
Storm, R.K. (2011), Winners and losers in Danish football: commercialization and developments in European and Danish first-tier clubs, *Soccer & Society*, **16** (6), 737–53.
Sullivan, L. (2009), 2010: the year social marketing gets serious, *Media Post Publications*, available at: www.mediapost.com/publications/?fa=Articles.showArticle&art_aid=119493 (accessed 20 November 2009).
Thompson, J.L. (2001), *Strategic Management. Awareness and Change*, 4th edn, London: Thomson.
Thwaites, D. (1995), Professional football sponsorship – profitable or profligate?, *International Journal of Advertising*, **14** (2), 149–64.
Troussier, P. (2002), *Passion*, Tokyo: Japan Times Press.
Urawa Reds (2006), In the world. FC Bayern Munich Partnership, available at: http://www.urawa-reds.co.jp/english/club-in_the_world.html (accessed 14 December 2011).
Vargo, S.L. and Lusch, R.F. (2004), Evolving to a new dominant logic for marketing, *Journal of Marketing*, **68** (1), 1–17.

Walters, G. and Hamil, S. (2013), Regulation and the search for a profitable business model: a case study of the English football industry, in S. Söderman and H. Dolles (eds), *Handbook of Research on Sport and Business*, Cheltenham, UK and Northampton, MA, USA: Edward Elgar, pp. 126–41.

Williams, J., Hopkins, S. and Long, C. (eds) (2001), *Passing Rhythms: Liverpool FC and the Transformation of Football*, Oxford: Berg.

Wolf, M.J. (1999), *The Entertainment Economy. How Mega Media Forces Are Transforming Our Lives*, New York: Random House.

Woodman, C. (2011), *Underground. Overground*, 23 May, available at: http://conorwoodman.com/index.php/2011/05/underground-overground/ (accessed 14 December 2011).

Woratschek, H. and Popp, B. (2010), Branded communities as an alternative branding concept to brand communities: the case of a German football community, University of Bayreuth, Discussion Paper, available at: http://www.fiwi.uni-bayreuth.de/de/download/WP_07–10.pdf (accessed 14 July 2011).

Zimmermann, D. (1997), Subsidizing stadiums. Who benefits, who pays?, in R.G. Noll and A. Zimbalist (eds), *Sports, Jobs and Taxes. The Economic Impact of Sports Teams and Stadiums*, Washington, DC: Brookings Institution Press, pp. 119–45.

21 Panel econometrics in sports economics research: player remuneration and sporting performance
Bernd Frick

1 INTRODUCTION

More than ten years ago, labor economist Lawrence Kahn (2000: 75) emphasized that:

> professional sport offers a unique opportunity for labor market research. There is no other research setting than sports where we know the name, face, and life history of every production worker and supervisor in the industry. Total compensation packages and performance statistics for each individual are widely available, and we have a complete data set of worker-employer matches over the career of each production worker and supervisor in the industry. . . . Moreover, professional sports leagues have experienced major changes in labor market rules and structure . . . creating interesting natural experiments that offer opportunities for analysis.

Since then, the number of publications in 'mainstream' economics journals has increased rapidly. Moreover, the *Journal of Sports Economics* and the *International Journal of Sports Finance* have attracted the attention of a wide (academic) audience. Today, many researchers with a solid background in industrial organization, labor and personnel economics as well as econometrics use data from the professional (team) sports industries in the United States (US) and in (Western) Europe applying 'state-of-the art' techniques to study various issues:[1] what are the main determinants of player remuneration and of contract length? What are the determinants of player mobility and career length? To what extent do individuals respond to (changes in) incentives? What is the relationship between team wage bills and (sporting) performance? Does the distribution of salaries affect team performance? To what extent are 'fairness considerations' important? What is the impact of organizational 'constraints' such as draft rules, roster restrictions and salary caps on the behavior of (win maximizing versus profit maximizing) clubs? Do the clubs use the available resources (for example playing and coaching talent) efficiently?

Advanced quantitative methods are used in this chapter to analyse the very detailed and reliable longitudinal data that are available both, at the club and the individual level (many of the recent studies are based on hundreds of team-year-observations and even thousands of player-year-observations, see Tables 21.A1 and 21.A2 in the Appendix to this chapter). The purpose of this chapter is twofold. First, I summarize a selection of recent papers on team wage bills and sporting performance (section 2) and then present one study that uses data from German football in more detail. In a second step (section 3) I again first summarize a selection of empirical papers on the determinants of player remuneration and the issue of discrimination before presenting a particular study that uses longitudinal information on individual players in the first division of the German professional football league (Bundesliga). Section 4 concludes with a short summary and some implications for further research.

2 TEAM WAGE BILLS, PAY STRUCTURES, AND PLAYING SUCCESS

The constraint set faced by professional teams in football (soccer), basketball, baseball, American football and hockey is constant across clubs and is time invariant (if rule changes occur, all the clubs are affected in the same way). Moreover, the teams are identical in many ways: they produce an identical output, use the same units of skills, compete under the same rules, employ the same production function and share a common technology. More specifically, it is player quality, on the one hand, and the quality of managers and head coaches, on the other that is crucial for the clubs' performance. First, the degree of interaction among player skills determines the nature of the production function. Since the production technology is not additive, but exhibits complementarities among inputs, the individual player's contribution to output (wins and/or revenues) cannot be measured accurately even though his 'productivity' (scoring and defensive behavior) can be easily assessed. Second, managers and head coaches share the responsibility for the coordination of player skills and the transformation of these in outputs. In the classical principal–agent model the principal (management) observes the output of the agent (the player) precisely, but cannot tell to what extent that output reflects effort (which reduces player utility) and random factors (which do not directly affect the player's utility). In the case of professional athletes, an important source of uncertainty is just how productive the players will turn out to be. Another source of uncertainty for the players is the errors made by their head coaches in assessing performance, particularly in situations where precise measurement is either too costly or even impossible.

The question, whether and to what extent expenditures on playing talent – as measured by team wage bills – translate into playing success, is perhaps the one that has received most attention in the literature on the economics of professional team sports. The seminal theoretical contributions by Rottenberg (1956), Neale (1964) and El-Hodiri and Quirk (1971) assume the relationship to be statistically significant and robust: in general, large market teams will dominate small market teams because they can hire more talent and they actually do hire more talent because wins are more valuable to them. This chain of reasoning (see also Simmons and Forrest, 2004) depends entirely on the assumption that greater spending on talent will translate into more wins.

Early studies using data from the US Major Leagues, however, found weak – if any – empirical links between team payrolls and playing success (for example, Sanderson and Siegfried, 1997: 10; Scully, 1995: 94; Zimbalist, 1992: 96). The puzzle of a weak correlation between team wage bills and sporting success can potentially be resolved: first, there is always the potential for mistakes in assessing player talent. Having signed a number of mediocre players to long-term contracts is certainly detrimental to team performance. Second, institutional restrictions on player mobility (such as the draft system and a salary cap) have the potential to create a monopsonistic labor market, breaking the relationship between team wage bills and team performance (see, for example, Simmons and Forrest, 2004: 123).

Recent empirical studies indeed suggest that the pay-performance relationship is closer in the European football leagues than in the US Major Leagues (including baseball, basketball, American football and hockey). Since it is unlikely that managers of US teams make more mistakes when evaluating talent than their European counterparts, only the latter of the two explanations remains: while the US leagues all have a highly regulated labor market (drafts, salary caps and floors, roster restrictions, and so on) restricting player mobility for most of their careers, players in Europe enjoy freedom of movement with few – if any – restrictions in place. However, the most recent evidence suggests the existence of a statistically significant and positive relationship between team payrolls and team performance also in the US Major Leagues (see Table 21.A1 in the appendix).

The particularly close pay–performance relationship in European football is documented by, for example, Frick (2005). Using a hitherto unavailable unbalanced panel with detailed information on team wage bills and head coach remuneration in the First German Football League (covering the seasons 1981/82–2002/03) the author not only includes as right-hand side variables the wages of players and head coaches, but also tests for complementarities between the two inputs.

The data used to estimate the models presented come from a German sunday newspaper (*Die Welt*) that publishes team wage bills and head coach salaries immediately before the start of the new season. The data on the playing success of the teams as well as the information on coach dismissals come from a highly respected German football magazine (*Kicker*). In all but one of the 22 seasons 18 teams were playing in Germany's first football division 'Bundesliga'. At the end of each season the three weakest teams are relegated and replaced by the three best-performing teams from the second division. In 1991/92, when the two best teams from the first division of the former German Democratic Republic (Oberliga) were admitted to the Bundesliga, the number of teams was temporarily increased to 20. After that season, four teams were relegated to division 2 while only two were promoted to division 1, resulting in the well-known size of the league again.

The estimated models are of the following general form:

(1) $p_{it} = \beta_0 + \beta_1 (wb_{it}/wb_t) + \beta_2 (wb_{it}/wb_t)^2 + \beta_3 (cs_{it}/cs_t) + \beta_4\, ncd + \beta_5\, tpr + \varepsilon$

(2) $p_{it} = \beta_0 + \beta_1 (wb_{it}/wb_t) + \beta_2 (wb_{it}/wb_t)^2 + \beta_3 (cs_{it}/cs_t) + \beta_4\, ncd + \beta_5\, tpr + \beta_6\, tt *$
$(wb_{it}/wb_t) + \varepsilon$

where p_{it} denotes the number of points (a team is awarded three points for a victory, one point for a tie and zero points for a loss. Until the end of the season 1994/95 a win was worth only two points) of team i at the end of season t, (wb_{it}/wb_t) the relative wage bill of team i in season t, (cs_{it}/cs_t) the relative salary of team i's head coach in season t, ncd the number of head coaches dismissed by team i (the maximum number of dismissals per team and season is three. Estimating the models with three dummies instead of the ordinal variable used here leaves the coefficients of the other variables unaffected), tpr is a dummy representing the three point regime for a victory. Finally, the interaction term $tt * (wb_{it}/wb_t)$ in model (2) is included to test whether the pay–performance relationship is invariant over time (tt denotes a linear time trend).

To test for complementarities the estimations also include a Translog- (model 3) and a CES-specification (model 4) of the first model:

(3) $p_{it} = \beta_0 + \beta_1 (wb_{it}/wb_t) + \beta_2 ((wb_{it}/wb_t)/2) + \beta_3 (cs_{it}/cs_t) + \beta_4 ((cs_{it}/cs_t)/2)$
$+ \beta_5 ((wb_{it}/wb_t) * (cs_{it}/cs_t)) + \beta_6\, ncd + \beta_7\, tpr + \varepsilon$

(4) $p_{it} = \beta_0 + \beta_1 (wb_{it}/wb_t) + \beta_2 (cs_{it}/cs_t) + \beta_3 ((wb_{it}/wb_t) - (cs_{it}/cs_t)) + \beta_4\, ncd + \beta_5 + \varepsilon$

Table 21.1 Basic specifications: team wage bills, head coach salaries and team performance in German professional football (Cobb–Douglas specification; observation period 1981/82–2002/03)

Dep. variable: p_{it}	Model (1)		
	b	se b	T
(wb_{it}/wb_t)	15.506	2.014	7.70***
$(wb_{it}/wb_t)^2$	−2.324	0.639	−3.63***
(cs_{it}/cs_t)	3.967	0.885	4.48***
ncd	−5.482	0.470	−11.66***
tpr	12.652	0.773	16.37***
const	19.922	1.381	14.42***
N of observations		398	
$R^2 * 100$		67.3	
F-value		163.7***	
LM-test		1.36+	

	Model (2)		
	b	se b	T
(wb_{it}/wb_t)	15.008	1.991	7.54***
$(wb_{it}/wb_t)^2$	−2.614	0.681	−3.84***
(cs_{it}/cs_t)	3.750	0.892	4.21***
ncd	−5.574	0.480	−11.62***
tpr	11.476	1.013	11.33***
$tt * (wb_{it}/wb_t)$	0.114	0.063	1.80*
const	20.164	1.366	14.76***
N of observations		398	
$R^2 * 100$		67.5	
F-value		137.5***	
LM-test		1.45+	

Notes:
+ not significant; * $p < .10$; *** $p < .01$.
# OLS-estimation with heteroskedasticity-consistent standard errors (White, 1980).

Looking at Table 21.1 it appears that higher relative player salaries raise performance significantly – but at a decreasing rate (the latter finding is at odds with Simmons and Forrest, 2004: 132 who find decreasing marginal returns only for the English Premier League and the Italian Serie A, but not for the German Bundesliga). According to the estimates, the turning point is inside the sample range. An increase in player salaries beyond that point (3.336 in model (1) and 2.871 in model (2)) is detrimental to team performance in the sense that it reduces the number of points per season. The small number of cases in the range in which negative returns to relative wage bills are encountered (n = 4 in model (1) and n = 6 in model (2)) seems to suggest that managers are usually well aware of the negative effects of increasing wages. Relative coach salary, in turn, has a strictly linear positive and significant impact on team performance (inclusion of a quadratic term renders the linear as well as the quadratic term insignificant).

Moreover, each dismissal is accompanied by two additional losses, and the three-point regime increases the number of points won by about 12 per season (prior to the 1995/96 season, a team winning 28 points usually avoided relegation; since then about 40 points are required to survive in the first division).

Finally, it appears that the pay–performance relationship is getting closer over time (see the respective coefficient in model (2), Table 21.1) – again a finding that is at odds with the existing literature (see Forrest and Simmons, 2002: 228, 233). Although the coefficient is significant only at the 10 per cent level, this finding may have important implications with regard to what has been termed the 'rat race character' of league championships: if the ability to pay high wages to players and coaches is getting more important for sporting success, we may end up in the not so distant future with some far-reaching regulation of either the player or the product market (via, for example, a salary cap or a redistribution of revenues). Estimating models (1) and (2) with team fixed effects leaves the coefficients of the wage and salary variables unchanged, but has a considerable impact on the R^2: Adding team dummies to model (1), for example, increases the variance explained from 67.3 per cent to 72.3 per cent. Previous studies estimating a reduced form equation (with the team wage bill, the squared wage bill, a promotion dummy and a dummy for the three point regime, as in Simmons and Forrest, 2004) suggest that the inclusion of team fixed effects tends to increase the R^2 even more. This increase is most likely due to an omitted variable bias, because including head coach salary and the number of coaches dismissed during the season reduces the impact of the team fixed effects (and, therefore, the omitted variable bias) considerably.

Since player and coach talent may be complements rather than substitutes it is certainly advisable not only to estimate models of the traditional Cobb-Douglas form, but also to look at other specifications. Surprisingly, however, neither a Translog- nor a CES-specification reveals a statistically significant coefficient of any of the interaction terms (Table 21.2). The fact, that from a purely econometric point of view the coefficient of the interaction term (player talent and quality of the head coach) is of minor importance for the teams' sporting performance does not imply that the 'composition' of the club's playing and coaching staff is irrelevant. Most importantly, management is well advised not to increase relative player salaries beyond a certain turning point (somewhere around three times the mean value) whereas no such optimum can be found for coaches' salaries.

While in accordance with many of the findings reported in recent empirical analyses of the pay–performance relationship using data from other European football leagues, some of the findings reported above are apparently at odds with the existing literature. First, the study finds decreasing marginal returns to player salaries. Second, including head coach salaries and head coach dismissals in the estimation reduces the omitted variable bias considerably. Finally, the pay–performance relationship is getting closer over time. Since the estimates presented above are based on a much longer panel and include more explanatory variables than previous studies, the findings are likely to be very robust. However, the partial incompatibility with the evidence available so far implies that further research is still urgently required.

Table 21.2   *Further specifications: team wage bills, head coach salaries and team performance in German professional football (Translog- and CES-specification; observation period 1981/82–2002/03)*

Dep. variable: p_{it}	Model (3)		
	b	se b	T
(wb_{it}/wb_t)	15.860	2.253	7.04***
$(wb_{it}/wb_t)/2$	−3.793	3.074	0.93 +
(cs_{it}/cs_t)	2.854	2.338	−1.62 +
$(cs_{it}/cs_t)/2$	2.009	3.367	0.60 +
$(wb_{it}/wb_t) * (cs_{it}/cs_t)$	−1.225	2.032	−0.60 +
ncd	−5.504	0.471	−11.70***
tpr	12.530	0.824	15.20***
const	20.354	1.705	11.94***
N of observations		398	
R² * 100		67.3	
F-value		118.0***	

	Model (4)		
	b	se b	T
(wb_{it}/wb_t)	8.240	0.962	8.57***
(cs_{it}/cs_t)	4.460	0.919	4.85***
$(wb_{it}/wb_t) - (cs_{it}/cs_t)$	−0.566	1.010	−0.56 +
ncd	−5.379	0.799	−11.34***
tpr	12.117	0.474	15.17***
const	23.979	1.004	23.89***
N of observations		398	
R² * 100		65.8	
F-value		148.1***	

Notes:
+ not significant; *** $p < .01$.
# OLS-estimation with heteroskedasticity-consistent standard errors (White, 1980).

3   PLAYER REMUNERATION, DISCRIMINATION, AND INDIVIDUAL PERFORMANCE

Economic theory predicts that in the absence of labor market restrictions (such as salary caps, reserve clauses and/or draft rules) players will be paid according to their marginal product, that is, the wage an individual player receives is a function of his talent and his experience (Rottenberg, 1956). However, since the clubs differ with respect to their drawing potential – there are 'small market' and 'large market' teams – they also differ with respect to their 'ability to pay'.

Since it rests on a number of critical assumptions (such as player mobility, complete information and risk neutrality) the neoclassical model of wage determination has often been rejected not only by sports fans, but also by some highly respected economists: 'the elementary classical model presents a very poor description of employment relations in advanced economies' (Milgrom and Roberts, 1992: 329).

However, the problems that are characteristic for most – if not all – 'real life' labor contracts (information asymmetries, incompleteness, and importance of implicit elements) are clearly less important in professional team sports. Here, an individual player's performance can easily be measured, 'shirking' can be detected at low cost, and effort and talent can be evaluated not only by a player's current club but also by other teams. It is, therefore, plausible to assume that in the German Bundesliga – as in other professional team sports leagues with an unregulated labor market – players are paid mainly according to their (recent) performance. Contrary to the findings reported by Horowitz and Zappe (1998) for baseball veterans, this suggests that 'nostalgia effects' will be of minor importance only.

Moreover, professions in which talent is highly valued by consumers are usually characterized by a highly skewed distribution of earnings: small differences in talent translate into large differences in pay (Rosen, 1981). Player reputation not only attracts (additional) spectators, but advances in technology facilitate the reproduction of matches at low cost. Together, these two effects lead to a considerable expansion of the market. In general, players are neither completely homogenous nor completely specialized. This, in turn, creates a situation of bilateral monopoly in which players and teams share a surplus or economic rent. Only a few players who are sufficiently differentiated can shift surpluses (rents) completely into salaries; these players will tend to be the 'superstars' of their sports.

Several empirical studies examine the remuneration of players in European football. These include, inter alia, Frick (2007), Huebl and Swieter (2002), Lehmann and Schulze (2008), Lehmann and Weigand (1999) and Lucifora and Simmons (2003). The model structure of these studies is quite similar. In standard Mincer-style, player salaries are influenced by age, (career) games played, (career) goals scored, international caps, player position, assists and tackles, 'superstar status' and contract duration. While age and experience have a positive, yet decreasing effect, the influence of contract duration is strictly linear. Midfielders and forwards earn a premium relative to defenders. Higher productivity also has a positive and linear influence on wages (see Table 21.A2 in the Appendix).

Significant impacts of experience, performance and peer reputation on salary can also be found in studies of North American sports, see Hamilton (1997) on basketball, Kahn (1993) for baseball, Berri and Simmons (2009) and Simmons and Berri (2009) on American football and Idson and Kahane (2000) for hockey. These papers show that the salaries of professional sports players are influenced systematically by factors such as age, experience and performance in very similar ways to those found in other occupations. Where sports teams differ is in the distribution of salaries which is even more highly skewed than in standard occupations. Also sports teams apply more stringent selection procedures to occupations. For example, poor performance by a player results in being dropped from the team squad and very quickly being discarded; there are high levels of mobility within the industry (between teams) and into and out of the industry, with shorter careers than in most occupations. The large skewness of the salary distribution and high degree of player mobility appear to apply to all team sports, including North American major leagues as well as European football (see Table 21.A2 in the Appendix).

The most recent study by Frick (2010) includes an ordinary least squares (OLS) model (with robust standard errors), a random effects (RE) model as well as a median regression (MR) model followed by various quantile regressions (.10, .25, .75, .90) with and without bootstrapped standard errors (200 repetitions). Although the Hausman-Test suggests using the results from the fixed effects (FE) estimation, the findings of the random effects estimation are reported. The problem is that region of birth is a constant for each player and cannot be used in a fixed effects estimation. However, the differences between the remaining coefficients in the RE- and the FE-estimations are negligible. The results are comparable to those obtained from OLS as well as RE and MR estimations. However, few of the coefficients remain constant over the percentiles.

The model to be estimated is of the following general form:

$$lnPAY = \alpha_0 + \alpha_1 AGE + \alpha_2 AGE^2 + \alpha_3 GPL + \alpha_4 CGP + \alpha_5 CGP^2 + \alpha_6 CGP^3$$
$$+ \alpha_7 IAL + \alpha_8 IAL^2 + \alpha_9 IAL^3 + \alpha_{10} IAP + \alpha_{11} IAP^2 + \alpha_{12} IAP^3$$
$$+ \alpha_{13} GSL + \alpha_{14} CGS + \alpha_{15} CGS^2 + \alpha_{16} CGS^3 + \alpha_{17} TEN + \alpha_{18} CAP$$
$$+ \alpha_{19} FDD + \alpha_{20} PD + \alpha_{21} RD + \alpha_{22} TD + \alpha_{23} YD + \varepsilon$$

where AGE: player age
GPL: number of appearances in Bundesliga in last season
CGP: number of career appearances in Bundesliga
IAL: international appearances last season
IAP: international appearances in career
GLS: goals scored last season in Bundesliga
CGS: career goals scored in Bundesliga
CAP: captain of team (0 = no; 1 = yes)
FDD: previous team in first division abroad (0 = no; 1 = yes)
PD: position dummies (ref.: goalkeeper)
RD: region of birth dummies (ref.: Germany)
TD: team dummies (ref.: Borussia Moenchengladbach)
YD: year dummies (ref.: 2001/02)

Thus, the models distinguish between a player's career performance and his most recent (that is, last season) performance. The most recent performance (measured by, *inter alia*, the number of games played, the number of international appearances and the number of goals scored) is, of course, not included in the career performance (the results of the OLS, RE and MR estimations are displayed in Table 21.3). Contrary to the situation in most American team sports' leagues with their abundance of performance figures, measurement of individual player performance in European football can be problematic especially for defenders whose task it is to prevent the opposing team's forwards from scoring goals. While counting the number of goals scored, shots on goal and assists is straightforward, it is far more difficult to assess the performance of defensive players. In future work the models should, therefore, be estimated separately for the different groups of players.

Most studies of pay determination in football rely on the standard conditional expectations model. However, the focus on the conditional mean is likely to misrepresent the relationship between pay and performance if there are differences in the returns to

Table 21.3   *Estimation results I: various methods*

Variable	Random effects		Robust OLS		Median regression	
	B	T	B	T	B	T
AGE	.5121	22.43***	.4559	18.99***	.4361	23.71***
AGE²	−.0092	−21.48***	−.0083	−18.69***	−.0079	−23.12***
GPL	.0191	25.66***	.0240	31.95***	.0226	33.12***
CGP	.0042	7.48***	.0056	11.27***	.0057	12.46***
*CGP²*100*	−.0021	−5.97***	−.0028	−9.18***	−.0030	−10.26***
*CGP³ * 10000*	.0033	5.46***	.0043	8.07***	.0046	9.06***
IAL	.0848	6.86***	.0903	6.04***	.0909	8.02***
IAL²	−.0071	−3.56***	−.0081	−2.79***	−.0094	−5.01***
IAL³	.0002	2.19 **	.0002	1.74*	.0003	4.09***
IAP	.0118	4.19***	.0125	5.36***	.0131	5.94***
IAP²	−.0003	−3.40***	−.0003	4.17***	−.0003	−4.48***
*IAP³ *1000*	.0017	2.99***	.0016	3.67***	.0016	3.67***
GSL	.0444	14.24***	.0465	16.28***	.0513	18.26***
CGS	−.0129	−4.71***	−.0114	−4.69***	−.0077	−3.56***
CGS²	.0002	4.13***	.0002	4.38***	.0001	3.31***
*CGS3 * 1000*	−.0011	−3.68***	−.0011	−4.15***	−.0007	−3.11***
TEN	−.0142	−4.43***	−.0187	−6.46***	−.0153	−6.53***
CAP	.2692	6.60***	.3406	10.17***	.3718	10.50***
FDD	.5910	12.46***	.6159	11.41***	.6346	15.11***
DEF	.2113	5.17***	.0990	3.20***	.0539	2.24**
MID	.2677	6.65***	.1667	5.34***	.0965	4.04**
FOR	.3157	7.14***	.2167	5.97***	.1020	3.68**
S_AM	.4494	8.23***	.3778	9.87***	.3824	11.91***
N_AM	−.0822	−0.73 +	−.1785	−1.92*	−.1510	−2.10**
W_EU	.2442	6.62***	.1848	7.00***	.1969	8.53***
E_EU	.0774	2.23**	.0329	1.36*	.0200	0.95 +
AFR	.0654	1.24 +	−.0117	−0.30 +	−.0166	−0.52 +
AS_AU	.0928	1.28 +	.0099	0.20 +	.0185	0.42 +
CONST	5.8725	19.30***	6.8245	21.14***	7.1631	29.21***

Team dummies		Included		
Season dummies		Included		

N of obs.	6147	6147	6147
Obs. per player	1–13	–	–
N of players	1993	–	–
R²*100	61.7	62.7	40.5
F-value	–	164.5***	–
Wald chi2	6672.0***	–	–
LM-test	392.0***	–	–
Raw sum of dev.	–	–	4656.6
Min. sum of dev.	–	–	2772.6

Note: + not significant; * p < .10; ** p < .05; *** p < .01.

performance along the conditional distribution. Several studies of salary determination in other professional (North American) team sports use quantile regression estimation since log salary measures tend to have even greater kurtosis values than standard occupations (Berri and Simmons, 2009; Simmons and Berri, 2009; Vincent and Eastman, 2009). Ordinary least squares salary regressions are sensitive to the presence of outliers and can be inefficient if the log salary measure has a highly non-normal distribution, as is often the case in professional team sports. In contrast, quantile regression estimates are more robust. Presence of non-normality is indicated by a large kurtosis value and the D'Agostino et al. (1990) test is performed by the sktest command in Stata 10.1. In the panel used here, the *p*-value for the test statistic of the null hypothesis that kurtosis does not depart from the value associated with a normal distribution is 0.000 and hence the log salary data depart from normality, a result that is similar to those found in some studies of North American sports. One further advantage of quantile regression is that it facilitates examination of salary returns to characteristics at different points in the salary distribution.

That is, we can investigate the impacts of the available performance measures at any quantile of the salary distribution, not just the conditional mean. Moreover, the quantile regression approach is semi-parametric in that it avoids assumptions about the parametric distribution of the regression error term, an especially suitable feature where the data are heteroskedastic as in our case. To ensure robustness of standard errors, bootstrapping is performed with 200 replications. Quantile regression estimates are displayed in Table 21.4.

The main findings can be summarized as follows (see Tables 21.3 and 21.4):

- First, age, career games played, international appearances over the entire career and international appearances in the last season all have a statistically significant non-linear influence on salaries. The statistically significant coefficient of the cubic term suggests existence of 'superstar effects' (Rosen, 1981).
- A strange result is obtained for career goals scored: the coefficient of the linear and the cubic term are significant and negative, while the coefficient of the squared term is positive and significant. This unexpected result 'survives' a number of different specifications: interaction of the number of career goals with the position dummies leaves the finding virtually unaffected. Moreover, estimating the model separately by position yields the same result for forwards and midfielders, but not for defenders. Estimating the model only for position players (that is, without the goalkeepers) yields again the 'strange' coefficients.
- Second, goals scored last season as well as games played last season have a significantly positive and strictly linear influence on annual income, that is, there seem to be no decreasing returns to either goals scored or games played.
- Comparing the returns to career performance and to performance in the last season, it appears that 'historical merits' do not count very much, that is, recent performance is – as expected – far more important than past performance.
- Third, defenders, midfielders and forwards earn significantly higher salaries than goalkeepers. The premiums for these positions, however, differ considerably across estimations: the effect is most pronounced in the RE estimation and weakest in the MR model.

Table 21.4   Estimation results II: quantile regressions

Variable	.1 Quantile	.25 Quantile	.75 Quantile	.9 Quantile
AGE	.5415***	.5485***	.3660***	.2829***
AGE^2	−.0097***	−.0099***	−.0068***	−.0055***
GPL	.0347***	.0271***	.0173***	.0124***
CGP	.0050***	.0058***	.0047***	.0030***
CGP^2*100	−.0027***	−.0034***	−.0021***	−.0001**
CGP^3 * 10000	.0042***	.0057***	.0030***	.0013 +
IAL	.0340**	.0568***	.1241***	.1129***
IAL^2	−.0003 +	−.0034*	−.0149***	−.0114***
IAL^3	.0000 +	.0000 +	.0006***	.0004***
IAP	.0108***	.0119***	.0126***	.0122***
IAP^2	−.0002**	−.0003***	−.0002***	−.0002*
IAP^3 *1000	.0014**	.0019***	.0013***	.0009 +
GSL	.0453***	.0511***	.0486***	.0425***
CGS	−.0094**	−.0038 +	−.0132***	−.0077*
CGS^2	.0002***	.0000 +	.0003***	.0002**
CGS^3 * 1000	−.0014***	.0000 +	−.0001***	−.0009**
TEN	−.0134***	−.0181***	−.0201***	−.0177***
CAP	.3662***	.3742***	.3114***	.3296***
FDD	.7485***	.6895***	.5848***	.4772***
DEF	.2154***	.1049***	−.0002 +	−.1560***
MID	.2414***	.1458***	.0756***	−.0537 +
FOR	.2832***	.1634***	.1111***	−.0170 +
S_AM	.3010***	.3086***	.3863***	.4230***
N_AM	−.1989 +	−.0509 +	−.2002***	−.2519*
W_EU	.1999***	.1992***	.1637***	.1627***
E_EU	.0635 *	.0690***	−.0344 +	.0085 +
AFR	−.0153 +	.0538 +	−.0389 +	−.0320 +
AS_AU	.1296 +	.1042**	−.2022***	−.1494*
CONST	4.6571***	5.1341***	8.6862***	10.4911***
Team dummies		Included		
Season dummies		Included		
N of cases	6147	6147	6147	6147
Pseudo R^2*100	43.6	42.4	39.2	39.2
Raw sum of dev.	2196.5	3891.5	3577.2	1934.0
Min. sum of dev.	1239.1	2240.8	2139.6	1175.5

Note: + not significant; * $p < .10$; ** $p < .05$; *** $p < .01$.

- Fourth, region of birth is also important: players from South America and Western Europe receive a considerable pay premium while players from the rest of the world are neither favored nor discriminated against. The pay premium for South Americans and West Europeans is not surprising: other things equal, players from these regions attract larger crowds (Wilson and Ying, 2003) and contribute more to merchandising revenues (Kalter, 1999).

- The longer a player has been active for his current club, the lower is c.p. his annual salary. Whether this is the result of an adverse selection process (better players are traded while less talented players remain with their old club) or whether some players are willing to forfeit money to 'stay at home' is not yet clear. Anecdotal evidence seems to support the argument that some players suffer from 'home sickness' once they are traded to another club.
- Finally, team captains and players who moved from a first division club abroad to Germany are paid a significant premium, too. In the former case this is obviously due to leadership skills that are required for the job and that are, therefore, particularly rewarded in the market (Kuhn and Weinberger, 2005).

Few of the coefficients retain their magnitude across the different quantiles of the salary distribution. Estimating the models with the lagged annual salary to control for unobserved heterogeneity reduces the sample size considerably (from 6100 player-year observations to 4700). Although most of the coefficients retain their statistical significance, their magnitudes are somewhat reduced:

- Generally, the maximum income is reached at an age of about 27 or 28 years. The age–earnings profile, however, is much flatter for the players with the highest incomes.
- The impact of games played last season as well as career games played on annual salaries is much stronger for players at the bottom of the income distribution.
- International appearances (past as well as current) seem to have a much stronger influence on the salaries of the players at the top of the income distribution.
- Goals scored (past as well as most recent season), tenure with the current club and being a team captain seem to have a more or less constant impact on player salaries, that is, the coefficients are quite similar for the different quantiles.
- The coefficients of the position dummies change considerably across the income distribution, indicating that goalkeepers are the 'real superstars' in the business. It should be noted that the term 'real superstars' has first been used by Alan Krueger (2005) who analyses the revenues generated by particularly successful rock bands and musicians.
- The pay premium enjoyed by players from South America increases across the pay distribution while the premium of players from Western Europe decreases. In further research subjective evaluations of a player's performance (that is, school grades) will also be used to estimate the hedonic wage equations.

4 IMPLICATIONS FOR FUTURE RESEARCH

Building on the seminal theoretical contributions by El-Hodiri and Quirk (1971), Neale (1964) and Rottenberg (1956), a large number of empirical studies on the economics of the team sport industry have been published over the last three to four decades. For various reasons, however, the growth rate of this type of literature is likely to accelerate: first, new data becomes available every once in a while and, second, the statistical software for panel-econometric analyses becomes more and more user-friendly. Third, and most important, the number of talented and ambitious PhD candidates working in that particular field continues to grow rapidly.

The evidence presented in this chapter convincingly demonstrates the potential of econometric analyses to answer two particularly important questions that arise in the context of the team sports industry: first, is it possible to field a championship team by outspending the competitors and, second, what are the (main) determinants of player salaries? The answers are not only of academic value, but have obvious managerial implications. Team owners and/or presidents wishing to maximize the sporting performance of their clubs are well advised to take the results into account when purchasing talent in the relevant labor market.

The growing acceptance of sports economics research in the 'mainstream' of the discipline is certainly due to the high standards of both, the theoretical contributions as well as the empirical papers. The combination of rigorous modeling and state-of-the-art econometrics is required to gain the recognition of the social science community. Presenting the findings in a way that is accessible to the public is another step that has yet to be taken. Since the first examples (see, for example Berri et al., 2006; Kuper and Szymanski, 2009; Szymanski, 2009) are quite encouraging (they all quickly became bestsellers), the future of sports economics is likely to be a bright one. Research in sports economics has in the mean time also resulted in a number of highly entertaining textbooks (see, for example, Fort, 2003; Leeds and von Allmen, 2002; Sandy et al., 2004), and many of the 'stylized facts' produced by sports economists have made their way into 'classical' textbooks in fields such as personnel economics and industrial organization. Moreover, student interest in applied econometrics can be considerably increased by using data from the professional team sports industry.

However, a lot of research still needs to be done: individualistic sports (such as tennis, boxing, and track and field athletics) are interesting subjects to study, comparative analyses (across leagues and countries) are still scarce and the (economic) consequences of many rule changes (such as the de-regulation of the labor market following the Bosman Ruling) still need to be analysed and documented.

NOTE

1. Some of those issues are also addressed in this Handbook by applying a qualitative approach, ref. e.g. to players as a value capture in professional team sports management by Dolles and Söderman (2013, in this volume), or to governance structures influencing the sports labour market, see Gammelsæter and Senaux (2013, in this volume).

REFERENCES

Berri, D.J. and Jewell, R.T. (2004), Wage inequality and team performance: professional basketball's natural experiment, *Atlantic Economic Journal*, **32** (2), 130–9.
Berri, D.J. and Simmons, R. (2009), Race and the evaluation of signal callers in the National Football League, *Journal of Sports Economics*, **10** (1), 23–43.
Berri, D.J., Schmidt, M.B. and Brooks, S.L. (2006), *The Wages of Wins*, Stanford, CA: Stanford University Press.

Bloom, M. (1999), The performance effects of pay dispersion on individuals and organizations, *Academy of Management Journal*, **42** (1), 25–40.

Bodvarsson, O.B. and Brastow, R.T. (1999), A test of employer discrimination in the NBA, *Contemporary Economic Policy*, **17** (2), 243–55.

Conlin, M. and Emerson, P.M. (2003), Multidimensional separating equilibria and moral hazard: an empirical study of National Football League contract negotiations, *Review of Economics and Statistics*, **85** (3), 760–65.

D'Agostino, R.B., Belanger, A. and D'Agostino Jr, R.B. (1990), A suggestion for using powerful and informative tests of normality, *The American Statistician*, **44** (4), 316–27.

Depken, C.A. (2000), Wage disparity and team productivity: evidence from Major League Baseball, *Economics Letters*, **67** (1), 87–92.

Dolles, H. and Söderman, S. (2013), The network of value captures in football club management: a framework to develop and analyze competitive advantage in professional team sports, in S. Söderman and H. Dolles (eds), *Handbook of Research on Sport and Business*, Cheltenham, UK and Northampton, MA, USA: Edward Elgar, pp. 367–95.

El-Hodiri, M. and Quirk, J. (1971), An economic model of a professional sports league, *Journal of Political Economy*, **79** (6), 1302–19.

Forrest, D. and Simmons, R. (2002), Team salaries and playing success in sports: a comparative perspective, *Zeitschrift für Betriebswirtschaft*, **72** (supplement issue, no. 4, 'Sportökonomie'), 221–38.

Fort, R. (2003), *Sports Economics*, Englewood Cliffs, NJ: Prentice Hall.

Franck, E. and Nüesch, S. (2007), Wage dispersion and team performance. An empirical panel analysis, Working Paper, no. 73, Zurich: Institute for Strategy and Business Economics, University of Zurich.

Frick, B. (2005), '. . . und Geld schießt eben doch Tore': Die Voraussetzungen sportlichen und wirtschaftlichen Erfolges in der Fußball-Bundesliga ['Money scores': the conditions for sporting and economic success in the football Bundesliga], *Sportwissenschaft*, **35** (3), 250–70.

Frick, B. (2007), Salary determination and the pay-performance relationship in professional soccer: evidence from Germany, in P. Rodriguez, S. Késenne and J. Garcia (eds), *Sports Economics after Fifty Years: Essays in Honour of Simon Rottenberg*, Oviedo: Ediciones de la Universidad de Oviedo, pp. 125–46.

Frick, B. (2010), The football players' labor market: recent developments and econom(etr)ic evidence, mimeo, Paderborn: Department of Management, University of Paderborn.

Frick, B., Pietzner, G. and Prinz, J. (2007), Career duration in a competitive environment: the labor market for soccer players in Germany, *Eastern Economic Journal*, **33** (3), 429–42.

Frick, B., Pietzner, G. and Prinz, J. (2009), Team performance and individual career duration: evidence from the German 'Bundesliga', in P. Andersson, P. Ayton and C. Schmidt (eds), *Myths and Facts about Football: The Economics and Psychology of the World's Greatest Sport*, Cambridge: Cambridge Scholars Press, pp. 327–48.

Gabriel, P.E., Johnson, C. and Stanton, T.J. (1995), An examination of customer racial discrimination in the market for basketball memorabilia, *Journal of Business*, **68** (2), 215–30.

Gabriel, P.E., Johnson, C. and Stanton, T.J. (1999), Customer racial discrimination for baseball memorabilia, *Applied Economics*, **31** (11), 1331–5.

Gammelsæter, H. and Senaux, B. (2013), The governance of the game: a review of the research on football's governance, in S. Söderman and H. Dolles (eds), *Handbook of Research on Sport and Business*, Cheltenham, UK and Northampton, MA, USA: Edward Elgar, pp. 142–60.

Goddard, J. and Wilson, J.O.S. (2009), Racial discrimination in English professional football: evidence from an empirical analysis of players' career progression, *Cambridge Journal of Economics*, **33** (2), 295–316.

Groothuis, P.A. and Hill, J.R. (2004), Exit discrimination in the NBA: a duration analysis of career length, *Economic Inquiry*, **42** (2), 341–9.

Hamilton, B.H. (1997), Racial discrimination and professional basketball salaries in the 1990s, *Applied Economics*, **29** (3), 287–96.

Hanssen, A. (1998), The cost of discrimination: a study of Major League Baseball, *Southern Economic Journal*, **64** (3), 603–27.

Hanssen, F.A. and Andersen, T. (1999), Has discrimination lessened over time? A test using baseball's all-star vote, *Economic Inquiry*, **37** (2), 326–52.

Harder, J.W. (1992), Play for pay: effects of inequity in a pay-for-performance context, *Administrative Science Quarterly*, **37** (2), 321–35.

Hoang, H. and Rascher, D. (1999), The NBA, exit discrimination and career earnings, *Industrial Relations*, **38** (1), 69–91.

Horowitz, I. and Zappe, C. (1998), Thanks for the memories: baseball veterans' end-of-career salaries, *Managerial and Decision Economics*, **19** (6), 377–82.

Huebl, L. and Swieter, D. (2002), Der Spielermarkt in der Fußball-Bundesliga [The player transfer market in the German Bundesliga], *Zeitschrift für Betriebswirtschaft*, **72** (supplement issue, no. 4, 'Sportökonomie'), 105–25.

Idson, T.L. and Kahane, L.H. (2000), Team effects on compensation: an application to salary determination in the National Hockey League, *Economic Inquiry*, **38** (2), 345–57.

Kahane, L.H. (2009), Salary dispersion and team production: evidence from the National Hockey League, mimeo, East Bay: Department of Economics, California State University.

Kahn, L.M. (1992), The effects of race on professional football players' compensation, *Industrial and Labor Relations Review*, **45** (2), 295–310.

Kahn, L.M. (1993), Free agency, long-term contracts and compensation in Major League Baseball: estimates from panel data, *Review of Economics and Statistics*, **75** (1), 157–64.

Kahn, L.M. (2000), The sports business as a labor market laboratory, *Journal of Economic Perspectives*, **14** (3), 75–94.

Kahn, L.M. and Sherer, P.D. (1988), Racial differences in professional basketball players' compensation, *Journal of Labor Economics*, **6** (1), 40–61.

Kalter, F. (1999), Ethnische Kundenpräferenzen im professionellen Sport? Der Fall der Fußballbundesliga [Ethnical customer preferences in professional sports? The case of the German Bundesliga], *Zeitschrift für Soziologie*, **28** (3), 219–34.

Koch, J.V. and Vander Hill, C.W. (1988), Is there discrimination in the 'Black Man's Game'?, *Social Science Quarterly*, **69** (1), 83–94.

Krueger, A.B. (2005), The economics of real superstars: the market for rock concerts in the material world, *Journal of Labor Economics*, **23** (1), 1–30.

Kuhn, P. and Weinberger, C. (2005), Leadership skills and wages, *Journal of Labor Economics*, **23** (3), 395–436.

Kuper, S. and Szymanski, S. (2009), *Soccernomics*, New York: Nation Books.

Leeds, M. and von Allmen, P. (2002), *The Economics of Sports*, Boston, MA: Addison-Wesley.

Lehmann, E.E. and Schulze, G.G. (2008), What does it take to be a star? The role of performance and the media for German soccer players, *Applied Economics Quarterly*, **54**, 59–70.

Lehmann, E. and Weigand, J. (1999), Determinanten der Entlohnung von Profifußballspielern – Eine empirische Analyse für die deutsche Bundesliga [The determinants of professional football players' salaries – an empirical analysis on the German Bundesliga], *Betriebswirtschaftliche Forschung und Praxis*, **51** (2), 124–35.

Lucifora, C. and Simmons, R. (2003), Superstar effects in sports: evidence from Italian soccer, *Journal of Sports Economics*, **4** (1), 35–55.

Milgrom, P. and Roberts, J. (1992), *Economics, Management, and Organization*, Englewood Cliffs, NJ: Prentice-Hall.

Nardinelli, C. and Simon, C. (1990), Customer racial discrimination in the market for memorabilia: the case of baseball, *The Quarterly Journal of Economics*, **105** (3), 575–95.

Neale, W.C. (1964), The peculiar economics of professional sport, *The Quarterly Journal of Economics*, **78** (1), 1–14.

Rosen, S. (1981), The economics of superstars, *American Economic Review*, **71** (5), 845–58.

Rottenberg, S. (1956), The baseball players' labor market, *Journal of Political Economy*, **64** (3), 242–60.

Sanderson, A. and Siegfried, J.J. (1997), The implications of athlete freedom to contract: lessons from North America, *Economic Affairs*, **17** (3), 7–12.

Sandy, R., Sloane, P.J. and Rosentraub, M.S. (2004), *The Economics of Sport: An International Perspective*, Basingstoke: Palgrave Macmillan.

Scully, G.W. (1995), *The Market Structure of Sports*, Chicago, IL: University of Chicago Press.

Simmons, R. and Berri, D.J. (2009), Gains from specialization and free agency: the story from the gridiron, *Review of Industrial Organization*, **34** (1), 81–98.

Simmons, R. and Forrest, D. (2004), Buying success: team performance and wage bills in U.S. and European sports leagues, in R. Fort and J. Fizel (eds), *International Sports Economics Comparisons*, Westport, CT: Praeger, pp. 123–40.

Szymanski, S. (2000), A market test for discrimination in the English professional soccer leagues, *Journal of Political Economy*, **108** (3), 590–603.

Szymanski, S. (2009), *Playbooks and Checkbooks: An Introduction to the Economics of Modern Sports*, Princeton, NJ: Princeton University Press.

Szymanski, S. and Kuypers, T. (1999), *Winners and Losers: The Business Strategy of Football*, London: Viking.

Vincent, C. and Eastman, B. (2009), Determinants of pay in the NFL. A quantile regression approach, *Journal of Sports Economics*, **10** (3), 256–77.

White, H. (1980), A heteroskedasticity-consistent covariance matrix estimator and a direct test for heteroskedasticity, *Econometrica*, **48** (4), 817–38.

Wilson, D. and Ying, Y.-H. (2003), Nationality preferences for labour in the international football industry, *Applied Economics*, **35** (14), 1551–9.

Zimbalist, A. (1992), *Baseball and billions*, New York: Basic Books.

APPENDIX

Table 21.A1　*Wage bills, pay distribution, and team performance in professional team sports leagues*

Author(s) and year of publication	Setting (league and time period) and estimation technique	Results
Team payrolls and performance		
Szymanski and Kuypers (1999)	English Professional Football 1996/97, 96 clubs 1978–97, 40 clubs 1950–60, 28 clubs	78% of variation in league position can be explained by differences in wage bills. 92% of variation in league position can be accounted for by wage expenditure. 50% of variation in league position is due to differences in team wage bills. Thus, wage expenditures did matter in the 1950s as well, but were less important than they have been in the era of free agency
Simmons and Forrest (2004)	English Premier League 1977/78–2000/01 (364 team-year observations) German Bundesliga 1981/82–1995/96 (246 team-year observations) Italian Serie A (214 team-year observations) MLB 1985–2001 (441 team-year observations) NBA 1985–2001 (429 team-year observations) NFL 1981–2000 (574 team-year observations) NHL 1995–2001 (263 team-year observations) OLS regression with team fixed effects	Higher relative spending on team salaries generates higher win percentage or higher points ratio in any of the leagues, regardless of league design or specific measures to regulate the player market. However, overall $R2$ values are lower for regressions in North American leagues. This reflects the greater extent of regulation of player markets in the US compared to Europe. For most leagues, spending on player salaries that outstrip rivals' expenses is subject to diminishing returns In Europe, a higher relative wage bill is associated with increased probability of a top-six place in the respective league and qualification for supra-national cup competition. In the US, a higher relative wage is associated with an increased probability of playoff qualification
Pay distribution and team performance in professional team sports leagues		
Harder (1992)	MLB, 1976–77 and 1987–88 (320–406 different players), NBA, 1987–88 (301 players) Ordinary least squares (OLS)	Overpaid- and underpaid players respond differently to inequity: while underpaid individuals tend to behave more selfishly, overpaid players are more team-oriented

Table 21.A1   (continued)

Author(s) and year of publication	Setting (league and time period) and estimation technique	Results
	Pay distribution and team performance in professional team sports leagues	
Bloom (1999)	MLB, 1985–93 (29 teams, 1644 different players) Individual level: OLS team level: autoregressive procedure to control for serial dependence and cross-sectional heteroscedasticity	A more unequal/hierarchical pay distribution has a statistically significant and negative impact on player performance, i.e. the performance of players on teams with greater pay dispersion is lower. However, greater dispersion is negatively related to the performance of those lower in the dispersion and positively related to the performance of those higher in the dispersion. Finally, a more hierarchical pay dispersion leads to poorer team performance
Depken (2000)	MLB, 1985–98 (n = 378 team-year observations, unbalanced panel due to expansion teams) Random- and fixed-effects models	Controlling for the teams' wage expenditures, a more unequal intra-team pay distribution (as measured by the Herfindahl-Hirschman Index) is associated with a poorer team performance
Berri and Jewell (2004)	NBA, 1996/97–2000/01 (with 199 team-year observations). Fixed effects estimation	Salary dispersion (measured by Herfindahl-Hirschman Index) has no statistically significant impact on team performance (win percentage in regular season games)
Franck and Nüesch (2007)	German Bundesliga, 12 seasons (1995/96–2006/07) with 216 team-year observations 2SLS estimation with team fixed effects	The relationship between pay inequality and team performance follows a u-shaped pattern, i.e. teams do better by either deciding for an equal or an unequal pay structure. To be 'stuck in the middle' is, however, detrimental to team performance
Kahane (2009)	NHL, 2001/02–2007/08 (excluding the 2004/05 lockout season), balanced panel with 30 teams (180 observations) Fixed effects regression	Conditional salary dispersion has a negative and statistically significant impact on team performance (i.e. the number of regular season wins and the probability of making the playoffs)

Table 21.A2   *Individual performance, superstar effects, discrimination and remuneration in professional team sports leagues*

Author(s) and year of publication	Setting (league and time period) and estimation technique	Results
Superstar effects and remuneration		
Horowitz and Zappe (1998)	MLB, 123 position players who had played at least 1000 games with at least 500 appearances at one position, 1986–90 OLS regression	Peak end-of-career salaries are strongly influenced by career performance while the most recent performance is irrelevant. Apart from lifetime achievements the principal determinant of peak end-of-career salaries is commitment to the team that brought a player 'to the show'
Lucifora and Simmons (2003)	Italian Serie A and B, 1995/96 (n = 533 different outfield players) OLS regressions	Player salaries are a function of the individuals' experience, performance, and reputation. International status and goal-scoring rate are the most important determinants. The fact that the marginal effects on earnings of these performance variables are increasing steeply suggests existence of 'superstar effects'
Lehmann and Schule (2008)	German Bundesliga, 1998/99 and 1999/2000, 651 player-year observations OLS and quantile regressions	Popularity (as measured by the number of Google hits) has a positive and statistically significant, yet decreasing impact on player remuneration. This finding is not consistent with the theory of superstars
Discrimination and remuneration		
Kahn and Sherer (1988)	NBA, 1985/86, 226 players OLS and 2SLS regression	White players earn a statistically significant premium of about 20%. Replacing one black player with an identical white player raises the respective club's home attendance by 8000–13 000 fans per season. The two results together are consistent with the idea of 'customer discrimination'
Koch and Vander Hill (1988)	NBA, 1984/85, 278 players OLS regression, Chow test	Controlling for player and team characteristics as well as the size and the racial composition of the city a franchise is located in results in a statistically significant pay penalty for black players. A Chow test reveals that black players earn significantly less per unit of performance than white players (depending on the specification about 5–7%)
Kahn (1992)	NFL, 1989 season, 1363 players OLS regressions	Controlling for performance and other (potential) determinants of player salaries the difference between black and white players' remuneration is small (at most 4%) and statistically insignificant in most specifications

Table 21.A2   (continued)

Author(s) and year of publication	Setting (league and time period) and estimation technique	Results
Discrimination and remuneration		
Hamilton (1997)	NBA, 1994/95 season, 332 players OLS, Tobit and quantile regressions	Controlling for player and team characteristics, 'standard regression approaches' indicate no difference between black and white salaries. However, more elaborate estimation techniques show that whites receive a considerable pay premium of 18% at the upper end of the salary distribution, suggesting a form of consumer discrimination in which sports fans prefer to see white star players
Bodvarsson and Brastow (1999)	NBA 1985/86 (n = 236 players) and 1990/91 (n = 263 players) OLS regression	The black/white player salary differential that existed until the late 1980s completely disappeared in the early 1990s due to the 1988 NBA collective bargaining agreement fostering the mobility of players and the arrival of four new teams. These developments increased labor market competition which, in turn, made it more costly for employers (i.e. team owners and managers) to indulge tastes for discrimination
Szymanski (2000)	English Premier League, 1978–93, 39 clubs, unbalanced panel Arellano-Bond dynamic panel estimator	A club with a higher than average percentage of black players could expect a systematically better league position than the wage bill would appear to justify. This gain would be achieved at no extra financial expense, suggesting that black players receive a lower return on their talent than white players of equal ability. A club hiring no black player would have to pay a 5% premium in terms of its total wage bill to maintain any given league position compared to a non-discriminating team
Berri and Simmons (2009)	NFL, 1995–2006 with 530 player-year observations (quarterbacks only) Quantile regressions	Black quarterbacks are more likely to run with the American football than their white colleagues. Yet, they are not rewarded for their distinctively greater rushing contributions. This is suggestive of salary discrimination against black quarterbacks and is particularly important in the top half of the income distribution
Discrimination in the market for memorabilia		
Nardinelli and Simon (1990)	MLB, 344 hitters and 233 pitchers active in the 1970 season Tobit and probit regressions	Trading cards for nonwhite hitters (pitchers) sold for about 10% (13%) less than the cards of whites of comparable ability. Cards featuring black players (Hispanics) sold for 6% (16%) (pitchers) and 17% (16%) (hitters) less.

Table 21.A2   (continued)

Author(s) and year of publication	Setting (league and time period) and estimation technique	Results
Discrimination in the market for memorabilia		
		Pitchers are the most visible players in baseball and discrimination may be greater, the more visible a player
Gabriel, Johnson and Stanton (1995, 1999)	MLB, rookie cards issued from 1974–82 MLB, rookie cards issued from 1984–90 OLS regression	Controlling for past player performance and expected future performance, the prices of trading cards are not affected by a player's race (the possibility of a bias that could occur because race influences expectations of future performance is ruled out). However, over time rookie card prices are to some extent influenced by ethnicity as performance expectations become less important towards the end of a player's career
Kalter (1999)	German Bundesliga in the season 1997/98, 422 different players	Judged by the number of replica shirts sold fans have a clear preference for players from South America and, to a lesser extent, those from Western Europe. Significantly fewer shirts are sold with the names of players from Eastern Europe (controlling, of course, for individual performance)
Discrimination in hall of fame and all star votes		
Hanssen (1998)	MLB, 1950–1984, 16 teams that existed for the entire period, i.e. balanced panel with 400 team-year observations Instrumental variables approach	In the early 1950s, a higher percentage of black players in the starting lineup was associated with a significantly higher win percentage. This impact declined as the average number of black players on major league rosters increased. Due to differences in fan preferences the rate of integration was significantly lower in the 'American League' as compared to the 'National League' (i.e. each black player reduced attendance significantly more on an AL team than he would have done on an NL team)
Hanssen and Andersen (1999)	MLB, all star votes 1970, 1971, 1973, 1975, 1977, 1979, 1980, 1985, 1990 and 1996 Robust OLS regression	Controlling for individual performance, African Americans received significantly fewer votes for the annual 'All Star Game' than comparable white players in the early and mid-1970s, suggesting the existence of considerable customer discrimination. Since the early 1980s, however, discrimination disappeared completely and even reversed itself in the more recent years (i.e. since the mid-1990s)

Table 21.A2   (continued)

Author(s) and year of publication	Setting (league and time period) and estimation technique	Results
	Discrimination in professional team sports leagues (entry barriers, game appearances and career length)	
Hoang and Rascher (1999)	NBA, 1980–86, all players selected in the first two rounds of the annual draft (n = 275 players who received a contract and played at least one year in the NBA) Event history analysis (piecewise constant rate model)	Controlling for individual performance and team characteristics, white players have a 36% lower hazard rate than black players of being cut from the league. Thus, while a black player can expect to play 5.5 years, career length for a comparable white player is 7.5 years. The career earnings effect of exit discrimination in the 1980s is, therefore, considerably higher than the career earnings effect of wage discrimination ($808 000 vs $329 000)
Conlin and Emerson (2003)	NFL, 1986–91, 1827 out of 2016 drafted players OLS regressions, probit and ordered probit estimations	Controlling for player and team characteristics, white players have, on average, a 0.107 lower probability of making the team and start, on average, 0.837 games per season less than non-white players. These results suggest that NFL front offices discriminate against non-white players in their hiring practices and/or that that NFL coaching staffs discriminate against white players in their cutting, training and playing decisions
Groothuis and Hill (2004)	NBA, 1989–99 (n = 1113 different players with 4476 player-year observations) Estimation of semi-parametric hazard functions	Controlling for individual performance (games played, points, assists, blocks, steals, turnovers), tenure, height, weight, and draft number a player's race has no impact on career duration
Frick, Pietzner and Prinz (2007, 2009)	German Bundesliga, 1963/64–2002/03 (n = 4116 different players and 15 299 player-year observations). Cox survival models	Controlling for the individual player's performance, athletes from South America, Western Europe as well as Eastern Europe have a higher probability of exiting the league than German players. Most of the exits are voluntary, i.e. the players leave the Bundesliga to sign more lucrative contracts in either England, Italy and Spain. Only in the case of Eastern Europeans, the majority of the exits may be involuntary, i.e. these players may suffer from 'discrimination'

Table 21.A2   (continued)

Author(s) and year of publication	Setting (league and time period) and estimation technique	Results
\multicolumn{3}{l}{Discrimination in professional team sports leagues (entry barriers, game appearances and career length)}
Goddard and Wilson (2009)	English professional football, 1986–2001 (four divisions, n = 11 182 observations) Simulated maximum likelihood estimation, probit and ordered probit regression	Retention depends mainly on player age, divisional status, number of first-team appearances, playing position, and place of birth. Divisional transition depends an player age, number of first-team appearances, and playing position. Black players tend to be employed by teams of higher divisional status and have higher retention probabilities, suggesting a particular form of hiring discrimination that affects the process of becoming a professional football player

22 Examining corporate social responsibility in football: the application of grounded theory methodology

Christos Anagnostopoulos

1 INTRODUCTION

Grounded theory is a systematic inductive and comparative methodology for conducting inquiry with the purpose of developing theory (Bryant and Charmaz, 2007). Jones and Noble (2007) refer to Locke (2001) in giving three main reasons why grounded theory has proved popular in management research: (a) it is useful for developing new theory or fresh insights into old theory; (b) it generates theory of direct interest and relevance for practitioners, and (c) it can uncover micro-management processes in complex and unfolding scenarios. Notwithstanding its increasing popularity as a research methodology within the management discipline, its application in the sport management field has been relatively sparse. Such is the dearth of grounded theory in sport business and management research that, for their publication *Qualitative Research in Sport Management*, Edwards and Skinner (2009: 347) had to make reference to two postgraduate theses and two conference papers in order to illustrate the application of grounded theory in various sport management contexts. The reasons behind the methodology's failure to penetrate the sport management field of study remain a 'curious paradox', as Sotiriadou and Shilbury (2010: 185) point out.

The present chapter attempts to address this shortfall. Of course, this is not a manual for conducting a grounded theory-based empirical project. Specific books that provide such step-by-step guidance can be found in most university libraries. Instead, this chapter hopes to encourage more grounded theory-based research projects from sport management researchers by providing an example of an empirical study employing the methodology. Its emphasis is on the broader philosophical difficulties associated with the different variants of grounded theory which have often brought early-career researchers up short; addressing these difficulties should remove this potential stumbling block. By way of illustration, all these philosophical arguments are contextualized with reference to a project that looked at how managers in English football make decisions regarding their corporate social responsibility (CSR) strategy. This provides the methodological approach under discussion with a practical application.

The chapter is structured as follows. The scene is set by offering some reasons for focusing on the concept of corporate social responsibility. This scene-setting also has the benefit of outlining the study's context, namely, English football. Next, an explanation of the reasons for grounded theory's employment over other qualitative research methodologies is provided. We then turn our attention to the place of the traditional literature review in grounded theory studies. This is a controversial issue within the methodology, and so it is addressed in some depth. This discussion is in dialogue with a consideration of the researcher's role when employing grounded theory. The chapter then goes on to discuss the need to observe basic philosophical and methodological consistencies when conducting grounded theory-based research, and concludes by highlighting three key issues that prospective researchers intending to employ grounded theory must take into account.

2 CSR AS AN AREA FOR SPORT MANAGEMENT RESEARCH: THE CONTEXT OF ENGLISH FOOTBALL

The concept of corporate social responsibility has, particularly in its abbreviated form CSR, become a widely used shorthand term to cover a multitude of corporate activities. These range from business philanthropy to the responsible management of a company's external impacts on society, including community investment (Marsden, 2006: 39). In this research project, the concept of CSR was used to describe the way in which football clubs in England's top two tiers have mobilized resources in the service of a variety of outreach and environmental-related programmes. Football clubs in England have a relatively long history of engaging in community-based work, especially since the establishment of the national 'Football in The Community' (FiTC) programme in the mid-1980s (Russell, 1997). As Mellor (2008: 319) points out, on the arrival of a New Labour government in 1997 the community work in which football clubs were expected to engage expanded beyond traditional children's coaching schemes and player appearances. Indeed, under the ideological dogma of the 'Third Way', the party introduced a number of reforms in welfare and other areas of public policy that focused on creating a strong sense of responsibility across society. According to Mellor (2008: 318), the football sector was also part of this political agenda; this was because football had been identified by the British Government as a potential key deliverer of a range of policy objectives as diverse as health, education, community cohesion, regeneration and crime reduction. Even after the spending review ordered by the new coalition government in 2010, the football sector continued to be seen as a crucial delivery mechanism for various social programmes aiming to tackle these issues.

English football in particular has been subject to a growing body of analysis on the grounds of governance, commercialization and management and business practices. Despite this, empirical works that look explicitly at the business side of English football and its coupling with socially responsible practices have been few and far between. Notable exceptions include Brown et al. (2010), McGuire (2008), Slack and Shrives (2008), Walters and Tacon (2010) and Walters and Chadwick (2009). Useful though these empirical studies are, none of them has tried to identify and understand managers' interpretations associated with the strategy in regards to CSR programmes within the English football sector. The study this chapter draws on, therefore, was based on the premise that the approach taken by empirical researchers reflects an oversimplification of the decision-making process in regards to CSR in this particular business sector. It neglects, *inter alia*, (1) the managers' cognitions and interpretations of the job they do, (2) how managers construe the football club's internal organization as a means of facilitating the strategy behind the formulation and implementation of CSR, (3) possible external factors that may shape the managers' decisions on the formulation and implementation of CSR, and thus ultimately (4) the ways in which the espousal of CSR in the football sector are being manifested by the managers who oversee its application. There was, then, no theoretical framework available within which these points could be addressed. It was the researcher's wish to do so by drawing on the cognitive perspective of organizational theory's social context. This required a certain amount of theory building, and grounded theory was selected as the means of accomplishing this.

In this empirical research project, theory development was employed in the hope of arriving at a better understanding of the decision-making process in regards to CSR in English football. Having said that, the aim was not to seek out relationships which could then predict the conditions of CSR; rather, this study's power of explanation was associated with the context from which it emerged. In other words, the research related to a specific 'phenomenon' (that is, the decision-making process in regards to CSR) in the context of a clearly identified group of individuals (that is, managers in English football). This contextual specificity means that the research at hand yielded a substantive theory, limited in origin and application to a specific kind of human experience or interaction (Kearney, 2007: 148). These limitations differentiate it from formal theories, which depict the predictors and dynamics of social actions and interactions general enough to be applied across a wide range of instances and contexts (cf. Birks and Mills, 2011: 156; Corbin and Strauss, 2008: 55–6; Glaser and Strauss, 1967: 32–4; Kearney, 2007: 148).

From my point of view, it is important for sport management researchers to keep this differentiation between substantive and formal theory in mind. This is for two main reasons. First, undertaking theory development may present itself as a grandiose task, especially for novice or early career researchers. This should not be the case. Without wishing to underplay the challenges encountered by those working on theory development, a clarification of their inquiries' contextual specificities might help to alleviate some of the expectations attaching themselves to 'theory development'. Secondly, theory development should be seen as an opportunity (a) to discern (possible) differences highlighted by the sport context, and thus to answer the need for theory development while acknowledging the various particular characteristics associated with sport (Chalip, 2006), or (b) to explore synergies (Wolfe et al., 2005) between mainstream management formal theories and substantive theories derived from the sporting context.

Reflection on all the above-mentioned points raised the question: 'How do managers in English football make strategic decisions regarding CSR?' This subject, while perhaps very broad, nevertheless lent itself well to a qualitative research study that employed grounded theory methodology; a reader may infer from it that the study investigated the decision-making process in regard to CSR through the meanings attached to it by those overseeing its application within a specific business context. Corbin and Strauss (2008: 25) suggest that when employing qualitative research methodologies – and grounded theory in particular – researchers need to frame their research question in a manner that provides them with sufficient flexibility and freedom to explore a topic in some depth. The point of departure of this research, therefore, was that the way managers themselves interpret the decision-making process is key to understanding the strategy English football clubs have adopted with regard to the concept of CSR.

The study was populated by the top two divisions of English football. Thirty-two CSR managers were interviewed through snowball and purposive sampling. The sample provided a good mixture of football-playing status as it consisted of 12 clubs from the

Premiership, given the code Pr-FC, and 13 clubs from the Championship, given the code Ch-FC. Of those CSR managers, six were working directly for the club, 16 were engaged with the club's charitable trust, and three had dual capacity in both organizations. In two cases I interviewed more than one member of the respective club or trust. In addition, four managers of the two respective football leagues also took part in this empirical research. Further interviews were conducted with the CSR manager of the governing body of European football (UEFA) and with the community director of the English Professional Footballers' Association (PFA). The selected interviewees were considered key participants as they were directors, heads of departments and senior managers directly responsible for setting strategic goals and overseeing the general CSR work being done. The choice of participants, therefore, was made on the basis that these were individuals specializing in this area and consequently possessing the maximum amount of information as far as the formulation and implementation of CSR was concerned.

Given, however, that 'those undertaking qualitative studies have a baffling number of choices of approaches to inquiry' (Creswell, 2007: 6), a sport management researcher might question why grounded theory was judged the most suitable methodology for investigating this particular topic. The following section attempts to answer this question by explaining the reasons behind grounded theory's adoption within the example study. In doing so I hope that researchers will discern the fit between the study's scope and the chosen methodology. The discussion then moves on to address some key philosophical issues which sport management researchers will need to consider when embarking on a grounded theory-based study.

3   OPTING FOR GROUNDED THEORY

While this inquiry into football managers' interpretations of CSR was conducted using grounded theory, the choice was not a foregone conclusion. Other qualitative-oriented methodologies such as ethnography, phenomenology and the case study were also considered. Although it is far beyond the scope of this chapter to provide an exhaustive list of the similarities and differences evidenced in these methodologies, this section will touch upon some points that, ultimately, confirmed grounded theory as the best choice for the task at hand.

First, ethnography, which advocates the collection of data through participant observation (see, for example, Dibben and Dolles, 2013, in this volume), could have proved a very fruitful methodology for this study given that it examines how a culture-sharing group works. As Stern (1994: 215) points out, however, one stream of ethnographic reseach starts out from a given theoretical perspective, often based on much preceding work undertaken by previous anthropologists. Another stream, for example, Dibben and Dolles (2013) however point out, going into the field without a pre-determined theory or set of theories is central to a sound account of observations. One of the weaknesses identified in the 'pre-field' work analysis for this study was that empirical research on CSR in sport – and in football in particular – was informed by certain theoretical perspectives such as stakeholder theory (Hamil and Morrow, 2011; Walters and Tacon, 2010), corporate citizenship (Walters and Chadwick, 2009) and legitimacy theory (Babiak and Trendafilova, 2011; Slack and Shrives, 2008). The current research therefore, although not 'a-theoretical', aimed to extend theoretical knowledge of CSR by moving away from those theoretical perspectives that have dominated examinations of the subject. In addition, other academic commitments would not have allowed me to gain the necessary access – both in terms of scope and time – that participant observation ideally requires. So it is that in the quest for a suitable methodology, practicalities can have a major role to play in deciding between schools that have a good deal of epistemological crossover (see, for example, the Straussian variant of grounded theory explained further along with some forms of ethnography).

The approaches of both phenomenology and case study were considered to methodologically 'inform' this study. Phenomenology describes the meaning certain individuals (for example, managers in the football sector) attribute to their lived experiences of a concept or 'phenomenon' (for example, CSR). Furthermore, this approach treats culture with a good measure of caution and suspicion. That is, phenomenology requires researchers to engage with phenomena in the world and make sense of them directly and immediately. 'Inherited understanding' must be left aside – to the best of our ability – in order for the experience of phenomena to speak to us first hand (Crotty, 1998). As will be discussed further, and avoiding the temptation to delve into too complex a sociological or philosophical discussion here, it was difficult to imagine how I could have 'bracketed' my personal biography (that is, this 'inherited understanding') from the topic I was researching.

Case study methodology (refer, for example, to Skille, 2013 in this volume) also involves the study of an issue explored (for example, the decision-making process with regards to CSR) through one or more cases within a bounded system (for example, English football) and its results take the form of a case description as well as reporting case-based themes (Creswell, 2007: 73). These two methodologies could, indeed, address my process-related questions of 'how' and 'why' (without placing too much emphasis on 'what', that is, the content of the CSR programmes), but would have provided a 'thick description' of what I was trying to explore. Although Pratt (2009: 857) acknowledges that 'thick description' has not only a venerable history, but it can also contribute to theory, he suggests that limiting an analysis to simply describing what one found is often inadequate. The current research sought for theory development and not an in-depth description of the decision-making being the formulation and implementation of CSR in the football context. Strauss and Corbin (1990: 29) clearly differentiate theory from description by saying that:

> Theory uses concepts. Similar data are grouped and given conceptual labels. This means placing interpretation on the data. The concepts, then, are related by means of statements of relationship. In description, data may be organised according to themes. These themes may be conceptualisations of data, but are more likely to be a précis or summaries of words taken directly from the data. There is little, if any, interpretation of data. Nor is there any attempt to relate the themes to form a conceptual scheme.

This distinction became evident in my study while collating data through interviews: the ongoing analysis influenced the questions that were asked, and the direction of the interview became driven by the emerging theory, that is, through theoretical sampling. From a phenomenological perspective, in contrast, 'openness remains irrespective of the number of interviews; the emphasis is on "the experience of . . . " and is driven from the individual account as opposed to the emerging theory' (Wimpenny and Gass, 2000: 1489).

The preceding reasons should of course be read as indicative rather than comprehensive. It was however upon reflection of the above mentioned 'attributes' that some widely used qualitative-oriented methodologies possess that grounded theory was judged as the most suitable methodology to inform the empirical study in question. The upshot of all this is that a sport management researcher should be aware that the justification of a chosen methodology goes hand-in-hand with the purpose of the research or, as Crotty (1998: 2) puts it, 'with the research question that our piece of inquiry is seeking to answer'. To complicate matters, the most appropriate methodologies often contain a good deal of overlap. Nevertheless, a researcher should pay attention to the factors determining the choice of methodology throughout the entire research process.

By employing grounded theory, the researcher is often faced with a number of issues that will need to be resolved in order to ensure methodological consistency. The place of the traditional literature review, for example, is a source of controversy in grounded theory-based studies, and here I will take the opportunity to explain how I dealt with this matter in my empirical research project. Furthermore, Fendt and Sachs (2008: 450) contend that to engage in grounded theory is to venture into a maelstrom of 'realities' and contradictions. One could argue that this maelstrom is characterized by a philosophical divergence as well as various procedural discrepancies. What variant of grounded theory, for example, should the prospective grounded theory sport management researcher adopt? Glaser's emergent type of theory development, epistemologically informed by the positivist tradition? Or perhaps Strauss's highly complex and systematic coding techniques, associated with symbolic interactionism, might fit the study better? Alternatively, Charmaz has recently found both 'Glaserian' and 'Straussian' versions of grounded theory, the sharp distinctions between them notwithstanding, to be mired in positivist rhetoric. Should the researcher answer her call for a more constructivist grounded theory? Discussion of these procedural discrepancies between variants of grounded theory uncovers some philosophical chasms and, in the interests of methodological rigour, these divergences must be addressed. First, though, we need to consider the role of the literature review within grounded theory research along with observations of our own potential influence on the reviewing process.

4 RESEARCHER'S ROLE AND THE REVIEW OF THE LITERATURE IN GROUNDED THEORY

Strauss and Corbin (1990: 48) hold the view that 'we all bring to the inquiry a considerable background in professional and disciplinary literature'. At this point then it is right to acknowledge that I have been personally involved with football in various capacities. I played at professional level in my home country and I worked on a part-time basis for almost five years in one of the Premier League's top-tier football clubs. Moreover, my academic qualifications have not only afforded me a good level of familiarity with 'theories' that underpin the professional practices adopted by today's top-tiers English football clubs but have also helped me to direct my research interest towards the investigation of CSR and the role managers play within it. Thus, both my strong 'sporting' background and a general familiarity with the football sector itself formed a personal biography that fostered an element of 'sensitivity'. In grounded theory parlance, sensitivity means having insight, being tuned in, and being able to pick up on relevant issues, events, and happenings in data. My personal experience in this context may be taken for what Gummesson (2000: 14) refers to as the 'pre-understanding' of a specific problem or social environment before one embarks upon a research project. In doing grounded theory, this type of researcher's 'exposure' may increase the trustworthiness of the study outcome. Research access, for example, was partly achieved through my contact at the club where I used to work; the CSR manager there served as my 'gatekeeper', at least at the initial stages of my research. Johns (2011: 32) calls such clarifications 'methodological context'. I would encourage all sport management researchers to clarify their position when venturing into a grounded theory study, whether their personal biographies have a bearing on their chosen topic or not.

This need for researcher disclosure is intimately related to the role of the literature review within the application of grounded theory methodology. Reading for the purpose of reviewing is a 'taken for granted' exercise through which the researcher sensitizes his or her study to the pertinent issues extant in the relevant literature (Charmaz, 2006; Hart, 1998). However, within grounded theory this is a somewhat controversial activity. Classic grounded theorists (Glaser, 1978; Glaser and Strauss, 1967), for example, advocate delaying the literature review until after the analysis has been completed. Charmaz (2006: 165) explains that this practice hopes to prevent the researcher's seeing his or her data through the lens of earlier ideas. The obvious problem here is that classic grounded theory tends to view the researcher as a *tabula rasa*, while, as we have seen, Strauss and Corbin (1990: 48) suggest otherwise. Based on the premise that grounded theory is an appropriate methodological path where the researcher has little extant knowledge of the topic they wish to investigate, the question becomes: how can a productive 'lack' of knowledge be acquired unless a preliminary review of the relevant literature is undertaken? One of my earlier arguments was that empirical studies have not looked at the managers' decision-making process with regard to the formulation and implementation of CSR programmes in the English football sector. How did I reach such a conclusion, if not by reading around the topic area?

Strauss and Corbin (1990: 42) counsel researchers to familiarize themselves with previous works in the field of inquiry so that they may acquire 'a rich background of information that "sensitises" you to what is going on with the phenomenon you are studying'. Theoretical sensitivity can be a rich source of stimulation for the researcher, including (but certainly not limited to) the generation of initial research questions. Equally important is the fact that familiarity with existing literature and thus with the 'phenomenon' under study (in my case, the decision-making behind CSR) helps researchers to understand what actors (here managers) are saying and doing (Corbin and Strauss, 2008; Strauss and Corbin, 1990, 1998). Ultimately, an understanding of *what* such actors do and say should lead to understanding of *why* they do what they do.

In consideration of the above, the process of 'reviewing the literature' in this study took place in two separate phases differing in both time and scope. The first phase took place before I entered the field and started talking with managers from the football sector who make strategic decisions about CSR programmes. The scope here was to seek a broad understanding of the notions of strategy and CSR in mainstream management literature in general and, subsequently, in the sport/football sector in particular. The basic goal, therefore, was to gain an appreciation of the range of conditions in which football clubs have espoused the concept of CSR. The second phase of the literature review took place after the intended substantive theory had been developed. The scope at this phase was to place my study's findings in critical conversation with the literature as Strauss and Corbin (1998) suggest and by doing so to establish a new substantive theory within the body of knowledge already existing in the field.

If reviewing the literature has been a controversial 'exercise' for those who employ grounded theory, the different variants of the methodology emerging since the seminal work of Glaser and Strauss (1967) have often constituted a stumbling block for researchers wishing to work in the area. Fendt and Sachs (2008) advise a researcher to position the different variants of grounded theory in such a way as to make clear which stance is being deployed for his or her research and on what grounds. I followed this advice in my own research, motivated by a desire for coherence and methodological rigour, and the resulting discussion of the procedural discrepancies between different versions of grounded theory is given below. These procedural discrepancies will be seen, in turn, to shed light on ontological and epistemological divergences. Prospective sport management researchers must engage with these divergences in order to ensure that their own research endeavours demonstrate philosophical consistency.

5   DEALING WITH DIVERGING VARIANTS OF GROUNDED THEORY

The purpose of this section is, in deference to Fendt and Sachs (2008), to position the different variants of grounded theory by making clear which stance was deployed by the study under discussion and on what grounds. Corbin (Corbin and Strauss, 2008) recognizes the influence that contemporary thought on grounded theory (for example, Charmaz, 2006; Clarke, 2005) has had on her own thinking in this area. Accordingly, although reference will be made to these latest thoughts on grounded theory (for example, Charmaz's constructivist approach in 2006) the emphasis is on the two most popular variants of grounded theory used in organization and management research (Jones and Noble, 2007). The intention here is not to resurrect the old Glaser-versus-Strauss debate, nor to revisit the argument over who can claim ownership of the methodology. Rather, aligning this study with the work of Jones and Noble (2007), I will briefly examine the different emphases and variations between the two schools which have hampered the ongoing development of grounded theory methodology. It has already been noted that these differences often put (sport) management researchers off employing this particular methodology. It is therefore hoped that an apprehension of these differences may lead to a basic, but sensible, articulation of the link between the adopted methodology, the scope of the research and its underlying philosophical roots.

According to Charmaz (2006), grounded theory gained a wider audience with the appearance of Strauss's 1990 co-authored book with Juliet Corbin, *Basics of Qualitative Research: Grounded Theory Procedures and Techniques*. This book also led Strauss and Glaser to take grounded theory in divergent directions and contributed to a major split between them (Kelle, 2007: 198). Easterby-Smith et al. (2008) ask researchers to look at the ontology and epistemology of these authors in order to make sense of differences between what they advocate. For them Glaser comes across as a realist in ontological terms whereas Strauss and Corbin (1990) (as well as Charmaz, 2006) have a more nominalist ontology, assuming as they do that the social world is created through the interaction of agents. Epistemologically, Strauss and Corbin (1990) adopt a more relativist position which emphasizes systematic and reductionist approaches to the analysis of data. Glaser, in contrast, promotes a more 'relaxed' epistemology, insisting that the data should be analysed in its entirety and not reduced to discrete elements. Easterby-Smith et al. (2008) add that in some respects this is similar to the constructivist perspective seen in Charmaz (2006), although the latter goes further in emphasizing the primacy of the stories and experiences of her research subjects (ibid.).

Moreover, Glaser continues to regard grounded theory as a methodology of discovery where categories emerge from a continuous comparison of the data: 'We do not know what we are looking for when we start . . . we simply cannot say prior to the collection and analysis of data what our study will look like' (Glaser, 2001: 176). In accordance with this approach, the researcher enters the field with only a broad topic in mind, without specific preconceived research questions or a detailed reading and understanding of the extant literature in the area (Jones and Noble, 2007: 86). Glaser, therefore, chooses an area of organization or activity and, through the course of the research, the researcher is able to specify the phenomenon to be studied. For the opposing camp of grounded theorists, the phenomenon is the 'central idea, event, happening, or incident about which a set of interactions or actions are directed at managing or handling, or to which the set of actions is related' (Strauss and Corbin, 1990: 96). The core category is then 'inductively derived from the study of the phenomenon it represents' (Strauss and Corbin, 1990: 23). The Straussian school of grounded theory, therefore, identifies a specific phenomenon to be studied before the researcher enters the field. In addition, Strauss and Corbin's (1990) techniques encourage researchers to use their own personal and professional experiences and acquired knowledge as a positive advantage in the grounded theory process, to enhance theoretical sensitivity rather than obscure vision: 'if you know an area, have some experience . . . you don't tear it out of your head, you can use it' (Strauss, 1987: 84). Readers may recall that this 'experience' proved to be significant while I was trying to develop a substantive theory of how managers make decisions with regard to CSR in English football. The Straussian variant of grounded theory's emphasis on the need to 'identify the phenomenon to be studied' (Strauss and Corbin, 1990: 96) contrasts with the Glaserian school in which the core category is the theoretical formulation that represents the 'continual resolving of the main concern of the participants' (Jones and Noble, 2007: 89). The current study adopted the Straussian version of grounded theory as its guiding methodological principle. This choice perhaps requires a little more philosophical justification, which the section below attempts to provide.

6   SYMBOLIC INTERACTIONISM AND 'STRAUSSIAN' GROUNDED THEORY

There is a general consensus, not always explicitly articulated, that grounded theory methodology is the product of symbolic interactionism (Bryant and Charmaz, 2007;

Charmaz, 2006; Corbin and Strauss, 2008; Strübing, 2007; Weed, 2009). This theoretical perspective did indeed inform the pertinent study, and represented the philosophical stance behind its methodology. An examination of the roots and premises of symbolic interactionism should demonstrate its particular relevance to Straussian grounded theory. This, in turn, could demonstrate to perspective sport management researchers considering this particular methodology the ideal seamlessness that should exist between the research question, philosophical underpinnings and methodological choices in the execution of a sound grounded theory empirical study.

Strübing (2007: 582) posits that the Straussian variant of grounded theory is deeply rooted in both the theoretical perspective of symbolic interactionism and the intellectual tradition of American pragmatism. The theoretical perspective of symbolic interactionism essentially stems from pragmatism as it assumes that people are active and creative. Meanings emerge through practical actions that solve problems and through the actions by which people come to know the world. For pragmatist philosophers, therefore, 'knowledge' is created through action and interaction and as Dewey (1929: 138) puts it: 'ideas are not statements of what is or has been but of acts to be performed'. Strübing (2007: 583) firmly states that this line of thinking does not preclude the possibility that 'something out there' might exist independently of social actor(s) any more than it holds reality-in-action to be an idealistic concept of 'the real' existing, produced and manipulated exclusively in cerebral form. Reality *becomes* reality only in so far and as long as it is part of the environment within which actors act (ibid.). Mead (1934: 162) contends that 'a person is a personality because he belongs to a community, because he takes over the institutions of that community into his own conduct'. To contextualize Mead's point with the empirical research I draw on in this chapter: even if a single person (rather than a team or organization) discovers or creates some new understanding of reality (that is, the formulation and implementation of CSR in his or her respective football club), this person does so having already been socialized according to inherited perspectives. In this example those perspectives might be the football club's history, local social needs and so forth. 'Neither inquiry nor the most abstractly formal set of symbols can escape from the cultural matrix in which they live, move and have their being' (Dewey, 1938: 20). Strübing (2007: 584) articulates the same thing with a slightly different emphasis, writing that 'whenever humans act with reference to their social or physical environments, they reflect their doing in light of what actions these environments might evoke in other actors'. Here, it is worth taking the unusual step of referring to the study's results to offer a further contextual illustration of the crucial point. The following quotation is taken from a participant talking about CSR in the club for which he or she works:

> We are talking about the club here; so you have people who have been here for long time and have built up an ethos, philosophy . . . this allows you, this gives you wings to go out and do things . . . so I walk in the footsteps of legends and I am looking after that while I am here [. . .] my job here is . . . working at the roots where the club has been. (Own sample: interview with Pr-FC)

The respondent's comments illustrate Mead's (1934) contention that the concept of 'community' emphasizes the hold our culture has on us: it provides the way in which we see things and gives us a definite view of the world. Yet, the nature of *human responses* creates conditions that impact upon, restrict and contribute to a restructuring of the varieties of action/interaction that can be observed in societies (Corbin and Strauss, 2008: 6); in this research project 'societies' (or communities) were the football clubs and the 'people-legends' to whom the quoted CSR manager refers might constitute 'human responses'. As Corbin and Strauss (2008) have already noted, humans shape their institutions (that is, the football clubs) as much as the institutions shape them; they create and change the world around them through action/interaction. This point, too, is evident in the responses of the above-mentioned participant:

> So we had, before I came in two years ago, a team of coaches who went around the area and worked with schools for six weeks; they ticked all the 'CSR' boxes, you know. But what have they done really? No longevity to the programme no reason doing it. So [we] changed all that and this 'football community coach' – as we call them – he now stays with a school for three years; he knows the community, he knows little Johnny, his sister, his older brother . . . and this is not false credibility. (Own sample: interview with Pr-FC)

Thus, there is a bond between the actor (the CSR manager) and the environment or, to use Mead's term, 'the community' (in this case the football club). It is this bond that creates the 'situation' (Mead, 1908: 315). I regarded this premise as particularly important for my investigation into how managers make decisions regarding the CSR strategy in English football. It is, of course, the manager's engagement with social issues in the areas where their football clubs reside (action–interaction) that gives 'meaning' to the formulation and implementation of CSR programmes. At the same time, however, each manager's cultural heritage, biography, education, past experiences and so forth guide his or her life, decisions and overall 'interpretation' of the task (that is, to formulate and implement CSR) with which he or she is engaged. This cultural heritage – or 'inherited understanding' as Crotty (1998) prefers to call it – is a central concept of symbolic interactionism. Within the current study, 'inherited understanding' informed both how managers regarded the matter of CSR and subsequently answered my questions, and how I – as a researcher – gave meaning to their responses.

This 'inherited understanding' was not a matter that could be excluded from my discussion of theorising of CSR strategy in football. Crotty (1998), for instance, talks about the phenomena of reification and sedimentation. The former refers to our propensity to mistake 'the sense we make of things' for 'the way things are'. This could be read as 'the sense CSR managers make of CSR strategy', but also as 'the sense I make of what CSR managers said'. This blithely undertaken process is what Crotty calls the 'tyranny of the familiar'; the expression implies that our understanding of the world's realities is built upon pre-existing theoretical deposits. In this way, Crotty (1998: 59) writes, we become further and further removed from reality with our sedimented cultural meanings serving as a barrier between us and the world as it really is. That was indeed the most challenging methodological exercise involved in the development of the substantive theory executed in this research. How do I deal with two simultaneous 'inherited understandings' in the quest of theorising on CSR strategy in football? The first of Mead's 'situations' in this research, that is, the 'situation' created by the CSR managers in their respective football clubs, could be dealt with only by extensive memo-writings while formulating the substantive theory. Part of an example of this process is given in Table 22.1.

Table 22.1   Part of an early-stage memo

Research Question: *What does CSR mean for you?*	Memo #5: 29/01/2010 (15:05)
For me . . . it's an interested one, because obviously you have already got what I do as a community scheme, so we have 27 full-time staff, we have got another 20 part-time staff, all these things, already doing great work around the council, and what I keep telling the football club is that we are not the club's CSR policy; it doesn't really work like that, we can deliver on the club CSR policy but we are not their CSR policy. It would be easy for the directors to just come and say: 'you coach 30 000 children a year, you are working with adults with mental health problems, reducing health inequalities, all these kind of things, we are just going to say that you are our CSR and we will stand up and go we have got the best CSR'; but what I try to say is actually they have a corporate social responsibility, we are already doing this so they should be doing a little bit more, that's where I come from . . . (Own sample: interview with Ch-FC)	*'at arm's length'*: it refers to what the manager believes the relationship between the charitable trust and the football club is all about. [He or she] firmly states that his or her team's efforts should not be seen as the club's CSR agenda. What does it mean, I wonder? Does the manager imply that the club should not be capitalising on the trust's actions, because the club's actual contribution on the formulation and implementation of these programmes is disproportional from the indirect benefits the latter gets? What if, [he or she] gets more support from the club? Then what? But again, would the trust be possible without the club? Some conflict of interests here??? Control issues, also??? Perhaps, I will have to dig more into the relationship between the trust and the parent club and find out how this relationship between these two organisations affect the strategy and in particular the decision-making process regarding CSR. What is the picture in other clubs?

The second-level 'situation' – that is, between me (actor) and the data (environment) – could be dealt with by recognizing the impossibility of 'bracketing' my personal biography from the concept I was studying. Once one has acknowledged this, however, the need to make explicit what one brings to a study acquires an urgency; this is why I made clear from the outset the 'theoretical sensitivity' that I brought in while trying to develop the substantive theory in question. Again, it is this type of 'openness' and 'exposure' to which prospective sport management researchers need to commit themselves in order that their grounded theory-based inquiry is as transparent as possible.

7   EMPLOYING GROUNDED THEORY: THREE KEY POINTS AND CONCLUSION

As mentioned at the beginning of this chapter, the utilization of grounded theory methodology by researchers into the business side of sport has not been widespread. Elements of grounded theory, of course, such as data coding and analysis can be seen more frequently in the sport management literature. Warnings have recently been put forward, however, that researchers should not claim to have adopted grounded theory unless they have utilized *all* the elements that characterize a grounded theory methodology (Weed,

2009). Weed illustrates his point with a useful analogy of a motor car: although a steering wheel and an engine may *belong* to a motor car, they cannot be described *as* a motor car if four wheels, seats, bodywork and so on are absent.

Moreover, sport management researchers should take notice that a grounded theory-based inquiry (in particular one that adopts the Straussian variant) is not an a-theoretical research engagement. The example used throughout this chapter, for instance, located itself in the broad field of organizational strategy. The decision-making with regards to CSR strategy was, therefore, closer to what Roome and Jonker (2005: 3) have put forward; for them, it is seen as 'an emerging sense making process developed over a period of time, shaped by a series of (non)intentional choices and actions by various actors and influenced by changing set of conditioning and intervening factors'. Thus sport management researchers must always keep in mind that their 'substantive theory' lies in a broader field of study and this is why, for example, a modest review of the literature can be justified; it can actually provide the platform upon which further 'knowledge' on the matter can be acquired.

Building on the previous point, those who wish to employ grounded theory methodology will also need to specify from the outset the unit of analysis their inquiry will use. For the research discussed in this chapter, for example, although the goal was to develop a substantive theory that was grounded in the way managers make decisions regarding CSR strategy in English football, the focus was on decision-making and not on the individuals who facilitated this process. In other words, I sought for similar interpretations among managers in the English football sector while not losing sight of the fact that the unit of analysis was the decision-making behind the formulation of CSR.

To conclude, the aim of this chapter has been to discuss some basic philosophical and methodological issues associated with grounded theory by drawing on a research project concerning (broadly speaking) the decision-making process and the strategy behind CSR in English football. That project was a context-specific exercise and this is how it should be regarded and treated. I do not claim any authority over how one should philosophically or methodologically go about his or her grounded theory research. It would be, at the very least, an arduous task to support such a grandiose claim. The message here is simple, though not simplistic: in order for a grounded theory-based research project to be regarded as 'scientifically' legitimate as well as transparent as possible, the philosophical issues surrounding it should be thoroughly addressed at the outset. That way, a sound methodology for inquiry may be laid down in advance of the empirical research itself.

ACKNOWLEDGEMENTS

This chapter has benefited from the careful reading and constructive criticism of Sudi Sharifi (Salford Business School, University of Salford) and Benoît Senaux (Coventry Business School, Coventry University). I would also like to especially acknowledge Mark Dibben (School of Management, University of Tasmania) who raised important questions and challenged me to clarify my position; much appreciation, also, to Barbara Cooke for her sharp editorial advice.

REFERENCES

Babiak, K. and Trendafilova, S. (2011), CSR and environmental responsibility: motives and pressures to adopt green management practices, *Corporate Social Responsibility and Environmental Management*, **18** (1), 11–24.

Birks, M. and Mills, J. (2011), *Grounded Theory: A Practical Guide*, London: Sage.

Brown, A., McGee, F., Brown, M. and Ashton, A. (2010), *The Social and Community Value of Football*, Manchester: Substance.

Bryant, A. and Charmaz, K. (2007), Grounded theory in historical perspective: an epistemological account, in A. Bryant and K. Charmaz (eds), *The SAGE Handbook of Grounded Theory*, London: Sage, pp. 31–57.

Chalip, L. (2006), Toward a distinctive sport management discipline, *Journal of Sport Management*, **20** (1), 1–21.

Charmaz, K. (2006), *Constructing Grounded Theory. A Practical Guide through Qualitative Analysis*, London: Sage.

Clarke, A. (2005), *Situational Analysis: Grounded Theory after the Postmodern Turn*, Thousand Oaks, CA: Sage.

Corbin, J. and Strauss, A. (2008), *Basics of Qualitative Research*, 3rd edn, Thousand Oaks, CA: Sage.

Creswell, J. (2007), *Qualitative Inquiry and Research Design: Choosing among Five Approaches*, 2nd edn, London: Sage.

Crotty, M. (1998), *The Foundations of Social Research: Meaning and Perspective in the Research Process*, Sydney: Allen and Unwin.

Dewey, J. (1929), *The Quest for Certainty: A Study of the Relation of Knowledge and Action*, New York: G.P. Putnam's Sons.

Dewey, J. (1938), *Logic: The Theory of Enquiry*, New York: Henry Holt & Co.

Dibben, M. and Dolles, H. (2013), Participant observation in sport management research: collecting and interpreting data from a successful world land speed record attempt, in S. Söderman and H. Dolles (eds), *Handbook of Research on Sport and Business*, Cheltenham, UK and Northampton, MA, USA: Edward Elgar, pp. 477–94.

Easterby-Smith, M., Thorpe, R. and Jackson, P. (2008), *Management Research*, 3rd edn, London: Sage.

Edwards, A. and Skinner, J. (2009), *Qualitative Research in Sport Management*, Oxford: Butterworth-Heinemann.

Fendt, J. and Sachs, W. (2008), Grounded theory method in management research: users perspectives, *Organisational Research Methods*, **11** (3), 430–55.

Glaser, B. (1978), *Theoretical Sensitivity*, Mill Valley, CA: Sociology Press.

Glaser, B. (2001), *The Grounded Theory Perspective: Conceptualisation Contrasted with Description*, Mill Valley, CA: Sociology Press.

Glaser, B. and Strauss, A. (1967), *The Discovery of Grounded Theory*, Chicago, IL: Aldine.

Gummesson, E. (2000), *Qualitative Methods in Management Research*, 2nd edn, London: Sage.

Hamil, S. and Morrow, S. (2011), Corporate social responsibility in the Scottish Premier League: context and motivation, *European Sport Management Quarterly*, **11** (2), 143–70.

Hart, C. (1998), *Doing a Literature Review: Releasing the Social Science Research Imagination*, London: Sage.

Johns, G. (2001), In praise of context, *Journal of Organizational Behavior*, **42** (1), 31–42.

Jones, R. and Noble, G. (2007), Grounded theory and management research: a lack of integrity?, *Qualitative Research in Organisations and Management: An International Journal*, **2** (2), 84–103.

Kearney, M. (2007), From the sublime to the meticulous: the continuing evolution of grounded formal theory, in A. Bryant and K. Charmaz (eds), *The SAGE Handbook of Grounded Theory*, London: Sage, pp. 127–50.

Kelle, U. (2007), The development of categories: different approaches in grounded theory, in A. Bryant and K. Charmaz (eds), *The SAGE Handbook of Grounded Theory*, London: Sage, pp. 191–213.

Locke, K. (2001), *Grounded Theory in Management Research*, London: Sage.

Marsden, C. (2006), In defence of corporate responsibility, in A. Kakabadse and M. Morsing (eds), *Corporate Social Responsibility: Reconciling Aspiration with Application*, Basingstoke: Palgrave Macmillan, pp. 24–39.

McGuire, B. (2008), Football in the community: still 'the game's best kept secret'?, *Soccer and Society*, **9** (4), 439–54.

Mead, G. (1908), The philosophical basis for ethics, *International Journal of Ethics*, **18** (3), 311–23.

Mead, G. (1934), *Mind, Self and Society*, Chicago, IL: University of Chicago Press.

Mellor, G. (2008), The Janus-faced sport: English football, community and the legacy of the 'third way', *Soccer and Society*, **9** (3), 313–24.

Pratt, M. (2009), For the lack of a boilerplate: tips on writing up (and reviewing) qualitative research, *Academy of Management Journal*, **52** (5), 856–62.

Roome, N. and Jonker, J. (2005), Whistling in the dark: the enterprise strategies of European leaders in corporate [social] responsibility, *ICCSR Research Paper Series*, no. 30-2005, Nottingham: Nottingham

University Business School, University of Nottingham, available at: http://www.nottingham.ac.uk/business/ ICCSR/ (accessed 27 December 2011).

Russell, D. (1997), *Football and the English: A Social History of Association Football in England, 1863–1995*, Preston: Carnegie.

Skille, E.Å. (2013), Case study research in sport management: a reflection upon the theory of science and an empirical example, in S. Söderman and H. Dolles (eds), *Handbook of Research on Sport and Business*, Cheltenham, UK and Northampton, MA, USA: Edward Elgar, pp. 161–75.

Slack, R. and Shrives, P. (2008), Social disclosure and legitimacy in Premier League football clubs: the first ten years, *Journal of Applied Accounting*, **9** (1), 17–28.

Sotiriadou, K. and Shilbury, D. (2010), Using grounded theory in sport management research, *International Journal of Sport Management and Marketing*, **8** (3/4), 181–202.

Stern, P. (1994), Eroding grounded theory, in J. Morse (ed.), *Critical Issues in Qualitative Research Methods*, Thousand Oaks, CA: Sage, pp. 212–24.

Strauss, A. (1987), *Qualitative Analysis for Social Scientists*, Cambridge: Cambridge University Press.

Strauss, A. and Corbin, J. (1990), *Basics of Qualitative Research: Grounded Theory Procedures and Techniques*, London: Sage.

Strauss, A. and Corbin, J. (1998), *Basics of Qualitative Research*, 2nd edn, Thousand Oaks, CA: Sage.

Strübing, J. (2007), Research as pragmatic problem-solving: the pragmatist roots of empirically-grounded theorising, in A. Bryant and K. Charmaz (eds), *The SAGE Handbook of Grounded Theory*, London: Sage, pp. 580–601.

Walters, G. and Chadwick, S. (2009), Corporate citizenship in football: delivering strategic benefits through stakeholder engagement, *Management Decision*, **47** (1), 51–66.

Walters, G. and Tacon, R. (2010), Corporate social responsibility in sport: stakeholder management in the UK football industry, *Journal of Management and Organisation*, **16** (4), 566–86.

Weed, M. (2009), Research quality considerations for grounded theory research in sport and exercise psychology, *Psychology for Sport and Exercise*, **10** (5), 501–10.

Wimpenny, P. and Gass, I. (2000), Interviewing in phenomenology and grounded theory: is there a difference?, *Journal of Advanced Nursing*, **31** (6), 1485–92.

Wolfe, R., Weick, K., Terborg, J., Porro, L., Murrell, A., Dukerich, J., Crown Core, D., Dickson, K. and Simmons, J. (2005), Sport and organisational studies: exploring synergy, *Journal of Management Inquiry*, **14** (2), 182–210.

PART VI

SPORT BRANDING AND SPONSORING

23 A review of fan identity and its influence on sport sponsorship effectiveness

Torsten Schlesinger

1 INTRODUCTION

Sport fans – as opposed to sport spectators – have a high emotional solidarity and an abiding interest in their sport team or club. Therefore, they are often characterized by loyal consumer behaviour toward product of their club (for example, tickets, merchandising products). Fans consume their sport clubs' products on a regular basis admitting that price and quality only play a secondary role. It is therefore inconceivable that fans with high emotional solidarity are likely to change to another club only because tickets are cheaper, the stadium is nicer or there is a wider range of merchandising products offered. Even the attractiveness of the athletic performance or the success of a team/club does influence the fans' loyalty only insignificantly. Indeed, sport fans are a highly attractive target group for marketers of sport clubs. However, it could not be clarified so far if this is only the case for products connected directly with the club or if these effects are also related to offers indirectly associated with the club. This especially concerns the products of club or team sponsors. Companies hope that the passion fans feel toward a sport team or club are transferred to or 'rub off' on their brand (Madrigal, 2004). The results of market research indicate the potential of top sport sponsorship in increasing awareness of brands (Johan and Pham, 1999; Lardinoit and Derbaix, 2001; Rifon et al., 2004; Speed and Thompson, 2000). Awareness as an isolated parameter only shows a marginal positive correlation with parameters crucial for success, like the purchase intention. The awareness of products is only a necessary though not a sufficient condition for the purchase intention. On the contrary, the influence of certain product specific associations or attitudes is more decisive than the influence of awareness (Keller, 2008). Cornwell (2008, 2013 in this volume) states that there is still a lack of research on how sponsorship works in the mind of sport spectators and how it might be more effective. In the light of the invested sponsoring budgets of companies in top-level sports, the effects of sport sponsorship influenced by the relationship between fans and their club is a matter for sponsors with regard to the decision for or against a commitment in top-level sports. Yet with regard to their negotiating position for future sponsorships, sport clubs are also interested in the effect of sponsorship on their fans in order to further legitimate their relationships with sponsors. This chapter draws on the following question: does the fans' identification with their sport team or club influence the sport sponsorship effectiveness?

The procedure for dealing with this question is as follows: to begin with, the state of research results will be outlined and discussed. In the next step, a theoretical model of the influence of fan identity on the attitude toward sponsors and the intention of purchasing the sponsors' products will be developed and research hypotheses will be derived from them. This is followed by the introduction of the research method and the presentation of empirical findings by two different case studies. Finally, a discussion of the results and implications for sport sponsoring practice concludes the chapter.

2 LITERATURE REVIEW

The following literature review is divided into two sections: the first, which briefly addresses the question of how the construct 'team identification' can be explained and delimited, and the second, on current research results of the relationship between fan identity and sponsor effects.

2.1 Delimitation of the Construct Team Identification

In the sports fans literature there is a large number of several concepts and models which analyse different psychological (attitudinal and behavioural) facets and components for assessing the connection between spectators and fans with their team or club. Therefore researches have used various terms to describe this psychological association. Such terms include team identification (Dolles and Söderman, 2008, 2013 in this volume; Kerr et al., 2011; Wann and Branscombe, 1993; Wann et al., 1999, 2001, 2003), fan loyalty (Bee and Havitz, 2010; Heere and Dickson, 2008; Tapp, 2004; Theysohn et al., 2009; Wakefield and Sloan, 1995), psychological commitment (Mahoney et al., 2000), fan attitude network (Funk and James, 2004, 2006) or fan attachment (Kwon and Armstrong, 2004; Kwon et al., 2005; Robinson and Trail, 2005).

In this study the focus lies on the construct 'team identification'. Team identification refers to the extent to which a fan feels psychologically attached to a team (Wann and Branscombe, 1993). Analysing the fan identity literature, the strong bond between fans and their teams or clubs can be described by different dimensions: emotional achievement, self-connection and intimate commitment. Emotional achievement represents the feeling of personal achievement and pride of the fans when their team is successful. Self-connection reflects the degree to which a team delivers important identity concerns, tasks or themes expressing a significant aspect of a fan's identity. Self-connection is seen, for example, when people state that they are fans of a specific team or clubs (for example, 'I am a FC Barcelona fan!') or say that their team expresses what is important to them. Intimate commitment refers that the connection between the fan and the team or club has been found to be relatively stable and shows little fluctuation either from game to game or from season to season.

2.2 Sport Fans and Sponsorship Effectiveness

Multitudes of parameters have already been examined within the effect analytical oriented sponsoring research (see Cornwell, 2008, 2013 in this volume; Cornwell et al., 2005; Walliser 2003). In the following the focus lies mainly on studies, which deal with the influence of fan identity on sponsoring effects. In sponsorship research, the fan identity construct plays an important role in the processing of sponsorship stimuli (Crimmins and

Horn, 1996; Meenaghan, 2001). Team identification is related to team loyalty, improved sponsor recall and recognition, improved attitude toward and satisfaction with sponsors, as well as increased preference for the sponsor's products (Gladden and Funk, 2001; Sutton et al., 1997). It has been found that fans with a high identification reach higher recall and recognition scores concerning the sponsors than those fans with lower identification (Levin et al., 2001; O'Roark et al., 2009; Pavelchak et al., 1988; Wakefield et al., 2007). Yet, recall and recognition scores only marginally correlate positively with critical success factors like consumer intention. Rather, the emotional commitment between fans and their clubs, teams and athletes needs to be focused on when exploring attitudes and consumer intention toward the sponsors' products (Meenaghan, 1999). Using the example of the National Association for Stock Car Auto Racing (NASCAR) confirms the empirical findings, that sponsors of the favourite racers are very popular among NASCAR fans, while those sponsors of the less-liked racers are perceived rather negatively. Moreover, it becomes apparent that the interviewees often prefer the brands of the NASCAR because of the sponsorship commitment (Dalakas and Levin, 2005; IEG, 1994).

When investigating university sport teams Madrigal (2000, 2001), Gwinner and Swanson (2003) provide proof, that fans with high fan identity show a positive attitude and a higher consumer acceptance toward the sponsors than the spectators with lower fan identity. This research suggests the existence of a positive correlation between consumers' team identification levels and attitudes toward the team sponsor, sponsor recognition and sponsor purchase intentions. Schlesinger et al. (2009), using the example of a German football club in the first division, the Bundesliga, illustrated that with an increasing fan identity the fans' disposition to buy products of a sponsor rises, whereas the price sensitivity decreases. Cornwell and Coote (2005) were able to verify a positive correlation between the disposition to buy products of a sponsor and the identification with the respective sport club, using the example of a sport club (Voluntary Sports Club). Thereby, the prestige of the sport club and the duration of membership function as moderating variables. On the other hand, Huber and Matthes (2007) could not show any effects on sponsors depending on fan identity. This can, among other things, be traced back to methodological problems in the realization of the empirical study since the research object was a virtual sponsorship. Even though fictitious scenarios enjoy an increasing popularity in recent sponsoring research (Becker-Olsen, 2003; Rifon et al., 2004; Roy and Cornwell, 2003), it seems appropriate to revert to real identification objects in order to gather effects of fan identity in the context of sport sponsoring. Only in that case a positive attitude toward the sponsor can be generated.

Summarizing the state of research, we have to keep in mind that the effect of sponsorship might well be influenced positively by the fan identity. In this context the effective influence of fan identity on parameters crucial for success like attitude or purchase intention is of special interest. In addition, criteria which possibly boost or obstruct the process need to be identified. Given the ambivalent results, further research contributions within the field of sponsorship research are necessary.

3   THEORETICAL FRAMEWORKS

3.1   Sport Fans – a Unique Consumer Group

Classic economic explications for consumer behaviour do not take external effects like passion, solidarity and identification as parameters into account, since they can be observed among spectators (Gratton and Taylor, 2000). In order to explain the impact of the fan identity on the purchase intention for products of a sport club such parameters are particularly relevant because they suppress rational cost–benefit considerations. Particularly, socio-economic approaches accentuate that individual preferences are integrated in a wide context of social conditions and social behaviour. Thereby, the basis of reference for this study is provided by social identity theory, following Tajfel (1978) and Tajfel and Turner (1986). Social identity theory proposes that individuals classify themselves into various social categories in order to facilitate self-definition within their own social environment. Social identity has to be distinguished from personal identity, which comprises individual characteristics which in turn make people distinguishable from each other. Social identity is therefore the part of the self-concept that evolves from group relationships (Ashforth and Mael, 1989). This attribution to a group is connected to behavioural and attitudinal decisive consequences, because such communities possess a common thought-style which determines what and how the group members 'see'. Hence, such collectively shared thought-styles lead to selective observation and specific evaluations and behavioural patterns in given situations and on particular occasions. In conclusion, identification with a sport team or club is a special form of social identity. It has to be noted that the attribution of fans to their club is not only effected through identification but also through the demarcation from other fan groups (Richardson and Turley, 2006).

Research on fan identity has continuously attracted the interest of researchers from two sport domains – sport psychology and sport marketing. According to the extent or strength of this identification, fan identity has different effects on consumer behaviour (see Funk and James, 2006; Trail et al., 2000). Team identification is one of the most important aspects for sport clubs to foster because highly identified fans are more likely to have a strong sense of attachment and belonging to the team or club (Fink et al., 2002; Mitrano, 1999; Wann et al., 2003). Fans with a high identity usually attend more games (Wakefield and Sloane, 1995; Wann et al., 1999) and invest a large amount of money and time watching their team play (Depken, 2000; Derbaix et al., 2002; Laverie and Arnett 2000; Wann et al., 1999). At this point, it is important to mention that a high fan identity stands for a high frequency of stadium visits even during periods of poor performance (Fisher and Wakefield, 1998; Parker and Stuart, 1997; Richardson and Turley, 2006) as well as for a decreased price sensibility (Sutton et al., 1997). Thus, fans' identification with a sport team or club is vital for a club's economic success. Beyond the economic benefits, understanding team identification with a sport team or club has important managerial applications, as also elaborated upon in this volume by Dolles and Söderman (2013, in this volume) and O'Reilly (2013, in this volume). With regards to marketing communication, fans' level of identification with a team can be utilized as the basis for targeted communication to influence fan behaviour.

3.2 Fan Identity as Determining Variable of Sponsorship Effect

Taking these points into consideration, one can expect influences of fan identity on the attitude toward the club's sponsors. Cornwell and Coote (2005) applied the social identity theory to sport sponsorships. In order to explain the sponsorship effect on the purchase intention of potential customers with a high identification toward certain objects the social exchange is referred to (see Emerson, 1976). Social exchange implies that every exchange reflects a direct or indirect give and take with the aim to generate a benefit for all. Such exchange processes can be observed particularly in groupings which show a high emotional connectivity (Lawler, 2001). In sport sponsorship such exchange processes also take place within sponsor, sponsored and fan (see Becker-Olsen, 2003). Thus, the stronger the relationship with the club is developed, the more the fan might feel it is his duty to repay the sponsors for their support by purchasing their products (Crimmins and Horn, 1996). A corresponding purchase behaviour of the fans would hence be linked for instance to the expectation that the sponsor permanently sustains his commitment to the respective club. The repayment of the sponsors' investment by consuming their products has to be seen as a gesture of gratitude of the fans. Thus, the purchase of the sponsor's products indirectly supports the particular sports club in the end.

A glance at the praxis of sponsorship exemplifies which influence the fan identity may exert on the process of purchase decision. However, possible negative effects of sponsorship also need to be taken into consideration: What inspires loyalty and sympathy on the one hand, may also cause backlash on the other. A famous example for this occurred in the English Premier League. Shortly after it had become known that Vodafone took up the sponsorship for Manchester United, the Liverpool Vodafone dealers suffered a significant decline in sales. The reason for this is easily identified: Liverpool fans scorn their rivals from Manchester. Such fans behaviour can be comprehended as a typical example of a 'rational handling of irrationality'. Analogue to the intention toward club products, a higher consumer acceptance can be assumed for the sponsors' products as opposed to the products of other competitors. This leads to the following first hypothesis:

Hypothesis 1 The stronger the fans' identification with the sport club, the higher their purchase intention toward the products of the club sponsor.

Fans cannot be characterized only by a high interest in the sporting events, but also increased attention toward the sponsors of their sport club can be imputed to them (Levin et al., 2001; Wakefield et al., 2007). This can positively affect the response toward the sponsors, but only if the fans' attitude toward the sponsors is positive. Such responses, however, only appear if there is a positive attitude of the fans toward the sponsor on hand. Goodwill plays an important role here (Meenaghan, 2001). It arises when the fans realize the support of the sponsor for their sport club and results in a higher commitment toward these sponsors. By supporting a sport club with which fans identify, sponsors are able to tap into a reservoir of goodwill that 'rubs off' onto their products (Madrigal, 2004). An individual's implicit memory for the sponsor creates many connections and leads to the formation to the fans' positive attitude toward their club's sponsors. The narrower the connection of a fan with the club, the bigger should the sympathy toward the sponsor for his commitment be. The fans with a high identity most probably show a positive attitude toward the sponsors supporting their clubs (Gwinner and Swanson, 2003; Madrigal, 2000, 2001). This leads to the following hypothesis

Hypothesis 2   The stronger the fans' identification with the sport club, the more positive their attitude toward the club sponsor.

3.3   Purchase Intention as Resulting Parameter

So far the direct influence of fan identity on the purchase intention and the attitude toward the products of sponsors has been conceptualized. Furthermore, the purchase intention is also influenced by the attitude toward the club sponsor. That is to say, the purchase intention is downstream to the attitude. The attitude toward the ad-model verified the influence of the attitude toward a product to the purchase intention (Brown and Stayman, 1992; MacKenzie et al., 1988). The behavioural intentions concerning certain objects are determined through the individual's attitude and/or through the perceived attitudes in the environment (for example the fan club). Thereby it is imperative that the more vivid, emotional and independent product-specific associations are anchored in the awareness of the consumer, the bigger is the influence on purchase behaviour (Keller, 2008). Transferred to the sponsorship context this implies: if fans are aware of the clubs' support of the sponsor, this can lead to a positive attitude toward the sponsor. A positive attitude toward the sponsor supports the fans' purchase intention toward the sponsor's products (Madrigal, 2001; Speed and Thompson, 2000). This leads to the following hypothesis:

Hypothesis 3   The more positive the fans' attitude toward the club sponsor, the higher is their purchase intention toward products of the club sponsor.

3.4   Further Variables Influencing the Sponsorship Effectiveness

The positive effect of fans' attitude toward the sponsor occurs only if the commitment between the sport club and the sponsor seems credible (Rifon et al., 2004). A lot of studies show that corporate credibility determines the intentions and attitudes of the consumers (Goldsmith et al., 2000; Newell and Goldsmith, 2001). Although sports clubs benefit from the revenue of sponsorships these are not always accepted by the fans, especially if they are perceived as not authentic or inappropriate. Depending on whether a sponsor is judged as altruistic-seeking or self-serving and follows commercial interests, the attitude towards the sponsor will change in a positive or negative way. Yet, it is assumed that the attitude toward the sponsor is not influenced or is even negatively affected, if the sponsors' commitment does not seem credible. Hence we can act on the assumption that the credibility of a sponsoring activity in sport sponsoring can positively influence the attitude toward the sponsoring enterprise. This leads to the following hypothesis:

Hypothesis 4   The higher the credibility of the sponsorship commitment, the more positive the fans' attitude toward the sponsor.

Furthermore, also the fans' attitude toward sport sponsorships in general might have an influence. In the background is the excessive commercialization and the dangers

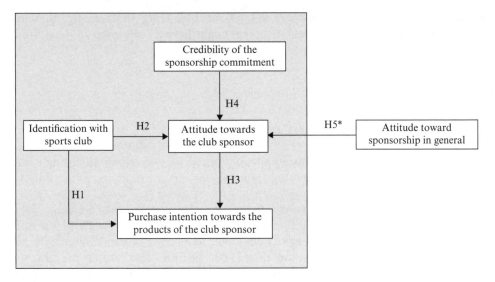

Note: *Only in case study 1 football.

Figure 23.1   System of hypotheses for the sponsorship effect model

associated with it: on the one hand, the club becomes very dependent on the sponsoring enterprise and, on the other, there is a possible erosion of the traditions and values of the club. The consumers' attitudes reflect their response to the marketing activities, which in turn affects the attitude toward the sponsors. Sport fans can take both – a tolerant as well as a critical position toward sport sponsorships. In a study by Easton and Mackie (1998) more than 75 per cent of the participants agreed that sponsoring is done purely for commercial purposes. However, they were aware, that the support provided by sponsors is ultimately the enabling element for major events and the most important way of financing sport. Consequently, the question that arises is how far the fans' attitude toward sport sponsorship in general also influences the attitude toward the single sponsor. It is presumed that the general attitude toward sport sponsoring indicates the attitude toward the single sponsor. This leads to the final hypothesis:

Hypothesis 5   The more positive the fans' attitude toward sponsorship in general, the more positive their attitude toward the single sponsor.

An overview of the developed model for the analysis of sponsorship effect on dependency of fan identity with the postulated hypotheses is summarized in Figure 23.1. Considering, to begin with, the parameter in the centre of the analysis, the fan identity (in grey), it is presumed that, depending on its level of specificity, the final action quantity purchase intention (H1) and attitude toward the sponsor (H2) are directly influenced. Moreover, a direct link between the attitude toward the sponsor and the purchase intention is postulated as a downstream parameter (H3) so that an indirect influence of fan identity via attitude toward the sponsor on the purchase intention can be presumed. The positive effect of fans' attitude toward the sponsor occurs only if the commitment between the sport club and the sponsor seems credible (H4). Furthermore, the fans' attitude toward sport sponsorships in general might have an influence on the attitude towards the club sponsor (H5).

4   METHOD

4.1   Contextual Setting of the Two Case Studies

The sponsorship effect model was empirically tested by two quantitative single case studies with sport clubs in different top sport leagues and one of its sponsors (sponsors are dealt with anonymously).

The first case study was carried out with regard to the sponsorship of a German football club of the highest division in football – the Bundesliga during the 2007/08 season. The football club, 1. FC Nürnberg (1.FCN), was founded in Nuremberg in 1900 and today has over 380 fan clubs with more than 15 000 members, that is to say the 1.FCN is a really traditional club. In the 2007/08 season an average of 30 000 spectators attended the team's home games. The greatest sporting success celebrated by the 1.FCN had been in the 1920s and 1960s. During this period the 1.FCN won the German football championship nine times. In the past years the biggest success had been the winning of the German Cup Final (DFB-Pokal) in 2007 and participation in the UEFA Cup in the following season. However, the 1.FCN periodically gets into financial problems due to poor management, which has led to the threat of licence revocation by the league. At the time of study the 1.FCN had a big sponsorship pool with one main sponsor, seven exclusive partners, six club partners and more than 50 other official sponsors (see http:// www.fcn.de for details, accessed 12 July 2011). The selected sponsor of the case study is a clothing company, the jersey sponsor of the club. This clothing company is located in the region around Nuremberg. The chosen sponsorship between the clothing company and the 1.FCN can be characterized as a long-term partnership.

The second case study is of SC Bern, a Swiss ice hockey club of the highest division (National League A) in the season 2008/09. Ice hockey is counted among the most attractive sports in Switzerland, along with football and alpine skiing. According to a ranking list published by the International Ice Hockey Federation (IHHF), the Swiss National League A occupies the second position following Sweden's 'Elite Series' with regard to average spectators per game. The Swiss National League A consist of 12 teams. SC Bern (SCB) is one of the largest ice hockey clubs in Europe and possesses an enormous fan potential. The 'PostFinance-Arena', which is where the SCB's home games are played, is one of the largest ice hockey arenas. Indeed, an average of 16 200 spectators per game was present in the 2008/09 season – in Europe the peak value. The SCB's club history boasts 12 Swiss National Championship triumphs, the last being in 2010. From an economic aspect, the club has developed excellently since its change into a public limited company in 1998. Owing to its growing number of spectators, together with its successful sport development in recent years, the club has become increasingly attractive for sponsors. The sponsorship-related revenue currently makes up about 28 per cent of the club's total income. At the time of study, the club had a 'main sponsor', four 'gold sponsors', 19 'silver sponsors' and 52 'partners' (see http://www.scb.ch/sponsoren.aspx for details,

Table 23.1   Random samples of both case studies differentiated by age and gender

Criteria	Study 1: football random sample (N = 1594)		Study 2: ice hockey random sample (N = 904)	
	N	%	N	%
Age:				
< 21 years	435	27.3	164	18.1
21–30 years	405	25.4	320	35.4
31–40 years	356	22.3	218	24.1
41–50 years	274	17.2	137	15.2
51–60 years	91	5.7	91	4.1
> 60 years	33	2.1	28	3.1
Sex:				
Female	223	13.9	229	25.3
Male	1371	86.1	675	74.7

accessed 12 July 2011). Furthermore, all available advertisement space and all of the 21 company boxes are sold on long-term contracts. The chosen sponsorship between the company for electric energy supply and the SCB can be characterized as a long-term partnership and belongs to the gold sponsors.

4.2   Data Collection and Samples

The fans and sympathizers of the football club (N = 1594) were questioned in the 2007/08 season, the fans and sympathizers of the ice hockey club (N = 904) were questioned in the 2008/09 season. The data was collected via online questionnaire on the official homepage of the football club and the ice hockey club, since these are the most frequently visited pages by the fans. An advantage of the online survey in this connection is that it is possible to generate a big sample within a very short time. However, it is only possible to question persons with a specific interest in a discipline and specific habit of media use, so that a control on representativeness with regard to age and sex was limited (see Table 23.1). The number of female and older participants is comparatively low. The reason for the unequal distribution of sexes lies in women's commonly lower interest in football and ice hockey. The reason for the slightly lower amount of older respondents can be explained by their less frequent use of the Internet.

4.3   Measuring Instrument

Operationalization of the independent variables
All multi-item measures are provided in Table 23.2. The measurement of the independent variables was specified as follows: the operationalization of team identification was carried out according to the Sport Spectator Identification Scale (SSIS) by Wann and Branscombe (1993) as a valid and reliable measuring instrument. The SSIS is unidimensional and comprises seven items assessing various aspect of the team identification construct. For both case studies a German adaption of the SSIS by Strauss (1995) has

Table 23.2 *Evaluation of the measurement model*

Construct/item	Convergent validity				Discriminant validity
	Factor loading* (≥0.707)		Cronbach's alpha (α ≥0.7)	AVE (≥0.5)	Fornell/Larcker AVE > Corr²**
	Study F	Study I			
Fan identity			Study F:.86	.62	.62 > .28
			Study I:.85	.57	.57 > .16
FI1: When I talk about the Club A/B I usually say 'we' rather than 'they'	.854	.730			
FI2: My friends believe that I'm a fanatic fan of Club A/B	.830	.826			
FI3: The Club A/B successes are my personal successes	.765	.822			
FI4: It is very important for me to support the Club A/B	.932	.846			
FI5: I follow nearly every game and all reports about Club A/B	.769	.859			
FI6: When someone praises Club A/B, it feels like a personal complement (*only study F*)	.731				
Attitude toward the club sponsor			.82	.61	.61 > .56
			.91	.65	.65 > .60
AS1: That . . . sponsors my favourite club is very good	.854	.875			
AS2: I hold a sympathetic opinion of the company . . . who sponsors my favourite club	.898	.926			
AS3: I have a positive attitude to . . .	.812	.926			
AS4: The . . . that sponsors my favourite club is nice	.798	.915			
Purchase intention			.82	.63	.63 > .45
			.74	.55	.55 > .36
PI1: To buy a product from . . . that sponsors Club A/B is likely for me	.882	.901			
PI2: To buy a product from . . . that sponsors Club A/B is impossible for me	.791	.821			
PI3: I probably will buy a . . .	.776	.913			

Credibility of the sponsorship			.78 / .92	.64 / .68	.64 > .55 / .68 > .60
CS1: The sponsorship between . . . and Club A/B is believable	.802	.928			
CS2: The sponsorship between . . . and Club A/B is convincing	.725	.947			
CS3: The commitment between . . . and Club A/B is biased	.734	.942			
Attitude toward sponsorship in general (only study F)			.79	.54	.54 > .24
SG1: Sport clubs need the financial support by companies	.802				
SG2: Sponsoring is done purely for commercial purposes	.744				
SG3: The support provided by sponsors is the important way of financing sport	.780				
SG4: Sponsorships are absolutely unnecessary	.727				

Notes:
* All factor loadings were significant (p<.001).
** Corr^2 = highest squared correlation between the model constructs.
Study F: football; study I: ice hockey.
Club A = 1. FC Nürnberg; club B = SC Berne.

been used. A multitude of other measuring scales can be found in the available literature: 'Psychological Attachment to the Team Scale' (James, Kolbe and Trail, 2002; Trail and James, 2001), 'Psychological Commitment to the Team Scale' (Mahony et al., 2000), 'Psychological Attachment to the Sport Team Scale' (Kwon and Armstrong, 2004) and 'Attitudinal Loyalty to the Team Scale' (Heere and Dickson, 2008). In comparative studies, however, no important differences among the different measuring scales relating to the power of explaining a construct could be discovered (Michalski and Helmig, 2008). Beyond that, in other impact studies in the area of sport sponsorship the use of the SSIS as a measuring scale has proven its worth (for example, Gwinner and Swanson 2003; Madrigal, 2000, 2001).

The measurement of the sponsorship commitment's credibility was based on experience in the field of advertising impact. This was measured utilizing a five-point semantic differential similar to MacKenzie and Lutz (1989). Specifically, items indicating the credibility of the sponsorship were: 'convincing/unconvincing', 'believable/unbelievable' and 'unbiased/biased'. As effects of publicity are definitely suitable as an explanatory approach for the effect of sponsorship a transfer seems to make sense. Here too a modification for a five-point Likert scale was conducted. The attitude toward sponsorship (general) was measured utilising the operationalizations by Easton and Mackie (1998) through a four-item, five-point Likert-type scale.

Operationalization of the dependent variables
In order to measure the construct attitude different approaches can be found in marketing literature. For assessing attitude toward sponsors we asked spectators to rate their impressions for the company sponsoring the football club and the ice hockey club. This was measured using a five-point Likert scale similar to MacKenzie and Lutz (1989). In comparison to other measuring approaches this one is best transferable for the exploration of the hypothesis model. Further, this kind of attitude measurement prevails in sponsorship research (for example Madrigal, 2001; Rifon et al. 2004; Roy and Cornwell 2003).

Compared with attitude there are fewer differences in operationalization for the measurement of purchase intention. For this measurement we revert to operationalizations by MacKenzie, Lutz and Belch (1988) through a three-item, five-point Likert-type scale: 'likely/unlikely', 'possible/impossible' and 'probable/improbable' (for sponsorship research, see Madrigal, 2000, 2001; Rodgers, 2004). In the present study, this operationalization with the modification to a five-point Likert scale was also applied.

5   RESULTS

The data was tested in a two-stage process. First, the measurement model was assessed via confirmatory factor analysis (CFA) to evaluate the reliability and unidimensionality of the scales used in the studies. Once we were satisfied with the measurement model, a structural model was estimated. This allowed for an assessment of the overall model fit and the hypothesized relationships. Owing to the fact that there are two different sponsoring situations on hand, the established model had to be analysed for each sport club separately.

5.1 Measurement Model (Measurement Validity)

The entire measurement model was subjected to the confirmatory factor analysis. To test the measurement model using the structure equation modeling (SEM) technique in AMOS 6 (Analysis of Moment Structures). Table 23.2 summarizes the statistic of the measurement model. Five different subscales were included in the confirmatory factor analysis: fan identity (five items), attitude toward the club sponsor (three items), purchase intention (three items), credibility of the sponsorship (three items) and the attitude toward sponsorship (general) (four items). To examine the model fit the following types of validity were consulted: (a) content validity provides information about how far the individual items reproduce the content of a construct. In order to determine the content validity the factor loading (recommended minimum value ≥ 0.70) of the individual indicators were consulted (Johnson et al., 2006). Owing to lower factor loadings, five items (two in the football study and three in the ice hockey study) were deleted from further analysis. All other indicators showed acceptable to high factor loadings and were significant ($p < .001$). (b) The convergent validity required that indicators belonging to the same construct have a sufficiently strong relation among each other.

The composite reliability (alpha coefficients) and the average variance extracted (AVE) help to determine the convergent validity (Hair et al., 2006). Composite reliability meets or exceeds 0.7 (Chin, 1998). Average variance extracted values were calculated to determine whether each of the items contributed to the scale's underlying theoretical construct, and AVE values which meet or exceed 0.5 indicate that the items represent the construct well (Fornell and Larcker, 1981). Composite reliabilities in both studies ranged from .74 to .91 The AVE values ranged from .54 to .68 for the five subscales indicating that the items represent the constructs well. Factor loadings, composite reliability and AVE showed values above the required thresholds. Based on these results, we conclude that the measures are both unidimensional and reliable. Therefore, the measurement models seem to have both high reliability and convergent validity. (c) In the assessment of discriminant validity we followed the advice of Fornell and Larcker (1981) by assessing whether the AVE estimates associated with each possible construct pair is greater than the square of the correlation between the two constructs. Once again, evidence of discriminant validity is provided as all variance extracted estimates exceed the appropriate squared factor correlation. Overall, then, we concluded that the scales had adequate measurement properties, and proceeded to test the hypothesized structural relationships.

5.2 Structural Model (Hypotheses Testing)

In order to assess the quality of the structural model the AMOS provides a multitude of fit indices. The model was tested using the maximum likelihood method of parameter estimation. Since there is no best index for the overall assessment of the model, multiple indices have to be consulted. Hair et al. (2006) recommend the use of at least three indices of the reporting measures of quality. The following fit indices were used to examine the model fit: the chi-square per degree of freedom ratio (χ^2/df), the root mean square error of approximation (RMSEA) and the comparative fit index (CFI). A χ^2/df in the range

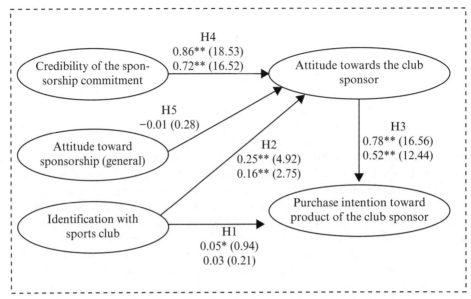

First Line: path coefficient and t-values (in the parentheses) football study.
Second Line: path coefficient and t-values (in the parentheses) ice hockey study.
*p ≤ 0.05, **p ≤ 0.001.

Summary of Overall Fit Indices for the Proposed Models Tested

Model	X²/df	CFI	NFI	RMSEA
Structural model football study	4.82	0.947	0.942	0.51
Structural model ice hockey study	3.41	0.936	0.925	0.58

Figure 23.2   The structural models with path coefficients (standardized values) and model fit

of 2–4 indicates an acceptable fit (Arbuckle and Wothke, 1999; Backhaus et al., 2006). Those RMSEA values less than .05 indicate that a model has a close fit, those of .08 or less would indicate a reasonable fit and RMSEA values higher than .10 should not be considered (Browne and Cudeck, 1993). Hu and Bentler (1999) have suggested that values less than .06 instead of .05 indicate that a model has a close fit. Whereas CFI values closer to 1 are indicative for a very good fit (Bentler, 1990). The fit indices for both structural models revealed reasonable fit (see Figure 23.2). The results revealed that the chi-square per degree of freedom ratio χ²/df = 4.82/3.41 (football model/ice hockey model), the RMSEA = .051/.058 and the CFI = .947/.936 indicated acceptable to adequate fit.

For testing the hypotheses, in the next step a structural equation modelling was estimated, which illustrates the correlation between the constructs in a path diagram. The path coefficients inform about the influence of a construct on a causally following construct. Height and significance of the parameter are crucial here. The hypotheses test reveals that in both case studies only one of the two assumed effects of fan identity can be proved. This implies that the exogenous variable fan identity does not influence the endogenous variable purchase intention. The path indeed has the expected direction, but the path coefficient (β = .05 football study and β = .03 ice hockey study) deviates only marginally from zero and only in the football study is statistically significant. As hypothesized, for the influence of fan identity on the attitude toward the club sponsor a significant path coefficient was deduced. The findings show that identifying with a sport club has a significant direct effect on the attitude toward the club sponsor (β = .25 football study; β = .16 ice hockey study). As expected, the direct path of the attitude toward the sponsor and the purchase intention produced a positive path coefficient of β = .78 in the football study and β = .52 in the ice hockey study. An advantage of the structural equation modelling in contrast to multiple regression analysis lies, among other things, in that, besides these direct effect relationships, indirect effects and total effects can also be estimated. There are indirect effects of the fan identity via the attitude toward the sponsor, finally culminating in the purchase intention (β = .20 football study; β = .08 ice hockey study). Taking the total effect into account as well, the fan identity culminating in the purchase intention amounts β = .25 in the football study and β = .11 in the ice hockey study.

Analysing the paths, further important findings can be presented: the variable 'attitude toward the sponsor' is influenced by credibility of the sponsorship. Results indicated that the credibility of the sponsorship commitment contains the strongest predictor of the variable attitude toward the sponsor (β = .86 football study; β = .72 ice hockey study). The variable 'attitude toward sponsorship (general)' shows no significant effect on the 'attitude toward the sponsor' in the football study. The assumption, that the general attitude toward sport sponsorship gives direction to the attitude toward the single sponsor could not be confirmed. An overview on the calculated path coefficients and t-values is provided in Figure 23.2.

5.3 Comparing the Different Sponsorships

Comparing the results of the two case studies no differences in terms of the direction of influence can be stated. At the most, there are considerable differences in the strength of the postulated interdependencies. In both studies only a smaller direct influence between fan identity and intention to buy can be observed, and this circumstance is only significant in the football study. This result is probably due to a smaller sample size. Furthermore it can be shown that the correlation between fan identity and attitude towards the sponsor is a little bit stronger in the football study than in the ice hockey study. Again, the impact of credibility on the attitude towards the club sponsor and the intention to buy is stronger in the football study. The results indicate a higher sponsoring effectiveness in football. For a statistical foundation of this statement it would be necessary to conduct a follow-up study for measuring and verifying the sponsoring efficiency in different sports. Moreover the impact of the sponsoring is related to the level of sponsorship, which goes along with the study by Wakefield et al. (2007), who show that higher-level sponsorships outperform lower-level sponsorships.

6   DISCUSSION, LIMITATIONS AND IMPLICATIONS FOR MANAGEMENT AND FURTHER RESEARCH

The starting point of this study was the answer to the question in how far the fans' loyal consumer behaviour toward their favourite sport club's products is also true toward the products of the club sponsor. The path models in both case studies are not able to verify the hypotheses H1 and H5, while the hypothesized paths H2, H3 and H4 are supported. This implies that the fan identity has no direct effect on the purchase intention but positively influences the attitude toward the club sponsor. The attitude toward the club sponsor correlates in turn very strongly with the purchase intention. The results of these studies support the premise that highly identified fans are more likely to exhibit several positive effects related to sponsorship. Thus it becomes clear, that fan identity may not be underestimated in the sponsorship effect context in top sports. Furthermore, the credibility of a sponsorship commitment shows a high relevance for the success of sponsorships. The results show that, especially in times of fans' increasing mistrust toward companies, the functional chain of credibility is highly relevant to the attitude toward the sponsor.

As with any study, some limitations must be acknowledged. At the same time, this opens up research perspectives for future studies: first, this research considered the simple purchase intention as an endpoint, not the actual consumer behaviour. Future research should investigate how far fan identity exerts influence on the actual behaviour. Second, the results are limited by the distinctiveness of the two sponsor's products since these are only low-involvement products. For this reason, further research about product involvement should incorporate a more differentiated approach than in both these studies. Future studies should also attach more importance to other moderating factors of sponsorship effects (for example, sponsorship level, prominence of sponsors, duration or history of the commitment between sponsor and club). In this way, the influences of fan identity in relation to the different kinds of sponsoring activities could be investigated. Based on this, companies can decide more accurately to what extent sponsorship is an effective communication tool for them. In this context comparative studies about single sponsorships of several sports clubs – as well as comparisons within different sport disciplines – would be of interest in this field of research in order to detect possible correlations or differences. Additionally, the online questionnaire is acknowledged to have some advantages (for example, sample size) and disadvantages (sample selectivity), compared with alternative questionnaire methods. In future research, the problem of the sample selectivity of the online questionnaire can be solved by additional questioning strategies, for instance, interviews in the stadium.

These findings underline the importance of a high fan identity in order to achieve direct and indirect sponsoring effects. Hence, developments in top-level sport clubs conductive to the maceration or even the dissolution of traditional identity patterns need to be discussed. The identification seems to be thus less endangered by the high fluctuation within the team arrangement as a consequence of the players' so-called mercenary mentality or through the sporting success. The fans observe far more sceptically the increased commercialization of club activities and the transformation of their club toward brand or event organizations linked to this. Identification always seems in danger when the clubs' only concern is about earning money because of increasing commercialization

(Riedl, 2006). This can create the impression among fans that the club is degrading them to a medium for the acquisition of profit. The latest trends in sport clubs, such as the rising dependence on private investors, the establishment of expensive VIP boxes instead of inexpensive standing room, may have a negative effect on the emotional bonds of the fans toward their club. In these cases, it is unlikely that fans develop a positive attitude toward the sponsors. Therefore, the sport marketers of the clubs must find creative ways to strengthen the fan identification with their club. The fans' sense of identification can be increased when sport clubs: (1) create opportunities for their fans to feel like they are affiliated with the club through, for example, fan clubs; (2) increase the public's accessibility to the team, and (3) hold events such as autograph and picture sessions to create accessibility for fans. There the fan can interact with players and other team personnel. This can help to stabilize or increase the connection between the club, the community and the fans (see, for example, Dolles and Södermann, 2011, 2013 in this volume; Sutton et al., 1997). Beyond that, sponsors should, with a view to the effect of their sponsorships, also be aware of the significance of a high emotional bond of the fans with their club. Therefore, sponsors should also proactively and conceptually support the club's activities for stabilizing the fan identity with the club. This does not only help to permanently stabilize their relationship with potential target groups, but also highlights their interest in supporting the club explicitly.

Furthermore, these findings reveal that the credibility of the sponsoring commitment has a positive effect on the attitude toward the single sponsor. From the company's point of view for generating credibility it needs to consider, that the fans' solidarity is primarily with the sport club. Companies which want to make their mark in business at the expense of sport clubs, and consider fans merely as consumers, will probably not evoke any sympathy among the fans toward their products. Thus the following is imperative: 'Sponsors must find where the emotional linkage is and attach themselves to that' (IEG, 1999: 2–3). Credibility can be reached through an appropriate fit between sponsor and the sponsored. This refers above all to the value fit between sponsor and club. The fit is not synonymous to congruence. Although the credibility of the sponsorship is lessened with too low a fit, this leads to a too large a distance between club and sponsor. Therefore, the consistency and reciprocal connectivity have to be kept in mind when designing the sponsorship portfolio and selecting the sponsorship object. Such a value fit is possible if both partners possess similarly stored denotative and/or connotative features. On the one hand, the sponsor has to verify to what extent their own brand essence value exhibit matches with the values and the image of the club. On the other hand, the club has to reflect to what extent certain sponsorships are compatible with their philosophy. Furthermore connectivities can be established through regional relations, a product fit or through thematic connections. In order to establish credibility the importance of a consistent and permanent sponsorship commitment has to be emphasized. In reference to the first case study, the 1.FCN has changed its jersey sponsor in the meanwhile to a French conglomerate, heavily involved in nuclear power plants. The club has received criticisms from its fans for this sponsorship. The reason for this is easily identified: the operation of nuclear power plants is criticized harshly in Germany. Hence the fans consider the sponsorship unsuitable for the 1.FCN, which stands for a family-friendly image. Thus the attitude toward the sponsor is negatively affected.

Furthermore, within the scope of sponsorship it also needs to be made clear to fans how the relationship between club and sponsor has to be interpreted, and the advantages to the club which emerge from the partnership with the sponsors. This demands a corporate communication strategically adjusted to the sponsoring commitment and containing thematic reference points to the sport club (morals, tradition). On this basis a symbiosis can develop between the club and the sponsor which can be seen as authentic by the fans.

To conclude, companies take up sport sponsoring with the expectation that the potential consumers' passion for their club will rub off onto their products. Both studies partially confirm this expectation. Support for the sport club by the consolidation of its relationship with the fans gives the sponsor both the unique opportunity for stable links with potential consumers as well as the chance to distinguish itself from other competitors. This study's findings offer further ways to create successful sponsorships. Nevertheless more research within the sponsoring effectiveness field is needed to clarify unresolved questions.

REFERENCES

Arbuckle, J.L. and Wothke, W. (1999), *AMOS 4.0 User's Guide*, Chicago, IL: Small Waters.
Ashforth, B.E. and Mael, F. (1989), Social identity theory and the organization, *Academy of Management Review*, **14** (1), 20–30.
Backhaus, K., Erichson, B., Plinke, W. and Weiber, R. (2006), *Multivariate Analysemethoden* [*Multivariate Analysis Methods*], Berlin: Springer.
Becker-Olsen, K.L. (2003), And now, a word from our sponsor, *Journal of Advertising*, **32** (2), 17–32.
Bee, C.C. and Havitz, M.E. (2010), Exploring the relationship between involvement, fan attraction, psychological commitment and behavioural loyalty in a sports spectator context, *International Journal of Sports Marketing & Sponsorship*, **11** (2), 160–77.
Bentler, P.M. (1990), Comparative fit indexes in structural models, *Psychological Bulletin*, **107** (2), 238–46.
Brown, S.P. and Staymann, D.M. (1992), Antecedents and consequences of attitude toward the ad: a meta-analysis, *Journal of Consumer Research*, **19** (1), 34–51.
Browne, M.W. and Cudeck, R. (1993), Alternative ways of assessing model fit, in A.K. Bollen and J.S. Long (eds), *Testing Structural Equation Models*, Thousand Oaks, CA: Sage, pp. 136–61.
Chin, W.W. (1998), The partial least squares approach to structural equation modeling, in G.A. Marcoulides (ed.), *Modern Business Research Methods*, Mahwah, NJ: Erlbaum, pp. 295–336.
Cornwell, T.B. (2008), State of the art and science in sponsorship-linked marketing, *Journal of Advertising*, **37** (3), 41–55.
Cornwell, T.B. (2013), State of the art and science in sponsorship-linked marketing, in S. Söderman and H. Dolles (eds), *Handbook of Research on Sport and Business*, Cheltenham, UK and Northampton, MA, USA: Edward Elgar, pp. 456–76.
Cornwell, T.B. and Coote, L.V. (2005), Corporate sponsorship of a cause: the role of identification in purchase intent, *Journal of Business Research*, **58** (3), 268–76.
Cornwell, T.B., Weeks, C.S. and Roy, D.P. (2005), Sponsorship-linked marketing: opening the black box, *Journal of Advertising*, **32** (2), 21–42.
Crimmins, J. and Horn, M. (1996), Sponsorship: from management ego to marketing success, *Journal of Advertising Research*, **36** (4), 11–21.
Dalakas, V. and Levin, A.M. (2005), The balance theory domino: how sponsorships may elicit negative consumer attitudes, in G. Menon and A.R. Rao (eds), *Advances in Consumer Research*, Urbana, IL: Association for Consumer Research, pp. 91–7.
Depken, C.A. (2000), Fan loyalty and stadium funding in professional baseball, *Journal of Sport Economics*, **1** (2), 124–38.
Derbaix, C., Decrop, A. and Cabossart, O. (2002), Colors and scarves: the symbolic consumption of material possessions by soccer fans, *Advances in Consumer Research*, **29** (4), 511–18.
Dolles, H. and Söderman, S. (2008), The network of value captures: creating competitive advantage in football management, *Wirtschaftspolitische Blätter Österreich* [*Austrian Economic Policy Papers*], **55** (1), 39–58.
Dolles, H. and Söderman, S. (2011), Learning from success: implementing a professional football league in

Japan, in H. Dolles and S. Södermann (eds), *Sport as a Business: International, Professional and Commercial Aspects*, Basingstoke: Palgrave Macmillan, pp. 228–50.

Dolles, H. and Söderman, S. (2013), The network of value captures in football club management: a framework to develop and analyse competitive advantage in professional team sports, in S. Söderman and H. Dolles (eds), *Handbook of Research on Sport and Business*, Cheltenham, UK and Northampton, MA, USA: Edward Elgar, pp. 367–95.

Easton, S. and Mackie, P. (1998), When football came home: a case history of the sponsorship activity at Euro '96, *International Journal of Advertising*, **17** (1), 99–144.

Emerson, R.M. (1976), Social exchange theory, *Annual Review of Sociology*, **2** (3), 335–62.

Fink, J.S., Trail, G.T. and Anderson, D.F. (2002), An examination of team identification: which motives are most salient to the existence?, *International Sports Journal*, **6** (2), 195–207.

Fisher, R.J. and Wakefield, K. (1998), Factors leading to group identification: a field study of winners and losers, *Journal of Psychology & Marketing*, **15** (1), 23–40.

Fornell, C. and Larcker, D.F. (1981), Evaluating structural equation models with unobservable variables and measurement error, *Journal of Marketing Research*, **18** (1), 39–50.

Funk, D.C. and James, J.D. (2004), The fan attitude network (FAN) model: exploring attitude formation and change among sport consumers, *Sport Management Review*, **7** (1), 1–26.

Funk, D.C. and James, J.D. (2006), Consumer loyalty: the meaning of attachment in the development of sport team allegiance, *Journal of Sport Management*, **20** (2), 189–217.

Gladden, J.M. and Funk, D.C. (2001), Developing an understanding of brand associations in team sport: empirical evidence from consumers of professional sport, *Journal of Sport Management*, **16** (1), 54–81.

Goldsmith, R.E., Lafferty, B.A. and Newell, S.J. (2000), The impact of corporate credibility and celebrity credibility on consumer reaction to advertisements and brands, *Journal of Advertising*, **29** (3), 45–54.

Gratton, C. and Taylor, P. (2000), *Economics of Sport and Recreation*, New York: Spon Press.

Gwinner, K. and Swanson, S.R. (2003), A model of fan identification: antecedents and sponsorship outcomes, *Journal of Services Marketing*, **17** (3), 275–94.

Hair, J.F., William, C.B., Barry, J.B., Rolph, E.A. and Ronald, L.T. (2006), *Multivariate Data Analysis*, Upper Saddle River, NJ: Prentice-Hall.

Heere, B. and Dickson, G. (2008), Measuring attitudinal loyalty: separating the terms of affective commitment and attitudinal loyalty, *Journal of Sport Management*, **22** (2), 227–39.

Hu, L. and Bentler, P.M. (1999), Cutoff criteria in fix indexes in covariance structure analysis: conventional criteria versus new alternatives, *Structural Equation Modeling*, **6**, 1–55.

Huber, F. and Matthes, I. (2007), Sponsoringwirkung auf Einstellung und Kaufabsicht [Sponsoring effects on attitude and purchase intention], *Marketing ZFP – Journal of Research and Management*, **29** (2), 90–104.

IEG (eds) (1994), Performance research quantifies NASCAR impact, *IEG Sponsorship Report*, **13**, 3–6.

IEG (eds) (1999), Sponsor loyality . . . it's not just for NASCAR anymore, *IEG Sponsorship Report*, **18**, 2–3.

James, J.D., Kolbe, R.H. and Trail, G.L. (2002), Psychological connection to a new sport team: building or maintaining the customer base?, *Sport Marketing Quarterly*, **11** (4), 215–25.

Johan, G.V. and Pham, M.T. (1999), Relateness, prominence and constructive sponsor identification, *Journal of Marketing Research*, **36** (4), 299–313.

Johnson, M.D., Herrmann, A. and Huber, F. (2006), The evolution of loyalty intentions, *Journal of Marketing*, **70** (2), 122–32.

Keller, K.L. (2008), *Strategic Brand Management. Building, Measuring and Managing Brand Equity*, Upper Saddle River, NJ: Prentice-Hall.

Kerr, A., Smith, N.F. and Anderson, A. (2011), 'As American as mom, apple pie and Dutch soccer?': the team identification of foreign Ajax FC supporters, in H. Dolles and S. Söderman (eds), *Sport as a Business: International, Professional and Commercial Aspects*, Basingstoke: Palgrave Macmillan, pp. 15–34.

Kwon, H.H. and Armstrong, K.L. (2004), An exploration of the construct of psychological attachment to a sport team among college students: a multi-dimensional approach, *Sport Marketing Quarterly*, **13** (2), 94–103.

Kwon, H.H., Trail, G.T. and Anderson, D.F (2005), Are multiple points of attachment necessary to predict cognitive, affective, conative, or behavioural loyalty?, *Sport Management Review*, **8** (3), 255–70.

Lardinoit, T. and Derbaix, C. (2001), Sponsorship and recall of sponsors, *Psychology & Marketing*, **18** (2), 167–90.

Laverie, D.A. and Arnett, D.B. (2000), Factors affecting fan attendance. The influence of identity salience and satisfaction, *Journal of Leisure Research*, **32** (2), 18–27.

Lawler, E.J. (2001), An affect theory of social exchange, *American Journal of Sociology*, **107** (2), 321–52.

Levin, A.M., Joiner, C. and Cameron, G. (2001), The impact of sports sponsorship on consumers' brand attitudes and recall: the case of NASCAR fans, *Journal of Current Issues and Research in Advertising*, **23** (1), 23–31.

MacKenzie, S.B. and Lutz, R.L. (1989), An empirical examination of the structural antecedents of attitude toward the ad in an advertising pretesting context, *Journal of Marketing*, **53** (2), 48–65.

MacKenzie, S.B., Lutz, R.L. and Belch, G.E. (1988), The role of attitude toward the ad as a mediator of advertising effectiveness: a test of competing explanations, *Journal of Marketing Research*, **23** (5), 130–43.

Madrigal, R. (2000), The influence of social alliances with sports teams on intentions to purchase corporate sponsors' products, *Journal of Advertising*, **29** (4), 13–24.

Madrigal, R. (2001), Social identity effects in a belief-attitude-intentions hierarchy: implications for corporate sponsorship, *Psychology & Marketing*, **18** (2), 145–65.

Madrigal, R. (2004), A review of team identification and its influence on consumers' responses toward corporate sponsors, in L.R. Kahle and C. Riley (eds), *Sports Marketing and the Psychology of Marketing Communication*, Mahwah, NJ: Erlbaum, pp. 241–58.

Mahony, D.F., Madrigal, R. and Howard, D. (2000), Using the psychological commitment to team (PCT) scale to segment sport consumers based on loyalty, *Sport Marketing Quarterly*, **9** (1), 15–25.

Meenaghan, T. (1999), Commercial sponsorship – the development of understanding, *International Journal of Sports Marketing and Sponsorship*, **1** (1), 19–31.

Meenaghan, T. (2001), Understanding sponsorship effects, *Psychology & Marketing*, **18** (2), 95–122.

Michalski, S. and Helmig, B. (2008), Fan identification: towards a common understanding of the conceptualization and measurement of the construct, paper presented at the 16th EASM European Sport Management Conference: Management at the Heart of Sport, 15–18 September, Heidelberg.

Mitrano, J.R. (1999), The 'Sudden Death' of hockey in Hartford: sports fans and franchise relocation, *Sociology of Sport Journal*, **16** (2), 134–54.

Newell, S.J. and Goldsmith, R.E. (2001), The development of a scale to measure perceived corporate credibility, *Journal of Business Research*, **52** (3), 235–47.

O'Reilly, N. (2013), Portfolio theory and the management of professional sports clubs: the case of Maple Leaf Sports and Entertainment, in S. Söderman and H. Dolles (eds), *Handbook of Research on Sport and Business*, Cheltenham, UK and Northampton, MA, USA: Edward Elgar, pp. 333–49.

O'Roark, J.B., Wood, W.C. and DeGaris, L. (2009), Brand identification among stock car racing fans in the USA, *International Journal of Sport Management and Marketing*, **6** (1), 35–51.

Parker, K. and Stuart, T. (1997), The West Ham syndrome, *Journal of the Market Research Society*, **39** (3), 509–17.

Pavelchak, M.A., Antil, J.H. and Munch, J.M. (1988), The Super Bowl: an investigation into the relationship among program context, emotional experience and ad recall, *Journal of Consumer Research*, **15** (3), 360–67.

Richardson, B. and Turley, D. (2006), Support your local team: resistance, subculture, and the desire for distinction, in C. Pechmann and L.L. Price (eds), *Advances in Consumer Research*, Duluth, MN: Association for Consumer Research, pp. 175–80.

Riedl, L. (2006), *Spitzensport und Publikum [Top Sports and Audience]*, Schorndorf: Hofmann.

Rifon, N.J., Choi, S.M., Trimble, C.S. and Li, H. (2004), Congruence effects in sponsorship, *Journal of Advertising*, **33** (1), 29–42.

Robinson, M.J. and Trail, G.T. (2005), Relationships among spectator gender, motives, points of attachment, and sport preference, *Journal of Sport Management*, **19** (1), 58–80.

Rodgers, S. (2004), The effects of sponsor relevance on consumer reactions to internet sponsorships, *Journal of Advertising*, **32** (4), 67–76.

Roy, D.P. and Cornwell, T.B. (2003), Brand equity's influence on responses to event sponsorships, *The Journal of Product and Brand Management*, **12** (6), 377–93.

Schlesinger, T., Nagel, S. and Günnel, F. (2009), Zum Einfluss der Fanidentität auf das Kaufverhalten gegenüber Produkten der Vereinssponsoren [The influence of fan identity on consumer behaviour toward products of a club's sponsors], in H. Dietl, E. Franck and H. Kempf (eds), *Fußball – Ökonomie einer Leidenschaft*, Schorndorf: Hofmann, pp. 153–72.

Speed, R. and Thompson, P. (2000), Determinants of sports sponsorship response, *Journal of the Academy of Marketing Science*, **28** (2), 226–38.

Strauss, B. (1995), Die Messung der Identifikation mit einer Sportmannschaft: Eine deutsche Adaption der 'Team Identification Scale' von Wann und Branscombe [Measuring identification with a sports team: a German adaption of the 'Team Identification Scale' by Wann and Branscombe], *Psychologie und Sport: Zeitschrift für Sportpsychologie*, **2** (2), 132–45.

Sutton, W.A., McDonald, M.A. and Cimperman, J. (1997), Creating and fostering fan identification in professional sports, *Sport Marketing Quarterly*, **6** (1), 15–22.

Tajfel, H. (1978), *Differentiation between Social Groups: Studies in the Social Psychology of Intergroup Relations*, London: Academic Press.

Tajfel, H. and Turner, J.C. (1986), The social identity theory of intergroup behavior, in S. Worchel and W.G. Austin (eds), *Psychology of Intergroup Relations*, Chicago, IL: Nelson-Hall, pp. 7–24.

Tapp, A. (2004), The loyalty of football fans – we'll support you ever more?, *The Journal of Database Marketing & Customer Strategy Management*, **11** (3), 225–46.

Theysohn, S., Hinz, O., Nosworthy, S. and Kirchner, M. (2009), Official supporters clubs: the untapped potential of fan loyalty, *International Journal of Sports Marketing & Sponsorship*, **10** (4), 302–24.

Trail, G.T. and James, J.D. (2001), The motivation scale for sport consumption: a comparison of psychometric properties with other sport motivations scales, *Journal of Sport Behaviour*, **24** (2), 108–27.

Trail, G.T., Anderson, D.F. and Fink, J.S. (2000), A theoretical model of sport spectator consumption behavior, *International Journal of Sport Management*, **1** (3), 154–80.

Wakefield, K.L. and Sloane, H.J. (1995), The effects of team loyalty and selected stadium factors on spectator attendance, *Journal of Sport Management*, **9** (2), 153–72.

Wakefield, K.L., Becker-Olsen, K. and Cornwell, T.B. (2007), I spy a sponsor. The effects of sponsorship level, prominence, relatedness, and cueing on recall accuracy, *Journal of Advertising*, **36** (4), 61–74.

Walliser, B. (2003), An international review of sponsorship research: extension and update, *International Journal of Advertising*, **22** (1), 5–40.

Wann, D.L. and Branscombe, N.R. (1993), Sports fans: measuring degree of identifications with their team, *International Journal of Sport Psychology*, **24** (1), 1–17.

Wann, D.L., Roberts, A. and Tindall, J. (1999), The role of team performance, team identification, and self-esteem in sport spectators game preferences, *Perceptual and Motor Skills*, **89** (3), 945–50.

Wann, D.L., Melnick, M.J., Russell, G.W. and Pease, D.G. (2001), *Sport Fans: The Psychology and Social Impact of Spectators*, New York: Routledge.

Wann, D.L., Pierce, S., Padgett, B., Evans, A., Krill, K. and Romay, A. (2003), Relations between sport team identification and optimism, *Perceptual and Motor Skills*, **97** (3), 803–4.

24 State of the art and science in sponsorship-linked marketing
T. Bettina Cornwell

Sponsorship of sports, arts, and charitable events is a mainstream marketing activity no longer in need of extensive introduction or justification. There is, however, a need to account for the progress made to date in integration of sponsorship-linked marketing into management, theory, and research. Moreover, there is a need to open a discussion of realignment in our thinking regarding the role that sponsorship and other indirect marketing communications play and will play in the future. Up to this point, we have tended to consider sponsorship, product placement, advergaming, and other new approaches as uniquely interesting areas at the intersection of advertising and entertainment. It is time to consider these trends holistically as a move toward a new era in communications, one that could be called 'indirect marketing.' There are many perspectives that can be taken on sponsorship. In this chapter, the perspective of the firm or organization that might use sponsorship in a marketing and communications program is considered.

1 HISTORY OF DEVELOPMENT AND GROWTH

Over the past two decades, sponsorship-linked marketing growth has outstripped advertising growth by several percentage points (see Figure 24.1), with the 2007 figure for sponsorship topping $37 billion worldwide (IEG, 2007). Moreover, this figure only represents the packaged sponsorship fee and does not include the leverage or activation that accompanies most sponsorship at a debated dollar for dollar ratio. Despite rapid growth, the area still suffers from lack of a strong understanding of how sponsorship works in the mind of the consumer and how it might be made more effective. Sponsorship and other indirect marketing communications (such as product placement) have also suffered from being free-standing areas of inquiry, sometimes thought of as sales promotion techniques or communication gimmicks, sometimes as consumer promotions, and very often as 'other' in the communications budget.

1.1 Sponsorship's Hand in the 'Death of Advertising'

Rust and Oliver predicted the death of traditional advertising fourteen years ago.

> Mass media advertising as we know it today is on its deathbed, and its prognosis is poor. . . . direct marketing is stealing business from traditional advertising; and the growth of sales promotion and integrated marketing communications both come at the expense of traditional advertising. The reason for advertising's impending demise is the advent of new technologies that have resulted in the fragmentation of media and markets, and the empowerment of consumers. . . . the era of producer–consumer interaction will dominate by 2010. (1994, p. 71)

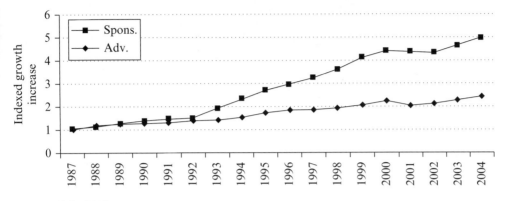

Source: Sisily (2005).

Figure 24.1 *Advertising expenditure versus sponsorship expenditure*

Clearly, the future is here. It has been over a decade since Rust and Oliver (1994) predicted the death of advertising at the hand of new technologies. It has also been over a decade since Fox and Geissler (1994) countered that advertising was not dying. It was simply having a crisis – a crisis that was decidedly driven by the changing business environment that focused on the bottom line. It seems that not much has changed. A recent feature in *Fortune* magazine, 'Nightmare on Madison Avenue' (Burke and Leonard, 2004), again suggests that the old rules of marketing must be abandoned due to technological advancements and harsh control of spending. Admittedly, the rules have changed, but it is not only technology and economics driving the change; it is the intersection of these drivers with changed lifestyles and values of individuals and communities that is making this trend irreversible.

Around the world, countries wealthy enough to have discretionary income show increasing levels of out-of-home activities. In the United States, trends show increased spending on performing arts, and spectator sports in particular (Figure 24.2). While increased spending may partially reflect an increase in prices for these activities, participation in out-of-home activities figures more and more into the typical budget. The magnitude of these changes is significant. In the United States, expenditure on performing arts events increased by almost 50 per cent between 1989 and 2000, adjusted for inflation, and admissions to major sporting events have almost doubled since the 1960s (Woudhuysen, 2001). In England and Wales, participation in sports has increased since the 1980s among adolescents and adults (Green et al., 2005). Likewise, among Swedish adolescents, sports participation has increased between 1974 and 1995 (Weserståhl et al., 2003). This trend toward out-of-home activities holds multifaceted implications: People have growing emotional connections to events of their choosing; individuals are away from in-home television, and their engagement with communication technologies is typically self-selected. With cell phones argued to outnumber both television sets and personal computers as of 2005 (Townsend, 2000), 'wirelessness' supports the trend to be away and yet connected.

Furthermore, the expansion of corporate involvement in readily sponsored out-of-home activities is evident in several areas. For example, the advent of 'extreme sports'

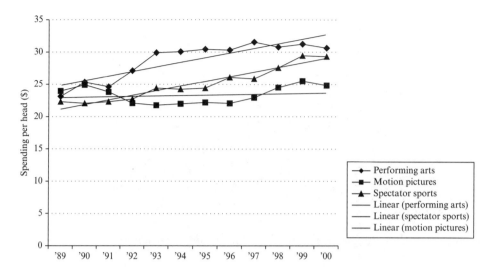

Note: Figures at constant 1996 dollars.

Source: National Endowment for the Arts (2002).

Figure 24.2   Spending on performing arts, motion pictures, and spectator sports

has been an image field day for marketers wanting to distinguish themselves from competitors (Puchan, 2004). Likewise, expansion of music tours (Waddell, 2005), sport tourism (Kurtzman and Zauhar, 2003), local festivals (Felsenstein and Fleischer, 2003), and mega events such as the Olympics and World Cup Soccer correlate neatly with the expansion of sponsorship.

In addition to the expansion of potentially to-be-sponsored activities, the support for these and traditional activities figures into the long-term nature of this trend. Much sponsored activity is fueled, or at the minimum endorsed, by communities, governments, and nations as vital to economic prosperity (Felsenstein and Fleischer, 2003; Matheson and Baade, 2004). Large-scale and community event initiatives bind community and sponsors together and the glue is rather hard to undo. For example, it is almost unimaginable that community development or refurbishment of a major sports arena would be accomplished without corporate sponsorship. Taxpayers have learned that they can avoid at least part of the bill by selling the communications potential of the venue (Sillars, 1995; Vadum, 2004).

1.2   The State of the Industry

Yet another perspective on the irreversible trend toward sponsoring would come from the firms themselves and the developing infrastructure surrounding sponsorship activities. While early on, firms in many industries, especially those even tangentially related to sport, sought out sponsorship opportunities, many other firms were drawn into sponsorship by the 'properties,' that is, athletes, teams, events, and organizations that sought them out for sponsorship support. In response, many firms have some kind of sponsorship policy regarding, at the minimum, what investments they will and will not make and the type of information they need for this decision. A recent study of Fortune 500 firms found that one-third of these firms has made their sponsorship policy available on the Internet (Cunningham, et al., 2009). Firms have invested in people and processes to deal with sponsorship and other indirect marketing initiatives. They have also begun to outsource these activities.

As sponsorship-linked marketing began to take off in the late 1980s and early 1990s, the response from the advertising industry was mixed. It ranged from embracing excitement to disdaining detachment, with some agencies feeling forced to deal with the often thematically incompatible (and seemingly financially incomprehensible) investments of their clients. As sponsorship investments have grown, so has the supporting infrastructure. With some advertising agencies slow to reinvent themselves to accommodate the rapid growth in sponsorship, the door for start-up service providers was left open and inviting. Early entrants, such as Joyce Julius (see Table 24.1 for a summary of this intermediary and others mentioned in this section), provided some much-needed measurement of the quantity of sponsorship exposures. Although measuring sponsorship investments in seconds of exposure time and comparing this to the cost of advertising in a similar time slot continues to be problematic because these exposures are not equivalent in quality to an advertising message (see Cornwell, 1995), it is clear that this measurement does provide some comfort to practitioners wanting to put a value on their investment. The next identified need in sponsorship support was for some sort of matching service where sponsors and sponsees could locate each other readily. Several matching services have begun and many have faltered. Two that appear to be flourishing are found in the United Kingdom: Sponsorshiponline, which provides a database of sponsors and sponsorship seekers, and the government-funded Sportsmatch.

The most recent addition to the sponsorship infrastructure has been proposal manager services. No matter their size, firms experience regular and sometimes overwhelming numbers of requests to sponsor sports, events, charities, the arts, and individuals. The task of managing requests has become a full-time job for many, since these groups and individuals see some relationship to the firm, and to rebuff or ignore them is tantamount to telling them never to buy your product again. Proposal management services are an intermediary employed by the firm. They accept applications from properties seeking sponsorship either in a standard template or using a customized proposal submission form. They may either forward all applications for sponsorship as received or they may screen and develop received proposals under some guidelines. For example, Sponsorwise helps shape on-line sponsorship proposal submissions to meet corporate decision-making needs.

Another evolution is the development of sports marketers such as Velocity Sports and Entertainment based in the United States, and Sportfive in Europe. Velocity tends to emphasize strategy and planning for sponsorship and event marketing, while Sportfive focuses more on an intermediary role between football clubs and leagues and potential sponsors. While these firms have broadened their offerings over time in recognition of the need for communications integration, they are decidedly centered on sport properties and property rights, an area where their expertise differs from that of the traditional advertising agency.

This is not to say that traditional advertising agencies have not risen to the occasion.

Table 24.1   Examples of sponsorship intermediaries

Name, URL, and year founded	Type	Description of example product offering
IEG www.sponsorship. com 1984	'Information house' with multiple products	IEG has numerous products, including their biweekly *Sponsorship Report* and the Return on Sponsorship (ROS) service, which quantifies the link between expenditures and investment returns. They model the factors that tie back to client objectives and calculate returns in each area
Joyce Julius www.joycejulius. com 1985	Research supplier	Joyce Julius and Associates, Inc., provides independent sports, special event, and entertainment program evaluation. Key products include the Sponsors Report®, which provides documentation of in-broadcast brand exposure during sports, special event, and entertainment television programming, and the National Television Impression Value (NTIV®) Analysis, which provides impression measurement of sponsorship programs. Joyce Julius and Associates' Survey Analyses provide quantitative and qualitative research feedback to gauge a sponsorship's success
Omnicom Group's Element 79 Sports www.element79. com 2006	Sports-marketing consulting and analysis	'Element 79 Sports will use a proprietary process called SportsSynch, which attempts to find the intersection of sports, target, and brand. The process is intended to differentiate the shop's work from other sports marketing companies' (Baar, 2006)
Sponsor Direct www.sponsor direct.com 2000	Proposal management intermediary	Sponsor Direct is focused on developing Web-based applications for the sponsorship industry. SponsorPort is their sponsorship proposal and portfolio management software, which helps corporate sponsors and agencies manage new sponsorship proposals as well as current sponsorship portfolios
Sponsorshiponline www.sponsorship online.co.uk 2000	Matching service	Sponsorshiponline provides a database of sponsors and sponsor seekers to help match sponsors and sponsorship seekers
Sponsorwise www.sponsorwise. com 2002	Proposal management intermediary	Sponsorwise is an on-line service that helps corporations and agencies manage sponsorship proposals and requests

SPORTSMATCH www.sportsmatch.co.uk 1992	Government matching program	Sportsmatch is a government-funded program that supports the development of grassroots and community sports in England by matching commercial sponsorship money invested in community sport with Sportsmatch funding
(The) Sponsorship Report www.sponsorship.ca 1988	Newsletter and conference organizer	The Sponsorship Report is a Canadian publication focused on corporate sponsorship of the arts and entertainment, sports, charitable causes, festivals, and events. The aim of the newsletter is to foster partnerships between Canadian corporations and potential sponsees
SPORTFIVE sportfive.com 2001	Sports rights marketing company	SPORTFIVE specializes in sports rights marketing, with headquarters in Hamburg and Paris, and offices throughout Europe and worldwide. SPORTFIVE also offers consulting services and publishes market-media studies, feasibility studies, and market research reports
Starcom Mediavest Group's Relay www.relayworldwide.com 2000	Agency	Relay is a sports and event-marketing company focusing on sports, sponsorship, lifestyle, and event marketing. Services offered by Relay's sponsorship consulting division include strategy development, sponsorship evaluation, activation plan development and implementation, negotiation, sponsorship management, licensing, and consumer promotions. Relay SponsorVision is a digital monitoring system that uses image recognition technology to compute sponsorship exposure value
Velocity www.teamvelocity.com 1999	Sport and entertainment agency	Velocity is a sponsorship- and lifestyle-marketing agency with services including consulting, brand promotions, retail marketing, event management, customer entertainment, meeting planning, municipal marketing, property alliances, and research and evaluation

Note: Unless otherwise noted, information and descriptions were drawn from the URLs provided in the table, and in some instances, from personal communications with representatives from the firms listed.

Most large agencies have a division that deals with sponsorship. At Starcom Mediavest Group's Relay, they manage the development of sport sponsorship and event-marketing projects for clients. Moreover, on the client side, firms are seeking to find agencies with specialized services for event planning and sponsoring (Maddox, 2005). Thus, new entrants, such as Omincom's Element 79 Sports in 2006 (Baar, 2006), are appearing on a regular basis. It should therefore be emphasized that Table 24.1 is only illustrative of the developing infrastructure. Trends in the industry taken together show a worldwide network of sponsors, sponsees, and intermediaries forging a long-term business communications platform.

1.3   The Art of Management

As philanthropy gave way to strategic investing in sports, arts, and charities, the guardians of wealth were questioned for their intentions. Was it the CEO's love of tennis that moved Volvo into sponsorship or was it a match between the drivers of their cars and the tennis demographic? A paper that was perhaps a watershed in this regard was titled 'Sponsorship: from management ego trip to marketing success.' Written by industry practitioners James Crimmins and Marty Horn (1996) at DDB Needham, it endorsed overtly the possibility that sponsorships could be a reasoned business investment and need not be an emotional action of a sports enthusiast CEO.

While commentators in the business press continue to suggest that management egos or agency effects overly influence sponsorship decision making, empirical evidence is mixed. Agency effects are said to exist when nonowner managers put their own interests above those of the shareholders in decisions involving corporate assets of the firm. That is to say, managers, with no cost to themselves, would invest corporate funds in activities such as sponsorship of sport or the arts that yield, for example, season box seats for their own use.

Cash flow within a firm is often considered a proxy for potential agency expropriations by managers within sponsoring firms. The thinking is that in firms with abundant cash, there is less monitoring of activities such as sponsorship investing. So-called agency costs (Jensen and Meckling, 1976) are incurred when sponsorships benefiting the CEO are placed above sponsorships that are of benefit to the firm and its shareholders. Since manager motives for sponsorship investment are difficult to study, cash flow has become a proxy variable for this potential. A study of the National Association for Stock Car Auto Racing (NASCAR) showed a significant negative influence of the cash flow proxy variable (Pruitt, et al., 2004), suggesting that managers take advantage of the benefits of sponsorship at no cost to themselves. In an event study of major league 'official' sponsorships, no influence of the cash flow proxy variable was found, suggesting no agency effects (Cornwell et al., 2005). Using a slightly different approach to discovery of any agency effects, Farrell and Frame (1997), in a study of the 1996 Summer Olympic Games in Atlanta, found a positive relationship between ownership by large investors and securing abnormal returns. The researchers explain this result to be consistent with a monitoring hypothesis where shareholders are powerful enough to discipline managers. Conversely, they did not find negative abnormal returns for 'entrenched' managers, that is, those operating without significant shareholder pressure to maximize firm value (p.179). One interpretation of these various but limited event-study findings is that sponsorships with more public fee negotiations may be less subject to agency effects than those with clandestine decision making. NASCAR is known for very quiet negotiations. Alternatively, perhaps some contexts lend themselves more to agency effects than others – adequate evidence is not yet available.

Another perspective on management decision making could be that some ostensible agency conflicts may be misconstrued. Take, for example, an industrial firm in Belgium that had a sponsorship portfolio of typical large-scale sports properties and one curiously small sponsorship of a church choir. When queried about this latter sponsorship while visiting the manufacturing plant, on exiting the building, the manager simply pointed to the church across the street and said, 'That is why we sponsor the choir.' While it popped to mind that local civic responsibility would indeed be a reason for sponsorship, he explained that the reason for the sponsorship was far more pragmatic: the churchgoers did not need their parking spaces Monday through Friday and his firm did. Thus, while the managerial motives for sponsorship investments are important in understanding practice, it seems that we may need to borrow frameworks from management and marketing to better understand their complexity. Sponsorship decision making is thick with negotiation, barter, and deal making, and research is yet to unravel these complexities.

1.4 Researching Managerial Decision Making

If advertising, as an area of study, embraces sponsorship as part of the domain of advertising, which it has, then sponsorship decision making must be embraced as part of the domain of advertising management, but this has not yet happened. The old set of advertising relationships focused largely on the relationship between the agency and the client (see, for example, Gould et al., 1999), and were focused on the transactional perspective of buying advertising exposure. For many clients, advertising agencies were the gateway to media. In contrast, sponsorship-linked marketing may take many forms and include many intermediaries, such as those noted in Table 24.1, but may also include direct alliances between the firm and the property (Farrelly and Quester, 2005); sponsoring is almost always relational in orientation. Intermediaries may play a pivotal role in sponsoring, but sponsorship is characterized by 'go/no go' managerial decisions involving the property and activation of the relationship to it. Thus, sponsorship decision making must come to the fore of the advertising management research agenda.

In studying managerial decision making in sponsorship, it seems that choice-modeling approaches would be most useful. With choice modeling we could better understand how managers make trade-offs when considering sponsorship opportunities with differing characteristics. Similar methods such as choice-based conjoint (Pracejus and Olsen, 2004) and conjoint analysis (Bloom et al., 2006; Dean, 2004) have been utilized to understand how consumers make choices when sponsorship or cause-related elements are involved. A developing gold standard in this methodological vein is best/worst scaling (see Finn and Louviere, 1992, for an example and Marley and Louviere, 2005, for the underlying theory). With this approach, managers would evaluate choice sets (sponsorship alternatives, perhaps three or four at a time, with various characteristics) and indicate for each set the 'best choice' and the 'worst choice.' This approach has several advantages over traditional discrete choice tasks (Marley and Louviere, 2005, p. 464). First, it yields a good deal of information (with information about rankings derivable from the task). Second, the approach takes advantage of a person's propensity to respond more consistently to extreme options. Last, and perhaps most attractive of all, best/worst tasks are easy for people to do. Of course, a major challenge would be finding adequate samples of managers willing to participate in such studies.

2   HOW SPONSORSHIP WORKS: THEORETICAL PROPOSITIONS

Underlying many marketing communications theories is more basic psychological theory on information processing. Key to an understanding of what happens in the mind is the idea of associative networks (Anderson and Bower, 1973) and spreading activation (Collins and Loftus, 1975). Briefly summarizing from this literature, knowledge is stored in memory in the form of linked nodes of information; activation of a node through some stimulation spreads, and in doing so, supports retrieval of stored information. Researchers in advertising and marketing have utilized this conceptualization extensively. For example, Keller (1993, 2003) shows sponsorship activities as resulting in brand knowledge, which is linked to the brand node in memory in an associative network. It is generally accepted that experience with the brand, and thus a large set of linkages, results in greater associative strength, which is a good thing in the main. Even so, Keller notes (2003, p. 597) that a deeper understanding of how knowledge for a brand and other linked entities interact is paramount. Understanding interactions with other linked entities and other linked information generally is important to sponsorship because sponsorship embeds the brand in a vast field of possible information nodes (for example, player jerseys, time clocks, scoreboards), often with little direction on how to meaningfully link them to the brand.

Henderson, et al. (1998) have noted that while research on associative networks has progressed in psychology, these developments have not been adequately leveraged in advertising and marketing. While some research in consumer behavior, such as work on interference (Jewell and Unnava 2003; Kumar and Krishnan, 2004), is making use of recent advances in psychology, there is still room for improvement. The need to consider theory is particularly important in sponsorship since little is known about how sponsorship-linked communications are remembered. Unlike traditional advertising, where a rich depiction of the brand may be (but is not always) made, sponsorship is an impoverished media, with media being broadly construed as the context through which messages pass. Sponsorship without leverage is a logo or brand name briefly displayed – a title sponsor mentioned by an announcer, but not a complete message. Although sponsorship may increase brand awareness and transfer event image elements to a brand or company, it accomplishes these things and others in an entirely different way. The question is then: What theories might be useful in consideration of sponsorship? Two of the more thought-provoking areas are now discussed.

2.1   Theory on How Sponsorship Might Not Be Working as We Expect

How sponsorship information is encoded and later retrieved depends not only on the nature of the exposure, but also on the nature of the receiver. Previous research suggests that the knowledge a person holds about a sport influences his or her perception of the congruence of a sponsor–event pairing (Roy and Cornwell, 2004). This research only captured event knowledge – what is the role of other information held in memory? What influence does it have on a new sponsorship relationship?

The pairing of a brand or corporate name with an event or activity is similar to the paired-associate learning task found in numerous studies in psychology. In the paired associate paradigm, two words are presented at study and then individuals are asked to recall one given the other. In the memory literature, Nelson and his colleagues (Nelson et al., 2003; Nelson et al., 1998; Nelson et al., 1992) have provided the most comprehensive account of how pre-existing memories might contribute to recall. Their work accepts the associative networks of Anderson and Bower (1973), and then focuses on understanding one word's relationship to another and the way in which these relationships influence memory. They now have convincing evidence that when recall is cued with an associate of a to-be-remembered word, the network of associations emanating from both the cue and the target are involved in the recall process (Nelson et al., 1997; Nelson and McEvoy, 2002). For example, if you ask individuals, 'Is the brand TELUS a sponsor of amateur hockey?' the associates of TELUS as well as the associates of amateur hockey are activated in memory. This activation of associates might allow an implicit mediator such as 'Canadian' to naturally arise and influence memory since TELUS is a Canadian company and hockey is a popular sport in Canada. This leads us to the following testable proposition:

Proposition 1 Natural mediators arise and influence memory for sponsorship-linked communications.

The results of Nelson et al. (1997) suggest that the provision of a mediator concept (or word) would be most important when the associative pathway involves an intermediate link between the cue and the target, as would often be the case in sponsorship. That is to say that in practice, communication managers could supply a concept to support the link between the sponsor and activity instead of relying on individuals' pre-existing memory networks. Consider the example mentioned previously, 'TELUS sponsors amateur hockey' (a hypothetical associative network is shown in Figure 24.3). In most past research, this pairing would not be considered to be highly congruent since telecommunications equipment is not typically featured or demonstrated during amateur hockey play, nor is there an obviously strong strategic relationship between the target market for telecommunications and the audience for amateur hockey (Cornwell, 1995). For Canadian citizens, the hypothetical associative network shown might be cryptic, with their actual networks being much richer because TELUS is a Canadian firm and hockey is a national pastime for many. On the other hand, this hypothetical network might hold more information than the typical non-Canadian has in memory. With regard to supplied mediation (supplied by the communications manager of the firm), a plausible chain linking TELUS and amateur hockey could involve the intermediate links of 'young people' and 'cold.' By emphasizing young people as the link between TELUS and hockey, one might activate a pathway that would otherwise not be activated. It should also be noted that associations are not limited to words and concepts, but might include visual images (for example, the Telus lizard made popular in advertising and available

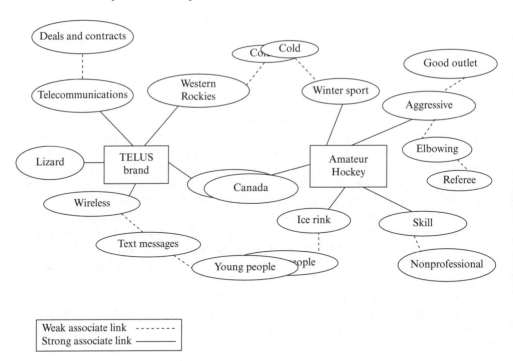

Figure 24.3   Hypothetical associative network

as a free download from www.telusmobility.com), or referents to places (like Canada) or people. This suggests a second testable proposition:

Proposition 2   Plausible (yet distinctive) supplied mediating associations can help individuals form better memories for sponsor–event linkages and may also influence formation of positive attitudes.

An extended network perspective – one that considers natural mediators and second-ary associations – would account for the superior memory results typically found for congruent sponsor–event pairs. An athletic shoe manufacturer would have numerous weak and strong links with a running event and would, in general, benefit from them. Without articulation or reasons to form an explicit memory for the sponsor–event rela-tionship (Cornwell et al., 2006), however, implicit or unintentional memory for both the sponsor and event may make many connections available. These connections might be parallel and may activate resonant connections from the sponsor to the event and back, or they may traverse to other similar associations such as competitors, especially ones that have sponsored this or a similar event. This also suggests that a direct competitor might be picked up in the activation of weak intermediate links, even if it is not a sponsor of the particular event under consideration. Thus, the following proposition is offered:

Proposition 3   Providing a link of information relating to the sponsor and event may help establish memory for the sponsor as contrasted to any direct competitors.

The idea of providing additional information to support memory for a relationship between two entities is straightforward enough; however, the question of what type of information to provide in a given situation is still an open empirical question.

2.2   Why Use Item or Relational Information?

In a competitive marketplace where many brands are sponsors and many in the same category are sponsoring similar events, linking associations or relational information might not be enough. Weeks et al. (2006a) suggest that consideration of both item information and relational information might be instructive. This thinking, summarized here, combines the work of organizational memory theorists and levels-of-processing theorists. Organizational memory theorists (for example, Bower, 1970; Mandler, 1967; Puff, 1979) argue that good memory performance requires that an episode be encoded in an organized manner. They argue that similar features across various items produce overlap in memory, and overlap results in the various related items within an episode being encoded as a single, organized representation. Alternatively, levels-of-processing theorists argue that good memory is based on the encoding of differences (Craik and Lockhart, 1972; Craik and Tulving, 1975). Items are stored as unique representations in memory, identifiable through a lack of overlapping features or lack of integration across representations. It is this lack of overlap that assists retrieval, with the distinctiveness of a particular item allowing discrimination.

Einstein and Hunt (1980; Hunt and Einstein, 1981) bring these two ideas together. They argue that distinctiveness encoding, as suggested by levels-of-processing theorists, applies to the processing of item information, whereas similarity encoding, as suggested by organizational theorists, applies to the processing of relational information. Relational information serves primarily a generative function, by activating the general class or category to which a specific stimulus belongs. Item information may then be used to search within this limited group of representations. In this way, Einstein and Hunt propose that relational and item information each contribute to memory retrieval processes, but in different ways.

To put this in the context of sponsorship, if someone is asked the question 'Which brand is the major sponsor of World Cup Soccer?' both relational and item processing may be used to provide an answer. Relational processing is required to activate memories related to the category 'World Cup Soccer.' This information alone may not be enough to provide a precise response, however, and so the use of item processing is also needed. Item processing would be used to discriminate among all those activated representations in the 'World Cup Soccer' category, to identify the one with the distinctive feature of 'major sponsor.' Thus, if a congruent sponsor for an event might be confused with other congruent sponsors, it may be more important to emphasize the distinctiveness of the sponsor (provide item information) than to further develop the sponsor's relationship to the event. (For preliminary results in support of this proposition, see Weeks et al., 2006b.) This theorizing leads to the following two propositions:

Proposition 4   A brand with a diffuse image (and many varied associations) might be congruent with and fit with more sponsorship opportunities, but memory for sponsorship relationships would be expected to be poor.

Proposition 5   A brand with a very distinctive image might have to work to develop fit with a sponsorship opportunity, but would then be expected to have a stronger relationship in memory due to the distinctiveness of the association.

2.3   Sponsorship Theory and Generalizability

The above-mentioned arguments for the growth and entrenchment of sponsorship also apply to other nontraditional or 'indirect' forms of marketing communication. Advances in technology and changing lifestyles are also related to the growth of activities such as product placement, viral marketing, buzz, ambient marketing, and even guerrilla marketing. All these approaches stem from the need to be where consumers are and the need to be embedded in experience, thus circumventing technologically enabled avoidance on the part of the consumer. These approaches then result in a similar pattern of communication and loose memory networks. Brand names flit by in a video game or come in the form of an audio or visual mention in a sitcom, but they do not form rich advertising messages. We need to know more about the knowledge networks developed by indirect marketing and the ways that they contribute to consumer understanding and behavior.

The other major player in indirect marketing is brand placement, and one of the lifestyle changes it follows is growth in cinema attendance. For example, in the United Kingdom during the years 1984 to 2001, cinema viewing increased rather dramatically (www.statistics.gov.uk/STATBASE/ssdataset.asp?vink=6484/). For individuals age 7 to 14, those reporting monthly viewing increased from 10 to 38 per cent, and for those in the 15–24 age group it increased from 16 to 50 per cent (along with lesser but significant increases across other age groups). Karrh (1998, p. 33) defined brand placement as the 'paid inclusion of branded products or brand identifiers, through audio and/or visual means, within mass media programming.' While the payment might be some kind of value exchange (barter is big in both brand placement and sponsorship), the idea is to connect with consumers by being embedded in media.

Here, several points of integration are worth noting. In a recent review of the theory explanations for sponsorship effects (Cornwell et al., 2005), the following mechanisms were found in the literature: mere exposure effects, low-level processing, reactivation, matching/congruence, articulation, balance or meaning transfer, social identification, classical conditioning, prominence heuristics, and attribution theory. Following are examples that demonstrate the overlapping theory and research implications that suggest the need for bridging among indirect marketing communication areas.

As mentioned, one explanation for sponsorship effects is that the mere exposure of a brand name or logo during an event has the potential to influence affect, as suggested by Zajonc (1968, 1980). This has been explored in several papers on sponsorship (for example, Bennett, 1999; Olson and Thjømøe, 2003). Similar theorizing was used by Auty and Lewis (2004) to explore children's choice of a soft drink following exposure to a movie clip with the soft drink brand name embedded in it. The contribution of Auty and Lewis's work with application to sponsorship research is the role of previous exposure in producing a reminder effect for the brand. Although the best starting point for future research on mere exposure might be to view it as processing fluency (Reber, et al., 2004), where aesthetic pleasure is thought to be a function of the individual's processing dynamics, it is clear that in most instances the substantive differences in information processing are few across sponsorship and brand placement.

Again, focusing on brand placement, we find that several of the theory explanations for sponsorship are similar to those found in brand placement. Russell and Stern (2006) use balance theory to explain how consumers align their attitudes toward brands with those of the story characters. Likewise, congruence between brand and plot influence memory (Russell, 2002), as is the case in sponsorship where congruence between brand and event influence memory (Cornwell et al., 2006).

Blogging, brand pushing, and word-of-mouth communication also operate in a loose web of associations that might be studied in the same ways as sponsorship and brand placement. Thus, it would be beneficial to take a more integrative approach to the various forms of indirect marketing. As Gilbert says with regard to buzz and related custom communication approaches, 'While advertising remains a vital tool, it is increasingly becoming one element among equals in the marketing mix' (2005, p. 294). It is useful theoretically and practically to group techniques using experience-embedded exposure together as indirect marketing and to learn to what extent they differ from traditional advertising. Thus, a starting point would be to examine the following proposition empirically.

Proposition 6 Indirect marketing communications result in context-dependent associations that are more variable and idiosyncratic than associations developed via traditional advertising messages.

3 MANAGERIAL IMPLICATIONS

If we were to conduct a similar analysis of industry activities for each of these indirect approaches to marketing as was done for sponsorship in Table 24.1, we would find fledgling firms reminiscent of where sponsorship was only a decade ago. Already, the established firms are capitalizing on core capabilities established in sponsorship analysis, namely, capabilities in choosing the best opportunity for a brand or organization and of measuring effects. Consider the expansion of Joyce Julius, known for sponsorship exposure analysis, to include products such as 'Television Product Placement Analysis,' 'Motion Picture Product Placement-Rental/Sales Analysis,' 'Opportunity Assessment-Projection Analysis,' and 'On-Site Theater Surveys.' Likewise, the major agencies are on top of these trends. For example, in addition to a Sport and Event Marketing division, Starcom Mediavest Group has one devoted to Entertainment Marketing for entertainment tie-ins and Gaming Communications to reach video-game players.

While sponsorship should have an elevated status in advertising and marketing, it must reckon with traditional views of the promotions mix. Given the above discussion regarding the similarities between sponsorship and other indirect marketing approaches, and given the need for a term that is flexible for use into the future, the new element should be described with a term such as 'indirect marketing.' At this time, spending on sponsorship dominates indirect marketing budgets, but other areas, particularly brand placements, are expanding rapidly. This suggests that definitional work is needed to set indirect marketing apart from advertising, public relations, personal selling, and sales promotion.

4   FUTURE RESEARCH

In writing this review of the state of the art and science in sponsorship-linked marketing, a number of areas in need of research were brought to the fore. Several have already been addressed, but others seem noteworthy. Therefore, a research agenda seems a fitting note on which to conclude.

4.1   Sponsorship and Reconstructive Memory

Advertising has been shown to influence consumer memory for past product experiences (Braun, 1999). Braun's finding that 'consumer recall of past experience is subject to distortion and can be guided by marketing communications' (p. 332) could certainly be applied to sponsorship. A simple extension would examine the potential of sponsorship to elevate recall of past brand experience, but other extensions could be even more interesting. While Braun focused on postexperience communication, attendees during sponsored events might also be influenced by contemporaneous product experience (for example, through sampling and pouring rights at events) and exposure to signage, as well as postexperience advertising. This multifaceted potential to refashion brand experience has not been explored.

4.2   Leveraging and Activation of Sponsorship

One of the most needed areas of research concerns spending that occurs in addition to the sponsorship contract. This spending typically results from efforts to build awareness of the link between the brand and event through advertising and promotion. Recently, Weeks et al., (2008) distinguished *leveraging* as all marketing communications collateral to the sponsorship, whereas *activation* relates to those communications that encourage interaction with the sponsor. The term 'sponsorship-linked marketing' as the orchestration and implementation of marketing activities for the purpose of building and communicating an association (link) to a sponsorship was coined to reflect the required coordination of interacting employees, audiences, volunteers, events, activities, sales promotions, merchandise, cosponsors, and media (Cornwell 1995, pp. 15–16). Very few papers have attempted to address the integrative effects of sponsorship in combination with leveraging (consider Becker-Olsen and Simmons, 2002; McCarville et al., 1998). Researchers know little about how each possible element in the sponsorship arsenal communicates, and we know next to nothing about how they communicate in combination. Practitioners also face challenges in managing them. For example, are logos able to communicate in a meaningful way on football jerseys, rotational signage, on a field, or when superimposed on broadcast scoring? Based on the findings of Janiszewski and Meyvis (2001), we know that logo meaning, familiarity, and presentation schedule are important for processing fluency, and in turn, for consumer decision making. Moreover, in focused experiments, it seems that processing fluency is not a monotonically increasing function of the number of exposures (Janiszewski and Meyvis, 2001). Thus, with logos, more is not necessarily better. In fact, targeted logo presentations might be balanced with efforts to provide other meanings that would improve processing fluency and, arguably, memory.

4.3   Sponsorship Portfolios

In addition to the management and measurement required in activating a sponsorship, one must also consider the firm's portfolio of sponsorships. Managing a large sponsorship portfolio might be considered simply another integrated marketing communications challenge. On the other hand, there are at least two aspects of sponsoring that deserve additional research. First, there is a practical and strategic need to understand the value of integrating sport and charity sponsoring to gain reach (with sport) while at the same time avoiding perceptions of commercialization (via charity). This portfolio strategy seems commonplace in practice but is underresearched. Theoretically, it is important to understand how the addition of a new sponsorship to an existing portfolio changes the knowledge network of consumers. Keller (2001) argues that for any communications element, it is important to consider the trade-off between commonality and complementarity, in other words, the extent to which the same associations are reinforced or the extent to which new associations are added by any new communications element. Clearly, the theory presented in the previous section could be applied to the development of sponsorship portfolios.

4.4   Sponsorship's Role in Market Entry

The ever-increasing internationalization of sport (Amis and Cornwell, 2005) is making sponsorship a truly international communications vehicle, rivaled only by the Internet. Global and local objectives can be united in sport sponsorship, and a consistent brand image can be presented across multiple global markets (Rines, 2002). In fact, large-scale sponsorships 'amortized' across markets makes the most cost-effective use of sponsoring sport ('Sports marketing' 2004). What, then, is sponsorship's role when brands seek to enter new markets? Because sponsorship is only able to carry a rather cryptic message, it seems that it would be most useful where new markets can already make the link between the product category and the brand name. This would suggest that sponsorship would be helpful in brand line extensions, but would not be as useful as advertising for an entirely new entry for the brand in a category. Nonetheless, it seems that sponsorship may have an expanding role to play if it can be effectively combined with traditional advertising in market entry because it builds awareness for the brand (Schulz et al., 2005).

4.5   Social Considerations

Controversial sponsorships, such as those for tobacco brands, have been receiving academic attention for some time (Cornwell, 1997; Dewhirst and Hunter, 2002; Dewhirst and Sparks, 2003), but only recently have the issues surrounding obesity forced fast food vendors into a similar unwelcome limelight (Barrand, 2004). The main policy issue involves the combining of unhealthy consumption choices with seemingly healthful sport images. Does pairing sport and fast food implicitly communicate that one can eat these foods and still look like an athlete? In this regard, gambling, food, and alcohol may all deserve more researcher attention. Other more subtle social issues also merit investigation. It seems that in keeping with the commercialization of sport, holding celebrities in check may actually kill the goose that lays the golden egg. In NASCAR experience, for example, sponsorship is forcing drivers into the same corporate mold, thus reducing their 'wild' appeal (Macur, 1999). Also noted is a preference for decidedly attractive athletes for sponsorship. This is one point in the broader set of issues regarding people and sports included and excluded from sponsorship opportunities.

4.6   Sponsorship Policy as a Company Instrument

Sponsorship policies are a curious element as a corporate instrument. A sponsorship policy is the document a company crafts that typically explains what a company will (and will not) sponsor, which audiences should be targeted, the quantity of sponsorships that should be undertaken over a given period, and the level of sponsorship devoted to each. Unlike policies on marketing, advertising, and public relations, sponsorship policies are the most likely to be made public. Because sponsorship engagement has historically hinged on some rather unsophisticated, nearly random matching of sponsor and sponsee, policies have been made public to support this process. It seems that some publicly available policies show a missed opportunity to communicate positively and effectively with important audiences. Many sponsorship policies on the Web are deeply embedded in a tangle of links (Cunningham et al., 2009). Thus, the state of the art could be described as a bit Jackson Pollock-esque.

4.7   Sponsorship Termination

We have failed to give adequate attention to the end of the sponsorship relationship. A starting point is a paper by Olkkonen and Tuominen (2006) on relationship fading: 'The concept of relationship fading refers to the phase in which a relationship seems to be permanently or temporally weakening and declining. Relationship fading can precede an enduring relationship ending, but it can also represent a temporal weakening of the relationship without leading to ending' (p.67). One obvious challenge is to begin to understand carryover effects in sponsorship. When a sponsorship is taken over by a firm, in particular a competitive firm in the same industry, how significant are the carryover recollections of the previous sponsor? This suggests the need for additional research on sponsorships as relationships or strategic alliances (Farrelly and Quester, 2005) rather than tactical decisions.

4.8   Ambushing

No chapter on sponsorship-linked marketing would be complete without some mention of ambushing. Ambushing is typically thought of as the efforts of an organization to associate itself indirectly with an event in the hope of reaping the same benefits as an official sponsor (Sandler and Shani, 1989). Past thinking on policies and strategies regarding ambushing needs to be reconsidered. Since legal protections for true sponsors have expanded, ambushers tend to come close to stepping over the legal line, but do so less often. Strategy research needs to consider how to incorporate would-be ambushers and form alliances, thus avoiding bothersome legal fees as well as painful and expensive surveillance. Communication research needs to consider the positive and negative outcomes for all parties involved. Perhaps an outrageous ambushing actually helps establish memory for the sponsorship in general, and moreover, for the true sponsor as contrasted with the ambusher.

Sponsorship-linked marketing is a decidedly interesting and multifaceted area of research. While worthy of examination in its own right, it is also a leader in the sweeping trend toward greater investment in indirect marketing activities. There is a need to better understand the differing communication capabilities of sponsorship, product placement, ambient marketing, and other indirect forms of promotion. There is also a corresponding need to identify areas of overlap and synergy.

ACKNOWLEDGEMENTS

The author thanks Helen Katz and Michael Humphreys for insightful comments and Russ Laczniak for his invitation to write on this topic. She also thanks Chanel Stoyle and Emerald Quinn for their research assistance.

REFERENCES

Amis, John and T. Bettina Cornwell (2005), *Global Sport Sponsorship*, Oxford: Berg.
Anderson, John R. and Gordon H. Bower (1973), *Human Associative Memory: A Brief Edition*, Hillsdale, NJ: Lawrence Erlbaum.
Auty, Susan and Charlie Lewis (2004), Exploring children's choice: the reminder effect of product placement, *Psychology and Marketing*, **21** (9), 697–713.
Baar, Aaron (2006), Element 79 forms sport division, *Adweek* (September 25), available at www.vnuemedia.com/aw/national/article_display.jsp?vnu_content_id=1003156478/ (accessed 5 January 2007).
Barrand, Drew (2004), Sport's biggest sponsors fight their corner, *Marketing* (18 March), 15.
Becker-Olsen, Karen and Carolyn J. Simmons (2002), When do social sponsorships enhance or dilute equity? Fit, message source, and the persistence of effects, in *Advances in Consumer Research*, vol. 29, Susan M. Broniarczyk and Kent Nakamoto (eds), Provo, UT: Association for Consumer Research, 287–89.
Bennett, Roger (1999), Sports sponsorship, spectator recall and false consensus, *European Journal of Marketing*, **33** (3/4), 291–313.
Bloom, Paul N., Steve Hoeffler, Kevin Lane Keller and Carlos E. Basurto Meza (2006), How social-cause marketing affects consumer perceptions: a market research technique called conjoint analysis can help managers predict what kind of affinity marketing program is likely to offer the best return on investment for their brand, *MIT Sloan Management Review*, **47** (2), 49–55.
Bower, Gordon H. (1970), Organizational factors in memory, *Cognitive Psychology*, **1** (1), 18–46.
Braun, Kathryn A. (1999), Postexperience advertising effects on consumer memory, *Journal of Consumer Research*, **25** (1), 319–34.
Burke, Doris and Devin Leonard (2004), Nightmare on Madison Avenue, *Fortune*, **149** (11), 42–9.
Collins, Allan M. and Elizabeth F. Loftus (1975), A spreading-activation theory of semantic processing, *Psychological Review*, **82** (6), 407–28.
Cornwell, T. Bettina (1995), Sponsorship-linked marketing development, *Sport Marketing Quarterly*, **4** (4), 13–24.
Cornwell, T. Bettina (1997), The use of sponsorship-linked marketing by tobacco firms: international public policy issues, *Journal of Consumer Affairs*, **31** (2), 238–54.
Cornwell, T. Bettina , Stephen W. Pruitt and John M. Clark (2005), The relationship between Major League

sports' official sponsorship announcements and the stock prices of sponsoring firms, *Journal of the Academy of Marketing Science*, **33** (4), 401–12.

Cornwell, T. Bettina, Clinton S. Weeks and Donald P. Roy (2005), Sponsorship-linked marketing: opening the black box, *Journal of Advertising*, **34** (2), 21–42.

Cornwell, T. Bettina, Michael S. Humphreys, Angela M. Maguire, Clinton S. Weeks and Cassandra L. Tellegen (2006), Sponsorship-linked marketing: the role of articulation in memory, *Journal of Consumer Research*, **33** (3), 312–21.

Craik, Fergus I. and Robert S. Lockhart (1972), Levels of processing: a framework for memory research, *Journal of Verbal Learning and Verbal Behavior*, **11** (6), 671–84.

Craik, Fergus I. and Endel Tulving (1975), Depth of processing and the retention of words in episodic memory, *Journal of Experimental Psychology: General*, **104** (3), 268–94.

Crimmins, James and Martin Horn (1996), Sponsorship: from management ego trip to marketing success, *Journal of Advertising Research*, **36** (4), 11–20.

Cunningham, Stephanie, T. Bettina Cornwell and Leonard V. Coote (2009), Expressing identity and shaping image: the relationship between corporate mission and corporate sponsorship, *Journal of Sports Management*, **23** (1), 65–86.

Dean, Dwane Hal (2004), Evaluating potential brand associations through conjoint analysis and market simulation, *The Journal of Product and Brand Management*, **13** (7), 506–13.

Dewhirst, Timothy and A. Hunter (2002), Tobacco sponsorship of formula One and CART auto racing: tobacco brand exposure and enhanced symbolic imagery through co-sponsors' third party advertising, *Tobacco Control*, **11** (2), 146–50.

Dewhirst, Timothy and Robert Sparks (2003), Intertextuality, tobacco sponsorship of sports, and adolescent male smoking culture: a selective review of tobacco industry documents, *Journal of Sport and Social Issues*, **27** (4), 372–98.

Einstein, Gilles O. and R. Reed Hunt (1980), Levels of processing and organization: additive effects of individual-item and relational processing, *Journal of Experimental Psychology: Human Learning and Memory*, **6** (5), 588–98.

Farrell, Kathleen A. and W Scott Frame (1997), The value of Olympic sponsorships: who is capturing the gold?, *Journal of Market-Focused Management*, **2** (2), 171–82.

Farrelly, Francis and Pascale Quester (2005), Examining important relationship quality constructs of the focal sponsorship exchange, *Industrial Marketing Management*, **34** (3), 211–19.

Felsenstein, Daniel and Aliza Fleischer (2003), Local festivals and tourism promotion: the role of public assistance and visitor expenditure, *Journal of Travel Research*, **41** (4), 385–92.

Finn, Adam and Jordan J. Louviere (1992), Determining the appropriate response to evidence of public concern: the case of food safety, *Journal of Public Policy and Marketing*, **11** (1), 12–25.

Fox, Richard J. and Gary L. Geissler (1994), Crisis in advertising?, *Journal of Advertising*, **23** (4), 79–84.

Gilbert, Josh (2005), Jazz, gestalt, and the year ahead for marketers, *Journal of Advertising Research*, **34** (3), 294–5.

Gould, Stephen J., Andreas F. Grein and Dawn B. Lerman (1999), The role of agency–client integration in integrated marketing communications: a complementary agency theory-interorganizational perspective, *Journal of Current Issues and Research in Advertising*, **21** (1), 1–12.

Green, Ken, Andy Smith and Ken Roberts (2005), Young people and lifelong participation in sport and physical activity: a sociological perspective on contemporary physical education in England and Wales, *Leisure Studies*, **24** (1), 27–43.

Henderson, Geraldine R., Dawn Iacobucci and Bobby J. Calder (1998), Brand diagnostics: mapping branding effects using consumer associative networks, *European Journal of Operations Research*, **111** (2), 306–27.

Hunt, R. Reed and Gilles O. Einstein (1981), Relational and item-specific information in memory, *Journal of Verbal Learning and Verbal Behavior*, **20** (5), 497–514.

IEG (2007), Projection: sponsorship growth to increase for fifth straight year, *Sponsorship Report* (January), **1** (4).

Janiszewski, Chris and Tom Meyvis (2001), Effects of brand logo complexity, repetition, and spacing on processing fluency and judgment, *Journal of Consumer Research*, **28** (1), 18–32.

Jensen, Michael C. and William H. Meckling (1976), Theory of the firm: managerial behavior: agency costs and ownership structure, *Journal of Financial Economics*, **3** (4), 305–60.

Jewell, Robert D. and H. Rao Unnava (2003), When competitive interference can be beneficial, *Journal of Consumer Research*, **30** (2), 283–91.

Karrh, James A. (1998), Brand placement: a review, *Journal of Current Issues and Research in Advertising*, **20** (1), 31–49.

Keller, Kevin Lane (1993), Conceptualizing, measuring and managing customer-based brand equity, *Journal of Marketing*, **57** (1), 1–22.

Keller, Kevin Lane (2001), Mastering the marketing communications mix: Micro and Macro Perspectives on Integrated Marketing Communications Programs, *Journal of Marketing Management*, **17** (7/8), 819–47.

Keller, Kevin Lane (2003), Brand synthesis: the multidimensionality of brand knowledge, *Journal of Consumer Research*, **29** (4), 595–600.

Kumar, Anand and Shanker Krishnan (2004), Memory interference in advertising: a replication and extension, *Journal of Consumer Research*, **30** (4), 602–11.

Kurtzman, Joseph and John Zauhar (2003), A wave in time: the sports tourism phenomena, *Journal of Sports Tourism*, **8** (1), 35–47.

Macur, Juliet (1999), NASCAR is shifting from wild to mild, *Orlando Sentinel* (14 August), B1.

Maddox, Kate (2005), Clients seek agencies with specialized services, *BtoB*, **90** (3), 38.

Mandler, George (1967), Organization and memory, in *The Psychology of Learning and Motivation*, Kenneth W. Spence and Janet T Spence (eds), New York: Academic Press, pp. 327–72.

Marley, A.A.J. and Jordan J. Louviere (2005), Some probabilistic models of best, worst, and best-worst choices, *Journal of Mathematical Psychology*, **49** (6), 464–80.

Matheson, Victor A. and Robert A. Baade (2004), Mega-sporting events in developing nations: playing the way to prosperity?, *South African Journal of Economics*, **72** (5), 1085–96.

McCarville, Ronald E., Christopher M. Flood and Tabatha A. Froats (1998), The effectiveness of selected promotions on spectators' assessments of a nonprofit sporting event sponsor, *Journal of Sport Management*, **12** (1), 51–62.

National Endowment for the Arts (2002), Admission receipts to performing arts events, motion pictures, and spectator sports: 1989–2000, Research Division Note No. 79, U.S. Department of Commerce, Bureau of Economic Analysis.

Nelson, Douglas L. and Cathy L. McEvoy (2002), How can the same type of prior knowledge both help and hinder recall?, *Journal of Memory and Language*, **46** (3), 652–63.

Nelson, Douglas L., David J. Bennett and Todd W. Leibert (1997), One step is not enough: making better use of association norms to predict cued recall, *Memory and Cognition*, **25** (6), 785–96.

Nelson, Douglas L., Cathy L. McEvoy and Lisa Pointer (2003), Spreading activation or spooky action at a distance?, *Journal of Experimental Psychology: Learning, Memory and Cognition*, **29** (1), 42–52.

Nelson, Douglas L., Thomas A. Schreiber and Cathy L. McEvoy (1992), Processing implicit and explicit representations, *Psychological Review*, **99** (2), 322–48.

Nelson, Douglas L., Vanesa M. McKinney, Nancy R. Gee and Gerson A. Jancurza (1998), Interpreting the influence of implicitly activated memories on recall and recognition, *Psychological Review*, **105** (2), 299–324.

Olkkonen, Rami and Pekka Tuominen (2006), Understanding relationship fading in cultural sponsorships, *Corporate Communications: An International Journal*, **11** (1), 64–77.

Olson, Erik L. and Hans Mathias Thjømøe (2003), The effects of peripheral exposure to information on brand performance, *European Journal of Marketing*, **37** (1/2), 243–55.

Pracejus, John W and G. Douglas Olsen (2004), The role of brand/cause fit in the effectiveness of cause-related marketing campaigns, *Journal of Business Research*, **57** (6), 635–40.

Pruitt, Stephen, T. Bettina Cornwell and John Clark (2004), The NASCAR phenomenon: auto racing sponsorships and shareholder wealth, *Journal of Advertising Research*, **44** (3), 281–96.

Puchan, Heike (2004), Living 'extreme': adventure sports, media and commercialisation, *Journal of Communication Management*, **9** (2), 171–8.

Puff, C. Richard (1979), *Memory Organization and Structure*, New York: Academic Press.

Reber, Rolf, Norbert Schwarz and Piotr Winkielman (2004), Processing fluency and aesthetic pleasure: is beauty in the perceiver's processing experience?, *Personality and Social Psychology Review*, **8** (4), 364–82.

Rines, Simon (2002), Guinness Rugby World Cup sponsorship: a global platform for meeting business objectives, *International Journal of Sports Marketing and Sponsorship*, **3** (4), 449–65.

Roy, Donald P. and T. Bettina Cornwell (2004), The effects of consumer knowledge on responses to event sponsorships, *Psychology and Marketing*, **21** (3), 185–207.

Russell, Cristel Antonia (2002), Investigating the effectiveness of product placements in television shows: the role of modality and plot connection congruence on brand memory and attitude, *Journal of Consumer Research*, **29** (3), 306–18.

Russell, Cristel Antonia and Barbara B. Stern (2006), Consumers, characters, and products: a balance model of sitcom product placement effects, *Journal of Advertising*, **35** (1), 7–21.

Rust, Roland T. and Richard W. Oliver (1994), The death of advertising, *Journal of Advertising*, **23** (4), 71–7.

Sandler, Dennis M. and David Shani (1989), Olympic sponsorship vs. 'ambush' marketing: who gets the gold?, *Journal of Advertising Research*, **29** (4), 9–14.

Schulz, Oalf, T. Bettina Cornwell and Ursula Weisenfeld (2005), The role of sponsorship in market entry strategy, in *Advertising and Communication, Proceedings of the Fourth International Conference on Research in Advertising* (ICORA), S. Didhl, R. Terlutter and P. Weinberg (eds), Saarbruecken: Saarland University, pp. 223–30.

Sillars, Les (1995), Name-dropping is big business, *Western Report*, **22** (35), 14.
Sisily, Andrew (2005), New and traditional media: the unfolding revolution, working paper, UQ Business School, The University of Queensland, Brisbane, Australia.
'Sports marketing: global deal, local glory' (2004), *Marketing* (11 August), 36.
Townsend, Anthony M. (2000), Life in the real-time city: mobile telephones and urban metabolism, *Journal of Urban Technology*, **7** (2), 85–104.
Vadum, Matthew (2004), D.C. stadium bill may allow private financing, officials say, *The Bond Buyer* (12 November), 7.
Waddell, Ray (2005), Tour sponsorship growth expected, *Billboard*, **117** (6), 5–18.
Weeks, Clinton S., T. Bettina Cornwell and Judy C. Drennan (2008), Leveraging sponsorships on the Internet: activation, congruence, and articulation, *Psychology and Marketing*, **25** (7), 637–54.
Weeks, Clinton S., T. Bettina Cornwell and Michael Humphreys (2006a), Conceptualizing sponsorship: an item and relational information account, in *Creating Images and the Psychology of Marketing Communications*, Lynn R. Kahle and Chung-Hyun Kim (eds), Mahwah, NJ: Lawrence Erlbaum, pp. 257–76.
Weeks, Clinton S., T. Bettina Cornwell and Michael Humphreys (2006b), Empirical support for an item and relational conceptualization of sponsorship, in *Advances in Consumer Research*, vol. 33, Connie Pechmann and Linda Price (eds), Duluth, MN: Association for Consumer Research, pp. 312–13.
Westerståhl, M., M. Barnekow-Bergkvist, G. Hedberg and E. Jansson (2003), Secular trends in sports: participation and attitudes among adolescents in Sweden from 1974 to 1995, *Acta Paediatrica*, **92** (5), 602–9.
Woudhuysen, James (2001), Play as the main event in international and UK culture, *Cultural Trends*, **11** (43/44), 95–154.
Zajonc, Robert B. (1968), Attitudinal effects of mere exposure, *Journal of Personality and Social Psychology*, **9** (2), 1–27.
Zajonc, Robert B. (1980), Feeling and thinking preferences need no inferences, *American Psychologist*, **35** (2), 151–75.5

25 Participant observation in sport management research: collecting and interpreting data from a successful world land speed record attempt
Mark Dibben and Harald Dolles

1 MOTORSPORTS AS A FIELD OF SPORT MANAGEMENT RESEARCH

Motorsports and motorsports management is more commonly associated with the multimillion dollar big business of for example Formula One, the World Rally Championship, or motorcycling's MotoGP and World Superbikes. Each of these sub-industries – or 'circuses' as they were euphemistically known because of their arrival en masse at one venue, their performance to a paying audience, and their subsequent departure to the next venue – is a grouping of increasingly highly professional corporatized teams headed by charismatic archetypal entrepreneurs, competing under the regulations of the World Motorsport governing bodies of the Fédération Internationale de l'Automobile (FIA) and the Fédération Internationale de Motocyclisme (FIM). They are almost without exception located geographically and culturally in Europe; only the CART and NASCAR racing series dominate the North American market. The barriers to entry to these sub-industries are extremely high and the politics surrounding entry are notorious (Dolles and Söderman, 2008; Henry et al., 2007). This is in contrast to most motorsports activity, which has historically been characterized by artisans, small businessmen, a genuine family atmosphere and a culture of 'run what you bring' and 'make do and mend', in which competitors would help each other with problems, both technical and personal (for example, Dibben, 2008; Stewart, 2007; Pearson, 1965 [2002]).[1] The values of motorsport here are, arguably, richer, where spectators are not excluded from the paddock and so can experience not only the racing as a spectacle but participate to a certain extent in the human side of the 'circus'; the emphasis is more on the fostering and enjoyment of social capital as opposed to the garnering of economic wealth.

While such values as trust, camaraderie, cooperation and reputation are still present in the upper echelons of motorsport like Formula One, they are subsumed or hidden under a 'cloak of institutionalization' (formal rules, roles, systems, procedures, policies, hierarchies, and so on) and difficult to access for the purposes of study (Dolles and Söderman, 2008). One area of world-class motorsports in which the entrepreneurial, pioneering spirit of creating and extracting value from an environment (Anderson, 1995, 2000a, 2000b) can still be seen, however, is in world land speed records (WLSRs). In many respects, WLSR attempts are similar to other forms of motorsport activity. They are very closely regulated by the governing body (FIA/FIM), they have uncertain outcomes and evoke strongly emotional and often patriotic responses from their audiences, which are considered by Dolles and Söderman (2011a) to be crucial elements of sport. They can also be very expensive to put on. In other respects, however, they are quite different: there may be just one competitor who is responsible not only for developing his machine and driving it but also for fundraising, preparing the course and organizing the event. Those drivers or riders are less corporatized, more 'shoestring', and thus readily accessible to an observer willing to offer a hand as a volunteer.

This chapter introduces the participant observation technique as a method taken from ethnography into the field of research on sports management. The vast majority of sport management research uses questionnaires and interviews or relies on secondary data. A careful observation of ongoing behaviour by the researcher is often ignored, in most cases due to the lack of access. Vidich (1955) has emphasized that what an observer will see shall be conditioned by his personal knowledge, and will depend largely on his particular position in a network of not purely academic relationships. Another reason why participant observation has not been accepted as a method in sport management research might be that the methodology of participant observation is sometimes considered epistemologically suspect (Bouchard, 1976; Bruyn, 1963, 1966). We do not look to unpack this reservation in detail in this chapter, but we do emphasize how participant observation could be meaningfully applied in sport management research to provide new insights not easily revealed by other research approaches.

The chapter begins with a description of the research setting – the case of Flying Kiwi Promotions Limited established in 2002 by Phil Garrett for the sole purpose of breaking the world land speed record for motorcycle and sidecar combinations (that is, sidecars; Figure 25.1). Next we introduce participant observation as a research method and how it is applied in this research. In the analysis we highlight insights gained by applying participant observation in regard to aspects of finance, promotion, organization and entrepreneurial coordination in the case. The chapter concludes with a discussion of issues raised in terms of their existing understanding in the sports management literature. We also suggest other fields in sport management research, where this method could be meaningfully applied.

2   THE RESEARCH SETTING – FLYING KIWI PROMOTIONS LIMITED

Flying Kiwi Promotions Limited[2] (FKP) was established in 2002 as a 'loss attributable qualifying company' by Phil Garrett, an amateur sidecar racer who worked at a DIY store in Christchurch New Zealand, for the sole purpose of breaking the world land speed record for sidecars. The company was founded to separate the risk of the venture from the family finances. Garrett had spotted anomalies in the FIM rules for this land speed record which meant that it stood at only 222 km per hour (137 miles per hour) while the New Zealand record was 260 km per hour (162 miles per hour); he reasoned these were easily achievable. Other FIM regulations, apart from the technical specifications for the machine, included a requirement for a particular type of road, very straight and with a limited gradient (Figure 25.2). He spent months in his spare time searching land survey maps of New Zealand and found only one which, as luck would have it, happened to be only an hour's drive from his house. The idea seemed feasible.

*Figure 25.1   Phil Garrett (right) and the team's second driver after breaking the world
land speed record*

In these early stages, the project was nothing but an idea on the wall in his home garage.
By the time the record attempts were made in July 2005, the company had over 300 volunteers, raised over NZ$200 000 in sponsorship and built a bespoke land speed record
vehicle that it ran over two days to establish a new world land speed record. These two
days were intended to be just one day. The costs of building the bespoke machine (Figure
25.3) and surveying the road as suitable, meant that there was only enough funding for
one day's hire of the fire engine, ambulance, 'chase car', their respective crews and the
officially certified timing equipment – not to mention the catering for all the volunteer
marshals needed to patrol the road which had been closed by permission of the local
council, and its perimeter, to ensure no member of the public strayed onto the course.
However, the timing equipment failed early on the first day, which meant that new
timing equipment had to be procured and everyone had to turn up the following day for
a repeat attempt. This second day Garrett was forced to pay for out of his own pocket.
Throughout, however, the ethos was the epitome of the never-give-up Kiwi can-do attitude, being a 'good bastard', and a sense of fun; the company's logo was a cartoon Kiwi
bird (the national icon of New Zealand) spinning its wheels.

Figure 25.2   Early work: evaluating the suitability of the road

In total, the personal costs of the project for Garrett were significant. Although FKP did not go overdrawn, neither did it make a profit and, indeed, the opportunity costs to Garrett of lost work income were estimated at NZ$150000. In addition, since as in all land speed records (LSRs), the record is 'held' by the driver, the project's second driver (whose company built the engine) was the person who in fact broke the world record at 272 km per hour (Figure 25.4), not Garrett himself (Garrett got the New Zealand record, achieving an average speed of 264 km per hour, a mere 8 km per hour/5 miles per hour slower). Nevertheless, the record still stands, and the machine itself was sold to an American paraplegic (the bike used an innovative pneumatic gearbox actuator and required hand controls only) who used it to set an American Land Speed Record at Utah in 2006.

3   THE PARTICIPANT OBSERVATION TECHNIQUE

Ethnographic methods enjoy a long tradition in social sciences and have been widely employed in various ways by scholars from a variety of disciplines. Contemporary sport studies, with their emphasis on multinational institutions, state-level agencies, commercial and media conglomerates, clubs as firms and mass publics of interpreting consumers as the most visible social actors would appear to be well suited to ethno-

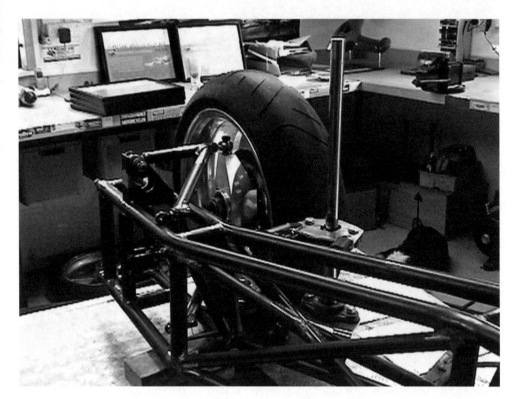

*Figure 25.3   Constructing the machine in the workshop. In the background can be seen
320 Club certificates as well as some of the manufacturing tools used*

graphic approaches to data gathering. In his 1992 critique of extant sports management research, however, MacAloon argued little attention has thus far been given to using a longitudinal participant observation as a formal fieldwork method in sports management research. We will not here attempt a comprehensive overview of historical and contemporary applications of the participant observation technique. Rather, we will focus on central issues in the methodological literature and emphasize its value as a research method to be applied in sport management research.

Atkinson and Hammersley (1994) start with the misleading distinction drawn between participant and nonparticipant observation made in the literature (for example, by Gold, 1958; Junker, 1960), asking (a) how much, and what is known about the research by whom; (b) whether the researcher is known to be a researcher by all those being studied, or only by some, or by none; (c) what sorts of activities the researcher in the field is or is not engaged in, and how this locates her or him in relation to the various conceptions of category and group membership used by the participants; (d) what the orientation of the researcher is, and (e) how completely he or she consciously adopts the orientation of insider or outsider (Atkinson and Hammersley, 1994: 249). Notwithstanding these detailed issues, in a sense *all* social research is a form of participant observation because we cannot study the social world without being part of it (Hammersley and Atkinson, 1995). From this point of view participant observation is not a particular research

*Figure 25.4   A world record attempt in action! Almost all the sponsorship was in-kind
supply of materials and equipment*

technique but 'a mode of being-in-the-world characteristic of researchers' (Atkinson and
Hammersley, 1994: 249). We assume this argument is explicitly of value to research in the
field of sport management as most of the researchers are in one way or the other engaged
with sports themselves.

The participant observation technique is commonly associated in the literature (for
example, Baker, 2006; Becker and Geer, 1970; Bouchard, 1976; Bryman, 1989; Friedrichs
1975; Janesick, 2000; Jorgensen, 1989; Pearsall, 1970; Spradley, 1980; Williams and
Rodsakoff, 1989) with the following six strengths that compensate the weaknesses of
other methods:

First, it needs to be mentioned that participant observation focuses the researchers'
attention on the behaviour of individuals rather than simply on comments received in
verbal interviews or an individual person's (a group's) test-taking behaviour. Kluckholn
(1940) for example argues that active participation increases the range, relevance and
reliability of data. Range is increased because discussions are much freer and the nature
of the relationships are relatively open. Relevance is increased because questioning
is often tied up to the current situation rather than being retrospective. Reliability is
increased because higher levels of depth and intimacy can be achieved that are inaccessible to interviewing or by using questionnaires. Bouchard (1976: 385) even concludes,
'it is difficult to understand why researchers have held so tenaciously to paper and pencil

methods rather than turning to a systematic examination of the structure of the behaviour of interest'.

Second, participant observation tends to force the researcher to look at individuals, groups of people, institutions or organizations and the surrounding social and physical environment in a holistic, integrated network perspective. Williams and Rodsakoff (1989: 248) see participant observation as 'ideally suited for examining reciprocal relationships between individuals'. It is this specific advantage of the technique that might also be seen to be in line with the argumentation of the Nordic School in management research, where relationships, networks and interaction appear as central concepts (for example, Dolles and Söderman, 2011b; Gummesson, 1994, 1999; Gummesson et al., 1997).

Third, observers often see things that respondents take for granted or are unaware of. Recognizing differences is the necessary first step to anticipating potential threats and opportunities for research encounters emphasized by Dolles (1997). But in order to go beyond awareness and to create useful interaction these differences need to be the subject of discussion. The 'Johari window' developed in psychology and first described by Jourard (1964) might be applied as a tool to discover differences.

Fourth, participant observation demands a change of perspective by the researcher as highlighted by Dolles (1997: 277). He sees the strength in this technique, particularly in cross-cultural research, as the focus of attention shifts from describing observation from an outsider's perspective to a hermeneutic portrayal based on understanding from an insider's perspective of common shared experiences between researcher and the subject under investigation.

Fifth, and according to Bouchard (1976) a good reason why a researcher should try participant observation in at least one study, is that this technique puts him or her in the context of discovery and facilitates what Merton (1949) calls the 'serendipity pattern' of social research (also Merton and Barber, 2004). This refers to the experience of observing an unanticipated, anomalous strategic datum which becomes the mechanism for developing a new theory or extending an existing theory (Merton, 1949: 98).

Sixth, the participant observation technique centres around 'the participant observer gather[ing] data by participating in the daily life of the group or organization he studies. He watches the people he is studying to see what situations they ordinarily meet and how they behave in them. He enters into conversation with some or all of the participants in these situations and discovers their interpretations of the events he has observed' (Becker, 1958: 652). In using this technique, Kluckholn (1940) argues it is essential not only that the investigator views himself as a participant, but also that the other members of the group being studied regard him as a participant. Otherwise the observer will not be regarded with sufficient legitimacy as a member of the group for the group to behave in any way ordinarily. 'This means that he must achieve status within the community organization, [and] must play his part in a constellation of roles' (ibid.: 331–2).

4   ABOUT COLLECTION OF DATA AND PARTICIPANT OBSERVATION

The last argument of engaged participation in the activities of the group under study was certainly the case with our study of Flying Kiwi. One of the authors was told of the

Figure 25.5   Mark Dibben with Phil Garrett during testing of the machine

idea first via a mutual friend. A family background in motorcycle racing was of immediate interest and there was an informal agreement to help in whatever way seemed possible; the family background immediately gave the researcher a level of legitimacy in the
group that otherwise would have taken a great deal of time to achieve. The participant
role initially involved business mentoring and informal consulting, and eventually grew
to assisting in project planning and an involvement in official timekeeping during the
record attempt (Figure 25.5). All those roles call for conscious and systematic engagement with the needs of the project leader. This is in line with Kluckholn's (1940) argument: we as researcher must survey the field for roles, the playing of which will lead us to
be regarded as participants. We need to analyse these roles for the data and insights they
afford, and we need to examine them for the biases inherent in them.

Over the course of the three-year project once a fortnight one of the authors went to the workshop in Christchurch to see how they were getting along. He also had a number of evenings acting as an executive coach/mentor for Phil Garrett to just talk things through. During the course of the final year, he visited the workshop more than 25 times, spending an average of two hours each visit. He also became a member of the land speed record project as part of the track team, where he went down to the road together with the team to plan it. He also organized five planning meetings at his university to work up the concept of a one-off rally special stage, which in essence is what the record attempt was. On the day of the attempt, he was a member of the road team working the timing system and confirming the course was safe.

In his various roles, it was understood that the first author was also observing the project; he occasionally took photographs to supplement journal notes of the meetings. This is based on Becker's (1958) suggestion that participant observers should maintain a natural history of their research and report it pretty much as it occurs. Only accurate and comprehensive descriptions of behaviour and facts will enable the researcher later on to deal with the criterion problem in a meaningful way (Bouchard, 1976, and above). This method was certainly adopted in our case, although since the involvement started by personal interests, it was only after the world land speed record attempt was success-fully concluded that the first author sat down and thought 'now, what have I got here?' At the time, when making the notes he had no idea how they might be pulled together. This is, in fact, an important aspect of the approach; it is only in this way that one does not 'drive' the data as one is gathering it. In this respect, participant observation also adheres to a principle of grounded theory (refer, for example, to Glaser and Strauss, 1967; Anagnostopoulos, 2013 in this volume). Taken in this way, grounded theory is linked with the technique of participant observation as a method of discovery, where categories emerge from a continuous comparison of the data. As Glaser (2001: 176) has noted, 'we do not know what we are looking for when we start . . . we simply cannot say prior to the collection and analysis of data what our study will look like'. Jones and Noble (2007) have emphasized in this regard that the researcher enters the field with only a broad topic in mind, without specific preconceived research questions or a detailed reading and understanding of the extant literature in the area.

This leads to the methodological problem of classifying situations or interpreting certain behaviour as one of the most important concerns for field researchers, as the development of an adequate taxonomy would allow the comparison of the data gath-ered in the light of existing theory. This allows comparison with other researchers' work in order to facilitate the development of empirical generalizations, or to highlight new findings found in the observed empirical setting. There are many coding and analysis schemes available in the literature (for example, Creswell, 2003; Mayring, 1995; Miles, 1979; Miles and Huberman, 1994; Silverman, 1989 just to emphasize a few) and it there-fore might be doubtful that any recommendation will be widely applicable across all settings where the participant observation technique can be meaningfully applied. In this chapter we exemplify the results by focusing on two interlinked issues for analysis – finance and promotion of the project.

It needs to be emphasized with Bouchard (1976: 391) that 'data collected by par-ticipant observation is open to *more validity threads* than that obtained by any other method' (emphasis added). Based on the summary of methodological concerns gathered by Bruyn (1963, 1966), Bouchard proposed the following ways adopted in this study, by which the *objectivity* of participant observation data can be increased (1976: 391–2):

1. Bolster interpretations with data from other sources, such as other observers, structured and unstructured interviews, recordings, pictures, archival data, etc.
2. Separate facts from interpretations. Indeed, this distinction should be maintained at all times. The data base for an interpretation should be recorded at the time the interpretation is made.
3. Distinguish carefully between informant and respondent data.
4. Be aware of your own prejudices, defences, biases, stereotypes, etc.
5. Be sensitive to your own position in the social structure.
6. Be aware of the motivations, biases, and prejudices of your respondents and informants.
7. Examine all counter positions carefully and openly. The plight of the worker may indeed be miserable, but it must be understood in the context of management's situation.
8. Observe your subjects in as many different contexts as possible.
9. When quantitative terms are used, such as 'many', it is important to indicate the percentage of the total group to which you are referring and how you arrived at the figure.
10. Be sensitive to changes in your own attitudes, beliefs, and emotions. Such changes are often cues to a lack of objectivity.
11. Recognize that your subjects are not a random aggregate, but rather a social network. People live, work, and function in groups.
12. Avoid over-rapport and do not identify symbolically or emotionally with any subgroup unless it is tactically necessary. Maintain sufficient distance so that your implicit commitments to individuals will not proscribe your movements.
13. Be sure that your informants know you will be gathering data from others. If they know you will be checking on them they are less likely to lie.

The authors agree with this approach to achieving validity in participant observation, and thus do not themselves follow an increasing, and indeed interesting, trend towards auto-ethnography – where the ethnographer uses what he observes to reflect on himself – as a mode of social scientific inquiry in management research (see, for example, Down, 2006). Further, in their view, not going into the field with a pre-determined theory or set of theories is central to a sound account. In using participant observation, therefore, we argue there is considerable truth in Sir Arthur Conan Doyle's fictional character Sherlock Holmes' assertion, that 'it is a capital mistake to theorize before one has data. Insensibly one begins to twist facts to suit theories, instead of theories to suit facts' (Doyle, 1992[1892]: 5).

5   RESEARCH FINDINGS

The chapter will now explore behaviour and activity as it was recounted and observed during the WLSR attempt, by focusing on two interlinked issues for analysis – finance and promotion of the project. It might also be added, by way of a prefatory remark to the subsequent discussion, that the case in question is a WLSR attempt made in New Zealand, a country limited in infrastructure, expertise, and technological and financial resources in comparison with Europe or America.

5.1 Insights into Financial Issues

Finance was always a core concern for FKP. Garrett had established a membership club to bring in donations from interested members of the public. Although this was successful, at one point FKP had NZ$16 in the bank and NZ$5000 of bills to pay. Garrett had a meeting with his bank manager, at which he outlined his idea for a WLSR vehicle and asked whether the bank would be interested in sponsoring the project through a small short-term overdraft facility of NZ$10 000 for four months. The interview was brief, but insightful:

> 'How many of these bikes do you plan to make, Mr Garrett?'
> 'One. It's a one-off.'
> 'So why do people give you money then?!'
> 'Well, because they want to.'
> 'I'm sorry?'
> 'Err, because they *want* to give me money.'
> 'Oh, I see!'

Throughout the four years of the project, FKP never went overdrawn, because it couldn't.

5.2 Insights into Promotional Issues

The problem of finance was dealt with in two ways. First, from the outset, Garrett used every opportunity to raise awareness about the project. He covered his four-wheel-drive vechicle in stickers with the name of the company, the expected speed and his mobile phone number. Second, he set up a website detailing everything about the project, with a supporters club that people could join on the website, coupled with displays of his racing sidecar at local motor shows and other public events, and the usual range of merchandise such as caps, T-shirts and jackets. He would ultimately give away over 2500 posters.

The Flying Kiwi 320 Club would have a major hand in allowing supporters to feel included, as well as helping to raise some of the estimated NZ$250 000 that the undertaking would require. NZ$320 would supposedly 'purchase' members 1 kph of the targeted 320 kph and a sense of ownership of the event. In addition, members would receive posters, a certificate and a video, discount on merchandise, regular updates on progress, their name on the website, their name in the supporter's chapter of the book being written about the record attempt, and the chance to be involved in the actual running of the event itself, which would not be open to the public (primarily for safety reasons). In this way, the club would provide a unique opportunity to help make history and return a sporting record to Canterbury.

Garrett received e-mails of support from as far away as the United States and the UK. The project even attracted the support of a former world champion sidecar racer, who wore a Flying Kiwi T-shirt to a race meeting in Belgium at which he was guest of honour. Word spread quickly. Soon TV3, one of the free-to-air broadcasters in New Zealand, had agreed to include Flying Kiwi on their Sunday afternoon sports programme. Garrett was always thinking how he could make the project work on television, to the extent he put cameras in the workshop to film everything that went on. Regular news spots followed and, in due course, TV3 agreed to make an hour-long documentary for prime-time viewing.

6   DISCUSSION: FINANCE, PROMOTION, STRUCTURE AND ORGANIZATIONAL CULTURE AS CRITICAL SUCCESS FACTORS OF A SUCCESSFUL WLSR ATTEMPT

The above-mentioned interview with the bank manager is almost stereotypical. One view is to argue that this is the response of a bank manager who cannot see a clear possibility for the business to be able to clear its debt – it is not making a product that it can sell, much less lots of products it can sell. The problem with FKP's product was that it is not immediately replicable or tangible (at the time of the meeting). Having said this, there is clearly a value to what FKP is doing, because people did indeed give Garrett money. However, this value is about a feelgood factor that is the value-added 'product' people are buying into (Chatziefstahiou, 2007; Funk and James, 2004). Garrett himself remained ever-scornful of the bank manager's attitude, on the grounds that the overdraft facility was not exactly enormous and the bank manager seemed to lack vision. In fairness, bank managers have to justify their lending to their head office, which is obviously looking for a reasonable return on the investments their bank managers make on their shareholders' behalf. This is an illustration of different perceptions of value among different company's stakeholders (Friedman et al., 2004).

Gaining the means by which to build the vehicle and run the event was achieved in part by FKP having a very clearly defined mission from its inception – a mission that drove the company forwards and involved a wide range of stakeholders. The name of the company was a purposeful signal that it was primarily conceived to 'promote' the idea of breaking the world land speed record for sidecars, create an impression of substance and credibility, and involve as many people as possible in the record bid (Friedman et al., 2004; Psarvero and Chalip, 2007). The website was marketing an aura of success, an ethos of Kiwi can-do never-say-die persistence, the glamour of a world record bid, the dream of a successful outcome, all 'values' (Stinson and Howard, 2008). In so doing, FKP overcame a lack of financial and physical assets to (a) develop distinctive competencies in the efficient use of what tangible resources were available, (b) focus on quality (both marketing and production) and (c) innovation. Lastly, FKP has created a perceived value from achieving a world land speed record.

There were long periods when FKP seemed doomed to failure as a result of a lack of funds. Even hiring the airfield to test the machine (Figure 25.6) occurred very late as a result of a lack of funds. Garrett kept all this to himself and always claimed things were 'excellent'. Even though entrepreneurs must balance a range of stakeholder interests to keep their businesses afloat through the maintenance of sufficient social capital (Anderson, 2007; Jack et al., 2004; Low and Srivatsen, 1995; Lynch et al., 2007), we

Figure 25.6   Phil Garrett tests the machine, minus its fairing, at a local airfield in Canterbury, New Zealand

might question whether such lies are morally justifiable. Ultimately, however, Garrett was very aware that if the volunteers and supplying companies knew themselves just how close FKP was to collapse on occasions, the support would have evaporated and the company and its mission would have foundered. This is indicative of the need to maintain the psychological contract with the volunteers and sponsors (Taylor et al., 2006) in terms of the impression of impending success (Stinson and Howard, 2008).

What became obvious during the coding and data analysis was that the structure and organizational culture of FKP was a further critical success factor. These were essentially designed to achieve high levels of organizational learning (Marrioti, 2007), and facilitated by a charismatic entrepreneur (arguably another critical success factor) who – unusually for entrepreneurs, and especially 'novice' entrepreneurs with little experience – recognized the need to empower his 'staff' and let other people make decisions that would or could have a very drastic effect on the success or otherwise of his venture. With an all-volunteer workforce, and difficult challenges to overcome, considerable personal and group learning needed to take place and be communicated throughout the organization (this communication was mainly done by Garrett himself as he regularly liaised with each of the teams and passed on news and developments), engendering trust between himself and the volunteers and acting as a fulcrum for trust development among the volunteers themselves.

This in turn generated a close-knit team identity and a clear goal that translated vision, communication, planning, feedback and learning. Ongoing evaluation of goal achievement was a significant aspect of organizational learning and thus strategy development in FKP which 'morphed' successfully from a marketing organization (to gain sponsorship) into a manufacturing organization (to build the vehicle) and then an event management organization (to actually run the attempt), all to deliver a unique and ultimately tangible 'product' of a world land speed record. In this regard, FKP can be seen to exhibit many of the factors identified as engaging volunteers and fans to a sport (Funk and James, 2004), including vicarious achievement, aesthetics, drama, the need for social interaction, entertainment, escape or diversion, group affiliation and self-esteem enhancement.

7   CONCLUSION

These sorts of insights, we argue, are not readily available from more traditional studies of sports business; there is a degree of intimacy required to yield such sensitivities. The implications of the hard financial reality for the project were felt every day in FKP; there was no prospect of obtaining materials without having the necessary cash and it was being run on a 'hand-to-mouth' basis. Yet to the outsider there would be nothing to suggest anything other than a paid team working in a well-funded environment. Indeed, it was not in the interests of Garrett to make the privations known; this would have caused sponsors and officials to doubt the potential success of the project to the extent it would have ceased to retain the necessary credibility. As such, it seems to us that it is only through a participant observation that one is able to discern just precisely what the drivers are behind a sports project or event; the data is not as readily available from more traditional methods as it is in other ventures with, for example, publicly available financial information. Such insights as those presented in the foregoing analysis only arise by working with the individual(s) and getting to know them well enough for them to bring the academic into their confidence.

Further, sports events, teams and projects exist precisely as a result of a camaraderie among the individuals that is not fully observable from the outside. Particularly in motorsport, the true *raison d'être* is held within the team; it is a fallacy to believe that all teams are only there to win, because teams are realistic as to their chances. Getting behind the sponsorship and the vehicle, to sit 'inside the caravan' of the team and, indeed, each member of the team in 'the circus' is the only way to access the personal lived reality of the participants and their families. It is for this reason that we suggest participant observation is a valid method for sports management research and argue that the standard normative scientific methodological questions regarding 'objective validity' and 'replicability' are rendered obsolete.

Sports management scenarios require access to the ephemeral and the personal precisely because that is where the value that is inherent within them resides. It is for this reason we suggest the technique may usefully be applied to other related topics of interest. These include events, such as the studies on the Exstremsportveko in Voss, Norway by Gyimóthy (2009) and Mykletun (2009), or on the 1995 World and 2006 European Athletics Championships in Gothenburg, Sweden (Larson, 2009), or on the Coca-Cola Masters Surfing event in Western Australia (O'Neill et al., 1999 – evaluating service quality). Participant observation is also valuable in research on fans and spectators such as that by Shimizu (2002) on Japanese football fans motivation and behaviour, or insights into the 'dark side' of sport such as football hooliganism in the UK by Pearson (2009), Armstrong (1998) and Giulianotti (1995); the latter studies also explore the limits of the method, when participant observation comes close to breaking the law. It further encompasses investigations into sports brand communities and consumption cultures, such as McAlexander et al.'s (2000) study of Judo in Japan and the United States, or Schouten and McAlexander's (1993) and McAlexander et al.'s (2002) studies of Harley Davidson motorcyclists. It enables studies of sports organizations and their relations with the communities they represent, such as Steen-Johnsen's (2008) study of the Norwegian Snowboard Federation's attempts to establish legitimacy within the snowboard community and Soares et al.'s (2010) study of political factors in the decision-making process in sports associations in Portugal. Finally, as this chapter has also shown, participant observation allows access to the complexities of volunteerism, entrepreneurship and the competitor's perspective in sport, such as Terjesen's (2005, 2008) study of female runners, ultrarunning and the IAU World Cup in Korea, and addresses calls for increased attention to and the subsequent understanding of sport volunteerism (for example, Doherty, 2006). We further suggest the method has applications in other growing fields of management research interest such as environmental or humanitarian activism.

In sum, each of these topics concern the implicit, intangible and inestimable personal 'feelgood' value that the athlete, fan, spectator, volunteer or organizer gets out of participating in and being associated with the event. Only participant observation, we argue in conclusion, can connect the academic researcher to the topic of study in a manner that allows an otherwise unavailable rich engagement with and insight into the nature of that value on a human level, and thus as a lived experience.

NOTES

1. Mark Dibben has a strong interest in motorcycle racing and deep-rooted family connection to motorsports; both his father and grandfather were world champion motorcycle road racers in the 1950s. Harald Dolles is active in classic motorcyle and sidecar racing.
2. This participant observation study was conducted with Flying Kiwi Promotion's permission. The photographs were given to Mark Dibben by Phil Garrett, while an earlier version of parts of this chapter were first published by Wiley & Sons as parts of a strategy case study (Dibben and Garrett, 2006); the authors are grateful for copyright permissions held therein.

REFERENCES

Anderson, A.R. (1995), The Arcadian enterprise: an enquiry into the nature and conditions of rural small business, PhD thesis, University of Stirling.

Anderson, A.R. (2000a), The Protean entrepreneur: the entrepreneurial process as fitting self-circumstance, *Journal of Enterprising Culture*, **8** (3), 201–34.

Anderson, A.R. (2000b), Paradox in the periphery: an entrepreneurial reconstruction?, *Entrepreneurship and Regional Development*, **12** (2), 91–109.

Anderson, A.R. (2007), Entrepreneurial social capital, *International Small Business Journal*, **25** (3), 245–72.

Anagnostopoulos, C. (2013), Examining corporate social responsibility in football: the application of grounded theory methodology, in S. Söderman and H. Dolles (eds), *Handbook of Research on Sport and Business*, Cheltenham, UK and Northampton, MA, USA: Edward Elgar, pp. 418–32.

Armstrong, G. (1998), *Football Hooligans: Knowing the Score*, Oxford: Berg.

Atkinson, P. and Hammersley, M. (1994), Ethnography and participant observation, in N.K. Denzin and Y.S. Lincoln (eds), *Handbook of Qualitative Research*, Thousand Oaks, CA: Sage, pp. 248–61.

Baker, L.M. (2006), Observation: a complex research method, *Library Trends*, **55** (1), 171–89.
Becker, H.S. (1958), Problems of inference and proof in participant observation, *American Sociological Review*, **23** (6), 652–60.
Becker, H.S. and Geer, B. (1970), Participant observation and interviewing: a comparison, in W.J. Filstead (ed.), *Qualitative Methodology: Firsthand Involvement with the Social World*, Chicago: Markham, pp. 133–42.
Bouchard Jr, T.J. (1976), Field research methods: interviewing, questionnaires, participant observation, systematic observation, unobtrusive measures, in M.D. Dunnette (ed.), *Handbook of Industrial and Organizational Psychology*, Chicago, IL: Rand McNally, pp. 363–413.
Bruyn, S. (1963), The methodology of participant observation, *Human Organization*, **22** (3), 222–35.
Bruyn, S. (1966), *The Human Perspective in Sociology: The Method of Participant Observation*, Englewood Cliffs, NJ: Prentice Hall.
Bryman, A. (1989), *Research Methods and Organisation Studies*, London: Unwin Hynman.
Chatziefstathiou, D. (2007), The history of marketing an idea: the example of Baron Pierre de Coubertin as a social marketer, *European Sport Management Quarterly*, **7** (1), 55–80.
Creswell, J.W. (2003), *Research Design. Qualitative, Quantitative, and Mixed Methods Approaches*, 2 edn, Thousand Oaks, CA: Sage.
Dibben, M.R. and Garrett, P. (2006), Flying Kiwi Promotions Ltd: The story of a world land speed record breaker, in C.W.L. Hill and G.R. Jones (eds), *Strategic Management: An Integrated Approach*, 6th edn, Milton, Queensland: John Wiley & Son, pp. 513–19.
Dibben, S.J. (2008), *Hold On!*, High Wycombe: Panther.
Doherty, A. (2006), Sport volunteerism: an introduction to the special issue, *Sport Management Review*, **9** (2), 105–9.
Dolles, H. (1997), *Keiretsu: Emergenz, Struktur, Wettbewerbsstärke und Dynamik japanischer Verbundgruppen.* [*Keiretsu: Emergence, Structure, Competitive Strengths and Organizational Dynamics of Corporate Groupings in Japan*], Frankfurt am Main: Peter Lang.
Dolles, H. and Söderman, S. (2008), Formula One in the US. Interview with Joie Chitwood III President and Chief Operating Officer Indianapolis Motor Speedway LLC, *International Journal of Sports Marketing & Sponsorship*, **10** (1), 11–14.
Dolles, H. and Söderman, S. (2011a), Sport as a business: introduction, in H. Dolles and S. Söderman (eds), *Sport as a Business: International, Professional and Commercial Aspects*, Basingstoke: Palgrave Macmillan, pp. 1–12.
Dolles, H. and Söderman, S. (2011b), Learning from success: implementing a professional football league in Japan, in H. Dolles and S. Söderman (eds), *Sport as a Business: International, Professional and Commercial Aspects*, Basingstoke: Palgrave Macmillan, pp. 228–50.
Down, S (2006), *Narratives of Enterprise: Crafting Entrepreneurial Self-identity in a Small Firm*, Cheltenham, UK and Northampton, MA, USA: Edward Elgar.
Doyle, A.C. (1992 [1892]) *The Adventures of Sherlock Holmes*, London: Harper Collins.
Friedman, M.T., Parent, M.M. and Mason, D.S. (2004), Building a framework for issues management in sport through stakeholder theory, *European Sport Management Quarterly*, **4** (3), 170–90.
Friedrichs, J. (1975), *Participant Observation: Theory and Practice*, Lexington, MA: Saxon House.
Funk, D. and James, J. (2004), The fan attitude network model: exploring attitude formation and change among sports consumers, *Sport Management Review*, **7** (1), 1–26.
Giulianotti, R. (1995), Participant observation and research into football hooliganism: reflections on the problems of entree and everyday risks, *Sociology of Sport Journal*, **12** (1), 1–20
Glaser, B.G. (2001), *The Grounded Theory Perspective: Conceptualisation Contrasted with Description*, Mill Valley: Sociology Press.
Glaser, B.G. and Strauss, A.C. (1967), *The Discovery of Grounded Theory*, Chicago, IL: Aldine.
Gold, R. (1958), Roles in sociological field observation, *Social Forces*, **36** (3), 217–23.
Gummesson, E. (1994), Marketing according to textbooks: six objections, in D. Brownlie, M. Saren, R. Wensley and R. Whittington (eds), *Rethinking Marketing: New Perspectives on the Discipline and Profession*, Coventry: Warwick Business School, pp. 248–58.
Gummesson, E. (1999), *Total Relationship Marketing*, Oxford: Butterworth-Heinemann.
Gummesson, E., Lehtinen, U. and Grönroos, C. (1997), Comment on Nordic perspectives on relationship marketing, *European Journal of Marketing*, **31** (1), 10–16.
Gyimóthy, S. (2009), Casual observers, connoisseurs and experimentalists: a conceptual exploration of niche festival visitors, *Scandinavian Journal of Hospitality and Tourism*, **9** (2), 177–205.
Hammersley, M. and Atkinson, P. (1995), *Ethnography: Principles in Practice*, 2nd edn, London: Routledge.
Henry, N., Angus, T., Jenkins, M. and Aylett, C. (2007), Motorsport Going Global. The Challenges Facing the World's Motorsport Industry, Basingstoke: Palgrave Macmillan.
Jack, S.L., Dodd Drakopoulou, S. and Anderson, A.R. (2004), Social structures and entrepreneurial networks: the strength of strong ties, *International Journal of Entrepreneurship and Innovation*, **5** (2), 107–20.

Janesick, V. (2000), The choreography of qualitative research design: minuets, improvisation, and crystallization, in N.K. Denzin and Y.S. Lincoln (eds), *Handbook of Qualitative Research*, Thousand Oaks, CA: Sage, pp. 379–400.

Jones, R. and Noble, G. (2007), Grounded theory and management research: a lack of integrity?, *Qualitative Research in Organisations and Management: An International Journal*, **2** (2), 84–103.

Jorgensen, D.L. (1989), *Participant Observation: A Methodology for Human Studies*, Thousand Oaks, CA: Sage.

Jourard, S. (1964), *The Transparent Self*, Princeton, NJ: Van Nostrand Reinhold.

Junker, B. (1960), *Field Work*, Chicago, IL: University of Chicago Press.

Kluckholn, F.R. (1940), The participant observer technique in small communities, *American Journal of Sociology*, **46** (3), 331–43.

Larson, M. (2009), Joint event production in the jungle, the park, and the garden: metaphors of event networks, *Tourism Management*, **30** (3), 393–9.

Low, M. and Srivatsen, V. (1995), What does it mean to trust an entrepreneur?, in S. Birley and I. MacMillan (eds), *International Entrepreneurship*, London: Routledge, pp. 59–78.

Lynch, P., Johnson, P. and Dibben, M. (2007), In whom do we trust? Relationships of trust in adventure recreation, *Leisure Studies*, **26** (1), 47–64.

MacAloon, J.J. (1992), The ethnographic imperative in comparative Olympic research, *Sociology of Sport Journal*, **9** (2), 104–30.

Mariotti, F. (2007), Learning to share knowledge in the Italian motorsport industry, *Knowledge and Process Management*, **14** (2), 81–94.

Mayring, P. (1995), *Qualitative Inhaltsanalyse. Grundfragen und Techniken [Qualitative Content Analysis. Basic Questions and Techniques]*, 5th edn, Weinheim: Deutscher Studienverlag.

McAlexander, J.H., Fushimi, K. and Schouten, J.W. (2000), A cross-cultural examination of a subculture of consumption: judo in Japan and the United States, in R.W. Belk, J.A. Costa and J.W. Schouten (eds), *Research in Consumer Behavior*, vol. 9, Stanford, CT: JAI Press, pp. 47–70.

McAlexander, J.H., Schouten, J.W. and Koenig, H.J. (2002), Building brand community, *Journal of Marketing*, **66** (1), 38–54.

Merton, R.K. (1949), *Social Theory and Social Structure*, Glencoe, IL: Free Press.

Merton, R.K. and Barber, E. (2004), *The Travels and Adventures of Serendipity: A Study in Sociological Semantics and the Sociology of Science*, Princeton, NJ: Princeton University Press.

Miles, M.B. (1979), Qualitative data as an attractive nuisance: the problem of analysis, *Administrative Science Quarterly*, **24** (4), 590–601.

Miles, M.B. and Huberman, A.M. (1994), *Qualitative Data Analysis*, 2nd edn, Thousand Oaks, CA: Sage.

Mykletun, R. (2009), Celebration of extreme playfulness: Ekstremsportveko at Voss, *Scandinavian Journal of Hospitality and Tourism*, **9** (2), 146–76.

O'Neill, M., Getz, D. and Carlsen, J. (1999), Evaluation of service quality at events: the 1998 Coca-Cola Masters Surfing event at Margaret River, Western Australia, *Managing Service Quality*, **9** (3), 158–66.

Pearsall, M. (1970), Participant observation as role and method in behavioral research, in W.J. Filstead (ed.), *Qualitative Methodology: Firsthand Involvement with the Social World*, Chicago, IL: Markham, pp. 340–52.

Pearson, G. (2009), The researcher as hooligan: where 'participant' observation means breaking the law', *International Journal of Social Research Methodology*, **12** (3), 243–55.

Pearson, J. (1965), *Bluebird and the Dead Lake*, repd 2002, Melbourne: Text.

Psarvero, E. and Chalip, L. (2007), Professional teams as leverageable assets: strategic creation of community values, *Sport Management Review*, **10** (1), 1–30.

Schouten, J.W. and McAlexander, J.H. (1993), Market impact of a consumption subculture: the Harley-Davidson mystique, in G.J. Bamossy and W.F. van Raaij (eds), *European Advances in Consumer Research*, Provo, UT: Association for Consumer Research, pp. 389–93.

Shimizu, S. (2002), Japanese soccer fans. Following the local and the national team, in J. Horne and W. Manzenreiter (eds), *Japan, Korea and the 2002 World Cup*, London: Routledge, pp. 133–46.

Silverman, D. (1989), The impossible dream of reformism and romanticism, in J.F. Gubrium and D. Silverman (eds), *The Politics of Field Research: Beyond Enlightenment*, Thousand Oaks, CA: Sage, pp. 30–48.

Soares, J., Correia, A. and Rosado, A. (2010), Political factors in the decision-making process in voluntary sports associations, *European Sport Management Quarterly*, **10** (1), 5–29.

Spradley, J.P. (1980), *Participant Observation*, New York: Holt, Rinehart and Winston.

Steen-Johnsen, K. (2008), Networks and the organization of identity: the case of Norwegian snowboarding, *European Sport Management Quarterly*, **8** (4), 337–58.

Stewart, J. (2007), *Winning Is Not Enough*, London: Headline.

Stinson, J. and Howard, D. (2008), Winning does matter: patterns in private giving to athletic and academic programs at NCAA Division I-AA and I-AAA institutions, *Sport Management Review*, **11** (1), 1–20.

Taylor, T., Darcy, S., Hoye, R. and Cuskelly, G. (2006), Using psychological contract theory to explore issues in effective volunteer management, *European Sport Management Quarterly*, **6** (2), 123–47.

Terjesen, S. (2005), A history of major milestones in women's athletics and ultrarunning, *Ultrarunning*, **25** (March), 10–11.

Terjesen, S. (2008), Venturing beyond the marathon: the entrepreneurship of ultrarunning and the IAU World Cup in Korea, *Asian Business and Management*, **7** (1), 225–41.

Vidich, A.J. (1955), Participant observation and the collection and interpretation of data, *The American Journal of Sociology*, **60** (4), 354–60.

Williams, L. and Rodsakoff, P. (1989), Longitudinal field methods for studying reciprocal relationships in organisational behaviour research: towards improved causal analysis, in L. Cummings (ed.), *Research in Organisational Behaviour*, vol. 11, London: JAI Press, pp. 211–46.

26 Brand equity models in the spotlight of sport business

Tim Ströbel and Herbert Woratschek

1 INTRODUCTION

Consumers are confronted with brands throughout their daily life. One could easily say that the number of brands has exploded in recent years. Thus, it is nearly impossible to get an overview of all the offered brands in every area of daily life. For example, consumers are no longer used to normal toothpaste that helps cleaning teeth. Nowadays, toothpaste must offer several flavours, special dental prophylaxis, fancy designs and a number of methods to turn the colour of teeth shiny white again. These features are offered by many different producers, all promising similar effects. How do consumers then make their choice? Consequently, how can a toothpaste company increase its sales? Well, the company has to fulfil two crucial tasks: to position its brands visibly and to endow its brands with important attributes from the consumers' perspective (Esch, 2008: 25–7).

At the same time the relevance of service brands has increased. Since the beginning of the twenty-first century, so-called brand awards are given, media regularly publish rankings of the best brands, and the equity of a brand dominates the preparation of financial statements. In the case of Germany, this can be proven by 72 321 new registrations in the German Patent and Trademark Office (DPMA) solely in 2006. In this context, it is quite apparent that almost every second brand registration was related to a service (DPMA, 2007: 64). Scientific literature has already seized on this development as it deals in several publications with the importance of service brands (for example, Benkenstein and Uhrich, 2008; Bruhn and Stauss, 2008). In the course of the increased attention and investigation of new application fields in brand management, more and more publications deal with branding applied to tourism destinations, media, celebrities and sport organizations. This development was recognized by Gladden et al. (2001: 289) as they stated: '2000 to 2010 will be the decade in which team management activities evolve from a focus on winning as a means of realizing short-term profits to a focus on strategic management of the team brand as a means of realizing long-term appreciation in franchise value'.

2 HOW IS BRAND AND BRAND EQUITY DEFINED?

2.1 The Definition of a Brand

Although there is an enormous variety in applications and publications it seems almost impossible to find one consistent definition. Nevertheless, it is absolutely necessary to find a terminological distinction because already the usage of the term 'brand' in the literature is in a mess (Welling, 2006: 15). This mess becomes obvious by taking a closer look on the different brand definitions.

Aaker (1991: 7) summarizes the role of brands as: 'A brand is a distinguishing name and/or symbol (such as a logo, trademark, or package design) intended to identify the goods or services of either one seller or a group of sellers, and to differentiate those goods or services from those of competitors.' Furthermore, a brand could be defined as a deeply established and distinctive picture of a product or a service in the mind of the customer and other peer groups (Meffert et al., 2002: 6). With regard to differentiation as one of the core brand issues, a brand could also be seen as an individual sign or sign bundle that is capable of being protected and can be used in competition in order to differentiate its offers from those of other competitors. Additionally, it realizes positive effects with actual and potential exchange partners that help in achieving the brands' goals (Welling, 2006). In sport management, professional sports teams and sporting events could serve as concrete examples for sport brands. Brand issues even play a major role in professional sports teams' marketing strategies, since a strong sport brand leads to trust and fan loyalty which then leads to higher economic success (Richelieu and Pons, 2006).

2.2   The Definition of Brand Equity

In order to get a better differentiation of the term 'brand equity', the following paragraphs seize upon the definitions above. In this context we will take a detailed look at the relationship between brand equity and brand strength as these two expressions are used frequently in the literature.

The term 'brand equity' has been discussed diversely in research and practice for decades. In general, practitioners are more or less split over the approach brand equity. On the one hand, they discuss brand equity by explaining the financial power of a brand. On the other, they often seek for brand equity in the sense of a strategic aim and not a monetary figure. We come to the conclusion that the decision between a quantitative and a qualitative evaluation plays a minor role. The focus should be on a comprehensive approach that especially seizes on the determination of latent variables, such as image or awareness, rather than on the pure financial value of a brand.

With regard to research in the German-speaking community, one finds a basic understanding of brand equity already existed in the early 1960s. Kern (1962: 26) stated that the value of trademarks must be interpreted as the sum of additional earnings discounted to the present point of time. This focus on investment analysis prevailed for a long time, and researchers struggled to find a consistent definition and conceptual classification of brand equity.

In the USA, American research, mainly by Aaker, gained acceptance of his understanding of brand equity. Even today, Aaker is one of the most cited authors in this research area:

> Brand Equity is a set of brand assets and liabilities linked to a brand, its name and symbol that add to or subtract from the value provided by a product or service to a firm and/or to that firm's customers. . . . The assets and liabilities on which brand equity is based will differ from context to context. However they can be usefully grouped in five categories: Brand loyalty, name awareness, perceived quality, brand associations and other proprietary brand assets. (Aaker, 1991: 15–16)

Keller takes up this basic and widespread definition and connects it with the relevant discussion at that time: 'In a general sense, brand equity is defined in terms of the marketing effects uniquely attributable to the brand – for example, when certain outcomes result from the marketing of a product or service because of its brand name that would not occur if the same product or service did not have that name' (Keller, 1993: 1). Furthermore, according to Keller (1993: 1–2) a brand has both an accounting and a commercial value. From the accounting perspective brand equity must be determined as exactly as possible because it can be seen as a financial figure being implemented in financial statements or being needed for mergers and acquisitions (see also Barwise et al., 1989). The commercial value of a brand can be seen in additional sales. Therefore, in times of rare financial resources and budgets cut, marketing executives must have a comprehensive understanding of how customers perceive the brand.

We follow this separation and consider brand equity from a monetary perspective as well as from a customer-oriented perspective. In that regard, we define brand strength as a driving force that emerges from the subjective appreciation of the brand. A brand possesses high brand strength when customers have unique and relevant associations of the brand in their minds that are more than only related to the product or the branch.

Consequently, we have to differentiate between those approaches that create brand strength in the customers' minds and those that evaluate the monetary brand equity. This differentiation can be summarized in three steps: first, brand strength is an indicator for the reason of high or low brand equity (diagnosis). After the diagnosis, one can derive useful strategies to increase brand equity (therapy). Finally, the monetary brand equity is important as its detailed number makes the brand comparable (evaluation). These three steps can be seen as independent, but the value drivers of the brand are decisive for the remaining process. The diagnose, that is, the determination of brand strength, must be done before the evaluation, that is, the determination of monetary brand equity (Esch, 2008: 627–8).

In summary, German language literature shows a relatively clear separation between brand strength and brand equity. In this separation, brand strength takes the part of the qualitative valuation of the brand, whereas brand equity stands for the quantitative valuation of a brand. This clear separation cannot be found in English language literature, which uses the term 'brand equity', according to the occasion, so it has to be defined in more detail. In this respect, Keller (1993: 8) coined the term 'customer-based brand equity' and defined it as follows: 'Customer-based brand equity is defined as the differential effect of brand knowledge on consumer response to the marketing of the brand.' This definition with emphasis on the customer perspective shows some considerable similarities to the above-mentioned brand strength. Keeping that in mind, one could draw the conclusion that in both German and English language literature there is evidence of two main constructs that either are called brand equity and brand strength or show quite close similarities to them.

To summarize that discussion, brand equity should be divided into (financial) brand equity and brand strength, as shown in Figure 26.1.

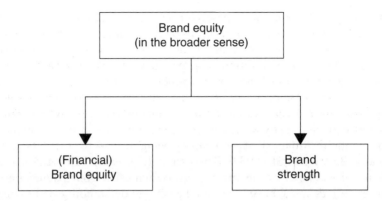

Figure 26.1   Understanding of brand equity

3   WHAT ARE THE REASONS FOR EVALUATING BRAND EQUITY?

In general, the way of evaluating brand equity mainly depends on the interests and goals of the evaluators. According to these evaluation reasons the used brand equity models must be adjusted. The evaluation reason finally represents the central starting point for the development of different brand equity models.

3.1   External Evaluation Reasons

Mergers and acquisitions can be seen as the most important reason for evaluation nowadays. For this purpose, brand equity represents the crucial factor for determining the price. This connection is supported by the fact that the actual purchase price often differs from the financial data. The acquired brands of a company or a sport club mostly serve as justification for the surplus paid price beyond the net asset value. That means that brand equity serves as a reference for price negotiations or as a guarantee for external investors. In the case of an external licence, the brand owner grants to the licensee the use of the brand for his or her products or services. In order to work out the corresponding contracts, information concerning the value of the brand is needed as well.

The evaluation of brand equities in the course of determining licence prices takes an important role especially in Germany as in 2001 revenues of about 24 billion euro were generated in that context (Sattler and Völckner, 2007: 181). The so-called product or trademark piracy also led to an increased interest in the evaluation of brands. The awareness of trademark piracy rose with the abusive use of the Rolex and Lacoste brands that led to losses in the millions. Until now legislation has needed to rely on special reviews in order to estimate the compensation. A more objective evaluation of brand equity would help tremendously. In addition, the purchase of brands has an effect on the financial reporting of the acquiring party.

3.2 Internal Evaluation Reasons

From inside the company or the sport organization brand equity is often seen as a target figure. The increase of this brand equity is the only goal of all marketing activities. Besides that, this figure represents a controlling instrument of a success factor. All strategic activities in the context of planning, managing and controlling the brand must be oriented to this factor. In particular, companies that have several brands in their portfolio have to decide regularly which brands are worthwhile to invest in and which brands should be dismantled.

Furthermore, the internal transfer of brand rights (internal licensing) can be the reason for calculating brand equity, especially for multinational corporations consisting of many different companies which transfer licenses, for example for logo and naming rights, according to the corporate strategy. This procedure needs to be included in the financial statements. In order to find realistic prices for those licence rights the calculation of brand equity is necessary as the buying company has to list this brand equity as an immaterial asset in the financial statements.

4 WHY IS BRAND EQUITY RELEVANT FOR SPORT BUSINESS?

Gladden and Funk (2002: 54) stated that sport managers begin to view their organization as brands that must be managed. Consequently, those sport managers need to understand the components of brand equity in order to enhance it. Only then will they be able to increase the image, awareness and revenues of their organization (Gladden et al., 1998: 2). More and more consultancies in sport management have started to measure the brand equity of football clubs. In 2004 a study revealed the brand equity of Real Madrid CF as 278 million euro (FutureBrand, 2004). Three years later, in 2007, its brand equity was calculated as 1063 billion euro (BBDO consulting, 2007). Furthermore, this difference is not only related to Real Madrid CF, but to all other top European football clubs included in these studies (for example, FC Barcelona 141 versus 948 million euro, Chelsea FC 80 versus 828 million euro) as illustrated in Figure 26.2.

In the course of commercialization and professionalization in sports the perspectives of sport organizations change. Especially marketing perspectives get more and more attention in the sense of strategic decisions. This goes along with the increased relevance of sport brands and the detailed knowledge of their value. For example, latest research results show that the development and the implication of branding strategies are critical for long-term marketing success in French football (Couvelaere and Richelieu, 2005). Strong brands guarantee added value that is consequently reflected in economical success. Strategic brand management in sport leads to enhanced sympathy and further fan potential, which finally lead to increased media awareness and marketing profits. These profits refer to higher revenues in ticketing and merchandising, the liquidation of marketing rights, as well as media rights.

Spectators are in the core of this discussion because they represent the origin of nearly every revenue source. The existence of a certain number of spectators is the basic

	Future Brand (2004)	BBDO (2007)
Club	Brand equity (mio. €)	Brand equity (mio. €)
Real Madrid CF	278	1063
FC Barcelona	141	948
Manchester United	288	922
Chelsea FC	80	828
AC Mailand	197	824
FC Bayern München	149	727
Inter Mailand	97	715
Arsenal FC, London	111	712
JuventusTurin	131	709
Liverpool FC	84	645

Figure 26.2   Ranking of European football clubs

requirement for successful marketing strategies with media, sponsors, agencies and licensees. In this context Bauer, Sauer and Schmitt (2005) verified empirically the relation of a strong brand and the average numbers of spectators. An established sport brand offers decisive added values for customers since it conveys values, associations and images. The sport organization must try to expand this relationship in order to intensify brand loyalty, for example. Furthermore, strong brands get more public attention and are more often seen in the media. Television rights, in particular can be seen as important revenue sources, as a decentral marketing of television rights would follow directly the brand strength of the sport organization.

Sponsors have become increasingly more aware of the opportunities of a strong sport brand. Especially in times of smaller budgets, sponsors look for reasonable business facts that justify a sport sponsorship. In that sense sponsor and sport organization establish a brand partnership in order to achieve common goals. This strategic partnership can be summarized by the expression 'from sponsoring to co-branding'. Also, merchandising is one of the most important revenue sources for sport organizations. This area is dominated by strong brands as, for example, in the German Bundesliga in 2002/03 just five clubs were responsible for 60 per cent (about 90 million euro) of all the merchandising revenues (Ernst and Young, 2005: 17).

To conclude, brand management and the detection of brand strength and brand equity is absolutely relevant for the economical success of sport organizations.

5   WHAT IS THE STATE OF RESEARCH CONCERNING BRAND EQUITY MODELS?

5.1   Importance of Brand Equity Models

Since the middle of the 1980s, companies' business strategies have been changing. Up until then, companies justified purchase prices of acquired companies by their financial results. Usually this led to prices that were eight to ten times more than the company's profits. This guideline became obsolete when amounts being paid were up to 25 times higher than the company profits or three to four times higher than the stock exchange value. Prices at this level were justified by the financial value of the brand that was purchased at the same time. These developments made obvious that the need for a financial evaluation of brands was more necessary than ever before (Kapferer, 1992). If one keeps in mind that in those times the practice of evaluating brands was in its early, stages, it is not surprising that three decades later plenty of diverse approaches to brand equity models exist. In this regard, agencies, research institutes and consultancies now compete to such an extent in the development of new brand equity models that the German community already counts more than 30 considerable brand equity models (Schimansky, 2004: 15). Based on that result, it is no surprise that there is a huge range of analytical approaches. But this huge variety is not the only reason for ever-increasing criticism in this area. It is, rather, the uncertainty of the results deriving from this model diversity that supports the critics. Thereby, the evaluation of monetary brand equity actually cannot be fulfilled by any of the existing models (Esch, 2008: 642). This dilemma can be shown by the example of the brand evaluation of Coca-Cola from 1988 until 1992.

Figure 26.3 shows in a very impressive way the dilemma of brand evaluation. Over a period of only four years several experts calculated brand equities for Coca-Cola that differ by a factor of 165. For a responsible manager this situation leads immediately to the question, which brand equity model should be chosen?

What aspects could help answering this question? Of course, the above-mentioned evaluation reasons play a role, but even if this question is clarified there is still a wide range of potential methods. So, would you choose the brand equity model that promises the highest possible brand equity or would you prefer to rely on the reputation of the evaluators?

In order to shed some light on this topic, this chapter presents a categorization of brand equity models as well as a closer analysis of particular representative models. For this purpose, the following paragraphs are divided into the three main categories of finance-oriented, customer-oriented and integrative brand equity models (Figure 26.4).

These three categories represent the current state of brand evaluation in research and practice. The first category finance-oriented brand evaluation, follows the classical understanding of financial calculation of brand equity. The second category, customer-oriented brand evaluation, takes up the ambiguous discussion about brand strength in respect of customer-based brand equity. The third category, integrative brand equity, brings the first two categories together by considering brand equity as an immaterial value with customer orientation, but also showing a financial part that consists of monetary and non-monetary data.

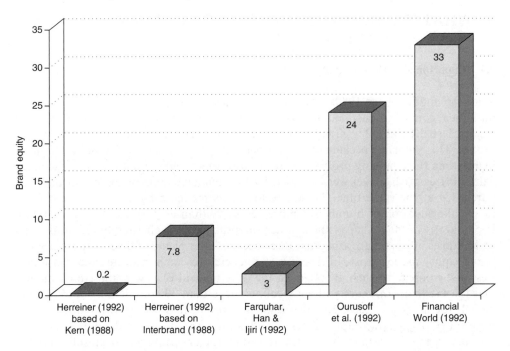

Source: Graph based on Bekmeier-Feuerhahn (1998: 62).

Figure 26.3   Brand equities of Coca-Cola

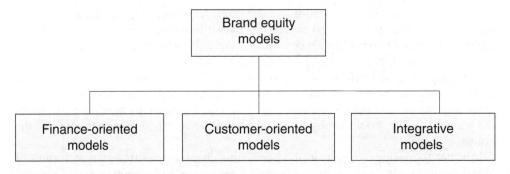

Figure 26.4   Classification of brand equity models

5.2   Finance-oriented Brand Equity Models

This chapter presents two selected finance-oriented brand equity models in order to give an insight into this area of brand evaluation. We focus on the net value-oriented brand equity model and on the capital market-oriented brand equity model.

5.2.1 Net value-oriented brand equity model of Kern

Kern (1962) ascertains that it is almost impossible to conduct a brand evaluation on the basis of all factors that compose the so-called trademark value. In the end one would be confronted with numerous indicators which, on the one hand, influence each other and, on the other, mostly cannot be quantified. Kern finally reduces all indicators to two components: the revenue-based and the risk-based indicators. On the basis of the analysis of these factors he points out that it is at least possible to conduct an approximate brand evaluation with reference to the revenues driven by the brand. However, he acknowledges that a calculation based on revenues is problematic, because only the past revenues are known and, consequently, estimated values cannot be avoided.

In general, Kern assumes that the brand equity always depends on the original purpose. If the purpose was to realize additional profits with the brand, then the brand evaluation should concentrate on future additional profits being realized by the brand. However, Kern excludes future profits from the beginning, considering revenues indirectly by calculating the return on sales as about 4 to 6 per cent. In the same context he confesses that it is impossible to determine the revenues only generated by the brand. As a consequence he suggests focusing on the total revenues. In addition he concludes, based on practical experience, that, on the supposition of rising revenues, brand equities only increase on a diminishing scale. This effect is explained by the assumption that other indicators, such as quality, price or distribution channels, are more important for the revenue increase than the brand.

According to these reflections, Kern finally comes to the conviction that the brand equity (BE) is composed of a function of the average revenue expectations per year (R), the typical licence rate per branch (L), the time frame of revenue expectations in years (n) and the typical interest rate per country (i), which can be expressed by the relation of $q = 1 + i/100$. Altogether, Kern comes to the following formula for calculating brand equity:

$$BE = \sqrt[3]{R^2} * L * \frac{q^n - 1}{q^n * (q - 1)} \qquad 26.1$$

5.2.2 Capital market-oriented brand equity model of Simon and Sullivan

The financial market value of a company represents the basis of the capital market-oriented brand equity model of Simon and Sullivan (1993). The market value results, in this context, from the immaterial assets of a company. Simon and Sullivan focus on the stock market value because, in their opinion, this value is an undistorted estimation of future cashflows that themselves reflect again on the assets of the company. In general, they divide their brand equity model into two perspectives: the macro and micro perspective. At the macro level they look for an objective value of all company brands. In contrast, the micro level isolates the single brands and their influences on the brand equity. At this level one is mainly interested in the influences on the brand equity being derived from marketing decisions. At that point Simon and Sullivan confess that their model is not appropriate for companies with several brands because the brand equity is always calculated for the whole company, including all brands. That means that there is no allocation of the brand equity among the single brands.

In general this model is based on three assumptions:

1. The brand equity is an immaterial asset of the company and can be separated objectively from other assets. The taken assets are the result of the due diligence of listed companies. In addition, the immaterial assets can be divided into three categories: (a) brand equity; (b) factors reducing costs in comparison to competitors, for example, research and development or patents and (c) customary factors.
2. The brand equity is calculated future-oriented as the calculation is based on the market values being confirmed by the stock market. It is assumed that the development on the stock market reflects the future chances of the company.
3. The brand equity changes as soon as new information is available on the market, like new product introductions or new sales campaigns.

Summing up, it can be ascertained that Simon and Sullivan (1993) restrict mainly to the capital market and the effects of marketing decisions. Finally, the brand equity results from the current stock market value of the company deducting the material and immaterial assets that are not relevant to the brand equity.

5.3   Customer-oriented Brand Equity Models

This chapter deals with customer-oriented brand equity models that in general have in common that the customers represent the core of the model. The differences arise solely from the structure and the indicators used. The following paragraphs give an insight into this category of brand equity models.

5.3.1   The five determinants of brand equity according to Aaker

Aaker is considered as the pioneer in the area of customer-oriented brand evaluation. In his book *Managing Brand Equity* (Aaker, 1991) he presents his frequently cited qualitative view of brand equity. He assumes that the assets that are the basis for brand equity differ from company to company. Although he ascertains this inconstancy, Aaker defines five decisive determinants for brand equity:

1. Brand loyalty
2. Name awareness
3. Perceived quality
4. Brand associations
5. Other proprietary brand assets (for example, patents and brand rights).

Aaker also states that these five determinants or the brand equity itself create value for the customers as well as for the company. Moreover, he mentions that the single determinants might depend on, or influence, each other. Furthermore, these five issues cannot only be seen as determinants, but also as a consequence of the brand equity. Altogether, Aaker's approach is often criticized as it does not offer an established method, but a theoretical framework. This makes it hard to reconstruct and interpret results.

5.3.2 The determination of brand knowledge according to Keller

Keller (1993) attaches his concept of customer-based brand equity to Aaker's perspective by concentrating on the brand effects on the customers as well. The aim of his approach is to find out how specific marketing strategies can affect the value of the brand. In order to achieve this it is absolutely necessary to create knowledge about the brand in order to ensure that the customer reacts accordingly to the strategy. Keller summarizes this idea with the term 'brand knowledge'. In this regard the customer-based brand equity is a result of the following context: 'Customer-based brand equity is defined as the differential effect of brand knowledge on consumer response to the marketing of the brand' (Keller, 1993: 8). Keller especially highlights the terms 'differential effect', 'brand knowledge' and 'consumer response to marketing' as decisive components in this definition. Differential effect means the comparison of the customer reactions to the marketing strategy with the reactions to similar strategies of unbranded goods or services. Brand knowledge consists of brand awareness and brand image from customers' perspective. Consumer response to marketing' finally subsumes the perceptions and concrete reactions of customers to the marketing strategy. Keller concludes that brand equity will be positive if customers evaluate marketing strategies of the brand as more valuable than those of an unbranded good or service. The general premise to achieve positive brand equity must be seen in the high brand knowledge of the customers. This high brand knowledge results from brand awareness and positive, strong and unique brand associations. In comparison with Aaker's approach, Keller is confronted with the same criticisms with regard to the general question of feasibility of the brand equity analysis.

5.4 Integrative Brand Equity Models

The literature in the area of integrative brand equity models is characterized by the responsible persons or institutions who represent those models. That is why the following descriptions cope with two models of consultancies, one of Interbrand and the other one of BBDO.

5.4.1 Basic understanding

The integrative brand evaluation represents the most current development in this specific area. The core of this category lies in the combination of the finance-oriented and the customer-oriented approaches. In the broader sense there is a combination of quantitative and qualitative data. Consequently, the integrative brand equity models try to evaluate brands in the most comprehensive way as the criteria are determined from the company perspective as well as from the customer perspective. But the aim of integrative brand equity models is not only the combination of finance-oriented and customer-oriented approaches. Most authors try to transfer the qualitative data together with the financial data to achieve a monetary value. Usually this is made on the basis of a two-staged method. In the first step, a scoring model is used for calculating the brand strength. Then the brand strength is aggregated to an overall score that can be interpreted as the measure of brand strength. In the second step, the detected brand strength serves as a component of the monetary evaluation.

5.4.2   Brand evaluation according to Interbrand

At the end of the 1980s the consultancy, Interbrand, developed an integrative brand equity model that is based upon a scoring model. The model tries to identify determinants that influence brand strength. Then those determinants get weighted and, with the help of a transformation function, converted into an index value. This index value is then linked with the brand profits that finally leads to the brand equity (Penrose and Moorhouse, 1989).

The starting point of this approach is the scoring model, including seven factors that are operationalized by 80 to 100 criteria. The seven factors – brand leadership, brand stability, marketplace, internationality, trend, marketing support and legal protection – are responsible for the brand strength. The investigated brand gets conversion points for each criteria. By doing so, each of the seven determinants gets a certain sum of conversion points. Subsequently, each sum gets weighted according to its relevance to the brand strength (Sander, 1994: 69–70). Table 26.1 gives a summary of this procedure.

According to Interbrand statements the brand strength is a measure scale of the brand potential to realize future profits. That is why the consultants try to connect brand strength with profits. But this step is not done by multiplying brand strength by a financial figure with respect to an appropriate interest rate. There is still a step in between. Interbrand states that they transfer the brand strength, which can have an index value of 0–100, with the help of a function into a multiplier. However, this function, and especially its derivation, are not explained further. Interbrand refers to long-term experience and self-conducted research. Finally, a brand-index function is determined that shows a multiplier from 0 to 20 according to the brand strength (Birkin, 1991: 43). Figure 26.5 shows this context and the resulting s-shaped function.

Finally, this value is multiplied by the average after-tax earnings of the last three periods. The result of this calculation is the monetary brand equity. One of the most obvious criticisms concerning this model is based on its subjectivity as there are significant doubts within the determination of the brand strength both on the arbitrary

Table 26.1   Determinants of brand strength

Determinants	Weighting	Selected criteria
Brand leadership	25%	Market share, market position, relative market share, market structure, future aspects
Brand stability	15%	History, current position, future developments
Marketplace	10%	Competition structure, market segment, market value, market size, trend, future perspectives
Internationality	25%	Representation of foreign markets, relevance in those markets, exports, advertisement, future perspectives
Trend	10%	Sales development, status towards competitors, strategic plans, future chances
Marketing support	10%	Advertisement, trade support, brand personality, consistency of message and image, future strategies
Legal protection	5%	Naming rights, registration

Source: Table based on Sander (1994: 72).

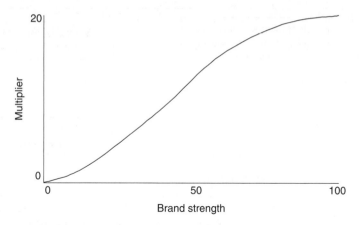

Source: Graph based on Birkin (1991: 43).

Figure 26.5   Transformation of a brand

selection and weighting of the determinants and its criteria, and on the definition of the transformation function. In addition, the model depends on the tax system being used in the relevant country. This makes the comparability of different brand equities on an international level very difficult.

5.4.3   Brand equity valuation for accounting (BEVA) according to BBDO

The integrative model brand equity valuation for accounting (BEVA) was developed by the consultancy, BBDO, and can be considered as the latest advancement in the line of brand equity models from BBDO. With reference to BBDO's tradition, this BEVA model is based on the preceding brand equity evaluation system (BEES). The BEES model mainly deals with general data of the consolidated annual reports, whereas the advancement of the BEVA model is substantiated in the use of internal data from accounting, business development and market research. This focus on internal data makes the BEVA model more flexible towards its use for different brands.

The core of the model consists of the connection of aspects such as image or loyalty and finance-oriented data in one model. In general, BBDO refers to the relief-from-royalty method that proceeds on the assumption that the owner of a strong brand can abandon paying licence rates for other successful brands. These savings of licence rates are declared as royalty savings. Also, the BEVA model consists of two modules. First, the brand strength must be detected with the help of the BBDO 5-step model. Here, the brand strength is again the result of a scoring model that mainly concentrates on the measurement of several image factors. Then, all brand-related revenues must be isolated including future revenues which are estimated for a certain period of time. The link between these two modules is guaranteed by the brand profit rate. This rate is identified by a transformation function. The determined point value of the brand strength module is transferred into a licence rate with the help of this function.

The scale of this licence rate refers to actual licence rates of comparable brands. As a guideline, one can ascertain that the stronger the brand is evaluated from the customer

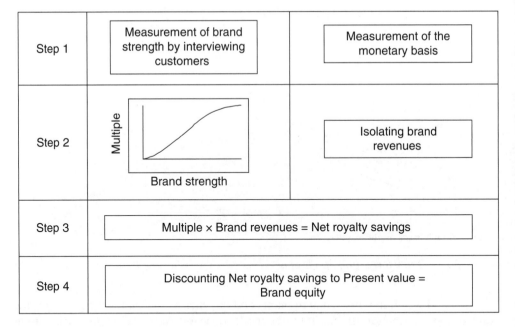

Figure 26.6   The four steps of the BEVA model

perspective the higher is the corresponding licence rate. In the next step, the resulting brand profit rate must be adjusted to the brand relevance of the relevant branch. This figure is then multiplied by the brand-related revenues. Finally, this figure must be discounted on the net present value, which then represents the brand equity in the BEVA model (Granz and Schmidt, 2009; Klein-Bölting et al., 2007). The whole procedure of the BEVA model is summarized in Figure 26.6.

Most of the critical issues discussed previously for the Interbrand model could be repeated here for the BEVA model, especially the subjectivity within the determination of brand strength. Furthermore, the isolation of brand revenues would be another issue that is strongly criticized in the literature.

6   WHAT ARE THE CONCLUSIONS?

In general, the discussion about the evaluation of brand equity should refer to two main issues:

1. One should always differentiate between brand equity and brand strength. Although this separation is not entirely consistent in the literature and the expression 'brand equity' dominates the discussion, there is a common understanding of the existence of both finance-oriented and customer-based brand equity.
2. Based on that first conclusion, one should distinguish between the three main models of brand evaluation: finance-oriented models, customer-oriented models and integrative models.

In summary, with reference to these two main issues and the preceding text in the chapter's the evaluation of brand equity belongs to one of the most discussed and most important management topics. This development has also become more apparent in sport business. Owing to several reasons shown above it is extremely important for sport organizations to evaluate both brand strength and brand equity. This is proven in practice by the increasing numbers of evaluations done in several sports. By following that discussion, one should keep in mind that finance-oriented models usually ignore the influence of different stakeholders, especially the sport spectators' perspective. In that case, psychological variables such as fan loyalty or image are completely out of scope. Customer-oriented models, however, include those psychological variables, but more or less ignore financial figures. These two perspectives are combined in integrative models, which measure brand equity by scoring models where the weights of brand key drivers are subjectively determined. This is the reason why the results of different brand evaluations of one and the same brand usually differ significantly. Therefore, it is important to differentiate brand strength and brand equity.

Furthermore, the drivers of brand strength and brand equity should be identified and integrated into a model showing clear cause–effect relationships of those drivers. In that sense, brand strength would lead to brand equity. Following that idea, brand equity could not finally be calculated, but financial indicators could serve as a measurement scale. Besides that, in sport business it is also necessary to include sport specific variables. The most obvious variable might be sporting success of the sport brand. But there could also be other variables, such as sport involvement, that are still not sufficiently discussed in brand equity literature.

REFERENCES

Aaker, D. (1991), *Managing Brand Equity: Capitalizing on the Value of a Brand Name*, New York: The Free Press.

Barwise, P., Higson, C., Likierman, A. and Marsh, P. (1989), *Accounting for Brands*, London: London Business School.

Bauer, H., Sauer, N. and Schmitt, P. (2005), Customer-based brand equity in the team sport industry: operationalization and impact on the economic success of sport teams, *European Journal of Marketing*, **39** (5/6), 496–513.

BBDO Consulting (2007), Real Madrid ist der Fußballclub mit dem höchsten Markenwert in Europa [Real Madrid is the football club with the highest brand equity in Europe], press release, http://www.bbdo-consulting.com/cms/de/news/pressemappe/Pressemitteilungen/PM_Fussballclub_Ranking_2007.pdf, accessed 27 November 2009.

Bekmeier-Feuerhahn, S. (1998), *Marktorientierte Markenbewertung: Eine konsumenten- und unternehmensbezogene Betrachtung [Market-oriented Evaluation of Brands: A Consumer- and Business-focused Analysis]*, Wiesbaden: Deutscher Universitäts-Verlag.

Benkenstein, M. and Uhrich, S. (2008), Wertorientierte Führung von Dienstleistungs-marken [Value oriented management of service brands], in H. Bauer, F. Huber and C.M. Albrecht (eds), *Erfolgsfaktoren der Markenführung – Know-how aus Forschung und Management*, Munich: Vahlen, pp. 445–58.

Birkin, M. (1991), Valuation of trade marks and brand names, in J. Murphy (ed.), *Brand Valuation*, London: Business Books, pp. 33–46.

Bruhn, M. and Stauss, B. (2008), Dienstleistungsmarken [Service brands], in M. Bruhn and B. Stauss (eds), *Forum Dienstleistungsmanagement – Dienstleistungsmarken*, Wiesbaden: Gabler, pp. 3–33.

Couvelaere, V. and Richelieu, A. (2005), Brand strategy in professional sports: the case of French soccer teams, *European Sport Management Quarterly*, **5** (1), 23–46.

Deutsches Patent- und Markenamt (DPMA) (eds) (2007), *Jahresbericht 2006 [Annual Report 2006]*, Munich: DPMA.

Ernst and Young (eds) (2005), *Bälle, Tore und Finanzen* [*Balls, Goals, and Finances*], Essen: Ernst and Young.
Esch, F.-R. (2008), *Strategie und Technik der Markenführung* [*Strategy and Technique of Brand Management*], Munich: Vahlen.
Farquhar, P.H., Han, J.Y. and Ijiri, Y. (1992), Brands on the balance sheet, *Marketing Management*, **1** (4), 16–22.
Financial World (1992), in Mega-Markenwert für Marlboro – Das US-Magazin Financial World beziffert den Wert von US-Top-Marken [Mega brand equity for Marlboro – US magazine Financial World quantifies the equity of US-top brands], *Horizont*, 17 Septemper 1993.
FutureBrand (eds) (2004), *The Most Valuable Football Brands in Europe – the 2004 Report*, London: Future Brand.
Gladden, J. and Funk, D. (2002), Developing an understanding of brand associations in team sport: empirical evidence from consumers of professional sport, *Journal of Sport Management*, **16** (1), 54–81.
Gladden, J., Irwin, R. and Sutton, W. (2001), Managing North American major professional sport teams in the new millenium: a focus on building brand equity, *Journal of Sport Management*, **15** (4), 297–317.
Gladden, J., Milne, G. and Sutton, W. (1998), A conceptual framework for assessing brand equity in Division I College Athletics, *Journal of Sport Management*, **12** (1), 1–19.
Granz, A. and Schmidt, A. (2009), Brand equity valuation for accounting (BEVA), in U. Klein-Bölting and A. Schmidt (eds), *Insights Special*, Düsseldorf: BBDO Consulting, pp. 7–13.
Interbrand (1988), in Herreiner, T. (1992), Der 'Wert' der Marke – Darstellung und kritische Würdigung von Verfahren der Markenevaluierung [The value of the brand – presentation and critical reflection of brand evaluation models], *Arbeitspapier zur Schriftenreihe Schwerpunkt Marketing*, **37**, Augsburg: Augsburg University.
Kapferer, J.-N. (1992), *Strategic Brand Management: New Approaches to Creating and Evaluating Brand Equity*, New York: Kogan Page.
Keller, K.L. (1993), Conceptualizing, measuring, and managing customer-based brand equity, *Journal of Marketing*, **57** (1), 1–22.
Kern, W. (1962), Bewertung von Warenzeichen [Evaluation of trademarks], *Betriebswirtschaftliche Forschung und Praxis*, **14** (1), 17–31.
Kern, W. (1988), in Herreiner, T. (1992), Der 'Wert' der Marke – Darstellung und kritische Würdigung von Verfahren der Markenevaluierung [The value of the brand – presentation and critical reflection of brand evaluation models], *Arbeitspapier zur Schriftenreihe Schwerpunkt Marketing*, **37**, Augsburg: Augsburg University.
Klein-Bölting, U., Granz, A. and Beerlink, A. (2007), Monetäre Markenbewertung: Erfolgsfaktor für Markenmanagement und Unternehmensführung [Monetary brand evaluation: success factor for brand management and corporate governance], in U. Klein-Bölting (ed.), *Insights*, Düsseldorf: BBDO Consulting, pp. 39–48.
Meffert, H., Burmann, C. and Koers, M. (2002), Stellenwert und Gegenstand des Markenmanagement [Status and type of brand management], in H. Meffert, C. Burmann and M. Koers (eds), *Markenmanagement – Grundfragen der identitätsorientierten Markenführung*, Wiesbaden: Gabler, pp. 3–15.
Ourusoff, A., Ozanian, M., Brown, P.B. and Starr, J. (1992), What the world's top brands are worth, *Financial World*, 1 September, 32–49.
Penrose, N. and Moorhouse, M. (1989), The valuation of brands, *Marketing Intelligence & Planning*, **7** (11/12), 30–33.
Richelieu, A. and Pons, F. (2006), Toronto Maple Leafs vs Football Club Barcelona: how two legendary sports teams built their brand equity, *International Journal of Sports Marketing & Sponsorship*, **7** (3), 231–50.
Sander, M. (1994), *Die Bestimmung und Steuerung des Wertes von Marken: Eine Analyse aus Sicht des Markeninhabers* [*Determination and Controlling of Brand Equity: An Analysis from the Perspective of the Owner of the Brand*], Heidelberg: Physica.
Sattler, K. and Völckner, F. (2007), *Markenpolitik* [*Brand Politics*], Stuttgart: Kohlhammer.
Schimansky, A. (2004), Markenbewertungsverfahren aus Sicht der Marketingpraxis [Brand equity models from the perspective of marketing practice], in A. Schimansky (ed.), *Der Wert der Marke – Markenwertungsverfahren für ein erfolgreiches Markenmanagement*, Munich: Vahlen, pp. 14–27.
Simon, C. and Sullivan, M. (1993), The measurement and determinants of brand equity: a financial approach, *Marketing Science*, **12** (1), 28–52.
Welling, M. (2006), *Ökonomik der Marke: Ein Beitrag zum Theorienpluralismus in der Markenforschung* [*Brand Economics: A Contribution to Pluralism in Brand Research*], Wiesbaden, Deutscher Universitäts-Verlag.

PART VII

REFLECTION

27 From outside lane to inside track: sport management research in the twenty-first century
Simon Chadwick

The history of sport is arguably richer than any other form of human activity. Sport has variously developed across the world as a ceremony, a celebration, a physical pursuit, a leisure activity and now, increasingly, a business. As an illustration, consider the case of football in England: some people believe the sport emerged over centuries, therefore giving it a depth and context that are unsurpassed by any other current industrial sectors. In its earliest form, myth has it that during the Viking invasions, victorious battlers among the resident population would cut off the heads of the invaders and kick them around their villages. From these origins, the game most notably began to thrive during the nineteenth century in the English independent schools system, as a puritanical form of healthy activity for young men. Thereafter, the onset of the Industrial Revolution led both to an upsurge in the popularity of football as a diversion for the masses away from their harsh industrial lives, and to the emergence of the professional game. Throughout the twentieth century, as people's leisure time increased and communication links improved, regular international football began, the game developed and the popularity of football began to take hold. By the turn of the century, and in the light of technological and media change, regulatory influence from bodies such as the European Union, internationalization and globalization, and the prevalence of free market economics, business oriented thinking began to pervade across a large number of sports. Beech (2004) has generally characterized such an overall transition as having being comprised of seven phases:

1. foundation;
2. codification;
3. stratification;
4. professionalization;
5. post-professionalization;
6. commercialization; and
7. post-commercialization.

While English football is not necessarily typical of all developments across the sporting world, it does help to show a very important characteristic of sport: that it is deeply socio-culturally embedded, which creates highly distinctive, and often unique, challenges for sport managers.[1] When we consider one of the current developments evident in sport, we can see that in the intensity of fan loyalty to certain sports brands, managers simultaneously face the juxtaposition of major commercial and managerial opportunities and the constraints of history and heritage. Many other brand managers can do little more than crave the strength of loyalty, affiliation and identification displayed by some sports fans towards 'their team'. The problem is, in seeking to target new customers, secure new market entry, or build a global fan base, such loyalties often pose a serious challenge to what business managers might normally expect to achieve in such branding activities elsewhere in industry. For academic researchers too, there are consequences for them in sport's socio-cultural embeddedness. In philosophical terms, serious questions must be raised about whether sport business management is a rational economic activity. Such an observation is borne out by the involvement of corporate benefactors in sport across the world, and the continuing predilection of some executives for engaging in sport sponsorship on the basis of the 'hobby motive'. This implies that sport management is as likely to have a social-psychological foundation as much as it does an economic one. As yet though, the management literature has not got to grips with such a fundamental debate. Indeed, an overall sport management paradigm has yet to meaningfully emerge, while prevailing generic management theory/practice is often parachuted in to sport in order to explain what are often highly untypical situations. While it might be too early or too naive (or actually completely unnecessary) to propose that we need a general theory of sport management, a greater understanding of sport management's philosophical foundations is required.

The allusion being made here is that sport management is actually different to mainstream management, that somehow the knowledge base, skill set and practice of management is distinct from managing in other sectors. Such an allusion is not unintentional, begging the question: what makes sport so different to management in other industrial sectors? In short, sport managers are in the business of uncertainty; as Neale (1964) noted, the essence of sport is the uncertainty of outcome associated with a contest between two individuals or teams. That is, one never really knows who is going to win the game, the race or the championship, and this is what draws so many people, groups and organizations too sport, each for their own reasons. The heritage of uncertainty in sport can be traced from Neale's work through to more recent work published by people such as Downward and Dawson (2000). For sport management scholars, we clearly owe these people a debt of gratitude. The challenge for us now is to really start thinking about how uncertainty impacts upon how we research, study, and practice sport management. There is also a much broader debate in which we need to engage: what is the appeal of uncertainty? Although the psychology of uncertainty has received attention in the literature (for instance, Grether, 1978; Morgan, 1978), we do not seem to know how or why watching an uncertain contest may lead one to become a lifetime fan or affiliate of, say, a rugby team. For countries and sports that do not operate a franchise model, a particularly interesting debate would also be the relationship between uncertainty and the geographic identity that is implicitly bound up sports fan's decision to 'support' a team.

If uncertainty of outcome constitutes the fundamental basis of sport, then preserving the strength of uncertainty becomes the essence of sport management. Once more, it has been economists who have led the way, competitive balance being advocated as the central element of maintaining competitive balance (for instance, see Fort and Quirk, 1992). Established debate has tended to consider the relative merits of highly regulated models (synonymous with United States sport) in which salary caps, draft picks and franchise location are used to maintain uncertainty, versus more *laissez-faire* approaches where sport independently functions and issues of uncertainty are addressed through the periodic interventions of governing bodies. Such interventions implicitly direct us to a management challenge that has thus far received scant attention in the literature. That is, how games, leagues, competitions and tournaments can be managed to ensure that uncertainty, balance and, indeed, equity are promoted. There is evidence both of new sports (for example, Indian Premier League cricket) being managed to fulfil these principles, and of existing sports (for example, recent rule changes in Formula One motor racing) being managed by governing bodies in response to competitive pressures by, for instance, changing points structures or qualifying formats. However, both of these approaches have either been predicated on US-type models or have been reactive in nature. The management and structuring of contests really needs to become higher profile, with a greater emphasis on progressive, proactive and strategic management, as well as more innovative approaches to managing the promotion of uncertainty.

The way in which contest management might ascend to a new level of importance is an interesting issue in itself. Even in sports where more commercial modes of operation are evident, the sports themselves have historically been product-led. In other words, it has been what happens on the field of play, the athletes involved in this and the management of them, that have largely dictated the product offering. This explains why in many sports, fans and customers often appear as being subservient to teams, clubs and governing bodies. In many respects, this must continue, especially given the importance of the finite resource that is talented athletes. However, the notion that sport should become a more market-led industry is an interesting one. This immediately implies a clear split between managing on-field and off-field activities. For off-field activities, such as stadium/capacity utilization, the relevance of being led by the market place is both more obvious and more justifiable. In the case mentioned, utilizing stadium capacity is both a financial and an ethical imperative: how to make best use of a valuable finite resource and one that can potentially generate important revenue flows.

The argument that on-field activities should have a stronger market focus is rather more challenging, if not unpalatable for some. Contest management has already been highlighted as the biggest challenge facing managers, which can clearly be driven by the demands of a dynamic, rapidly changing industry. Yet developments that challenge the fundamental nature of a sport pose much greater managerial problem. The failure of X-treme Football in the USA, where World Wrestling Entertainment re-packaged American Football in order to target new consumers, is a case in point (Willoughby and Mancini, 2003). In a similar vein, a proposal made by US officials prior to the FIFA World Cup in 1994, that goal sizes should be increased to enhance the appeal of soccer to consumers, was dismissed by football purists. The tension in sport between product and market is therefore an important one, and understanding the nature of their inter-relational dynamics is significant for researchers and practitioners alike. Central to this understanding would surely be the question: should sport be market-led, or should the product always come first?

Although uncertainty is the fundament of sport and contest management a means of preserving it, neither can exist without a third element: competitors. Without one or more individuals, teams or groups, the execution of sport would be impossible (and sport would cease to be sport, and simply be a leisure pursuit). Central to managing the successful execution of sporting contests is the notion that individuals/teams/groups will need to coordinate their activities. This is a further feature that marks out sport as being significantly different to other industries, as sport organizations actively need to engage with one another in order to fulfil their central purpose. The notion of collaborating to compete is something that has been acknowledged across a range of literatures and sectors since the late 1980s (Bleeke and Ernst, 1993). However, the heritage of sport in this regard was established far longer ago. Yet despite the imperative of joint action, sporting contests have yet to be considered as a form of collaboration, strategic or otherwise, in the management literature. The way in which competitors collaborate in the scheduling of contests is one important issue for researchers to address, especially if uncertainty (and the attendant tensions associated with it) is to be maximized for the full duration of, for example, a tournament or a season.

Scheduling is only one form of collaboration, there are many other forms including: teams collaborating with one another as part of a league, both for individual and collective benefit (such as the National Basketball Association); and teams collaborating across international boundaries (such as the alliance between Arsenal FC and Colorado Rapids football teams). Identifying the full range of collaborative arrangements, the specific nature of them, the management issues they raise and the intended/actual outcomes of such arrangements are all important issues that have yet to receive detailed attention from researchers. Clearly there are opportunities for researchers to apply generic models of collaboration in a sporting context. However, in the light of the juxtaposition of uncertainty, collaboration and competition, there would also appear to be a tremendous case for establishing a sport-specific approach to the notion of collaborating to compete.

Despite the need for collaboration, competition remains at the heart of sport raising some interesting issues of performance measurement. The most obvious form of performance measurement are the league tables of points scored or medals won. This exposes sport to a level of scrutiny not evident in other industrial sectors, which is exacerbated even further by the media coverage and general interest in sport. Allied to this, as technology has developed so too has our ability to measure increasingly specific details of sporting performance. The epitome of this has been the 'Moneyball' phenomenon in which team selection decisions are entirely data driven (Lewis, 2003). In such cases, sport managers face some interesting challenges for, while they may be responsible for a team notionally comprised of the strongest individuals, the science of selection may be undermined by problems such as the group dynamic. As such, one clearly has to question whether an entirely statistical or an intuitive approach to team selection is the best approach. One senses nevertheless that there is likely to be an optimum combination of the two; one challenge for sport management researchers would therefore appear to be the determination of this optimum.

Measuring on-field performance rather deflects attention away from the measurement of off-field performance, a matter that has become an increasingly contentious one in recent years. As a commercial view of sport has emerged, the debate about the importance of financial measures of performance and the extent to which they might undermine on-field performances have grown. This is most aptly highlighted in English football's Premier League where teams have had to deal with the conundrum of an inflationary labour market, in which clubs have had to spend heavily on player acquisition and remuneration in order to successfully compete, while simultaneously trying to adopt a commercial approach to financial management; that is, achieving break-even, if not actually making a profit. Reconciling the 'on-field/off-field' dichotomy is not easy, although there is already partial recognition that on- and off-field performances may be linked (for instance, Cornwell et al., 2001). To advance our understanding of this new reality, establishing how the two are connected and the ways in which the relationship between them should be managed would represent a major development in the sport management literature.

At present, the performance measurement debate is seen as being one involving a tension between the effectiveness of on-field performances and the effectiveness of off-field financial performance. However, sport is distinctive in the way that it binds together a broad, unique, socio-cultural, economic and commercial constituency. Sport often has a profound impact on communities, social cohesion, identity and self-esteem, health, lifestyles and, as is increasingly being accepted, the environment. As such, the need to establish and employ other measures of performance in sport is something that many commentators have yet to truly appreciate. In some respects, sport is already exemplary in the way it conducts, for instance, its community relations. Developing measures for this would help sport create its own performance benchmarks, that would also serve to help other industries establish a stronger approach to their corporate social responsibilities. At the same time, environmental concerns have thus far received scant attention in sport; incorporating such elements into the performance measures associated with sport would help in creating a impetus for sports organizations to take a more focused and serious approach to the wider obligations that sport has. If further evidence of this is required, consider the controversy that often accompanies the development of new golf courses, or the very basis for motor sport.

While uncertainty of outcome, competitive balance, collaboration, the on-field and off-field products, and performance measurement are fundamental elements of sport, how the configuration of these elements is managed remains one of the biggest challenges facing sport. In the USA, arguably – and ironically – the largest free market in the world, sport managers have adopted what is in essence a centrally planned, almost socialist, model of sport. Typically, this entails a governing body or association using a multiplicity of strategies for ensuring that sport retains its essential features while still serving the needs of the increasingly dynamic markets in which sport operates. The strategies variously involve employing a combination of franchising whereby team location decisions are made, the implementation of a draft system for acquiring players, and salary capping to ensure equity in player remuneration decisions. There is evidence that other sports elsewhere in the world are beginning to adopt the American model of sport; for instance, in Asia the recently instigated Indian Premier League utilized a similar approach, albeit without the use of a draft system, which was replaced by a player auction that was held across all constituent members of the league. What the organizers of the competition recognized however, was that the on-field product needed to be comprised of commercially attractive performers and so special dispensation was given to pay larger salaries to 'icon players'. These players are intended to be leading world stars who are paid outside salary restrictions centrally imposed by the competition's governing body. This is similar to the 'Designated player rule' that is now being used in North American Major League Soccer.

What might generally be called the 'American model' of sport is starkly different from that which predominates in Europe. In a continent generally characterized as having more socially democratic political and economic systems, approaches to the macro-management of sport are essentially *laissez-faire*. That is, the historical development of sport as a socio-cultural phenomenon has resulted in custom and practice dominating the way in which sport operates. Moreover, the principles of the European Union, most notably the promotion of freedom of movement, means that franchising and salary capping, as two examples, are either socially unacceptable or else illegal under European law. As such, a debate has emerged about what constitutes the 'European model' of sport, especially as a number of sports are experiencing problems of uncertainty and competitive balance. The way in which sport should be managed has therefore risen to the top of the political agenda in Europe, with sport becoming one of the main provisions of the, still to be ratified, Lisbon Treaty. In a similar way, as sport across the world develops, especially in rapidly emerging markets such as China and India, the debate about how to macro-manage sport so that it retains its essential, and most attractive, features will continue to be important.

The academic community has an important role to play in this debate by helping to identify the optimum model for managing sport. At the present time, there is little analysis of the most effective, or efficient form, of sporting model, nor of the management implications of employing existing models. Moreover, given the diversity of constraints facing sport across the world, determining alternative, possibly hybrid, sporting models that account for local conditions, could be advocated by the academic community. Ideally, academic researchers should underpin their work in the area [with] strong methodologies drawn from a range of research philosophies. Nevertheless, such is the conundrum facing the macro-management of sport in some parts of the world, most notably Europe, that well informed opinion leadership also has a key role to play in advancing the understanding and application of appropriate sporting models.

Sharpening the debate about the sporting model are the ongoing processes of internationalization and globalization. The uncertainty of outcome and competitive balance are being fundamentally affected by these phenomena, particularly as larger sports organizations that can operate on a international/global scale are able to gain access to new markets and resources, which consequently reinforces and strengthens their playing, and their market, positions. This raises numerous issues, most notably of power and control. Hence, their has been intense debate surrounding recent developments such as the English Premier (Soccer) League's proposed '39th Game' which, it is intended, will be staged each year in strategically important overseas markets. Added to this, we have also seen the National Basketball Association (the NBA) targeting markets such as China using leading Asian players like Yao Ming (of the Houston Rockets). This raises an array of sporting issues ranging from competitive balance and the governance of league structures, through to the way in which teams and competitions should be regulated and managed. Yet even at the micro-management level, there are some highly pertinent matters to address: how the sport product can most effectively be transported to new markets in which there is no socio-cultural heritage relating to the sport; ensuring that specific local needs are satisfied by the international growth of sporting franchises, rather than diverse populations being culturally homogenised by these franchises; issues of scheduling and media coverage across the world; and the 'corporatization' of sport to the detriment of the core sport product (uncertainty of outcome), are all major issues that managers and researchers have yet to truly get to grips with.

As both a driving force for the internationalization/globalization of sport, and also as a leading beneficiary of the phenomena, the media is becoming an increasingly significant member of the sport network (Woolfe et al., 2002). With the emergence of satellite television, mobile technology, the Internet and digital television over the last decade or so, the size and value of the global media market has grown considerably. At the same time, the market has proliferated and fragmented as the number of media outlets has grown. Indeed, the development in technology has been such, that there has been a culture change among consumers who now demand relevant content delivered on-demand. This is posing some challenges at both the macro- and micro-management levels, many of which have the potential to change the fundamental nature of sport. At the macro-level, the global nature of the technology means that the sport product on offer has to be attractive. In sport, this normally means teams that win or performers who are, in some way, attractive. The market dynamics in such cases nevertheless means that resources flow to a small group of sports and sports people, delivering strategic and financial benefits to them, while crowding out others. A major issue around this dynamic is that we are beginning to see the strong emergence of resource rich sports, sports organizations and athletes. This is, in turn, affecting competitive balance and uncertainty of outcome thereby posing major challenges for the managers of sporting contests. Moreover, how organizations manage their activities in the face of a rapidly changing technological environment, and the implications of it, is something that is likely to be central to their survival. Even for those organizations that are prospering, there is a significant concern; that is, rather than being associated with sport, they are now effectively in the process of managing their evolution from sport businesses to entertainment businesses.

At the micro-management level, gaining some degree of control over technology is an imperative. Sport appears to be responsive to technology, rather than controlling and managing it for its own purposes, therefore understanding the processes underpinning technological change, and being creative in the ways in which it is used, are arguably the two biggest issues for sport managers. As mobile technology proliferates, the need to populate electronic media space with meaningful content will grow. Sport can readily provide such content in the form of, for example, game coverage or the presentation of statistical and game information. However, the key challenge for sport managers will be to create other, more creative, content that enables their organization to secure a differential advantage over their rivals, both within and outside sport. Being close to the market, understanding one's customers and adopting an innovative approach to content generation, all of which are currently anathema to some sports organizations, will be paramount if sport is to take full advantage of the opportunities that new media provides.

As for the role that academics and researchers can play in the macro- and micro-management, there are clear opportunities for them to make a contribution. The need to think in a creative, value-adding is one way in which academics can help, as well as in providing opinion leadership on the subject of managing technology. Harnessing the power of mobile media, among elite professional sports as well as other levels of sport poses some interesting questions that scholars can help to answer. This may include how phenomena such as social networking and viral marketing can contribute to the organizational and commercial development of sport. Underpinning this are issues pertaining to the ways in which customers – fans, spectators or otherwise – actually consume sport and what motivates them to do so. As the sport market fragments into a multitude of clear and distinct segments, the need for customer understanding will grow. The closeness to market that this implies is something that academic researchers are particularly adept at achieving. Otherwise, sport management academics must devote time to understanding the mega-shifts that increasingly appear to characterize the sporting environment. The growth of social networking, for instance, is something that has taken many organizations aback. Being able to predict such developments, identifying how sport organizations should respond, and the way in which technology can help to accentuate and enhance the fundamental features of sport can become a route through which academia makes a growing contribution to the management literature.

In the main, this chapter has addressed management issues that are central both to the existence of sport and to the overall health of it. Although analysis and debate in these areas are more strongly established in North America, the literature elsewhere is at best formative. As such, there is tremendous potential for further future research, especially as sport moves from being a peripheral interest of academics and researchers to being part of the management mainstream. At the micro-management level, the full range of functional areas in the management literature has strong links to contemporary developments in sport, and therefore clearly has a roll to play in helping us understand them. The constraints facing a chapter of this nature nevertheless are such that a broad, deep commentary on these developments cannot be provided. For the convenience of readers, Table 27.1 therefore summarises some of the management areas, emerging issues in sport and challenges facing sport managers. This is not intended to be definitive, although it is anticipated that the table's content will help in establishing a stronger focus for the sport management research agenda.

One important issue underlying the content of the table nevertheless, is a debate about the extent to which sport should draw from the existing management literature. At one level, this implies that sport is an industrial sector similar to any other and that the generic implications of the established management literature are equally as applicable in a sporting context. Adopting such a viewpoint would clearly be beneficial, as it then would allow those with an interest in sport to engage in a process of applying established management theory to sport. However, this rather denies the specificity of sport, most notably the importance of managing in the essential context of uncertainty [of outcome]. Given this core characteristic of the sector, some argue that sport requires special attention and is not a vehicle to which one can simply apply management theory that is evolved in other, often less distinctive, settings. The richness of sport may therefore be best served by the continuing development of a specialized sport management literature. A major concern in this case is that sport will never be more than a management outpost, a ghetto in which highly specific work is undertaken by academics and researchers working outside the mainstream management literature. A debate about the relative merits of both viewpoints would certainly help in developing the credibility of sport management research. However, there is a third way, one that involves a more consensual relationship between the generic and the sport management literatures. That is, the servicing of sport management literature by the mainstream, and vice versa. There is already evidence of this having happened (see for instance the *European Journal of Marketing*'s special edition on sport marketing), although the extent, coherence and credibility of such work remains underdeveloped. The opportunity therefore remains for a truly compelling case to be made that there are bilateral lessons for sport and generic management to be learned.

Table 27.1 Summary of potential research areas and foci for academic researchers

Area of management affected	Focus of emerging issues	Management challenges posed by such issues
Ownership model of organizations	The most appropriate form of ownership for sports organizations, particular clubs; whether ownership model adopted by, e.g. Manchester United v FC Barcelona is the most effective	Which is the most appropriate and effective ownership model? An assessment needs to be made of the following: private ownership; public ownership; state ownership; membership clubs; supporter-led initiatives
Ethics in sport	Reconciling the need for fair, equitable, balanced and open competition with the competing demands of a diverse range of stakeholders in sport, e.g. gambling and match fixing	Establishing and implementing mechanisms to ensure that activities including money laundering, match-fixing, and general corruption do not impinge upon uncertainty of outcome and competitive balance
Governance in sport	Establishing, regulating and monitoring sport; ensuring good governance, notably transparency, equity, accountability, equity and responsibility, e.g. determining fit and proper owners in sport	Creating benchmarks, standards and best practice for the management of teams, clubs, leagues, competitions and governing bodies; ensuring that core principles of sport are not compromised by, e.g. corporate interests
Role of public sector versus private sector	Determining the extent to which sport should function within the private sector domain, be controlled by the state, or be an alliance of both, e.g. funding and staging of sporting mega events	Assessing whether private sector is the most effective way of creating and delivering the sport product or if state involvement is required; addressing issues of public/private sector partnership, and strategic alliances
Organizational management	Determining most appropriate structural form that enables reconciliation of on-field/off-field performance, e.g. signing best players while controlling costs	Creating culture where on-field and off-field can co-exist; creating structures that promote, enhance on-field performance, while enabling off-field efficiency; establishing responsive, apolitical organizations
Human resource management	Acquisition, reward, remuneration of players and managers; management of multicultural teams; managing highly skilled individuals and teams, drawn from small pool of labour, e.g. footballers	Building networks for recruiting and developing playing talent; development of reward and remuneration strategies promoting loyalty/rewarding performance; managing cultural differences within teams
Marketing	Change from product orientation to market orientation; internal culture change leading to market focus; acquiring and retaining customers, e.g. given competition of rival leisure products	Enabling culture change; reconciling differences between product-led and market-led organizations; maintaining core appeal of sport; addressing issues relating to fans and lifetime value of customers

Table 27.1 (continued)

Area of management affected	Focus of emerging issues	Management challenges posed by such issues
Sponsorships, endorsements and image rights	Fragmentation of the rights market; effective management and protection of sponsorship, endorsements and image rights; issues of ambushing and clutter, e.g. the Beckham brand	Development of sponsorships, endorsements and image rights as form of partnership/collaboration rather than a transaction; optimum, most effective form of activation and leveraging of value in such deals
Public relations and the media	Relationship between sport and media; extent to which media drives sport, and vice versa; nature of power and influence between the two; media representation of sport, e.g. portrayal of players	Need for sport to adopt a strategic approach to PR and media; need to adopt open, collaborative, constructive approach to such activity while managing relationship and protecting sport performers
Operations	Creation of networks of partners; delivering products of an appropriate quality; scheduling and delivery in order to reconcile disparate interests, e.g. in relation to TV coverage	As sport globalizes, ensuring needs of multiple market places are met through appropriate scheduling of games and events; building supply links that enable prompt and economic identification of playing talent. Creating well researched and carefully developed
Merchandising, retailing and distribution	Development and extension of sport-related retail and merchandising activity; role as a source of additional revenue; management of a portfolio of off-field products, e.g. replica shirts	product offerings that serve the needs of spectators, fans and other customers; developing supply chains that best serve various categories of sport consumer
Finance	Accessing and securing finance to sustain teams, clubs and franchises; generating new streams; cost control; building liquidity and sustainable financial performance, e.g. the case of Leeds Utd	Given high costs of player acquisition/remuneration, and cost of staging sporting events — cost control issues managing liquidity when revenue streams are seasonal/ irregular; realizing revenue potential of sport
Internationalization and globalization	Development of international/global activities; influence of internationalization and globalization; relationship with global customers and suppliers, e.g. tour games, tailored products	Consideration of market entry strategies; issues pertaining to the export and overseas delivery of cultural products; adapting/responding to local market requirements; issues of monitoring and control

Agents and representation	Balancing need for player representation with financial pressures facing sports clubs; role and regulation of player representatives; reward and remuneration of agents, e.g. extent of agents fees	System for monitoring and controlling role and influence of agents, especially in sports where power has shifted towards agents/players; establishing benchmarks and best practice for agents
Legal, ownership and property issues	Extent to which sport falls within the jurisdiction of the law, e.g. with regard to European freedom of movement, on-field violence; issue of who owns sport, e.g. in cases of ambush marketing	Fundamental issue of who owns sport; extent to which sports people, clubs, teams, governing bodies, media et al. can claim property rights; how global freedom of movement will impact upon resource decisions
Risk and security	Given prevailing economic conditions and costs of staging sport, assessment of risks associated with sport; managing safety and security of sporting events given, e.g. terrorist threats	Developing strategies for generating large crowd size while simultaneously ensuring safety and security of crowds and performers; guarding against terrorist threat; mitigating/managing possible effects of threat
Media and technology	Way new media and technology drives sport; proliferation and fragmentation of media rights and product offerings; impact on sport and sport consumers, e.g. provision of mobile content	Ensuring sport utilises and drives technology rather than relationship being entirely driven by technology; way in which technology helps serve existing markets and creates new market opportunity
Event management	Bidding for, securing, organizing, staging and evaluating the outcome of sports events; recognition of multiple functions that events fulfil, e.g. assessing costs and benefits of events	Ensuring events are strategically planned to ensure effectiveness, efficiency and overall success; reconciling multiplicity of effects events can have commercial, economic, social, health, psychological
Impact and legacy of sport	Size, extent and nature of sport economy; extent to which sport impacts on aspects of economy, society, psychology, health and culture, e.g. contribution to workplace well being	Way sport can be used as a basis for driving development of economic and commercial activity; managing balance of sporting impacts and event legacy to include economic as well as socio-cultural legacy

CONCLUSIONS

Sport has now emerged as an industrial sector in its own right, with a number of studies and estimates that it makes a major contribution to economic and commercial activity both within and across national boundaries. At the same time, sport continues to have a profound influence on the social, cultural, health and psychological spheres of human existence. The prevailing appeal of sport is such that a wide range of institutions, organizations, bodies, clubs, teams and individuals are both affected by and involved in sport. As such, there is a multitude of challenges facing managers in sport, many of which have only emerged over the last ten to twenty years. There is a real need to understand the challenges faced by sport managers, and what the most effective ways of managing them are. It is therefore reasonable to anticipate that the sport management literature will develop apace over the next decade. While the literature stock already displays signs of health and diversity, scholars will have a major role in moving sport management research and the literature from the margins to the mainstream: from the outside lane to the inside track. . . . [I]t is hoped that this chapter contributes in promoting the importance of sport management. . . .

FURTHER READING

Arnault, J.-L. (2006), Independent European sport review, European Union, available at: www.independent-footballreview.com/ (accessed 12 February 2007).

NOTE

1. For an accessible introduction to the socio-cultural and psychological foundations of sport, readers are directed to Barnes (2006) and Smith (2008).

REFERENCES

Barnes, S. (2006), *The Meaning of Sport*, London: Short Books.
Beech, J. (2004), Introduction: the commercialisation of sport, in Beech, J. and Chadwick, S. (eds), *The Business of Sport Management*, Harlow: Pearson Education.
Bleeke, J. and Ernst, D. (eds) (1993), *Collaborating to Compete*, New York: Wiley.
Cornwell, T.B., Pruitt, S.W. and van Ness, R. (2001), The value of winning in motorsports: sponsorship-linked marketing, *Journal of Advertising Research*, **41** (1), 17–32.
Downward, P. and Dawson, A. (2000), *The Economics of Professional Team Sports*, London: Routledge.
Fort, R.D. and Quirk, J. (1992), *Pay Dirt – The Business of Professional Team Sports*, Princeton, NJ: Princeton University Press.
Grether, D.M. (1978), Recent psychological studies of behavior under uncertainty, *Psychology and Economics*, **68** (2), 70–75.
Lewis, M. (2003), *Moneyball: The Art of Winning an Unfair Game*, New York: W.W. Norton.
Morgan, J.N. (1978), Multiple motives, group decisions, uncertainty, ignorance and confusion: a realistic economics of the consumer requires some psychology, *Psychology and Economics*, **68** (2), 58–63.
Neale, W.C. (1964), The peculiar economics of professional sports, *Quarterly Journal of Economics*, **78**, 1–14.
Smith, E. (2008), *What Sport Tells Us about Life: Bradman's Average, Zidane's Kiss and Other Sporting Lessons*, London: Viking.

Willoughby, K. and Mancini, K. (2003), The inaugural (and only) season of the Xtreme Football League: a case study in sports entertainment, *International Journal of Sport Marketing and Sponsorship*, **5** (3), 227–35.

Woolfe, R., Meenaghan, T. and O'Sullivan, P. (2002), The sports network: insights into the shifting balance of power, *Journal of Business Research*, **55** (7), 611–22.

28 The special features of sport: a critical revisit
Aaron C.T. Smith and Bob Stewart

1 INTRODUCTION

Sport has an ambiguous history when viewed from a management perspective. As Stewart and Smith (1999) noted, the management of sport has traditionally been divided between two contrasting philosophical approaches. At one extreme, sport is viewed as a unique cultural institution with a host of special features wherein the reflexive application of standard business practices not only produces poor management decision making, but also erodes its rich history, emotional connections, tribal links, and social relevance. At the other extreme, sport is seen to be nothing more than just another generic business enterprise subject to the usual government regulations, market pressures and customer demands, and is best managed by the application of standard business tools that assist the planning, finance, human resource management and marketing functions.

Over time these divisions have been blurred because of sport's corporatization, and through the emergence of sport management as an academic discipline. Sport is additionally complicated by the fact that it exists in both commercial and not-for-profit forms like other cultural services such as theatre, art, music, health care and education. On the other hand, it is also distinctive in the sense that despite its growing commercialization and corporatization, it ostensibly possesses many special features. This chapter will focus on these 'distinct and special features which make sport a unique institution' (Stewart and Smith, 1999, p. 87). In particular, it seeks to (1) critically review the features of sport considered special or unique, (2) consider whether these features are genuinely distinctive in the current environment, and (3) decide whether they are sufficiently distinctive to warrant a situational or customized approach to sport's management.

2 ARGUMENTS FOR DEMARCATING SPORT FROM BUSINESS

The special features of sport, its demarcation from business, and its implications for effective management are considered either explicitly or implicitly by most authors when writing about sport's social and cultural development. As Slack (2003) observed, an indicator of the strength of an academic discipline like the study of sport is the quantity and quality of the literature it wields. Sport's unique nature and context have been highlighted by Mangan and Nauright (2000), and developed in Hess and Stewart's (1998) book, *More than a Game*, as well as in their most recent analysis of Australian Rules football's commercial and cultural evolution, *A National Game* (Hess et al., 2008). The theme in these commentaries is that sport is a unique cultural institution that operates in a commercial environment. A decade earlier, Slack (1998) indicated that the management of sport was differentiated from general management due to a belief in the social value of sport, rather than on the exclusive basis of its economic value. Around the same time, Slack (1996) emphasized the importance of connecting contemporary management issues and theories to the management of sport by not only bolstering the credibility of sport management, but by also using sport as a testing ground for broader management theory development.

Foster et al. (2006) tackled the sport-as-a-unique institution issue by compiling a list of features professional sport and business have in common, and areas where they differ. They concluded that whereas sport and business share a common concern for value creation, branding, funding new sources of revenue, product innovation and market expansion, sport is significantly more concerned with beating rivals, winning trophies, sharing revenue, and channelling the passions of both players (the employees), and fans (the customers).

The other important point made by Foster et al. is that athletes are now business assets, who are instrumental in attracting fans, sponsors and media exposure. It therefore comes as no surprise that unlike business, a sport's service deliverers, the players, earn far more than their immediate supervisors, the club managers.

Similarly, Hoye et al. (2008) suggested that sport has a number of distinctive features, which they argue are most clearly played out in different ways across sports' three sectoral landscapes, the corporate, the not-for-profit, and the public. They contend that the unique attributes of sport organizations influence how theories, principles, and strategies are applied by sport managers. The unique attributes included 'consumer behavior, the relationship between sport and government, regulatory regimes, strategy, organisational structure, human resource management, organisational culture, governance, and performance management . . .' (p. 507). In other words, the management of sport invokes the same basic considerations as any other form of business management, but the specific application is subject to a range of contextual quirks that demand customised adjustments.

The idea that sport is not the same as the for-profit, commercial business sector was addressed in the 2000 Nice Declaration on Sport (European Council, 2000), when it introduced the term 'specificity of sport' in reference to sport's special characteristics. In doing so it made it clear that sport was not just a convenient or casual way of filling in leisure time, but was also an important cultural institution that delivered significant social benefits to a diverse spread of communities. The Declaration urged that the European Community should, despite an absence of direct power in the area, take account of the social, educational, and cultural function inherent in sport that makes it special. The more recent White Paper on Sport (Commission of the European Communities, 2007) confirmed sport's unique status when it announced that the specificity of European sport can be approached through two prisms, the first in the form of the specificity of sporting activities and rules including the provisions for preserving competitive balance and outcome uncertainty, and the second, the specificity of the sport structure, in the form of its pyramidal representation and peak authorities.

The specificity of sport has been recognized by the European Commission in numerous ways, the most notable being the Bosman case, which led to a 1995 European Court of Justice decision regarding the freedom of association of workers. The case had a profound influence on the player transfer system by removing the restrictions placed on player movements within the European Union, allowing them to move freely to other clubs at the end of their contractual terms. While the Bosman case exemplifies the specificity of sport, it does not lead to a general exemption from European Union law. It does, however, lead to some fluidity and grey area where some of the features of sport's organization are overlooked to the extent that they do not contravene European Union Competition Law and that any anti-competitive effects are legitimate in the context of sports' rules. As a result, sporting competitions in Europe enjoy relative freedom in determining the rules concerning the technical features of games, the composition of competitions, and the regulation of transfer periods. On the other hand, governing bodies of sport have less control over rules preventing multiple ownership of clubs in the same competition, the enforcement of anti-doping regulations, and cartel-like collusion.

The special features, or specificity, of sport have also been mired in a high degree of structural ambiguity, and a cursory review of different governance systems in sport around the world reveals that the push toward corporatization has delivered a range of substantially different business models. As Foreman (2003) observed, there are numerous facets of sport's organizational structure to consider that go well beyond its legal status. They include systems of governance, patterns of ownership, the mix of stakeholders, corporate partnerships, and sport's regulatory context (Hoye and Cuskelly, 2007). Even where the imperative of commercial success is at its most powerful in professional team sport, there is considerable diversity, ranging from the membership based clubs of Australia, New Zealand, South Africa and sub-continental Asia, to the listed public shares of European football clubs, and the privately owned franchises of the US 'big four' leagues (NFL, NBA, MLB, NHL). Foreman's suggestion that this suite of elements also affects the management practices undertaken is supported by Noll (2003), who argued that different governance and business models have a significant influence on management practice.

Of all the contextual forces observed to affect sporting structures and practices over the last decade, it has been the impact of commercialization that has received the greatest attention. Szymanski and Kuypers (1999) emphasized sport as an entertainment business capable of generating prodigious sums of money and imposing into the lives of billions of people across the globe. Accordingly, the problems of running a sporting business are much like those found in any other business. To Szymanski and Kuypers, clubs like any other commercial enterprise, must generate revenues by selling their product to the paying customers; they must engage in advertising, marketing and promotion, and they have to invest in facilities which enable them to distribute and sell their product in the right environment (Szymanski and Kuypers, 1999). Subsequent to Szymanski and Kuypers analysis of professional team sports in the UK, a raft of scholarly monographs appeared that dealt with the so-called peculiar economics and business arrangements of large scale sport with a focus on North American and European sport leagues. Three of them used the title 'The business of sport(s)' (Foster et al., 2006; Humphreys and Howard, 2008; Rosner and Shropshire, 2004), while others like Lewis' (2004) 'Moneyball', were designed to stun the reader with stories of rampant commercial excess, extravagant power, and shady deals. They all agreed that sport had an immense power to generate cash, and there seemed to be little to differentiate it from a casino, theatre or shopping mall. Add in the moral uncertainties associated with outsourcing the manufacture of sporting wear to developing nations and the deleterious effect that sport has on the environment, and you are left with what Thibault (2009) described as the 'inconvenient truth'.

If there is indeed a difference between sport business and other forms, then sport economists like Szymanski (2009), might argue that it is to be found in sport's idiosyncratic structures. Clubs, Szymanski observed, are the 'fundamental units of modern sport' (2009, p. 9), having emerged from civil societies under freedom of association. As a result, an organizational model of sport developed that was based on an alliance of independent clubs within associations and federations, and established largely on amateur, not-for-profit principles. However, variations of this model have also taken hold. At one extreme are those spectator sports that become vulnerable to commercial entertainment, and therefore become heavily modified by broadcasters and other commercial interests like sponsors. At the other extreme are sports restrained under the hand of political doctrine such as in communist states and centrally planned economies, or underpinned by strong cultural values advocating amateurism, with the United States collegiate sport system being a good example. For Szymanski (2009, p. 26), the commercial pressures are not only producing a class of highly paid sport entertainers, but are also challenging the viability of traditional sporting structures and the very 'soul' of sport.

Although the special features of sport appear in a variety of works associated with sport and its management, with Foster et al. (2006) being a good recent example, there have been only a few attempts to systematically address their importance and implications for good management practice. Hoye et al. (2008) recently reviewed what they described as the unique features of sport management, but their discussion was narrowly grounded in conventional aspects of management, like strategy and human resources. Hoye et al. argued that the best way to tackle sport management was to inject sport's idiosyncrasies with a healthy dose of business management practices. While this approach was useful, it did not have much to say about what it is that makes sport qualitatively different from other products and services. For this reason, the following critical analysis will examine whether it is plausible to maintain the argument that sport has many distinguishing special features. We contend that the claim for unique status has eroded substantially commensurate with sport's increasing corporatization and heterogeneity. In pursuing sport's special features, we observe some difficulty in defending any characteristics on the basis of their generalizability across all sport. As a result, we note the relative ease with which any putative special feature can be falsified by contrary examples. On the other hand, we are not comfortable with the claim that sport at the professional level is just another form of business, and that its so-called special features are nothing more than a reactionary attempt to preserve the myths that support, for example, the view that sport has to be regulated in a way that other businesses should not, in order to secure the best quality experience for fans and customers. Neither are we convinced that sport has no more social benefit than a visit to a cinema, an expedition to a local shopping complex, or a holiday in the West Indies. With these conflicting propositions in the back of our minds, we will proceed to examine the claims made about sport's idiosyncratic features, and see if they have indeed been washed away by the tide of corporatism and hard-nosed pragmatism.

3   A REVIEW OF SPORT'S SPECIAL FEATURES

A challenge of any analytical approach to assessing sport's special features lies in the selection of suitable organizing principles. In this instance, we have determined to shadow the features of sport articulated by Stewart and Smith (1999), with the intention of providing a critical review of their current status, and assessing their relevance to contemporary sport management practice.

In 1999, Stewart and Smith specified ten distinctive features of sport they claimed impact upon its management. For the purposes of this chapter, the ten features have been conflated to four interrelated dimensions. First, sport is a *heterogeneous and ephemeral experience* mired in the *irrational passions* of fans, commanding high levels of *product and brand loyalty, optimism* and *vicarious identification*. Second, sport favours on-field *winning over profit*. Third, sport is subject to *variable quality*, which in turn has implications for the management of *competitive balance* and *anti-competitive behaviour*. Fourth, sport has to manage *a fixed supply schedule*. Each of the four dimensions is reviewed next.

4   THE FUSION OF LOYALTY, IDENTIFICATION AND IRRATIONAL OPTIMISM

Stewart and Smith originally described this first set of features as four separate characteristics. They began their analysis by noting that professional sport is a highly intangible product where satisfaction comes from experiences that centre on watching others engage in various forms of structured physical activity. When looking at spectator sport they note that its core feature is its capacity to intimately engage fans and deliver intensely emotional and loyal attachments to their favourite teams and clubs. Underpinning loyalty is a powerful sense of identification, where fans experience belonging and vicarious emotions. Such strong identification with the sporting product produces a low cross elasticity of demand, which means that one form of sporting product cannot easily be replaced by another. This low degree of substitutability also means that a team can regularly under-perform, but still not sacrifice its fans to a better performing team. For Stewart and Smith, sport's ability to arouse strong passionate attachments, unstinting loyalty, vicarious identification, and blind optimism, makes it a special experience that markedly differentiates it from both consumer goods like plasma TV screens, motor vehicles, and cosmetics, and even the more service-based products like airline travel, cinema-watching and supermarket shopping (Pine and Gilmore, 1999).

But, is the distinction now as marked as Stewart and Smith declared ten years ago? On the one hand there is little doubt that sport elicits intense vicarious pleasure, lifelong personal attachments, and highly charged memories. The volume of empirical literature that supports this contention is vast, and a range of persuasive work in multiple cultural contexts has demonstrated sport's power to incite, arouse and connect (Giulianotti, 2002; Hardy, 1999; Hornby, 1995). It was even found that some sport consumers are passionate to the point of addiction (Queenan, 2003; Rein et al., 2006; Stewart et al., 2003).

On the other hand, the mechanisms of attachment are not unique to sport, and the psycho-emotional benefits of sport consumption are not particularly distinctive from those conferred through other patterns of consumption. While sport fan experiences meet a number of important psychological, social and cultural needs ranging from escapism, stimulation, and entertainment, to national pride, cultural celebration, and a sense of community and personal identity (Armstrong, 2002; Chen, 2007; Crawford, 2004;

Fink et al., 2002; Funk et al., 2001; Hinch and Higham, 2005; Milne and McDonald, 1999; Zhang et al., 2001), they are not peculiar to sport. Moreover, a number of contextual variables mitigate the psychological, social and cultural drivers of sport consumption, including demographic factors like age and gender, the expected quality of the game, and the venue in which it is played. As a result, such factors moderate individual fan motivation and the resulting degree of emotional attachment held by fans to teams and events. In a recent work, Smith and Stewart (2007) identified in excess of 30 different factors impacting upon fan behaviour, but they concluded that most of them are merely proxies for more fundamental needs, such as cultural connections, collective identity, entertainment and excitement. At the same time, these needs can be met by a range of consumption experiences that have little to do with sport. Shoppers who salivate over a $1000 Gucci handbag have much in common with sport consumers, since they too are prepared to pay good money to secure some vicarious identification and reflected status.

Neither are shoppers necessarily any less superficial, ephemeral or irrational than their sporting counterparts. Consider the fact that consumers seek variety in their use of hedonic, or pleasure-eliciting, products (Ratner et al., 1999). In addition, more options not only lead to positive consumer reactions because of the value placed on choice, but more options also makes it increasingly difficult for consumers to make up their minds, leaving them confused and indecisive. Kahneman (2000a, 2000b) explained this paradox in terms of an inability to predict future satisfaction. Consumers fail to choose optimally because they either fail to accurately predict which option will generate the best experience, or because they ignore their own predictive calculus. In short, the fewer the options the easier it is to work out which one is best (Hsee and Hastie, 2006). Consumers generally like to predict the consequences of their choices and then act on them, but as Heath and Tversky (1991) and Kahneman and Tversky (2000) have demonstrated, not only are consumers poor at predicting the consequences of their decisions, they are also poor at acting on them even if they are initially sound. As a result, people still eat to obesity, smoke cigarettes despite the health warnings, consume alcohol and binge-drink excessively, buy uncomfortable sports-cars, ride dangerous motorbikes, pay exorbitant prices for imported shoes and cosmetics, and watch reality television when they could quite easily do something real themselves.

It thus becomes clear that sport consumers use sport to meet their needs and extend their personal sense of self in the same ways that all consumers use discretionary leisure and luxury products to build self-esteem and confirm their identity (Ahuvia, 2005; Belk, 1988; Timothy, 2005). Sport consumers are no more irrationally optimistic than any other kind of consumers, and their exuberance, passion and pleasure-seeking behaviour is similar to the behaviours described in studies on the fashion industry, luxury goods, cigarettes, alcohol, hospitality and tourism (Belk et al., 2003; Ratneshwar and Mick, 2005). Sport consumption is not so much the exception as the exemplar of contemporary consumer behaviour.

In consequence, the key question is not so much a matter of what it is about sport that is unique in cultivating ardent consumers, but rather what mechanism is responsible for building powerful relationships between consumers and products. Many theorists believe that the answer is found in social identity theory (Tajfel, 1981,1982; Tajfel and Turner, 1986), which has been used to explain group and individual behaviours (Platow et al., 1999). Central to this theory is the concept of identification where sport consumers employ social categories to define others and locate themselves in the social world (Cornwell and Coote, 2003). Identification with a team, club or athlete may be a means of constructing or bolstering the self-concept (Ferrand and Pages, 1996; Jones, 2000; Wiley et al., 2000), and can be motivated by factors including the need to maintain and enhance positive personal and social self evaluations, the need to belong, and a sense of self-efficacy through vicarious achievement (Fink et al., 2002; Hughson, 1999; Morris, 1981; Platow et al., 1999; Wann, 1995; Wann and Branscombe, 1993). A critical conclusion is that emotional attachment is more strongly implicated when an individual is motivated to construct a sense of self through identification (Fink et al., 2002). Although sport commands identification through heightened emotional attachment, so too do other consumption-based behaviours. While indigenous to sport, emotionally charged identification is not exclusive to sport, and it would therefore be misleading to conclude that this constitutes a special feature.

Comparisons between conventional consumers and sport consumers are also complicated by the tendency of researchers to study extreme forms of sport fandom. While 'die-hard' and passionate fans are obviously an appealing cohort to examine, the elucidation of their motivations and behaviours provides an imbalanced picture of sport consumption. Like all consumption, sport is subject to a 'bewildering array of values, attitudes and behaviors' (Stewart et al., 2003, p. 206). Sport consumers are not all passionate and fanatical, and nor do they all live vicariously through their favourite team or player in order to bolster their personal identities. Equally, their loyalty can be variable, their attendance irregular, and their interest erratic (Stewart et al., 2003).

5   THE TENSION BETWEEN WINNING AND PROFIT-MAKING

The passions associated with sport fandom, according to Stewart and Smith (1999), not only produce blind and unswerving loyalty, but can at times also override commercial imperatives. That is, consumers and clubs will, for the most part, weight wins and trophies more highly than a healthy balance sheet. On the other hand, they also asserted that commercial pressures can instigate the demise of longstanding traditions if they are thwarting future success. At the same time, they argued that fans who value tradition will often use it to resist club attempts to commercialize the management process. While Stewart and Smith considered these tensions between performance and tradition, and profits and winning, to be indicative of a special feature, their analysis did not fully explain the nuances of on- and off-field performance, and the variance between different sporting competitions and leagues.

Separating the rhetoric and bright-lights of professional sport from its prosaic position as just another product in the entertainment marketplace is a challenging managerial exercise. The difficulty in grasping the common threads running through sport is compounded by the fact that while professional sport is a form of business, most volunteer-driven participation sport is not. The complexities of sport management are exaggerated by the vast chasm that divides the pay-per-view world of corporatized global-sport-entertainment from the parochial, kitchen-table world of preparing for a Saturday afternoon match at the local sports ground. Moreover, the global, revenue-maximization orientation of some professional sports (Chadwick and Arthur, 2007) such as Formula-1 motor racing and boxing, can be contrasted with other teams and clubs in professional sports, that while enveloped by profit-seeking owners, do not overtly pursue profit, but rather sacrifice an operating surplus to secure an on-field advantage. The extravagance of European professional football salaries is a case in point, and in general, participants in professional sport will use whatever marketing and management tactics are required to achieve success. While proper funding is as important for sport organizations as it is for other commercial enterprises, financial resources are most often deployed towards competitive success rather than returned to shareholders in the form of dividends. In the United States there are still no definitive conclusions about whether teams are profit-maximizers where the balance sheet rules, or utility maximizers where a high win–loss ratio is the true measure of superior performance (Fort and Quirk, 2004). In the end, according to Zimbalist (2003a), it is difficult to distinguish profit-maximizing behaviour from any other organizational practice. As Szymanski and Kuypers (1999, p. 7) commented about the imperative sport organizations share, 'Above all they have to pay wages to players and invest in the development of talent in order to achieve winning performances, perhaps for their own sake, but also to keep the public interested in the club and willing to pay for its product.' In other words, success is a function of a strong stream of revenue.

6   TRANSFORMING THE SPORT-FIELD INTO A WORKPLACE

On balance, the dichotomy between winning and profitability, as well as performance and tradition, has been eroded with sport's commercial expansion. As Stewart and Smith (1999) somewhat tritely observed about the transformation of sport into sport business, 'The subsequent focus on rationalisation and productivity has forced sport managers to translate their human and material resources, particularly players, into economic equations in which the division of labour, efficiency, regulation, rational work practices and management control become crucial management issues' (p. 88). In fact, this focus on improving the efficiency of human capital has become endemic to all elite sport. In Olympic sports like track and field and swimming, nationally determined macro variables such as demographics and elite development pathways play a significant role in improving performance in international sport events (Digel, 2002). In fact, Oakley and Green's (2001) analyses revealed that close to a decade ago national elite sport development systems around the world were starting to look more homogenous as a result of adopting business models to manage their sporting enterprises. In their analysis of the changes in professional sport between 1970 and 1997, Cousens and Slack (2005) similarly found that sport's structures had converged commensurate with the drive for higher levels of performance.

Despite the managerial drive in sport for more revenue and improved efficiency, many sport fans still argue for the prioritization of on-field success, and the celebration of competitive ideals which privileges it above conventional profit-seeking endeavours. And, for the critics of contemporary sport, the increasing focus on financial imperatives has eroded the inherent value of sport and its social utility. As Stewart and Smith (1999) cautioned, some fans have been marginalized by the corporatization of sport's management practices, with such warnings having been prominent for a decade (King, 1998;

Nash, 1997). In a similar critical vein, Milton-Smith (2002) lamented that there has been a failure of major sporting global institutions in dealing with the consequences of globalization: 'Disillusionment with the Olympic Games mirrors the disenchantment with the perceived values of globalisation, including winning at any price, commercial exploitation by MNCs, intense national rivalry, cronyism, cheating and corruption and the competitive advantage of advanced nations' (Milton-Smith, 2002, p. 131). Gems (1999) also warned that professional sport had canalized meaning for its consumers through an American 'ideological imperialism' that emphasizes the homogeneity and commodification of the sport product, however culturally precious. Belk (1996) and Ritzer (1998) also predicted that sport business would take a McDonald's approach, emphasizing standardized products punctuated by the 'hyper-reality' of over-zealous marketing. From an economic perspective, Ross and Szymanski (2006) suggested – perhaps wryly – that a McDonald's structural franchise system presented an illustrative model challenging the conventional wisdom that sport leagues should be organized and operated by stakeholding clubs. Sport McDonald's is more like NASCAR, which is an entity independent of the competing teams and drivers, and can therefore impose broadcasting, marketing and other commercial arrangements in the best interests of consumers without the competing and inefficient agendas of individual owners.

On the other hand, Rein et al. (2006) would probably approve of NASCAR's positioning, since they emphasized the need for constant adaptation in order for sports to remain competitive in a cutthroat and competitive marketplace. To achieve this they favour a strategic approach that features segmentation through fan identity leading to brand-building. Noteworthy in their modelling of the sport industry is the presence of seven characteristics of the marketplace: (1) a pressurized competitive environment; (2) higher fan expectations; (3) the paradox of commercialism; (4) new technology; (5) individualism; (6) changes in family structure and behaviour; and (7) time pressure.

7   THE DILEMMA OF CORPORATE SPORT

Of most interest to our analysis of sport's special features is the paradox of commercialism. To Rein et al. (2006), although their strategic marketing advice is geared towards bolstering the commercial success of sport brands, they acknowledge a tension between sport as a business and sport as a game-centred and social institution. In this uneasy balance, sports are faced with the challenge of extracting commercial value from their brands without compromising the intrinsic 'integrity' and spirit of the game. Fuelled by a celebrity ethos and the centrality of entertainment, it is easy to undermine the brand and diminish its status as a heroic form of human endeavour. As a consequence, sport's quintessential nature is at risk whenever it commercializes itself to secure a larger share of the market. However, it also means that unless sport commercializes itself, it will be unable to survive in the contemporary competitive landscape. This commercial paradox, which Stewart and Smith addressed only fleetingly, constitutes a genuine special feature of professional sport.

The appeal of this paradox is amplified when taken in tandem with the Rein et al. (2006) assessment of sport's twin advantages. The first advantage is its attractiveness as a live product-experience capable of commanding significant advertising and broadcasting interests, while the second advantage is the increasing ability for sport brands to become their own content providers and media distributors. However, these emerging features of sport are not without their problems. The live product, which means the at-game-experience, is the beating heart of sport, but is offset by its potential to become a tacky vehicle for selling other, often banal products. In addition, the vertical integration of the sport and its distribution offers great scope for control of the product but risks the introduction of vertical restraints that could lead to anti-competitive behaviour. Moreover, when the lines blur between the contest, its participants and its distribution, there is also the potential for a serious loss of emotional attachment of fans to teams, and a fall-off in fan interest.

Despite the dire pronouncements linked to sport's rampant commercialization, fears that traditional and so-called authentic fans will abandon professional sport have proved to be unfounded. The evidence indicates that professional sport enjoys a greater following than ever before (Westerbeek and Smith, 2003), and this is precisely because sport managers have wielded commercial business practices to bolster the watching and viewing experiences of fans.

In fact, professional sport has effectively ridden on the back of international broadcasting and new media into the twenty-first century, and in doing so has strengthened its position in the entertainment marketplace (Smith and Westerbeek, 2004; Wenner, 1998; Wright, 1999). If consumers of sport are somehow more traditionalist or ideologically pure than other kinds of consumers, it has not translated into diminished ratings for 'McSport'. While some fans have bemoaned the loss of traditional values and practices, far more fans want comfortable seating, easily available merchandise, game statistics at their fingertips, replays and expert commentary, interactive technology, and a steady supply of nachos, hot-dogs and Coke. Sport has been transformed into a fast-moving consumable experience that fits neatly into the 'iPod society', and as a result has gone well beyond being a symbol of a pleasant Saturday afternoon at the neighbourhood sports ground.

This transformation has also cut through the tension between the need to make a profit and the desire to achieve on-field success. In the contemporary sports world it is now acknowledged that winning is most likely to come from having both a large revenue stream and a surplus of income over expenditure (Foster et al., 2006; Gerrard, 2005; Szymanski and Kuypers, 1999). In other words, the wealthiest sport organizations, which include teams sent to the Olympic Games as well as sport clubs, associations, and leagues, are generally speaking also the best on-field performers.

8 THE NEED TO BALANCE VARIABLE QUALITY AGAINST COMPETITIVE BALANCE

Another pervasive claim about the sport product is that its quality is variable, and its levels of performance are unpredictable. Stewart and Smith (1999) argued that this phenomena is not only troublesome, but also an unavoidable feature of professional sport. Try as they might to perform consistently at the highest level, the same athletes and players will not always win, and even Tiger Woods, the greatest golfer in the history of the game, has off-days when his name fails to appear on the leader board. The news is not all bad, however, because, unlike other parts of the service and entertainment indus-try, inconsistency and uncertainty become important product features for sport. Stewart and Smith declared that sport is one of the few products that actually depend upon unpredictability for success, and the result is another paradoxical relationship. In this case, whereas clubs, teams and players aspire to win by the largest margin possible, the popularity of sport leagues rely on high levels of competitive balance in order to ensure close and exciting contests.

Of all the special features of sport identified by Stewart and Smith, the issue of quality is the most vexing, since it is so multi-dimensional and subjective. At the outset, it has to be conceded that winning does not always equate to quality in the eyes of many sport consumers, who will rank sport's aesthetic appeal, excitement, atmosphere, social inter-action, and camaraderie more highly (Fink et al., 2002; Zhang et al., 2001). However, unlike other competing entertainment products with similar commercial realities, like theatrical performances, musical groups, and artistic creations, where so much time is spent rehearsing in order to guarantee consistent and reliable service delivery, sport actually puts resources into ensuring an unpredictable result. Again, unlike professional wrestling, where every move and incident is choreographed, and every result is acutely stage-managed, competitive sport relies on unscripted and uncertain outcomes to build tension, excite the fans, and consequently deliver a quality consumer experience.

While one-sided contests and long-term on-field domination by a few clubs can lead to declining attendance and shrinking television audiences, the jury is still out on the precise role of competitive parity. The evidence about the relative importance of outcome uncertainty remains ambiguous (Borland and Macdonald, 2003; Szymanski, 2003), even though it is used as a key indicator of a quality sport experience.

To compensate for the variable quality of the core, on-field sport product, sport organizations also offer a range of supplementary products and services like merchan-dise and hospitality that can be more easily controlled for quality. Since these augmented products are important for cross-subsidizing the core on-field activities of sport organi-zations, they have to be handled with a careful awareness of customer satisfaction and service quality. Consistency and ongoing performance improvement for auxiliary serv-ices are even more important to sport organizations than they are to other organizations because of the dramatic fall in quality that can come from poor weather, an overwhelm-ingly one-sided contest, injury to star players, and a half-empty stadium devoid of any atmosphere.

Although the conventional wisdom says there is too little competitive balance in most sport leagues as evidenced by the tendency of the same clubs and teams to dominate, it has also been suggested that from an attendance and revenue-maximization viewpoint, the strongest and most popular clubs do not win enough (Szymanski, 2006). However, this remains true only until such point as the strong become too dominant and the assumption amongst consumers becomes that the strong never lose.

Despite the evidence that strong teams attract big crowds even where the result is not seen to be in doubt, sports leagues continue to allocate significant resources to the con-struction of regulatory mechanisms aimed at maintaining competitive parity and ensuring outcome uncertainty. While these regulations are for the most part effective, they intro-duce a further special, but complicating feature in the form of anti-competitive behav-iour. As Stewart and Smith (1999) and Stewart et al. (2005) argued, most professional sport leagues operate as cartels. That is, a collective of firms which through collusion act as a single supplier to a market; a point re-enforced by Downward and Dawson (2000), Sandy et al. (2004), Dabscheck (2007), Macdonald and Booth (2007) and Stewart and Dickson (2007). Sport leagues gravitate toward cartel-like behaviour because they rely on the cooperation of teams and collective agreements on areas like salary ceilings, player recruitment and drafting, admission pricing, game scheduling, income-redistributions, and broadcasting arrangements to maintain an equitable competition and to maximize marketing and licensing opportunities (Davenport, 1969; Demmert, 1973; Gratton and Taylor, 1986; Schofield, 1982; Stewart et al., 2005; Szymanski and Kuypers, 1999). Teams and clubs depend on the continued on- and off-field success of their opponents, but in most industries, organizations are not permitted to cooperate in this way as it is considered anti-competitive behaviour and is typically prohibited by law. This produces a third paradox, or conundrum for sport. Clubs must compete in a hostile environment against numerous, aggressive rivals while at the same time cooperate with these rivals to the degree necessary to benefit the entire group (Szymanski and Kuypers, 1999).

The incentive to operate as a cartel is therefore powerful in sport, since restraining the desire of a few clubs and teams to dominate a league or competition can actually increase revenue and profits for all members of the league or competition. Professional sport has used forms of anti-competitive behaviour to amplify its commercial impact, protect its brands, and increase revenues through collective marketing efforts. Anti-competitive behaviour is a distinctive feature of contemporary professional sport (Noll, 2002). And, like other industrial clusters that manage to create cartel-like structures, such as the Organization of the Petroleum Exporting Countries (OPEC), it presents both opportunities and challenges for its management.

9   THE CRUCIAL IMPORTANCE OF SETTING UP STRUCTURES FOR COLLABORATIVE BEHAVIOUR

Morgan (2002) observed that key stakeholders in sport, such as spectators, club officials, the organizing body, clubs, and broadcasters, rarely have congruent interests. The corollary is an ongoing disagreement about the best way to structure, govern and regulate a sporting competition, as well as arguments over the management of teams, the movement of players and the distribution of revenues. While broadcasters favour interventions that maximize viewer interest club officials seek resources to bolster their team's talent pools, and organizing bodies want to maintain strict custodianship of the game. The complexities of collaborative behaviour are compounded when different political systems are used to frame the structure and operation of professional sport leagues. In Barros et al. (2002), there is a detailed exploration of the dichotomy between what is described as the North American profit-maximizing model and the European 'utility maximizing' model. There is also a discussion of the ways in which North American and European anti-trust legislation delimits the potential for what economists like Szymanski and Ross refer to as horizontal and vertical restraints. Horizontal restraints exist between competing firms supplying rival products to suppliers, while vertical restraints exist between firms that each play a role in the delivery of a particular product in the market (Szymanski and Ross, 2007). In sport the primary focus is on horizontal restraints, particularly cartel-like behaviour where anti-competitive collusion may allow clubs to limit competition or fix prices at the expense of the consumer. However, Szymanski and Ross (2007) point out that vertical restraints are also potentially anti-competitive where member clubs of a league control its organization and the movement of players. The issue lies in the distinction between a contest organizer and a contest participant. A blurring of the two is not only ambiguous in terms of the interests of consumers, but may also be economically inefficient (Szymanski, 2003) For example, a governance system independent of the league or competition's participants can have significant implications on the deployment of revenue. In the cases of Union of European Football Associations (UEFA), the governing body of European soccer, and the Australian Football League (AFL), the governing body for Australia's indigenous football code, some resources are diverted into developmental activities for the long-term benefit of the sports; financial decisions which would not be sanctioned by owner clubs.

The differences between the North American and European governance models are also highlighted in their league structures. Whereas the North American leagues are closed systems where the same teams participate no matter what their league standing in the previous year, the European governance model extols the benefits of a promotion and relegation system. It can bolster interest in championship standings at the top and bottom of the competitive ladder, provide the opportunity for numerous teams from a single city to compete for a place in the highest league, and remove incentives for team relocation given that it is less expensive to buy more talent in order to win promotion (Noll, 2002; Zimbalist, 2003b). Professional sport has been forced to grapple with a range of challenges over the last decade, with Compton and Howard (2002) noting that both North American and European sport have had to regularly confront rising player salaries, vastly different levels of operating revenue between teams, fierce sponsorship rivalry, and heavy-handed broadcasters.

10   USING TECHNOLOGY TO MANAGE SUPPLY

According to Stewart and Smith (1999), sporting clubs and competitions are traditionally restricted to what economists would call fixed short-run supply, or a highly inelastic production curve. The supply of the core sport product – for example the on-field performance – cannot be increased in the same way that a manufactured good like a motor car, or a generic service like dental work can. Only a certain number of games can be played during a season, and irrespective of the spectator demand, attendance is always limited by the number of games scheduled and the seating capacity of the venue. Conversely, when there is limited demand, unsold seats represent revenue lost forever. In these instances the sport product cannot be stored and re-sold another day.

Stewart and Smith (1999) went on to claim that professional sport is in the vanguard of technological development as a means of increasing product supply. Subsequent developments have largely born this claim out, although it would be more accurate to say that professional sport became a notable vehicle for the commercial utilization of new technology without being a special case. There are now a myriad of mechanisms for reproducing, repackaging and reselling sport, as there are for other information and entertainment services. They include World Wide Web platforms, such as blogs and social networking sites, email, web video, podcasts, vodcasts, websites, pop-ups, spam, virtual worlds, wikis, electronic commerce (such online and mobile payments), MySpace and Facebook. Add to these mobile communications technologies like Bluetooth, mobile phones, personal digital assistants, wireless, SMS (short message service), MMS (multi-media messaging service), 4G mobile/cellular phones and handheld gaming devices, all of which are free from the restrictions of traditional land-based connections and offer new distribution channels. They offer fans an additional forum by which to experience, and indeed, re-experience their favourite sport event, but they do nothing to differenti-ate sport from a whole array of service-based products that are equally as effective in providing content through repackaging and re-presenting. The handset presence of sport provides a convenient and novel experience for sport fans, but does nothing to give sport its own special or unique positioning.

11 MANAGING THE FISHBOWL EXPERIENCE OF PLAYERS

Players and athletes are at the heart of professional sport, and they are a fundamental reason why fans pay good money to attend games and events. The history of sport dem-onstrates that sporting heroes, particularly when they perform at the very highest level, will attract enormous crowds who come just to watch them perform. Examples include Babe Ruth in American Major League Baseball, Stanley Matthews in English soccer, Donald Bradman in Australian and international cricket, Pele in Brazilian and interna-tional soccer, and Michael Jordon in American basketball (Cashman, 1984; Goldblatt, 2006; La Feber, 1999).

There are many equivalent examples in contemporary sport, including Tiger Woods in international golf, and David Beckham in world soccer. With the growing profession-alization of sport at the local level around the world, there is now considerable interest in players in all sports of inter-city and provincial leagues. Even in these local competi-tions there is an insatiable media interest in not only what players do on the field, but also what they do off the field. In becoming the centre of media attention they have also become local celebrities, and every misdemeanour, and ever so slightly social deviant behaviour is allocated front page headlines (Hess et al., 2008).

This development means that players live a fishbowl existence where their behaviour is scrutinized on a daily basis. Moreover, clubs, teams and leagues have become increas-ingly sensitive to any negative publicity that arises from player misbehaviour, and have put in place a raft of rules and codes of conduct that provide sanctions for players in contravention. Sport organizations have hired lawyers, counsellors, agents and psy-chologists to assist players in managing their behaviour, and when players go outside of the narrowly proscribed limits, a team of experts and specialists is invariably there to guide them through the maze of media scrutiny and commentary that inevitably follows. The pressures on players to behave appropriately, and not to make fools of themselves or undermine the reputation of their clubs are more onerous than in nearly any other occu-pation. Whereas music, film and television celebrities are almost expected to flaunt illicit drug use, sexual impropriety and financial extravagance, sports stars are expected to be exemplary citizens and solid role models for impressionable children. The media scrutiny becomes breathtakingly intense when sexual assaults or drug use is involved. In respect of drug use, one of the most discussed cases involved Ben Cousins, an elite Australian Rules footballer who played for the Perth West-Coast Eagles in the Australian Football League. In 2007, he admitted he had taken numerous illicit drugs during his football career, and was barred from the game after admitting he was a drug addict (Stewart et al., 2008).

But it is not just the media spotlight which has applied pressure on athletes to conform to behavioural guidelines. Sport organizations have begun to introduce conduct-related clauses in player contracts, which are also appearing in an increasing number of collective bargaining agreements (Dabscheck and Opie, 2003). Nowhere are assumptions about sport's fishbowl more obvious than in the World Anti-Doping Agency's (WADA) rise to power, and the control they aim to exert over the lives of players and athletes. The prevailing policy approach to substance use in sport rests on the proposition that punitive sanctioning will deter drug use and remove 'drug cheats' from competition. This policy position is driven by WADA, supported by the International Olympic Committee and the United Nations Educational, Scientific and Cultural Organization, and followed by national and international sporting bodies all over the world. Current global drug management policy aims to regulate drug use by (1) specifying a list of prohibited drugs, being careful to distinguish between those drugs that demonstrably improve on-field performance, and those drugs that are illicit and undermine the health and well-being of players and athletes as well as tarnishing the reputation of sport itself, (2) listing a raft of suspensions and fines for players and athletes who have been found to have used, possessed, supplied or trafficked any banned substances, and (3) providing for a tribunal-style process whereby allegations are heard, judgements made, and penalties imposed where appropriate.

Stewart and Smith (1999) were silent on the 'fishbowl' experience of players, and the omission represents a substantive gap in their list of sport's special features. The experiences of players have now not only become the one constant in the weekly reporting cycle of professional and elite level sport by the media, but also fall under the watchful eye of anti-violence campaigners, equal opportunity proponents, anti-discrimination officials, gender equity activists, doping agency officers, and drug investigators.

12   MANAGING PLAYERS AS INCOME EARNING ASSETS

Another feature of contemporary sport that Stewart and Smith (1999) failed to adequately grasp was the massive increase in player salaries and recruiting costs, and how they impact on the management process in professional sport. Clubs are now confronted by the issue of how to not only deal with players who earn more than the club's chief executive officer and senior management team, but also how transfer fees should be dealt with. In these instances players are increasingly counted as assets, and indeed given a value in the same way that an item of machinery or office equipment is listed as an asset and allocated a value.

In theory, an increased payroll for a team should have a causal impact on competitive success. That is, it should pay to pay, at least in terms of on-field performance. However, the economic modelling of Hall et al. (2002) revealed an unimpressive correlation between team performance and payroll in US Major League Baseball and for English

Football between 1980 and 2000, although it was seen to be increasing since the mid-1990s. For European football on the other hand, Forrest and Simmons (2004) concluded that relative spending on team payroll is a good predictor of team league standings.

The player-as-asset issue arises especially in professional sport leagues where teams are able to trade players through a transfer market. In English Premier League football, where large transfer fees are standard, this issue is dealt with by listing the transfer fee as an asset, and amortizing the fee over the contract life of the player. Take for instance former Manchester United Football Club player Cristiano Ronaldo, who transferred from Porto, in Portugal in 2003. His transfer fee was just under GBP 12 million, and he signed with Manchester United for five years. Using the straight-line method of depreciation his fee was amortized at around GBP 2.4 million a year, and charged as an expense against revenue for each of the five years of his contract. After two years he was valued at around GBP 7.2 million (i.e. 12 less 4.8). At the end of his five-year contract his value would technically be zero. However, in practice his value and his potential transfer price is likely to be positive, unless he was cut down by injury. In fact as a result of his impressive on-field performances, his real 2009 value and transfer fee were significantly higher than his 2003 purchase price. In fact, Ronaldo moved to Real Madrid in 2009 at a record GBP 80 million transfer.

The bonus here is that unlike other assets that lose value over time and are depreciated, many players will in fact have increased in value. However, in some countries, and in those sports where there is no transfer market, the balance sheet will show players as having zero value at the end of their contract. Under these conditions clubs' assets will be seriously undervalued, and this peculiar feature constitutes another management issue to be dealt with.

Stewart and Smith (1999) said little about this issue, and it now constitutes a problematic oversight from their analysis. Treating players as assets means that like any other part of the club's capital stock, they need to be fully maintained and given maximum support to ensure their optimal performance. The implication is that players have enormous bargaining power, but players can also be treated like cattle and traded at the whim of coaches, managers, and team owners, not to mention the unobserved but not-so-subtle influence of sponsors and broadcasters.

13 THE CONFOUNDING INFLUENCE OF LEAGUE STRUCTURES

The fact that many of the above so-called special features are not exclusive to sport is additionally complicated by the growing disparity of sporting organizations and structures. There are four major trans-national models for the governance of sport at the highest level (Morgan, 2002). First, there is the traditional national governing body pyramidical *hierarchy* exemplified by traditional European sports like swimming, badminton and collegiate sport in the United States. Second, there is the distinctive North American *cartel* structure operating in its 'Big Four' national leagues. Third, there is the *oligarchy* model illustrated in English Premiership football. Finally, there is the *promoter-led* structure found in boxing. While these broad classifications can illuminate the presence of common special features, they are also becoming increasingly blurred and fragmented as a consequence of sport's commercial and competitive pressures. For example, NASCAR functions somewhere between a monopoly and a promoter-led licensed franchise. Tennis and golf are strictly committed to an international, hierarchical model but the power and money resides with its tournaments, which are owned and operated by nationally sanctioned venues. Cricket and rugby are also organized within an international and national hierarchical framework, but have been vulnerable to the forays of new commercial ventures like Super-league rugby and the Indian Premier League.

These four governance structures make for differing management outcomes, but there is little evidence that they fundamentally change the fan experience. They all view sport as a contest where highly skilled teams of relatively equal strengths will produce the highest quality outcomes. And, where these performance differences are inappropriately wide, they will for the most part act to create greater levels of parity. The common managerial assumption is that sport is at its best when there is collaborative intervention to ensure a quality experience for fans.

14   CONCLUDING COMMENTS

Over the last 10 to 20 years professional sport has been interrogated from various perspectives, with sociologists, historians, lawyers and management theorists leading the charge. On balance they found that sport is both commercially special and culturally unique. Our review of these special and unique features indicates that (1) the distinctiveness of some of them have been overstated, (2) a number of new and novel features have emerged, while (3) other features have been eroded in line with sport's relentless corporatization. While it is inappropriate to conclude that the features discussed above demand a specialized form of management practice, our analysis suggests that sport leagues and competitions still have many idiosyncrasies that demand considered and strategic responses.

In the first place, sport is still characterized by fierce, loyal and passionate fans who experience a strong, vicarious identification with their favourite players and teams. It remains one of the few products that delivers engaging experiences that become part of our collective memory. However, even the most strident sport fans are also motivated by other benefits of the sport product, including aesthetic appeal, entertainment, and social interaction. As a result, the needs of sport fans are similar to those sought by consumers for a range of other discretionary leisure products like the cinema, the art gallery and the theatre.

In addition, some of the distinctive features of sport have been eroded as a consequence of the pressures for homogenization arising from commercial development, global expansion and cultural marginalization. Traditionally, the major difference between business and sport was the importance of profit and return-on-investment for business, and the preference for winning and on-field success for sport. While it is clear that winning is sovereign in professional sport, there is a growing recognition that revenue and profits, and the resources that money attracts, are the keys to successful performance. Moreover, the evidence suggests that winning is also the fastest route to profitability. This means that it is no longer a case of either or, but of both aims being met through an interdependent managerial strategy that builds a strong platform of quality resources from which to launch a high win–loss ratio.

While the corporatization of sport over recent years may have resolved the dilemma of how to balance profits against performance, no such solution has been secured for the issue of quality in sport. The ambiguous nature of sport product quality is exemplified in the ways in which different stakeholders approach it. For example, many club officials and die-hard fans view quality primarily in terms of consistent winning, whereas regulators and the run-of-the-mill sports follower are more likely to perceive quality in terms of competitive balance and outcome uncertainty. Added to this ambiguity is the complicating fact that the core sport product is now surrounded by services and merchandise that are used to provide a more consistent and multi-faceted sport experience.

The capacity of sport to adjust supply by broadening the delivery platform is an important strategic development, but it is not unique to sport, and is now commonplace with a whole range of information and entertainment experiences. On the other hand, the corporatization of sport has brought players to centre stage, both on and off the field. As a result their fishbowl existence and integral contribution to the commercial progress and asset growth of clubs and associations is something that sets sport apart from more prosaic businesses and industries.

Finally, professional sport is embedded in a fundamental structural and operational paradox which complicates its management at every strategic turn. It arises out of the fact that sport's commercial progress and subsequent corporatization is a two-edged sword. While on one hand it allows sport to tap into new markets by changing its shape and features, on the other hand it fractures all those traditions that made it attractive to fans in the first place.

Overall, the evidence suggests that the special features of sport identified by Stewart and Smith in the late 1990s are now less distinctive. Many of the eclectic features associated with any given sport structure or system may be novel, complex, and even contradictory, but they are no more so than the services delivered by the arts (Cray and Inglis, 2008) or the hospital and health management sectors (Somers and Perry, 2008). When added to the changes that have taken place to sport over recent years, the special features of sport are in need of wholesale revision.

While professional sport is still both similar to and different from so-called conventional business, their key features and contextual weightings have changed. Both business and sport are concerned with widening their market share, building profits, and strengthening the brand. At the same time, the view that sport has a monopoly over the delivery of passion, loyalty and strong identification is difficult to defend. There are now only four features that clearly distinguish sport from business, instead of the ten that Stewart and Smith had initially marked-out. First, sport performance is fundamentally unstable, and as a result is in constant need of hands-on management in order to engineer a level playing field, and guarantee a minimum level of quality. Second, sport can get away with a number of anti-competitive practices that would normally put the CEOs of business enterprises in jail. Third, sport players and athletes are put under a level of scrutiny and held up to standards that would not be tolerated in other spheres of commercial endeavour. Finally, the constant rating of players, their perception as income earning assets, and the tight constraints that are placed on their behaviour and movement between clubs would rarely take place in any other business enterprise or industry. So, in short, while professional sport has undergone significant structural and operational change over the last ten years, it still has enough idiosyncratic features to justify a customized set of management practices.

At one extreme, even at its most hard-core professional level, sport has been re-badged and re-organized as a not-for-profit cultural practice that delivers a range of memorable experiences and social benefits that the commercial for-profit sector under-supplies. At the other extreme it is built around a set of market-driven forces that make it just another product situated in a competitive marketplace delivering just another package of ephemeral, banal and for the most part, forgettable, experiences to its customers At the same time, and under both of these extreme structural circumstances there are still a number of idiosyncratic features that give sport its special character, and that reveal themselves in both the profit and nonprofit sector as well as in its different forms of governance, be it pyramidal/hierarchical, cartel-based, an oligarchy, or promoter-led.

In summary, despite the changing face of sport over the last ten years, and despite the severe, indeed sometimes fundamental weaknesses contained in the Stewart and Smith (1999) model of sport's special features, some of their broad conclusions are worth revisiting. Although the details of their 1999 analysis are, for the most part, outdated, there are three general points that are difficult to refute. First, '. . . a failure to recognise sport as a business will produce poor performance, and second, management strategies that "gives no recognition to its special features"' (p.97), will fail to deliver optimal outcomes. So too does their pronouncement that '. . . it is precisely these special features which demand the application of sophisticated and 'professional' business principles' (p.98).

REFERENCES

Ahuvia, A.C. (2005), Beyond the extended self: loved objects and consumer's identity narratives, *Journal of Consumer Research*, **32** (1), 171–84.

Armstrong, K.L. (2002), Race and sport consumption motivations: a preliminary investigation of a black consumers' sport motivation scale, *Journal of Sport Behavior*, **25** (4), 309–30.

Barros, C., Ibrahimo, M. and Szymanski, S. (eds) (2002), *Transatlantic Sport: The Comparative Economics of North American and European Sports*, Cheltenham, UK and Northampton, MA, USA: Edward Elgar.

Belk, R. (1996), Hyperreality and globalization: culture in the age of Ronald McDonald, *Journal of International Consumer Marketing*, **8** (3–4), 23–37.

Belk, R.K. (1988), Possessions and the extended self, *Journal of Consumer Research*, **15** (2), 139–68.

Belk, R., Ger. G. and Askegaard, S. (2003), The fire of desire: a multisited inquiry into consumer passion, *Journal of Consumer Research*, **30** (3), 326–51.

Borland, J. and Macdonald, R. (2003), Demand for sport, *Oxford Review of Economic Policy*, **19**, 478–502.

Cashman, R. (1984), *Ave a go yer mug! Australian cricket crowds from larrikan to ocker*, Sydney: Collins.

Chadwick, S. and Arthur, D. (eds) (2007), *International Cases in the Business of Sport*, Oxford: Elsevier.

Chen, P. (2007), Sport tourists loyalty: a conceptual model, *Journal of Sport and Tourism*, **11** (3–4), 1–37.

Commission of the European Communities (2007), *White Paper on Sport*, Brussels.

Compton, J. and Howard, D. (2002), The growth and financial status of professional sports in North America: insights for English soccer leagues?, *Managing Leisure*, **7** (3), 145–63.

Cornwell, B. and Coote, L. (2003), Corporate sponsorship of a cause: the role of identification in purchase intent, *Journal of Business Research*, **58**, 268–76.

Cousens, L. and Slack, T. (2005), Field-level change: the case of North American major league professional sport, *Journal of Sport Management*, **19** (1), 13–42.

Crawford, G. (2004), *Consuming Sport: Fans Sport and Culture*, London: Routledge.

Cray, D. and Inglis, L. (2008), Issues of managing nonprofit arts organizations in the 21st Century, in C. Wankle (ed.), *Sage Handbook of 21st Century Management*, Los Angeles: Sage, pp.482–90.

Dabscheck, B. (2007), Moving beyond ethnicity: soccer's evolutionary progress, in B. Stewart (ed.), *The Games*

Are Not the Same: The Political Economy of Football in Australia, Carlton: Melbourne University Press, pp. 198–235.

Dabscheck, B. and Opie, H. (2003), Legal regulation of sporting labour markers, *Australian Journal of Labour Law*, **16**, 259–83.

Davenport, D.S. (1969), Collusive competition in Major League Baseball – its theory and institutional development, *The American Economist*, **13**, 6–30.

Demmert, H.G. (1973), *The Economics of Professional Team Sports*, Lexington: Lexington Books.

Digel, H. (2002), A comparison of competitive sports systems, *New Studies in Athletics*, **17** (1), 37–50.

Downward, P. and Dawson, A. (2000), *The Economics of Professional Team Sports*, London: Routledge.

European Council (2000), *Nice Declaration: Declaration on the Specific Characteristics of Sport and its Social Function in Europe*, Nice: European Council.

Ferrand, A. and Pages, M. (1996), Football supporter involvement: Explaining football match loyalty, *European Journal for Sport Management*, **3** (1), 7–20.

Fink, J.S., Trail, G.S. and Anderson, D.F. (2002), An examination of team identification: which motives are most salient to its existence?, *International Sports Journal*, Summer, 195–207.

Foreman, J. (2003), Corporate governance issues in professional sport, available at: http://www.commerce.adelaide.edu.au/apira/papers/Foreman172.pdf (accessed 15 February 2008).

Forrest, D. and Simmons, R. (2004), Buying success: team performance and wage bills in U.S. European sports leagues, in R. Fort and J. Fizel (eds), *International Sports Economics Comparisons*, Westport, CT: Praeger, pp. 123–40.

Fort, R. and Quirk, J. (2004), Owner objectives and competitive balance, *Journal of Sports Economics*, **5** (1), 20–32.

Foster, G., Greyser, P. and Walsh, B. (2006), *The Business of Sports: Texts and Cases on Strategy and Management*, New York: Thomson.

Funk, D.C., Mahony, D.F., Nakazawa, M. and Hirakawa, S. (2001), Development of the sport interest inventory (SII): implications for measuring unique consumer motives at team sporting events, *International Journal of Sports Marketing and Sponsorship*, September/October: 291–312.

Gems, G. (1999), Sports, war, and ideological imperialism, *Peace Review*, **11** (4), 573–78.

Gerrard, B. (2005), A resource utilization model of organizational efficiency in professional team sports, *Journal of Sport Management*, **19** (2), 143–69.

Giulianotti, R. (2002), Supporters, followers, fans, and flaneurs: a taxonomy of spectator identities in football, *Journal of Sport and Social Issues*, **26** (1), 25–46.

Goldblatt, D. (2006), *The Ball is Round: A Global History of Football*, London: Viking Penguin.

Gratton, C. and Taylor, P. (1986), The economics of professional football, *Leisure Management*, 29–30.

Hall, S., Szymanski, S. and Zimbalist, A. (2002), Testing causality between team performance and payroll: the cases of Major League Baseball and English soccer, *Journal of Sports Economics*, **3** (2), 149–68.

Hardy, M. (1999), *Saturday Afternoon Fever: A Footy Fan's Memoirs*, Sydney: Harper Collins.

Heath, C. and Tversky, A. (1991), Preference and belief: Ambiguity and competence in choice under uncertainty, *Journal of Risk and Uncertainty*, **IV**, 5–28.

Hess, R. and Stewart, B. (1998), *More Than a Game*, Melbourne: Melbourne University Press.

Hess, R., Nicholson, M., Stewart, B. and De Moore, G. (2008), *A National Game: A history of Australian Rules Football*, Camberwell: Viking Penguin.

Hinch, T. and Higham, J. (2005), Sport, tourism and authenticity, *European Sport Management Quarterly*, **5** (3), 243–56.

Hornby, N. (1995), *Fever Pitch*, London: Longman.

Hoye, R. and Cuskelly, G. (2007), *Sport Governance*, Oxford: Elsevier.

Hoye, R., Nicholson, M. and Smith, A. (2008), Unique aspects of managing sport organizations, in C. Wankle (ed.), *Sage Handbook of 21st Century Management*, London: Sage Publications, pp. 501–9.

Hsee, C. and Hastie, R. (2006), Decision and experience: why don't we choose what makes us happy?, *Trends in Cognitive Science*, **10** (1), 31–7.

Hughson, J. (1999), A tale of two tribes: expressive fandom in Australia's A-League, *Culture, Sport Society*, **2** (3), 11–30.

Humphreys, B. and Howard, D. (2008), *The Business of Sport*, Westport, CT: Praeger Perspectives Series.

Jones, I. (2000), A model of serious leisure identification: the case of football fandom, *Leisure Studies*, **19**, 283–98.

Kahneman, D. (2000a), Experienced utility and objective happiness: a moment-based approach, in D. Kahneman and A. Tversky (eds), *Choices, Values and Frames*, Cambridge: Cambridge University Press, pp. 673–92.

Kahneman, D. (2000b), New challenges to the rationality assumption, in D. Kahneman and A. Tversky (eds), *Choices, Values and Frames*, Cambridge: Cambridge University Press, pp. 758–74.

Kahneman, D. and Tversky, A. (2000), *Choices, Values and Frames*, Cambridge: Cambridge University Press.

King, A. (1998), *The End of the Terraces: The Transformation of English Football in the 1990s*, Leicester: Leicester University Press.

La Feber, W. (1999), *Michael Jordan and the New Global Capitalism*, New York: W.W. Norton.

Lewis, M. (2004), *Moneyball: The Art of Winning an Unfair Game*, New York: W.W. Norton.

Macdonald, R. and Booth, R. (2007), Around the grounds: a comparative analysis of football in Australia, in B. Stewart (ed.), *The Games Are Not the Same: The Political Economy of Football in Australia*, Carlton: Melbourne University Press, pp. 236–331.

Mangan, J.A. and Nauright, J. (2000), *Sport in Australasian Society: Past and Present*, London: F Cass.

Milne, G.R. and McDonald, M.A. (1999), *Sport Marketing: Managing the Exchange Process*, Sudbury, MA: Jones and Bartlett.

Milton-Smith, J. (2002), Business ethics in Australia and New Zealand, *Journal of Business Ethics*, **35** (2), 131–42.

Morgan, M. (2002), Optimising the structure of elite competitions in professional sport – lessons from rugby union, *Managing Leisure*, **7** (1), 41–60.

Morris, D. (1981), *The Soccer Tribe*, London: Jonathan Cape.

Nash, R. (1997), Research note: concept and method in researching the football crowd, *Leisure Studies*, **15**, 127–31.

Noll, R. (2002), The economics of promotion and relegation in sports leagues: the case of English football, *Journal of Sports Economics*, **3** (2), 169–203.

Noll, R. (2003), The organization of sports leagues, *Oxford Review of Economic Policy*, **19**, 530–51.

Oakley, B. and Green, M. (2001), The production of Olympic champions: international perspectives of elite sport development systems, *European Journal for Sport Management*, **8** (1), 83–105.

Pine, B.J. and Gilmore, J.H. (1999), *The Experience Economy*, Boston, MA: Harvard Business School Press.

Plarow, M.J., Durante, M., Williams, N., Garrett, M., Walshe, J., Cincotta, S., Lianos, G. and Brautchu, A. (1999), The contributions of sport fan identity to the production of prosocial behaviour, *Croup Dynamics: Theory, Research and Practice*, **3** (20), 161–9.

Queenan, J. (2003), *True Believers: The Tragic Inner Life of Sports Fans*, New York: Henry Holt and Co.

Ratner, R.K., Kahn, B. and Kahneman, D. (1999), Choosing less-preferred experiences for the sake of variety, *Journal of Consumer Research*, **26**, 1–15.

Ratneshwar, S. and Mick, D. (2005), *Inside Consumption: Consumer Motives, Goals and Desires*, Oxford: Routledge.

Rein, I., Kotler, P. and Shields, B. (2006), *The Elusive Fan: Reinventing Spores in a Crowded Marketplace*, New York: McGraw-Hill.

Ritzer, G. (1998), *The McDonaldizatian Thesis*, London: Sage.

Rosner, S. and Shropshire, K. (2004), *Business of Sports*, Sudbury, MA: Jones and Bartlett.

Ross, S.F. and Szymanski, S. (2006), Antitrust and inefficient joint ventures: why sports leagues should look more like McDonald's and less like the United Nations, *Marquette Sports Law Review*, **16** (2), 213–59.

Sandy, R., Sloane, P. and Rosentraub, M. (2004), *The Economics of Sport: An International Perspective*, Basingstoke: Palgrave Macmillan.

Schofield, J. (1982), The development of first-class cricket in England: an economic analysis, *The Journal of Industrial Economics*, **30** (4), 337–60.

Slack, T. (1996), From the locker room to the boardroom: changing the domain of sport management, *Journal of Spore Management*, **10**, 97–105.

Slack, T. (1998), Is there anything unique about sport?, *Journal for Sport Management*, **5** (2), 21–9.

Slack, T. (2003), Sport in the global society: shaping the domain of sport studies, *International Journal of the History of Sport*, **20** (4), 118–29.

Smith, A. and Stewart, B. (2007), The travelling fan: understanding the mechanisms of sport fan consumption in a sport tourism setting, *Journal of Sport Tourism*, **12** (3–4), 155–81.

Smith, A. and Westerbeek, H. (2004), *The Sport Business Future*, London: Palgrave Macmillan.

Somers, S. and Perry, R. (2008), Hospital planning for weapons of mass destruction incidents, in C. Wankle (ed.), *Sage Handbook of 21st Century Management*, Los Angeles: Sage, pp. 491–500.

Stewart, B. and Dickson, G. (2007), Crystal-ball gazing: the future of football, in B. Stewart (ed.), *The Games Are Not the Same: The Political Economy of Football in Australia*, Carlton: Melbourne University Press, pp. 71–113.

Stewart, B., Dickson, G. and Nicholson, M. (2005), The Australian Football League's recent progress: a study in cartel conduct and monopoly power, *Sport Management Review*, **8** (2), 145–66.

Stewart, B., Dickson, G. and Smith, A. (2008), Drug use in the Australian Football League: a critical survey, *Sporting Traditions*, **25** (1), 57–74.

Stewart, B., Smith, A. and Nicholson, M. (2003), Sport consumer typologies: a critical review, *Sport Marketing Quarterly*, **12** (4), 206–16.

Stewart, R. and Smith, A. (1999), The special features of sport, *Annals of Leisure Research*, **2**, 87–99.

Szymanski, S. (2003), The economic design of sporting contests, *Journal of Economic Literature*, **41** (4), 1137–87.

Szymanski, S. (2006), Competitive balance in sports leagues and the paradox of power, *International Association of Sports Economists*, Working Paper number 0618, 1–12.

Szymanski, S. (2009), *Playbooks and Checkbooks: An Introduction to the Economics of Modern Sports*, Princeton, MA: Princeton University Press.

Szymanski, S. and Kuypers, T. (1999), *Winners and Losers: The Business Strategy of Football*, Harmondsworth: Viking Press.

Szymanski, S. and Ross, S.F. (2007), Governance and vertical integration in team sports, *Contemporary Economic Policy*, **25** (4), 616–25.

Tajfel, H. (1981), *Human Groups and Social Categories: Studies in Social Psychology*, Cambridge: Cambridge University Press.

Tajfel, H. (1982), Social psychology of intergroup relations, *Annual Review of Psychology*, **33**, 1–39.

Tajfel, H. and Turner, J. (1986), An integrative theory of intergroup conflict, in G. Austin and S. Worchel (eds), *The Social Psychology of Intergroup Relations*, Monterey, CA: Brooks/Cole, pp. 33–47.

Thibault, L. (2009), Globalization of sport: an inconvenient truth, *Journal of Sport Management*, **23** (1), 1–20.

Timothy, D.J. (2005), *Shopping, Tourism Retailing and Leisure*, Buffalo: Channel View Publications.

Wann, D. (1995), Preliminary validation of the sport fan motivation scale, *Journal of Sport and Social Issues*, **19** (4), 377–96.

Wann, D. and Branscombe, N. (1993), Sports fans: measuring degree of identification with their team, *International Journal of Sports Psychology*, **24** (1), 1–17.

Wenner, L (ed.) (1998), *MediaSport*, New York: Routledge.

Westerbeek, H. and Smith, A. (2003), *Sport Business in the Global Marketplace*, London: Palgrave Macmillan.

Wiley, C.G., Shaw, S. and Havitz, M. (2000), Men's and women's involvement in sports: an examination of the gendered aspects of leisure involvement, *Leisure Sciences*, **22** (1), 19–31.

Wright, G. (1999), Sport and globalization, *New Political Economy*, **4** (2), 267–81.

Zhang, J.I., Pease, D.G., Lam, E.T., Bellerive, L.M., Pham, U.L., Williamson, D.P. and Lee, J.T. (2001), Sociomotivational factors effecting spectator attendance at Minor League Hockey games, *Sport Marketing Quarterly*, **10** (1), 43–56.

Zimbalist, A. (2003a), *May the Best Team Win: Baseball Economics and Public Policy*, Washington: Brookings Institute.

Zimbalist, A. (2003b), Sport as business, *Oxford Review of Economic Policy*, **19** (4), 503–11.

29 Outlook: sport and business – a future research agenda

Harald Dolles and Sten Söderman

1 OPENING THE FIELD FOR FUTURE RESEARCH

The purpose of the handbook is to present the current frontier of research on sport and business in theory and in practice. It would not be complete without opening the field for future research at the end of this endeavour. The handbook is divided into five thematic clusters 'Governance and performance', 'Media and technology', 'Place, time and spectators', 'Club management and teams', 'Sport branding and sponsoring'. We use the cluster structure to summarize the insights gained from the experts in the field and some of our own thoughts to develop an agenda for further research on the nexus between sport and business (see also Figure 29.1 on the next page providing a selection of the proposed topics for further research) in the following.

In the beginning we emphasize that it is the research topic and what the researcher wants to achieve by conducting her or his research that leads to the choice of the theoretical approach and a suitable research method. When we designed the handbook we had no fixed preference or predefined evaluation of what is a 'good' or 'appropriate' and a 'bad' or 'inappropriate' theory and research method. No theoretical reasoning and no research method, qualitative or quantitative, is intrinsically better than the other, and in some cases the researcher will end up with a struggle to choose between different theoretical approaches and between multiple, competing methods. The chapters in the handbook therefore represent a rather broad introduction into various theories and research methods. There is one obvious implication of this distinctiveness: although a lot of advice about various theories and research methods is provided in the chapters of this handbook, it should not be seen as definitive. The researcher must be prepared to continually use her or his own judgement by designing her or his own research project by taking advantages of the insights and experiences gained from this volume. To support this might be one of the most important outcomes of this handbook.

2 SUGGESTIONS FOR FURTHER RESEARCH WITHIN THE THEMATIC CLUSTER ON 'GOVERNANCE AND PERFORMANCE'

The chapters assembled in this thematic cluster inform managers and researchers about new and alternative ideas in order to design elite sport systems and operational processes within them. Benchmarking, qualitative comparative analysis and the SPLISS model are featured research methods in the handbook to support comparisons between institutions of different sports and/or between different national settings. Thus those

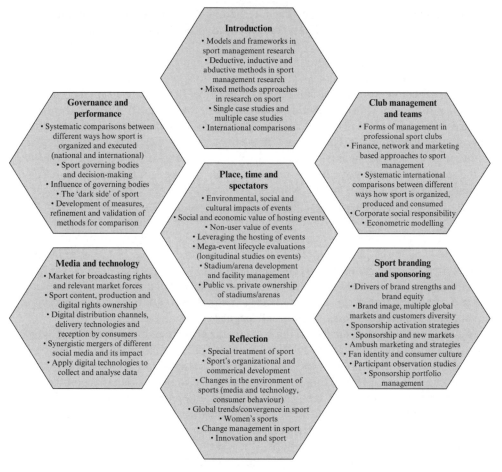

Introduction
• Models and frameworks in sport management research
• Deductive, inductive and abductive methods in sport management research
• Mixed methods approaches in research on sport
• Single case studies and multiple case studies
• International comparisons

Governance and performance
• Systematic comparisons between different ways how sport is organized and executed (national and international)
• Sport governing bodies and decision-making
• Influence of governing bodies
• The 'dark side' of sport
• Development of measures, refinement and validation of methods for comparison

Club management and teams
• Forms of management in professional sport clubs
• Finance, network and marketing based approaches to sport management
• Systematic international comparisons between different ways how sport is organized, produced and consumed
• Corporate social responsibility
• Econometric modelling

Place, time and spectators
• Environmental, social and cultural impacts of events
• Social and economic value of hosting events
• Non-user value of events
• Leveraging the hosting of events
• Mega-event lifecycle evaluations (longitudinal studies on events)
• Stadium/arena development and facility management
• Public vs. private ownership of stadiums/arenas

Media and technology
• Market for broadcasting rights and relevant market forces
• Sport content, production and digital rights ownership
• Digital distribution channels, delivery technologies and reception by consumers
• Synergistic mergers of different social media and its impact
• Apply digital technologies to collect and analyse data

Sport branding and sponsoring
• Drivers of brand strengths and brand equity
• Brand image, multiple global markets and customers diversity
• Sponsorship activation strategies
• Sponsorship and new markets
• Ambush marketing and strategies
• Fan identity and consumer culture
• Participant observation studies
• Sponsorship portfolio management

Reflection
• Special treatment of sport
• Sport's organizational and commerical development
• Changes in the environment of sports (media and technology, consumer behaviour)
• Global trends/convergence in sport
• Women's sports
• Change management in sport
• Innovation and sport

Figure 29.1   Selected topics to be considered for future research on the nexus between sport and business

methods provide the potential to investigate other sport contexts as well. They also allow systematic comparisons, for example why the quality of organization and delivery of one sport might be higher in one sport than another, or to advance understanding how a professional league increases its spectators when another is experiencing a reduction. Although benchmarking is a valuable methodology for understanding the nature and complexity of the structures of elite sport systems, Leigh Robinson and Nikolai Böhlke admit it does not necessarily mean that the descriptive benchmarks generated by the research can be directly utilized by managers of other elite sport systems. Thus, from a management perspective, process benchmarking should not be carried out in an attempt to identify a ready-made solution for a specific benchmarking object. Rather, managers should understand process benchmarking as a method for innovation, idea generation and general inspiration based on the descriptive benchmarks that emerge from the research exercise.

Medal tables in the Olympic Games or world rankings in certain sports, such as the

FIFA ranking in football, suggest that international comparisons are standard procedures in the world of sports. However, when advocating international comparisons, we need to take into account how sport is organized differently across the globe. In the United States, for example, sport is highly embedded in the school system that is designed to feed athletes into the university system. There is no sport club tradition in the United States that is comparable to the kind found in Europe. In Japan, we found community-based institutions of sport competing with corporate-based sport. These and other differences between nations make international comparison of sport determinants, and (not only elite) sport systems or (elite) leagues in particular, a very rich field for future research. Cultural factors shape the environment surrounding sports, as for example emphasized in the chapter on sports governance in Ireland (Ann Bourke), on English football (Geoff Walters and Sean Hamil) or on Norwegian sport policy implementation (Eivind Å. Skille). Cultural factors are integrated with the determinants and not isolated from them. Cultural factors change only gradually and are difficult for outsiders to fully understand. Hermeneutics and case study approaches are used in the handbook in order to understand and explain the phenomenon of study in a national setting. But how to introduce such factors in cross-cultural sport management research? Research examples might be the effects on sports governance in Belgium of the distinct language and culture divide in the country or the transfer of best practices taken from abroad to create, implement and advance the Japanese professional football league (Dolles and Söderman, 2013).

Another similarly neglected research topic in comparative research on sport governance are lateral and multilateral relations between national associations of sports and how these connect to politics in regional confederations and supranational bodies, such as the IOC or FIFA. Hallgeir Gammelsæter and Benoit Senaux point out, for example, that voting in the UEFA general assembly and representation on the Executive Committee before 1990 reflected the Cold War divide as well as a north–south split in Western Europe. This might have created an environment which slowed down the decision-making capacity of the associations. But what happened after 1990? Are there still powerful blocks in UEFA? How do they operate (and shift?) and what are the processes like? What issues have been (and are) at stake here, and what has been the upshot of such processes? An interesting question is also how football (but we might take other sports as well) through the hosting of the final round of international tournaments affects the governance of the sport in the hosting countries as well as the question of a larger socio-cultural impact? During FIFA's deliberations over the choice of host countries for the World Cup in 2018 and 2022, there was much comment as to the governance procedures in FIFA amid accusations of corruption. These claims were exacerbated in 2011 when FIFA (re-)elected its president. Many journalists and commentators were asking of governance procedures adopted by supra-national sports organizations: are such institutions in sport responsible to no overall authority other than themselves?

Governance in sports itself needs further research attention. It is argued by Hallgeir Gammelsæter and Benoit Senaux that the understanding of governance in sports often comes from disciplines that are dedicated to pursue research questions other than governance, such as ethnography, cultural sociology, sport history and, in part, sport marketing, and not by typical governance disciplines such as sport management and organization studies. Rather it reflects that many of them are not primarily directed to studying governance but happen to fill a vacuum by providing descriptions and analyses that are relevant for the research field. Straightforward outlines are needed of how different sports are structured and how the structure changes at different levels. Just to take football as an example, do the membership-based national associations defend the interests of the sport's members, whoever these are – amateurs or professionals, or if football's superior bodies, notably FIFA and UEFA now operate as commercial corporations, not to say conglomerates, in the disguise of voluntary non-profit organizations. Do the enormous amounts of revenue that pass through football's organizations compromise the sport to the extent that it no longer represents its diverse actors? And do the seemingly increased commercial orientations of the traditional governance bodies and the increased relative power of professional clubs undermine the 'one member, one vote' principle so entrenched in the governance of the game? It has also been asserted that the decisive moments of European football have been provoked by clubs more than by national associations, and that many national associations increasingly have seen their influence over professional clubs and leagues decrease. Thus, the current context is characterized by systemic governance; the new interest groups which short-cut the traditional bottom-up hierarchical process, provide direct guidance to their members at the national and international level. Although these organizations are increasingly important, there is very little research, if any, analysing their emergence and highlighting their role in the governance of the game. More research is welcomed in how actors, structures and processes evolve in this industry and regarding the outcomes of the interaction between the actors. Is football's allegedly new network structure and the partnership with the European Union equipped to combat economic doping, corruption, match-fixing, hooliganism, racism and promote more equal competition on and off the pitch?

The methods itself used by the authors in the chapters might also be fields of further studies. Veerle De Bosscher, Jasper Truyens, Marten van Bottenburg and Simon Shibli suggest econometric approaches in future research in order to identify the most important success determinants, and to identify the weights to be used for each of them. Using additional questionnaires, factor analysis or principal component analysis might offer alternative methods to determine weights for each critical success factor in the research model. Furthermore, in order to aggregate variables into a composite indicator the variables need to be normalized or standardized to a common scale. To date however, in economic studies as well as in the SPLISS model, there has been limited critical interrogation of how valid and useful these measurements are with respect to their ability to provide insights into what drives competitiveness and robust predictions of future performance. Thus, the SPLISS model needs to be explored in more nations and for specific sports (or 'industries'). Mathieu Winand and Thierry Zintz state that a qualitative comparative analysis builds upon a rigorous and transparent selection of conditions made by the researcher and supported by theory. The reliability is considered according to the theoretical validation (that is, ratio between variables and number of cases, absence of contradictory configuration showing the coherence of the data and absence of contradictory simplifying assumption when using logical remainder(s)) and the proper interpretation of the solution (that is, confronting the solution with the narratives of cases and, when possible, with individuals' own interpretation). The authors suggest for future research, that combinations of factors leading to phenomena of interest and not only the net effects of variables should be analysed. Indeed, factors are interconnected and thus affect each other to produce results. Their presence (or absence) might lead to different results according to the factors with which they are combined. It is argued that this is particularly relevant for complex organizations such as sport organizations growing in a complex internal and external environment.

Generally speaking, and as a conclusion of the chapters in this thematic cluster, it is also a recommendation to researchers to engage in mixed method designs. The combination of quantitative and qualitative data could be useful to strengthen researchers' analysis/studies. Benchmarking, qualitative comparative analysis, the SPLISS model and multiple case studies – just to mention the research methods applied by the authors in the respective chapters in the handbook, but not exclusively – have proven to be adequate methods to explore the link between sport governance and various factors. Relevant aspects of culture needs to be systematically introduced in future research – thus single or multiple case study research might advance the knowledge in the field. The development of scoring systems is a supportive and tangible way of advancing the understanding of sport policies and strategic action more broadly in relation to sporting success, rather than an isolated competitiveness measurement or ranking system on its own. In this respect scoring systems as research methods are merely a guiding system as part of an overall qualitative and quantitative evaluation.

3   SUGGESTIONS FOR FURTHER RESEARCH WITHIN THE THEMATIC CLUSTER ON 'MEDIA AND TECHNOLOGY'

The impact of information technology and media over the past decades on the development of the relationship between sport and business is the core issue in this thematic cluster. The fast-paced, constantly changing, networked, integrated and relentlessly competitive (but simultaneously cooperative) business and media environment of today has changed how sport is performed, delivered and consumed. Those obvious changes also demand a change in thinking in order to more successfully navigate through the current milieu in order to collect data, address problems and capitalize on opportunities.

With this development, media has become a major source of income for all kinds of sports – including events, and the proliferation of information technology has made it possible to serve the needs of sports fans all over the world. The broadcasting landscape may be changing, affecting the way major sporting events are perceived – a research question in itself. More important, though, is to explore how the market for broadcasting rights has changed over recent years, substantially escalating the price of these rights. Chris Gratton and Harry Arne Solberg argue, if national governments want to continue to see certain events remain on terrestrial television in the future they may have to compensate the sports affected in order to meet other public objectives in sport. This issue is equally relevant to other countries with listed events legislation and it is an issue likely to become more important with the escalation in the price of broadcasting rights for sport events. The listed events legislation, particularly in the European Union where it is backed up by an EU Directive, provides one of the few opportunities for governments to have some control over supra-national organizations in sport, which seem to lack any other form of control mechanisms (a research question which also fits into the thematic cluster on aspects of governance and performance).

Harry Arne Solberg and Kjetil Kåre Haugen consider that the major reason behind the strong inflation of revenue generation from the sale of media rights has been the fierce competition between commercial broadcasters. In order to analyse types of competitive situations that are common in the market for television sports rights, game theory is applied to illustrate how stakeholders involved in sport management could better analyse the consequences of alternative strategies. It is advocated, that game theoretic approaches should receive more attention in research, as they can help sport governing bodies, event organizers, sports clubs and other stakeholders involved in sport activities to better understand how market forces can affect the outcome of their own decisions. It can also help them to better analyse the strategies of their rivals as well as their counterparts, for example, in sale processes. Using the language of mathematics might limit the possibilities in analysing 'real-world' game situations, but the authors believe that relevant simplifications may already provide valuable managerial information. The most significant conclusion drawn is that simple games already indicate a great complexity in seemingly simple television-rights gaming situations. As such, a promising future is predicted for game theoretic applications in sport management research.

Readers interested in sport marketing and social media will find the chapter by James Santomier and Patricia Hogan to be a very worthwhile reference that could stimulate a number of ideas for research. It is argued that the unstoppable development of information technology opens the field for using specific digital technologies (Internet, mobile, and so on) to conduct sport business research in social media, such as: (1) new designs or methods, in form of new ways of collecting or generating quantitative or qualitative data (for example, on-line interviews or observations, enhanced use of photography and other audio/visual methods, sensory ethnography, soundscapes, eliciting creative writings from respondents) or new representations of qualitative research (for example, visual 'texts', using hypermedia, ethnographic fiction, multi-layered and multi-vocal texts); (2) new concepts by generating new ways of thinking about research (for example, drawing on autobiographical practices, practitioner-led research, multi-modal research practices), and (3) responding to the changing research landscape (for example, enhanced information and communication technology (ICT) capacities, new ethical challenges and guidelines).

An example of innovative research methodology using social media and an integrative, cross-organizational (that is, university business schools, sport business, research companies) format introduced by James Santomier and Patricia Hogan could be based on the ESPN XP project. ESPN XP provides a vehicle to introduce new techniques and innovative methodologies (cross-media measurement) to sport marketing research: the commercial goal of most sport enterprises regarding their digital initiatives is to leverage as much of their sport content across as many multi-media platforms as possible in order to aggregate as many consumers as possible. Therefore, researchers may want focus on any one or more of these dimensions at any point in the digital media value chain, which includes: (1) various types of sport content and digital rights ownership; (2) the technical aspects of digital production; (3) distribution channels including sport specific portals, websites, and so on; (4) delivery technologies, such as broadband, satellite and cable, and (5) reception by consumers via specific digital devices. In addition, there may soon be synergistic mergers of different social media to build partnerships (for example, iTunes + Facebook + ?) to accomplish business or social responsibility goals, and the impact of such synergy on sport marketing would be an interesting study. In conclusion, it must be recognized that social media and the techniques and processes related to marketing using social media are changing at an incredible rate and will require continual monitoring for those involved in social media research. As such, the authors emphasize the need for sport marketing researchers who are abductive thinkers who can design, combine and use innovative research methodologies as stimulated by the continually evolving technology. Ultimately, however, research prospects related to social media and sport marketing are vast for scholars and marketing professionals alike, and are replete with opportunities for designing new research methodologies.

4   SUGGESTIONS FOR FURTHER RESEARCH WITHIN THE THEMATIC CLUSTER ON 'PLACE, TIME AND SPECTATORS'

The growth of sport events in numbers, diversity and popularity has been enormous in recent years. Numerous communities developed or have been active in developing new sport events as leisure and cultural pursuits for residents, as well as aiming for economic and community development benefits. Despite the growth and popularity of sport events, researchers have been very slow in directing research on events beyond their economic impacts and motivations. Tangible impacts, such as improvement of local sporting facilities, infrastructure or urban regeneration, are commonly associated with large-scale sport events, but intangible effects of hosting large-scale sporting events may be at least as important. Large-scale sport events are also manifestations and often celebrations of sport values such as competitiveness, fairness and loyalty. Given the fact that such values are important and have an impact on social life not only in the short run but also on the accumulated social capital of the community, it opens up for research questions regarding the social and cultural impact of sporting events. A part of the community, however, might not have any interest in the event as such, exploring the non-user value of events is therefore an important research question. In addition the idea of environmentally friendly sporting events has become a major issue in the planning and operation of sporting events, and might also be an important element to study.

The triple bottom line approach has a split focus on three types of impacts of events, that is, economic, sociocultural and environmental. The triple bottom line is a tool under development for general business activities that also provides a suitable framework for analyses of the sustainability of sport events. A development of this approach comprises *ex post* analyses of sociocultural and environmental impacts as in Tommy Andersson's fruitful research to learn more about both how correct and how stable over time triple bottom line results are. Another issue is the fact that in the triple bottom line approach certain impacts are described by perceptions of impacts, especially sociocultural impacts, whereas other impacts are described in concrete technical (environmental) or financial (economic) units. A theoretical development of social capital and measurements of social and cultural capital can in the future hopefully be integrated in the triple bottom line framework. Theoretical developments in the field of measuring willingness-to-pay may also influence the development of economic impact assessments of sport events. When sociocultural impacts can be given an economic value this will certainly increase the relevance of analytical results not only for the community and politicians but also for the event managers in their strategic decisions. Similarly, a well-functioning emission rights market is most probably not too far away in the future. Sport events will then be able, just like other industries, to work with market prices for environmental emissions and integrate an environmental strategy with an overall economic and sociocultural strategy. A fully fledged cost–benefit analysis will then be feasible and impact assessments of sport events can be integrated not only in the long tradition of cost–benefit analyses from a wide range of industries, but also in the well-established theoretical framework of welfare economics.

Sport economists produced significant literature questioning the supposed economic impact of new sports facilities and the lasting effects of facilities in terms of spectator attendance. Boris Helleu and Michel Desbordes address the research problem of 'public cost for private gain' when researching French football arenas and discussing how public support could be legitimized. They introduce the organizational model of sport in France as a research problem, by arguing that the state is involved in sport through economic and legal regulation, and stands as the guarantor of the interdependence between amateur and professional sport. If the state makes a decision to support the refurbishment of run-down stadiums in order to host a mega-sporting event such as the final round of the European football championships, regional governments whose budgets are not inexhaustible will be forced to make a choice. The authors indicate that a systematic introduction of a commercial and marketing policy designed to retain the loyalty of existing spectators and attract new ones is missing. Customer relationship management research is missing, aimed at collecting a set of data that will optimize customer understanding and satisfaction. Another research question is, whether the private financing and operation of stadiums by the clubs might be an alternative to public ownership? What can be the role of local government in this new situation? At the moment French clubs do not have the property holdings required for the construction of new stadiums. Thus, making a site available requires the intervention of local government, which also has the power to issue the administrative documents necessary for the construction or renovation of the stadium.

Follow-up studies are important in order to understand the long-term effect of hosting similar major sport events. Anne-line Balduck, Marc Maes and Marc Buelens draw the following important practical implications resulting from this proposition. Besides diminishing the negative impacts for residents when hosting major sport events, it is time to leverage major sport events. Cities should take the hosting of major sport events into the overall strategy of the city in order to maximize the long-term benefits. The event is an opportunity to foster and nurture long-term outcome. The importance of the social value of hosting major sport events is a central outcome of the study. Although there are studies that focused on the leveraging of events, research on social leveraging of major sport events is only in its preliminary phase. Impact studies are needed to provide useful information on environmental issues of hosting major sport events. Further research should also focus on the most effective ways to implement, create and maintain the leverage of major sport events.

In summary, the phases or stages of the sport mega-event lifecycle vary considerably in length of time. For the football World Cup, the bidding alone takes one to two years, seven years for preparation, 40 days of competition and potentially decades for the legacy stage. To host the Olympic Games, the cycle is similar but the event takes place over 17 days. Public perceptions of the event shift across the lifecycle: from elation and euphoria at the bid stage; concerns over readiness, costs, anxiety and 'wait-and-see' in the preparation stage; relief and joy during operations, and then pride, appreciation and satisfaction following the Games. Longitudinal studies following this process are seldom found in the literature and should be supported. The research by Alessandro 'Chito' Guala and Douglas Michele Turco is one example of this type of study, reflecting the attitudes of the Torino residents toward the 2006 Winter Olympic Games. The authors propose that such research is useful for future Olympic Games, particularly for developing nations (such as, India, the UAE and South Africa) keen to bid for the Games. These surveys not only serve the purpose of data collection and information, but also are an opportunity for knowledge transfer to initiate discussion on the future of the Olympics and their impacts on host countries. Event organizing committees and host governments need to seek the voices of residents before, during and after a sport mega-event, as their perceptions will change over time. Periodic resident perception research should be featured in event legacy planning as residents will encounter the legacy on a daily basis and can therefore offer intimate perspectives on the event.

It must be remembered that field research on sport events is fluid and dynamic, and requires, at times, flexibility by the researchers. This lesson came across loud and clear for Douglas Michele Turco at the 2010 FIFA World Cup in South Africa. Fans blaring the vuvuzelas made match-day interviews at the stadium precincts extremely difficult and survey schedules as well as location had to be altered. The author emphasizes that technology will play an increasingly important role in conducting and advancing sport business research. Smart phones and other small portable electronic devices will permit sport consumer research that is less intrusive and can collect data immediately.

5   SUGGESTIONS FOR FURTHER RESEARCH WITHIN THE THEMATIC CLUSTER ON 'CLUB MANAGEMENT AND TEAMS'

The reasons why sport clubs make profits or losses are among the central questions in sport management research. The causes of a club's success or failure are inextricably tied to questions such as: why clubs differ, how they act on and off the pitch, how they choose strategies for performance on the pitch and within the club on different levels, and how they are managed. While much of research on sport clubs has a more national focus, it also has become increasingly apparent that any quest for the causes of a clubs success must also confront the reality of international competition, the difference in governance structures of the game between different countries (see the thematic cluster 1) and the striking differences in the performance of clubs in different nations. It is therefore not surprising that research on management models in professional sport are dominating this thematic cluster. An asset-based approach to management is advocated by Norm O'Reilly, defining a professional sport club as a series of assets forming the basis for applying portfolio theory as a foundation for professional sport club management. Hans Jansson and Sten Söderman suggest a conceptionalization of club management based on relationship marketing and networking to create a fit with the mix of rules of the institutional set-ups faced by clubs. The resource-based view and the concept of co-creation of value is applied by Harald Dolles and Sten Söderman to develop professional team sport management as a network of value captures to create sustained competitive advantage on and off the pitch.

In conclusion, all three approaches set an important agenda for future research and provide management frameworks for consideration by practitioners in professional team sport. All approaches to management have considerable potential for improved organizational performance, but also need to be developed further. For example, as portfolio theory is related to the management of risk and reward through an efficient portfolio of assets, the conceptualization of risk requires further clarification. Specifically, questions such as 'what is the relative risk of high versus low return?', 'what is the specific relationship between time left on a player's contract and the club's risk?', 'what are the variables that determine management's determination of a player's risk?' and 'what is the impact of industry (sport) and geographical setting (one city) on the club's investment strategy?' The 'customer focused relationship marketing' theory caters to a too narrow range of stakeholders and activities. Pivotal attention is only aimed at relationships and making profits through them. Access to 'multiple markets' would enable a club to cover a broader spectrum of stakeholders and activities. In the 'institutional-network theory' the logic of appropriateness and logic of consequence go hand in hand. The logic of appropriateness is used to find alternatives to a problem as the word 'appropriate' suggests. Conversely, the logic of consequence plays a critical role in solving the problems outlined and maximizing the social values from an economic point of view. This logic therefore goes a step further by translating social values into economic consequences, for example the competitiveness of the club, but this needs to be explored in further research.

The 48 value-capturing relations, as identified in the network of value captures for professional team sport management, show the competitive scope of a club. The authors emphasize that not all value-capturing activities are equally important in every situation, which needs further exploration. The challenge for future research in this field will be both conceptual – where recent approaches into marketing and networks might be used to align this approach – and empirical. The research tasks in the latter might prevent developing measurements, creating scores and describing exchange standards to further analyse the relationships between the value captures. There is thus a need to further operationalize each of the value captures and combined strategies using bundles of value captures. It is also important to further investigate how to measure the size of these value captures (in monetary and non-monetary terms), the importance of value-capturing activities and their growth potential. We thus suggest research on perceived value for each customer group and how specific value can be created. What might be a value for one customer group might not be perceived as valuable for another customer group, see, for example, acceptance of jersey sponsors and selling the naming rights of the stadium. There might also be tensions between the different value captures, for example, individual players versus the team spirit or the development of VIP lounges versus standing rows. It also needs to be explored how value is to be co-created between sets of value captures. Is there empirical evidence – exemplified in single and multiple case studies or by large-scale quantitative surveys – to show whether certain combinations of value captures are more successful than others, measured by a clubs' success during one season or longitudinal. Are we able to define 'minimum standards' to each value capture or to each value-capturing activity of our framework, thus enabling the club management to benchmark with other clubs (developing an expert system) – nationally or internationally? The speed of commercialization as well as internationalization also needs to be elaborated for each value capture and value-capturing activity.

Furthermore, all three proposed conceptualizations of professional club management draw on the condition that sport club management is embedded in the sociocultural environment in which the sport and its organizational forms have evolved, are performed and are consumed. Research questions in this regard might be focusing on international comparisons. Do such concepts equally apply to the setting of sport across the globe? A further question remains on the industry level or the level of broader generalization. We thereby encourage studies to compare professional team sports within only one global region or worldwide, such as football, ice hockey, basketball, American football or cricket.

The chapter by Bernd Frick addresses one specific aspect in professional team sport management, namely, the relation between team wage bills, pay structures and playing success. Questions that are asked within this field of research are: what are the main determinants of player remuneration and of contract length? What are the determinants of player mobility and career length? To what extent do individuals respond to (changes in) incentives? What is the relationship between team wage bills and (sporting) performance? Does the distribution of salaries affect team performance? To what extent are 'fairness considerations' important? What is the impact of organizational 'constraints' such as draft rules, roster restrictions, salary caps, and so on, on the behaviour of (win maximizing versus profit maximizing) clubs? Do the clubs use the available resources (for example, playing and coaching talent) efficiently? The question, whether and to what extent expenditure on playing talent – as measured by team wage bills – translates into playing success, is perhaps the one that has received most attention in the literature on the economics of professional team sports. As mentioned by the author, early studies using data from the US Major Leagues found weak, if any, empirical links between team payrolls and playing success. The puzzle of a weak correlation between team wage bills and sporting success can potentially be resolved: first, there is always the potential for mistakes in assessing player talent. Second, institutional restrictions on player mobility (such as the draft system and a salary cap) have the potential to create a monopsonistic labour market, breaking the relationship between team wage bills and team performance. It is suggested by Bernd Frick, that a lot of further research needs to be done: individualistic sports (such as tennis, boxing, and track and field athletics) are interesting subjects to study, comparative analyses (across leagues and countries) are still scarce and the (economic) consequences of many rule changes (such as the de-regulation of the labour market following the 'Bosman-ruling') still need to be analysed and documented. Lastly, presenting the findings in a way that is accessible to the public is another step that has yet to be taken.

Another important aspect club managers need to consider is the concept of corporate social responsibility in sport, nowadays covering a multitude of corporate activities, ranging from business philanthropy to the responsible management of the club's external impacts on society, including community investment. By applying grounded theory Christos Anagnostopoulos explores how English football clubs mobilized resources and its managers' decision-making with regard to corporate social responsibility (CSR). He concludes that the utilization of grounded theory methodology by researchers into the business side of sport has not been widespread. Elements of grounded theory, of course, such as data coding and analysis, can be seen more frequently in the sport management literature. Warnings have been put forward, however, that researchers should not claim to have adopted grounded theory unless they have utilized all elements that characterize a grounded theory methodology. Those who wish to employ grounded theory methodology will also need to specify from the outset the unit of analysis their inquiry will use. For example, although the goal in the research by Christos Anagnostopoulos was to develop a substantive theory on the way managers make decisions regarding a corporate social responsibility strategy, the focus was on decision-making and not on the individuals who facilitated this process. In other words, the author sought similar interpretations among managers in the English football sector while not losing sight of the fact that the unit of analysis was the decision-making behind the formulation of CSR.

6   SUGGESTIONS FOR FURTHER RESEARCH WITHIN THE THEMATIC CLUSTER ON 'SPORT BRANDING AND SPONSORING'

The relevance of branding has increased tremendously during the last decade, as to identifying name and/or symbol (such as a logo, trademark, or package design) of either one seller or a group of sellers, and to distinguishing those goods or services from those of competitors. In the course of the increased attention and investigation of new application fields in brand management, more research is addressing branding applied to tourism destinations, media, celebrities and sport organizations – just to mention a few areas. The measurement of brand equities has become one of the 'hottest topics' in business administration literature during the last few years, as mentioned by Tim Ströbel and Herbert Woratschek. Their chapter presents a broad categorization of brand equity models (finance-oriented, customer-oriented and integrative), where each category is discussed by the underlying theoretical background to give a basic understanding and introduces representative models of each category. For further research in the field, the authors suggest identifying the drivers of brand strength and brand equity, and integrating them into a model showing clear cause–effect relationships of those drivers. In that sense, brand strength would lead to brand equity, and following that idea, how to calculate brand equity, by using – among others – financial indicators as a measurement scale. In the field of sport, as the most obvious this might be sporting success. But there might also be other variables like sport involvement that are still not sufficiently discussed in brand equity literature.

An extensive research agenda on sponsorship-linked marketing is provided by T. Bettina Cornwell: (1) advertising has been shown to influence consumer memory for past product experience. Such consumer recall could certainly be applied to sponsorship. A simple extension would examine the potential of sponsorship to elevate recall of past brand experience. (2) One of the most needed areas of research concerns spending that occurs in addition to the sponsorship contract. This spending typically results from efforts to build awareness of the link between the brand and event through advertising and promotion. (3) The term 'sponsorship-linked marketing' as the orchestration and implementation of marketing activities for the purpose of building and communicating an association, a link to a sponsorship, was coined to reflect the required coordination of interacting employees, audiences, volunteers, events, activities, sales promotions, merchandise, co-sponsors and media. (4) Researchers know little about how each possible element in the sponsorship portfolio communicates, and we know next to nothing about how they communicate in combination. (5) Practitioners also face challenges in managing the sponsorship portfolio. For example, are logos able to communicate in a meaningful way on football jerseys, rotational signage, on a field or when superimposed broadcast scoring? (6) In addition to the management and measurement required in activating a sponsorship, one must also consider the firm's portfolio of sponsorships. Managing a large sponsorship portfolio might be considered simply another integrated marketing communications challenge.

The ever-increasing internationalization of sport is making sponsorship a truly international communications vehicle, rivalled only by the World Wide Web, thus leading to the next challenge for sponsorship-linked marketing research: (7) Global and local objectives can be united in sport sponsorship and a consistent brand image can be presented across multiple global markets. In fact, large-scale sponsorships amortized across markets makes the most cost-effective use of sponsoring sport. What, then, is sponsorship's role when a brand seeks to enter new markets? One suggestion is that sponsorship would be helpful in brand line extension, but would not be as useful as advertising for an entirely new entry for the brand in a category. (8) Sponsorship policies are a curious element as a corporate instrument. A sponsorship policy is the document a company crafts that typically explains what a company will (and will not) sponsor, which audience should be targeted, the quantity of sponsorships that should be undertaken over a given period and the level of sponsorship devoted to each. Unlike policies on marketing, advertising and public relations, sponsorship policies are the most likely to be made public. (9) Ambushing is typically thought of as the efforts of an organization to associate itself indirectly with an event in the hope of reaping the same benefits as an official sponsor. Strategy research needs to consider how to incorporate would-be ambushers and form alliances, thus avoiding bothersome legal fees as well as painful and expensive surveillance. Communications research need to consider the positive and negative outcomes for all parties involved.

Sport fans – as opposed to sport spectators – have a high emotional solidarity and an abiding interest in their sport team or club is the starting point for the research by Torsten Schlesinger. Therefore, sport fans are often characterized by loyal consumer behaviour toward product of their club (for example, tickets and merchandising products). Fans consume their sport clubs' products on a regular basis, admitting that price and quality only play a secondary role. It is therefore inconceivable that fans with high emotional solidarity are likely to change to another club only because tickets are cheaper, the stadium is nicer or there is a wider range of merchandising products offered. The author suggests further research on this topic, for example, to investigate how far fan identity exerts influence on the actual consumer behaviour. Future studies should also attach more importance to other moderating factors of sponsorship effects (for example, sponsorship level, prominence of sponsors, and duration or history of the commitment between sponsor and club). In this way, the influences of fan identity in relation to the different kinds of sponsoring activities could be investigated. Based on this, companies can decide more accurately to what extent sponsorship is an effective communication tool for them. In this context comparative studies about single sponsorships of several sports clubs – as well as comparisons within different sport disciplines – would be of interest in this field of research in order to detect possible correlations or differences. Additionally, the online questionnaire is acknowledged to have some advantages (for example, sample size) and disadvantages (sample selectivity), compared with alternative questionnaire methods. In future research, the problem of the sample selectivity of the online questionnaire can be solved by additional questioning strategies – thus applying a multiple methods research design.

The challenging task for researchers to develop a suitable research method is also emphasized by Mark Dibben and Harald Dolles. It starts with asking why motorsport is, despite its economic value, the vast amount of investment by industry and the huge interest by spectators, only covered very rarely in research. The values of motorsport are, arguably, richer, as spectators are not necessarily excluded from the paddock and so can experience not only the racing as a spectacle but participate to a certain extent in the human side of the 'racing circus'; the emphasis is more on technical aspects, the driving or riding competence of drivers/riders and the fostering and enjoyment of social capital, what makes in sum research in motorsport probably more demanding. Ethnographic methods enjoy a long tradition in social sciences and have been widely employed in various ways by scholars with a variety of disciplines. Little attention, however, has thus far been given to using a longitudinal participant observation as a formal fieldwork method in sports management research. Sports management scenarios require access to the ephemeral and the personal precisely because that is where the value that is inherent within them resides. It is for this reason the authors suggest the technique may usefully be applied to other related topics in sport and event management research: research on fans and spectators, insights into the 'dark side' of sport like football hooliganism. Those studies also explore the limits of the method, when participant observation comes close to breaking the law, or investigations into sports brand communities and consumption cultures. It enables studies of sports organizations and their relations with the communities they represent. Participant observation also allows access to the complexities of volunteerism, entrepreneurship or the athlete's perspective in sport. The authors further suggest the method has applications in other growing fields of management research interest, such as environmental or humanitarian activism.

It is concluded by Mark Dibben and Harald Dolles that each of the above-mentioned topics concern the implicit, intangible and inestimable 'personal feel good value' that the athlete, fan, spectator, volunteer or organizer gets out of participating in and being associated with the event. Only participant observation can connect the academic researcher to the topic of study in a manner that allows an otherwise unavailable rich engagement with and insight into the nature of that value on a human level, and thus as a 'lived experience'.

7   SUGGESTIONS FOR FURTHER RESEARCH WITHIN THE CONCLUDING CLUSTER 'REFLECTION'

Traditionally, the major difference between business and sport was the importance of profit and return-on-investment for business, and the preference for winning and on-field success for sport. While it is clear that winning is sovereign in professional sport, there is a growing recognition mentioned by Aaron C.T. Smith and Bob Stewart that revenue and profits, and the resources that money attracts, are the keys to successful performance. Moreover, the evidence suggests that winning is also the fastest route to profitability. This means, according to the authors, that it is no longer a case of either or, but of both aims being met through an interdependent managerial strategy that builds a strong platform of quality resources from which to launch a high win–loss ratio. While the corporatization of sport over recent years may have resolved the dilemma of how to balance profits against performance, no such solution has been secured for the issue of quality in sport. The ambiguous nature of sport quality is exemplified in the ways in which different stakeholders approach it. For example, many club officials and die-hard fans view quality primarily in terms of consistent winning, whereas regulators and the run-of-the-mill sports follower are more likely to perceive quality in terms of competitive balance and outcome uncertainty. Added to this ambiguity is the complicating fact that the core sport product is now surrounded by services and merchandise that are used to provide a more consistent and multi-faceted sport experience. Finally, professional sport is embedded in a fundamental structural and operational paradox which complicates its management at every strategic turn. It arises out of the fact that sport's commercial progress and subsequent corporatization is a double-edged sword. While, on one hand, it allows sport to tap into new markets by changing its shape and features, on the other, it fractures all those traditions that made it attractive to fans in the first place. While professional sport is still both similar to and different from so-called conventional business, their key features and contextual weightings are changing. Both business and sport are concerned with widening their market share, building profits and strengthening the brand. At the same time, the view that sport has a monopoly over the delivery of passion, loyalty and strong identification is difficult to defend.

In short Aaron C.T. Smith and Bob Stewart conclude, while professional sport has undergone significant structural and operational change over the past ten years, it still has enough idiosyncratic features to justify a customized set of management practices. At one extreme, even at its most hardcore professional level, sport has been reorganized as a not-for profit cultural practice that delivers a range of memorable experiences and social benefits that the commercial for-profit sector under-supplies. At the other extreme it is built around a set of market-driven forces that make it just another product situated in a competitive marketplace delivering just another package of ephemeral, banal and, for the most part, forgettable experiences to its customers At the same time, and under both of these extreme structural circumstances, there are still a number of idiosyncratic features that give sport its special character, and that reveal themselves in both the profit and non-profit sector. To conclude: first, a failure to recognize sport as a business will produce poor performance and, second, management strategies that give no recognition to its special features, will fail to deliver optimal outcomes. The authors state that it is precisely these special features which demand the application of sophisticated and professional business principles.

The prevailing appeal of sport is such that a wide range of institutions, organizations, bodies, clubs, teams and individuals are both affected by and involved in sport. As such, and emphasized by Simon Chadwick, there is a multitude of challenges facing managers in sport, many of which have only emerged over the past 10 to 20 years. There is a real need to understand the challenges faced by sport managers and what the most effective ways of managing them are. It is therefore reasonable to anticipate that the sport management literature will develop apace over the next decade.

As for the role that academics and researchers can play in this development, Simon Chadwick notes there are clear opportunities for them to make a contribution. To think in creative, value-adding, innovative terms is one way in which academics can help, as well as in providing opinion leadership on the subject of managing complexity. Harnessing the power of mobile media among elite professional sports as well as other levels of sport poses some interesting questions that scholars can help to answer. This may include how phenomena such as social networking and viral marketing can contribute to the organizational and commercial development of sport. Underpinning these are issues pertaining to the ways in which customers – fans, spectators or others – actually consume sport and what motivates them to do so. As the sport market fragments into a multitude of clear and distinct segments, the need for customer understanding will grow. The closeness to market that this implies is something that academic researchers are particularly adept at achieving.

We conclude and emphasize that sport management researchers must devote time to understanding the mega-shifts that increasingly appear to characterize the changing nature of sport and its environment. The growth of social networking, for instance, is something that has taken many organizations aback. Diminishing gender differences in sporting achievements and the growing interest in women's sport might be another megatrend. For example, after becoming world champions in women's football in Germany in 2010 Nadeshiko Japan is the most successful Asian team in women's football and is now attracting crowds that could not previously have been dreamt of for female football in Japan. Missing important product or management innovations might be one of the reasons for losing the competitive edge in sport. While the expected positive effects of innovation strategies are well documented and supported empirically within industry and services, research in the field of innovation and sports is still very limited; just consider the development and implementation of enhanced sports products (like the new football for the Football World Cup in Germany, or performance-aiding swim suits as used during the Beijing Olympic Games and the Rome World Championships or advanced swimming goggles to allow for 180-degree peripheral vision underwater), aspects of the 'dark-side' of sports (like using drugs and innovative ways of drug-testing), the development of sporting facilities (like wave-crushing lane ropes to diminish and deflect waves in the pool, which helps swimmers to swim faster as they do not need to battle the waves), or the development of new forms of sports (like long-boarding, kite-surfing or T20 cricket). Being able to predict such developments, identifying how sport organizations should respond, and the way in which technology can help to accentuate and enhance the fundamental features of sport can become a route through which researchers are able to make significant empirical and theoretical contributions to the advancement of research on sport and business.

REFERENCE

Dolles, H. and Söderman, S. (2013), 20 years of development of the J-League: analysing the business parameters of professional football in Japan, *Soccer & Society*, **14** (June) (in press).

Index

Index notes: this index focuses on research methods and subjects. All country names are included.